INSIGHT GUIDES

New England

D0166934

Discovery
CHANNEL

APA PUBLICATIONS L
Part of the Langenscheidt Publishing Group

INSIGHT GUIDE
New England

Editorial

Edited by
Brian Bell
Updated by
Kay and Bill Scheller

Distribution

UK & Ireland
GeoCenter International Ltd
Meridian House, Churchill Way West,
Basingstoke, Hampshire RG21 6YR
Fax: (44) 1256 817988

United States
Langenscheidt Publishers, Inc.
36–36 33rd Street, 4th Floor
Long Island City, NY 11106
Fax: 1 (718) 784 0640

Canada
Thomas Allen & Son Ltd
390 Steelcase Road East
Markham, Ontario L3R 1G2
Fax: (1) 905 475 6747

Australia
Universal Press
1 Waterloo Road
Macquarie Park, NSW 2113
Fax: (61) 2 9888 9074

New Zealand
Hema Maps New Zealand Ltd (HNZ)
Unit D, 24 Ra ORA Drive
East Tamaki, Auckland
Fax: (64) 9 273 6479

Worldwide
**Apa Publications GmbH & Co.
Verlag KG (Singapore branch)**
38 Joo Koon Road, Singapore 628990
Tel: (65) 6865 1600. Fax: (65) 6861 6438

Printing

Insight Print Services (Pte) Ltd
38 Joo Koon Road, Singapore 628990
Tel: (65) 6865 1600. Fax: (65) 6861 6438

©2007 Apa Publications GmbH & Co.
Verlag KG (Singapore branch)
All Rights Reserved

First Edition 1984
Seventh Edition (updated) 2007
Reprinted 2007

CONTACTING THE EDITORS
We would appreciate it if readers
would alert us to errors or out-
dated information by writing to:
**Insight Guides, P.O. Box 7910,
London SE1 1WE, England.
Fax: (44) 20 7403 0290.
insight@apaguide.co.uk**
NO part of this book may be reproduced,
stored in a retrieval system or transmitted
in any form or means electronic, mechanical, photocopying, recording or otherwise, without prior written permission of
Apa Publications. Brief text quotations
with use of photographs are exempted
for book review purposes only. Information has been obtained from sources
believed to be reliable, but its accuracy
and completeness, and the opinions
based thereon, are not guaranteed.

www.insightguides.com

ABOUT THIS BOOK

A region with such a rich history and culture as New England lends itself especially well to the approach taken by the 190-title Insight series. The first Insight Guide pioneered the use of creative full-colour photography in travel guides in 1970. Since then, we have expanded our range to cater for our readers' need not only for reliable information about their chosen destination but also for a real understanding of that destination. Now, when the Internet can supply inexhaustible – but not always reliable – facts, our books marry text and pictures to provide that much more elusive quality: knowledge. To achieve this, they rely heavily on the authority of locally based writers and photographers.

How to use this book

The book is carefully structured to convey an understanding of New England and its culture and to guide readers through its sights and attractions:

◆ The Features section, with a yellow colour bar, covers the region's history and culture in lively

The contributors

This edition builds on earlier ones edited by **Jay Itzkowitz** and **Sue Gordon**. Nothing stands still, even in such a tradition-saturated region, and the text has been thoroughly overhauled and expanded by **Kay and Bill Scheller**, a Vermont-based husband-and-wife team who have also written new features on literature and education (two areas in which New England excels). In addition, many fresh photographs have been added.

The editor was **Brian Bell**, Insight Guides' editorial director, whose exploration of New England over the years has been guided by his Connecticut-born wife.

The writers whose text has been adapted from earlier editions are **Mark Bastian, Marcus Brooke, Tom Brosnahan, Kay Cassill, Kimberly Grant, Inez and Jonathan Keller, Molly Kuntz, Tim Locke, Sandy MacDonald, Julie Michaels, Mark Muro, Adam Nossiter, Norman Sibley, Mark Silber, Bryan Simmons** and **Peter Spiro**.

Zoë Goodwin was cartographic editor and **Hilary Genin** handled the picture research. **Elizabeth Cook** compiled the index.

A note on public holidays

The dates when many summer attractions open and close are linked to public holidays. Visitors from overseas should note that the principal ones are: *Memorial Day*, last Monday in May; *Labor Day*, first Monday in September; and *Columbus Day*, second Monday in October. There's a full list on page 330.

authoritative essays written by specialists.

◆ The Places section, with a blue bar, provides full details of all the sights and areas worth seeing. The chief places of interest are coordinated by number with specially drawn maps.

◆ The Travel Tips section, with an orange bar, at the back of the book, offers a point of reference for information on travel, accommodation, restaurants and other practical aspects of the region. Information may be located quickly using the index printed on the back cover flap, which also serves as a bookmark.

Map Legend

—‥‥	International Boundary
‒ ‒ ‒ ‒	State Boundary
‒‥•‥‒	National Park/Reserve
‒ ‒ ‒ ‒	Ferry Route
❶	Subway
✈ ✈	Airport: International/Regional
🚌	Bus Station
P	Parking
❶	Tourist Information
✉	Post Office
🏛 † ⛪	Church/Ruins
†	Monastery
☾	Mosque
✡	Synagogue
🏰 🏚	Castle/Ruins
∴	Archeological Site
∩	Cave
1	Statue/Monument
★	Place of Interest

The main places of interest in the Places section are coordinated by number with a full-colour map (e.g. ❶), and a symbol at the top of every right-hand page tells you where to find the map.

INSIGHT GUIDE

New England

Contents

Maps

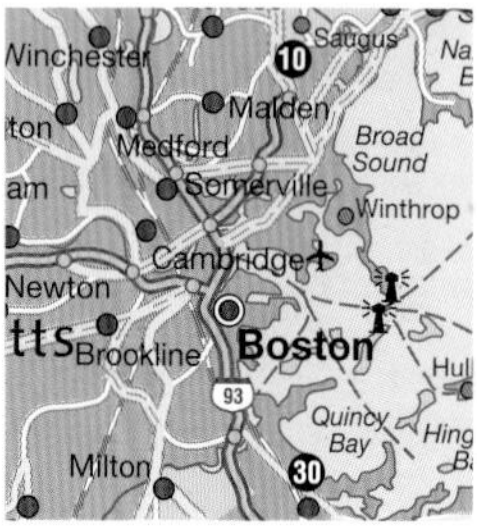

A map of New England is on the inside front cover and a map of Boston on the inside back cover.

Introduction

History

Features

Dune-backed
beach at Truro,
Cape Cod

Insight on....

Information panels

Travel Tips

Places

THE BEST OF NEW ENGLAND

Setting priorities, the sights worth seeing,
best hiking and skiing, unique attractions...
here, at a glance, are our recommendations,
plus tips even the locals may not know

In 1775 the Minute Men were ready to fight the British at a minute's notice.

THE TOP HISTORIC SITES

● **Freedom Trail, Boston**. Follow the red brick path that links Boston's most important Revolutionary sites, including the Old State House, Paul Revere's Home, the Old North Church, and the 1797 frigate *Constitution*, "Old Ironsides." *Pages 132–3.*

● **Lowell National Historical Park, MA**. With many of its massive textile mills still intact, the city's core is now a National Historical Park. Tour downtown by canal boat or trolley, and visit a mill where power looms still turn out cloth. *Pages 145–6.*

● **Salem National Historic Site, MA**. This was the cradle of America's first mercantile fortunes. An old waterfront quarter contains an 1819 Custom House, the home of a merchant prince, and a replica sailing ship. *Page 143.*

● **Minute Man National Historical Park, MA**. The events of April 18 and 19, 1775, are brought to life on Lexington Green, where Minute Men and British soldiers first exchanged fire, and at Concord's North Bridge, where hostilities began in earnest. *Page 146.*

● **Coolidge State Historic Site, VT**. The preserved birthplace of President Calvin Coolidge isn't just a single home, but all of Plymouth Notch village. You can visit the house where Coolidge took the oath of office by kerosene lamp on learning of President Harding's death. *Page 256.*

THE BEST PARKS

● **Baxter State Park, ME**. This wilderness tract deep in Maine's interior is crowned with Mt. Katahdin, the northern terminus of the Appalachian Trail. This is the place to look for moose, black bear... and supreme solitude. *Pages 328–9.*

● **Acadia National Park, ME**. Nowhere is the famed "rock-bound coast of Maine" better exemplified – and better preserved – than in this rugged parkland. *Pages 324–6.*

● **Boston Harbor Islands**. A short boat ride away from downtown Boston, these varied islands offer old forts, historic lighthouses, wilderness hiking and surf fishing. Some islands have overnight camping facilities. *Page 152.*

LEFT: the 1797 *Constitution*, preserved in Boston.

THE FINEST MUSEUMS

● **Museum of Fine Arts, Boston**. One of the world's great museums, whose collections include some of the best Impressionist paintings outside Paris. *Pages 134–5.*

● **Shelburne Museum, VT**. This peerless collection of Americana, folk and fine art,

ABOVE: the Museum of Fine Arts in Boston.

and vernacular New England architecture features the restored 1906 Lake Champlain steamer *Ticonderoga*. *Pages 268–9.*

● **Old Sturbridge Village, MA**. A striking recreation of a New England village circa 1840. Costumed artisans demonstrate their skills. *Page 189.*

● **Isabella Stewart Gardner Museum, Boston**. A Venetian palazzo with fine art, antique furniture, and a flower-filled interior courtyard. *Pages 124–5.*

● **Sterling and Francine Clark Art Institute, MA**. The small but superb Clark houses a fine American collection and first-rate Impressionists from Europe. *Page 200.*

ABOVE: Mystic Seaport re-creates the maritime past.

BEST FOR FAMILIES

● **Mystic Seaport, CT**. In this re-creation of a 19th-century waterfront community, shops and chandleries line the narrow streets and the *Charles W. Morgan*, the last surviving American whaling vessel to sail under canvas, rests at wharfside. *Page 222.*

● **Mount Washington Cog Railway, NH**. An improbable artifact of Victorian technology, the railway climbs to the roof of New England, the 6,288-ft (1,917- meter) Mount Washington, using steam locomotives that push coaches up a narrow-gauge track laid in 1869. A ride to remember. *Page 297.*

● **Museum of Science, Boston**. Five stories of

science and technology made fun, ranging from natural history to computers, from the human body to space flight. On site are an Omni Theater, planetarium, and laser-light show. *Page 125.*

● **The "Big E", MA**. There are state and county fairs all over New England, but the biggest is the region-wide Eastern States Exposition in West Springfield. Animal exhibits and judging, amusement rides, and big-name entertainment fill the 175-acre (71-hectare) fairgrounds in September. *Page 195.*

● **Ben & Jerry's Factory Tour, VT**. The tour tells the story of how two unlikely entrepreneurs created the famous ice cream, revealing the alchemy behind flavors such as Cherry Garcia and Phish Food. *Page 261.*

THE BEST HIKES

● **Appalachian Trail**. Linking every state except Rhode Island, the Georgia-to-Maine Appalachian Trail's northernmost portion offers opportunities for day or overnight hiking. *Page 164.*

● **The Long Trail**. Vermont's rugged trail, which overlaps the Appalachian, scales the Green Mountain peaks. *Page 164.*

● **Appalachian Mountain Club Huts,**

RIGHT: hiking in the Green Mountains.

NH. The staffed huts offer White Mountain ramblers meals and lodging in the heart of the lofty Presidential Range. *Page 292.*

THE TOP COLLEGE TOWNS

● **Cambridge, MA**. Home to Harvard and the Massachusetts Institute of Technology (MIT); both have specialized museums, with Harvard's Fogg Art Museum and Peabody Science museums among the region's finest. Harvard Square bustles with shops, bookstores, restaurants, and clubs; Central Square, near MIT, offers inexpensive eateries and eclectic shops. *Pages 127–30*.

● **Northampton, MA**. This compact city is a hub for five colleges. Right in town is the renowned Smith College of Art; the main street is a festival of art galleries, ethnic restaurants, craft shops, book stores, and art cinemas. *Pages 191–2*.

● **Hanover, NH**. Here is one of the region's loveliest town greens, surrounded by the stately buildings of Dartmouth College.

The school's Hood Museum of Art and Baker Memorial Library are cultural highlights. *Page 289*.

● **Burlington, VT**. The architectural treasures of the University of Vermont dominate the hilltop above the state's largest city. Church Street Marketplace is lined with boutiques, bars, and restaurants, and the waterfront sparkles with marinas, a natural history museum, and a bike path. *Pages 267–8*.

● **New Haven, CT**. New Haven is home to some of America's most spectacular collegiate Gothic architecture on the campus of Yale University. Yale's array of museums include a center for British art, a rare book and manuscript library, a museum of natural history, and even a collection of musical instruments. *Page 216*.

ABOVE: Harvard overlooks the Charles River.

THE FINEST HISTORIC HOUSES

● **Gillette Castle, CT**. A medieval stone mansion on a site overlooking the Connecticut River in East Haddam. *Page 220*.

● **Salem, MA**. The homes preserved by the Peabody-Essex Museum and Salem Maritime National Historic Site represent the pinnacle of the austerely beautiful Federal style of architecture. *Pages 143–5*.

● **Longfellow House, Cambridge, MA**. This spacious Georgian mansion was George Washington's HQ early in the Revolution, and was later the home of Henry Wadsworth Longfellow. *Page 130*.

● **Portsmouth, NH**. A treasure trove of Georgian and Federal architecture, including the one-time home of naval hero John Paul Jones. *Pages 282–3*.

● **Newport, RI**. The greatest monuments to America's Gilded Age are the wildly extravagant mansions along Bellevue Avenue. The Breakers, Rosecliff, The Elms, and other monuments to untaxed riches were, amazingly, used only for a few weeks each summer. *Pages 234–9*.

LEFT: The Elms in Newport, a copy of a French château.

THE BEST BEACHES

● **Block Island, RI**. It's worth the ferry ride to enjoy these uncrowded strands – remote Mohegan Bluffs, calm State Beach, and Surfers Beach. *Pages 240–1.*

● **Crane's Beach, MA**. A beautifully preserved stretch of sand with views reaching from Cape Ann right to the distant shores of New Hampshire and Maine. *Page 140.*

● **Plum Island, MA**. Parking is limited, so there are never towel-to-towel crowds. A bonus: the island is one of the East's premier birding destinations. *Pages 139–40.*

● **Cape Cod National Seashore**. Options for sunning and (brisk) swimming range from easy-to-reach Nauset in the south to the dune-circled Pilgrim Heights and Province Lands beaches in Truro and Provincetown. *Page 165.*

● **Hammonasset State Beach, CT**. The gentle, generally warm waters of Long Island Sound wash this broad, superbly maintained beach that has plenty of parking, and changing facilities. *Page 219.*

ABOVE: snowboarding at Sunday River Ski Resort.

THE TOP SKI AREAS

● **Stowe Mountain Resort, VT**. Some trails, including the famous "Front Four" on Mt. Mansfield, date from the 1930s. The resort boasts spectacular terrain, aerial gondolas, and superb lodging. *Page 262.*

● **Killington, VT**. New England's biggest ski area has 200 trails and nearly three dozen lifts. The resort is a study in superlatives – steepest mogul run, a 3140-foot vertical drop, and a 10-mile downhill trail. *Page 256.*

● **Jay Peak, VT**. The most reliable snow cover and a variety of trails: harrowing steeps, long cruising runs, and even a slow skiing zone. *Page 265.*

● **Sugarloaf, ME**. Plenty of intermediate runs, but nearly half the trails are black dia-monds. Glade action is terrific. *Page 330.*

● **Sunday River, ME**. Offers great grooming, high-speed quad lifts, and a double-diamond mogul run as foil to its more forgiving cruisers. *Page 332.*

ABOVE: a pristine Cape Cod beach near Truro.

PICK OF THE PERFORMING ARTS

● **Boston Symphony Orchestra and Boston Pops** perform at the Symphony Hall and the Hatch concert shell, and in Tanglewood's sylvan setting. *Pages 124, 199.*

● **Vermont Mozart Festival**. Indoor and outdoor summer venues for concerts of works by Mozart and other favorites. *Page 268.*

● **Jacob's Pillow Dance Festival, MA**. Indoor and outdoor theaters showcase classic works in a lovely Berkshires setting. *Page 362.*

● **Goodspeed Opera House, CT**. This 1876 theater by the Connecti-cut River is the venue for professional musical revivals and original productions. *Page 220.*

● **American Repertory Theater, Cambridge, MA**. Harvard's Loeb Drama Center puts on revivals and original works. *Page 360.*

ABOVE: Tanglewood picnic.

AMERICA'S ATTIC

The blending of Old England traditions and New World values
created six distinctive states, each with its own character

New England "is a finished place," wrote the Pulitzer Prize-winning author Bernard De Voto in 1936. "Its destiny is that of Florence or Venice, not Milan, while the American empire careens onward towards its unpredicted end... It is the first American section to be finished, to achieve stability in its conditions of life. It is the first old civilization, the first permanent civilization in America."

De Voto was only partly right; in the decades since he wrote, New England has changed and changed again – like the rest of America, it's hardly ever finished. But as America's first old civilization, New England has done more than most places to preserve its most cherished touchstones of memory: Paul Revere's almost medieval house, the battlefields of Lexington and Concord, cobblestone streets that whaling captains trod, the haunts of the Adamses and Kennedys – even the most beloved baseball park in the land. New England never forgets that it was here that the first cries of American Independence were heard, here that the movement to abolish slavery found fertile ground, here that education achieved its fullest flowering, here that American art and literature attained their greatest refinement.

This is America's attic, crammed with marvelous antiques of every description. Here are the homes of Hawthorne, Emerson, Dickinson, and Melville; souvenirs of seafaring from centuries past; houses and churches in whose gables and steeples can be read a national architectural history. The countryside abounds with inspiring vistas, enchanted with the bright golds and reds of fall, slumbering beneath winter's heavy snows, bursting with the green rebirth of spring, and joyful in summer's ceaseless flowering.

The alluring variety embraces Maine's coast, its rocky promontories pointing to adventure; New Hampshire's forest-encircled lakes and gaunt granite peaks; Vermont's mountains, rising above a green patchwork quilt of dairy farms and woodlands; the gentle Berkshire Hills; Connecticut's trim colonial towns; Newport's well-preserved luxury; the charming villages and rolling dunes of Cape Cod and the islands; and Boston's vibrant cityscape.

If Boston is a state of mind – a remark variously attributed by the city's contentious academics to Mark Twain, Ralph Waldo Emerson, and Thomas G. Appleton – so is New England, to an even greater degree. And it is a state of mind well worth embracing. ❑

PRECEDING PAGES: sleigh ride on Come Spring Farm, Union, Maine; Newfane, Vermont, once described as the prettiest village in New England; Back Cove, Maine.
LEFT: history re-enacted on Hampton Beach, New Hampshire.

Decisive Dates

9000 BC Earliest evidence of human activity in New England, at Shawville, Vermont.

AD 1000 The Viking Leif Erikson discovers Vinland the Good, the location of which remains unknown.

14th–15th centuries The Algonquin Indians arrive in the region.

EARLY COLONISTS

1497 John Cabot explores North American coast.

1524 Giovanni da Verrazano, sailing under the French flag, journeys as far north as Narrangansett Bay.

1602–6 Bartholomew Gosnold, Martin Pring, and George Weymouth lead successful expeditions to the region. Weymouth returns with five Indians abducted from the coast of Maine.

1607 One hundred adventurers, funded by the Plymouth Company, build Fort St George on Parker's Island, Maine, where they spend the winter.

1614 British Captain John Smith returns laden with furs and fish from what he calls "New England."

1620 The Plymouth Company finances a group of 66 Puritans to establish a permanent settlement in North America. They leave on the *Mayflower*, and sight Cape Cod on November 11. In mid-December they found Plymouth Colony.

1630 The Massachusetts Bay Colony is founded by John Winthrop on the Shawmut Peninsula, where the settlement of Boston begins.

1635 The country's first secondary school, the Boston Latin School, is established.

1636 Harvard College is established. Reverend Roger Williams is banished from the Massachusetts Bay Colony and founds Providence, Rhode Island. War erupts with the Pequots.

1639 The first printing press is set up, in Cambridge.

1675–76 King Philip's War sees the demise of Indian society in New England.

1692 Salem witch trials: 400 stand accused of sorcery and other crimes. Of the guilty, 20 are executed.

1701 The Collegiate School (later Yale) is founded.

1712 Captain Christopher Hussey of Nantucket bags the first sperm whale taken by New Englanders.

THE ROAD TO INDEPENDENCE

1764 The Revenue Act, imposed by Britain on the colonists, taxes sugar, silk, and some wines.

1765 The Stamp Act is passed, taxing commercial and legal documents, newspapers, and playing cards. Demonstrations are held throughout New England.

1767 The Townshend Acts place harsh duties on paper, glass, and tea. Two regiments of British troops land at Boston to impose order.

1770 On March 5, five colonists are killed outside the Custom House by Redcoats in what becomes known as the "Boston Massacre."

1773 On December 16, in the "Boston Tea Party," 60 men (disguised as Mohawk Indians and blacks) dump tea over the railings of three ships in Boston Harbor in protest against taxes on tea.

1774 Britain retaliates against the Boston Tea Party by imposing the Coercive Acts, including the Boston Port Act which closes Boston Harbor. On September 5 the First Continental Congress convenes at Philadelphia and starts to organize an army.

1775 On the night of April 18, Paul Revere and William Dawes ride from Boston to warn of the impending arrival of 700 British troops sent to destroy an arms depot in Concord. The following day the two sides engage at Lexington in the first battle of the Revolution. On June 17 the British force an American retreat at the Battle of Bunker Hill near Boston (actually fought on Breed's Hill), but only after massive casualties.

1776 In March, George Washington drives the British from Boston. On July 4, the Declaration of Independence is adopted.

BOOM AND BUST

1789 Samuel Slater is engaged by financier Moses Brown to set up a cotton mill at Pawtucket.

1791 Vermont, briefly an independent republic, is admitted to the Union.

1800 Poor working conditions at Pawtucket lead workers to strike in the nation's first industrial action.

1820 Maine, formerly part of Massachusetts, is admitted to the Union as a state.

1826 The growing community surrounding the Merrimack Manufacturing Company's showpiece cotton mill is renamed Lowell after its founder.

1831 The Abolitionist William Lloyd Garrison founds the weekly *Liberator* newspaper.

1833 New England's first steam railroad opens between Boston and Lowell, Massachusetts.

1845–50 More than 1,000 Irish immigrants fleeing for payroll robbery and murder; their execution in 1927 causes widespread protests.

1929 The Wall Street Crash and the resultant Great Depression hit New England hard.

1938 A hurricane in September is New England's worst natural disaster.

1930s–1950s Decline of New England manufacturing economy, especially textiles and shoes.

MODERN EVENTS

1960 Masssachusetts Senator John F. Kennedy is elected US President.

1960s–1980s New England's economy transformed by high-technology industries.

from the Potato Famine arrive in Boston each month.

1852 *Uncle Tom's Cabin*, by Harriet Beecher Stowe, encourages the Abolitionist movement.

1854 The Boston Public Library becomes the world's first free municipal library.

1861 Whaling declines as kerosene replaces whale oil for lighting.

1871 Boston's Museum of Fine Arts opens.

1880s Irish immigrants start to control Boston politics.

1881 Debut of the Boston Symphony Orchestra.

1920 Italian anarchists Sacco and Vanzetti arrested

1980s–1990s New England cod fishery collapses as a result of declining stocks.

1990 Vermont elects the nation's only Independent congressman, socialist Bernie Sanders.

1992 The Mashantucket Pequot Indians open the controversial but highly profitable Foxwoods Casino in Connecticut. It is soon followed by Mohehan Sun.

2005 America's biggest ever public works project, the "Big Dig," is completed. It sinks Boston's Central Artery and adds a third harbor tunnel.

2006 Vermont's Independent congressman Bernie Sanders elected to US Senate. Massachusetts elects its first African-American governor, Deval Patrick. Edward Kennedy, JFK's only surviving brother, is elected to his 8th full term as Massachusetts senator. ❏

PRECEDING PAGES: an early English map of the region.
LEFT: the Pilgrims come ashore in the New World.
ABOVE: a harpooned whale overturns a whaleboat.

EARLY DAYS

The first Indians arrived in the region around 12000 BC, but it was the landing of the Pilgrim Fathers in 1620 that changed the face of America for ever

A crumbling stone wall in the middle of a forest: this is New England. Separating trees from other trees, this wall stands as a reminder of what man can and cannot do, of what the pioneers accomplished and what nature has reclaimed, of what New England was and what it is. The frontier no longer faces guide the nation, the engineer to create new technology, and the scholar to study the lessons of the past and plan for the future.

And so the stone wall stands as a symbol of work well done, and work yet to be accomplished. New England's people – the newly arrived and those with centuries of American

the rolling hills and woodlands; the Indians no longer hunt and fish undisturbed; the white man no longer clears the forest to eke out a precarious life. Now, spruces and firs tower over this crumbling stone wall, dwarfing the achievements of those pioneers who toiled so hard in the excitement and uncertainty of a new land.

The rough work of building New England has long since been finished; its physical frontiers have been conquered. But the spirit of its pioneers lives on to grapple with the intricacies of a different age. The same urge that impelled the explorer to chart an unknown land, the freeman to stake his claim, and the immigrant to make his fortune, now lead the politician to lineage – embody the strength of diversity. Its history – a long trail of advance and retreat – provides an enduring inspiration. And its landscape – the elegance of time-worn peaks, the tranquility of forests as dense and majestic as ever, the lulling crash of the ocean waves – draws countless visitors.

Lay of the land

New England encompasses 66,672 sq. miles (172,680 sq. km), including the states of Massachusetts, Connecticut, Rhode Island, Vermont, New Hampshire, and Maine. It is bounded by Canada to the north, the Atlantic Ocean to the east, Long Island Sound to the south, and New

York to the west. Moving inland from the coastal lowlands in the south and east, the terrain gradually rises to forested hills and culminates in the weather-beaten peaks of the Appalachian system, represented by the White Mountains to the north and the Green and Taconic Mountains and Berkshire Hills to the west.

Perhaps 2 billion years ago, a vast ocean trough, under the pressure of more than 500,000 cubic miles (2 million cubic km) of sediment, was convulsed upward by an upheaval of the earth's crust. The mountains thus created were ancestors of the Appalachians. Its foundation a great buckling fold, the chain continued to shift and shudder. The intense heat generated metamorphosed sandstone and limestone deposits into the schists and marble now found in the southeastern lowlands and Berkshire Hills of Massachusetts and in Vermont's Green Mountains. Later, streaks of intrusive rocks formed, represented by the granite of Rhode Island, New Hampshire, and Maine, and the reddish rocks of the Connecticut River Valley.

About 200 million years ago, the thrusts from below the earth's crust stopped. The geologic revolution complete, the Appalachians towered about 30,000 ft (some 9,000 meters), the Himalayas of another time.

The elements went to work on the jagged landscape, until much of southern and central New England was no more than a featureless plain. Some outcroppings fared better against the wind and rain than others, accounting for the few scattered mounts that stand unescorted out of the lowlands – now called monadnocks after New Hampshire's Mount Monadnock. About 8 million years ago, meanwhile, the rest of the flats were gently folded one final time into the hills we see today.

Legacy of the Ice Age

The marauding glaciers of the Ice Age added the finishing touches to the landscape. About a million years ago, a sudden drop in the world's average summer temperature thickened existing ice masses to 200 ft (60 meters). Under this pressure, their foundations spread outward, grasping for new ground, until the glaciers eventually claimed more than one-third of the globe's total area. Ice swallowed up northeastern America on four different occasions

LEFT: a prehistoric inhabitant.
RIGHT: primitive tools unearthed in forests.

during the Pleistocene Era, retreating and readvancing over the millennia, finally leaving New England about 10,000 to 12,000 years ago.

This last flooding etched the New England landscape we admire today. Although the glaciers left unchanged the land's basic geologic make-up, they did leave reminders of their former supremacy. Working like steel wool, the glaciers – by now often more than 2 miles (3 km) deep – rounded out slopes and valleys.

Carving scratches (glacial striations) on exposed rock, the glaciers left behind evidence of the path they traveled. Glacial till, the chaff that the ice scraped off the ground, was carried

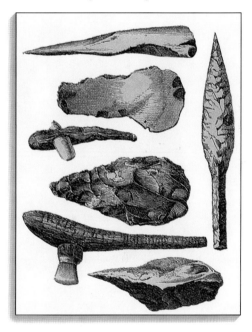

TRIASSIC PARK

During the Triassic period, the great swamplands that surrounded the Appalachian core and the hot climate created a perfect habitat for dinosaurs, the rulers of the day. Between 200 and 300 million years ago, dinosaurs roamed the Newark Bed, which runs more or less along what is now the Connecticut River Valley. Such primitive dinosaurs as *coelophysia* (an early two-legged herbivore), *rhychosaurus* (a tusked four-legger with an eerie rodent look), and more than 150 other species of reptiles and amphibians, left tracks by the thousands in Smith's Ferry and South Hadley in central Massachusetts, and, of course, at Dinosaur State Park in Rocky Hill, Connecticut.

south. As the glaciers receded, this material was left behind; much of New England's bedrock is blanketed with a thin layer of this till, composed of clay, sand, and broken rock. Rounded hills of glacial till, called drumlins, are found scattered throughout New England.

A similar process created Cape Cod, and the islands of Martha's Vineyard and Nantucket. Other dramatic legacies of the Ice Age include glacial cirques (large bowl-shaped depressions on mountainsides),

> **BEACHED WHALE**
>
> In 1848, workers laying railroad tracks in Charlotte, Vermont, a distance of over 150 miles (240 km) from the Atlantic Ocean, unearthed the skeleton of an improbable resident: a whale.

km) worldwide. The floods were great, and the oceans claimed many areas that are landlocked today. In parts of Maine, Atlantic waves crashed against shores up to 75 miles (120 km) inland from the present coastline; Lake Champlain was an arm of the sea which transformed northern New England into an Atlantic peninsula. Evidence of marine activity has been found at more than 500 ft (150 meters) above today's sea level. Hundreds of lakes once thrived where there are none now.

glacial erratics (boulders, weighing as much as 5,000 tons, dragged for miles by the moving ice), and kettle lakes (crater-like indentations, of which Walden Pond is a good example).

Like the towering Appalachians millions of years ago, many of these features are slowly wearing away. The erosion can only be measured in thousands of years, however, and the distinctiveness these features lend to New England's landscape will survive far into the future.

When the glaciers melted in force, they released a vast amount of water, perhaps as much as 8 million cubic miles (33 million cubic

The waters gradually receded, and the land, relieved of its burden of ice, rebounded slowly upward. New England assumed its present configuration. Tundra plants and, later, trees took hold. A flourishing fauna could live once again on the land but, this time, with a new creature in its midst: man.

The earliest explorers

Although, as the name suggests, it was the English who sowed the seeds of New England's fortune, they were not the first to gaze on these northern shores. Anthropologists generally agree that the first pilgrims reached North America overland from Asia via the then-frozen Bering

Straits, arriving on the continent between 12,000 and 25,000 years ago.

The oldest fossil finds of human activity in New England, uncovered in Shawville, Vermont, and Wapunucket, Massachusetts, date respectively to 9000 and 4000 BC and include a variety of spear points, knives, pendants, and ancient house floors. These early settlers were to witness the landing of the Vikings, the first documented European visitors to North America. In AD 1000, King Olaf of Norway commissioned young Leif Erikson to bring Christianity to the new Viking settlement in Greenland, founded only 15 years ear-

The skraelings

But the natives proved too strong for the small band. Initial relations between the two groups were good; Viking cloth was cordially traded for local furs. All was well, says one saga, until the *skraelings* (the etymology is uncertain; it may mean wretches or dwarves) were startled to martial frenzy by a bellowing Viking bull. A fierce battle ensued in which several Vikings fell. Concluding that "although the country thereabouts was attractive, their life would be one of constant dread and turmoil" because of the natives, Karlsefni and his followers headed home to Greenland. The Vikings did not return.

lier by Eric the Red, Leif's father. Despite the winds that blew his *knarr* (Viking cargo ship) south of his appointed mission, Leif the Lucky lived up to his name and discovered a new land where grapes and wheat grew wild: Vinland the Good.

A few years later Thorfin Karlsefni set sail with several families and a few cattle, intending to establish a permanent settlement in Vinland. At first, the new frontier treated them well. They were impressed by the fertile land, the fish-filled streams, and the game-packed forests.

LEFT: Viking longboats arrived around AD 1000.
ABOVE: an 1876 painting of a native New Englander.

VINLAND'S LOCATION

The Vikings' visit to North America is well documented, but precisely where Vinland the Good lies on a contemporary map of North America is a matter of much debate. Some claim the stump of a stone tower in Newport, Rhode Island, marks the southernmost extent of their explorations. Other evidence pointing to an 11th-century visit to New England includes a Viking axe found at Rocky Nook, Massachusetts (near Plymouth Rock); early English accounts of blue-eyed natives; and reports that Karlsefni and his band wintered in a place without much snow. Other historians refuse to believe the Vikings ventured south of Nova Scotia.

The Algonquins

The Algonquins were the Indians of the real Age of Discovery and the Indians who were first befriended and then destroyed by European fortune hunters and refugees. Represented as far west as the Rockies and as far south as the Carolinas, the Algonquin tribes were related to one another approximately as the French are to the Spanish. Although intertribal communication often demanded an interpreter, the two languages shared basic grammatical and phonetic constructions.

The Algonquins seeped into the New England forests probably sometime during the

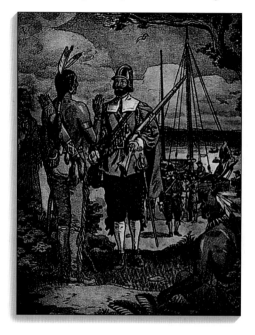

Everyone contributed to the efficient workings of the typical Algonquin community. While the men took care of the chase, the women sowed and harvested the fields, tended the children, and maintained the portable family wigwams. The Algonquins were, in fact, dumbfounded by the inequity of European sex roles. As one Englishman reported the Indians' reaction to the white female's social function: "They say *Englishman* much foole, for spoiling good working creature meaning women. And when they see any of our English women sewing with their needles, or working coifes, or such things, they will cry out Lazie *Squaes!*"

14th or 15th centuries. They did not come in droves; by 1600, no more than 25,000 Indians populated New England, fewer than one for every 2 sq. miles (5 sq. km). Nor did this population comprise a unified culture: the Algonquins broke down into at least 10 tribal divisions. Tribes included the Narragansetts of present-day Rhode Island, the Abenaki of Maine, the Pennacooks of New Hampshire, and the Massachusetts of their namesake, as well as lesser groups such as the Nipmucs, Nausets, Pocumtucks, and Niantics. Some tribes could boast no more than 200 or 300 members.

Far from being the nomads of later characterizations, the Algonquins were agricultural and semi-sedentary, wandering little more than the fashionable Bostonians who summer on Cape Cod. Tribal communities moved with the seasons, following established routes restricted to particular tribal domains. In the winter they occupied the sheltered valleys of the interior, in the warmer months the fertile coastal areas.

But the Indians had to toil year round to feed and clothe themselves. With an excellent understanding of agricultural techniques, they grew crops such as beans, pumpkins, and tobacco, but relied most heavily on maize, the Indian corn. Meat and fish sufficiently balanced the vegetable fare. Plentiful moose and beaver, turkey and goose, lobsters and clams, salmon and bass, along with other delectables, made for an enviably varied menu.

Politics and state affairs were left in the charge of the *sachem*, a hereditary chief who commanded each tribe in much the same way that monarchs ruled medieval Europe. Although men usually controlled the sachemships, there were many cases of women filling the top posts. Sub-*sachems* and war captains, the Indian equivalents of lords and knights, paid material tribute to these rulers and were nominally subject to their will.

The *powwows*, or medicine men, gained considerable political might as the vicars of Indian religion. They combined healing with religion and enjoined their parishioners in intense mystical rites.

In no sense did the Algonquins comprise a nation in the modern European style. Unlike their Iroquois neighbors to the west, no council, senate, or chief-of-chiefs disciplined the Algonquin tribes toward unified action. Divided into sachemships, New England's Indians were not simply disunited; they were constantly at each other's throats. "The savages... for the most part," reported the merchant-adventurer George Peckham, "are at continuall warres with their next adjoyning neighbor." These conflicts could be extremely vicious, typified by the grotesque torture of prisoners and the parading of a slaughtered adversary's head and hands.

Tribal animosities so hardened by generations of battle would later contribute to the Algonquins' downfall by preventing the tribes from unifying against the advancing white settler, a formidable common enemy.

Columbus's countryman Giovanni Caboto (John Cabot), searching for the Northwest Passage to the East, received slightly better treatment from his patron, Henry VII of England. The first European since the Norse to visit America's northern shores (at Labrador, historians believe), Cabot was blessed with a huge royal pension of £20 a year after his 1497 expedition. It was a good bargain for the Crown, considering that England based its claim to all America east of the Rockies and north of Florida on the extent of Cabot's exploration.

For most of the 16th century, Spanish conquistadors dominated the New World, where

Path to settlement

The early European explorers were not mere adventurers, but determined fortune hunters seeking an easier passage to the Orient and its treasures – and, incidentally, seeking to save heathen souls. When the Genoese sailor Cristoforo Colombo (better known by the latinized Christopher Columbus) was trying to finance his expedition, he spoke of riches and trade. So when he returned with a new continent, but with no gold or spices, he was ridiculed and disgraced.

LEFT: contact is established with the natives.
ABOVE: French explorer Jacques Cartier.
RIGHT: the Italian Giovanni da Verrazano.

they profitably exploited resource-rich Central and South America. After Cabot's venture, the less inviting and accessible north was largely neglected and the Northwest Passage remained no more than a merchant's dream.

Sailing for the French, Giovanni da Verrazano traveled the Atlantic seaboard in his *Dolphin* as far north as Narragansett Bay. Jacques Cartier laid the foundation for what would later become New France by navigating the important St Lawrence River. The Portuguese joined the French in fishing the teeming waters of the Grand Banks. But, as yet, there was very little talk of settling the then unchristened land of New England.

The English take over

In the closing decades of the 16th century, Elizabeth I's England eclipsed Spain as master of the seas. Recognizing conquest and colonization as a path to power, the late-starting English were to take over from the conquistadors as pioneers of the New World.

In 1583, equipped with a royal charter to discover "remote heathen and barbarious land not actually possessed by any Christian prince or people… and to have, hold, occupy and enjoy" such territories, Sir Humphrey Gilbert was the first Englishman to attempt the settlement of North America. Sailing from Plymouth with

his flagship *Delight* and three other vessels, Gilbert intended to establish a trading post at the mouth of the Penobscot River. But after reasserting English control of Newfoundland, he sailed south to disaster: three out of the four ships sank and Gilbert himself lost his life.

The misfortune of Gilbert proved only a temporary inhibition to other pathmakers. The first years of the 17th century saw a renewed interest in exploration. Between 1602 and 1606, expeditions led by Bartholomew Gosnold, Martin Pring, and George Weymouth went smoothly and, although not ambitious enough to plant settlements, these voyages did discover a commercial lure to New England – plentiful sassafras bark, then considered a powerful cure-all. Weymouth also had another interesting cargo – five Indians abducted from Maine.

In 1606, James I granted charters for two new ventures, the Virginia Companies of London and Plymouth, giving the latter rights to found a colony somewhere between North Carolina and Nova Scotia. Directed by luminaries such as Sir Ferdinando Gorges, Raleigh Gilbert (son of Sir Humphrey), and the veteran Pring, 100 adventurers set out from Plymouth in early 1607. Loaded with the usual arms and foodstuffs, some livestock, and trinkets to trade with the natives, the crew built Fort St George on Parker's Island in Maine. There they wintered but, finding no evidence of precious metals, and the weather "extreme unseasonable and frosty," the group left the following spring.

Recognizing the need to plan more carefully, the Plymouth Company next commissioned the experienced surveyor John Smith to take a critical look at the region's potential for settlement and profit. Smith is credited as the first to give the region its name of "New England."

Answering a higher call

The explorers of the 16th century were driven by the profit motive. Since they discovered neither the coveted Northwest Passage nor gold and diamonds, they couldn't discern the promise of the New World. Decades of work produced no more than a few crude maps and travelogues. The Cabots and Gosnolds and Weymouths were not interested in settling New England; only a higher call would people the new land.

Renaissance Europe could not imagine religious tolerance. Dissent was treason, and heretics mounted the same scaffolds as did traitors. To the Puritans, devotees of more extreme Protestant beliefs than their Church of England (Anglican) countrymen, the symbols of papal domination – jeweled miters, elaborate rituals, and power-hungry bishops – were the Devil's work, from which the Anglican establishment had not sufficiently distanced itself.

Perhaps even more disturbing to the Puritans was the persecution they suffered under Catholic sympathizer James I. The Puritans had enjoyed years of respectability during Elizabeth I's reign. Their followers included highly placed academics and public officials, many merchants, and local clergymen. The

In 1602, a group of several hundred Puritans from Lincolnshire migrated to the college town of Leyden, Holland, but they did not prosper. The exacting Puritans found their travel along the True Path hindered by the fact that "the morals of the people in the Low Countries were loose." And so, the Puritans struck a deal with the Plymouth Company to finance a settlement in the unpopulated north of America. In the early summer of 1620, 66 of the Leyden community sailed with the *Speedwell* to Southampton to prepare for the trials ahead. "They knew they were pilgrims," Bradford wrote, and so they are remembered by history.

shock of disgrace under James I, therefore, was all the more frightful. The new king wasn't lopping off any heads, but harassment went beyond mere inconvenience. "Some were taken, & clapt up in prison, others had their houses besett & watcht night and day, & hardly escaped their lands," related Puritan leader William Bradford in his oft-quoted *History of Plimoth Plantation*, "and ye most were faine too flie & leave their houses & habitations; and the means of their livelihood."

LEFT: eight-year-old Anne Pollard, the first white woman to set foot in Boston (1630).
ABOVE: "Pilgrims" at Plimoth Plantation today.

Leaving from Plymouth on the 180-ton *Mayflower*, the Pilgrims packed everything they needed to start and maintain a self-sufficient community. The trip itself was no luxury cruise, and after more than two months at sea the travelers "were not a little joyful" to sight Cape Cod on November 11. Deciding that the sandy cape lacked fresh water and arable land, the group dispatched Captain Miles Standish (who was nicknamed "Captain Shrimp" because of his height) to find a more fertile site. In mid-December, the Pilgrims disembarked at Plymouth Rock.

The first winter was a miserable ordeal, testing fully the hardened Puritan will. Scurvy, pneumonia, and other infections killed more than half of the settlers, including Governor John Carver and the wives of Bradford and Standish. At any one time, no more than six or seven remained in good health. But spring brought better times and the critical cooperation of the local Indians.

As luck would have it, Squanto, one of those brought back to England by George Weymouth, had returned to his homeland and was there to greet the Pilgrims. Squanto persuaded Massasoit, the local *sachem*, to help the beleaguered English pioneers. A treaty of friendship was signed.

A PURITAN ACHIEVEMENT

Like the Pilgrim Fathers, the later Puritan arrivals were determined not only to establish themselves permanently in the New World but also to live fully their religious ideals. "For wee must consider that wee shall be as a Citty upon a hill," Governor Winthrop declared. "The eies of all people are upon us; so that if we shall deale falsely with our god in this worke… wee shall shame the faces of many of God's worthy servants, and cause their prayers to be turned into Cursses upon us till wee be consumed out of the good land." Driven by such heavenly aspirations, these religious refugees fared well with their worldly pursuits. The founding of New England was a Puritan achievement.

Heavenly aspirations

Acknowledging the native contribution, the Pilgrims hosted a feast of celebration nearing the first anniversary of their arrival. In this first Thanksgiving, natives and newcomers enjoyed a meal of roasted game (including turkey), eel, fruits, vegetables, and cornbread. A few weeks later, 35 freedom-seekers, well stocked with provisions, joined the *Mayflower* survivors, and by the spring of 1624, Plymouth was a thriving village of more than 30 cottages.

With tracts such as Edward Winslow's *Good Newes From New England* making their way back to the mother country, more settlers overcame an understandable timidity to join the religious migration.

In 1628 another group of Puritans, led by Thomas Dudley, Thomas Leverett, and John Winthrop, obtained a royal charter as the "Company of the Massachusetts Bay in New England." The next summer, 350 hopefuls arrived at Salem, followed by another 1,500 in 1630. Not only more numerous than the Plymouth Pilgrims but also better financed, the Massachusetts Bay Company founded the town of Boston that year on the Shawmut peninsula – a neck of land whose only prior English inhabitant had been the scholarly hermit William Blaxton, who promptly removed himself to Rhode Island.

As Charles I and Archbishop William Laud tightened the screws of persecution back home, the Massachusetts Bay Colony grew quickly despite primitive conditions. Some 2,000 immigrants joined the settlement each year between 1630 and 1637, and, to accommodate these arrivals, new communities such as Ipswich, Dorchester, Concord (the first inland village), Dedham, and Watertown sprang up.

In 1636, the Puritan clergy established Harvard College to train future ministers. The Great and General Court – to this day the name of the Massachusetts legislature – was formed to manage administrative and judicial affairs, a governor and deputy governor being indirectly chosen by the colony's freeholders (those who owned Bay Company stock). At the town level, landowners convened to confront problems of general interest; this was an entirely practical mechanism of administration given that, even as late as 1700, the average town included no more than 200 or 300 families.

Growth was not limited to the area of the first landings on the Massachusetts shore. The reverends Thomas Hooker and Samuel Stone, along with former Bay governor John Haynes, left Cambridge for Connecticut, where they settled the towns of Hartford, Wethersfield, and Windsor. Londoners Theophilus Eaton and John Davenport soon after established themselves at New Haven. The Plymouth Colony had been operating a trading post on Maine's Kennebec River since 1627, and New World magnates John Mason and Sir Ferdinando Gorges tried to develop vast property grants in New Hampshire and Maine, but these ventures were humbled by the region's inhospitality.

Elsewhere, groups of New Englanders helped

could not only enjoy their own religion, but could prevent everybody else from enjoying his." Dictating rules of conduct not just for the church but for all worldly pursuits, the Puritans were far less tolerant of social or theological deviation than their oppressors back in England had been. Indeed, in 1661, the king himself intervened to protect Quakers in the Bay Colony after several were hanged publicly on Boston Common. As has often been the case in American history, injustice belied the slogans of liberty.

Such intolerances did, however, bear an unwanted but ultimately productive child in the

pave the frontiers outside the region. Puritan communities transplanted to New York, North Carolina, and Georgia maintained ties with their old homes. One such group, originally from Westmorland, Connecticut, continued to send representatives to the Connecticut Assembly long after moving to Pennsylvania.

The 19th-century social satirist Artemus Ward (real name: Charles Farrar Browne) once observed: "The Puritans nobly fled from a land of despotism to a land of freedom, where they

LEFT: Pilgrims give thanks for their safe landing.
ABOVE: early settlers barricading their house against Indian attack.

new colony of Rhode Island. In the early years of Massachusetts Bay, the Reverend Roger Williams took it upon himself to condemn the shackles of imposed religion, preaching from his pulpit in Salem that "forced worship stinks in God's nostrils." Williams' compatriots in the General Court banished him from the colony in 1636.

But Williams did not return to England. He turned instead to Canonicus and Miantonomi, the two Narragansett *sachems* whom he had befriended in the course of studying the native population. The chieftains saw fit to grant him, *gratis*, a large tract on the Pawtuxet River. Here, Williams founded Providence. Fellow exiles joined him over the next few years – Anne Hutchinson and William Coddington on nearby Rhode Island (so named because someone thought it resembled the Greek island of Rhodes), and Samuel Gorton in Warwick.

Though the new settlement grew slowly – from fewer than 20 families in 1638 to no more than 1,000 individuals three decades later – the Providence and Rhode Island plantations proved an unholy thorn in Massachusetts' underbelly. No kind words here: Hutchinson,

racial prejudice against the Indians (one contemporary theory held that they were descended from a lost tribe of Israel), the Puritans soon assumed the task of converting their new-found neighbors from their heathen ways.

Missionary efforts did show some initial promise. The Bible was translated into the Algonquian language. The Reverend John Eliot set up a string of "Praying Towns" of Christian Algonquins. During the 1660s and early 1670s, these communities may have accounted for as

> ### SANCTUARY FOR ALL
>
> Aside from outcast Puritans, the new community of Rhode Island welcomed New England's first Jewish émigrés in 1662, along with scores of Quakers and French Huguenots.

with her "very voluble tongue," lambasted her former parish with "Call it whore and strumpet not a Church of Christ;" while back in Massachusetts, the ordinarily restrained Cotton Mather continually insulted the colony as the "fag end of creation," "the sewer of New England," and, ever so cleverly, "Rogue's Island." But Rhode Island lived up to its intent, and religious freedom was guaranteed by a 1663 royal charter.

A much worse oppression than Williams had suffered was imposed upon the Indians. Although the Puritans owed much to the Algonquins for their cooperation in the early days of settlement, and although they professed no

many as one-fifth of all New England Indians. But the Puritans were looking for more than religious fellow-travelers; they sought to create nothing less than a breed of neo-Englishmen.

Cultural suicide

As the historian Alden T. Vaughan concluded, the natives would have had to "forsake their theology, their language, their political and economic structures, their habitations and clothing, their social mores, their customs of work and play" – in short, commit cultural suicide – to please the Puritans sufficiently.

Several Algonquins were sent to Harvard to receive ministerial training, but only Caleb

Cheeshahteaumuck graduated. Many natives took to drinking the "strong water" introduced by the English, and were chastised for their supposed indolence, a cardinal Puritan sin. A few might have made the crossing to "civilization," but to expect all to do so was unreasonable and typical of a profound disrespect for a proud society.

Soon empire-building replaced missionary zeal and led to bloodshed. At first, there was plenty of room for the natives and settlers to coexist peacefully. About a third of the Algonquin inhabitants had fallen victim to a great plague in the early 1600s, leaving their lands

Wampanoag forces, nominally led by Philip (whose real name was Metacomet), suffered from chronic tribal disunity and were outnumbered by at least five to one. At the "Great Swamp Fight" near present-day South Kingston, Rhode Island, 2,000 Narragansetts were slain (many of them women and children trapped in burning wigwams) in one of the fiercest battles ever fought on New England soil. The Indian will was broken; for them, the war had been a holocaust.

For the settlers, whose initial ascetic zeal had been diluted, politics, not religion, would be the rallying call of a new era. ❑

underpopulated when the *Mayflower* landed. But, as the English settlements expanded and pushed south, friction between the two peoples was the inevitable result.

In 1636 war erupted with the Pequots (a fearsome tribe whose name means "destroyer" in Algonquian), and battles at Fort Mystic and Fairfield, Connecticut, saw several hundred lives lost on both sides. It was King Philip's War (1675–76), however, that marked the demise of Indian society in most of New England. The Nipmuc, Narragansett, and

LEFT: Roger Williams, founder of Providence.
ABOVE: King Philip's War broke the Indians' will.

LAST OF THE WAMPANOAGS

Following the Narrangansett massacre at the Great Swamp Fight in December 1675, King Philip and his allies formed raiding parties, looting and burning towns and garrisons. These attacks spread terror across New England until the settlers began to learn the art of forest warfare and Indian tactics.

These new methods, combined with a policy of withholding food supplies from all but friendly Indians, reduced Philip's forces dramatically until only a few weakened warriors remained. Philip himself was captured in July 1676 and beheaded. Wampanoag land was confiscated and the tribe ceased to exist.

BIRTH OF A NATION

The famous "shot heard around the world" signaled the start of the
American Revolution and the fight for independence

Captain Preston, a veteran of the Revolutionary War, was interviewed in 1842 by a certain Mallen Chamberlain:

Q: Were you not oppressed by the Stamp Act?
A: I never saw one of those stamps. I certainly never paid a penny for one of them.
Q: Well, then, what was the matter? And what did you mean in going in the fight?
A: Young man, what we meant in going for those Redcoats was this: we always had governed ourselves, and we always meant to. They didn't mean we should.

Struggles over home rule were not new to New England. But the northern colonies had, for the most part, been left to their own devices from the first landing at Plymouth until the dramatic Stamp Act crisis of 1765. When the mother country attempted to rein in her distant child, the reaction had been quick and biting, a portent of the more drastic rebellion that lay ahead.

Suffering serious political turmoil in the early 17th century, highlighted by the beheading of Charles I and the subsequent ascendancy of the Lord Protector, Oliver Cromwell, England had little time to attend to the governing of dissident settlers 3,000 miles from London. The Puritans gladly filled the vacuum and took on the responsibilities of *de facto* autonomy.

Even before reaching their destination, the Pilgrims signed the famous Mayflower Compact, creating a government "to enact, constitute, and frame such just and equal Laws, Ordinances, Acts, Constitutions, and offices, from time to time, as shall be thought most meet and convenient for the general good." John Winthrop and his followers carried with them their royal charter when they sailed to Massachusetts, and in 1631 the freemen of the new colony gave an oath of fidelity not to the king but to the Bay Company and its officers. The settlers agreed that if England tried to impose its own governor on them,

LEFT: the Battle of Bunker Hill, June 1776 – the first major engagement in the war with the British.
RIGHT: British colonial governor, General Thomas Gage.

"we ought not to accept him, but defend our lawful possessions."

Dominion days

Fifty-five years later, they were given the chance. In 1686, James II unilaterally revoked the northern colonies' sacred charters and con-

solidated English holdings from Maine to New Jersey into a vast Dominion of New England in America. The monarch justified his decision as a security measure, a benevolent protection from the French and Indians. The colonists knew better: who could presume that the Puritans would kowtow to a royally appointed governor? The king's first envoy, Joseph Dudley, an avid Anglican, was scorned as having "as many virtues as can consist with so great a thirst for honor and power."

His successor, Edmund Andros, was ridiculed as "the greatest tyrant who ever ruled in this country." When the new administration extorted taxes, "ill Methods of Raising money without a General Assembly," the disenfranchised populace grew more incensed.

A strong cue from England itself moved New England to action and revolt. At the "Glorious Revolution" of early 1689, William and Mary, in cahoots with Parliament, seized the throne from James II. New England spontaneously erupted; Andros and his cronies were dragged from state house to jail cell. The old powers of self-government were largely restored, along with a certain mutual respect between Crown

MOB RULE

Many of the demonstrations against the Stamp Act were peaceful, but in Boston, mobs ransacked the houses of stampman Andrew Oliver and Governor Thomas Hutchinson.

ridiculed at mock trials. Liberty was buried in symbolic funerals. Citizens of all stripes throughout New England, both of city and country, gathered to decry the new tax. Parliament, led by commoner William Pitt, took the hint and repealed the Stamp Act in March 1766.

But Britain had not learned a proper lesson. In the summer of 1767, with Prime Minister Charles Townshend boasting before the Commons, "I dare tax America," Parliament passed the Townshend Acts, impos-

and colonies. Though only three years long, the Dominion days had nonetheless decisively molded the New Englanders' political instincts.

But Hanoverian monarch George III would have a prostrate America or none at all. Britain's first *faux pas* on the road to losing its New World empire was the Revenue Act of 1764, which imposed duties on sugar, silk, and certain wines. The tax was duly denounced and boycotts proclaimed.

The infamous Stamp Act followed a year later, requiring that all commercial and legal documents, newspapers, and playing cards be taxed. The measure was fiercely assailed. Stamp distributors were hanged in effigy and

ing harsh duties on such imports as paper, glass, and tea. Two regiments of British troops landed at Boston to put some muscle behind Governor Hutchinson's waning control.

The Boston Massacre

The Redcoats were not pleasantly received. On the night of March 5, 1770, a crowd of several hundred rowdy Bostonians gathered to taunt a lone "lobster-back" standing guard outside the customs house on King Street (present-day State Street). When shouts turned to stones and snowballs, seven Redcoats came to aid the sentry. One fired into the melee without orders, others followed, and, after the smoke had cleared, three colonists lay dead (including a black man named Crispus Attucks) and two were mortally wounded. The American revolt had its first martyrs, and the growing anti-British element in New England had a field day with the nocturnal showdown.

Tempers cooled after the Boston Massacre. In the early 1770s, economic prosperity returned to the colonies. A once-again pragmatic Parliament struck down the Townshend Acts – all except one, that is. Just to make sure nobody questioned who was still boss – or king – Britain maintained the tax on East Indian tea, a not insignificant gesture given that tea was about as important as bread to the 18th-century diet.

American addicts turned to smuggled Dutch blends or to "Liberty Tea," a nasty brew made from sage, currant, or plantain leaves. The British responded by subsidizing their brand and, in September 1773, flooded the market with about half a million pounds of the "pestilential herb," with shipments to points all along the eastern seaboard. It didn't work.

Boston emerged once again as the focus of resistance. The Massachusetts Committee of Correspondence, an unofficial legislature, and the local chapter of the Sons of Liberty, a fast-growing secret society at the forefront of revolutionary activism, barred the piers and demanded that Governor Hutchinson send home the tea-laden *Dartmouth*.

When he refused, the protesters' reaction was swift and calculatedly theatrical. On December 16, 60 men (among them Sam Adams and John Hancock) disguised as Mohawk Indians and blacks descended on the *Dartmouth* and two sister ships. Boston Harbor was turned into a giant teapot as they dumped 342 crates over the railings.

The Boston Tea Party, as it came to be called, was a display of profound disrespect to Parliament and the king. Parliament responded with the so-called Coercive Acts. Most infamously, the Boston Port Act sealed off the city by naval blockade. This time, the colonies had had enough. The First Continental Congress convened in Philadelphia on September 5, 1774. Revolution was at hand.

LEFT: the British Redcoats retreat from Concord, defeated by the Minutemen.
RIGHT: the Battle of Lexington.

A shot heard round the world

An uneasy stalemate prevailed from the fall of 1774 to the spring of 1775. British garrisons controlled only the major towns. The countryside became virtually unpoliceable. New Englanders stockpiled arms and ammunition to prepare for the inevitable conflict.

The rebels didn't have to wait long for war. In early April 1775, London instructed Boston commander General Thomas Gage to quash seditious activities in rural Massachusetts, where a Provincial Congress had assumed de facto governmental control. Late on April 18, Gage accordingly dispatched a contingent of 700 soldiers to destroy

a makeshift arms depot in Concord, located 20 miles (32 km) west of Boston. At Lexington, 70 citizen soldiers, the original Minutemen (who could be summoned for duty at a minute's notice), lay in wait for the British by dawn's light, having been forewarned by the daring early morning rides of patriots Paul Revere and William Dawes.

The two forces met on the town common. A musket was fired. Minutes later, eight Americans lay dead. The unscathed Brits continued on to Concord, where the colonial militia triggered, in Ralph Waldo Emerson's words, "the shot heard round the world." The Minutemen made up for what they lacked in numbers by employing unconventional guerrilla tactics, harassing their enemies with crack sniper fire. By nightfall they had knocked off 273 British soldiers.

Sensational accounts of these skirmishes sent settlers reaching for their rifles. "The devastation committed by the British troops on their retreat," reported one, "is almost beyond description, such as plundering and burning of dwelling houses and other buildings, driving into the street women in child bed, killing old men in their houses unarmed." Among the dead bodies, the card of compromise lay discarded.

PAUL REVERE'S RIDE

Henry Wadsworth Longfellow immortalized Paul Revere's ride in his famous ballad: "Listen, my children, and you shall hear/ Of the midnight ride of Paul Revere…"

supply of ammunition. It was for this reason, and not out of bravery, that Colonel William Prescott issued his famous command: "Don't fire until you see the whites of their eyes, men."

Bunker Hill was a costly victory for the Crown, which suffered over 1,000 casualties. Optimism, seen in remarks like General John Burgoyne's "We'll soon find elbow room," was reduced to the doubting reflections of another British officer: "This victory has cost us very dear indeed… Nor do I see that we enjoy one

The first major engagement of the war, the Battle of Bunker Hill, broke out in June on the Charlestown peninsula, across the Charles River from Boston. To consolidate control of overland access to the port city, Continental Army General Artemus Ward ordered the fortification of Bunker's Hill (as it was then known), although it was actually on adjoining Breed's Hill that the Americans dug in.

The British could not allow such a build-up if they were to entertain even the faintest hope of holding Boston. On June 17, Redcoats scaled Breed's slopes twice but were rebuffed. In a desperate third attempt they succeeded, but only because the colonial force had exhausted its

solid benefit in return, or are likely to reap from it any one advantage whatever." Less than a year later, under siege by George Washington, Gage evacuated his troops to Halifax.

A few months later, on July 4, 1776, the Declaration of Independence was adopted by the Continental Congress. Of the proud signatories, 14 came from the charter states of Massachusetts, Connecticut, New Hampshire, and Rhode Island. Except for Newport, Rhode Island, not taken from the British until October 1779, the rest of New England had achieved its independence.

After the Treaty of Paris ended the Revolutionary War in 1783, the magnates of New England's prosperous cities turned to protect their newly established interests as the 13 independent colonies hammered out an integrated union. Concerned that a centralized federal government would prove as insensitive to local sentiment as had the Crown, revolutionary heroes Sam Adams and John Hancock gave only grudging support to the Constitution. Rhode Island, in more than a dozen votes between 1787 and 1789, voted down the Constitution and only ratified it after the Bill of Rights was added.

The industrial age

New England's leaders became increasingly reactionary as they went about guarding their seas and on the seas that New England's money was made. Codfish provided a lucrative export to Catholic Europe, while whaling provided oil for lighting and lubricants. New England was at the pivot of the profitable Triangular Trade: in harbors like Newport, a fleet of 350 ships unloaded West Indian molasses and reloaded with rum. From there, the rum was transported to Africa, where it was traded for slaves who were shipped to the West Indies and, in turn, traded for molasses. New England shipyards gained world fame for crafting swift, easily managed ocean-going vessels, a tradition launched even before Pilgrim settlement with

economic interests. In Massachusetts, poor hill farmers rose against the state government in Shays' Rebellion of 1786, demonstrating that genuine equality remained a dream. In 1812, fearing the loss of a thriving maritime trade, New England firmly opposed renewed and greater conflict with Great Britain.

When not calling comrades to religious or political barricades, the colonial New Englander attended to the more practical pursuit of commerce: it was both out of the

LEFT: whaling was an early source of wealth.
ABOVE: the 19th century saw improvements in transportation, including the Fall River paddle steamer.

the construction of the *Virginia* in the short-lived Popham, Maine, colony in 1607.

Although disrupted by the Revolution, maritime trade bounced back quickly, mining the riches of China and India so coveted by the early American explorers. In 1792, Boston's *Columbia* threaded the Straits of Magellan en route to Canton to trade for tea, spices, silk, and opium. The magnates of rival Salem – Elias Hasket Derby, Joseph Peabody, and Billy Gray – preferred to sail east, skirting the southern tip of Africa on frequent and successful ventures to the Orient.

But, unfortunately, the first two decades of the 19th century demonstrated how vulnerable maritime trade was to the whims of international politics. The Napoleonic Wars, President Thomas Jefferson's Embargo Acts, and the War of 1812 ("Mr Madison's War") severely hampered New England's chase after an honest, apolitical dollar. Recognizing that it is best not to put all one's commercial eggs in one flimsy basket, its merchants turned to the herald of a new industrial age.

The machine age

In the fall of 1789, a teenage Samuel Slater sailed from England to New York disguised as a common laborer. Slater departed in defiance

answer, so Quaker financier Moses Brown engaged Slater to come to Providence and put his knowledge to use. Together, they built America's first successful cotton mill on the Blackstone River at Pawtucket.

With underpaid workers kept at the grind for 70 hours a week, Pawtucket became the site of the nation's first strike in 1800. It was left to Bostonian Francis Cabot Lowell (from the family that would later produce a Harvard president, a celebrated astronomer, and three poets) to take a more enlightened approach.

During a two-year visit to England, Lowell became an avid industrial tourist and, on his

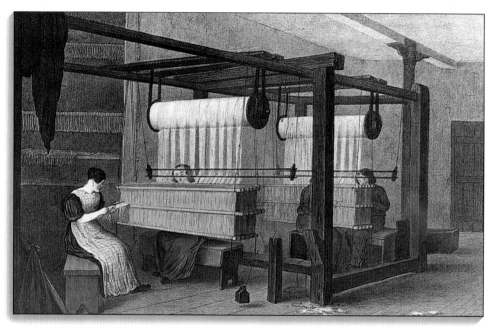

of British laws forbidding the emigration of skilled mechanics. For seven years Slater had apprenticed to Jedediah Strutt, a partner of the famed industrial innovator Richard Arkwright, and had carefully memorized the specifications of Arkwright's factory-sized, cotton-spinning machine.

In America, the reduction of raw cotton was still being done by the inefficient "put-out" system, where laborers worked in their own homes on individual looms. An early attempt at consolidating the process, a mill at Beverly, Massachusetts, had been a failure owing to the crudeness of its machinery. Arkwright's device, already proven across the Atlantic, was the

INDUSTRIAL CENTER

New England in the 19th century was the center of industrial America. The region boasted two-thirds of the nation's cotton mills, while tiny Rhode Island alone processed more than 20 percent of America's wool. In Connecticut, Sam Colt (of six-shooter fame) and Eli Whitney manufactured the first firearms to have interchangeable parts.

In the paper, shoe, and metal-working industries, New England also stood unchallenged. The Connecticut firm of Edward and William Pattison minted coins for South American governments, while Boston's Frederick Tudor made a fortune exporting ice to places as far away as India.

return to Massachusetts, he was determined to duplicate British weaving feats. Putting up $10,000 of his own money, he collected another $90,000 from the so-called "Boston Associates" – the families of Lawrence, Cabot, Eliot, Higginson, and others – to establish a small mill (with a power loom and 1,700 spindles) at Waltham.

A "commercial utopia"

Lowell died in 1817, but his plans were realized by his associates under the aegis of the Merrimack Manufacturing Company. In 1820, the mill was moved to a tract on the Merrimack River, just above the village of Chelmsford.

Paying dividends as high as 28 percent, the operation was wildly profitable. Sales went from a respectable $3,000 in 1815 to an unprecedented $345,000 in 1822. In 1826, the growing community was named after its founder.

The Merrimack Company took care of its people. Though grievously overworked by modern standards, "mill girls" enjoyed clean, safe dormitory housing and opportunities for cultural enrichment. New England's first company town was, in the words of the English novelist Anthony Trollope, "the realization of commercial utopia." Soon the efficient new factory system – if not its early paternalism – would spread up the Merrimack River to Lawrence, Massachusetts, and ultimately to the vast Amoskeag mills at Manchester, New Hampshire, destined to become the greatest producer of cotton cloth on Earth.

Life on the frontier

Not everybody shared in the boom. During the second half of the 18th century, the northern areas of New England had enjoyed a dramatic infusion of people, as land began to grow scarce in the densely populated coastal areas. More than 100 new towns were established in New Hampshire in the 15 years preceding the Revolution; between 1790 and 1800, the populations of Vermont and Maine nearly doubled.

On the craggy hillsides, the pioneers set up small farms, built their own houses and barns, and raised wheat, corn, pigs, and cattle to fill the dinner table. These rugged families

prided themselves on being almost completely self-sufficient; in fact, it used to be said of upcountry farms that all they needed to import were nails and salt. This was a new frontier, New England's frontier.

But this frontier's potential was limited by nature. The climate was inhospitable: in 1816, for instance, a June snowfall resulted in total crop failure. Agricultural machinery could not plough the irregular farmland. As for those famous New England stone walls, they were in actuality a practical by-product of what many disillusioned farmers called the region's prime produce: rocks. Property consolidation was dif-

ficult, as families jealously guarded original claims; small-scale production could not compete with more efficient new suppliers elsewhere in the United States and around the world. As far as agriculture was concerned, northern New England had seen its zenith by 1850.

After that, a slow, sapping decline attacked upland vitality. By the turn of the century, population growth had leveled and agricultural production dived. More than half of New Hampshire's farmland lay abandoned. Cheese production in Maine, New Hampshire, and Vermont fell by some 95 percent between 1849 and 1919. The California Gold Rush of 1849 drew young men from the farms. The

LEFT: new textile machinery made it possible to produce cheap cloth using low-skilled labor.
RIGHT: Old State House, Boston, around 1801.

Civil War took away even more, with veterans often heading west to seek their fortunes rather than returning to their fathers' stony acres. And girls went to the Massachusetts mills.

Cultural laurels

Long before the wheels of industry started to turn, New England minds had been establishing a cultural life unparalleled in the New World. In education, the media, the arts, and letters, America now looked to New England for guidance and inspiration. Boston led the way in the first flowering of American culture.

Colonial New Englanders had enriched their

intellectual life by founding such pioneer colleges as Harvard, Yale, Dartmouth, and Brown. As the 19th century progressed, and with the interest on their old China Trade money compounded tremendously via investment in the new manufacturing technologies, Boston's first families sponsored a new round of institutions that would lend weight to the city's position as "the Athens of America." The Handel and Haydn Society dates from 1815, the New England Conservatory of Music from 1867, and the Boston Symphony Orchestra – founded and supported for 40 years by the arch-Brahmin Major Henry Lee Higginson – from 1881. The BSO is the parent organization of the less classically-oriented Boston Pops, and makes its summer home at the renowned Tanglewood Music festival in the Berkshires.

Boston's magnificent Museum of Fine Arts (1871) evolved from a collection room on the top floor of the Boston Athenaeum – itself a great New England Institution, founded in 1807 and still one of America's premier privately-owned libraries (there are only 1,049 proprietary shareholders).

Athenaeums for all

Elsewhere in New England, Salem's Peabody and Essex Museum – founded in part as a repository of curiosities brought home by the city's far-faring merchant captains – now preserves historic homes as well. In Hartford, the Wadsworth Athenaeum was founded in 1842 by local businessman Daniel Wadsworth, and remains the nation's oldest public art museum in continuous operation ("athenaeum" was a cultural catch-all title in the 19th century; the Providence Athenaeum, once a haunt of Edgar Allan Poe, is still a private library). The future of American libraries, though, lay in the public domain. Here, too, New England was a leader: in 1854, the Boston Public Library became the world's first free municipal library.

Cradle of the Revolution, pioneer in commerce and industry, and now America's cultural capital – New England had shown its leadership in one realm after another. But as the 20th century approached, it would have to face a challenge not of invention, but re-invention. ❑

LEFT: society life in late 19th-century Boston.
RIGHT: a composite of portraits of the leaders of 19th-century manufacturing and industry.

DECLINE AND REVIVAL

Following the industrial and cultural zenith of the 18th and 19th centuries,
New England faced political corruption and economic recession

By the beginning of the modern era, New England had come to represent America's achievements and ideals – or, conversely, it could be said that America was New England writ large. The Yankee trader, the Yankee tinkerer, Yankee "know-how" were all archtypes that had their roots here. New England had been the conduit for high culture in America as well, bringing in the best of European art and ideas while helping the young republic create its own cultural persona. But no one looking at the American social and economic landscape in 1900 could doubt that the nation's energy and drive now found their sources in other places – in the dynamo of New York, in the raw busy cities of the Midwest, and even in upstart California. New England wasn't entirely played out. But its days at the vital forefront were over.

At the national political level, New England's influence diminished; locally, corruption and social divisions blemished the birthplace of American democracy and wellspring of the abolitionist and other reform movements.

Much of the trouble began with the vanishing of the ethnic and religious homogeneity which had aided the old political consensus. Uprooted by the Potato Famine of 1845–50, the Irish sailed to the land of opportunity, arriving in Boston at

land had been the conduit for high culture in America as well, bringing in the best of European art and ideas while helping the young republic create its own cultural persona. But no one looking at the American social and economic landscape in 1900 could doubt that the nation's energy and drive now found their sources in other places – in the dynamo of New York, in the raw busy cities of the Midwest, and even in upstart California. New England wasn't entirely played out. But its days at the vital forefront were over.

At the national political level, New England's influence diminished; locally, corruption and social divisions blemished the birthplace of

a rate of more than 1,000 a month. Immigrants from Quebec and throughout Europe followed: Catholics, Jews and Orthodox Christians upset Protestant homogeneity. The influx touched every corner of New England; even in backwater New Hampshire, one out of every five residents had adopted, not inherited, the American flag.

Electoral corruption

In the wake of this human shock wave, a predictable, if deplorable anti-immigrant backlash erupted among the established citizenry, whose forebears had fought so hard to achieve democracy and equal rights.

The doors of society were shut to even the

most successful of the new arrivals, and their children and grandchildren. Politically, anti-immigration groups campaigned for tightened entry requirements. In the 1850s, the openly racist Know-Nothing Party controlled governorships in Massachusetts, Rhode Island, Connecticut, and New Hampshire. Later organizations such as the American Protective Association and the Immigrant Restriction League gathered substantial memberships in their efforts to contain the electoral power of their upstart neighbors.

Collin represented Suffolk County with a congressional seat in Washington. By the turn of the century, all levels of government were being run by what was, after all, the majority of the population.

But with newfound responsibility came insidious corruption. Rhode Island, once again, was the object of biting criticism as Boss Charles Brayton and the *Providence Journal* ring bought their way to office. Individual votes cost the political machine between $2 and $5 in normal elections, as much

> **STATE FOR SALE**
>
> "The political condition of Rhode Island is notorious, acknowledged and it is shameful," deplored one journalist, Lincoln Steffens; "Rhode Island is a State for sale and cheap."

Their efforts failed. No matter how unfamiliar the immigrants were with the workings of democracy, they soon learned the power of votes well orchestrated – particularly the Irish. In 1881, John Breen of Tipperary became the first Irish-born politician to take high office as mayor of Lawrence, Massachusetts. His triumph launched fellow Irishmen not only to political influence but also to political domination. Hugh OBrien won the mayoral election in Boston three years later, and Patrick Andrew

as $30 in hotly contested ones.

Many leaders, vividly embodied in the figure of James Michael Curley, abused the privileges of solid ethnic support. Curley displayed enormous political staying-power: he was elected mayor of Boston five times in the first four decades of the 20th century; and governor of the state for one term, 1934–38. The Irish Mussolini, as his detractors tagged him, improved the economic welfare of his less privileged constituents. His imperious methods, however, were suspect. Curley doled out jobs and money to community leaders who in turn carefully steered their neighborhoods in the appropriate direction each time election day rolled around. There was

FAR LEFT: Mayor James Curley, a legend in Boston.
LEFT AND ABOVE: Boston's wharves, late 19th century.

some justification to the accusation of the critics: "This is a Republic and not a Kingdom." When the mayor went to a ball game at Fenway Park, howitzers trumpeted his arrival.

Cultural suppression

In Boston, cultural freedoms came under increasingly harsh attack as Irish Catholic activists and the Yankee heirs to the Puritan tradition found common ground. Led by Catholic leader William Cardinal O'Connell and the associated Watch and Ward Society, moralists lobbied successfully for prohibitions on

> ### BOSTON POVERTY
>
> In 1930, only 81 out of 5,030 apartments in the North End had refrigerators, and only one in two had bathrooms.

ers. It was a question of costs, specifically labor costs, and the South underbid New England. Hourly wages in New England averaged 16 to 60 percent higher than those below the Mason-Dixon line. The South also remained relatively free of labor unions, a distinct advantage to employers with bitter memories of the strikes that shut down textile mills in Lawrence, Massachusetts, in 1912 and at the Amoskeag mills in Manchester, New Hampshire, in 1922.

Owners gravitated to the cheaper workforce,

such classics as Theodore Dreiser's *An American Tragedy* and Ernest Hemingway's *The Sun Also Rises;* they also gained control over what could and could not appear on the Boston stage. "Banned in Boston!" became a double-edged term of opprobrium: the moral watchdogs took pride in it, while elsewhere in the land it actually sold books and helped pack theaters.

Migration of jobs and capital

Days of industrial glory passed. In much the same way that international competition now threatens American industrial jobs, other regions of the country challenged and overcame New England and its once-proud manufactur-

in an industrial exodus dramatically illustrated by statistical indices. Up from a mere 6 percent in 1880, the South wove almost half the nation's cotton goods by 1923. Industrial production in Massachusetts alone fell by $1 billion during the 1920s. Unemployment in factory towns left idle a quarter of the total labor pool. Gone, too, were the heady days of 28 percent dividends for the owners of Lowell's mills: expenditures in New England mills now surpassed the factories' earnings. Even the mighty Amoskeag was not immune: the great mills finally closed their doors in 1935.

New England felt the brunt of the Great Depression. In Boston it cramped even upper-class lifestyle; hardships were, of course, far more shocking in already squalid working-class quarters. Here, wages plunged by half, and unemployment jumped to almost 40 percent after the Wall Street stock market crash. By the end of 1935, nearly a quarter of Manchester's families were receiving public welfare.

Like the rest of the country, New England was jerked suddenly from the Depression by World War II. Shipyards hummed in Bath, Maine and Quincy, Massachusetts. In Hartford and Springfield and even Island Pond, Vermont, workers assembled guns for the Allied armies. But peace came to a New England that still hadn't solved its core economic difficulties – the migration of jobs to states where labor was cheaper, the aging of the manufacturing infrastructure, and a location that was at the outer corner of America's transporation network, instead of at its center.

The bulldozers move in

New England, to put it simply, was getting *old* – not merely its factories, but its cities and towns were showing their age. One remedy was renovation. Boston led the way in the 1950s, with the establishment of a redevelopment authority. Without sacrificing the charm of its venerable Beacon Hill and Back Bay neighborhoods, the Massachusetts capital set about remaking its downtown into a new landscape of civic structures, office buildings, and modern apartments.

Cities throughput New England followed suit, with greater and lesser degrees of success; from Portland, Maine to Rutland, Vermont, noble old train stations came crashing down, with the wrecker's ball tearing all too freely into the downtown streets around them. Often, the result was a bland city center of sterile office plazas and suburban-style malls. The smaller and more economically disadvantaged cities usually came out best in the long run: places like Newburyport, Massachusetts and New London, Connecticut saved their old downtowns by neglecting them until restora-

ANTIWAR RULING

The Massachusetts Supreme Court, heir to the nation's oldest democratic tradition, ruled in 1970 that its citizens couldn't be forced to fight in an undeclared war. They had the Vietnam conflict in mind.

tion and adaptive re-use had become popular. Urban renewal would have been mere window dressing without a revival of the regional economy. Salvation would have to come through exploitation of New England's particular resources – but just what might those resources be? They certainly weren't oil, gas, or minerals.

During the energy crisis of the 1970s the region was especially hard hit, and just about the only thing of value New England takes out of the ground is granite and marble

from the quarries of Vermont. Manufacturing hadn't disappeared altogether; the Bath Iron Works in Maine still builds ships for the Navy, and there are still specialty textile, footwear, and machinery factories scattered throughout the six states. But these are hardly growth industries. When New England searched for the key to future prosperity, it looked to its most protean and dependable resource of all, its people.

More precisely, it looked to people and to education, one of the oldest New England pursuits. When it became clear that the high technology and financial service sectors would become prime drivers of the American economy, New England was ready. The concentra-

LEFT: in the 1930s, many of the unemployed worked on Civilian Conservation Corps projects in camps such as this one in the Berkshires.

RIGHT: Ted Kennedy was elected to the Senate in 1962, using the slogan "I can do more for Massachusetts."

tion of colleges and universities in the Boston area provided a splendid resource at the dawn of the computer age.

This was the era of Wang laboratories and the Digital Equipment Company (now both subsumed into other corporations), of Edwin Land's Polaroid, and of Raytheon's growth in step with a military now dependent on sophisticated technology. By the 1970s, Route 128 – the beltway surrounding Boston and its inner suburbs – was touted on official road signs as "America's Technology Highway." In 1988, Michael Dukakis ran on the Democratic ticket for president, boasting of

the "Massachusetts Miracle" that had lifted his state to prosperity.

A need for new directions

In his incisive 1981 book *The Nine Nations of North America*, Joel Garreau offered a telling insight into the mentality of the boom years: "...at one point, if somebody came to the First National Bank of Boston to ask for money, and he had a government contract associated with a high-technology scheme, the loan officers had standing orders: No matter how crazy either this person or his idea seemed to be, neither could be turned down without authorization from a senior vice-president."

In a place where capital earned in the China Trade had been taught to weave cloth, and where the Harvard Business School looms large along the banks of the Charles River, those loan officers and their vice-presidents were part of another New England economic trend – the rise of the financial services industry. Boston became an investment banking capital, and the center of the mutual-fund business. Fidelity, Putnam, and MFS all headquartered here. And in Hartford, some two dozen insurance companies, dominated by titans such as Aetna, still call the Connecticut capital home.

High technology and finance, of course, have been at the core of the boom-and-bust cycle of the past two decades. Both industries flew high in the mid-1980s and late 1990s, and both caught cold when the economy sneezed in the early 2000s. Not all of the ill-fated dot-coms were based in California, and many of the dreams and fortunes that crashed with them belonged to New Englanders. But the region's economy has proven to be sufficiently broad-based to prevent the kind of protracted catastrophe that the exodus of the textile industry had created.

Of course, not everyone in New England designs computer chips or manages a mutual fund, just as the entire working population never ran power looms or shoe-stitching machines. The diversification of the region's economy ranges from the rise of "electronic cottages," in which individuals run publishing, consulting, and other businesses from their homes, to the traditional pursuits of farming, logging, and fishing.

Life hasn't been easy for people involved in those primary industries. Dairy farmers, mostly centered in Vermont, have seen their ranks dwindle as expenses spiral and milk prices stagnate. The forest products industry struggles against foreign competition; in 2003, the northern Maine town of Millinocket was shocked by the bankruptcy of its biggest employer, Great Northern Paper. And the men and women who sail out of Gloucester and other fishing ports have had nothing but bad news for the past 20 years or more – the cod stocks on Georges Bank have been drastically depleted, and restrictions on fishing mean that many boats no longer leave the harbor.

Plenty to argue about

Since the days of the earliest settlements, one of the best ways to learn what New Englanders are thinking has been to drop in at a town meeting. Naturally, these are an annual event only in smaller communities; but sometimes it seems as if all New England is one big town meeting. Every four years the debates take on a national dimension and, with the 1960 election of Massachusetts Senator John F. Kennedy as president of the United States, New England regained a place as a focus of national political attention that it hadn't enjoyed since the heyday of the Adamses, two centuries ago.

There haven't been any New England presidents since, although Massachusetts Senator John F. Kerry came close to winning the 2004

political labels worn by its leaders. (Several Maine governors in recent years have been *de facto* Independents. So is Vermont's lone congressman, Bernie Sanders, who has never made any bones about the fact that he is a socialist.)

Deep divisions

This independent streak reveals deep divisions over many issues. New Englanders have long led the way in protecting the environment, but an economic slump made jobs vs. development regulations an issue in state elections. Education is a time-honored priority, but tempers flare over financing schools via property taxes vs. broad-

election. But the New Hampshire presidential primary, always the first of the election season, forces contenders and voters alike to listen to what people are thinking about in this small corner of the nation. So do news bombshells such as the 2001 defection of Republican Senator Jim Jeffords of Vermont, who by declaring himself an Independent gave Democrats a temporary upper hand in the US Senate.

"Independent" is the operative political word in New England, regardless of the conventional

LEFT: antique tractor rally, New Hampshire.
ABOVE: famous faces from the Café du Barry mural on Newbury Street in Boston's Back Bay.

based levies. New Englanders, who provided leaders for the abolitionist and early feminist movements and sent "Freedom Riders" south during the 1960s Civil Rights struggle, now find themselves embroiled in the debate over gay rights. Vermont's 2000 establishment of "civil unions" (a form of virtual marriage) for gays and lesbians now sparks little local comment, but a Massachusetts Supreme Court ruling allowing gay marriage has met with considerable protest.

"We shall be as a city on a hill," wrote John Winthrop as his Massachusetts Bay Company embarked upon the founding of Boston in the 1630s. Winthrop felt that the world was watching, and many are watching still. ❏

THE PEOPLE OF NEW ENGLAND

New England's indomitable Puritan heritage is complemented by the pioneering spirit shared by the region's numerous immigrant ethnic groups

The product of centuries of "plain living and high thinking," New Englanders have long considered themselves the conscience of the nation. New England has contributed more distinguished legislators, writers, teachers, and thinkers to the United States than has any other region. It's true that it had a head start on the rest of America. But even after the other states had caught up in terms of population, the flow of outstanding people produced by this unpromising land never let up.

The Puritan heritage, and the region's harsh landscape and weather, have led New Englanders to view life a bit more seriously than do the residents of more forgiving cultures and climes. Although New Englanders have, as a rule, eschewed frivolity, they're quite in favor of individualism, provided that it enhances self-reliance and does not impinge on others' rights to pursue their own individual vision.

Most would consider this fierce independence to be a carryover from colonial days. However, the genius of the New England style is that it is an amalgam of all the disparate groups that have settled here and forged common bonds and goals: Native American, English, African-American, Irish, Italian, French Canadian, Latin American, Asian... The list continues to grow.

The Algonquins

New England has been inhabited for around 12,000 to 14,000 years. When the first English settlers arrived in the early 17th century, most of the native inhabitants were concentrated in Rhode Island, Connecticut, and Massachusetts. They were divided into tribes with well-established rivalries and territorial boundaries. All of Algonquin blood, they had two distinct but grammatically similiar languages, within which 13 different dialects have been identified.

PRECEDING PAGES: Red Sox legend Ted Williams (on left) and writer Bud Leavitt were avid fishermen.
LEFT: William Garrett and his Brahmin ancestor.
RIGHT: a Micmac from Connecticut.

These Algonquins were friendly to the first English settlers, who seemed far too few in numbers to represent any serious threat to their way of life. The Mohegans and Pequots of Connecticut, the Wampanoags of Massachusetts, and the Narragansetts of Rhode Island imparted their age-old hunting, fishing, farming, and

canoe-making skills to the newcomers.

But this honeymoon was to last only about 15 years. In 1636, the English waged war against the Pequots in revenge for some real or imagined Indian outrage. The Narragansetts took the fatal step of allying themselves with the English, destroying the possibility of a united native front. When the war was over, the Pequots had been obliterated. By 1670, there were 75,000 English settlers in New England and only about 10,000 Indians. The natives had sold much of their land, their settlements having been penetrated everywhere. A sizeable minority had been converted to Christianity and lived in what were called "Praying Towns."

The wars of 1675–76 marked the last desperate gasp of native resistance. In 1675, an alliance to fight the English – formed by the Wampanoag *sachem* Metacomet ("King Philip") with several smaller tribes – was crushed. Philip was caught in July the following year, and was beheaded, his body quartered, and the parts displayed in Plymouth for 24 years.

The English weren't content until the last threat of a native uprising had been eliminated. After the Pequots and the Wampanoags,

DEADLY DISEASE

In 1763, during one six-month period, 222 of the 358 natives living in Nantucket succumbed to an epidemic.

it was the Narragansetts' turn. By the time the English were through with them at the end of 1676, fewer than 70 were left out of the original 4,000 to 5,000.

Beginning of the end

The Algonquin's cultural integrity was shattered. Many fled west. Some native groups, like the Narragansetts on Rhode Island, were granted reservations. Those who stayed on the reservations never adopted European farming methods (the notion of private property was entirely foreign to their way of life); instead, they rented out their land, while eking out a meager existence from the manufacture of craft items.

These native-held territories steadily dwindled over the following two centuries; great tracts of land were sold off by the tribes or simply appropriated. Although the reservations were allowed some degree of self-government (they had, for example, their own magistrates or justices of the peace), they were also appointed nontribal overseers, who often administered to the natives' detriment.

In 1869 the Massachusetts legislature voted to end reservation status for those Indians still on reservations, and 11 years later the Rhode Island legislature abolished the Narragansett tribe as a legal entity. Their disenfranchised descendants became ordinary US citizens with no special rights – until recently, when activists began mobilizing for the restoration of tribal lands.

Most Indians did not live on reservations, however; they simply merged into the surrounding population at the lowest level of colonial society, assuming menial jobs as indentured servants or day laborers. Some signed on board whaling ships – a grueling and perilous, if colorful, livelihood. In Rhode Island, Indians gained renown for their skill in building stone walls.

For the most part, the 18th and 19th centuries saw a sad, slow decline of the old tribal associations. The colonists' diseases finished what their guns had begun, causing a continual attrition in population. The Algonquin dialects died out almost completely, and Indians in New England became so marginal that they faded out of public consciousness.

SAMSON OCCOM

Although Indians fought bravely in both the Revolutionary and Civil Wars, few outstanding figures emerged from their own ranks to guide and lead them.

An exception was Samson Occom, a Mohegan born in Connecticut in 1723. A brilliant student at Eleazar Wheelock's school for the "Youth of Indian Tribes" (which later became Dartmouth College), Occom became a vigorous Christian missionary. He was bitterly disappointed when his mentor Wheelock moved his school from Connecticut to its present location in rural New Hampshire, where, as Occom pointed out, few indigenous residents remained.

Native Americans today

According to the 2000 census, there are approximately 40,000 American Indians in New England; the number has increased in recent years as more individuals recognize their Indian ancestry. Only a minority live on the region's nine existing reservations. Indians in New England have long lived an unobtrusive, unnoticed life. In recent years, however, there has been something of a renaissance.

A new consciousness of tribal identity has taken hold in the region. It has found expression in cultural events and in attempts to right ancient wrongs. Since the 1960s, the annual 4th

now number approximately 1,500, have as yet had no success reclaiming any part of the 10,500 acres (4,250 hectares) which the Plymouth General Court accorded them in perpetuity in 1660. The Gay Head Wampanoags fared a bit better: in 1987, the federal government granted them $4.5 million for the repurchase of 475 acres (192 hectares).

The Narragansetts, a 2,400-strong tribe in southern Rhode Island, filed a similar suit in 1976; in an out-of-court settlement, they were awarded 1,900 acres (780 hectares). The 2,000 Penobscots of Maine sued the state in 1975 to recover 10 million acres (4 million hectares),

of July *powwow* of the Mashpee Wampanoag of Cape Cod, which previously had been a modest affair, has grown to include more dances, rituals, performances of music, and meetings with other tribes. In the 1970s, the Mashpee and Gay Head (Martha's Vineyard) Wampanoag communities brought suits against their respective New England towns contesting the 1869 law which, in effect, deprived Indians of their reservations. Recognized by Massachusetts but still denied their federal tribal status, the Mashpee Wampanoags, who

and reached a compromise settlement three years later. (Alone among New England tribes, the Penobscots have preserved their native tongue; about 100 speak it, and it is being taught.)

The most unusual case in recent years is of the Mashantucket Pequots in Connecticut, who in 1992 won a Supreme Court ruling to keep open their Foxwoods High Stakes and Bingo (now Foxwoods Resort Casino), which has since become the largest casino in the western hemisphere. The legal battles are far from done, but for the first time in 300 years, New England's Native Americans have begun to recoup some small portion of the losses they suffered at the hands of high-minded colonists.

LEFT: a park ranger, Ferry Beach State Park, Maine.
ABOVE: education is one of the region's big industries.

The proud Puritans

The world has rarely seen a group of immigrants quite like the New England Puritans of the 17th century. Fleeing religious persecution in England, they were fired by an extraordinary sense of mission. As the first immigrants to America, they would create a civilized society in the harsh, inhospitable New England wilderness, and they would set an example of purpose and industry for the rest of the world.

Because their motive for coming to New England was primarily religious and not economic, the Puritans were a socially diverse lot. Although most of these early comers were

peasants and artisans, an unusually large number of educated men – ministers, theologians and teachers – were among them. These learned men set a tone for the Puritan community of strict disciplined piety, with religion pervading every aspect of life.

For 200 years, New England's population consisted overwhelmingly of descendants of this tightly knit, homogeneous group and other Englishmen who followed. What Yale president Timothy Dwight said of Bostonians in 1796 could have been applied to *all* New Englanders: "They are all descendants of Englishmen and, of course, are united by all the great bonds of society – language, religion, government, man-

ners and interest." Having grown from a strictly controlled religious state to a cradle of revolutionary democratic ideas, this community was thought of as a distinctive nation-within-a-nation by other Americans at the end of the 18th century. According to Dwight, New Englanders were distinguished by their "love of science and learning," their "love of liberty," their "morality," "piety" and "unusual spirit of enquiry."

The rest of the country was more likely to characterize Yankees, as they became known, as speculators, entrepreneurs, inventors, or investors. They were men like early 19th-century Boston textile baron Francis Cabot Lowell, who established one of America's first modern factories, or members of the great Boston families that made their fortunes in Far East trade.

The "exalted" Brahmins

New Englanders considered themselves the national elite. The self-proclaimed heads of this elite were the Boston Brahmins – rich Boston families such as the Lowells, Cabots, Welds, Lodges, and Saltonstalls, who mostly secured their fortunes in the first half of the 19th century in shipping, and later in the railroad, banking, and textile industries. The name "Brahmin" is that of the priestly caste among the Hindus; it was first cited, if not originally applied, by the doctor, poet, and essayist Oliver Wendell Holmes, Sr., who wrote of a fellow Bostonian in 1860: "He comes from the Brahmin caste of New England. This is the harmless, inoffensive, untitled aristocracy."

The archetypal Brahmin attended Harvard and belonged to one of its exclusive "final clubs" such as the Porcellian or Fly; he lived on Beacon Hill or in the Back Bay, with a summer place at Beverly Farms or Manchester-by-the-Sea on the North Shore. And he (and she) is by no means extinct, but merely keeping a seemly low profile – except when called to politics like former Massachusetts governor William Weld.

Despite the fact that many of today's Brahmins hold exalted notions of the extent of their lineage, few descend from the *Mayflower* Pilgrims, from prominent Puritans of the 17th century, or even from rich merchants of the 18th century. It was the rise in trade and, eventually, industry that followed American independence that created most of their wealth. Some Brahmin families even have a few economic skeletons in their closets, having gotten rich, according to their their Irish nemesis, the late Boston mayor James Michael Curley, "selling opium to the Chinese, rum to the Indians, or trading in slaves."

Indomitable Yankees

The farther you get from from Boston, the more the Yankee image is likely to be that of a yeoman than an aristocrat. President Calvin Coolidge, a famous Vermonter, once declared at Vermont's Bennington College: "I love Vermont... most of all because of her indomitable people. They

> **HARVARD MEN**
>
> Boston Brahmin Edmund Quincy once said of the Harvard Triennial Catalog, which contained a list of all Harvard University graduates: "If a man's in there, that's who he is. If he isn't, who is he?"

torical one, although Vermont has a long tradition of idealism. When neighboring states were laying claim to its territory during the Revolution, Vermont declared itself an independent republic. It maintained this status for 14 years, during which time it declared universal suffrage (excepting women, of course) and prohibited slavery. It was the first state to do so.

New Hampshire Yankees are much like their cousins to the west, but have the reputation of being somewhat less tolerant than Vermonters,

are a race of pioneers who have almost beggared themselves to serve others. If the spirit of liberty should vanish in other parts of the Union and support for our institutions should languish, it could all be replenished from the generous store held by the people of this brave little state of Vermont."

The first inhabitants of the state were hardy trappers, and later farmers; and this has contributed to the independent characteristics of the modern Vermonter. Freedom is a personal issue for the Vermonter, not just an abstract his-

and more frugal and stubborn. Their politics are certainly more conservative: as playwright and part-time Vermonter David Mamet recently observed, early settlers traveling up the Connecticut River took a left into Vermont, and a right into New Hampshire.

The Maine Yankee was historically the most isolated inhabitant of the three northern states. Roads connecting Maine to the outside were traditionally poor. "Downeasters," as they have come to be called, had to put up with bad weather and unyielding terrain. This may explain why they're commonly characterized as crusty and quirky; they have a reputation for being down to earth and for saying little beyond what counts.

LEFT: Old Sturbridge Village guide in 1840s costume.
ABOVE: farming provides freedom but rarely wealth.

Rhode Island and Connecticut Yankees are perhaps less distinctive than other old New Englanders. The original populations of these states were the products of the first emigrations from Massachusetts, but they have since been influenced considerably – and had their own influence diminished – by their closer proximity to the Middle Atlantic states. Providence is heavily Italian; Newport became a preserve of New Yorkers; and, somewhere along the Connecticut coast, Red Sox loyalty gives way to a

> **MOTHER TONGUE**
>
> Until recently, a form of Elizabethan English was spoken in Washington County's Beals Islands in Maine, as well as in parts of Appalachia and the Ozarks.

passion for those other Yankees, pinstriped denizens of a place called The Stadium.

After the Civil War, old-line New Englanders knew their region was in decline and their numbers were dwindling. Nevertheless, they continue to think of themselves as the essential representatives of the nation's most cherished values and today remain convinced that they symbolize all that is best about their country.

African-Americans

The first African-Americans in New England came to Boston from the West Indies in 1638 as "perpetual servants." Within a century, slavery was well implanted in the region: by 1752,

Boston's 5,000 African-Americans constituted 10 percent of the population. That percentage declined dramatically during the Revolution, when Tory masters fled the region, removing their entire households. By the end of the 18th century, Massachusetts abolished slavery, and Connecticut soon followed.

In Boston, a thriving black community congregated on the northern slope of Beacon Hill. Though poor, it was organized and ambitious. About 2 percent of the population were doctors, ministers, teachers, or lawyers. Several fraternal organizations were founded to serve as a safety net for the indigent. The most famous, the African Society, founded in 1796 as a mutual-aid and charity organization, mirrored Puritan morality. Black-owned shops served as informal community centers, and black churches helped bring the community together. Ministers were looked up to as leaders, and towering above them were figures such as the anti-slavery activist Jehial C. Bemon.

Although blacks in 19th-century Boston rarely lived outside their own quarter, they did mingle freely. Black and white laborers drank together in North End taverns, and after 1855, when schools were desegregated, children of both races studied together. (Boston's tensions of the 1970s were the result of court-ordered busing to achieve racially balanced schools in otherwise homogenous neighborhoods.) Black students attended Harvard before the Civil War. Freemen laborers could be found in every New England industry, especially along the coast. Often half of crews of whaling vessels were African-American, and black labor contributed largely to the construction of Providence and New Haven.

As the vanguard of the Abolitionist movement, Massachusetts was unique in allowing blacks to stand for a political party (the Abolitionist Free-Soil Party in 1850) in elections to the state legislature. Their ability to excel was never in question, partly because of the accomplishments of such prominent figures as John Swett Rock, an abolitionist, doctor, and lawyer, and Charles Remond, the first black to argue a case before the Supreme Court. Over the past century, Massachusetts has produced an extraordinary number of Civil Rights activists.

Despite such efforts, the decline suffered by the region after the Civil War was particularly devastating to those struggling to subsist as porters, laborers, janitors and household domestics. Even well into the 1950s, few gains were made in improving the lot of this underclass. Although the number of blacks holding white-collar jobs in Boston more than doubled between 1950 and 2000, the vast majority remained poor and resolutely working class. In recent decades, Boston's black community – now representing roughly a quarter of the population – has made considerable strides, but inequities persist. Fortunately, Boston has no shortage of prominent black figures who can inspire through material success and civic accomplishment. And,

New London have neighborhoods in which blacks have lived since the 18th century.

Northern New England is overwhelmingly white, reflecting a historic absence of industrial jobs and the fact that slavery was virtually non-existent among the early settlers. In the 1990s, however, a small number of Africans, particularly Somalis in Portland and Lewiston, Maine, have settled in the region.

Irish power

The Potato Famine of 1845–50 killed at least a million people in Ireland, and drove another million to seek better conditions elsewhere.

in 2006, an African-American attained Massachusetts' top political prize when Deval Patrick was elected governor of the Commonwealth.

Connecticut and Rhode Island are the only other New England states with large and long-standing black minorities (respectively 9 and 4.5 percent of their total numbers). A small number arrived in the colonial days, and many relocated from the South in the 1870s to work on tobacco farms. Hartford, New Haven, and Bridgeport are the primary black population centers in Connecticut, but even smaller communities such as

Left: father and son at a Connecticut apple festival.
Above: Irish traditions are maintained in Boston.

Many came to Massachusetts. No precise figures are available, but one statistic claims that by 1860, 61 percent of Boston's population was foreign-born. Virtually all of these people would have been Irish, the only immigrant group to come in large numbers at that time.

The Irish did not receive a warm welcome. Not unlike the British oppressors back home, Yankees showed contempt for Catholicism, and, in turn, the Irish felt little sympathy for the idealism of the reform-minded Yankees. During the Civil War, Irish immigrants in Boston rioted when faced with a draft; the war, they felt. was about the freeing of slaves, a cause in which they had no specific interest.

The Irish community in Massachusetts grew at an extremely rapid rate. Before long, the Irish went into politics, with great success. The first Irish-born mayor of Boston was elected in 1884, and the first Irish governor took office in 1918. Between the world wars, the Irish controlled both Boston and state politics. A new economic as well as political clout was typified by Joe Kennedy, the father of the late President John F. Kennedy, who penetrated the Yankee stronghold of finance and banking on Boston's State Street.

> ### POLITICAL FAMILY
>
> The political life of the Kennedys began with John F. Fitzgerald, known as "Honey Fitz," grand-father of John F. Kennedy. He became mayor of Boston in 1905.

Middle-class Irish have long been assimi-lated into the mainstream of Boston and Massachusetts life. Especially in South Boston and Charlestown, though, blue-collar Irish have fiercely maintained the separateness both of their communities and of their ethnic iden-tity. To this day, many residents identify more with their neighborhoods than with the city as a whole.

These old patterns die hard, but if anything can change them, it is the increasing "gentrifi-cation" of the old ethnic quarters by young pro-fessionals – not necessarily Irish – and the tendency for even blue-collar workers to move to the suburbs.

French-Canadians

French-Canadians have been emigrating to New England since the middle of the 19th cen-tury. Although there are more French-Canadians in Massa-chusetts than in any other New England state, their influence is most evident in New Hamp-shire, where they make up as much as a quarter of the popu-lation; and in Maine, where – especially in the close-knit potato farming com-munities of far northern Aroostook County – 15 percent of the people are only one or two generations from Canadian birth.

The Canadians came to work in the textile mills, and (in the north) as lumberjacks and farmers. More than any other group in New England, they have clung to their ethnic identity and maintained a remarkable degree of distinc-tiveness. They are strongly Catholic, and there are still many who grew up speaking French at home. Use of the mother tongue is fading now, as is observance of traditional celebrations such as the June 24 feast of St. Jean Baptiste, patron saint of Quebec. But there is a renewed interest among the young in learning French, and in preserving folkways such as the characteristic Quebec styles of fiddling and clog-dancing.

The Italian and Jewish influx

Italians came to the United States in the first decades of the 20th century, most of them as poor peasants from southern Italy and Sicily. Many of them settled in Massachusetts and Rhode Island, and a distinctive community of mostly northern Italians brought their stone-cutting and carving skills to the granite center of Barre, Vermont. Despite the incursions of gentrification, Italians have managed to pre-serve a distinctive village subculture in certain areas, such as Boston's North End and East Boston and the Federal Hill neighborhood of Providence.

The Italians quickly climbed the economic ladder, making their money in law, real estate, construction, and a variety of other businesses. Like the Irish, they found their way into poli-tics. The success of the Italian community in Rhode Island is reflected in the career of the late John O. Pastore, the first Italian-American governor, later a senator. In Massachusetts, the Italian community has produced two governors,

Foster Furcolo and Paul Cellucci (later U.S. ambassador to Canada), and a mayor of Boston, Thomas Menino. Connecticut's first woman governor, the late Ella Grasso, was also of Italian descent.

Jewish settlers were among the earliest colonists: a community was established in Newport, Rhode Island, in 1658, with the help of Puritan dissident Roger Williams. The first families, from Holland, were Sephardics, descendants of exiles expelled from Spain at the end of the 15th century. Nineteen years after arriving in Newport, they organized North America's second congregation (the first was in New York). Free of the restrictions imposed on them in the Old World, they prospered in Newport.

The Newport community began to dissolve around the beginning of the 19th century as members emigrated to other parts of the country. For 100 years, there was little Jewish presence in New England, mainly because of the intolerance and rigidity of the Protestant Yankees. But by the end of the century, Boston had become a much more ethnically and religiously diverse place, and so Jews from Eastern Europe began to settle there in large numbers. Jews struck out for the New England hinterlands as well, often with hard-working peddlers in the vanguard. In the next generation, their families became shopkeepers, and Jewish names can still be seen on storefronts throughout small-town New England.

By 1910, 42,000 East Europeans, mostly Jewish, lived in the Boston area. Ten years later 10 percent of Boston's population was Jewish. Jews have made their mark in New England, notably in education: one-third of the Harvard faculty is Jewish.

Other late arrivals

New England has pockets of small ethnic groups which contribute greatly to the region's diversity. As in the rest of America, its new citizens are now drawn heavily from Asia, Latin America, and the Mideast. Every New England city has a sizeable Hispanic community; in

BRANDEIS UNIVERSITY

In 1948, Brandeis University was established in Waltham, near Boston. This was thanks largely to the fund-raising efforts of the Jewish business community.

Holyoke, Massachusetts, Hispanics make up more than 40 percent of the population. There has been a Chinese quarter in Boston for much of the past century, but today there are Chinese – and, increasingly, Vietnamese – immigrants in all parts of the region. There are Syrians and Lebanese in Rhode Island, Armenians in Worcester and Watertown, Massachusetts, and Bosnian and Sudanese immigrants in Burlington, Vermont. Greek-Americans live throughout the area, with particularly strong representation

in Lowell, Massachusetts, where a sizable Cambodian population has also helped transform the old mill town.

Portuguese communities exist along the coast, in such fishing ports as New Bedford and Provincetown. These Portuguese arrived in the middle of the 19th century from the Azores, as whaling hands picked up by American ships. When whaling foundered, they shifted to fishing and into the textile mills.

The social and economic transitions may not always be easy, but the presence of these groups signals how a region once regarded as inflexible has been enriched by an ever expanding ethnic diversity. ❑

LEFT: Italian immigrants have had a major impact on both outdoor and indoor catering.
RIGHT: Boston has a lively Chinatown.

THE PURITAN TRADITION

The Puritans regarded discipline and hard work as spiritual values, and it was those characteristics which laid the firm foundations of New England

The Puritans did more than settle New England; they created it. Out of the Calvinistic doctrines regarding humanity's inherent evil and the predestination of the soul grew a society that was stern and uncompromising. At its best, the Puritans' was a hard creed, an ultimate faith that required everyone

– from the most prominent minister to the humblest child – to strain toward an ineffable God. Puritans argued that humans, in their fallen state, could never know God and could thus never truly know the state of their own souls. Salvation came not through human action, but through God's mysterious grace. Abject though we human creatures may be, we must always examine our conscience, always repent our inevitable sin, always attempt to lead a just life.

Spiritual values

The Puritans' difficult faith stood them in good stead: regarding discipline and hard work as spiritual values, these early settlers labored long for the greater glory of God – and incidentally accumulated considerable wealth and built prosperous communities. At their worst, the Puritans came to identify worldly success with godliness, nonconformity with devil-worship. Their faith found little room for gentleness or pleasure.

In America, as in England, class distinctions were important. But the Puritans, eschewing such worldly signs of status as expensive clothes and fancy carriages, had to devise other more subtle ways of indicating social class. Thus, the title "Master" was reserved exclusively for educated men.

The search for perfection

Education was essential to the Puritans' vision of what their new society in America was to be. Most of the settlers were well educated; four officers of the Massachusetts Bay Colony – John Winthrop, Sir Richard Saltonstall, Isaac Johnson, and John Humphrey – had attended Cambridge University. For them, the journey to the New World was more than an adventure to a new frontier; it was a chance to transport their old society in purified form to a new land. Discontented in a country where they were persecuted for their religious practices, they came to America to build an ideal society, their "city on a hill." These men knew that unless they provided for the education of clergymen, they might quickly lose sight of the New (and perfect) England.

A society in which education established one's credentials before God and the world was destined to develop an impressive school system. As early as 1635, Boston voted a declaration that "our brother, Mr Philemon Pormont shall be intreated to become scholemaster for teaching and noutering of children with us."

Pormont established Boston Latin School, the country's first secondary school and still one of Boston's finest high schools. And with the goal of educating a native New England ministry still in view, Massachusetts Bay Colony officials chartered the institution that was to become

Harvard College in 1636. Harvard was the first of a succession of New England colleges founded upon strong religious foundations but destined to provide a secular education for future generations *(see pages 69, 127).*

Salem's obsession

A far less benign expression of Puritan didacticism emerged in the Salem witch trials of 1692. Since its founding in 1626, the town (whose name derives, ironically, from *shalom*, the Hebrew word for peace) had never been a bastion of tolerance and good will: it was from Salem that Roger Williams, the founder of Rhode Island, had been exiled for preaching religious freedom.

The townspeople's rigid ways took a destructive turn when Tituba, a Barbados slave serving the household of Salem's minister, Samuel Parris, began regaling his daughter, Elizabeth, and niece, Abigail Williams, with vivid accounts of voodoo. Fascinated, Elizabeth and Abigail invited a handful of their friends to listen to Tituba's tales.

Meetings of such a nature, being strictly forbidden in Puritan Salem, held an illicit appeal that the girls must have found difficult to resist, but no doubt they also found their guilty pleasure difficult to live with, for all soon began to exhibit bizarre behavior: they would crawl on the floor, making choking sounds, and cry out that needles were piercing their flesh. The town doctor was called in to examine the girls and, after medicine failed to cure them, he diagnosed them as victims of witchcraft.

The Rev. Mr Parris suggested that Tituba might be their tormentor, and the slave was charged with witchcraft. In confessing, under pain of torture, she gave a lurid account of how a tall man from Boston, accompanied by witches, had molested the girls.

Satan himself, she claimed, had ordered her to murder the girls, and other witches had beaten her for her refusal to comply; she merely tormented them, trying to abate her own pain. In her stories, she pointed a finger at two women unpopular in the village, Sarah Osborne and Sarah Good, who were charged

THE CRUCIBLE

Arthur Miller's celebrated 1953 play, *The Crucible,* is based on the Salem witch trials.

with everything from bewitching cattle to using voodoo dolls. Enflamed by the oratory of such self-promoting preachers as Cotton Mather, subsequent accusations spread like wildfire. Ultimately, 400 people ended up accused – many of them marginal members of society, whose lack of prosperity the Puritans took to mean a lack of godliness.

Imprisoned in cold, damp cells, several of the accused women died while awaiting trial. Of those found guilty in Salem, 19 were hanged and one man was pressed to death beneath a

wooden plank piled with rocks. These executions took place between June and September, and the terror might have continued through the fall had Governor General Sir William Phips not returned from the north woods, where he had been fighting an alliance of French and Native Americans, and put a stop to the madness. In December 1692, he ordered all the suspects released – including his own wife.

Always ready to discover depravity in someone else, the Puritans sat in eager judgment on the accused. Unrelenting in their desire to purge their world of evil and in their arrogant belief in their own righteousness, they sent innocents to their death. Too late, the Salemites repented

LEFT: guns and God – early settlers go to worship.
RIGHT: John Winthrop, the Cambridge-educated Puritan leader who aimed to build an ideal society.

of their actions: in 1693, the Salem jurors wrote that they begged the forgiveness of everyone who had been harmed by their actions.

A transcendentalist manqué

The gradual liberalization of New England's churches and colleges in the 18th century gave way to a true intellectual flowering in the 19th century. Flushed with the success of the Revolutionary War and the founding of the nation, growing prosperous from the lucrative China trade, the Puritan temperament was ready for a transformation. Many New Englanders were embracing the doctrines of Unitarianism, which

Thoreau's solitary retreat on Walden Pond, and short-lived communal farms at Brook Farm in Concord and Fruitlands in Harvard. Led by Ralph Waldo Emerson, the transcendentalist movement attracted some of the brightest minds of the day.

Cradle of reformation

As if to live down the small-mindedness of their predecessors, the New England philosophers and legislators of the 19th century stood in the very vanguard of political reform. Having abolished slavery themselves by the end of the 18th century, high-minded New Englanders

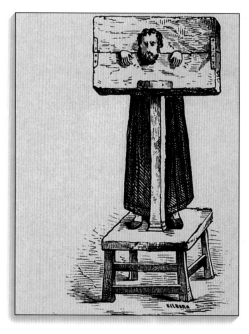

taught that God was a single rather than tripartite entity, and rejected such old Calvinist mainstays as predestination and the innate baseness of the human personality. Henry Ware, who founded Harvard's Divinity School in 1819, was a Unitarian, as was the great Boston pastor William Ellery Channing. Unitarianism's liberal cast of thought prepared the ground for the sweet optimism of transcendentalism, a mystical philosophy which argued the existence of an Oversoul unifying all creation, and which preached the primacy of insight over reason and the inherent goodness of humankind.

The movement spawned several experiments in living, the best known being Henry David

dedicated themselves to nationwide abolition. William Lloyd Garrison founded his weekly newspaper the *Liberator* in Boston in 1831 (not all shared his views at that time: he was nearly killed by a Boston mob in 1835) and persisted until 1865, when the 13th amendment was finally passed. Joining him in the struggle were writers such as Harriet Beecher Stowe, who delivered one of the Abolitionist movement's most effective tracts in the form of her best-selling 1852 novel, *Uncle Tom's Cabin*.

After the Civil War, New England's reformists turned their attention to the labor abuses brought on by the Industrial Revolution and to the role of women in society. The first women's college to open in the US was Vassar Female College, founded in Poughkeepsie, New York, in 1861. By 1879, four outstanding colleges for women had been established in Massachusetts: Smith, Wellesley, Mount Holyoke, and Radcliffe.

PURITANISM'S LEGACY

The early Puritans' moralism and sense of an elect people guided by God can still be sensed today.

Despite this growing willingness to entertain change – reinforced by decades of stability and prosperity – remnants of the Puritan strain persisted. For the most part, New England remained a deeply moral, and occasionally moralistic, society. At their worst, New Englanders banned books they

must wait till noon to be served at a bar, and liquor stores (called "package stores" hereabouts) must close on Sundays – except during the Thanksgiving to New Year's Day holidays season, and unless they are within 10 miles (16 km) of Vermont or New Hampshire, two states whose state-run liquor stores take a bite out of Massachusetts retailers' profits. Sound business practice, don't forget, is another Puritan desideratum.

What, then, is the true Puritan legacy? It's easy to grumble about arcane liquor laws, or to

deemed offensive to public taste (a practice their descendants now deplore among less enlightened, fundamentalist backwaters). They considered theater – and, worse yet, actors – a pernicious influence on impressionable minds.

Blue laws, first introduced in Connecticut in 1781 to control public and private conduct, especially on the Sabbath, enjoyed regular revivals in the 19th and 20th centuries and linger to this day in very watered-down form; in Massachusetts, for instance, would-be imbibers

FAR LEFT: a pillory, designed for public humiliation.
LEFT AND ABOVE: the trials of Mrs Hutchinson (left) and George Jacobs in the era of Puritan hysteria.

see the cold hand of Puritanism in each new dictum about what we should and shouldn't eat. And it's hard to argue with H. L. Mencken's famous quip that a Puritan is someone tormented by the fact that someone, somewhere, is having fun. But New England wasn't going to get settled by people out to have fun; the soil and the climate would not have cooperated.

As for the Puritan sense of rectitude and moral improvement, it survives today in activist movements – strong in new England – dedicated to social change and the environment. Ironically, the Puritans' conservative zeal lives on in what has become one of the country's most progressive regions. ❏

THE LITERARY TRADITION

The fascination with the supernatural that inspired Cotton Mather in the 17th century is echoed today in the work of Stephen King

The Massachusetts Bay Colony was barely 10 years old when its first printing press turned out a new edition of the Book of Psalms. The 1640 *Bay Psalm Book* represented not only the beginning of American printing, but, as it was a fresh translation, of American literature as well. Along with Scriptures and

sermons, 17th-century New England writers favored histories and biographies extolling the Puritan experiment. Governors William Bradford of Plymouth and John Winthrop of Massachusetts Bay both wrote the stories of their colonies. Edward Johnson called his 1653 history *The Wonder-Working Providence of Scion's Saviour*, reflecting the belief that America was a place reserved by God for his chosen people – the Puritans.

The religious strain in early New England writing is nowhere more pronounced than in Nathaniel Ward's *The Simple Cobbler of Agawam* (1647). Ward, a minister at the Massachusetts town of Ipswich (then Agawam),

sounded the clarion note of Puritan intolerance with his words: "If the devil have his free option, I believe he would ask nothing else, but liberty to enfranchise all false religions."

Increase Mather was a prolific writer who used historical narrative to elevate (or at least frighten) the New England faithful. In *An Essay for the Recording of Illustrious Providences* (1684) he told of the Devil tormenting Massachusetts villagers, and credited a Connecticut RIver flood as "an awful intimation of Divine displeasure." His son, Cotton Mather, was author of more than 400 works, and a dogged chronicler of supernatural manifestations. His 1689 *Memorable Providences, Relating to Witchcrafts and Possessions* helped set the stage for the 1692 Salem witch hysteria.

New England did produce two poets of merit in the 17th century. Anne Bradstreet, who arrived with the first settlers of Boston in 1630, collected her early work in *The Tenth Muse Lately Sprung Up in America* (1650). At first reliant upon contemporary British models and stock poetic themes laced with religion, she later found inspiration in her own life experiences.

Edward Taylor, a Massachusetts pastor, was the finest 17th-century American poet. His religious meditations have been compared to the English metaphysical poetry of his era; and his observations on commponplace subjects, as in "To a Spider Catching A Fly," reveal a talent for observation and terse description that transcends their purpose as religious metaphor.

Secular pressures

Although the early 18th century in New England is remembered as the age of Reverend Jonathan Edwards and his staunch religious orthodoxy – his famous 1741 sermon "Sinners in the Hands of an Angry God" must have made his congregation's blood run cold – it was also an era in which secular concerns became a part of the colonial life of letters. In Boston, James Franklin (brother of Benjamin) published one of New England's first successful newspapers, the *New England Courant*, beginning in 1721.

The *Courant* introduced the urbane essay style of Addison and Steele to the American colonies. Isaiah Thomas began publishing his *Massachusetts Spy* in 1770, largely as a vehicle for growing revolutionary sentiments.

The early Federal period in new England was the age of the "Connecticut Wits," a coterie noted for their Federalist politics and fondness for formal Augustan poetry. Among them were lawyers John Trumbull and Joel Barlow, and longtime Yale president Timothy Dwight.

> **QUOTES FROM EMERSON**
>
> There is properly no history; only biography.
>
> To be great is to be misunderstood.
>
> A foolish consistency is the hobgoblin of little minds.
>
> I hate quotations. Tell me what you know.

reflecting the new romantic feeling in English poetry, but for presaging the influential role that nature would play in the Transcendentalist movement of the coming decades.

The Golden Age

The era which critic Van Wyck Brooks called "the flowering of New England" began with the 1836 publication of an essay called "Nature," by Ralph Waldo Emerson, a young clergyman from Concord, Massachusetts. Emerson, a Unitarian,

The best remembered of their works is Barlow's *The Hasty Pudding*, a mock-heroic tribute to the simple cornmeal concoction that still appears on New England menus as "Indian Pudding."

Although he made his fame in New York City as a newspaper editor, Massachusetts-born William Cullen Bryant was still a New Englander when, in 1811, he wrote the first draft of his poem "Thanatopsis" (published 1817, expanded 1821) at the age of 17. "Thanatopsis" (Greek, "a view of death") is noteworthy not only for

---

LEFT: Cotton Mather, who wrote more than 400 works.
ABOVE: Ralph Waldo Emerson addressing a philosophy school in Concord and posing for a formal photograph.

found in that denomination's liberal humanism a cornerstone for the philosophy of Transcendentalism. The Transcendental movement emphasized the unity of the individual soul with the rest of creation and with the divine; its principles informed Emerson's poetry and essays such as "Self-Reliance," as well as the work of Bronson Alcott (father of *Little Women* author Louisa May Alcott), Margaret Fuller, and Jones Very.

Emerson owned land just outside Concord, on Walden Pond, and it was here that his friend Henry David Thoreau built a cabin and spent two years living the life of rustic simplicity and contemplation which he chronicled in *Walden* (1854). Thoreau coupled the Transcendentalist's near-mystical sense of the oneness of man and nature with a naturalist's eye for observation, as in *A Week on the Concord and Merrimack Rivers* and *The Maine Woods*; and with the fierce independence of conscience that blazes in his seminal essay "Civil Disobedience."

Even if no longer strictly Puritan in their theology, New Englanders like Thoreau brought the Puritan's moral rectitude to the greatest national drama of their day, the struggle over slavery. The abolitionist movement had deep roots in New England, home of William Lloyd Garrison and his uncompromising newspaper *The Liberator*, of *Uncle Tom's Cabin* (1852) author Harriet Beecher Stowe, and of John Greenleaf Whittier, a Quaker poet devoted to the cause. Whittier, though, is today remembered less as an abolitionist than as one of the "fireside poets" of the post-Civil War years. Working in genres such as the pastoral (Whittier's 1866 "Snow-Bound") and historical narrative (Henry Wadsworth Longfellow's "Evangeline" and "The Song of Hiawatha," published respectively in 1847 and 1855), these now largely neglected figures gave their contemporaries a common popular literature, often read aloud at the fireside. Theirs was a genteel tradition sustained by writers such as Oliver Wendell Holmes, Sr., a prolific poet and author of the droll essays collected in *The Autocrat of the Breakfast-Table* (1858), and poet James Russell Lowell, who with Holmes was a founder of Boston's still-influential *The Atlantic Monthly*.

One of the finest New England poets lived a secluded life in Amherst, Massachusetts, far from literary salons. Emily Dickinson had a gemcutter's way with language, crafting more than 1,000 short lyric poems in which sharp observation of the material world was a prism for the timeless and universal. She shunned publication, and the first volume of her work didn't appear until 1890 – four years after her death.

> **QUOTABLE HOLMES**
>
> Oliver Wendell Holmes, Sr, wrote:
> I found this great thing in this world is not so much where we stand, as in what direction we are moving.
> Old age is 15 years older than I am.

LEFT: Nathaniel Hawthorne.
RIGHT: *Moby-Dick* and its author, Herman Melville.

NATHANIEL HAWTHORNE

The descendant of Salem Puritans, Hawthorne (1804–64) grew up with a family legend of a Judge Hawthorne who, as a magistrate at the witchcraft trials, was cursed by a woman he convicted. Hawthorne would later use this story in *The House of the Seven Gables*. In fact, much of Hawthorne's work was drawn from real life. In the 1836 tale, *The Minister's Black Veil*, the protagonist explains: "If I hide my face for sorrow, there is cause enough, and if I cover it for secret sin, what mortal might not do the same." Hawthorne was no doubt familiar with the story of the Rev. Joseph Moody of York, Maine, who, after accidentally shooting and killing a friend on a hunting trip, became morbidly frightened of having his friend's family and fiancée look upon him, and therefore covered his face with a black handkerchief.

Young Goodman Brown, one of Hawthorne's greatest tales, also draws on his Salem heritage. In what may be a dream, Brown, wandering in the dark forest, comes upon the devil, who leads him to a clearing where villagers are engaged in devil-worship; among the congregation is Faith, Goodman's wife. In this tale, Hawthorne depicts a world sunk in evil: if Goodman Brown's vision is true, the devil rules; if not, and if Goodman has imagined innocent people in Satan's service, he reveals, like the Salem Puritans, the depth of his own corruption.

The two New England giants of American literature in the mid-19th century defy any association with a school or movement of their day. Nathaniel Hawthorne *(see panel)* had an early flirtation with Transcendentalism and radical communalism (his *The Blithedale Romance* is based in part on the Brook Farm commune is Massachusetts), but he was far too independent a figure to fit comfortably into the Concord where he spent part of his early career. Hawthorne mined the annals and mores of Puritan New England for the themes of guilt and consequence that inform *The Scarlet Letter* (1850) and *The House of the Seven Gables* (1851). Henry James wrote of *The Scarlet Letter:* "Something might at last be sent to Europe as exquisite in quality as anything that had been received, and the best of it was that the thing was absolutely American... it came out of the very heart of New England." Hawthorne's short stories, many in a deep allegorical vein, are often set in a mythic Puritan past.

Herman Melville *(see panel below)* was born in New York City, but spent much of his working life in New England. His masterpiece, *Moby-Dick*, employs the New England settings of New Bedford and Nantucket, both important whaling ports in the 19th century,

HERMAN MELVILLE

At the age of 20, Melville set sail on a packet to Liverpool in England, and two years later, in 1841, traveled to the South Seas on the whaler *Acushnet.* Although he later jumped ship to join the US Navy, it was to be a life-changing voyage, for it provided him with his first successful books, *Typee or a Peep at Polynesian Life* (1846) and *Omoo: A Narrative of Adventures in the South Seas* (1847).

He married Elizabeth Shaw, whose father was chief justice of Massachusetts, and they had four children. He continued to write sea stories, mostly because he needed to earn money, but he was inspired by the dark genius of Nathaniel Hawthorne to attempt the epic narrarive that

became *Moby-Dick, or The Whale* (1851). This masterpiece, written while he was living in Pittsfield, Massachusetts, draws upon the character of Yankee whalers Melville met during his own time in the "fishery" but the tale of Captain Ahab's relentless pursuit of the whale that had bitten off his legs assumes allegorical overtones as the crew of the *Pequod* are carried to their doom by Ahab's monomania.

Like much of his work, *Moby-Dick* was better received in England than in America. After a breakdown, Melville visited Hawthorne in Liverpool, where Hawthorne was serving as American consul. Later he worked as a customs officer in New York harbor. He died in 1891, his work largely forgotten.

Indian Summer

The post-Civil War "Indian Summer" of New England literature was the era of William Dean Howells, a midwesterner who edited *The Atlantic Monthly* and made Boston the setting of *A Modern Instance* (1882) and *The Rise of Silas Lapham* (1885), both of which deal with men on the make in a city flush with prosperity.

Henry James (1843–1916), who was in his mature period as much a British as an American writer, set many of his short stories in Boston's upper-class society, which also provided the milieu for *The Europeans* (1878) and for *The Bostonians* (1886), James's satire

on the city's radical and reformist circles.

The late 1800s also saw the rise of the Regional movement in American literature, represented in New England by figures such as Sarah Orne Jewett, a novelist of coastal Maine; and Rowland Robinson, a Vermonter with a sharp ear for the dialect of upcountry Yankees and French-Canadian immigrants.

And it was an age that saw one writer who belonged to a world far from New England happily set down roots in the region: Mark Twain built a sprawling mansion in Hartford, Connecticut, and transported a representative native of the state to medieval England in *A Connecticut Yankee in King Arthur's Court.*

Modern trends

By 1900, New England had long since ceased to be the most socially and economically vigorous part of the United States, but it still provided fertile ground for writers. Edward Arlington Robinson (1869–1935) drew upon characters of his native small-town Maine to create incisive portraits of often darkly conflicted individuals. Robert Frost (1874–1963), born in California of an old New England family but a resident of rural Vermont and New Hampshire for much of his life, created a universal language out of dry, economical Yankee speech. On the surface, his poems have the appeal of bucolic simplicity, but

he was no fireside poet – his was a spare and bittersweet estimation of life.

In the theater, Eugene O'Neill (1888–1953), brought up partly in Connecticut and associated as a young man with the Provincetown Players on Cape Cod, offered the bleak *Desire Under the Elms* and the uncharacteristically comic *Ah, Wilderness,* both with New England settings.

Local fiction in the 20th century ranged from John P. Marquand's skewering appraisal of the Boston Brahmin class run to ground in *The Late George Apley* (1937) to philosopher George Santayana's darker analysis of a similar scion of the old order in *The Last Puritan* (1936). John Cheever may have moved from his native

Massachusetts to New York, but his morally struggling suburbanites traded heavily in the old New England themes of guilt and redemption; John Updike, a New Englander by choice, presented the quandaries of his characters in early novels and stories set in the suburbs of Boston. And, far from the middle class of Cheever and Updike, Jack Kerouac set several autobiographical novels in the French-Canadian quarter of his native Lowell, Massachusetts.

Recent trends are more diffucult to trace, as the region – with its scores of colleges and universities, and its many writers' workshops – has attracted authors not necessarily rooted in the

decaying Maine mill town. John Irving, who lives in Vermont, made the quirks of New Englanders part of *The Hotel New Hampshire* (1981) and *The Cider House Rules* (1985). Howard Frank Mosher, also a Vermonter, lovingly portrays the vanishing world of the backcountry yeomen and eccentrics of the state's remote Northeast Kingdom in *Where the Rivers Flow North* (1978) and *Northern Borders* (1994).

And up in Bangor, in a big Victorian house behind an iron fence festooned with bats and spiderwebs, lives a native son who uses nondescript Maine settings while scaring his readers out of their wits. His name is Stephen King. ❏

region and its traditional concerns. Even a small state like Vermont can boast internationally recognized names such as Julia Alvarez, Jamaica Kincaid, and David Mamet. Native or not, though, many writers fasten quickly to New England locales and themes. Boston lawyer George V. Higgins gave us the rough side of his city's life and language via *The Friends of Eddie Coyle* (1972). In *Empire Falls* (2001) Richard Russo serves up his characters in the matrix of a

---

FAR LEFT: Mark Twain, master storyteller.
LEFT: John Irving with his Oscar for adapting *The Cider House Rules* for Hollywood.
ABOVE: Stephen King, pictured with bike in 1986.

STEPHEN KING'S MAINE

King has done for his native Maine, say critics, what Dickens did for Victorian London, and fans of the prolific writer have fun trying to identify the real-life locations that turn up, thinly disguised, in his creepy tales. Indeed, there's a nascent Stephen King Trail, taking in Kezar Lake, near Lovell (Dark Score Lake in *Bag of Bones*), Bridgton (setting for *The Mist* and *The Body*), Hampden (*Carrie*), Orrington (*Pet Sematary*), Long Lake (*The Shining*) and Durham (*Salem's Lot*). King has a summer lodge near Lovell and an old lumber baron's mansion near Bangor (a town disguised as Derry in *IT*). To locate the mansion, look for a locked gate decorated with a bronze vampire.

THE TRADITION OF EDUCATION

What cars are to Detroit, so colleges are to Boston. Not only do they help give
New England its character, they also bring in billions of dollars a year

New England is the cradle of American education, and the home of many of the nation's oldest and most distinguished institutions of higher learning. Four of the colleges and universities that make up the storied "Ivy League" – Harvard, Yale, Brown, and Dartmouth – are located here, as are scores of

smaller colleges and six respected state universities. But although the popular perception of education in New England tends to focus on the most elite collegiate institutions, the region's commitment to learning began at a far humbler level.

In an age when literacy was largely a luxury, the religious reformers who created the first settlements in New England firmly believed that every church member – every citizen, in other words – should be able to read Scripture. There was a secular tradition of education, as well. In post-Reformation England, grammar schools that taught Latin and some Greek were common, and many of the Puritan settlers had

attended them. One of the organizers of the Massachusetts Bay Colony, John White, had been the schoolmaster of the Free School at Dorchester, in the west of England, a place from which many of the colonists hailed.

By 1639, Boston and its neighboring communities of Charlestown and Dorchester (now both part of the city) had hired schoolmasters. The communities along the seacoast north of Boston followed, as did the towns the Plymouth colony and Connecticut. (Curiously, Rhode Island lagged well behind in establishing public schools.) New England's first school legislation was a 1642 act making parents and masters of indentured servants responsible for teaching their charges "to read and understand the principles of religion and the capital laws of the country."

Making it legal

Five years later, in 1647, the Massachusetts Bay Colony took the first step in institutionalizing public education. A new law required every town of 50 or more families to to appoint a schoolmaster, to be paid either by the parents or the town (either way, this legislation probably launched the ancient American tradition of grumbling about school taxes). Towns of 100 or more families had to "set upon a Grammar-School, the masters thereof being able to instruct youth so far as they may be fitted for the University." Where Massachusetts Bay led, the other colonies followed. By 1672, all – except Rhode Island – had adopted systems of compulsory elementary education.

It isn't easy to tell how effective the education statutes were in promoting literacy in New England. But measuring literacy in the simplest terms, as the ability of an individual to sign his or her name, one study of official documents from late 17th-century Massachusetts and Connecticut reveals that some 95 percent of the population could manage to put their signatures on deeds and court papers, as opposed to simply signing with an "X". Any such survey is skewed, of course, by the fact that poorer people, less likely to be educated, would have little reason to ever sign anything. And a much higher percentage of women "made their mark" instead of signing their names, since few girls were schooled outside the home.

Writing, though, was in those days taught after reading. It is fair to assume that a majority of early New Englanders were able to pick out passages from the big family Bibles that were often a household's only book.

When that 1647 Massachusetts statute required masters who could "instruct youth so far as they may be fitted for

TWAIN SPEAKING

In New York, said Mark Twain, they ask how much money a man has; in Philadelphia, what family he's from; in Boston, how much he knows. Twain bought a house in Hartford, Connecticut.

Rev. John Harvard left his personal library of 400 books and half of his estate to the new college, which would thereafter bear his name.

Although it was technically not a religious but a civic institution, Harvard College served primarily to train ministers throughout the 17th century – a century which saw only 465 documented graduates. It wasn't until 1708 that a layman was elected president. Harvard's greatest strides were taken during the four-decade presidency of Charles William

the University," there was only one "University" that the lawmakers had in mind. In October of 1636, the Great and General Court of Massachusetts Bay had appropriated the sum of £400 for "a schoale or colledge," which was established the following year at New Town, across the Charles River from Boston. The first class assembled two years later, and around the same time New Town was renamed Cambridge in honor of the English University city.

In that same year of 1638, a young minister in nearby Charlestown died of consumption.

LEFT: fencing at Yale in the early 20th century.
ABOVE: Cambridge colleges in 1743.

Eliot (1869–1909), who introduced the elective system, modernized the teaching of law and medicine, and created a graduate school of arts and sciences. Born into an old Boston family himself, Eliot did more than any Harvard educator to elevate the university beyond its one-time status as a school largely attended by the local Brahmin class.

In Connecticut, a group of 10 clergymen met in 1701 to found an institution called the "Collegiate School," which was located at first in Saybrook but in 1716 moved to the larger community of New Haven. Their impetus was in part a reaction against the perceived liberalization of the Harvard curriculum. The Collegiate

School, too, soon benefitted from a philanthropic gesture – not from the modest will of a churchman but from an immensely wealthy, Boston-born ex-governor of the East India Company. His name was Elihu Yale, and so generous were his donations to New Haven's fledgling school that it was named in his honor in 1718.

New England's third-oldest college was the fruit of a growing ecumenical spirit in a region once dominated by the Puritans' Congregationalist denomination. It isn't

surprising that a representative of the relatively new Baptist sect should have chosen to establish a college in Rhode Island, a colony devoted from its infancy to religious freedom. Rev. James Manning secured a charter for a "College of Rhode Island" in 1764, arranging that not only Baptists, but Congregationalists and Episcopalians would be represented in its corporation as well. Established on its College Hill campus in Providence by 1770, the college counted among its 1783 class of 15 graduates Nicholas Brown, Jr., son of one of the four Brown brothers who dominated Rhode Island commerce in that era. Nicholas Jr. would give his alma mater some $160,000 over his life-

time. Hence the institution's new name, from 1804 onward – Brown University.

> ### BUCKLEY ON HARVARD
>
> "William F. Buckley Jr. once remarked that he would rather be governed by the first 100 names in the Boston telephone book than by the faculty of Harvard University."
>
> —Richard Nixon, *The Real War* (1980)

One of the more unlikely locations for a college in the 18th century was the New Hampshire wilderness. In the 1760s, one Rev. Eleazar Wheelock was looking for a place to relocate a Christian school for Indians which he had established in Connecticut. Having secured a pledge of £11,000 and the patronage of the Earl of Dartmouth, Wheelock's next step was to find a community that wanted the school. The most eager candidate was tiny Hanover, New Hampshire, which offered 3,000 acres (1,200 hectares). Dartmouth College has called Hanover home ever since receiving its royal charter in 1769.

Years later, Dartmouth adopted as its motto the Latin phrase *Vox Clamantis in Deserto* ("A Voice Crying in the Wilderness"), an apt suggestion of what the place must have been like in its earliest years, when classes were held in a log cabin. Rev. Wheelock's Indians never showed up in significant numbers, but Dartmouth did attract upcountry New England boys, for whom Boston or New Haven might have been too far away. One of them, Daniel Webster (class of 1801), would one day defend Dartmouth in a charter dispute that threatened the school's existence. It was this case that inspired Webster's famous statement, "It is a small college, but yet there are those who love it."

Thinking small

New England is peppered with the campuses of small and not so small colleges beloved by many – Bowdoin in Maine, Middlebury in Vermont, and Amherst and Williams in Massachusetts are the nucleus of an informal "Little Ivy League" that shares the standards if not the breadth of graduate offerings of its larger counterpart. The region also pioneered in higher education for women, with Radcliffe (now largely integrated with Harvard), Smith, Wellesley, and Mt. Holyoke all having 19th-century roots. That century also saw the rise of the great public universities; each New England state supports one, with the University of Vermont (1791) occupying an unusual semi-private status. The Jesuit institutions Boston College and College of the Holy Cross (Massachusetts) and Fairfield University

(Connecticut) are among the leaders in church-sponsored higher education.

New England also played a major role in the development of scientific education, with the Massachusetts Institute of Technology enrolling its first students in 1865. Originally located in Boston, MIT now occupies an expansive campus along the Charles River in Cambridge. The Institute's graduates have been instrumental in making Boston a hub of the computer and other high-technology industries, an eastern counterpart to California's Silicon Valley.

Elementary and Secondary

It was, of course, at the elementary or "grammar school" level that formal education got started in new England, back when Boston hired its first schoolmaster in 1635. Long before the modern era of public education began in the late 19th century, New England's village schools had multiplied and followed settlement out into the hinterlands, where the legendary "one-room schoolhouses" offered the rudiments of mathematics, language skills, and civics to rural children. (An example of this type of school is preserved at the Bennington Museum in Bennington, Vermont; it's the one attended by folk artist Grandma Moses as a young girl in nearby New York State, c. 1870.) One-room schoolhouses are all but vanished today, although in many rural areas, seating two grades in the same classroom is not uncommon.

Especially at the middle school and high school level, "union" schools predominate in the sparsely populated countryside, as they do in other parts of rural America. Small towns seldom can individually bear the expense of secondary education, with all of its attendant government mandates and requirements. Riding a bus 20 miles to high school is a far cry from the days when a rural student graduating grammar school might have to board with townspeople at the "academy" in the nearest big town, as future President Calvin Coolidge did in the 1880s when he left tiny Plymouth, Vermont for the Black River Academy in Ludlow.

There are still boarding high schoolers in New England, but they mostly attend the prestigious private preparatory schools such as St Paul's (Concord, New Hampshire), Choate

Rosemary Hall (Wallingford, Connecticut), and the two Phillips academies (at Exeter, New Hampshire and Andover, Massachusetts) – traditional gateways to the Ivy League.

Even in an era when public education largely fits a national rather than a regional mold, one strong aspect of the old colonial legacy survives: a passionate grass-roots involvement in education issues. Drop in at any New England town meeting, and you'll likely hear spirited debates about school budgets, or state vs. community control. In the 1990s, politics in Vermont and New Hampshire were dominated by the problem of school funding, when courts ruled that

reliance upon local property taxes was unfair to children in towns with meager tax bases. Even in more populous and urban Massachusetts, where professional educators are more likely to insulate citizens from education policy decisions, there have been heated public discussions over issues such as teacher competency tests; and the question of English-only instruction reached the ballot box in 2002 (it won).

Ever since those first Massachusetts towns were enjoined to "set upon a Grammar-School," New England has been busy planning – and arguing – how best to educate its next generation of farmers, lawyers, computer engineers, and Nobel laureates. ❏

LEFT: commencement at Boston University.
RIGHT: Boston's research facilities are world-class.

THE TRADITION OF GOOD FOOD

*Seafood remains one of the New England classics, but the influence of
immigrants and new traditions are making their mark*

The Pilgrims would not have known what to make of our mania for lobster. They considered the crustaceans fit only for pig food, or bait; well into the 19th century, boatloads of lobsters sold for pennies, and prisoners rioted at the prospect of yet another lobster dinner. But lobster has long since gone upscale, and the har-

simmered their soups in a *chaudière* (cauldron). Such long, slow cooking is needed to render large hard-shell quahogs (pronounced "cohogs") palatable. Small and medium-size clams – cherrystones and littlenecks – are delectable served raw, on the half-shell. Soft-shell, longneck clams – commonly known as "steamers"

vest is today a lucrative enterprise. And while creative preparations abound, menus still feature traditional boiled lobsters and "lobster rolls" – toasted hot dog buns filled with chunks of lobster meat, tossed with celery and mayonnaise.

The settlers weren't quite so blind to the appeal of oysters, however. As early as 1601, Samuel de Champlain had singled out the area now known as Wellfleet, on Cape Cod, for its exceptional beds. He named the harbor "*Porte aux huitres.*" And to this day, Wellfleet and Cotuit, on Cape Cod, are world-renowned for their oysters.

New England's fabled clam chowder got its name from the French settlers of Canada, who

– are a favored repast all along the coast, dipped first in their own broth (to wash off the grit), then melted butter. Clam shacks fire up their fry-o-lators to prepare another favorite: clams batter-coated or simply rolled in cornmeal and fried.

Clambakes were once a New England tradition, especially on Cape Cod. The customary procedure was to dig a pit on the beach, line it with stones, build a driftwood fire, cover the hot stones with seaweed, add clams and their accompaniments (typically, lobsters, potatoes, corn on the cob), and then top it all off with more seaweed, a sailcloth tarp, and plenty of sand, leaving the whole to bake for about an hour. Most restaurants these days dispense with clambake *per se*, and just serve what's called a "shore dinner" – steamed.

It was the abundant cod, however, that initially lured English fishermen, and eventually settlers, to this land. Fillet of young cod, called scrod (from the Dutch *schrood*, for "a piece cut off"), still graces traditional menus.

Exposure to European traditions has introduced two relatively new seafood treats. Mussels, long ignored by New England restaurants, are now very nearly ubiquitous, usually served *marinière* or poached in white wine. Seasonal bay scallops have always enjoyed greater gourmet cachet than the larger, tougher sea roast, still found on the menus of traditional restaurants specializing in "comfort food." Made today with fresh beef, it's a throwback to the days when families got through winter by hunkering over hearth-simmered pots of preserved beef and root vegetables.

Boston has its famous baked beans, more commonly found nowadays on breakfast menus influenced by French Canadians in northern Maine and New Hampshire. For dessert, try Indian pudding, based on cornmeal and molasses, or grape-nut ice cream, made with the crunchy cereal. And New England might be the home of America's favorite comfort

scallop but, until recently, restaurants invariably threw away the tastiest part, serving only the adductor muscle. Bay scallops are now available year-round, and the more adventurous fine restaurants have begun serving them whole, on the half-shell or cooked.

Northern comfort

Not all New England culinary standards come from the sea. This is the land of Yankee pot

LEFT: interpreters at Plimoth Plantation prepare a meal the settlers would have eaten.
ABOVE: breakfast is a meal to be taken seriously during a canoe expedition.

food: Louis' Lunch in New Haven, Connecticut claims to have invented the hamburger.

Bright berries from the bogs

Cranberries – so named by Dutch settlers who thought the flowers resembled cranes – are one of the few fruits native to North America (among the others are Concord grapes and blueberries, a cash crop in Maine). Native Americans used the sassamanesh – "bitter berries" – as a dye, a poultice, and as food, pounded with fat and dried venison to make "pemmican" or sweetened with maple sap. Long before the need for Vitamin C was recognized, whalers would set off to sea with a barrel of cranberries to prevent scurvy. Today, visitors can tour Massachusetts cranberry bogs and celebrate fall festivals from Plymouth to Nantucket.

Maple syrup

New Englanders have also continued the Indian practice of boiling maple sap into syrup, and Vermont is America's leading producer of maple syrup. The trees of the "sugarbush" are tapped in early spring, when just the right combination of cold nights and warm days sets the thin sap rising. However modern the equipment, it still takes 40 gallons of sap to boil down to just one gallon of syrup. Visitors can

watch the process at dozens of commercial sugar houses.

Beer, wine, and cider

With safe drinking water no certainty in close-packed settlements, the Pilgrims – adults and children alike – drank beer (the alcohol content kept the microbes in check). Today they could travel around New England and never wander far from a microbrewery. Popular regional beer makers include Vermont's Long Trail, New Hampshire's Old Man Ale and Smuttynose, Maine's Allagash and Katahdin, and Massachusetts' Boston Beer Company (makers of Sam Adams), Ipswich, Harpoon, and Atlantic Coast

(home of Tremont brews). Many of these producers open their doors to visitors. In Boston, visitors can join Brew Pub Tours.

It's even possible to find good locally produced wine. Many vineyards are still in the fledgling stage, but several have a proven track record: Stonington Vineyards in Stonington, Connecticut; Sakonnet Vineyards in Little Compton, Rhode Island; Chicama Vineyards on Martha's Vineyard, Massachusetts; and Snow Farm in South Hero, Vermont.

Apple seeds, which came to New England with the Pilgrims in 1620, contributed another popular beverage – apple cider. This fresh-pressed apple juice was a favorite drink in colonial times and was also converted into "hard" or alcoholic cider. President John Adams claimed that a tankard of hard cider every morning calmed his stomach and alleviated gas. Hard cider has enjoyed a trendy revival in the 1990s, led by New England brands such as Woodchuck from Cavendish, Vermont. Sweet cider, often served hot with cinnamon or spiked with rum, makes a warming treat after a long day of leaf peeping or skiing.

The classic diner

New England is home to one of the original fast food restaurants – the diner. First created in Providence in 1872 as a horse-drawn lunch wagon, diners grew into a major manufacturing business in Worcester, Massachusetts, in the early 20th century. Many traditional New England diners serve breakfast all day – eggs any style, hash browns, pancakes – while waitresses circle with bottomless coffee pots, asking "Warm it up, hon?" Yet even diners have not escaped gentrification : some diner-style spots mix four types of cheese into the classic baked macaroni dish or spike their French toast batter with amaretto.

Specialty products

A new wave of "back-to-landers" has created a trendy land of plenty, raising deer for venison, goats for farmstead chèvre, trout and salmon for smoking. In Connecticut, the actor Paul Newman has followed up on his "Newman's Own" salad dressing success with lines of pasta sauce, popcorn, fig bars, and other foodstuffs – with all profits going to charity. In Vermont, specialty food producers whip up everything from "Putney pasta" to salsa and tortilla chips;

the entrepreneurs behind Ben & Jerry's ice cream empire, in Waterbury, parlayed a $5 correspondence school diploma into a business grossing more than $200 million a year. When Ben & Jerry's was sold to Unilever in 2000, many Vermonters reacted as if outsiders had bought Mt. Mansfield.

New traditions

Throughout New England, flavors once considered "exotic" have entered the mainstream, as waves of immigration have brought new

A NEW ENGLAND THING

The United States currently leads the world in per capita ice cream consumption, and New Englanders are said to eat 14 pints more of the stuff every year than the average American.

bread, spicy linguiça (pork sausage), and all manner of salt cod preparations are among the Portuguese contributions to New England tables.

Since 1960, almost 80 percent of immigrants to the US have come from Asia, Latin America, and the Caribbean. New England towns boast Chinese, Japanese, Thai, Vietnamese, Puerto Rican, Mexican, Haitian, and many other ethnic eateries, where clams in black bean sauce and lobster sautéed with ginger and scallions blend local ingredi-

culinary traditions to the area. The Italian immigrants of a century ago left an indelible stamp on the region's food. Pizzerias and spaghetti houses can be found in countless New England towns, while urban enclaves – including Boston's North End, Providence's Federal Hill, and Hartford's Franklin Avenue – add more contemporary Italian regional cooking.

In several Rhode Island and Massachusetts cities, Portuguese-Americans have transformed the land of the bean and the cod into the home of the feijão and the bacalhau. Doughy sweet

---

LEFT: fresh lobster on offer in Rhode Island.
ABOVE: creating a stir with cranberries.

ents into the classic cuisines of their home countries.

On the urban cutting edge, celebrity chefs transform traditional New England products into creative new "fusion" preparations. Adventurous eaters can have salad of Maine rock crab with lobster knuckles and fried taro, crispy squash risotto cakes, pumpkin ravioli with mussels *marinière*, lightly fried lobster with lemongrass and Thai basil, or seared scallops in cider sauce.

But tradition endures. Those boiled lobsters, that baked cod, and that paper cup overflowing with fried clams, washed down with a cool frappé (that's Massachusetts-speak for milk shake), remain New England culinary favorites. ❏

THE MARITIME TRADITION

The sea has always been important to New Englanders – first for transport

and trade and as a fishing ground, more recently for recreation

The little ship had been at sea for two months. It was November 1620, in the North Atlantic, not a kind season. The passengers and crew, more than 100 people, had squeezed into this one vessel after its sister ship had proven unseaworthy. They were headed for the tiny English colonies in America.

At last, the call came: "Land ho!" The weary passengers who crowded the railings could barely make out the tops of several small islands on the horizon. As the ship drew closer, they discovered that the "islands" were actually hills arising above a long bar of sand. Weary from the months at sea and eager to set foot in the New World, the Pilgrims disembarked at the tip of Cape Cod to rest and reconnoiter. After five weeks on land, they set sail again for Virginia. But, battered by storms that seemed endless, the tiny yet sturdy barque *Mayflower* was driven across Cape Cod Bay and into the mainland at a place the Pilgrims named Plymouth.

A path to the New World

The sea had allowed early New Englanders to escape the spiritual confines of the old country. It had brought them to the New World. But it had not given them any choice about their landing place. Down through the centuries, the sea has written the history of New England and determined its people's destiny. Of its six states, only Vermont is untouched by salt water.

The sea could move people speedily between continents – or condemn them to a watery grave. It has toppled granite buildings, even torn away the land itself, and it has turned fortunes upside-down overnight. A rich merchant, pillar of his community, might come into his warehouse on Boston's Long Wharf one morning only to find that his entire fleet and all its cargo had been swept away and lost forever, and that he was no better than a beggar. Or a lonesome beachcomber slowly tracing Cape Cod's sandy shores might come upon 100 gold doubloons washed up only minutes before by a whim of the sea.

The first generation of Europeans in America all had the same "baptism by sea:" a two-month voyage across the stormy North Atlantic. Most of the settlers who came were landlubbers; many had never seen the ocean before. But shipbuilding was one of the first enterprises the early colonists undertook. Ships maintained the connection to the homeland and provided an income from trade. The vast virgin forests of the New World supplied ready-at-hand materials for their construction. One hundred years after the Pilgrims stepped on Plymouth Rock, New England's coastal shipyards were launching a ship a day. With labor and lumber costs so cheap compared to those in England, American-made ships dominated the market.

For the early settlers, the sea brought news from home, fresh legions of colonists to do battle with the wilderness, and ships involved in the Triangular Trade (the transport of slaves, molasses, and rum between ports in Africa, the Caribbean, and New England). The vast virgin forests of colonial Maine seemed an inexhaustible storehouse of straight, lofty white pines for the masts of the Royal Navy. The fishing grounds along the coasts teemed with food for the taking.

One of the first important acts of the Great and General Court of Massachusetts was to set standards for the regulation and encouragement of the fishing industry. Early on, fishing was seen as a prime source of the region's prosperity. In fact, many settlers came not so much to enjoy religious freedom as to catch fish. Codfish, high in

be rendered, and the oil thus extracted would provide a clearer, brighter light.

Whales beached themselves frequently on the New England shores during the early colonial days, and whaling got its start as a shore activity. Teams of townsfolk gathered whenever they saw a whale, tethering the creature to a stake to prevent the tide from taking it out to sea. The blubber was cut away, rendered in the kettles of a "tryworks" set up on the beach and transformed into a high-quality oil which

THE "SACRED COD"

The "Sacred Cod" – a wooden effigy presented to the legislature by a Boston merchant in 1784 – was kept in the Massachusetts Colony House, and now hangs at the State House on Beacon Hill.

protein, iodine, and Vitamin A, nourished not just New Englanders, but colonists in Mid-Atlantic and Southern towns, and even many Europeans.

The whaling boom

The lamps of colonial New England were fired by vegetable and animal oils; candles were made from animal tallow. The light was dim and the lamps were smoky until someone made the discovery that blubber from a beached whale could

LEFT: the port of Boston in 1768, before areas of the harbor on either side of Long Wharf were infilled.
ABOVE: whalers pursued their quarry for months.

could be burned in the town's lamps or traded for other goods.

The demand for this excellent oil became so great that fishermen, hoping to get rich from the sale of oil, began actively to pursue whales along the shore, thus initiating New England's famous whaling industry. The trade took a great leap forward in 1712, when Captain Christopher Hussey of Nantucket was blown off course into deep water and accidentally bagged the first sperm whale. Although it had teeth in lieu of coveted baleen – bony upper jaw slats useful as stays for collars and corsets – the spermaceti oil proved far superior to that of the already endangered "right" whale (so called because it was the right one to pursue). Nantucket whalers came to specialize in the pursuit of this purer, lighter, and more profitable oil.

Whalers out of Nantucket and New Bedford pursued their mammoth quarry for months, even years, as far as the Pacific, until their holds were filled with barrels of the oil that would fire the nation's lamps and illumine the capitals of Europe. The whaling ships served as complete processing plants. Once a whale was sighted, men pursued it in small dories, harpooned it, and then braced

SCRIMSHAW

Sailors on the whaling ships whiled away the hours making intricate carvings in whale-bone or teeth, etched in black, known as scrimshaw.

Watery highways

The sea formed the path from England to America, and served as the road system from one point in America to the next. In colonial times, overland routes were expensive to build and maintain, so coastal freighters and passenger boats carried colonists and their wares from Boston to New York and Philadelphia. Dozens of boats out of Salem harbor headed for home with decks full of salt cod. The more enterprising captains headed south, where they unloaded

themselves for the "Nantucket sleighride" that followed. The hapless whale might drag the men in the dory many miles before exhausting itself. Tied up alongside the whaling ship, the whale carcass was stripped of blubber. Rendered in a tryworks right on deck, the oil was then stored in casks in the hold.

Until 1859, when petroleum was discovered in Pennsylvania and distillers began producing kerosene, the sea was the world's great proven oil reserve. For a closer look at this fascinating chapter in maritime history, see the last surviving whaler, the *Charles W. Morgan*, tied up at Mystic Seaport in Connecticut, or visit the whaling museums in Nantucket or New Bedford.

their cod at Philadelphia or Annapolis and took on corn and flour, beans, and barrels of pork, which could be sold at a greater profit at home than could codfish. New England never produced such goods in sufficient quantities; cod it had in great abundance.

Though a boon to New England's maritime economy, the coastal trade, like fishing and whaling, was not an easy way to make a living. Every trip between Boston and ports to the south involved a voyage around Cape Cod, and the weather that had so discouraged the Pilgrims was a constant threat. Ships and men were regularly lost to the ravages of the sea.

Though fishing and the coastal trade helped

New England employ its people and pay its bills, the region was not a rich one. Because it always imported more goods than it exported, ways had to be found to reduce the trade deficit.

Merchants and sea captains from New England towns saw themselves as the world's transport agents: if they couldn't produce the goods from their rocky soil and primitive industries, they reasoned, at least they could carry across the oceans the goods produced by others. New England merchant vessels undertook long and arduous voyages to Europe, Africa, and the Orient. And it was not only the cargoes that were put up for sale: the ships themselves were frequently on the auctioning block, bringing added revenue to their builders back home in New England.

Trade was good to the region. While the pioneer towns of inland America were primitive and rough, New England seaports took on the polish of wealth and culture. Fortunes made at sea were translated into fine mansions and patronage of the arts. From the profits of their voyages, captains brought home art treasures, luxury goods, and curiosities from exotic destinations. The Peabody-Essex Museum of Salem *(see page 144)* is filled with the wealth that came to New England on returning merchant ships, and that city's Salem Maritime National Historic Site *(see page 143)* preserves a custom house, a wealthy merchant's home, and other structures from the golden age of wind-borne commerce.

Clocks, shoes, and ice

As time went by, the new republic developed industries that produced goods for trade. Connecticut's household utensils, machines, clocks, pistols, and rifles, plus shoes and cloth from Rhode Island and Massachusetts, ultimately made their way around the world.

Perhaps the most ingenious export of all was ice. Cut from ponds, rivers, and lakes, ice was packed in sawdust, loaded into fast clipper ships and sent off to Cuba, South America, and beyond. The rulers of the British Raj in India sipped drinks cooled by ice from New England. In exchange for a commodity that was free for the cutting, New Englanders brought back spices, fine porcelain, silks, and other items.

The volume of New England's trade soon fell behind that of the Southern ports along the

Atlantic and Gulf of Mexico coasts. But trade continued to be important in maintaining the region's economy and its cosmopolitan outlook.

The taming of the sea

The war of 1812 sent New England's maritime commerce into depression, but by the mid-19th century its seaports returned to glory during the brief heyday of the clipper ship. "Never, in these United States, has the brain of man conceived, or the hand of man fashioned, so perfect a thing as the clipper ship," wrote the great Massachusetts historian Samuel Eliot Morison. Greyhound-lean, topped with acres of billowing

canvas, clippers such as those built by Donald McKay in his Boston and Newburyport yards set records in the race to bring tea and silks from the Orient to New England. But, like some creature evolved into over-specialization, the clippers were among the last of their kind. So were the larger, bulkier schooners carrying up to six masts, built to transport coal and other heavy loads that clippers, with their small holds, could never profitably carry.

Neither clipper nor schooner could go anywhere when the wind failed – but the new steamships could travel even in a dead calm, and even keep to schedule. They could sail around Cape Cod, ignoring the winds that had caused

LEFT: mural of Mystic Seaport, Connecticut.
RIGHT: a ship is launched at Bath Iron Works, Maine.

so much trouble since the time of the Pilgrims.

With the coming of steam, the Atlantic and Pacific coasts were linked by steel rails. Where once ships had sailed all the way around South America to reach California, rail transport steamed west in a straight line, undaunted by storms. Yet transport by sea, for both goods and passengers, hung on well into the 20th century. What finally laid it to rest was not the railroad but the highway.

Safer waves

Today, the sea is still a major source of income – and at a much lower price in lives lost to storms.

Although yachts, motorboats, and fishing fleets fill the harbors, disasters at sea are a relative rarity. A century ago whole families, even most of a town, might be lost to a single ferocious storm. There are still tragedies at sea – the 1991 foundering of the *Andrea Gail*, as recounted in Sebastian Junger's 1997 book *The Perfect Storm*, was a true story – but radar, radio, and stricter safety precautions help prevent many accidents.

The taming of the sea has allowed New Englanders to put it to other uses. Dependable passenger service by steamship opened up the coasts to vacation travelers. Newport and Bar Harbor turned into flourishing resorts as soon as they became accessible swiftly, comfortably,

and safely by sea. Today, reliable ferries carry vacationers to Nantucket, Martha's Vineyard, Block Island, and the outer islands along the Maine coast.

These resort communities are not the only ones to have benefited from the taming of the sea. Although the whalers and clipper ships have passed into history, the beautiful port towns built by the wealth of maritime commerce survive. Tourists stroll among the handsome sea captains' houses of Nantucket, Edgartown, Salem, and Newport, and explore in museums the world of the seafaring men who built them.

A salty playground

In other times, a New Englander either went to sea to earn a living, or remained a landlubber. But now New England's seacoast has become a major playground, and the variety of maritime sports seems limitless. As in so many other realms, the world of work has become the world of play, and places once associated solely with danger and hardship are visited just for fun. A hundred years ago, for example, "wreckers" used to trudge the beaches of New England with a keen eye for the remains of lost ships. Today, the beaches serve a distinctly different purpose. Forty miles (64 km) of Cape Cod's sandy beaches have been set aside as the Cape Cod National Seashore, one of the great tourist attractions of New England. The beaches of Connecticut, Rhode Island, New Hampshire, and Maine continue to attract visitors from near and far.

The whalers that sailed out of New Bedford and Nantucket are long gone. Or are they? Boats from a dozen New England ports still head out each day in search of whales, but now it's tourists' cameras, not the harpoon, that "captures" the whale for good. It's ironic, and heartening, that the leviathans that once made New England "oil-rich" should still be helping its economy.

Cruising the coast

Perhaps the clearest indication of the taming of the sea is this: the perilous voyage undertaken by the Pilgrims in 1620 is now done for sport. Transatlantic yacht racing began in 1866 when the *Henrietta* raced the *Vesta* to England. In 1851, the schooner *America* won the Royal Yacht Squadron Cup, and the America's Cup became the great event of yachting with the first race held in Newport in 1870. The beauty and science of yacht design and racing is pursued passionately in Newport and in dozens of other ports along the coast.

New England's waters are particularly suited to yachting: Long Island, off the coast of Connecticut, protects spacious Long Island Sound; and Cape Cod Bay has provided calm sailing ever since the days of the Pilgrims. With the cutting of the Cape Cod Canal and the establishment of the Intra-coastal Waterway, coastal cruising has been made safer and more enjoyable than ever before.

The high point of coastal cruising in New England is a run along the rocky shore of Maine. The jagged coast, cut with bays, inlets, coves, peninsulas, and islands, is some 3,500 miles (5,600 km) long, and blessed with exceptional beauty. One of the most thrilling ways to see it is aboard a windjammer out of Rockport or Camden. Since 1935, these sturdy sailing ships have taken amateur crews out into the cold waters to experience New England's maritime heritage at first hand.

Still a working sea

By the late 1980s it had become clear to lawmakers that the New England fishing industry was on its way to over-fishing itself out of existence. Massachusetts fishermen of New Bedford, Provincetown and Gloucester were forced to go farther and farther out to catch fewer and fewer fish. Although many fishermen – a fiercely independent lot – disagreed, laws were enacted to close and monitor the once fertile fishing banks. Some fishermen trained their sights on more abundant, less glamorous fish: formerly overlooked species began to show up in restaurants and supermarkets. Others reluctantly sold their boats, and took government subsidies for job retraining. Today, it looks as if the regulation is working, and mature stocks are starting to return. But government still imposes strict limits on catches, and the waterfront taverns of Gloucester are no place to praise the work of conservationists or fisheries biologists.

Northern New England's legendary lobster fleet, mostly hailing from ports in Maine, still finds a copious catch, though captains now must venture into deeper waters to fill their traps. (Long Island Sound's lobster populations,

though, have been sparse recently.) Boaters along the coast will often see the colorful bobbing floats that mark the location of the fish-baited traps on the bottom; each captain has his own float design. Captain Linda Greenlaw's 2002 book *The Lobster Chronicles* provides a first-hand account of of the lobster fishery.

New England's relationship with the sea is changing. The codfish has yielded to the computer as the most important element in New England's economic life; the schooner and whaler have yielded to the yacht. Over the years ahead New Englanders will no doubt discover new ways to enjoy and profit from the sea. ❑

LEFT: since the earliest days of settlement, New Englanders have turned to the sea for sustenance.
RIGHT: a young yachtsman enjoying the ocean.

SCIENCE OF THE SEA

Scientists say we have barely begun to tap the wealth of the sea, and the potential is enormous. To explore that potential, New England has its own world-class research facilities at Woods Hole, Massachusetts, just south of Falmouth. Woods Hole attracts tens of thousands of tourists each summer, most passing through to board the ferryboats to Martha's Vineyard. However, a knowledgeable few come to see what's new at the National Marine Fisheries Service, established in 1871; at the Marine Biological Laboratory, founded in 1888; or the Woods Hole Oceanographic Institute, begun with a $2.5 million Rockefeller grant in 1930.

THE ARCHITECTURAL TRADITION

Shingles and clapboards, gables and steeples – New England's buildings

reflect the beauty of its landscape and the practicality of its people

Buildings capture the essence of New England's character; they sum up what was at once noble and humble about the ambitions of generations of its inhabitants. And the charm of historic architecture is not lost on today's New Englanders, whose tireless efforts have preserved much of what was built in centuries past.

To learn New England, read its buildings, for they tell rich tales about the lives of their builders and inhabitants. Always aware of its heroic past, New England has retained enough of its architectural heritage to sketch a vivid picture of a distinguished history. Studying its buildings will not only stimulate the mind and seize the imagination; it will delight the eye.

Puritan practicality

Seventeenth-century New England homes were not built with an eye towards beauty, although there is something attractive about their stark simplicity. None of the earliest New England buildings survive, although they have been faithfully re-created at Plimoth Plantation in Plymouth, Massachusetts. Steep-gabled, almost toylike, these one-room houses look like peasants' huts in a fairy tale, and it is no wonder that their inhabitants built something more substantial as soon as they could.

What they did build – the "first period" houses, a number of which have survived – are heavy and medieval, a testament to the unaffected motivations of the Puritans. Stylistic vestiges of English country homes governed building design and construction, but none of these was applied solely for decorative effect: there is virtually no ornamental indulgence in the 1640 Whipple House in Ipswich or the *c.*1641 Wing Fort House in East Sandwich, both in Massachusetts. After all, when one was living for the glory of God and the common

---

LEFT: white paint was introduced in the 19th century, white being associated with Greek temples.
RIGHT: Hoxie House, Sandwich, a Cape Cod salt box dating from around 1675.

welfare, there was very little room for excess.

The Whipple and Wing Fort houses and the handful like them were nothing more than offspring of homes the Pilgrims had left behind in southeastern England. Simple oblong boxes, they were framed painstakingly and filled with the wattle-and-daub that on half-timbered Eng-

lish country homes was left visible. Clapboards, providing a blanket of protection against New England winters, created a stern look, relieved only by small, randomly placed windows. The steep roof and the massive central chimney, shared by the two lower and two upper rooms, crowned the house with an authoritative air.

In very early homes, the upper floor extended slightly beyond the lower. The 1683 Capen House in Topsfield, Massachusetts, offers a marvelous example. This overhang, recalling English townhouses where the lower floor stepped back in deference to the street, was a feature that was dropped as designs began to allow for expansion and reflect the colonists' growing sense of security. Diamond-paned casement windows were replaced by double-hung ones that brightened the interior and lightened the facade. Roofs were extended, giving additional space on the lower floor in the form of a lean-to addition. The *c*.1675 Hoxie House in Sandwich is a fine example of this "Cape Cod salt box."

Many 17th-century meetinghouses, also unadorned and otherwise simple, remain throughout New England. (The Old Ship Meetinghouse in Hingham is a fine example.) The large meetinghouses often served as the village's town hall and religious nucleus, reflecting early ties between church and state.

The Georgian style

The inspiration for the new Georgian style, as the pre-Revolutionary period of 18th-century design is known, stemmed from misfortune in England. London burned in 1666, and out of the ashes rose tributes to the ideas of the 16th-century Italian architect Andrea Palladio. Palladio's work recalled the classical architecture of antiquity, restating it in a refreshing, heroic way.

Christopher Wren, among others, championed this Renaissance spirit in London. In the United States, Palladian ideas spread in a new style that is as often termed Colonial as it is Georgian; the modern American landscape cer-

Coming of age

With a growing sense of confidence and prosperity, the colonists began adding flourishes to their humble homes. At the turn of the 18th century, commerce was growing beyond town borders, encouraging a more adventurous spirit and a weakening of the religious principles that had dampened individual expression.

The architectural symbols of this change vary according to place and time. Along the coast, where maritime trading and fishing were making their mark, money and exposure to influences from abroad combined to produce splendid mansions. Inland, changes in building style were more subtle and slower to peak.

tainly attests to its staying power.

Symmetry, a sense of strength and a quality of ease characterize the Georgian style. (The term Georgian was derived from the three English King Georges, 1714–1820.) The Georgian house was a simple two-story rectangle, but classical elements gave it definition: scrolled, often broken pediments capped centered doorways and windows; fluted attached columns marked the entrances of houses; and, in the grander examples, bulging cornerstones or "quoins" bracketed the corners of the structures from the eaves to the foundations. Mostly in wood, but sometimes in brick, the elements were precisely wrought by skilled New England carpenters.

Georgian homes, with wood-paneled walls and broad stairways, had larger rooms and more privacy. Four full rooms both upstairs and down were the norm. Two separate chimneys serviced the two, now larger, halves of the house. These two leaner towers added to exterior elegance and richness while leaving room for a deep hallway where the massive central chimney had been.

Wren-style steeples were added as a grace note on meetinghouses. For two opposite examples, from plain to elaborate, look to the Old South Meeting House in Boston and the Baptist Church in Providence.

absent in later painted facades. Indians were regularly raiding Deerfield, but when one's eyes rest upon these buildings, there is no sense of trepidation, and the marvelous doorways welcome visitors warmly.

Equally gracious is Deerfield's 1754 Dwight-Barnard House. This rambling residence is a fine example not only of Georgian architecture but also of the New England practice of connecting the house, the barn and any outbuilding that had to be reached during the bitter winter.

By mid-century, coastal ports were very profitable, as sea captains' and merchants' houses showed. Many of these were later remodeled

Old Deerfield, Massachusetts, has several charming renderings of early Georgian ideals. At the north end of a marvelous mile of 18th-century historical structures stand the 1733 Ashley House and the 1743 Hawks House. While the precise Georgian proportions and details exude a calm and assurance, their dark, unpainted clapboards suggest a ruggedness

FAR LEFT: the early colonial (1646) West Parish Meeting House, near West Barnstable on Cape Cod. **LEFT:** an 18th-century Georgian house on Benefit Street, Providence, Rhode Island. **ABOVE:** the impeccably Georgian Julius Deming House at Litchfield, Connecticut (1793).

to keep up with architectural fashions, making it difficult to find the purely Georgian. Portsmouth, New Hampshire, is blessed with unsullied originals in its 1763 Moffatt-Ladd House – as handsome as any – and the delightfully understated 1760 Wentworth-Coolidge House.

Aspects of Georgian architecture, particularly Palladian motifs, remained in the vernacular of New England design beyond the 18th century, but the style had almost run its course by the Revolutionary War. One exception is the handsome town of Litchfield, Connecticut, where pristine homes lining the village green compose the perfect picture of idyllic New England.

Some of the finest homes were built or

remodeled after 1780, when the Litchfield China Trading Company brought wealth to the town. The residence of one of the company's founders, a Mr Deming, and the remodeled Sheldon's Tavern are impeccably Georgian, down to the three-part Palladian window not commonly used before 1780. All other buildings in the borough of Litchfield are meticulously preserved, although not necessarily in their original state. The predominantly white exteriors date from a later 19th-century taste that conveys a feel quite different from that of the original yellow, blue or red hues that comprised a Georgian palette.

sion of trade brought the sea to many New Englanders as the coastal merchants commanded the goods and natural resources of the whole region. But no country carpenter could rival the skills of Salem's Samuel McIntire or Boston's Charles Bulfinch, whose combined work represents the finest of the period.

McIntire's work shows the clearest Federal style notations. While New England's roofs had lost some of their cant during the Georgian period, their Federal counterparts virtually disappeared behind delicately carved balustrades. The effect was urbane, as evidenced by the Peabody and Essex Museum's 1804 Gardner-

No style since the Georgian has lingered so long in New England. Deriving from familiar forms, but with more space and embellishments, New England builders adapted to it with ease. If the Georgian style took a long time to mature into its successor, the Federal, the lag was surely a result of the many preoccupations of a nation in adolescence, rather than an absence of active architectural acumen. The century that followed was to prove that.

The Federal style

Following the revolution, optimism was palpable in the harbors of Salem and Boston. Even inland, whaling, shipbuilding and the expan-

Pingree house in Salem, a neat summation of Federal motifs. Although primarily plain and boxy, its four-square facade is relieved by the semi-circular portico, its refined columns and the arching fanlight over the door – Federal era signatures. The front doorways of Federal houses are often distinguished by their narrow, leaded side windows, too.

McIntire's inspiration was Robert Adam, the Scottish architect who raised the art of interior decoration to exquisite heights with his dainty stucco reliefs. McIntire introduced these same embellishments to Salem, as can be seen inside the Gardner-Pingree house. Classical detailing, free-standing curved stairways and delicate fireplace mantels characterize Federal interior design.

The full impact of McIntire's work on the rest of Salem is best grasped on Chestnut Street, which in its entirety has been designated a National Historic Landmark. Up and down both sides of this majestic street are stunning Federal-style mansions, built in the early 1800s when the sea captains decided to move away a little from the noise and clutter of the port.

Elsewhere in Salem, a 1970s facelift not only turned around a declining city but, in doing so, reversed plans to topple many Federal-era buildings, which have been renovated and put

The brilliance of Bulfinch

The Federal era peaked with the work of Charles Bulfinch, who pursued architecture first as a leisure activity and then as a profession. Unfortunately, many of his more daring buildings have been destroyed, but the jewel among those standing, the Massachusetts State House, rests atop Beacon Hill. Here is as grand a composition as any Bulfinch realized, and to picture it surrounded by open land is to begin to appreciate what a dazzling paean to the promise of government it must have appeared to the Bostonian of 1798.

The classical State House, very Palladian in

to new use. A similar turnabout occurred in nearby Newburyport, where life and charm were reintroduced to the the the c. 1811 commercial district. Throughout the 1980s, 1990s, and early 2000s, preservation-minded private owners have bought up residential properties in these communities, bringing block after block of irreplaceable Georgian and Federal homes back to life – and taking real estate values into the stratosphere.

LEFT: an example of a wooden Federal-style house with typical semi-circular portico and roof balustrade.
ABOVE: a typical Adam-style Federal interior.
ABOVE RIGHT: Bulfinch's Massachusetts State House.

inspiration, has been extended twice in two contradictory styles. The 1890 addition to the back of the building is a lumpish but highly mannered baroque echo of its opposing side. The second addition of 1914 totally neutralized the first by blotting it out, at least from the front, behind two thoroughly impassive marble wings – dull perhaps, but a mute backdrop to the golden-domed Bulfinch original.

Bulfinch was in on the beginning of Beacon Hill speculation, and the three homes he built for the developer and politician Harrison Gray Otis summarize not only his growth but the maturation of the Federal residential style. The 1796 house, now the headquarters for the Society for the Preservation of New England Antiquities, is the least developed, a harmonious albeit basic expression of Federal-style concepts. In his 1802 house, Bulfinch took a few cautious steps to animate the street facade – the first-floor windows are recessed inside well-defined brick arches.

By his third house, completed around 1805, Bulfinch's confidence was established. This Beacon Street residence, of noble proportions and refined detail, set a tone of sophistication for the entire neighborhood, which Bulfinch also graced with several surviving row houses on Chestnut Street.

It was Benjamin who, in his final 1830 volume, judged New England ready for the Greek Revival style, a style that elsewhere in America was already vying with the newer Gothic Revival of architects such as Alexander Jackson Davis. The same sense of self-importance that had characterized the Federal era, along with the influence of learning and intellectualism, gave the imposing Greek style a certain snob appeal. New England allowed the style in without discarding the integrity of its previous architectural traditions. Particularly in non-residential examples, the Greek Revival style produced buildings that were a logical extension

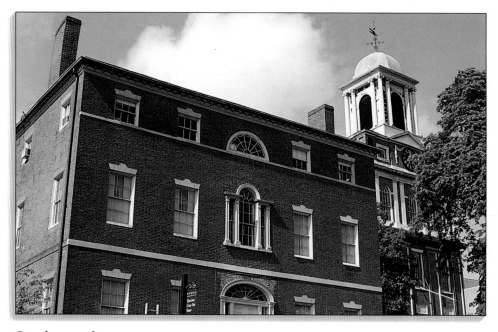

Greek grandeur

New England is a peaceful place, and among the emblems of this serenity are scores of white steeples, visible on every horizon as landmarks for travelers. This ubiquitous New England image can be traced back to Asher Benjamin, an influential force in New England architecture circa 1800. It was Benjamin's first of seven widely read architectural handbooks, in which he rendered a steepled church, that became the basis for decades of church design. The simple classicism changed little over time, but the detailing, particularly of the steeple, incorporated changing architectural fashions, giving a clue to the era in which a church was built.

of the refinements made during the Federal era. The tops of Greek Revival churches were squared-off or had multi-story steeples, but Greek Revival houses proved less successful.

The economy of Greek architecture gives it a superior air, and scale is the key to its grandeur. Civic buildings, institutions and halls of commerce lent themselves to the heroic Greek scale, usually constructed of either marble or granite; houses were dwarfed by it. (There were two residential benefits, however: tall windows and high ceilings.)

Although New England is not particularly rich in examples of the style, two exemplary Greek Revival buildings – both marketplaces, temples of commerce, if you will – are among the most clever and renowned examples of recently restored 19th-century buildings.

Providence's 1828 Arcade has been described as "something worthy of London or Paris," an apt compliment to its crisply colonnaded and handsomely detailed facade. Inside, the two-story, sky-lit interior has been beautifully restored, its cast-iron balconies once again offering an elegant setting for shops.

The most celebrated New England project of its kind, Boston's Faneuil Hall Marketplace, as restored by Ben Thompson & Associates, is now a consumer's cornucopia, with food and

well-proportioned Federal and Georgian homes. One of their fundamental features, however, was effortlessly assimilated into the vocabulary of vernacular New England design – the passion for white paint (white being associated with Greek temples). Some unusually fine examples of this style can be found in Grafton, Vermont, a quiet town remarkable less for its architecture than for its rescue by the Windham Foundation, which since 1963 has restored the entire core of this idyllic New England village. Another handsome Vermont example is Orwell's Wilcox-Cutts House, an 1840s remodeling of an existing farmhouse.

specialty stores galore. (The Marketplace occupies the arcaded structure called Quincy Market; Faneuil Hall itself is an adjacent Georgian structure.) The renovation was carried out with care and charisma; although the sober Greek references of Alexander Parris's 1826 domed building are generally overwhelmed by their surroundings, it seems fitting that this hive of activity be housed in such splendor.

The addition of heavy columns and crushing pediments did little, however, for otherwise

LEFT: Charles Bulfinch's first house for Harrison Gray Otis, 141 Cambridge Street, Boston.
ABOVE: Quincy Market, built in 1826.

Enlightened industry

Harrisville, New Hampshire, survives as an unchanged emblem of how pervasive the textile industry was in New England after 1830. The town comprises handsome granite and brick mills, boarding houses and storehouses. Today, these buildings house a weaving school and offer an abridged version of the rapid rise and fall of New England's mill towns, a story that began with cottage industries and climaxed with the building of entire towns designed around textile mills. The effects on the social fabric were profound and lasting.

In Lowell, Massachusetts, aggressive efforts preserved an extensive industrial architectural legacy. The Lowell National Historic Park and the Lowell Historic Preservation District celebrate factory buildings designed in the boxy, brick, frugal industrial version of the Federal style. They line the city's intricate canal system, with rows of boarding houses nearby.

Lowell is once again a healthy and active city, a rich visual lesson in the architecture of a tumultuous historical chapter. The mills are among many saved from the wrecking ball and reused for housing, commercial and retail purposes. Towns such as Fall River, Manchester and Pawtucket are the richer for these efforts.

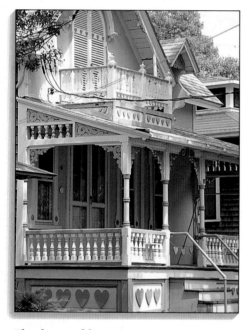

The loss of innocence

The opening of the industrial age marked the closing of an era of architectural innocence in New England. For 200 years, the principles of the region's architecture had been governed by function; form existed to serve the central purpose of shelter. While European ideas had clearly dictated design, they had been tempered by restraint. But by 1850, something had changed. Perhaps for no other reason than boredom with symmetry, scale and four-square plans, architecture took off in a riot of historicist revivals.

Gothic, Italianate, Renaissance and Romanesque are among the eclectic labels attached to the late 19th-century architectural revivals. The

Gothic Capitol building in Hartford is particularly asymmetrical, while the "gingerbread" carpenter Gothic style of Martha's Vineyard cottages represents a more quaint interpretation. Newport mansions exemplify a dizzying range of styles, from the shingled Hammersmith Farm "cottage" to the gilded Breakers (Italian Renaissance), the Victorian Château-sur-mer to the beaux-arts Marble House (*see pages 242–43*).

In the hands of architects such as Henry Hobson Richardson (who designed Boston's Trinity Church in a bold Romanesque style) and McKim, Mead and White (the Renaissance Revival Boston Public Library), these styles could be expressed with panache. But the spiritual link to early New England began growing remote, and these buildings – with massive stones and ornamentation – have only a distant kinship with the carefully proportioned, cautiously decorated creations of New England's early centuries. In effect, they represent mainstream trends in American architecture, rather than a homegrown New England school.

Further European grafts have been attempted, with varying degrees of success. Harvard University boasts the only LeCorbusier building in the United States (the Carpenter Center), and Gropius built a model Bauhaus house in the Boston suburb of Lincoln. At MIT, Eero Saarinen designed the striking Kresge Auditorium and Chapel. More recently, British architect James Stirling chose a postmodernist-Egyptian motif for Harvard's Sackler Museum of ancient, Islamic, and Asian art.

The future of New England architecture clearly lies in the hands of native architects such as Graham Gund of Cambridge, who acknowledge the contributions of their forebears even as they strive to break new ground. Particularly in his library work of the past decade – at the University of New Hampshire in Durham, at Mt. Holyoke College in South Hadley, Massachusetts, and at Berwick Academy in Berwick, Maine – Gund has accomplished a soaring simplicity that conjures nothing so much as the serene, light-filled spaces of New England's treasured meetinghouses. ❑

LEFT: well-preserved Carpenters Gothic cottages can be found at Oak Bluffs on Martha's Vineyard.
RIGHT: Boston's "Richardson Romanesque" Trinity Church contrasts with the 1970s Hancock Tower.

PLACES

*A detailed guide to New England, with principal sites
clearly cross-referenced by number to the maps*

*Meanwhile it occurs to me that by a remote New England fireside an
unsophisticated young person of either sex is reading in an old volume
of travels... The young person gazes in the firelight at the flickering
chiaroscuro of the future, discerns at last the glowing phantasm of
opportunity, and determines with a wild heart-beat to go and see it all –
twenty years hence.* —HENRY JAMES

There's no need to wait 20 years to see New England, no need to
delay at all, for its rewards are well established. It is a region
bursting with 300 years of historical sights and influence – considerably more than any other place in America. But it is also a
remarkably vital place: attend a town meeting in one of the superfi-
cially sleepy rural communities and you'll find that the robust tradition of democracy bequeathed by the founding fathers lives on,
making many a town manager's life little easier than the president's.

It is precisely this juxtaposition of past influence and present pres-
tige that is so compelling. Comprising six politically defined states,
New England has a thousand states of mind – Maine for solitude
and contemplation, Massachusetts for bustle and culture, Vermont for
beauty and peace, Connecticut for its carefully kept white clapboard
homes, Rhode Island for its renowned sailing, and tranquil New
Hampshire, whose bellwether presidential primary every four years
suggests the political fortunes that are about to be won and lost.

A trip to New England can mean finding a priceless antique in an
out-of-the-way backwoods store, or dining in a sophisticated Boston
bistro. It can mean rafting down a Maine river and skiing down a
New Hampshire mountain, lounging on a Nantucket beach or picnicking on the harbor in Newport, Rhode Island.

State delineations serve as convenient although somewhat artifi-
cial labels for New England's varied regions. In the following pages,
each state is explored in depth and treated as a self-contained unit. But
Massachusetts, the most populous, has been divided into sub-sections:
Boston, Boston Day trips, Cape Cod and the islands of Martha's Vineyard and Nantucket, Central Massachusetts and the Berkshires.

States of mind – calm, contentment, excitement, pride, surprise,
intrigue, enjoyment, pleasure – are to be found throughout New
England. From the scrub pines on Martha's Vineyard to the granite
outcroppings of Vermont's Green Mountains, from the cobbled
streets of restored Newburyport to the sleek Boston skyline, from
Rhode Island's natural wonderland, Block Island, to the country's
history that began in Lexington and Concord, this is New England,
home of American dreams, both real and still to be actualized. ❑

PRECEDING PAGES: winter in the White Mountains, New Hampshire; summer in the
White Mountains; Boston seen from the Charles River.
LEFT: Brant Point Lighthouse and Children's Beach, Nantucket.

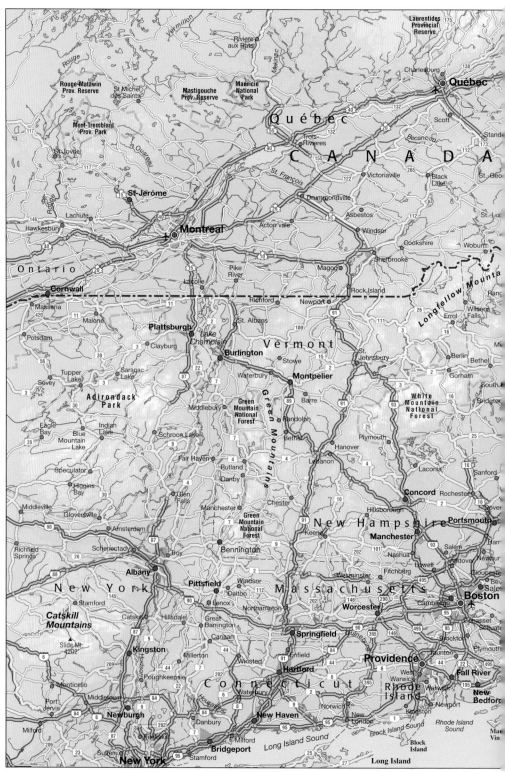

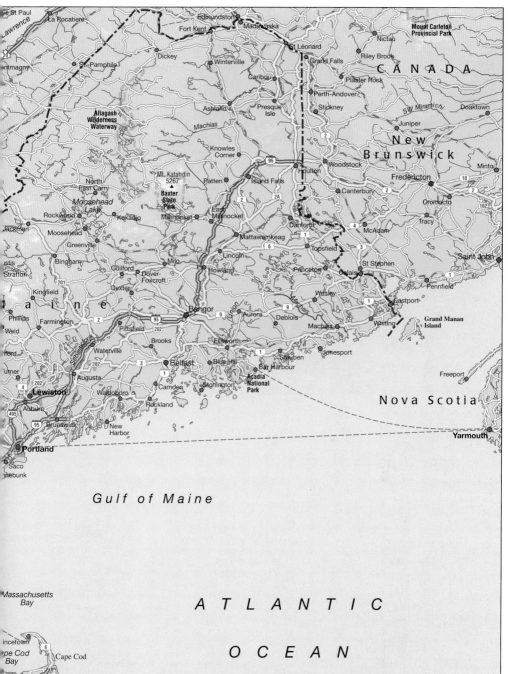

St Paul
Lawrence
La Pocatiere
Edmundston
Fort Kent
Madawaska
Mount Carleton
Provincial Park
Nictau
Riley Brook
St Léonard
Dickey
Winterville
Grand Falls
C A N A D A
St-Pamphile
Caribou
Plaster Rock
ntmagny
Perth-Andover
Ashland
Presque
Isle
Stickney
SW Miramichi
Doaktown
Allagash
Wilderness
Waterway
Machias
Juniper
N e w
Knowles
Corner
95
Woodstock
B r u n s w i c k
Minto
North
East Carry
Mt. Katahdin
5267'
Baxter
State
Park
Patten
Island Falls
Houlton
Fredericton
10
Moosehead
Lake
Kokadjo
Millinocket
2
2A
Canterbury
2
Oromocto
102
Rockwood
East
Millinocket
Danforth
4
McAdam
Tracy
Jackman
Moosehead
Mattawamkeag
6
Greenville
Lincoln
Topsfield
3
St Stephen
Saint John
ustis
Stratton
Bingham
Guilford
Dover-
Foxcroft
Milo
Howland
Princeton
Calais
Pennfield
201
Dexter
Wesley
1
Kingfield
Eastport
a i n e
Bangor
9
Aurora
Deblois
9
Whiting
Grand Manan
Island
Phillips
Farmington
2
95
Pittsfield
202
Brooks
Machias
Weld
Ellsworth
Jonesport
ford
Waterville
202
3
Steuben
1
Belfast
Blue Hill
Bar Harbour
Freeport
Augusta
1
Camden
Stonington
Acadia
National
Park
Lewiston
Waldoboro
Rockland
N o v a   S c o t i a
Auburn
495
95
Brunswick
New
Harbor
Yarmouth
Portland
Saco
nnebunk

G u l f   o f   M a i n e

Massachusetts
Bay

A T L A N T I C

ncetown
pe Cod
Bay
6
Cape Cod
Chatham
nnis
South
Yarmouth
Monomoy Island

O C E A N

Nantucket
Island
Nantucket

N

New England

0   50 miles

0   50 km

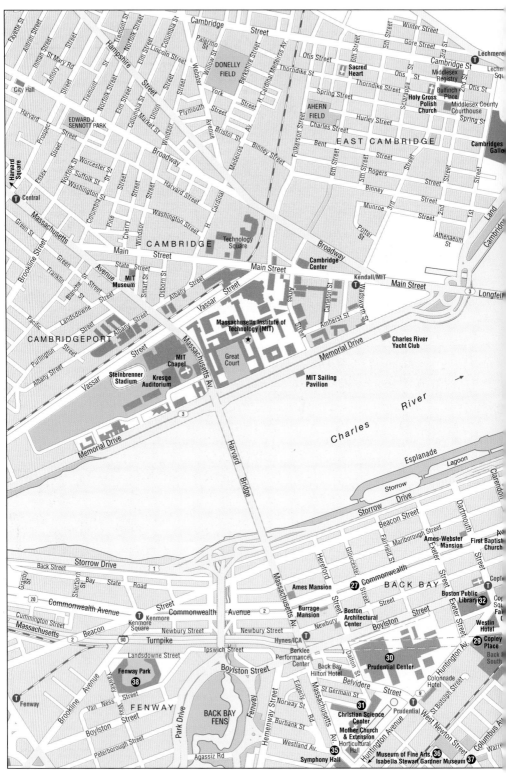

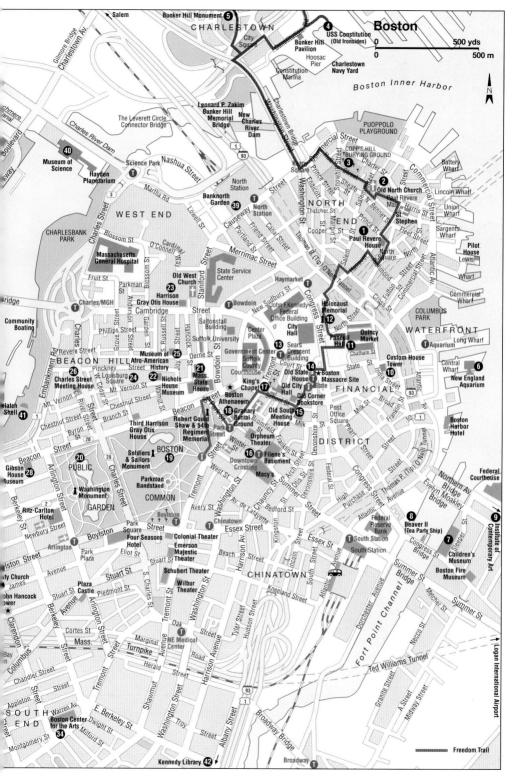

Boston

BOSTON

The city has always taken itself seriously. But it does, after all, all, have unequaled Revolutionary history, famed universities, vibrant arts, creative cuisine, and the Red Sox

Map on pages 102–3

T he poet and essayist Ralph Waldo Emerson wrote: "This town of Boston has a history… It is not an accident, not a windmill, or a railroad station, or a crossroads town, but a seat of humanity, of men of principle, obeying sentiment and marching to it…"

Oliver Wendell Holmes, Sr. was even more extravagant: "All I claim for Boston is that it is the thinking center of the Continent, and therefore of the Planet." He went on to christen his city "The Hub of the Universe." New York may be more dynamic, Washington more imposing, Seattle more beautiful, but no city in America so nobly mingles its past with its present, tradition with innovation.

Founded in 1630 when a band of Puritans who had landed in Salem (north of Boston) went searching for drinking water, Boston early on felt that "the eies of all people are upon us," as their first leader, John Winthrop, said. Driven by this relentless self-consciousness and the certainty that God, too, was watching, the little "Bible Commonwealth" quickly made something of itself.

Prosperity came from the sea. By 1700, thanks to cod fishing and the maritime trade made possible by Boston's natural harbor, the colony was booming: its fleet was the third largest in the English-speaking world, its population the largest in North America.

In the mid-18th century, the English Crown began to tighten its hold on its precocious offspring, imposing a series of tough new revenue measures which cooled relations between the colonies and the motherland. Tensions escalated; the Boston Massacre of 1770 and the Boston Tea Party (*see page 33*) three years later eventually flared into the American Revolution.

LEFT: Acorn Street, Beacon Hill.
BELOW: Ben Franklin turns up regularly in Boston's historical re-enactments.

The Athens of America

During the high noon of the 19th century Boston took its present-day form. Merchants and scholars alike created a great city that would eventually become known not only as "The Hub," but also as "The Athens of America."

During the decades following the Revolution, sea captains traded in ports farther abroad – Java, the West Coast and newly opened China. The Boston fishing fleet increased tenfold between 1789 and 1810, and created a "codfish aristocracy" of fortunes netted from the sea. A seemingly unending flow of riches lifted Bostonians with names such as Cabot, Lowell, and Forbes into a new American aristocracy. These were the "Boston Brahmins," a name borrowed from the Hindu priestly caste.

By 1850, industry had replaced trade as a maker of fortunes. And by 1900, in one of the great testimonies to the American knack for making something from nothing, Boston had tripled its size with landfill.

BELOW: Boston Public Library.

Boston was also expanding its mind. With its legacy of Puritan high-mindedness, its publishing houses and its fashionable literary salons, Boston suddenly found itself at the radiant center of intellectual America. Henry Wadsworth Longfellow, Robert Lowell, John Greenleaf Whittier, Ralph Waldo Emerson, Henry David Thoreau, Oliver Wendell Holmes, Bronson Alcott, Nathaniel Hawthorne: all were at one time or another citizens of the New England Parnassus; all could be found browsing at the Old Corner Book Store or meeting at the Parker House, where Emerson convened his luminous Saturday Club.

A whole slew of cultural institutions were nourished by Boston money and Boston brains. Among these were the Boston Public Library, the Boston Symphony Orchestra, the Massachusetts Institute of Technology (MIT) and Boston University, the first American university to admit women on an equal basis with men. Harvard had already become one of the world's great universities.

The great immigration

When the Irish Potato Famine began in 1845, Boston was at the apogee of its gleaming social and cultural pre-eminence. Suddenly, thousands of impoverished Irish immigrants arrived, promptly constituting a new underclass.

As the population exploded – swelled further by additional waves of Italians, Poles and Russians in the 1880s – census figures multiplied thirtyfold during the 19th century to about 560,000 people in 1900. Newcomers and incumbents clashed, and Boston was divided into two distinct cultures. Established Bostonians withdrew into their own carefully defended elite, distinguished by Harvard degrees and Back Bay addresses. The new citizens sweated in factories and did handwork, and remade Boston – and its politics – in their

own image. Once dominated by English names, the Puritan "City upon a Hill" became a predominantly Catholic metropolis of Irish and Italian names.

For all Boston's glory and growth during the 1800s, the century's end brought decline, a decline that would continue until the 1960s. New York superseded Boston as a port; the textile mills and shoe factories headed south for cheaper labor and lower taxes. By the 1940s and 1950s, Boston was shrinking.

But then the city woke up. For the first time, Boston's Protestant elite, representing wealth, and its Irish Catholics, representing political power, cooperated in a program of rejuvenation. Government Center, the Prudential and Hancock towers, and a score of downtown skyscrapers changed the face of the city; new hotels, sports facilities, and a convention center made Boston even more of a tourist draw. More recently, the ambitious multi-billion dollar "Big Dig," completed in 2005, eliminated downtown's unsightly elevated highway by diverting traffic underground.

The city further benefited as the Baby Boom generation grew up, went to college, then looked for jobs and apartments. Millions of young people have attended one of the three score colleges in Boston, Cambridge and environs, then stayed on to help transform the local economy.

Park Rangers have an educational role.

A walking city

Despite urban development, one of Boston's primary charms remains unchanged: its tangled streets and the art of walking them. Boston changes so abruptly in mood and nuance from one street to another that it cries out to be explored on foot. The city is charmingly, perversely bereft of a main drag, and its streets practice the old European vices of waywardness and digression. The visitor should, too. There's no telling what you'll find.

BELOW: George Washington's statue in the Public Garden.

Every day hundreds of visitors walk the red line on the sidewalk that marks the 2½-mile (4-km) **Freedom Trail** (tel: 617-242 5642; www.the FreedomTrail.org), a self-guided tour that takes in the major sites of the city's momentous Revolutionary history (*see pages 132–33*). The **Museum of African-American History** (tel: 617-725 0022; www.afroammuseum.org /trail), oversees the 1.6-mile (2.5-km) **Black Heritage Trail** which winds through Beacon Hill and Boston Common, past 14 historic sites relating to the life of the city's free African-Americans prior to the Civil War (*see page 118*).

The North End

This picturesque old neighborhood is Boston's original heart, and to walk its streets is to walk among legends. The Freedom Trail threads its way through the North End on its way between Boston Common and the Bunker Hill Monument in Charlestown.

The North End was the original nub at the end of the Shawmut peninsula where the first settlers planted their town. Later, it became the immigrant core of Boston: once Irish, then Jewish, and now Italian. Gentrification has homogenized this ancient quarter, but many older Italians remain — and people of all backgrounds still descend on the North End for its fragrant Italian grocery stores, restaurants, and festivals.

A stroll through the North End can start at the **Paul Revere House** ❶ (19 North Square; tel: 617-523 2338; open daily year-round; closed Mon Jan–March; entrance fee) in North Square. Built around 1680, it is the oldest building standing in the city, and the period furnishings on display include some items owned by the Reveres. From here, head north toward Hanover Street and the Revere Mall, with its equestrian statue of Revere. At the end of the tranquil, tree-shaded mall, also occupied by a fountain and old Italian men playing checkers, stands Boston's oldest church, the 1723 **Old North Church** ❷ (officially Christ Church, 193 Salem Street; tel: 617-523 6676; open daily), where beneath the graceful spire the sexton Robert Newman famously hung two lanterns on Apr 18, 1775, on the orders of Paul Revere, to signify to the citizens the British plan to move troops inland by boat rather than on foot. Inside, the stately pulpit and a bust of George Washington preside over the original box pews. The beauty of this space finds lovely accompaniment in the "royal peal" of its eight bells, considered the best and sweetest in America. One is inscribed, "We are the first ring of bells cast for the British Empire in North America, Anno 1774."

Behind Old North, between Hull and Charter streets, stand the weathered headstones of **Copps Hill Burying Ground** ❸ (open daily), where many early Bostonians are buried and where several gravestones bear evidence of British soldiers' musket practice.

Charlestown

Across Charlestown Bridge from the North End a famous bit of history lies at anchor: the **USS *Constitution*** ❹ (Charlestown Navy Yard; tel: 617-426 1812; open daily), the venerable frigate known as "Old Ironsides," built in 1797 and

BELOW: the Paul Revere House.

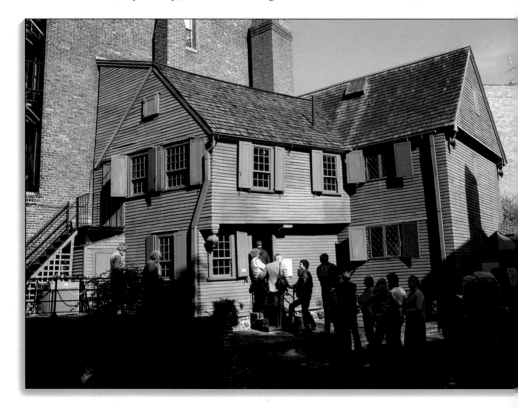

the oldest commissioned vessel in the world (she makes one voyage a year, a ceremonial "turnabout" on the 4th of July); she fought over 40 battles in the War of 1812 and never lost one. The majestic masts soar above the Charlestown Navy Yard, which opened during the War of 1812 and functioned until 1974.

The **USS *Constitution* Museum** tells the ship's story, while the **Boston Marine Society** within the Navy Yard's old octagonal Muster House contains an array of ship models and paintings. The **Commandant's House** is preserved as it was when last occupied in 1876. Also in dock, the **USS *Cassin Young*** is a World War II destroyer, open for tours. The Bunker Hill Pavilion has a multi-media extravaganza depicting the Patriots' heroic loss to the Redcoats in the second battle of the Revolution.

The Freedom Trail follows neighborhood streets from the Navy Yard to the **Bunker Hill Monument ❺** (Monument Square; tel: 617-242 5641; open daily), a granite needle 221 ft (67 meters) high, commemorating the battle. Climb this – be warned that there are 294 steps – and contemplate the complexity of the Harbor, speckled with dozens of islands. Many have odd histories, some linked with Native American legends, others with the deeds and demise of pirates (on tiny Nix's Mate, executed buccaneers were displayed as a warning). Two islands have supported hospitals, another a prison, and others have been fortified. During the Civil War, hundreds of soldiers trained for the Union Army at Fort Warren on George's Island, and more than 1,000 Confederates were jailed there.

The Waterfront

The eastern boundary of the North End is the Waterfront District. If the tall ships – or rather, their modern copies – now appear only sporadically, the great wharves remain, many now recycled as apartments, shopping arcades and upscale restaurants. At the center of it all is Columbus Park; with the completion of the "Big Dig," a much larger park than before links the Waterfront with the downtown area.

By Aquarium subway station, Long Wharf is the starting point for harbor cruises, or you can get harbor views for free by walking along the walkway southwards to Rowes Wharf. The **New England Aquarium ❻** (Central Wharf; tel: 617-973 5200; www.neaq.org; open daily; entrance fee) has the largest seawater fish tank in the world, a gargantuan three-story, 200,000-gallon (900,000-liter) cylinder in which sharks, sea turtles, moray eels and other tropical species glide in never-ending circles. By its base African and rockhopper penguins play on the Ocean Tray, while other highlights include The Edge of the Sea exhibit, a fiberglass re-creation of a New England shore. You can watch through the window on to the Aquarium Medical Center, a laboratory caring for injured and sick animals. The Aquarium operates "Science at Sea" and whale-watch cruises, with researchers and naturalists on board, and has an IMAX Theater.

Follow Harborwalk southwards past Rowes Wharf and cross Northern Avenue Bridge to find **Museum Wharf**, home of the **Children's Museum ❼** (300 Congress Street; tel: 617-426-8855; www.BostonKids.org;

Map on pages 102–3

TIP

In summer the MuSEAm Connection water shuttle links USS *Constitution*, the Aquarium, and Museum Wharf (for the Children's Museum and the Boston Tea Party Ship).

BELOW: "Old Ironsides".

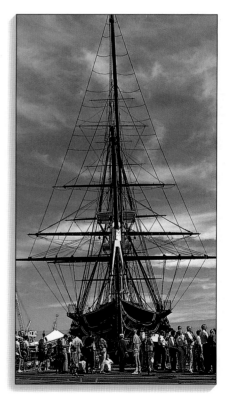

Wind-blown sculpture outside the Aquarium.

open daily; Fri till 9pm, reduced admission; entrance fee). Housed in a renovated warehouse, it is a hands-on adventure, where children can play shoppers at the Supermercado (based on a real Latino supermarket in Boston), climb a three-dimensional maze, and take their shoes off to enter an authentic Japanese house transplanted from Boston's sister city, Kyoto. New England's maritime traditions are reflected in hands-on boating exhibits and an environmental exhibit, Under the Dock, which simulates the underwater landscape of Fort Point Channel and includes a 14-ft (4-meter) fiberglass lobster.

Nearby, on Congress Bridge, is the **Boston Tea Party Ship & Museum** ❽ (Congress Street; tel: 617-338 1773; www.bostonteapartyship.com; entrance fee). Having been fully renovated and expanded after a fire, it will reopen in 2008 with full-size replicas of all three tall ships – the *Brig Beaver, Dartmouth* and *Eleanor* – whose cargo, on the chilly night of December 16, 1773, was thrown overboard in a protest against the English government's commercial practices. Visitors can explore the reasonably authentic decks, crews' quarters and cargo holds, and hurl a tea chest into the harbor. Various exhibits, video presentations and living history programs will elaborate on the mythic event.

The elegant, new four-story **Institute of Contemporary Art** building ❾, which cantilevers over the waterfront at 100 Northern Avenue (tel: 617-478-3100; www.icaboston.org; open Tues–Sun; entrance fee), provides 65,000 sq. ft (6,000 sq. meters) of exhibition and performing arts space, as well as a media center.

Faneuil Hall, Government Center and Downtown

BELOW:
Commercial Wharf, the Waterfront.

Just west of the New England Aquarium rises the **Custom House Tower** ❿, for many years Boston's tallest building, and today certainly the city's quaintest

high-rise (now converted into condominiums), with the 1915 clock tower placed somewhat incongruously on the Greek Revival-style Custom House of 1847.

Close by is **Faneuil Hall Marketplace** ⓫ (tel: 617-523 1300), also known as Quincy Market. Faneuil Hall, the fulcrum of the place, was donated to Boston by Peter Faneuil, a French Huguenot merchant who traded in slaves. This future "Cradle of Liberty," where Patriot orators would soon stir the embers of Revolution, was built in 1742 on a then-waterfront site (it was enlarged by Charles Bulfinch in 1805). Facing it is the domed granite arcade called Quincy Market, built by Mayor Josiah Quincy in 1826 to supplement the public markets on the lower level of Faneuil Hall. In 1976, the complex was reborn as Quincy Marketplace, the chic, wildly successful array of flower stalls, jewelry emporia and designer-clothing outfits you see today. In addition, several dozen food stands line the long hall of the central building, tempting strollers with an endless array of classic American and international snacks, from freshly shucked oysters to Italian sausage subs and exquisite French pastry.

The upper floor of Faneuil Hall itself, where meetings are still held, is open daily (tours every 30 minutes) and houses regimental memorabilia of the Ancient and Honorable Artillery Company. Two of Boston's landmark restaurants, **Durgin Park** and the **Union Oyster House**, are close by.

Street entertainment in Faneuil Hall Marketplace.

For those who wonder why all the shopping bags and restaurant menus bear an image of a grasshopper, just look to the weathervane atop Faneuil Hall. Theories abound as to why the creature was chosen, but it has long been a local icon.

Beside Union Street, six glass towers comprise the **New England Holocaust Memorial** ⓬, the "windows" etched with rows of numbers in memory of six million Jews murdered by the Nazis.

BELOW: reliving the past at the Boston Tea Party Ship (left) and at Faneuil Hall.

Map on pages 102–3

The New England Holocaust Memorial.

Looming just inland from Faneuil Hall, across Congress Street, is **Government Center** ⑬. Here, in the 1960s, the Boston Redevelopment Authority fired its most ambitious volley in its campaign to remake the old downtown. The designers razed buildings and removed streets to create a huge open space – some 56 acres (23 hectares). The centerpiece of this plaza is a massive concrete City Hall designed by Kallmann, McKinnell and Knowles, described as an "Aztec temple on a brick desert."

To the southeast rises the tall confusion of pin-striped Boston, the banks and office towers along Franklin, Congress, Federal, State and Broad streets. Rising confidently from a primitive warren of jumbled byways, these well-tailored behemoths constitute the Hub of Business. A resurrected early Bostonian might marvel at their architecture, but would nod appreciatively to learn that they are counting-houses.

Old State House

To the southwest lies downtown's retail heart, as well as some buildings illuminated brightly in history. At Washington Street's intersection with Court and State streets stands the **Old State House** ⑭ (tel: 617-720-1713; open daily; entrance fee), once the seat of British rule. The Bostonian Society has a museum inside, charting aspects of the city's history with changing displays. It was here, in 1761, that James Otis first fulminated against the British Writs of Assistance in a spellbinding speech that prompted John Adams to write that "then and there the child Independence was born."

In 1770, the infamous Boston Massacre took *(see pages 32–33)* place just outside the State House. After the Revolution, the building served as the meeting place for the Commonwealth Government until the present State House was built.

BELOW:
Quincy Market, which attracts over 10 million visitors a year.

The handsome brick building at the corner of School and Washington streets was once the Old Corner Bookstore, a sort of clubhouse for such writers and thinkers as Hawthorne, Emerson and Thoreau. Later it was the home of the *Atlantic Monthly* when it was launched in 1857, and of the *Boston Globe*, Boston's journal of record.

Continue down Washington Street to the **Old South Meeting House** ⑮ (617-482 6439; open daily; entrance fee), scene of scores of protest meetings denouncing British policy. From here on December 16, 1773, 60 whooping patriots dressed as Mohawk Indians set off for Griffin's Wharf and the Boston Tea Party. An audio historical display sets the scene.

Around the corner at 1 Milk Steet is the site of the now-vanished house in which Benjamin Franklin was born in 1706. Franklin left Boston as a teenager to seek his fortune in Philadelphia.

A little further on comes **Downtown Crossing** ⑯, where hordes of suburban shoppers stampede the city's major department stores. Probably the busiest intersection in Boston, it is the location of the phenomenal **Filene's Basement** (426 Washington Street; tel: 617-348 7848), the world's most celebrated bargain store. Every day, thousands of sharp-eyed professionals, discerning matrons, and blown-dry teen

Map
on pages
102–3

angels can be seen shoving and elbowing each other as they rummage frantically through this cut-rate El Dorado in search of designer seconds, men's suits, and household essentials. Goods are progressively marked down until they sell.

Alternatively, at the Globe Corner Bookstore, turn into School Street, pass the Old City Hall, a grand affair that out-Second Empires the French Second Empire, and at Tremont Street turn right to look into **King's Chapel ⓱** (tel: 617-227 2155; open daily in summer; limited hours rest of year; services Wed. 12:15 pm and Sun. at 11 am). Built in 1754 of Quincy granite, it retains its crisp white box pews as well as Paul Revere's largest bell; its burial ground is Boston's oldest.

Crossing over Tremont Street, head left to the **Granary Burial Ground ⓲**, a pleasant glade where Peter Faneuil, John Hancock, Samuel Adams, Paul Revere, six Massachusetts governors and the victims of the Boston Massacre are interred.

Overlooking the burial ground are the windows of the **Boston Athenaeum** (10½ Beacon Street; tel: 617-227-0270; www.bostonathenaeum.org. first floor open Mon–Sat; tours of entire building 3pm Tues, Thur; 24-hr. minimum advance reservation required), which in the 19th century became the private preserve of wealthy intellectuals and, although anyone is free to walk in and see the first floor art and book exhibits, it has retained that atmosphere virtually intact. There are reading rooms, marble busts, and prints and paintings, as well as books from George Washington's library.

A few more paces down Tremont lead to Peter Banner's elegant, magnificently-steepled 1809 **Park Street Church** (1 Park Street; tel: 617-523-3383; open for tours mid-June–Aug Tues–Sat; Sun services at 8:30am, 11am, 4pm and 6pm) on the corner of Boston Common. Henry James decided it was "perfectly felicitous"

Free, ranger-led tours of the Freedom Trail start from the Boston National Historical Park office, opposite the Old State House.

LEFT: the Old Corner Bookstore as it looked in 1909.
BELOW: the Old State House.

and "the most interesting mass of brick and mortar in America." On July 4, 1829, William Lloyd Garrison made his first anti-slavery speech here, launching his far-reaching emancipation campaign.

Boston Common and the Public Garden

Every American city has a great park somewhere in its outline, but only Boston can claim the oldest, the venerable **Boston Common ⑲**, a magical swath of lawn and trees and benches bounded by Tremont, Park, Beacon, Charles and Boylston streets. Sitting in the sun-mottled shade, watching pigeons strut and children frolic around Frog Pond, the out-of-towner can understand how Bostonians might mistake this spot for the very center of the world.

The land that was to become the Common originally belonged to Boston's first English settler, one Reverend William Blaxton, who had made his home in 1625 on the western slope of what is now known as Beacon Hill. There, he tended his orchard and read in peaceful solitude until his serenity was somewhat rudely interrupted in 1630 by the arrival of a band of new settlers led by Governor John Winthrop of the Massachusetts Bay Company. The new Bostonians were nobly determined, as Winthrop had written on the ship, to "be a Citty upon a hill," and their presence did not please Blaxton. In 1634, he sold his land to the town for around $150 and fled farther into the wilderness.

The 45 acres (18 hectares) he left behind quickly became a versatile community utility. During the next 150 years, it was used as a cattle and sheep pasture and as a militia drilling ground. And although, as an account written in 1663 says, "the Common was the beauty and pride of the Town, ever suggesting the lighter side of life," it also proved useful as a place to whip, pillory, or

The song "America" was first sung in Park Street Church on July 4, 1831.

BELOW:
the Granary
Burial Ground.

Map on pages 102–3

hang people – for stealing, for piracy, for being a Quaker, or a woman who snatched a bonnet worth 75 cents. As a military post, the Common put up the Redcoats all through the Revolution, and during the Civil War it provided a backdrop for the tears of recruiting and departures.

Now the Common is an urban oasis, a park and nothing else. Climb the little knolls and walk the meandering paths past bronze statues and dignified fountains. The Common is at its best all year – when the magnolias bloom, or when snow at sunset evokes the impressionist paintings of Childe Hassam.

West from the Common and across Charles Street, the elegant **Public Garden** ❷⓿ strikes a more formal pose. These variegated trees, meandering paths, and ornate beds of flowers were once part of the fetid Back Bay marshes; but by 1867, the Garden had taken its present graceful shape, complete with weeping willows, a bridge for daydreamers, and a shallow 4-acre (2-hectare) pond.

In summer, one can't overlook the swan boats (**www.swanboats.com**; open mid-Apr–mid-Sept daily; entrance fee), those fabled gondolas that carry happy tourists across the placid waters. At the Commonwealth Avenue entrance, an equestrian *George Washington* bronze by Thomas Ball presides, while a row of bronze ducks on the north side pays tribute to Robert McCloskey's children's story *Make Way for Ducklings*.

The Emerald Necklace is a 6-mile (9-km) corridor of forests, parks and ponds in and around Boston. Begun in 1881 by Frederick Law Olmsted, it links the Public Garden with Franklin Park in West Roxbury.

Beacon Hill

Back up at the east end of the Common, the gold dome of the **State House** ❷❶ (corner State and Washington streets; tel: 617-727-3676; open weekdays) gleams atop Beacon Hill. Completed in 1798 when the downtown building became too small, this design by Charles Bulfinch, with additions by several others,

BELOW LEFT: the dome of the State House seen from the Common.
BELOW: cooling down in Frog Pond.

symbolizes the eminence of politics in Boston. The approach to the legislative chambers passes through a series of splendid halls, beginning with the Bulfinch era Doric Hall and leading to the Senate Staircase Hall and the Hall of Flags, both symphonies of fin de siècle marble opulence supplied plentifully with statues, busts, flags and patriotic mottos.

But none of this dulls the eye to the House Chamber in the Brigham extension, a paneled hall under a two-stage dome. Great moments of Massachusetts' freedom decorate the walls in a series of Albert Herter paintings, while above circles a frieze carved with a roll-call of the state's super-achievers. The portentous codfish known as the "Sacred Cod," a sleek, stiff carving in pine that commemorates Boston's great Federal-era fishing industry, was first hung in the Old State House. Without this old mascot, the house refuses to meet.

The State House, now hemmed in by Beacon Hill residences, seems about as centrally located as a building can be, but it wasn't always that way. In 1797, residents of Boston thought that the Wild West itself began on the far side of the Common, hardly a quarter-mile from the State House site. Cows still grazed there, and much of the surrounding land had the bucolic air of pastures trailing off into forest. Even Beacon Hill rose, not as today's polite demi-hill, but as a rugged mass of wilderness, then called the Trimount because of its triple-peaked summit. The westernmost peak was isolated enough from the Puritan stronghold that it could be put to the purposes suggested by the name Mount Whoredom.

Predictably enough, moving the State House into this setting focused the city's attention on this area and changed things for good. While the Common became a true park, the Trimount became the subject of land speculation. It was quite ingeniously leveled and quickly became the idyllic gaslit neighbor-

Statues in the park include tributes to Edward Everett Hale, author of "The Man Without a Country" (at the Charles Street entrance opposite the Boston Common) and Charles Sumner, who led abolitionist forces in the Senate before the Civil War (at the Boylston Street perimeter).

BELOW:
a swan boat in the Public Garden.

Map on pages 102–3

hood of bow-fronted townhouses now known as "The Hill." At first, everyone expected that the new residences of Beacon Hill would be urban estates along the lines of Bulfinch's freestanding No. 85 Mount Vernon Street (1800) – his second house for developer and politician Harrison Gray Otis – which is to this day one of Boston's most majestic houses. But the mansion plans were quickly scaled down to the smaller blocks one sees today. At No. 55 Mount Vernon Street, the 1804 **Nichols House** ㉒ (tel: 617-227 6993; open May–Oct Tues–Sat pm; Nov–Apr Thurs–Sat pm; tours every half hour; entrance fee), the former home of philanthropist and landscape designer Rose Standish Nichols, offers a more typical example of Beacon Hill building. Also a Charles Bulfinch project, the house is now a small museum.

Federal-era tastes

The Boston window in the State House.

To get a sense of The Hill, walk west down Beacon Street from the State House. At numbers 39 and 40 Beacon stand twin 1818 Greek Revival mansions, one built for Daniel Parker, owner of the Parker House, Boston's oldest hotel. At numbers 42 and 43, the Somerset Club, built in 1819 as a mansion for David Sears, was acquired by the most exclusive of Boston social clubs in 1872. At number 45 Beacon stands the third of the houses designed by Bulfinch for Otis, built in 1805.

The first (1797) **Harrison Gray Otis House** ㉓ at 141 Cambridge Street, just outside Beacon Hill proper (tel: 617-227-3956; open Wed–Sun 11–4:30 pm; tours on the hour and half-hour; entrance fee), headquarters for Historic New England, offers an excellent glimpse of Federal-era tastes.

Louisburg Square ㉔, developed between Pinckney and Mount Vernon

BELOW: inside the State House.

At 66 Phillips Street is the Lewis and Harriet Hayden House, used in the 19th century to shelter fugitive slaves on their way to freedom in Canada. It was said that Hayden kept two kegs of gunpowder in the basement so that the house could be blown up if searched.

BELOW:
the gas lamps on Beacon Hill are permanently lit.
RIGHT:
Beacon Street.

streets around 1840, epitomizes the Beacon Hill style and its urban delicacy. The Square has long stood at the summit of Boston society. William Dean Howells, the novelist and *Atlantic Monthly* editor; Louisa May Alcott, author of *Little Women*; and Jenny Lind, the "Swedish Nightingale," all lived at one time or another in the houses surrounding the Square's elegant green. Lind married her accompanist Otto Goldschmidt at No. 20 during an American tour in 1852.

Another charming example of Beacon Hill's spirit is at numbers 13, 15 and 17 Chestnut Street, where Bulfinch built for the daughters of his client Hepzibah Swan three exquisite townhouses in a prim little row. Chestnut Street vies for the title of prettiest street on the Hill, so fetching is the gently animated conversation of its porches and windows, flower-box geraniums and romantic gaslights.

Museum of African-American History

During the 19th century much of Boston's free African American population lived in a neighborhood of Beacon Hill called North Slope. The 1.6-mile **Black Heritage Trail,** overseen by the **Museum of African-American History ㉕** (46 Joy Street; tel: 617-725 0022; open Mon–Sat year-round) encompasses four historic sites. Two are open to the public: the **African Meeting House** (8 Smith Court), dedicated in 1806 and the oldest black church building still standing in the United States, was where William Lloyd Garrison founded the New England Anti-Slavery Society in 1832. The **Abiel Smith School** (46 Joy Street), served as the country's first publicly-funded grammar school for African Americans from 1834 until 1855, when Boston's schools were integrated.

On the west side of Beacon Hill, Charles Street is a prime spot to stroll, shop and snack. Here is Boston's leading concentration of antique stores and a diverse

collection of coffee houses, bakeries, florists, cafes and boutiques. DeLuca's Market brims with the smells of ripe melons, fresh sausage and coffee beans. Nearby, Café Bella Vita serves coffee and pastries, but the real draw is people-watching.

The street's principal landmark is the **Charles Street Meeting House** at the corner of Charles and Mount Vernon streets. Built first for the Third Baptist Church in 1804, it served as the home of the African Methodist Episcopal Church and later the Unitarian-Universalist Church. At street level, this unpretentious building houses shops and a cafe.

Wander off Charles on to the shady, peaceful streets that trail toward the Charles River or lead back up the hill. Many of the houses here are noteworthy either for their former occupants. Polar explorer Admiral Richard E. Byrd lived in Nos. 7–9 Brimmer Street, while No. 44 in the same street was the lifelong home of the great historian Samuel Eliot Morison. The Victorian clergyman and philosopher William Ellery Channing lived at No. 83 Mount Vernon Street, next door to the second Otis mansion.

Back Bay

From Beacon Hill, it's an easy transition both in distance and architectural feeling to the handsome streets of Back Bay, the area that has come in recent years to epitomize "Old Boston." Don't be fooled by its old-money airs, though. Back Bay literally crawled from the mud into prominence, with a massive program of filling in a festering swampland that, in 1849, was declared "offensive and injurious" by the Board of Health.

The legislature's grand 1857 plan for Back Bay called for long vistas down

Map on pages 102–3

Charles Street has dozens of antiques shops.

BELOW: Louisburg Square.

dignified blocks, and a wide boulevard with a French-style park down the middle. In 1858 the first load of fill arrived by train from Needham, about 10 miles (16 km) to the southwest. During the next 20 years, some 600 acres (240 hectares) of dry land emerged from the muck that was Back Bay.

Despite the vagaries of individual taste and the piecemeal selling of lots, the new blocks went up with an architectural harmoniousness that from the beginning gave Back Bay the stately unity it still possesses. One young man who planned to build his bride a house in Back Bay was icily informed by his prospective father-in-law that he would never allow a daughter of his to live on "made ground." But such qualms were rare, and the new streets quickly became fashionable.

Commonwealth Avenue

Back Bay's imposing rowhouses present as great a showing of the successive revival styles of the late 19th century — from Italianate to Colonial — as Beacon Hill does of the earlier Federal period. The verdant mall of **Commonwealth Avenue** ㉗ centers things, and the houses along it, as well as those on Marlborough and Beacon, reveal choice architectural cameos. (Starting near the Charles River and going right to left, the axial thoroughfares are Beacon Street, Marlborough Street, Commonwealth, Newbury Street, and Boylson Street).

Head west to No. 137 Beacon Street, between Arlington and Berkeley (the cross-streets ascend in alphabetical order), to visit the **Gibson House** ㉘ (tel: 617-267 6338; open Wed–Sun, tours 1pm, 2pm and 3pm; entrance fee). Built at the start of Back Bay construction in 1859, the brick rowhouse has been left substantially as it was; it now houses a museum whose furniture, paintings, books, clocks and textiles recreate the feel of Back Bay living in its heyday.

In 1814 a developer, Uriah Cotting, built a dam across Back Bay, hoping to harness the tidal currents to power as many as 80 mills. But there was less tidal power than expected and only a handful of mills were built.

BELOW:
the rooftops
of Back Bay.

In the block between Clarendon and Dartmouth, Commonwealth Avenue (known as "Comm Ave" to most of the locals) displays its most memorable structures. The romantic houses that march down this stretch perfectly justify the avenue's reputation as America's Champs-Elysées.

Newbury and Boylston streets are the only part of the Back Bay zoned for commerce. On **Newbury Street**, which commences at the Garden with the stately Ritz-Carlton Hotel (lovely for tea or a martini, if you're not wearing jeans) pricey restaurants, sidewalk cafés and designer boutiques abound, and a number of fine galleries operate in sleekly converted townhouses. The best of the contemporary galleries – Alpha and Barbara Krakow – are located at No. 14 and No. 10, respectively. Vose's Gallery, at No. 238, specializes in American painting, 1669 to 1940.

Map on pages 102–3

Trompe l'oeil mural on Newbury Street.

Copley Place

The retail realm along Back Bay's southern commercial spine has long since outgrown its original streets. **Copley Place** ㉙ (100 Huntington Avenue; tel: 617-369-5000; www.shopsimon.com) is a megaplex occupying more than 9 acres (4 hectares) atop the Massachusetts Turnpike, with an 11-screen cinema, hotel, and dozens of inviting restaurants and upmarket shops. Although many of the latter are similar to those found in other upscale malls (Gucci, Tiffany, Neiman Marcus), a few are unique, such as the Artful Hand Gallery (exceptional crafts).

Connected to this complex by a "skyway," is Boston's original skyscraper, the **Prudential Center** ㉚ (800 Boylston Street), dating from the early 1960s and looking it. It has 52 stories and a 50th-floor **Skywalk Observatory** (tel: 617-859 0648; open daily 10am–9:30pm in summer, 10am–8pm in winter; entrance fee) which provides an exhilarating, map-like, four-way view of the city. An Antenna Audio Tour details points of interest far below.

Envisioned as a bold new look for the city, "The Pru" encompasses the John B. Hynes Veterans Memorial Convention Center (expanded in 1988 but with an uncertain future as a newer, larger venue has been built farther from the city center), a hotel, several department stores, and a lively mix of shops and restaurants. Hynes was Boston's mayor from 1950 to 1960.

BELOW: street café in Newbury Street.

The story of Christian Science

The **Christian Science Center** ㉛ (tel: 617-450 2000; www.tfccs.com; Sunday services at 10am, noon and 7pm; testament meeting Wed at noon and 7:30 pm) occupies the 22 acres (9 hectares) immediately south of the Prudential Center on Huntington Avenue. The complex includes three older buildings – the Romanesque Mother Church (1894), the Italianate Mother Church Extension (1904) and the Publishing Society (1933) – as well as I.M. Pei's 1973 additions. It all adds up to an impressive headquarters for a religious denomination scarcely a century old.

In the publishing wing, the **Mapparium** (tel: 617-450 7000; open daily except Mon; fee) is an extraordinary stained-glass walk-in representation of the globe, constructed between 1932 and 1935 to symbolize the Christian Science Publishing Company's

worldwide outlook. Illogical it may be – you stand inside the sphere surrounded by the map in concave form – but it is certainly one of the sights of Boston. The weird acoustics compound the hallucinogenic effect.

The founding of Christian Science dates to 1866 when a frail, impoverished 45-year-old woman named Mary Baker Patterson took a severe tumble on the ice as she was walking home from a temperance meeting in Lynn, north of Boston. Several days later, after turning to the New Testament for strength and inspiration, Mrs Patterson was suddenly healed, not only of the injuries she'd suffered in the fall, but of the chronic illness that had plagued much of her younger womanhood.

After several years of Bible study, she set out to heal others. In 1875, she posted a notice on her Lynn house designating it as a "Christian Science Home." After marrying a follower named Asa Eddy, she moved to Boston, where she continued teaching, writing (*Science and Health* is her great opus and the religion's founding text) and guiding the establishment of her church. Since then more than 3,000 Christian Science societies have been established in 50 countries.

Copley Square

Follow Dartmouth Street to Boylston for one of the city's most stimulating displays of architecture: Copley Square. First, Charles McKim's 1895 **Boston Public Library** ❸❷ (700 Boyston Street; tel: 617-536-5400; www.bpl.org; free art and architecture tours of the research library Mon at 2:30pm, Tues and Thurs at 6pm, Fri and Sat. at 11am, Sun at 2pm). This simple, serene and high-minded Parnassus might well be the center of the Boston that claims to be the "Athens of America." What better monument to a literary legacy populated by the likes

The Christian Science Monitor, a much respected daily newspaper that today claims hundreds of thousands of readers worldwide, was founded by Mary Baker Eddy in 1908, at the age of 87.

BELOW: the Christian Science Church Center.

Map on pages 102–3

of Emerson, Hawthorne, Thoreau and Alcott? (Bret Harte once observed that in these parts it was impossible to fire a pistol without bringing down the author of a two-volume work.) With more than 5 million volumes, this is one of the great libraries in the world. But it's more than a building of books. There's art everywhere – murals by Sargent, statues by Saint-Gaudens and Daniel Chester French – and, at the center of a maze of stairs and passages, a peaceful inner courtyard. Philip Johnson's massive 1972 addition "quotes" the original structure in a vastly simplified modern vernacular.

Across the square stands H. H. Richardson's masterpiece 1877 **Trinity Church ㉝** (206 Clarendon Street; 617-536 0944; www.trinitychurchboston.org; open daily 8 am–6 pm for self-guided tours; guided tours Mon–Sat at 11am and 1 and 2 pm; Sun, free tour after 11:15am service; fee for self-guided and guided tours), a tour de force in Romanesque inventiveness and a striking medievalist contrast to the Public Library's classicism. Inside, what impresses is the wealth of murals, mosaics, carvings and stained glass.

The John Hancock Tower

Above everything looms I. M. Pei & Partners' magnificent blue-green mirror, the **John Hancock Mutual Life Insurance Tower**, built in 1976. The Tower initially had a propensity in windy weather to lose the huge sheets of glass covering it; miraculously, no one was hurt when the glass fell. That problem was solved soon after the tower was completed, when all 10,344 panes – some 13 acres (5 hectares) worth – were replaced at a cost of $8.5 million, and the building's core stiffened. (Note: the once popular top-floor Observatory has been closed to the public since the terrorist attacks of September 11, 2001).

A "Duck Tour", by amphibious vehicle, includes a ride on the river. Tours start from the Museum of Science and the Prudential Center. Tel: 617-267 3825.

BELOW: Copley Square Park.

Every April, on Patriots' Day, Copley Square becomes the destination of the thousands who enter the celebrated Boston Marathon.

South End and The Fenway

The first Boston Marathon, staged in 1897, involved 15 runners. Today, about 8,000 line up for the starter's gun as 1½ million spectators look on.

To the south and east of the Christian Science Center and Copley Square sprawls the South End, an ethnically diverse but much gentrified quarter of Victorian bowfront townhouses. Particularly pleasing architecturally are the areas around Worcester Square, Rutland and leafy Union Park Square, where it's evident that London – rather than Paris, as in the Back Bay – was the developers' insprtration.

The **Boston Center for the Arts** ❸❹, at Clarendon and Tremont streets (tel: 617-426 5000; www.bcaonline.org), is almost always hopping: this lively complex encompasses the Mills Gallery (open Sun, Wed–Thurs noon–5pm; Fri and Sat. noon–10pm) and three theatres which present a total of 45 productions yearly. One of the city's favorite bistros, Hammersley's, is in the plaza complex.

From the South End, Huntington Avenue leads southwest past several of Boston's greatest institutions. At the northwest corner of Massachusetts Avenue ("Mass Ave") stands the majestic gable-roofed **Symphony Hall** ❸❺ (301 Massachusetts Avenue; tel: 617-266 1492 or, for tickets tel: 888-266 1200; www.bso.org; walk-up tours on the first Sat of the month at 1pm, except Dec, and Wed at 4:30pm from early Oct–early Dec and Jan–May), the acoustically impeccable 1900 building that is home to the renowned Boston Symphony Orchestra and, in spring and during the Christmas holidays, its less formal offshoot, the Boston Pops Orchestra. Tickets can be hard to come by.

BELOW: the John Hancock Tower.

Continue down Huntington Avenue to reach the **Museum of Fine Arts** ❸❻ (465 Huntington Avenue; tel: 617-267 9300; www.mfa.org; open Sat, Sun, Mon, and Tues 10am–4:45pm; special exhibits open Wed–Fri until till 9:45pm with reduced admission Thurs and Fri after 5pm; entrance fee). Built in 1909 and enlarged with an I.M. Pei-designed wing in 1981, this incredible museum is perhaps best known for its Impressionists – including the largest number of Monets outside France – but it also has the most complete assemblage of Asian art under one roof anywhere; the world's best collection of 19th-century American art; and the finest collection of Egyptian Old Kingdom objects outside Cairo. The latter includes what some consider one of the greatest portraits ever executed by the human hand – a limestone bust of Prince Ankh-haf (2520 BC) that is wholly unearthly in its magnificence.

Within sight of the Museum of Fine Arts stands the **Isabella Stewart Gardner Museum** ❸❼ (280 The Fenway; tel: 617-566 1401; www.gardnermuseum.org; open Tues–Sun, 11am–5pm; entrance fee) an exquisite 1903 neo-Venetian palazzo assembled by Boston's most flamboyant grande dame. The unstoppable "Mrs Jack" may have scandalized Brahmin Boston (she was known to parade two pet lions down Beacon Street), but she proved a generous and astute patron of the arts.

During the 1890s, she set her sights on such masterpieces as Titian's *Rape of Europa*, Rembrandt's *Storm on the Sea of Galilee*, and Vermeer's *The Concert*. In 1896, when her collection was bursting the seams of two adjoining Beacon Hill brownstones, she commissioned her fantasy palace at the very edge of town, alongside the marshes of the Fens.

The galleries that frame the four-story glass-roofed courtyard remained, by her posthumous order, unchanged until March 1990, when thieves, disguised as policemen, made off with works of art worth $300 million, including the Vermeer, three Rembrandts, five works by Degas and a Manet. To date, none has been recovered. There is still much to see, however, and this eclectic collection, displayed in a charmingly hodge-podge fashion, constitutes one of the great small museums in the world.

North of the museums broods another of Boston's great shrines, **Fenway Park ㊳** (4 Yawkey Way; ; tel: 617-267 8661 or 617-267 1700; www.redsox.com; behind-the-scene one-hour tours daily 9am-4pm, on the hour – if there's a game, the last tour is three hours before game time; entrance fee). Built in 1912, the Red Sox's home field is the oldest ballpark in the major leagues. Its survival appeared to be in doubt a few years back, but in 2002 new owners committed to updating its facilities while keeping its storied charm. As of October 2004, the World Series flag finally flew over the old ballpark.

The home of the Boston Celtics (tel: 617-624-1000; www.nba.com/celtics), who have been National Basketball Association champions 16 times, and the Bruins (tel: 617-624 1000; www.bostonbruins.com), Boston's major ice-hockey team is the state-of-the-art **Banknorth Garden ㊴**, near North Station.

On the banks of the Charles River

Like many great cities, Boston lies in the embrace of a great river. Here, before the townhouses of Back Bay, the Charles River, having meandered 40 miles (64

 Map on pages 102–3

 TIP

A delightful way to spend a Sunday afternoon in winter is to attend a concert in the Gardner Museum's Tapestry Room. Tickets at the door, or tel: 617-566 1401. www.gardnermuseum.org.

BELOW: the courtyard of the Isabella Stewart Gardner Museum.

Henry Moore's "Three-piece reclining figure, draped," on the MIT campus.

km) from its source, widens into a large basin, like a giant mirror held up to the city's profile. It was designed to do just that, by the civic-minded citizens who created the Charles River Dam in 1908. The dam itself is home to Boston's **Museum of Science** ❹ (tel: 617-723 2500; www.mos.org; open daily; Fri till 9pm; entrance fee). Here, visitors can watch simulated lightning, climb into a model of the Apollo lunar module, cower under a plastic Tyrannosaurus Rex, join "The Computing Revolution", and enjoy a wide variety of ever-changing hands-on exhibits. A combination ticket includes admission to the five-story, domed Omni Theater, planetarium, and laser show. On-site parking is available for a fee.

In ensuing decades after the construction of the dam, the **Esplanade** was landscaped, a winding park of lagoons, trees and walks. The river's edge is one of the city's favorite places to stretch its legs. Roller skaters wired for sound, joggers, bike riders and sunbathers all migrate here. So do the great crowds that turn out to hear the Boston Pops (tel: 617-266 1492) play under open summer skies at the **Hatch Memorial Shell** ❹.

Kennedy Library and Museum

Separate from central Boston sites, but a point of pilgrimage for many, is the **John F. Kennedy Library and Museum** ❹ (Columbia Point; tel: 617-514-1600 or 866-JFK-1960; www.jfklibrary.org; open daily; entrance fee; free parking; MBTA red line south to JFK/UMass and shuttle bus; or, in summer, boat from Long Wharf). Set dramatically beside the ocean, the museum, dedicated to the life and legacy of JFK, makes excellent use of film, videos and recreated settings (including the Oval Office). The building, designed by I.M. Pei, has a very large library and archive, and is surrounded by a 9½-acre (3.8-hectare) park.

BELOW: the Red Sox at Fenway Park.

Cambridge and Harvard Square

Elizabeth Hardwick once described Boston and Cambridge as two ends of the same mustache. Indeed, across the Charles lies a separate city that is absolutely inseparable from its companion metropolis. Neither suburb nor next town down the pike, Cambridge is the brains of the act, the nerve center of the body.

Just across Harvard Bridge is the **Massachusetts Institute of Technology (MIT)** . (Information Center open Mon–Fri at 77 Massachusetts Avenue; free tours at 10:45am and 2:45pm Mon–Fri; tel: 617-253-4795; www.mit.edu) Housed in solid neoclassical buildings with the trim logic of natural laws, MIT produces Nobel laureates, new scientific advances and White House science advisors with absolute reliability. The Finnish architect Eero Saarinen designed two of its highlights: the inward looking, cylindrical MIT Chapel, illuminated by light reflected from a moat, and the tent-like Kresge Auditorium which rises from a circular brick terrace, its roof apparently balanced by slender metal rods on three points. Exhibits at the **MIT Museum** (tel: 617-253-4444; open Tues–Fri; Sat and Sun pm; entrance fee) include paintings, scientific instruments, and "The Hall of Hacks", highlighting students' pranks over the years.

Harvard Square ❸, at the heart of Cambridge, is home to **Harvard University** (historic tours Mon–Fri at 10am and 2pm; Sat at 2pm – call 617-495 1573; www.harvard.edu) and the playground of book stores, coffee houses, and shops to the west and north of the Yard, with a menagerie of horn-rimmed professors, "B School" overachievers and fresh-looking undergraduates in evidence. At its center is the international **Out of Town News**, housed in a historic kiosk, and beside it, Dmitri Hadzi's gently humorous stone sculpture, *Omphalos*, suggesting that Harvard is, as its supporters have long held, the center (or navel) of the universe.

The JFK Library is one of 11 "presidential libraries," which hold the papers of nine of the presidents since Herbert Hoover. Presidents may establish a library in the location of their choice; this one was set up near the home of Rose Kennedy, JFK's mother.

BELOW: busking in Harvard Square.

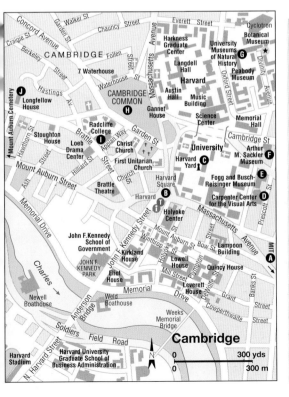

BELOW:
Harvard Square and its historic news stand.

Opposite Out of Town News is the venerable **Harvard Cooperative Society** ("Coop" for short), a Harvard institution founded in 1882 as an alternative to overpriced local shops; today the prices are pretty much at a par (except for affiliated students and faculty, who enjoy a discount), but the full-scale department store is a favorite with tourists for Harvard-seal mementos.

Every block presents some window or door to investigate. Browse the fine bookstores such as WordsWorth and the Harvard Book Store, check the movie schedules at the area's local collegiate-oriented theaters. There's even a great old tobacco store, a dark cave called Leavitt and Peirce, that has served generations of pipe-smoking academics and carries an collection of ruminative games.

Standing proudly above the red brick and green ivy are the spires of Harvard University, America's oldest institution of higher learning. Self-confident and backed by enormous wealth, Harvard has been a world index of intellectual accomplishment almost since that day in 1638 when the first 12 freshmen convened in a single frame house bordered by cow pastures. The alma mater of five American presidents to date, Harvard remains a formidable force.

The heart of the place is **Harvard Yard** ⓒ, withdrawn tranquilly behind the walls that separate it from Harvard Square outside. Passing through the gate that proclaims "Enter to Grow in Wisdom," the visitor enters a hallowed world of grass and trees, ghosts and venerable brick – a living, eminently walkable museum of American architecture from colonial times to the present.

Massachusetts Hall (1720), Harvard's oldest standing building, shows the beautiful simplicity of its period, but its history is complex. While it has always provided students with rooms, the Hall has also quartered Revolutionary troops, as well as housed a lecture hall, a famous drama workshop and, since 1939, the

offices of the University president. Nearby stands little Holden Chapel (1744), once described as "a solitary English daisy in a field of Yankee dandelions."

Map on page 127

At the Yard's center stands Charles Bulfinch's University Hall, built of white granite in 1815. In front is Daniel Chester French's 1814 statue of John Harvard, the young Puritan minister for whom the college was named after he left it half his estate and all his books. Since no likeness of John Harvard existed, French used a student as his model.

East of University Hall, three massive buildings set off the central green on which commencement is celebrated each June. These are H. H. Richardson's 1880 masterwork Sever Hall, with its subtle brick decorations; Memorial Church (1932), with its Doric columns; and the monumental Widener Library, fronted by a broad flight of steps and 12 stone columns. Given by the mother of alumnus and bibliophile Harry Elkins Widener, who died on the *Titanic*, the library is the center of Harvard's network of 92 libraries, which together house over 12 million volumes, America's third largest book collection.

Chess is traditionally played in Harvard Square.

Around this historic core, the university sprawls throughout central Cambridge. The Harvard Houses (1930), between the Yard and the Charles, represent a return to the Georgian traditions of the 19th century. These are the residences of sophomores, juniors and seniors. To the east of the Yard stands the **Carpenter Center for the Visual Arts** ❻ (1963), a cubist, machine-like design that represents the only American work of the great French architect Le Corbusier.

Of special interest to visitors are the university's museums. Just outside the Yard to the east are the **Fogg and Busch-Reisinger Art Museums** ❺ (32 Quincy Street; tel: 617-495-9400; www.artmuseums.harvard.edu; open Mon–Sat, Sun pm; entrance fee). The Fogg's massive holdings include such masterpieces

BELOW: a regatta at Cambridge Boat Club, on the Charles River.

Map on page 127

TIP

The Harvard University Art Museums are free daily after 4:30pm and on Saturday mornings 10–12pm. If you plan to visit all the Harvard museums, it's worth buying a Harvard Hot Ticket, sold at the Holyoke Center for $10.

BELOW: Longfellow House, Brattle Street.
RIGHT: students with original benefactor John Harvard.

as Van Gogh's *Self Portrait*, Renoir's *Seated Bather*, Fra Angelico's *Crucifixion* and several early Picassos. It also owns a world-class collection of Chinese cave paintings and archaic Chinese jade. Adjoining the Fogg, Werner Otto Hall houses central and northern European art. Housed in the same building, the Busch-Reisinger has outstanding examples of German expressionism and Bauhaus artifacts. Nearby, the **Arthur M. Sackler Museum ❻** (485 Broadway; tel: 617-495-9400; www.artmuseums.harvard.edu; open Mon–Sat, Sun pm; entrance fee) houses the Ancient, Islamic and Oriental collections.

A few blocks north on Oxford Street stands the **Harvard Museum of Natural History ❼** (26 Oxford Street; tel: 617-495-3045; www.hmnh.harvard.edu; open daily; entrance fee) a huge complex housing several museums. The displays are old-fashioned – they are university collections, after all – but a major draw is the **Botanical Museum** (tel: 617-495-3045; open Mon–Sat; Sun pm; entrance fee), with its famous "Glass Flowers," a collection of true-to-life models of more than 700 plant species executed by Leopold Blaschka and his son Rudolph in 19th-century Dresden. In the same building, the **Museum of Comparative Zoology** includes George Washington's stuffed pheasants as well as the world's oldest reptile eggs. Also on the site is the **Mineralogical and Geological Museum** (daily 9am–5pm), with a vast collection of rocks, meteorites and minerals.

The **Peabody Museum of Archaeology and Ethnology** (11 Divinity Avenue; tel: 617-496-1027; open daily; entrance fee) is one of the oldest museums of its type in the world (founded 1866). It exhibits collections from Native American and Central and South American cultures.

On July 4, 1775, George Washington assumed command of the Continental Army on **Cambridge Common ❽**. A trio of cannons abandoned by the British when they left Boston in 1776 stand close to a bronze relief of Washington on horseback under an elm tree; the elm enclosed by a fence is a token replacement of the original "Washington's elm." On the south side of the Common, just across Garden Street, Christ Church (1761) was used as a barracks by patriots, and its organ pipes were made into bullets. Close by is an entrance to **Radcliffe College ❾**, (www.radcliffe.edu) the women's college that merged with Harvard in 1975.

Longfellow's legacy

In the 18th century Brattle Street was home to so many British loyalists that it was known as Tory Row. There are numerous houses to be admired from the street, including No. 90, designed by H. H. Richardson of Trinity Church fame, and No. 94, the 17th-century Henry Vassal House. The yellow clapboard **Longfellow House** at the **Longfellow National Historic Site ❿** (105 Brattle Street; tel: 617-876-4491; www.nsp.gov/long; open May–Oct; tours Wed– Sun; entrance fee) was the idyllic wedding present given to the poet Henry Wadsworth Longfellow and his wife, Fanny, by her father in 1843. Little has changed inside; Longfellow's library and furniture are here, including a chair made from the "spreading chestnut-tree," which stood at No. 56 Brattle Street and was immortalized in his poem *The Village Blacksmith*. Unhappily, Fanny was fatally burned in the house in 1861. ❑

Map on pages 102–3

THE FREEDOM TRAIL

Given the dense traffic, it's simpler to walk in Boston than to drive. Taking advantage of that fact, this signed route provides an easy way of absorbing the city's revolutionary history

The shot heard round the world – the starting gun of the American Revolution – was fired in Lexington, just west of Boston, on April 18, 1775. In the months and years that followed, until the war for American independence from Britain ended in 1781, Boston would continue to play a leading role in the conflict. The "midnight ride of Paul Revere" (made famous in the poem by Henry Wadsworth Longfellow), the Boston Tea Party, the Battle of Bunker Hill – all are part of Boston's colorful Revolutionary past.

In Lexington and Concord, which today are suburbs of Boston, national parks preserve the legacy of the conflict's beginnings. And in the heart of Boston, a cleverly designed 2½-mile (4-km) footpath, the Freedom Trail, invites visitors to experience Boston as it was in the Revolutionary era, to visit historical sites associated with the war, and to walk where the founders of the country walked more than 200 years ago. It is estimated that some 3 million people visit the Freedom Trail each year.

Although most of the trail follows city streets, it is not advisable to drive it: Downtown Boston is famously hard to negotiate with a car, and parking spaces are hard to find and pricey. The Freedom Trail is easy to follow as a self-guided tour – just follow the red brick road (or more accurately in many places, the red painted line). At some sites, costumed interpreters and docents greet trail-walkers.

It takes an hour or so to walk the length of the trail at a brisk pace, but to appreciate the history of its 16 official sites, allow at least a half-day. Detailed brochures and guidebooks are available at the Boston National Historical Park Visitor Center (15 State Street, tel: 617-242 5642) or at the Boston Common Visitor Information Center (www.thefreedomtrail.org).

Walkers may begin anywhere along the Trail, but the logical starting point is the Common, itself a mustering ground for Colonial militia before and during the Revolutionary War. Today, the Common is one of the most beloved public spaces in Boston – a 45-acre swath of green that is overlooked by the gold dome of the State House.

From Boston Common, the Freedom Trail leads to the Granary Burying Ground adjacent to the Park Street Church on Tremont Street. Revolutionary heroes such as Samuel Adams, John Hancock, Paul Revere, and James Otis are buried here.

Nearby is King's Chapel, built of granite between 1749 and 1754, and containing the largest bell ever cast in Paul Revere's foundry. Revere, one of the best-known patriots of the Revolution, was a silversmith and later a foundry owner. Among those buried in the King's Chapel Burying Ground (the city's oldest graveyard) are Puritan governor John Winthrop; William

BELOW: Paul Revere as portrayed by John Singleton Copley in 1768.

Dawes, the lesser-known of the two Lexington messenger-riders who carried the warning that the British were on the march; and Elizabeth Pain, said to be the model for Hester Prynne in Nathaniel Hawthorne's *The Scarlet Letter.*

At the 1729 Old South Meeting House, one of the most notable sites of the Revolutionary era, a small historical museum includes a scale-model diorama depicting Colonial-era Boston. A crowd of 5,000 rallied at Old South on December 16, 1773 to oppose the British tea tax. Following the meeting, the Sons of Liberty headed off to dump a shipload of British tea into Boston Harbor in a famous protest, an incident later known as the Boston Tea Party.

From here the trail leads to the Old State House. Boston's oldest public building was built in 1713 to serve as the center of political life in the emerging Massachusetts Bay Colony. The proclamation of the Declaration of Independence was read to Boston citizens on July 18, 1776. Afterward, in a gesture of elated defiance, two leftover symbols of British rule – a lion and a unicorn – were removed from the roof of the State House and burned. They were replaced with replicas after the building was saved from demolition and restored in 1882.

Wending its way to Faneuil Hall (a key meeting point for Boston's revolutionaries), the Freedom Trail heads into the North End. The North End is the oldest section of Boston: its narrow, crooked streets were laid out over what were originally cow paths. Here, at 19 North Square, is the steep-roofed wooden house that belonged to Paul Revere. Already almost 100 years old when Revere bought it in 1770, the little peaked house where the patriot lived for some 30 years is the oldest structure in Boston.

Not far away, on Paul Revere Mall, a statue of Revere on horseback in front of the Old North Church is one of Boston's most-photographed sites. A pair of lanterns hung in the Old North on the eve of the war signaled that the British forces were leaving Boston (then almost an island) by sea, rather than by land. The church's original steeple, toppled in a 1954 windstorm, has been replicated.

From the North End, the Freedom Trail crosses the Charlestown Bridge to Charlestown. (An inexpensive water shuttle runs between Charlestown and Long Wharf, near the trail, making it possible to go one way on foot and the other by ferry.) Here a 221-ft (66-meter) granite monument commemorates the June 17, 1775 Battle of Bunker Hill. Here, on what is actually Breed's Hill, the Colonials hastily built an earthwork fort in anticipation of a British attack. During the ensuing battle, which was ultimately a British victory, the revolutionaries managed to strike a resounding blow by wounding or killing about half the British force.

"The Whites of Their Eyes," a half-hour multimedia presentation on the battle, is shown in the Navy Yard Visitor Center/Bunker Hill Pavilion near the Charlestown Navy Yard. Berthed nearby is the frigate USS *Constitution* – not part of Boston's Revolutionary past, but famous as the oldest commissioned warship afloat. Her first mission after being launched in Boston in 1797 was to guard the new country's commercial interests in the Caribbean against the French. During the War of 1812, she earned the nickname Old Ironsides, by which she has been known ever since. ❏

FANEUIL
HALL

The Freedom Trail is self-guided and can be joined at any point.

BELOW: the Bunker Hill Monument, Charlestown.

THE MUSEUM OF FINE ARTS, BOSTON

Few museums in the world rival the MFA for the quality and scope of its decorative and fine art collections. Every one has something exceptional

One of America's first museums, the MFA opened at Copley Square in 1870 and moved into its present building in 1909. Cyrus Edwin Dallin's bronze equestrian statue *Appeal to the Great Spirit* (left) was placed in the forecourt in 1913.

The highly cultured citizens of 19th-century Boston were keen collectors. Many were passionate about things Asian, and their treasures in due course came to the MFA, forming the nucleus of an outstanding collection. Others travelled to Europe, and the museum acquired one of the foremost holdings outside Paris of Impressionist painting, in particular works by Monet, Pissaro, Sisley, Renoir and Manet. It has nearly 70 works by Jean-François Millet. The American art collection is one of the best in the US; the European and American decorative arts rooms display superb silver, porcelain, furniture and musical instruments. The Nubian and Egyptian collections are unrivalled in the world.

There is so much to see, the first-time visitor would be well advised either to pick out just one collection, or take a (free) tour that highlights the best from all the collections. *See also page 124.*

▽ **AMERICAN DECORATIVE ARTS**
The museum is strong in decorative arts from pre-Civil War New England. Below: a Paul Revere teapot, *c.*1760–5.

△ **THE JAPANESE GARDEN**
Tenshin-en, "The Garden of the Heart of Heaven," is one of three gardens in which visitors may draw breath (beside the West Wing; open spring through early fall).

▷ **THE IMPRESSIONISTS**
Renoir's *Dance at Bougival* (1883) shares wall space with equally important works by such European painters as van Gogh, Degas, and Gauguin.

◁ **LANDSCAPE ART**
The New England landscape is captured in works by such American artists as Winslow Homer and Edward Hopper. Left: Edward Hopper's watercolour *Lighthouse and Buildings, Portland Head, Cape Elizabeth* (1927)

THE ANCIENT WORLD

For 40 years from 1905 Harvard University and the Museum of Fine Arts collaborated on an archeological excavation in Egypt, based at the Great Pyramids at Giza. From this, the museum acquired a world-famous collection of Egyptian treasures. Among many Old Kingdom sculptures is this beautiful statue of King Mycerinus, who built the Third Pyramid at Giza, and his queen, dated to *c*.2548–30BC.

Other treasures include gilded and painted mummy masks, and some amazingly well preserved hierglyphic inscriptions. The Giza expedition's director, Dr Reisner, also worked in the Sudan and brought home a dazzling collection of Nubian artifacts, the best in the world outside Khartoum. Particularly awe-inspiring is the exquisite gold jewelry, inlaid with enamel and precious stones, and the sculptures, varying in size from huge statues of Nubian kings to tiny shawabtis.

△ **AMERICAN ART**
The Letter by Mary Cassatt (1890). More formal are the portraits by colonial painters Gilbert Stuart and John Singleton Copley, and society portraitist John Singer Sargent.

▽ **THE ASIAN COLLECTION**
A highlight of the excellent Asian collection is this little 12th-century AD (Jin Dynasty) Chinese buddha, made of lacquered wood with painting and gilding.

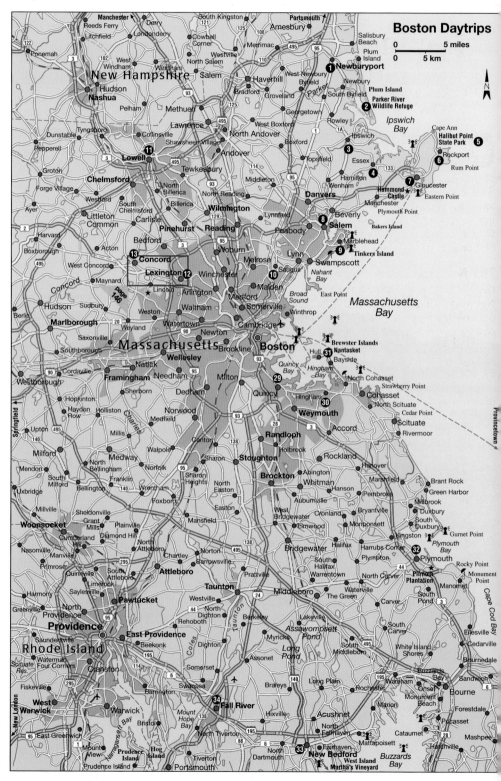

Boston Daytrips

DAYTRIPS FROM BOSTON

We've either read them or we've read about them: the witches of Salem, the Pilgrims of Plymouth, the Patriots of Lexington, and the writers – Alcott, Emerson and Thoreau – of Concord

Map on page 138

O ne of Boston's great advantages for visitors is its scope for daytrips, ranging from the obvious – Plymouth, or Lexington and Concord – to the decidedly offbeat delights. Public transportation from Boston makes many of the places described easy to reach; frequent commuter trains from North Station serve Concord, Salem (for buses to Marblehead), Rockport, Manchester, Gloucester, Ipswich and Newburyport, and there are buses from South Station to Plymouth, New Bedford, and Fall River ; the T Red Line goes to Quincy Center. Providence (*see page 229*) is another easy daytrip by train from South Station, and buses from South Station serve Newport (*see page 234*).

The North Shore

Once home to a magnificent merchant fleet and a thriving shipbuilding industry, **Newburyport ❶**, 35 miles (56 km) north of Boston, has benefited from careful preservation. The town survived a devastating fire in 1811; the rebuilding gave downtown its uniform Federal-era appearance. But by the early 20th century, the arrival of freighters had reduced the proud shipbuilding industry of "Clipper City" to an aging relic. **Lowell's Boat Shop** (495 Main Street; tel: 978 834-0050); tours by appointment) the country's oldest boatbuilding shop, is in nearby Amesbury.)

PRECEDING PAGES: Annisquam, Cape Ann. **BELOW:** Newburyport.

An exemplary renewal program begun in the 1960s has restored Newburyport's architectural beauty, and made it a popular destination. The **Market Square** district is a symphony of brick and bustle, with fine shops and restaurants, adjacent to a waterfront promenade and piers where whale watching tours embark.

On High Street successful sea captains built an imposing string of Federal-style mansions. **The Cushing House**, (tel: 978-462 2681; open May–Oct Tues–Sat; entrance fee) at No. 98 High Street, belonged to Caleb Cushing, a 19th-century lawyer (Newburyport's first mayor) and the first US Ambassador to China. Visitors to the 1808 house, now home to the Historical Society of Old Newbury, can view the exotic booty he brought back.

Parker River National Wildlife Refuge

On the way out to **Plum Island** along Water Street, the Massachusetts Audubon Society offers interpretive displays at their **Joppa Flats Education Center** (tel: 978 462-9888; open Tues–Sun and Mon holidays). Just across the road, the **Parker River National Wildlife Refuge** visitor center ❷ (open Mon–Fri; tel: 978 465 5753) offers a fine introduction to the refuge just 3 miles (5 km) away. Depending on the season, the 6 miles (10 km) of sand dunes and ocean beach yield a riot of false heather, dune grass, scrub pine and beach plums. Geese, pheasants, rabbits, deer, woodchucks, turtles and toads roam freely over the preserve. In March and October the skies are dark with migrating geese and ducks. Fishing, hiking and bird-watching are encouraged. Only a limited number of visitors (300 cars; parking fee) are allowed into the refuge at one time.

TIP

In the fall, after Labor Day, visitors to Plum Island are allowed to pick beach plums and cranberries – one quart per person, no rakes permitted.

The road to Ipswich

Heading south out of Newburyport on Route 1A, city and country meet about 4 miles (7 km) out of town in Newbury at the **Spencer-Pierce-Little Farm** (5 Little's Lane; tel: 978 462-2634; tours June–mid-Oct Thurs–Sun; entrance fee), a manor house built around 1675–1700 and now owned by Historic New England. A distinctively sturdy building for its day (built of stone and brick, instead of the customary wood), it is today, with its layers of structural alteration, a prime site for architectural archeology. Its farmland has been under three and a half centuries of continual cultivation.

Continue on Route 1A, a lazy, tree-lined road, into **Ipswich,** ❸ whose streets are lined with restored 17th- and 18th-century houses. On Main Street, the 1640 **John Whipple House** (tel: 978-356 2811; open Apr–mid–Oct Wed–Sat, Sun pm; entrance fee) is a fine example of a Puritan homestead, furnished in period style and with a colonial herb garden. Just out of town, the **Crane Wildlife Refuge** (tel: 978-356-4354; www.thetrustees.org) was part of a vast estate owned by plumbing fixture magnate Richard Crane. The **Great House at Castle Hill** (310 Arguilla Road; tel: 978-356-4351; open for tours mid-May–mid-Sept, Wed and Thur; entrance fee), Crane's opulent, 59-room 1927 Jacobean mansion, was his summer home. The refuge's 4-mile (6-km) **Crane's Beach** (tel: 978-356-4354; parking fee) is one of New England's finest.

BELOW: queueing for fried clams at Woodman's, Essex.

Ipswich is known for its clams, as is the neighboring town of **Essex ❹**, 5 miles (8 km) southeast on Route 133, where, folk legend has it, the fried clam was born. It was at **Woodman's** restaurant (tel: 978-768 6451) that clams were first dipped in cornmeal and fried. The **Essex Shipbuilding Museum** (28 Main Street; tel: 978-768 7541; open Jun–Oct Wed–Sun, Nov–May weekends pm; entrance fee) traces the region's rich boatbuilding history.

Cape Ann

Named for the mother of England's King Charles I, **Cape Ann** is practically an island, compact enough to explore in a day. From Annisquam, at the mouth of Ipswich Bay, to Pigeon Cove, the landscape is quintessential New England – quaint fishing villages and a rockbound coast.

The quarries at **Halibut Point State Park ❺** (Gott Avenue off Route 127, Rockport; tel: 978-546 2997; entrance fee) once provided granite for Boston's buildings. Within the granite-strewn dwarf woods, the original quarry is now a huge pool edged by sheer cliffs; trees open out into heathland and scrub to reveal views over the rocky shore towards Plum Island.

The granite was shipped to ports around the world in the 19th century, from **Rockport ❻**, a bustling former fishing village-turned-artists' colony and tourist attraction. The seagoers' cottages crowded on to Bearskin Neck have become tourist-oriented shops. The fishing shack on the harbor has become known as Motif No. 1 because it is said to be more frequently painted and sketched than any other building in America. Signposted off Curtis Street on the edge of the village, the **Paper House** (tel: 978-546 2629; 52 Pigeon Hill Street; open daily spring–fall; entrance fee) is an endearing oddity, built entirely of rolled-up news-

On a hot July day in 1915, restaurateur Lawrence Woodman was frying potato chips and complaining to a fisherman friend that business was slow. "Toss some clams in with those chips," suggested the friend. Woodman did, and thus created the first fried-clam.

BELOW: the much-painted Motif #1 at Rockport harbor.

Gloucester was the setting for "The Perfect Storm", Sebastian Junger's 1997 best-seller recounting the loss of the "Andrea Gail" fishing boat in 120-mile-an-hour winds.

TIP

See page 183 for more information on whale-watching trips.

BELOW: Gloucester's most famous fisherman.

paper reinforced with glue and varnish. Begun in 1924 by an inventor of office supplies, the project took 20 years, and includes a desk made of copies of the *Christian Science Monitor*, on which the print is still legible.

Take Route 127 or Scenic Route 127A to **Gloucester ❼**, one of the oldest seaports in the United States. Here, Leonard Craske's famous statue, *Fishermen's Memorial* (Route 127) grips the wheel and peers oceanward, a moving tribute with the legend "they that go down to the sea in ships." The city still has an active fishing fleet, and the catch is processed in plants near the waterfront. Every year, the fishermen, who are predominantly of Portuguese and Italian ancestry, participate in the Blessing of the Fleet ceremony.

Landlubbers get into the act, too, by taking one of the whale-watching cruises that leave daily from the Cape Ann Marina. To learn more about the heyday of whaling, visit the **Cape Ann Historical Museum** (27 Pleasant Street; tel: 978-283 0455; open Mar–Jan, Tues–Sat & Sun pm; entrance fee) for its small but select collection of furnishings and artwork, ranging from 19th-century painter Fitz Hugh Lane's luminist seascapes to semi-abstractions by modernist Milton Avery. To check out the work of living artists, visit the galleries and studios lining the narrow way along **Rocky Neck**, just off East Main Street.

Facing Gloucester across the harbor are two intriguing examples of monomaniacal nesting instincts. On Eastern Point Boulevard, the early 1900s **Beauport**, also known as the **Sleeper-McCann House** (tel: 978-283-0800; open Jun–Oct15; tours on the hour; entrance fee), is a romantic labyrinth of cottagey rooms, using architectural fragments from other buildings. The house served as a setting for the summer parties of collector and interior designer, Henry Davis Sleeper. The themes vary entertainingly: one bedroom is in chapel style, the

THEY THAT GO
DOWN TO THE SEA
IN SHIPS
1623 – 1923

belfry is rich in chinoiserie, and the book tower has wooden "damask" curtains salvaged from a hearse.

Just south of Gloucester, off Route 127 on Hesperus Avenue stands the imposing **Hammond Castle** (tel: 978-283 7673; open Memorial Day–Labor Day daily; after Labor Day–mid-Oct and Apr–Memorial Day, Fri–Sun; entrance fee), the 1920s fantasy abode of the prolific inventor John Hays Hammond Jr. Hammond plundered Europe for elements to work into his dreamhouse, including a medieval village facade to overlook the indoor pool. The entire castle was built around the monumental 8,200-pipe organ (the largest such instrument in the US in a private home) that Mr Hammond designed (although he is not the Hammond of Hammond Organ fame). Check the museum's website (www.hammondcastle.org) for a schedule of organ concerts.

Maps:
Area 138
City 143

Salem and Marblehead

Though the scandalous witch trials earned **Salem ❽** enduring notoriety (*see page 144*), the area has much else to recommend it. Salem (on Route 1A south of Route 128; 40 minutes' train journey from North Station) owes its grandeur, now carefully restored, to its former prominence as a seaport. A red line along the sidewalks marks the route linking the historic sites, which are also connected by trolley services.

Begin a tour with a visit to the **National Park Service Regional Visitor Center ❶** (2 New Liberty St.; tel: 978-740-1650; www.nps.gov/sama; open daily), which shows the excellent film, *Where Past is Present*. Nearby, the Park Service's **Salem Maritime National Historic Site ❷** at the Derby Street Waterfront airs another fine film, *To the Farthest Parts of the Rich East*, which

Bewitching Salem.

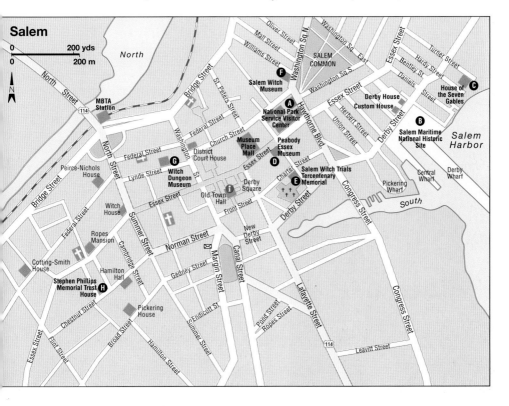

A ship's figurehead on display in the Peabody Essex Museum, Salem.

BELOW: Salem's Witch Museum.

explains how Salem opened up trade with the Orient. Here visitors may tour the Derby Wharf and a replica of a 19th-century brigantine, the *Republic*, the 1819 Custom House, and Derby House, a merchant's mansion built in 1761.

On Turner Street is the forbidding-looking 1668 **House of the Seven Gables** Ⓒ (tel: 978-744 0991; open daily; entrance fee), which inspired Hawthorne's novel of that name.

No visit should omit the **Peabody Essex Museum** Ⓓ (East India Square; tel: 800-745-4054; www.pem.org; open daily; entrance fee), which features excellent displays related to the maritime trade – particularly memorable are the ships' figureheads, maritime paintings, views of old Salem and a superb collection of artifacts brought back from the Far East. On Essex Street, the Museum preserves six houses that span two centuries of New England architecture. Salem's maritime glory notwithstanding, most visitors will want to tour the scenes of the infamous witchcraft trials of 1692, in which "hysteria," conveniently abetted political repression – the gentry, personified by the convicting judges, fell back on the time-honored method of attacking political and social upstarts as moral deviants.

Most moving is the **Salem Witch Trials Tercentenary Memorial** Ⓔ, a stark granite court adjoining Charter Street Burying Point, the final resting place of Witch Trials Court magistrate John Hawthorne. Incised along the paving stones and walls are passages from the accused women's pleas of innocence. The **Salem Witch Museum** Ⓕ (Washington Square North; tel: 978-744 1692; open daily; fee) reenacts, accurately if sensationally, key scenes to a recorded commentary, while the **Witch Dungeon Museum** Ⓖ (Lynde Street; tel: 978-741 3570; open Apr–Nov daily; entrance fee) is another live show evoking the persecutions.

THE SALEM WITCHES

There's a certain grim irony that Salem now makes sweet economic hay out of its dark and witchy past. All year round – but particularly during October, leading up to Hallowe'en – the old seaport touts occult events. Salem's web site (www.salem.org) provides gory details on attractions such as "Terror on the Wharf" and where to buy a "Fright Pass," for admission to three haunted houses.

Although Salem has a self-proclaimed "resident witch" (Laurie – she's easy to spot), and although the civil rights of witch practitioners have been upheld in Massachusetts, witches weren't always so welcome. Three hundred years ago, when Puritans were self-appointed arbiters of both law and religion, hysteria swept through Salem. Fourteen women and five men were executed (by hanging or pressing with stones) and hundreds were imprisoned. Several more died in jail. The trials grew from the feverish imaginations of adolescent girls who, in January 1692, became swept up in tales of voodoo and mysticism as told to them by Tituba, a slavewoman from Barbados.

Jealousy and greed between townspeople stoked the fire, as one after another pointed an accusing finger at his or her neighbor. The frenzy didn't end until May 1693, when the Governor issued a pardon to those still in jail.

Chestnut Street ranks among America's finest shows of domestic architecture. The **Stephen Phillips Memorial Trust House** ⓗ (34 Chestnut Street; tel: 978-744 0440; open late May–Oct Mon–Sat) is furnished with the belongings of five generations of the Phillips family.

Take a short detour from Salem on routes 1A south and 114 to **Marblehead** ➒, founded as a fishing village in 1629 and today the "Yachting Capital of America". The narrow streets are lined with more than 1,000 pre- and post-Revolutionary homes – many now chic B&Bs, shops, and galleries. The elegantly preserved **Jeremiah Lee Mansion** (161 Washington Street; tel: 781-631 1768; open June–Oct Tues–Sat; Sun pm; entrance fee) is one of the most opulent homes of the mid-1700s. The **Marblehead Museum & Historical Society** (170 Washington St.; tel: 781-631 1768; open June–Oct, Tues–Sat; entrance fee) exhibits a delightful collection of folk art. The original painting of the *Sprit of '76,* by Archibald Willard, is displayed in the selectmen's room of **Abbot Hall** (Washington Street; tel: 781-631 0000; open daily),

The word Salem derives from the Hebrew "shalom", meaning peace.

Echoes of the work ethic

The **Saugus Iron Works** ⓾ (244 Central Street; tel: 781-233-0050; open daily) have been reconstructed as they were from 1646 to 1668, with a blast furnace, forge, slitting mill, iron house, ironworks house, a blacksmith's shop, and a restored 17th-century house. The site was established by John Winthrop Jr, and, though ultimately unprofitable, launched America's ironworking industry.

The one-time model mill town of **Lowell** ⓫ is enjoying a renaissance as a major tourist attraction. Sightseeing ferries ply the old canals, trolleys clang through the streets, and looms pound again at the **Boott Cotton Mills Museum**

**Maps:
Area 138
City 143**

BELOW:
Salem Harbor.

(Market Street; open daily; entrance fee) operated with the **Lowell National Historical Park Visitor Center** (246 Market Street; tel: 978-897 5000; www.nps.gov/lowe; open daily; fee for walking and trolley tours), where a film and exhibits trace the town's history. The visitor center is the starting point for historic walking tours, including *Jack Kerouac's Lowell* : the Beat Generation icon was born, raised, and buried here.

Another famous American, the artist James Abbott Whistler, spent the first three years of his life in the **Whistler House Museum of Art** (243 Worthern Street; tel: 978-452-7641); open Wed–Sat; entrance fee), now home to the Lowell Art Association. Exhibits at the vast **American Textile History Museum** (491 Dutton Street; tel: 978-441-0400; open Thurs–Sun; entrance fee), housed in an 1860s canal-front factory, include the world's largest collection of spinning wheels and several recreated 18th and 19th-century mills.

The Minutemen were armed civilians who were prepared to fight at a minute's notice.

Lexington and Concord

The route of the British advance in 1775 through **Lexington ⑫** to **Concord ⑬**, where the opposing ranks met in battle, is designated the **Battle Road**, which although mostly a highway has a number of historical attractions along it, many part of the **Minute Man National Historical Park** (174 Liberty Street, Concord; tel: 978-369 6993; www.nps.gov/mima; open daily).

Chronologically, a visit to the Battle Road sites should go east to west. South of Lexington town center, the **National Heritage Museum ⑭** (33 Marrett Road, Route 2A; tel: 781-861 6559; open Mon–Sat; Sun pm) has permanent and rotating history exhibits. The **Munroe Tavern** (1332 Massachusetts Avenue; tel: 781-862 1703; open Jun–Oct, call for hours; entrance fee), a russet-colored

BELOW: a Memorial Day procession, Concord.

building (built 1695) on the left side of the Battle Road, served as headquarters for the Redcoats and as a hospital on their retreat from Concord. At the heart of Lexington a statue of Captain John Parker stands on **Battle Green** ⓯, where on Apr 19, 1775, the first shot was fired (possibly by a nervous 14- or 15-year-old Minuteman whose gun went off accidentally); of the Minutemen, vastly outnumbered, eight were killed. The **Lexington Visitor Center** (tel: 781-862 1450; www.lexingtonchamber.org; open daily) is next to the Green.

Maps: Pages 138 & below

The 1690 **Buckman Tavern** (1 Bedford Street; tel: 781-862 5598; 10am–4pm in summer; entrance fee; tours every half-hour), has been restored to its original appearance. Here, Captain Parker and his 77 Minutemen sipped beer while awaiting Paul Revere's warning; a bullet hole is visible in one door. The **Hancock-Clarke House** ⓰ (Hancock Street; open July–Oct; entrance fee), where John Hancock and Samuel Adams were woken by Revere on the eve of the battle with news of the British advance, contains period furnishings as well as the drum on which William Diamond sounded a warning to his fellow patriots.

At the **Ebenezer Fiske House Site**, a historical trail explains the course of the fierce fighting that broke out there; a section of the Battle Road here is unpaved and closed to traffic, giving an idea of its original appearance.

The **Battle Road Visitor Center** ⓱, part of the National Park, has a movie showing the events of 1775, and there are talks and guided walks. Just to the west is the **Paul Revere Capture Site**, where Revere was taken but a fellow rider, Dr Samuel Prescott, escaped to warn Concord. Restored to its condition at the time of the battle, the **Hartwell Tavern** ⓲ hosts re-creations of colonial life.

As you enter Concord the theme digresses into literature – it is remarkable that in the mid-19th century, so many American cultural giants made their homes

The American flag still flies on the Buckman Tavern in Concord, where the Minutemen were warned that the British troops were on their way.

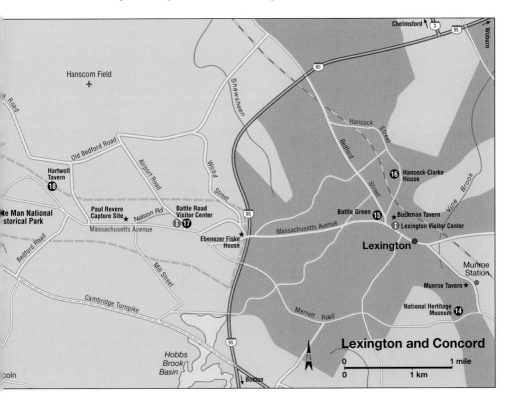

Lexington and Concord

Transcendentalist thinker Henry David Thoreau.

here. **The Wayside**  (455 Lexington Road, Route 2A; tel: 978-318 7825; closed Jan 1–15; exhibit center free, fee for tour) links the battle with the literary figures, for here Samuel Whitney, the muster master of the Concord Militia, lived during the Revolution. From 1845 to 1848 it was home to the Alcotts, and was purchased in 1852 by writer Nathaniel Hawthorne – he added the tower, but found it unsatisfactory for working in, and declared that he would happily see the house burn down.

Close by, the Alcott family lived from 1858 to 1877 at **Orchard House** (399 Lexington Road, Route 2A; tel: 978 369 4118; open Mon–Sat; Sun pm; closed Jan 1–15; entrance fee) where Louisa May Alcott penned her first novel, *Moods*, as well as the hugely popular *Little Women* and *Little Men*. The Alcotts' modest fortunes were reversed by the revenue from Louisa's writings; her father, Bronson Alcott, ran the far-from-lucrative Concord School of Philosophy, which functioned from 1880 to 1888. The building still stands next door.

Near the junction of the Battle Road with Route 2, **Concord Museum** (200 Lexington Road, Route 2A; tel: 978-369 9763; open Mon–Sat; Sun pm; entrance fee) has excellent displays relating to Revolutionary and literary Concord, including one of the two lanterns hung by Robert Newman in Old North Church in Boston. A gallery devoted to Thoreau has the largest collection of artifacts associated with the great author and naturalist, including furnishings from his cabin by Walden Pond. Ralph Waldo Emerson's study has been transferred here from the **Ralph Waldo Emerson House** (28 Cambridge Turnpike; tel: 978-369 2236; open mid-Apr–mid-Oct Thur–Sat; Sun pm; entrance fee) just across Route 2, where Emerson resided from 1835 until he died in 1882. Most of the furniture is his.

Sleepy Hollow Cemetery (Bedford Street, Route 62; tel: 978-318-3233) is the resting place of most of the Concord big names, among them Hawthorne, the Alcotts, Emerson and Thoreau. **The Old Manse** (269 Monument Street; tel: 978-369 3909; open Apr–Oct Mon–Sat; Sun pm; entrance fee) was built by minister William Emerson around 1770, and was used as a sanctuary for women and children in the battle. It became home to his grandson Ralph Waldo Emerson, who wrote *Nature* (1836) here, and was rented for three years to Nathaniel Hawthorne. It houses a huge book collection and Hawthorne's desk.

At **Old North Bridge** (a replica) where General Gage's British troops, crowded into the narrow pathway, were easily routed by the ragtag Americans, an obelisk marks where the first British soldier fell. Cross the bridge, pass Daniel Chester French's *Minute Man* statue, unveiled for the centennial of the famous fight, and walk up to the North Bridge Visitor Center.

South of Concord off Route 126, Thoreau spent 26 months in a one-room cabin (there's now a replica) by **Walden Pond** (tel: 978-369 3254; parking fee; open year-round) living in experimental self-sufficiency and recording the progress of nature through the year, all of which he recounted in *Walden* (1854). A state park surrounds the pond.

At **Lincoln**, off Route 126, the **Gropius House** (68 Baker Bridge Road; tel: 781-259 8098; open June–mid-Oct, Wed–Sun; Oct 15–May, weekends;

tours on the hour from 11am–4pm; entrance fee), designed in 1937 by the seminal Bauhaus architect, is now the most modern of the historic homes preserved by Historic New England. The **DeCordova Museum and Sculpture Park** ㉘ (off Route 2 or Route 128 at 51 Sandy Point Road; tel: 781-259 8355; open Tues–Sun; entrance fee) shows contemporary work in a turreted 1880 mansion; the outdoor sculpture garden is New England's largest, and a summertime jazz series is presented in the outdoor theater.

Maps
on pages
138 & 146

The South Shore

From Boston, head south on Route 1 for 8 miles (13 km) to **Quincy** ㉙ and the **Adams National Historical Park** (135 Adams Street; tel: 617-770 1175; www.nps.gov/adam; open mid-Apr–mid-Nov, daily; Visitor Center (not houses) open year-round with limited hrs; last tour at 3:15pm; entrance fee), home to five generations of Adamses from 1720 to 1927. The site includes the 1730 house that was home to four generations of the illustrious Adams family, among them America's first father-and-son presidential pair, John Adams (second President of the US), and his son, John Quincy Adams (the sixth). High points of the tour are J.Q. Adams's stone library, packed with 14,000 volumes, and the formal garden, especially appealing when the daffodils are in bloom. The Adams birthplaces, 17th-century saltbox farmhouses, also form part of the National Historical Site. A free trolley connects the houses, and tours are on a first-come, first-served basis.

The Minute Man *statue, by Daniel Chester French, at Old North Bridge, Concord.*

Further down the coast off Route 1, on Route 3A, is **Hingham** ㉚, beautified by Frederick Law Olmsted, creator of Boston's Emerald Necklace (*see page 115*) and Central Park, New York; his handiwork here is the **World's End Reservation** (250 Martin's Lane; tel: 781-740-6665; open daily; entrance fee),

BELOW: the Adams Homestead, Quincy.

a 250-acre (100-hectare) harborside preserve that is a protectorate of the Trustees of the Reservations. Walking trails provide views of the Boston skyline and Hingham Harbor. Also noteworthy, at the center of town, is the **Old Ship Meetinghouse** (Main Street) one of the oldest continuously-used wooden church structures in the country. Built by ship's carpenters in 1681, the interior (the pulpit and pews were built in 1755) resembles a giant hull turned upside down.

Enclosing Hingham Bay and curving toward Boston like a beckoning finger is the sandy spit of **Nantasket** ㉛, a long-time summer playground of which only a 1928 carousel has survived redevelopment. The classic **Paragon Carousel** (205 Nantasket Avenue; tel: 781-925 0472; open daily Memorial Day-Labor Day; weekends May–Memorial Day and Labor Day–Columbus Day; entrance fee) has 60 horses that still prance to the sounds of a Wurlitzer organ. It's the centerpiece of a festival museum complex.

From the tip of the peninsula is an optimal view of Boston Light, said to be the oldest operating lighthouse in America. The **Hull Lifesaving Museum** (1117 Nantasket Avenue; tel: 781-925 5433; open daily, year-round; entrance fee) gives a good idea of the heroic measures required when the lighthouse warnings didn't succeed in staving off disaster.

Plymouth

Directly southward, on Route 3, lies **Plymouth** ㉜, which styles itself "America's Home Town." Here **Plymouth Rock**, legendary 1620 landing place of the Pilgrims, enjoys a place of honor under an elaborate harborside portico.

A stone's throw from the monument over the **Rock** (claimed to be the stone the Pilgrims first stepped on when they came ashore) is the *Mayflower II* Ⓐ

Abigail Adams is remembered not only as the wife and mother of a president (a distinction shared with Barbara Bush), but as the mother of American feminism; in 1776, she urged her husband to "Remember the Ladies" at the fateful Continental Congress where independence was declared.

BELOW:
Mayflower II.

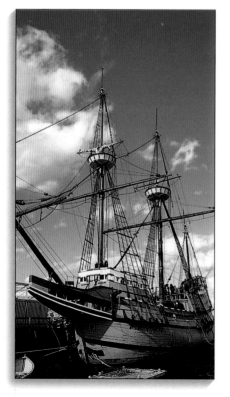

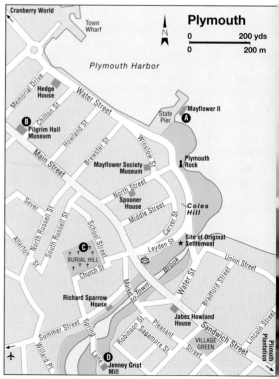

Plymouth

Maps
on pages
138 & 150

(State Pier, Water Street; tel: 508-746-1622; open April–Nov daily; entrance fee). A replica of the original *Mayflower*, this was built in England and sailed to Plymouth in 1957. Actors on board the 104-ft (32-meter) long vessel portray the original passengers and field visitors' questions with accuracy and wit, vividly conveying the hardships that its 102 passengers must have suffered on their 66-day voyage. (Note: a combination ticket with the Plimoth Plantation is available).

Across the road from the Rock is **Coles Hill**, where, during their first winter, the Pilgrims secretly buried their dead at night to hide the truth about their fast dwindling numbers from the Indians. Nearby is the site of the original settlement.

Pilgrim Hall Museum ❸ (75 Court Street; tel: 508-746 1620; open Feb–Dec daily; entrance fee), the first custom-built museum (1824) in the US, gathered the more outstanding memorabilia of Pilgrim life early on (though they are rather unimaginatively displayed). Relics include John Alden's halberd, Myles Standish's Bible and the cradle of Peregrine White, born aboard the *Mayflower*.

Playing the part at Plimoth Plantation.

Farther east, beyond Main Street, is **Burial Hill** ❸, with gravestones dating back to the colony's founding. "Under this stone rests the ashes of Willm Bradford, a zealous Puritan and sincere Christian, Governor of Plymouth Colony from April 1621–57 [the year he died, aged 69] except 5 years which he declined." The hill was the site of the Pilgrims' first meeting house, fort and watchtower. South of Burial Hill is the replica **Jenney Grist Mill** ❹, where corn is still ground.

Plymouth also possesses a number of historic houses to visit. The oldest is the **Richard Sparrow House** (42 Summer Street; tel: 508-747 1240; open Apr–Thanksgiving Day weekend Thurs–Tues; donations) built in 1640, and still retaining its diamond-shape leaded windows; the **Jabez Howland House** (33 Sandwich Street; tel: 508-746 9590; open late May–mid-Oct daily) originated in 1667 as a home for the son of one of the original Pilgrims. The **Mayflower Society House** (4 Winslow Street; tel: 508-746 2590; entrance fee) a house built in 1754, has a graceful flying staircase and a variety of period rooms.

Plimoth Plantation

About 3 miles (5 km) south of town, on Route 3, **Plimoth Plantation** (Warren Avenue; tel: 508-746 1622; www.plimouth.org; open April–Nov daily; entrance fee) is a painstaking reconstruction of the 17th-century Pilgrim village; its every detail has been meticulously researched. It is inhabited by actor/interpreters who so convincingly enact the quotidian rituals of the original village – and converse with visitors in Jacobean English – that visitors can easily lose themselves in the fantasy of those heady days full of hardship and dreams.

BELOW:
Plimoth Plantation.

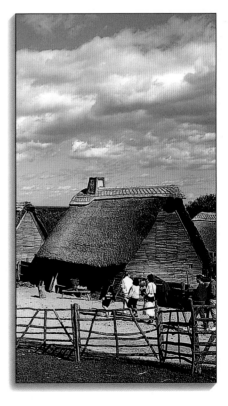

Southwest, via routes 3, 6, 495 and 195, is **New Bedford** ㉝, onetime whaling capital and today the East Coast's busiest fishing port. The narrow cobblestone streets and historic buildings of the old quarter have been incorporated into the **New Bedford Whaling National Historical Park** (tel: 800-508 5353; www.ci.new-bedford.ma.us). The big attraction is the **New Bedford Whaling Museum** (18 Johnny Cake Hill; tel: 508-996 4095; www.nps.gov/nebe; open daily year-round; entrance fee), the best place to find out

Map on page 138

TIP

A children's favorite is the **New Bedford Fire Museum** (51 Bedford St, open 9am–4pm Jun–Aug; tel: 508-992 2162; admission fee). Apart from ogling antique fire trucks, kids can try on uniforms, ring bells, and slide down poles.

BELOW:
going fishing.

about this aspect of New England's maritime past. In addition to informative sections evoking the lifestyles of the whalers and fishermen, there is a huge show of ship models – most memorably the *Lagoda*, a half-size replica of a whaling bark – and some fine paintings on the theme, plus a collection of scrimshaw, intricately carved out of whalebone by the sailors on their long voyages. Across from the museum is the **Seamen's Bethel** (tel: 508-992 3295; open May–Oct Mon–Sat and Sun pm) with the "Whaleman's Chapel" portrayed by Herman Melville in *Moby-Dick*. The 156-ft (57-meter) Grand Banks fishing schooner **Ernestina** (tel: 508-992 4900), launched in Essex in 1894, sails from the State Pier daily in season.

At the mouth of the Taunton estuary, 9 miles (6 km) west from New Bedford, **Fall River** ❸ is dominated by the huge mills that act as reminders of the city's long-defunct cotton industry. Some of these Victorian relics now house the thriving factory outlet stores that have put the town on the map. But the city had a life before outlets, and it's told at **Fall River Heritage State Park**, in Battleship Cove (tel: 508-675-5759; open daily).

Battleship Cove (tel: 800-533 3194; www.battleshipcove.org; open daily 9am–5pm; entrance fee) is also home to the world's largest collection of historic naval ships. Among them are the submarine USS *Lionfish;* the 46,000-ton battleship USS *Massachusetts*; and the world's only restored pair of PT boats on display. Virtually adjacent, the **Marine Museum** (700 Water Street; tel: 508-674 3533; open Wed–Fri, Sat pm, Sun am; entrance fee) traces the fascinating history of the Fall River Line from 1847 to 1937, and is packed with nautical paraphernalia, including a model of the doomed *Titanic* and more than 150 steamship models. ❏

BOSTON HARBOR ISLANDS

Until recently, few Bostonians even knew that their harbor had islands. But look on a map and there they are, some 30 of them, sprinkled within the embracing peninsular arms of Winthrop and Hull. They range from little more than piles of rock (The Graves) to 214-acre (85-hectare) Long, which stretches out into the middle of the harbor from the town of Quincy. For centuries, the islands served no more purpose than a dumping ground or shelter for Boston's sick or homeless. As for the harbor, it was little more than a cesspool for the city's waste. But thanks to a $3.5 billion clean-up, Boston Harbor is clean enough now on most days for swimming. And in 1996, Congress passed legislation to support ongoing local and state efforts to turn the islands into valuable recreational space for the city. Today, at Boston Harbor Islands State Park, you can catch a ferry from downtown Boston or Hingham to Georges Island, which serves as a nucleus for the recreation area. Water taxis travel to other islands, some of which feel as remote and unspoiled as those off the coast of Maine – except for that great view of the Boston skyline. For specific information about reaching the islands, or about camping, call 617-727 7676 or check the website www.mass.gov.

Outlet Shopping

Kittery and Freeport, in Maine, are both scenic coastal towns, but for many their names are more synonymous with outlet shopping than beaches. This was not always so. Factory outlets once referred to shops within factories that sold discounted wares to employees. The modern concept of New England factory outlets began in the mid-1970s in Fall River, Massachusetts, when the Anderson-Little clothing store opened a retail outlet.

Anderson-Little no longer exists, but outlets are here to stay. Fifty stores now occupy the original granite-faced Fall River mill buildings, and the popularity of outlet shopping has grown well beyond this industrial city. The outlet malls in Freeport and Kittery are now among Maine's most popular tourist destinations, and North Conway, New Hampshire, and Worcester, Massachusetts, also harbor large outlet malls advertising 20 to 70 percent discounts on products ranging from clothing to housewares to books. Many shoppers come armed with maps and strategies, and entire books have been written on the most productive way to shop.

There are three kinds of stores: national outlets for single brands selling in-season merchandise at a discount; regional value outlets carrying name-brand and designer merchandise; and manufacturer-owned clearance centers with discontinued and irregular merchandise at sharply reduced prices.

The Fall River Factory Outlet District, also known as the Heart District, consists of three independently owned malls. The huge Burlington Coat Factory takes up most of one. The district is at the junction of I-195 and Route 24 South, about one hour from Boston and 20 minutes from Newport and Providence, Rhode Island.

One hour north of Boston, at Kittery, Maine (888-KITTERY), more than 120 stores, including the megalithic Kittery Trading Post, line over a mile of Route 1 (Exit 3 from I-95). Farther north on I-95, at Exit 20, is Freeport, home to the never-closed headquarters of L.L. Bean. The outdoor outfitter's store is now flanked by 170 shops and outlets, but it's the L.L. Bean name that draws over 2½ million customers each year (800-341 4341). Founded in 1912 by Leon Leonwood Bean, an avid outdoorsman whose first product was a functional hunting boot, the company is still family-owned; it stocks more than 21,000 items and its global sales in 140 countries now exceed $1.5 billion a year.

L.L. Bean also has a store in North Conway, New Hampshire, two hours' drive north of Boston, along with 200 other outlet stores. Two large outlet malls, Settlers' Green (603-356 7031) and the Tanger Outlet Center (800–407 4078) are the anchors, with about 100 stores. Dozens of smaller outlet centers in stand-alone factory stores are also strung along Route 16, creating long traffic jams.

Vermont also has splendid opportunities for bargain shoppers. If the notion of a "perpetual sale" gets your heart fluttering, head to Manchester, where you'll be moved by such purveyors as Calvin Klein, Timberland, Baccarat, Giorgio Armani, Cole Haan, Dansk, and Brooks Brothers. ❑

RIGHT: L.L.Bean's "Maine Hunting Shoe."

CAPE COD AND THE ISLANDS

This is a sandy summer playground with fine clam shacks, historic B&Bs, undeveloped National Seashore beaches, and a lively arts scene – plus two sharply contrasting little isles

Map on pages 158–9

Shaped like a bodybuilder's flexed arm, Cape Cod extends 31 miles (50 km) eastward into the Atlantic Ocean, then another 31 miles to the north. Well forested up to about the "elbow," then increasingly reduced to scrub oak and pitch pine, this sandy peninsula is lined with more than 310 miles (500 km) of beaches. The crook of the arm forms Cape Cod Bay, where the waters are placid and free of often treacherous ocean surf. Lighthouses guide mariners plying the cold Atlantic waters. Geologically the Cape is relatively new, a huge mass of debris dumped after the melting of a vast ice sheet.

Bostonians consider Cape Cod their own private playground, but its fame has spread so far that it attracts international travelers. In high season (July and August), lodgings are filled to capacity, traffic on the Cape's few highways is heavy, and local merchants work hard to make the profits that will carry them through the all-but-dormant winters. (The pleasures of the Cape off-season, however, are much less of a secret than they were even a few years ago.) Even at the height of its summertime popularity, when the roads, restaurants, and beaches tend to be jammed, Cape Cod manages to preserve its wild charm and dramatic beauty.

Much of this quality is protected within the boundaries of the Cape Cod National Seashore, a vast 27,000-acre (11,000-hectare) nature reserve established by foresighted legislators in 1961. Precisely because it has not been commercially exploited, this huge expanse of untouched dunes survives as one of the Cape's most alluring features.

PRECEDING PAGES: old coastguard station at Eastham. **LEFT:** looking out to sea, at Douse's Beach. **BELOW:** rescue surfboard, Cape Cod.

Getting your bearings

Note the nomenclature. "Upper Cape" refers to the portion nearest the mainland; "Mid-Cape" is roughly from Barnstable County eastward to Chatham and Orleans, where the "arm" bends; "Lower Cape" is the "forearm" jutting northward to Eastham, Truro and Provincetown.

Itineraries on the Upper and Mid-Cape offer a choice of speedy, featureless highways or scenic, meandering roads. Those intent on reaching the Outer Cape in a hurry generally opt for Route 6, the four-lane, limited-access Mid-Cape Highway; those headed for Falmouth, Woods Hole, and points along Nantucket Sound can take the equally speedy Route 28. Anyone wishing to get a true sense of the Cape, however, will be well rewarded by taking the prettier non-highway counterparts. Roughly parallel to the Mid-Cape Highway, two-lane Route 6A starts in Sagamore and runs eastward along the Bay through old towns full of graceful historic houses, crafts and antique shops. The same can be said of Route 28A, hugging the shore en route to Falmouth. As Route 28 veers northeastward from Falmouth to Chatham it's marred by recurrent stretches

of overdevelopment but, again, one has only to venture off the main road a bit to discover such towns as Osterville and Centerville, Harwich Port and Chatham itself. Once Route 28 and Route 6 merge in Orleans, Route 6 north is pleasant all the way to Provincetown, if traffic-clogged in summer. For those wishing to avoid the drive, there are summer ferries between Provincetown and Boston, Provincetown and Plymouth, and flights into Hyannis and Provincetown.

Simple pleasures

The first hordes of tourists arrived in the late 19th century, brought by steamship, railroad and – eventually – automobile. Escaping the summer heat of Boston, Providence and New York for the cool sea breezes along the shore, they found low prices, inexpensive real estate and simple pleasures in abundance.

Before the advent of modern transport, Cape Cod was a hardscrabble area peopled by the Wampanoag tribes, hardy Yankees and industrious immigrants from the coasts and islands of Portugal. Since the land supported only subsistence farming, most people earned their living from the sea. Fishing, saltmaking, whaling, ship-building and "wrecking" – scavenging the beaches for the flotsam and jetsam of ships lost at sea – provided a livelihood, however uncertain.

In 1602, Bartholomew Gosnold, a British mariner sailing by this long arm of sand, noted a great many codfish in the waters and added the name "Cape Cod" to his map. In 1620, the *Mayflower* pulled into the harbor of what is now Provincetown and, before debarking to explore, its passengers drew up the Mayflower Compact for self-government. This early "constitution" grew into the government of the Commonwealth of Massachusetts.

The Cape Cod Canal

Purists could actually call Cape Cod an island, for in 1914, after five years

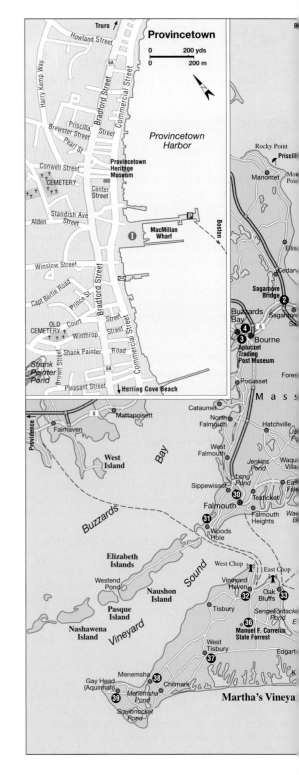

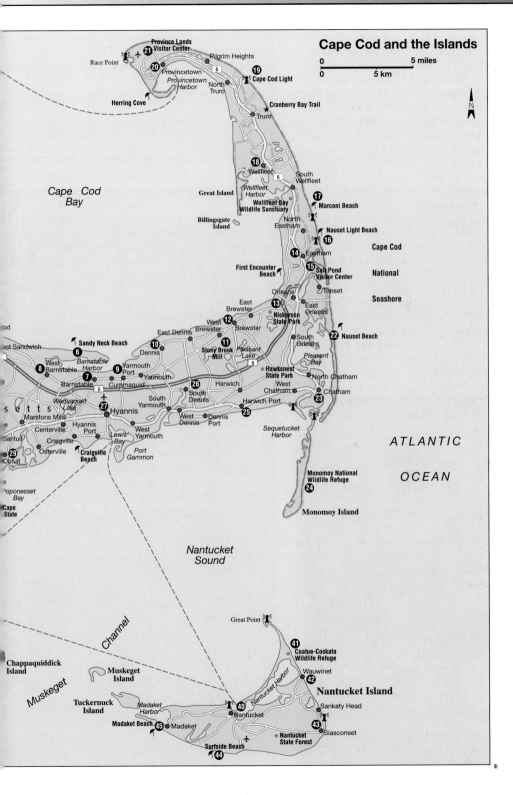

Cape Cod and the Islands

0   5 miles

0   5 km

N

Province Lands Visitor Center 21
Pilgrim Heights
Race Point
20 Provincetown
Provincetown Harbor
North Truro
19 Cape Cod Light
Herring Cove
Cranberry Bay Trail
Truro

Cape Cod Bay

18 Wellfleet
South Wellfleet
Great Island
Wellfleet Harbor
Billingsgate Island
Great Island
Wellfleet Bay Wildlife Sanctuary
17 Marconi Beach
North Eastham
Nauset Light Beach
16
Cape Cod
14 Eastham

First Encounter Beach
15 Salt Pond Visitor Center
National

Orleans
Tonset
Seashore

East Brewster
13 East Orleans
West Brewster
12 Nickerson State Park
Brewster
East Dennis
Sandy Neck Beach
6
10 Dennis
Stony Brook Mill
Pleasant Lake
South Orleans
Pleasant Bay
22 Nauset Beach

West Barnstable
8
Barnstable Harbor
9 Yarmouth Port
7 Barnstable
Yarmouth
Cummaquid
6
Harwich
West Chatham
North Chatham
Chatham
23
East Sandwich
od
Massachusetts
26 South Dennis
Harwich Port
25
Wequaquet Lake
27 Hyannis
South Yarmouth
West Dennis
Dennis Port
Sequetucket Harbor
ATLANTIC
Marstons Mills
Hyannis Port
Centerville
Lewis' Bay
West Yarmouth
Santuit
Craigville
Osterville
Craigville Beach
Port Gammon
OCEAN
29
Cotuit
Poponesset Bay
Cape State
Monomoy National Wildlife Refuge
24

Monomoy Island

Nantucket Sound

Great Point
Channel
Chappaquiddick Island
Muskeget Island
41 Coatue-Coskata Wildlife Refuge
Wauwinet
42
Nantucket Island
Muskeget
Tuckernuck Island
Madaket Harbor
Nantucket Harbor
40 Nantucket
Sankaty Head
Madaket Beach 45 Madaket
43 Siasconset
Nantucket State Forest
Surfside Beach
44

The Cape Cod National Seashore Trail, found at the northern tip of the Cape, is a spectacularly sculpted landscape of sweeping dunes descending into green hollows of scrub brush and stunted forest, with the sea all around to provide invigorating breezes.

of work, the Cape was effectively severed from the mainland by the **Cape Cod Canal** . Improved and widened in 1927, the canal eliminates the need for ships to round the Cape via the often stormy Atlantic. Two 7-mile (11-km) service roads which parallel the canal are great for bicycling or hiking. There are **visitor centers** (508-759 4431; www.capecodcanal.com) in Bournedale and Buzzards Bay.

Expressways funnel traffic to the two access bridges over the Canal. To the east is the **Sagamore Bridge** ❷, a graceful arched structure with one foot in the Cape town of Sagamore. Route 3 comes south from Boston and crosses the Sagamore Bridge to join Route 6, the Mid-Cape Highway.

Just past the bridge on the north side are the **Pairpoint Glass Works** (Route 6A; 800-899 0953; open daily in season), where glassblowers give demonstrations weekdays. Right nearby is the **Cape Cod Factory Outlet Mall** (Route 6; tel: 508-888 8417; open daily). With 20 stores, it's the largest on the Cape.

Near the southwestern end of the Canal is the Bourne Bridge, leading to Route 28, headed for Falmouth and Woods Hole. West of the bridge and by the canal, the Bourne Historical Society's **Aptucxet Trading Post and Museum** ❸ (Aptucxet Road, Bourne; 508-759 9487; open Tues–Sat Memorial Day/end-May–Columbus Day/Oct; entrance fee) is a replica of the first English-speaking trading post in North America, set up in 1627 to trade with the Wampanoag Indians, the Dutch in New York and the Plymouth settlement.

In nearby **Buzzards Bay** ❹ displays and animal exhibits at the **National Marine Life Center** (120 Main Street; tel: 508-743 9888; www.nmlc.org; open late May–early Sept, Mon–Sat and Sun pm) focus on the rescue and rehabilitation of the Cape's stranded marine animals.

BELOW:
going clamming.

CAPE COD RAIL TRAIL

In the Cape's early heyday, summertime visitors arrived by train – an option still available to a limited number of towns in July and August from New York City (Amtrak's Cape Codder, tel: 800-872 7245). Otherwise, with a singular lack of foresight, most of the train network has been dismantled. However, at least one lengthy section of roadbed has been put to an energy-saving, pleasure-making use: the Cape Cod Rail Trail is a 25-mile (40-km) paved recreational path ideal for bicycling, skating, walking and jogging. Along the way, it passes lakes and marshes, woods and a harbor. The most scenic or dramatic sections are the National Seashore spur trails in Eastham and Wellfleet that terminate at the Atlantic Ocean. The trail runs from just off Route 134 in South Dennis through Nickerson State Park and on to Wellfleet.

You can rent bicycles at a number of places along the way, including Barbara's Bike & Sport (tel: 508-760 4723) at the trailhead, Idle Times Bike Shop (tel: 508-896 9242) on the edge of Nickerson, and Little Capistrano Bike Shop (tel: 508-255 6515) across from the National Seashore headquarters in Eastham. If you forget to pack a lunch, there are a few places along the way where you can get a sandwich or fried seafood.

The Bayside: Sandwich to Brewster

This region gained world renown for its glass after Boston merchant Deming Jarvis founded a glass factory in **Sandwich ❺** in 1825. By taking advantage of local resources (sand shipped in from the Outer Cape, local timber to stoke the furnaces, and salt marsh to pack the delicate product) and using mass-production techniques, Jarvis made decorative glassware affordable.

Exhibits at Sandwich Glass Museum.

His Boston and Sandwich Glass Company factory thrived until threatened by coal-powered plants in the Midwest; that, and a strike by exploited workers, shut the enterprise down in 1888. However, examples of their output, in an astounding range of styles, can still be found in the **Sandwich Glass Museum** (tel: 508-888 0251; Main Street; open Apr–Dec daily; Feb–March Wed–Sun; entrance fee), and in the antique shops that line this historic old route.

Sandwich was the first town to be founded on the Cape, in 1637, and today – with the factories long since razed and the groves of trees regrown – it's one of the prettiest, and best-preserved. At its center stands the restored 1680 **Dexter Mill** (stone-ground cornmeal available in summer) and the c. 1637 **Hoxie House**, a remarkably well-preserved saltbox reputed to be the Cape's oldest dwelling (Water Street; tel: 508-888 1173; open mid-June–mid-Oct, Mon–Sat; Sun pm; entrance fee). Peter Rabbit, Reddy Fox, and all of the other whimsical characters created by author/naturalist Thornton Burgess come to life at the **Thornton Burgess Museum** (Water Street; tel: 508-888-6870; open mid-Apr–Oct Mon–Sat; Sun pm; entrance fee), housed in an 18th-century home once owned by his aunt Arabella.

Cooks at the 1903 Jam Kitchen, on the grounds of **Greenbriar Nature Center** (6 Discovery Hill Rd. tel: 508 888-6870; open year-round) in East Sandwich, prepare and sell jams and relishes.

BELOW: one of the exceptional vintage cars in Heritage Plantation.

TIP

You'll find more fine old houses lining the section of Route 6A around Yarmouth Port – once called Captains' Row – than anywhere else on the Cape. South Yarmouth was settled by Quakers in the early 1800s and many of their lovely houses remain.

For more glimpses into the American past, follow the signs – past a lovely historic cemetery overlooking **Shawme Pond** – to **Heritage Plantation** (67 Grove Street; 508-888 3300; www.heritageplantation.org; open Apr–Oct daily; Nov-Dec Fri–Sun, Jan–Mar by appointment; entrance fee), a spacious museum complex whose grounds, in spring, are awash in the vivid pinks and purples of flowering rhododendrons. Several buildings display extraordinary collections, from children's toys (including a working carousel) to military artifacts and folk art. A round stone barn (copied from the Shaker original in Hancock, Massachusetts) houses an outstanding array of early cars, including one particular beauty, Gary Cooper's 1931 Duesenberg.

Motoring east along Route 6A into Barnstable County you'll pass the turn-off for the 6-mile (9-km) barrier beach, **Sandy Neck** ❻, which is a favored habitat of the endangered piping plover. Hikers and swimmers are welcome to explore this sandy spit, provided they don't disturb the birds' nesting sites. **Barnstable** ❼ is also home to 4,000-acre (1,00-hectare) **Great Marsh**, the Cape's largest salt water marsh. **Hyannis Whale Watcher Cruises** (tel: 508-362-6088 or 888-942-5392) depart from Barnstable Harbor.

Just up the hill from the harbor is the **Trayser Memorial Museum** (3353 Route 6A; tel: 508-362 2092; open mid-June–Oct, Tues–Sun pm), the former Custom House, which now focuses on maritime life and culture. In **West Barnstable** ❽, West Parish Meetinghouse, built in 1646, is an outstanding example of early colonial architecture and has a Paul Revere bell cast in 1806.

East of Barnstable, **Yarmouth Port** ❾ is a delightful village with fine old houses to tour, including the **Captain Bangs Hallett House** (Strawberry Lane; tel: 508-362 3021; open June-mid–Oct Thurs–Sun; tours at 1, 2 and 3pm;

BELOW: the Town Hall and Dexter Mill, Sandwich.

Map on pages 158–9

entrance fee), an 1840 Greek Revival showcase house now owned by The Historical Society of Old Yarmouth, and the **Winslow Crocker House** (250 Route 6A; tel: 508-227 3957; open Jun–Oct, first Sat of month; tours on hour 11am–4pm; entrance fee), a 1780 Georgian manse moved here from nearby West Barnstable. For a pleasurable glimpse of more recent history, stop for an ice cream soda at **Hallett's** (139 Main Street; tel: 508-362 3362), a well-preserved 1889 drugstore with second-floor museum.

In the town of **Dennis ❿**, follow signs for the Scargo Hill Tower, a stone turret from which it's possible to see, on a clear day, Cape Cod laid out like a map, with Provincetown easily visible at the northern tip. Dennis is home to America's oldest, and most outstanding, professional summer theater: aspiring thespians such as Bette Davis (an ambitious usher) and Henry Fonda began their careers at the **Cape Playhouse** (Route 6A; tel: 508-385 3838 or 877-385 3911; performances mid-June–mid-Sept), founded in 1927 by Raymond Moore, a renegade from Provincetown's "little theater" movement. Productions here are skilled and lavish, and movies at the adjoining Cape Cinema are a sensory treat: the cinema features leather armchairs with antimacassars and Art Deco frescoes by Rockwell Kent. On the playhouse grounds, the **Cape Cod Museum of Art** (tel: 508 385-4477 open end-May–mid Oct, daily; rest of year, Tues–Sun; entrance fee) works devoted to interpreting the role of the Cape and islands in American art are exhibited in seven galleries and a sculpture garden.

The **Stony Brook Mill ⓫** (Stony Brook Road southwest off Route 6A) grinds cornmeal several days a week; there's a small museum upstairs. Each spring, from mid-April to early May, the mill hosts an eye-catching event: here, in a timeless ceremony similar to a salmon run, schools of alewives (a fish resembling

Vintage exhibit at the New England Fire and History Museum.

BELOW:
the New England Fire and History Museum, Brewster.

Summer Activities

New England's summer season may be short, but locals savor every balmy day that July and August bring. And although May/June and September/October may not qualify as "summer," the fine if less predictable weather of these "shoulder" months makes for excellent outdoor adventuring without the mid-summer crowds.

With 400 miles (640 km) of coastline, Rhode Island looks to the sea for recreation. Newport, known as "The Sailing Capital of the World" for its years hosting the America's Cup, is a good base for harbor sailing or learn-to-sail vacations.

At America's oldest sailing school, Boston's Community Boating, skiffs cruise the Charles River against a backdrop of brick bowfronts and downtown office towers. For longer adventures, many head for the Maine coast, where several outfitters offer multi-day sailing expeditions.

Maine has also become a center for sea kayaking, wiith over 2,000 coastal islands

and their protected waters, The Maine Island Kayak Company (see Travel Tips) offers sea kayaking lessons and tours. Rhode Island kayakers are rewarded with seaside views of Newport's grand Ocean Drive estates.

West of Boston, canoeists on the lazy Sudbury and Concord Rivers can visit Revolutionary-era sights, while on Cape Cod, naturalist guides lead canoe tours of salt marshes and tidal rivers. Along the Deerfield River in western Massachusetts, visitors can rent canoes and take whitewater rafting trips.

Connecticut's Housatonic River is a favored destination for canoeing and rafting. North American Outdoor Adventure (tel: 800-727 4379) organizes trips on the Housatonic and on Maine's Kennebec and Penobscot Rivers.

Swimmers will find beaches on Cape Cod or Nantucket Sound warmer and calmer than those on the Atlantic. The Atlantic, however, sometimes offers reasonable surfing, especially after an offshore storm.

Fishermen head for the trout-filled Battenkill River, near Manchester in Vermont, where the Orvis Company runs a fly fishing school. Orvis also teaches saltwater fishing on Cape Cod. Near New Hampshire's Mount Washington, Great Glen Trials (see Travel Tips) offers introductory fishing classes and arranges guided fly fishing excursions.

There's hiking for all abilities, from leisurely strolls on conservation land – such as the 11 self-guided nature trails within Cape Cod's National Seashore – to rugged mountain climbs. The 2,000-mile (3,200-km) Appalachian Trail crosses Maine, New Hampshire, Vermont, Massachusetts and Connecticut on its way south to Georgia. Serious hikers also follow the Long Trail (270 miles/ 435 km) across Vermont's highest peaks. The Appalachian Mountain Club has a network of overnight huts for walkers in New Hampshire's White Mountains.

Many ski resorts have become summer mountain biking centers, including Vermont's Mount Snow and Killington. The self-guided Franconia Notch Bike Tour in New Hampshire starts at Echo Lake, continues through the scenic notch, and ends at Loon Mountain's ski area. ❑

LEFT: Cape Cod and Acadia are two areas that offer excellent, easy cycling.

herring) leap up a series of ladders to spawn in the freshwater pond behind the mill. Besides its fine old houses and inns, **Brewster** ⓬ has a variety of attractions. The **Cape Cod Museum of Natural History** (869 Main Street, Route 6A; tel: 508-896 3867 or 800-479-3867 in Mass; open Oct–Mar, Wed–Sun; Apr–May, Wed–Sun; Jun–Sept, daily; entrance fee) explores the local habitat with hands-on exhibits and a small network of nature trails.

The **New England Fire and History Museum** (1439 Main Street; tel: 508-896 5711; open weekends mid-May-mid-Oct; entrance fee) has large collections of fire-fighting equipment used from the late 1700s to the early 1900s.

Railroad magnate Roland Nickerson once owned 2,000 acres (800 hectares) of open land in Brewster and held them as his personal hunting and fishing preserve. In 1934 his widow donated most of this tract to the state; today **Nickerson State Park** ⓭ (Route 6A; tel: 5908-896 3491), is a popular spot for camping, swimming, picnicking, and walks.

The National Seashore and the Outer Cape

The Cape Cod National Seashore extends along the Atlantic coast of the Lower Cape all the way to Provincetown. Its glorious sandy beaches are backed by high dunes; by contrast the (western) bayside has calmer, warmer waters and marshy inlets.

The town green at **Eastham** ⓮ has a 1793 windmill. For a deeper side trip into Cape Cod's history, head west to **First Encounter Beach**. It's here that a Pilgrim scouting party out of Provincetown first encountered a band of Indians, who, wary after earlier encounters with kidnappers, attacked the Pilgrims and were rebuffed by gunfire. This uneasy meeting is among the reasons the Pilgrims

Map on pages 158–9

TIP

The best beaches in the area are Nauset Beach and Skaket Beach, both in Orleans (see page 168), and Nauset Light, Coast Guard and First Encounter Beaches, all in the vicinity of Eastham.

BELOW: Nauset Light Beach.

Festival time in Provincetown can be a drag.

pressed on to Plymouth. Today the historic site is a peaceful town beach (which, like most, charges a parking fee in summer).

Further up Route 6A is the **Salt Pond Visitor Center** ⑮ (tel: 508-255 3421; www.nps.gov/caco; open daily) of the Cape Cod National Seashore. Interpretive films and exhibits explain the ecology of the Cape, and a bicycle trail (bikes can be rented nearby) winds through pine forests and marshes to end at **Coast Guard Beach**, where, in the 1920s, Henry Beston wrote his classic *Outermost House*; further north is **Nauset Light Beach** ⑯, graced with a picturesque lighthouse.

At **Marconi Beach** ⑰, Guglielmo Marconi set up the first wireless station in the United States and transmitted the first trans-Atlantic wireless message to Europe in 1903. (In 2003, Marconi's daughter marked the event's centennial by speaking with International Space Station astronauts via satellite from here.) The **Atlantic White Cedar Swamp Trail**, starting from the Marconi site, is especially beautiful.

Famous for its oysters, **Wellfleet** ⑱ is one of Cape Cod's most appealing towns, full of fine galleries and fun restaurants, and surrounded by inviting wildlife areas. Just south of town, off Route 6, the Audubon Society maintains the 700-acre (280-hectare) **Wellfleet Bay Wildlife Sanctuary** (tel: 508-349 2615; open 8am–dusk, Columbus Day–early May, Tues–Sun; entrance fee); a network of delightful walking trails leads from the visitor center, where there are natural history exhibits.

Farther north, the landscape becomes ever more wild and barren. Scrubby vegetation gives way to desert-like sand dunes. This is Truro, whose light and scenery led realist painter Edward Hopper to make his summer home here for some 30 years. East of Truro, the **Cranberry Bog Trail** (within the Cape Cod

BELOW:
Provincetown is a center for artists.

National Seashore) offers a look at the natural habitat of the tiny red fruit that proved such a boon to Cape Cod agriculture. Another road east leads to **Highland Light**, towering over **Head of the Meadow Beach**.

Cape Cod Light , also known as Highland Light, is one of the much-photographed landmarks of the Cape; erected in 1857, it is the peninsula's oldest lighthouse.

Provincetown

Contrast the subtle beauties and serenity of the National Seashore lands with the raucous and sometimes tawdry atmosphere along Commercial Street in **Provincetown ②**. Sidewalk artists will run off a pastel portrait, or perhaps a cartoon caricature. Shops emblazoned with advertisements sell fine works of art, bad works of art, kitsch souvenirs and an infinite variety of snacks. There are good restaurants and bad ones, delightful old inns and inexpensive guest houses, tacky shacks and beautiful landscaped captains' mansions. The artiness of "P-town" (a term *never* used by the locals) has coincided with its status of one of the most overtly gay capitals of the East Coast.

With its well-protected harbor, Provincetown started out as a natural fishing port – long before the Pilgrims came along. So it remains to this day. Portuguese fishermen, many from the Azores, came here in the heyday of the whaling trade and stayed on for the good fishing. Their descendants still make up a sizable proportion of the town's year-round residents. Led by painter Charles Hawthorne, who in 1899 founded the Cape Cod School of Art, hordes of artists and writers flocked to Provincetown in the early decades of the 20th century, drawn partly by the area's stark beauty and largely by the cheap rents and food to be found

Map on pages 158–9

TIP

A good way to see the principal sights is to take the Provincetown Trolley which runs along Commercial Street and continues on to the National Seashore. The main pick-up point is outside the Town Hall.

BELOW:
Provincetown Heritage Museum.

PROVINCETOWN ART COLONY

Bay and ocean, sand and sky: the natural beauty of Provincetown at the tip of Cape Cod has attracted artists since the town was little more than a fishing pier at the end of a sand spit. Today, Provincetown boasts dozens of art galleries, many of which specialize in contemporary works by local painters, photographers, and sculptors such as Joel Meyerowitz, Paul Bowen, and Paul Resika.

The artists who live and work in Provincetown today are drawn to the area by its pure, Mediterranean-like light – the same light that nearly a century ago inspired a group collectively known as the "Provincetown Art Colony," as renowned as those in Taos in New Mexico, Carmel in California, and East Hampton in New York State.

The colony began in the late 1800s, when a new railroad bed made Provincetown more easily accessible to artists in search of inexpensive lodging and studio space. In 1899, impressionist painter Charles Webster Hawthorne opened the Cape Cod School of Art, which was soon followed by the Summer School of Painting.

By the summer of 1916, more than 300 artists and students – associated with six schools of art – were thriving in the tolerant town, leading the *Boston Globe* to dub it "the Biggest Art Colony in the World."

Just keeping an eye on things.

here (thanks to the tourist boom they inspired, the latter are of course history).

Among the notables who passed through here, if only briefly, are dramatists Eugene O'Neill and Tennessee Williams, and writers Sinclair Lewis, John Dos Passos, and Norman Mailer. A dozen or more illustrious painters, such as Robert Motherwell, have left their mark, with new contenders cropping up year after year in such cutting-edge galleries as the Long Point and Bertha Walker. A number of galleries now specialize in Provincetown art going back to the early 1900s.

Other places to catch outstanding early work are the **Provincetown Art Association and Museum** founded in 1914 (460 Commercial Street; tel: 508-487 1750; www.paam.org; open May–end Oct. Mon–Fri and Sat & Sun pm; Nov–Apr, Wed–Sun pm; entrance fee); the **Provincetown Heritage Museum** (356 Commercial Street; tel: 508-487 7098; open daily in season; entrance fee).

The lofty Italianate tower looming above the town is the **Pilgrim Memorial** (off Winslow Street; tel: 508-487 1310; open Apr 15–Oct daily; weekends rest of year; entrance fee), built early in the century to ensure that Provincetown's place in colonial history would not be overlooked. The determined climber will be rewarded with a panoramic view of the town and the entire Cape. At the monument's foot is the **Provincetown Museum** (off Winslow Street from Bradford Street; open July–Aug, daily till 7pm; entrance fee), with intriguing local history exhibits. Spoils from the *Whydah*, a pirate ship discovered off Wellfleet in 1984, are displayed at **Exhibition Whydah** on MacMillan Wharf (tel: 508-487 8899; open May–Oct; entrance fee).

The very tip of Cape Cod – which is almost entirely within National Seashore boundaries – is a place of desolate beauty. Two vast beaches, **Race Point** and **Herring Cove**, invite exploration: by bike, on horseback, on foot, and off-road vehicle tours. For information, call in at the **Province Lands Visitors' Center ㉑** (Race Point Road; tel: 508-487 1256; open May–Oct, daily), which has a good viewing platform.

BELOW: waiting for the Hyannis ferry.

The Sound: Chatham to Falmouth

Orleans was called by its Indian name of Nauset until it was incorporated in 1797 and renamed for the Duke of Orleans (the future king of France), a recent visitor. Orleans has another "French connection" – it was the stateside terminus for a transatlantic telegraph cable to Brest in France. The cable performed well from 1891 to 1959 before it become obsolete, and is now commemorated in the **French Cable Station Museum** (41 South Orleans Road; tel: 508-240 1735; open Jun & Sept Fri & Sat pm; July & Aug, Wed–Sat pm). **Nauset Beach ㉒** is one of the Cape's finest stretches of coast; gentler **Skaket Beach** on the bay side is popular with bathers.

Cape Cod's southern shore, from Chatham to Falmouth, is a zone where the battle for – and against – commercialization has raged for the past few decades. Some pockets of subdued gentility still reign just off the honky-tonk stretches.

Chatham ㉓ is one of the aristocratic enclaves. The handsome Chatham Bars Inn was built as a private hunting lodge early in the 20th century. The nearby Fish Pier is a perfect spot to watch the fishing fleet

Map on pages 158–9

bring in the daily catch. The **Chatham Railroad Museum** (153 Depot Road; tel: 508-945-5199; Tues–Sat in season) is housed in the town's ornate Victorian railroad station, out of commission for several decades. **Chatham Light**, yet another picturesque Coast Guard lighthouse, overlooks South Beach.

Bird fanciers will want to make a visit to **Monomoy National Wildlife Refuge ㉔** (headquarters: Morris Island Road; tel: 508-945 0594; open daily), a narrow strip of land which is the stopping point for hundreds of species of birds traveling the Atlantic Flyway. It is accessible only by boat; the **Audubon Society** (tel: 508-349 2615) offers tours.

Picturesque Harwich and **Harwich Port ㉕** are the last peaceful settlements before the Cape's commercial belt. From West Harwich to Hyannis, Route 28 is lined with motels, restaurants, businesses and amusements. It's a long, tawdry stretch, where traffic usually crawls all summer.

South Dennis ㉖, perversely north of West Dennis, has on Old Main Street a typical shingled Full Cape house, built for a sea captain in 1801, known as **Jericho House** (tel: 508-394 9303; open mid-Jun–Sept Wed & Fri; Sept Sun pm). ("Full Cape" denotes a shingle-hung house with two windows either side of the door. Three-quarters Cape means two windows on one side and one on the other, while a Half Cape has the door on the left and two windows to the right.)

Look behind the house for the 1810 **Barn Museum** filled with farming implements, plus a remarkable "driftwood zoo" of carved flotsam created by Sherman Woodward in the 1950s.

Hyannis ㉗, the Cape's year-round commercial center, boasts more than a score of worthwhile restaurants and nightclubs, the **Cape Cod Melody Tent** fea-

Cranberries are a Cape specialty.

BELOW: Spohr's Garden, Falmouth.

A bird box in Trinity Park, Martha's Vineyard.

BELOW: Quissett Harbor, worth a detour off the road from Falmouth to Woods Hole.

turing top-name musicians and comedians (West Main Street; tel: 508-775 5630; www.melodytent.com), and, in the old Town Hall, the **John F. Kennedy Museum** (397 Main Street; tel: 508-790 3077; open Memorial Day–Columbus Day Mon–Sat, Sun pm; Nov–mid-April, Thurs-Sat, Sun pm; entrance fee) featuring photos and mementos of the President who summered in adjoining Hyannis Port. (Although the Kennedy Compound is the object of many a pilgrimage, it is not open to the public and very little of it can be seen from the road.) A small park dedicated to Kennedy's memory adjoins Veterans Beach, on Hyannis's harbor.

West of Hyannis, the tide of commercialism subsides occasionally to provide glimpses of Cape Cod's signature beauty. Make a southward detour for Centerville, where relatively warm-watered **Craigville Beach** (parking fee in summer) has drawn Christian "camp meetings" since the mid-19th century, and for affluent Osterville, a rarefied village surrounded by awe-inspiring seaside mansions.

Heading on toward Falmouth, take a side trip north to **Mashpee** ㉘, located amid Wampanoag tribal lands which in recent decades have been carved up by development. The **Old Indian Meetinghouse** (Meeting House Road at Route 28), the oldest church building on the Cape, built in 1684, and the burial ground next door, are well worth a look.

The primitive yet fanciful paintings of Ralph and Martha Cahoon are on exhibit, along with 19th- and early 20th- century American marine paintings, in **Cotuit** ㉙ at the **Cahoon Museum of American Art** (4676 Falmouth Road; tel: 508-428 7581; open Tues–Sat, Sun pm; closed Jan), housed in a 1775 colonial farmhouse.

Falmouth ㉚ is like a microcosm of Cape Cod life. The town green – a Revolutionary militia training ground – is among the prettiest on the Cape; it's ringed by fine old houses, including several delightful B&Bs, and the **Falmouth Historical Society Museums** (Village Green; tel: 508-548 4857; open early June–mid-Sept Tues– Sept; mid-Sept–late Oct Sat and Sun pm; entrance fee). Falmouth Harbor is filled with pleasure craft; swimmers and windsurfers favor the beaches and guest houses of Victorian-era Falmouth Heights, overlooking Nantucket Sound. Spring is the best time to visit **Spohr's Garden**, off Woods Hole Road in Falmouth. The town property borders a scenic oyster pond.

One of the most pleasant activities in Falmouth is to rent a bicycle and follow the old railroad bed, now a bike path, down to **Woods Hole** ㉛. This small town is devoted almost exclusively to maritime activities. Most travelers pass through here merely to board the ferry for Martha's Vineyard, a 45-minute voyage away, but Woods Hole itself warrants a stopover.

The world-famous **Woods Hole Oceanographic Institutution** (15 School Street; tel: 508-457 2180; www.whoi.edu; exhibit center closed Jan–Mar; open Apr by appointment; May–Oct Mon–Sat, Nov & Dec Tues–Fri) maintains a visitor center to describe its fascinating research. Weekdays from late June through early September, the intitution offers free 1¼-hr tours of the dock area and restricted village facilities (tours begin at 10:30am and 1:30pm from 93 Water Street; it's wise to reserve – tel: 508-289 2252).

With an advance reservation of at least a week, visitors can tour the **Marine Biological Laboratory** which houses marine organisms used in research (MBL Street at Water Street; tel: 508-289 7623; tours late June–Aug Mon–Fri at 1pm, 2pm and 3pm). Try to visit the small but intriguing **Woods Hole Science Aquarium** (Albatross and Water streets; tel: 508-495 2001; open weekdays) for the 11am and 4pm seal feedings. Though no larger than a couple of city blocks, this tiny town supports a number of superb casual restaurants, where the specialty, naturally, is seafood.

Map on pages 158–9

The island of Martha's Vineyard

Over the decades, Vineyard residents have grown blasé about the celebrities in their midst, and precisely because of that laissez-faire attitude, the roster just keeps growing. It took a Presidential visit – the Clintons' during the mid-1990s – to shake things up a bit, but, despite the hordes lining the roadways, most people went about their business, and leisure, as usual.

Islanders have worked too hard to create and preserve a relaxed way of life to let a little glitz and glamour throw them. For many, the island represents a true escape from the stresses of high-powered careers. Though the price of admission may be high, once one has arrived, a kind of barefoot democracy prevails.

Like Cape Cod, Martha's Vineyard is a geological remnant from the last Ice Age. Two advancing lobes of a glacier molded the triangular northern shoreline, then retreated, leaving hilly moraines, low plains and many-fingered ponds. And Martha herself? She was the daughter of Thomas Mayhew, who in 1642 bought a large tract of land, including Nantucket Island, for the sum of £40. (Mayhew named the nearby Elizabeth Islands after another daughter.) The "Vineyard" part of the name refers to once-abundant wild grapes.

Vineyard Haven, Oak Bluffs and Edgartown, the three protected harbor towns

Bikes and blades for rent.

BELOW: Oak Bluffs, Trinity Park.

of the northeastern portion of the island, have always been active and prosperous, although the main order of business is no longer shipping and whaling, but tourism and summer homes. By contrast, the sparsely populated "up-island" (i.e., to the west and south) towns of West Tisbury, Chilmark, Menemsha, and Gay Head remain determinedly rural.

It may come as a disappointment to many visitors to find that, as a rule, Martha's Vineyard's extensive beaches are not accessible to outsiders but have been reserved for homeowners; the major exception, beyond the placid Joseph Sylvia State Beach on the bay side, is South Beach, fronting the rolling Atlantic south of Edgartown; other public beaches are Katama (good for surfing and for strong swimmers), Moshpu, Oak Bluffs and Menemsha.

Vineyard Haven, Oak Bluffs and Edgartown

Known until 1870 as Holmes Hole, **Vineyard Haven** ❷ (the official name of the town is Tisbury, but everyone calls it by the name of its primary village) blossomed into a busy port during the 18th and 19th centuries, with both maritime businesses and farmers profiting from the constant movement of ships. Today, the homey **Black Dog Tavern** (Beach Street Extension; tel: 508-693 9223), with its offshoot bakery, store, and catalog business, enjoys a similar relationship with the legions of vacationers who arrive by ferry from Woods Hole.

Handsome houses dating from the years before the great fire of 1883 can be found on Williams Street, a block off Main Street. Nearby, the 1829 **Old Schoolhouse Museum** (110 Main Street), was the island's first schoolhouse; the building was also once a carpentry shop and a church. At the western end of Main Street (bicycle or take the car) stands the 52-ft-high (10-meter) **West Chop**

TIP

Martha's Vineyard Preservation Trust is also the steward of three lighthouse and offers sunsets tours of two of them from mid-June through mid-Sept. For information on Gay Head Light tour (Fri–Sun evenings) tel: 508-645 9954. For information on the East Chop light tour (Sun evenings) tel: 508-963 8104. The Trust also offers two-hour catboat charters.

BELOW: Edgartown.

Lighthouse, built in 1838. Across the way, **East Chop Lighthouse** was built just 10 years earlier.

Religion tinged with tourism produced an unusual community in **Oak Bluffs** ㉝, a town renowned for its engaging cottages built in "carpenter gothic" style. In 1835, Edgartown Methodists chose a secluded circle of oak trees here as a site for a camp meeting. Twenty years later, there were more than 320 tents at Wesleyan Grove, as it was named, and many thousands of people gathered here each summer. Small houses soon replaced the tents, laid out along circular drives that rimmed the large central "tabernacle" where the congregation assembled.

Today this camp meeting site is known as **Trinity Park**. Tiny gingerbread cottages are a riot of color and jigsaw carvery, with all manner of turrets, spires, gables and eaves. Yet the park remains remarkably serene and intimate. The huge cast iron-and-wood theater in the center of the campground, built in 1870, still hosts community gatherings. **Illumination Night**, held every August, recreates the camp's traditional closing-night ceremony, when colorful glowing lanterns were strung up throughout the park.

Circuit Avenue and Lake Street mark the hub of town and the site of the 1876, National Historic Landmark **Flying Horses Carousel**, one of America's oldest (Circuit Avenue; tel: 508-693 9481; open mid-Apr–mid-Oct, daily; fee).

South of Oak Bluffs on Beach Road, **Edgartown** ㉞ is the oldest settlement on Martha's Vineyard. In 1642, missionary Thomas Mayhew, Jr, son of the Watertown, Massachusetts, entrepreneur who bought the islands off the Cape for a pittance, arrived at Great Harbor, now Edgartown, and set about converting the island's native population. The town struggled along until the 18th century, when it became a capital in the worldwide whaling trade, vying with Nantucket and, later, New Bedford. The captains who made their fortunes from the sea left behind a treasure: their elegant Federal and Greek Revival houses, especially those lining North and South Water streets.

The Martha's Vineyard Preservation Trust operates **Martha's Vineyard Museum** (99 Main Street, www.mvpreservation.org; tel: 508-627 4440; entrance fee) and gives tours of severall historic buildings. Among them: the Federal-style Edgartown residence built in 1840 by whale-oil magnate **Dr Daniel Fisher**, who once supplied all US lighthouses with Edgartown oil.

Next door is the imposing Greek Revival **Old Whaling Church** of 1843, whose enormous pillars and soaring tower are a rare instance of monumental scale in Edgartown. The church is now the venue for concerts, a film series, and community events. Tucked behind the church is the **Vincent House Museum**, built in 1672 and the oldest house on the island. At the corner of Cooke and School streets is the **Martha's Vineyard Historical Society Museum** (tel: 508-627 4441; www.marthasvineyardhistory.org; open early June–early Oct Tues–Sat; early Oct–early June Wed–Fri pm and Sat 10–4; entrance fee), which also oversees historic buildings and sites including the **Ross Fresnel Lens Building**, housing a 19th-century first order Fresnel lens; the **Francis Foster Maritime Gallery**, exhibiting logbooks, ship models and other nautical treasures; and the c.1845 **Captain Francis**

Map on pages 158–9

TIP

Christmas visitors to the Old Whaling Church can attend Handel's "Messiah". Films, lectures and concerts are presented in the 500-seat church as well as services.

BELOW: the ferry to Chappaquiddick.

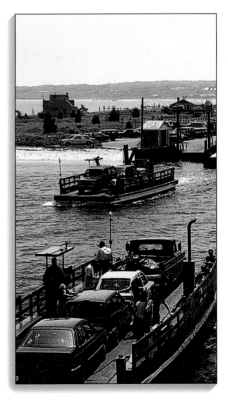

Pease House, with exhibits about the island's history, a Native American Gallery, a book shop, and local crafts.

A stone's throw away from Edgartown, across a narrow neck of the harbor, is **Chappaquiddick Island** ㉟. The island's native name means "The Separated Island," which it steadfastly remains, although the *On-Time III* regularly ferries cars (a few at a time) and clusters of pedestrians over the 200-yard (180-meter) crossing (tel: 508-627 9427). The main attraction on "Chappy," several miles from the ferry landing, is the **Wasque** (pronounced *wayce*-kwee) **Reservation** (east end of Wasque Road; tel: 508-627 7260; open year round; entrance fee Memorial Day-mid Sept), a 200-acre (80-hectare) preserve with walking trails and beach (be careful: there's a strong current). **Cape Poge Wildlife Refuge** at the island's eastern end, offers 6 miles (10 km) of dunes, woods, salt marshes, ponds, tidal flats, and beach. Naturalists offer jeep tours of the area (tel: 508-627 3599).

Up-island escape

To retreat to the tranquility of up-island life, drive west from Edgartown through forests of pine and oak, to a Vineyard where nature still decisively holds the upper hand. The 5,000-acre (2,000-hectare) **Manuel F. Correlus State Forest** ㊱ (tel: 508-693 2540) is laced with 15 miles (24 km) of walking and bridle paths, and brings the scent of pines to the outskirts of **West Tisbury** ㊲ center. The island's only youth hostel (25 Edgartown-West Tisbury Road; tel: 508-693 0309 or 888-901 2087 weekdays for reservations; www.hihostelsw.com) is on the edge of the forest. The modest and unassuming village traditionally has been a center of small industry (including woolen and flour mills). Quirky attractions

Playwright Lillian Hellman and actor John Belushi are buried in Chilmark Cemetery. Belushi's simple stone, which fans sometimes adorn with a beer can, is set up in front, but his body lies in an undisclosed plot.

BELOW:
Gay Head cliffs and lighthouse.

such as the Field Gallery (where Tom Maley's fanciful sculptures frolic in a field) and the Granary Gallery at the Red Barn Emporium (showcasing the historic photos of the late Alfred Eisenstaedt, a summer regular) draw more attention these days, but the county fair is still a high point of the summer.

Chicama Vineyards (Stoney Hill Road; tel: 508-693 0309; open year-round; tours mid-May–mid-Oct) offers free tours and tastings.

Of the three parallel roads traveling from West Tisbury to Chilmark, Middle Road traverses the most rugged, interesting glacial terrain. At **Chilmark Center** is Beetlebung Corner, a stand of tupelo trees from which "beetles" (mallets) and "bungs" (wooden stoppers) were once made.

Nearby **Menemsha** ❸ is a tiny fishing village on Vineyard Sound, famed for its appearance in Steven Spielberg's ever-popular 1975 movie *Jaws* and prized for its Technicolor sunsets.

The most spectacular natural sight on Martha's Vineyard is at its westernmost tip, looking out to the untamed sea. From Chilmark, follow the single hilly road that at several points offers breathtaking views of Menemsha Pond northward and Squibnocket Pond to the south.

At the end, **Aquinnah Lighthouse** (Lighthouse Road; tel: 508-645 2211; tours by appointment; entrance fee) marks the western terminus of the island and the location of the stunning, ancient geologic strata that compose the cliffs at **Aquinnah** ❸ (formerly Gay Head). Clays of many colors – from gray to pink to green – represent eons of geological activity: fossils found amid the ever-changing contours of this 150-ft (46-meter) promontory have been dated back millions of years.

Gay Head is one of only two Native American communities in Massachusetts;

Map on pages 158–9

TIP

The ferry to Nantucket leaves from Hyannis and the trip takes around two and a half hours. Call (508) 477 8600 for schedules. There is also a hydrofoil ferry (no cars) that takes only an hour. www.steamship authority.com

BELOW: cocktails by the harbor, Edgartown, Martha's Vineyard.

Old Mill,
Nantucket Town.

it has been more successful than the related Wampanaoag settlement at Mash-pee in asserting its rights, and remains a cohesive social entity, over three cen-turies since the advent of colonizing forces.

On Indian Hill Road, heading back toward Vineyard Haven, is the site of Christiantown, settled by "praying Indians" in 1659; a plaque fixed to a boul-der honors Thomas Mayhew's missionary efforts. At the end of the road, the **Cedar Tree Neck Wildlife Sanctuary** provides a commanding view of the Vineyard Sound, across to the Elizabeth Islands, and a fine spot for strolling and contemplating nature.

The island of Nantucket

In 1830 the whaling ship *Sarah* returned home to Nantucket island, carrying 3,500 barrels of valuable whale oil after a voyage of nearly three years. On the island, stately mansions, decorated with silks and china from faraway lands, awaited the returning captains. Schools, hotels, a library and the commercial activity on Main Street were indications of a prosperous people.

Nantucket's golden age was not destined to last much longer, but the hand-some little town that whaling fortunes had built would survive as if preserved in amber. Surrounded by pristine moors, broad beaches, and bluffs strewn with wild roses, it would live to see a new day of prosperity built on tourism.

Chasing the whales

Since its earliest days, Nantucket has been populated by determined and spir-ited people. The first colonists, who arrived in 1659, were emigrants who chafed at the Puritan severity of towns on the North Shore of Massachusetts. Taught

"onshore" whaling by the native Algonquins, they traveled out in open boats to chase and harpoon whales sighted from land. By the beginning of the 18th century, offshore whaling had begun and, with each generation of larger, more seaworthy craft, the whaling industry grew.

The natives, however, lost out. Although they sailed on whaling boats, their way of life on the island was irreversibly changed by the colonists. By 1855, disease (introduced to the country from Europe) and alcohol had taken the last of Nantucket's original residents.

Both the Revolutionary War and the War of 1812 battered Nantucket's whaling industry, but the islanders' tenacity brought it back to life. Nantucket ships again sailed throughout the world and brought back record quantities of oil. It was during this period that the town acquired much of its urbanity, but the islanders' prosperity was destined to be short-lived: the Great Fire of 1846 razed the port, and in the 1850s kerosene replaced whale oil. Too heavily dependent on whaling, Nantucket was left high and dry.

From a peak of around 10,000, Nantucket's population dropped to 3,200 in 1875. Those who remained applied their ingenuity to a new venture, one that thrives today and continues to capitalize on the gifts of the sea. Tourism took off toward the end of the 19th century, as steamboats made the island more readily accessible. Land speculators built hotels and vacation homes. Quaint Siasconset (pronounced "Sconset"), linked to the town by a narrow-gauge railroad built in 1884, was especially popular, drawing such luminaries as actress Lillian Russell. The railroad is gone now (it was used for scrap metal during World War I), but tourism lives on.

An Indian word meaning "that faraway land," Nantucket isn't too far away for

Map on pages 158–9

Information point for visitors.

BELOW: Nantucket Town.

the thousands of people who visit each year by ferry and airplane. The winter population of 7,000 increases sevenfold when the "summer people" take over the sidewalks of town.

In sharp contrast to Martha's Vineyard, Nantucket's mid-island moors and miles of beautiful, unspoiled beaches are open to visitors, most of whom use the preferred island mode of transportation: bikes (several shops stand ready to equip tourists near the ferry dock). Though smaller residential neighborhoods dot the island's coast, the harbor town of Nantucket, centrally located on the north shore, is unquestionably the focal point of the island and its only commercial center.

The pleasures of Nantucket town

One can spend days walking through the town of **Nantucket** ⓐ and always be sure of seeing something new. The community is a gem of 18th- and 19th-century architecture, from the dominant clapboard-and-shingle Quaker homes to the grandeur of the buildings lining **Upper Main Street**. It's best to tour with a street map (available from the bike shops, or in the free local newspapers distributed on the ferry), for the twists and turns can prove disorienting.

As in whaling days, the waterfront is the focus of life in Nantucket town. Several wharves extend into the harbor, the most central of which – **Straight Wharf** – is an extension of Main Street. First built in 1723, rebuilt after the 1846 fire, and renovated in the late 1950s to accommodate shops and restaurants, it's now like a small village unto itself, surrounded by luxury yachts and sailboats, some of which are available for charter. (The untouched barrier beach of Coatue is an ideal destination.)

Old South Wharf has also been spruced up and rendered tourist-friendly

TIP

A good rainy-day stop in summer is the Dreamland Theatre, on South Water, which shows first-run films. It started life in the mid-1800s as a Quaker meeting house.

BELOW: the tools of a gardener's trade, Nantucket town.

with boutiques and cafés; it's possible (for a tidy sum) to rent tiny but picturesque wharfside cottages here.

Along Main Street up from Straight Wharf, a picturesque shopping district lines the gently rising cobblestone street. Although the square-mile (2.5 sq. km) National Landmark Historic District contains 800 pre-1850 buildings, the red-brick facades lining Main Street are relatively "young," post-fire replacements. With its tree-lined, brick-paved sidewalks, Main Street is a hub of activity in summer, offering distractions from collectibles to edibles. Noteworthy emporia include the Main Street Gallery (actually, just off Main, on South Water Street) and Espresso Café, a lively place with the look of a classic ice-cream parlor.

Nantucket is proud of its history, especially its grand old homes and museums. The **Nantucket Historical Association** (tel: 508-228 1894; www.nha.org; fee) oversees more than a dozen properties, including several museums, in the historic district, and sells a Visitor Pass good for admission to all buildings, or individual tickets). Most are open daily from Memorial Day to Labor Day: call ahead for off-season hours. Among their properties is the **Whaling Museum** (13 Broad Street), housed in a former spermaceti candle factory, which commemorates Nantucket's seafaring days with impressive displays, including the skeleton of a 43-ft (13.1-meter) finback whale. The Association's **Peter Foulger Museum** (15 Broad Street), mounts temporary exhibits from its permanent collection.

Climb up the tower of the Association's **First Congregational Church** (50 Prospect Street; 508-228 1894) for a spectacular view of the island. The oldest house on Nantucket is the Association's 1686 **Jethro Coffin House** on the northwest edge of town on Sunset Hill Lane. This plain saltbox design reflects the austere lifestyle led by the island's earliest settlers. In contrast, the three-story

Map on pages 158–9

TIP

One of the island's better kept secrets is the subterranean Brotherhood of Thieves, an 1840s whaling bar at 23 Broad Street (tel: 508-228 2551). The restaurant/bar serves terrific mixed drinks, good pub food and chowder by candlelight.

BELOW: the Wauwinet inn, Nantucket.

Doorknocker, Jared Coffin House.

red-brick **Jared Coffin House**, at the corner of Centre and Broad streets, made its 1845 debut as the showiest dwelling on the island; within two years it became a hotel, and to this day it remains one of the island's finest inns.

Two more Coffin residences (the family was so prolific, it accounted for half the island's population by the early 19th century) stand at No. 75 and No. 78 Main Street, examples of the brick Federal style of architecture.

Farther up Main Street are the "**Three Bricks**," architectural triplets built by wealthy whaler Joseph Starbuck for his three sons. Across the street, and worlds apart in style, stand the "**Two Greeks**," Greek Revival mansions built by Frederick Coleman for two Starbuck daughters. One, the Association's **Hadwen House** (96 Main Street, showcases the affluent lifestyle of a wealthy whaling family.

Ralph Waldo Emerson gave the inaugural address at the 1847 Greek Revival **Nantucket Atheneum**, now a public library, at the corner of Lower India Street.

A few blocks out of town, at the corner of Vestal and Milk streets, is the **Maria Mitchell Science Center** (4 Vestal Street; tel: 508-228 9198; www.mmo.org; call for hours; entrance fee) honoring the local savant – and Atheneum librarian – who discovered a comet at the age of 29 in 1847, garnering international acclaim. She became the first woman admitted to the American Academy of Arts and Sciences, and America's first female college professor (she taught astronomy at Vassar). The somewhat scattered complex includes several facilities open to the public, including her childhood home, built in 1790 and showing what19th-century island Quaker life was like; and two observatories. The Center offers several field trips, including bird, wildflower, and marine ecology.

No. 99 Main Street, with its detailed and finely proportioned facade, is one of the most handsome wooden Federal-style buildings on Nantucket; it was

built by forebears of Rowland Macy, who left the island to seek his fortune and founded a well-known namesake store.

Overlooking the harbor from **Brant Point** is one of America's oldest lighthouses. Visitors departing by sea often toss the traditional penny into the water off Brant Point to ensure that they'll return to the shores of Nantucket.

The rest of Nantucket island

"Nantucket! Take out your map and look at it," urged Herman Melville in his whaling adventure classic *Moby-Dick*. An inspection of the map reveals an island with hamlets and hideaways sprinkled across its 14-mile (23-km) length. Despite some mid-island development in recent decades, about one-third of the island is under protective stewardship, Although environmental restrictions limit activities on dunes and moors, much of the land can be explored. Wear long pants and use insect repellent; deer ticks carry Lyme disease.

Stretching northeast from the town of Nantucket is a 6-mile (10-km) inner harbor, protected from Nantucket Sound by **Coatue**, a thin spit of land with flat white beaches accessible only by boat. This sweep of land, encompassing the 1,117-acre (453-hectare) **Coatue-Coskata Wildlife Refuge** ⓰ (Wauwinet Road; tel: 508-228 0006) extends north to **Great Point**, where a lighthouse – a solar-powered 1986 replica of the 1818 original, swept away by a 1984 storm – warns boats away from the sandbars of Nantucket Sound. The Trustees of Reservations (508-228 5646; www.thetrustees.org), which administers the refuge, offers three-hour naturalist-led excursions from June to October.

The **Nantucket Life Saving Museum** (158 Polpis Road; tel: 508-228 1885; open mid-June–mid-Oct; entrance fee), en route to Great Point, includes artifacts

Map on pages 158-9

TIP

The Nantucket Trustees of the Reservations (www. thetrustees.org; tel: 508-228 5646) offers several tours, including a trip to remote Cape Poge Lighthouse, an over-sand tour of the Coatue-Coskata Wildlife Refuge, and kayak and canoe trips.

BELOW: much of Nantucket is protected from development.

Map on pages 158–9

A seaside treat.

BELOW: a
Siasconset cameo.

from the Italian liner *Andrea Doria*, which sank not far from here in 1956.

Monomoy, the most populous settlement and the nearest to town, affords spectacular views from its bluffs. From here, the Polpis Road leads across the rolling and delicate **Nantucket Moors**, which are carpeted with bayberry, beach plum, heather and other lush vegetation – a lovely green and flowering pink in summer, brilliant red and gold in the fall.

Wauwinet ㊷, a tiny community of cottages tucked amid the beach grass at the head of the harbor, is home to the ultra-elegant (and ultra-expensive) Wauwinet, a finely refurbished 1850 hostelry within splashing distance of both ocean and harbor. (It's located on the "haulover" where fishing boats used to avoid the long trip around Great Point.)

Tourists discovered **Siasconset ㊸**, the easternmost and second-largest town on Nantucket, in the 1880s. Theater people from the mainland mingled with local fishermen; the resulting architecture ranges from Lilliputian cottages to large rambling shingle-style houses along the bluffs.

Nantucket's most popular beaches are located on the flat, windswept south shore, open to the cold, spirited waters of the Atlantic Ocean. At **Surfside Beach ㊹**, a colorful Victorian lifesaving station serves nowadays as the island's only Youth Hostel. Surfers favor the beach at **Cisco**, a bit more remote, at the end of Hummock Pond Road, while **Madaket Beach ㊺**, at the southwestern tip of Nantucket, is popular for swimming, fishing, and, especially, sunset-gazing.

The northern coast east of Madaket Harbor, heading back toward town, offers the gentle surf of **Dionis** and **Jetties** beaches. **Children's Beach**, tucked well inside the West Jetty, near Steamship Wharf, is especially placid and enhanced by a playground. ❑

Whale Watching

Destination: Stellwagen Bank, a shallow underwater deposit of sand and gravel off the coast of Massachusetts, to which pods of gentle humpback whales return each year between April and October after spending the winters breeding in the West Indies. Sightseers are hot on their tails, for it's truly breathtaking to see these huge (often endangered) spectacles lunge, breach and flipper in the open ocean.

It's so rare for visitors not to see whales during a trip that most companies offer a "rain check," good for another trip. More often than not, the boats approach to within 50 ft (15 meters) of these magnificent mammals.

The world's largest concentration of whales (both in numbers and in species) are drawn to the fertile feeding grounds of Stellwagen Bank by huge quantities of plankton and an infinite number of small sand eels. The vast majority of the 500 or so whales who summer here are humpbacks, but their number also includes minkes, finbacks and a few endangered right whales (so called because, being slow swimmers, they were the "right" whales to hunt). Hundreds of frolicking dolphins and immense basking sharks will be close by, too.

The humpback is basically a bulk feeder, diving deep below schools of sand eels and lunging upward through the school with its mouth open. On the way up, it engulfs large quantities of fish and water, while its rorquals (folds of skin that begin at the chin and stretch to the navel) balloon to double its oral capacity. This allows the whale to catch hundreds, perhaps thousands, of fish with every lunge.

Whales also breach – that is, leap from the water, and flipper-roll on to their sides and lift their long white flipper out of the water before slamming it down hard on the surface.

Experts recognize individual humpbacks, which often reach lengths of 40–50 ft (12–15 meters) and weights of 30 tons, by their body markings, especially those on their tail flukes.

Whale watching was popularized in 1975 by Captain Al Avellar, a deep-sea fisherman from Provincetown, who invited Charles Mayo, a Provincetown-based marine biologist, to act as a guide on his first trips. Today, whale-watching excursions, all with experts on board, attract over 100,000 visitors annually.

Sightseeing boats generally depart two or three times daily in summer and on weekends in spring and fall. Trips last about three hours. Take jackets and seasickness pills, even on calm and seemingly warm days.

Many companies are based in Provincetown on Cape Cod: the Dolphin Fleet (tel: 508-349 1900, 800-826 9300) has an on-board biologist from the Center for Coastal Studies. In mid-Cape's Barnstable Harbor, call Hyannis Whalewatcher Cruises (tel: 508-362 6088).

From Boston, the New England Aquarium (tel: 617-973 5200) sponsors whalewatching trips, as does Boston Harbor Cruises (Rowes Wharf; tel: 617-227 4321).

On the North Shore in Gloucester, call Cape Ann Whale Watch (415 Main Street; tel: 978-283 5110, 800-877 5110) and Yankee Fleet Whale Watch (Route 133; tel: 978-283 0313, 800-942 5464). In Plymouth, Captain John Boats (tel: 508-746 2643, 800-242 2469) and Captain Tim Brady and Sons (tel: 508-746 4809) leave from Town Wharf. ❑

RIGHT: dolphins frolic alongside.

CENTRAL MASSACHUSETTS AND THE BERKSHIRES

Map on page 188

Famed outdoor museums recall the past and students enliven the present. In the west, art, dance, music, literature, and crafts flourish like nowhere else in New England

Tucked between metropolitan Boston and the more tourism-oriented Berkshire Hills, Massachusetts' mid-section harkens back to an earlier era of agriculture and small-town industry.

The vigor and sincerity of early Americans' social vision is on display from mid-May to mid-October at **Fruitlands Museums** (102 Prospect Hill Road; 978-456 3924; openmid-May–mid-Oct daily; entrance fee) in the little town of **Harvard** ❶, an hour west of Boston via Route 2. In the mid-19th century, transcendentalist Amos Bronson Alcott, father of Louisa May Alcott (author of *Little Women*), left his Concord home with political activist Charles Lane and a group of followers to found an anti-materialist utopian community on the Fruitlands farm.

Vegetarianism, asceticism and a philosophical return to nature were their mandates but, despite the best intentions and an inspiring view of the beautiful Nashua River Valley, the commune soon dispersed. Today the farmhouse has been transformed into a museum with presentations on Alcott, Emerson, Thoreau and other transcendentalists. Also at the site are a 1794 Shaker house and an Indian Museum.

Farther west, off Route 62 between Westminster and North Rutland, **Wachusett Mountain Ski Area** (tel: 413-464 2300) in the **Wachusett State Reservation** ❷ has chair lifts and trails leading to one of the state's highest summits (2,006 ft/649 meters), with views of the Boston skyscrapers. It's the nearest ski and snowboard center to Boston, and transports leafpeekers in the fall.

PRECEDING PAGES AND LEFT: fall in the west of the state. **BELOW:** in the Indian Museum at Fruitlands Museums.

Worcester

To the southeast is **Worcester** ❸, the state's second-largest city. This gritty industrial center spawned the country's first park, first wire-making company, first steam calliope, first carpet loom, first diner manufacturer, first Valentine, and (suitably enough) first birth-control pill, not to mention the beginnings of liquid-fuel rocketry, female suffrage and the Free Soil Party, precursor of the Republican Party. Notable residents have included Dr Robert H. Goddard, born here in 1882 (a fine collection of his rocketry patents, drawings and other memorabilia is on exhibit at the **Goddard Library** at Clark University (tel: 508-793 7572; open Mon–Sat, Sun pm); composer Stephen Foster; socialist leader Emma Goldman; humorist Robert Benchley; and 1960s radical Abbie Hoffman. Sigmund Freud gave his only US lecture at Clark University.

Publisher Isaiah Thomas, a Son of Liberty who fled Boston in advance of the British Army in 1770 and continued to publish his rabble-rousing revolutionary newspaper, the *Massachusetts Spy*, was from Worcester. He

Central Massachusetts and the Berkshires

later established the American Antiquarian Society; its Worcester headquarters, on Salisbury Street, is now a research library (tel: 508-755-5221; tours Wed 2pm).

The city, despite its reincarnation as an educational and medical center, is itself a trove of antiquarian delights. The **Worcester Historical Museum** (30 Elm Street; tel: 508-753 8278; open Tues–Sat; Sun pm; entrance fee) traces the city's industrial and cultural history, and maintains the splendid 1772 Georgian Salisbury Mansion (40 Highland Street; open Thur–Sun pm; entrance fee). The **Higgins Armory Museum** features a vast collection of medieval armor, as well as armaments dating back to 6th-century BC Greece (100 Barber Avenue; tel: 508-853 6015; www.higgins.org; open Tues–Sat; Sun pm; entrance fee).

The **Worcester Art Museum** (55 Salisbury Street; tel: 508-799 4406; open open Wed–Sun; Thur until 8pm; entrance fee except Sat 10–noon) is the second largest in New England and perhaps the most adventurous: its sponsorship of excavations at Antioch, Syria, in the 1930s yielded a remarkable collection of 2nd-century AD Roman mosaics. It also has fine collections of European and Eastern art. But perhaps most appealing is the extensive gallery of 17th-, 18th- and 19th-century American art, including paintings by John Singleton Copley, Winslow Homer, and John Singer Sargent.

The best-known diner in the city where they were originally made is **The Boulevard** (155 Shrewsbury Street; tel: 508-791 4535). Built in 1936 and now open 24 hours a day, it has stained-glass windows and Formica-topped tables.

Higgins Armory Museum, Worcester.

Reliving the past

Off Route 20, **Old Sturbridge Village ❹**, a recreated community encompassing some 40 period buildings scattered over 200 acres (80 hectares), offers a "you are there" take on early 19th-century New England rural life (tel: 508-347 3362 or 800-733 1830; www.osv.org; open year-round Tues–Sun and Mon holidays; entrance fee includes two days' admission; tel: 508-347 3362).

BELOW: interpreting the past at Old Sturbridge Village.

Visitors are given illuminating explanations, couched in modern parlance, as the interpreters go about the daily business of farm and town life – from cobbling shoes, to making tin lanterns, to leading prayers.

Of special interest is the Pliny Freeman Farm, where, depending on the season, workers in period dress engage in making soap, shearing sheep, and laboriously building stone walls. Concepts of political freedom and discourse grew, in part, from the emergence of a free and vibrant press, and the activities of the Isaiah Thomas Printing Office are designed to show how printed communication became an integral part of the new nation's growth.

Lying northwest of Sturbridge amidst rolling hills that are especially beautiful in autumn, the huge **Quabbin Reservoir ❺** (Visitor Center; Route 9, Belchertown; tel: 413-323 7221; open daily) comprises 128 sq. miles (331 sq. km) of flooded valley that holds 412 billion gallons and supplies the drinking water to Greater Boston. Four towns were flooded in 1939 to create this great body of water. Quabbin is prized as a place to fish, hike and admire the rare bald eagles that breed by the reservoir.

The pioneer heritage

Farther west, in the well-preserved pioneer village of **Old Deerfield 6** – 15 museum houses make up **Historic Deerfield**, off Route 5 (Main Street; tel: 413-774 5581; www.historic-deerfield.org; open Apr–Dec daily; in Jan–Mar, Flynt Center of Early Life open weekends only; entrance fee good for two consecutive days). It has a fascinating history that dates from its settlement in 1669. The Pocumtuck Indians, who farmed the fertile valley, were not pleased to see their land usurped, and massacred the entire population (by then 125 strong) in 1675. That deterred settlers, but the lure of the land was irresistible, and the interlopers eventually won out, despite a French-instigated Indian raid in 1704 in which half the village was burned, 100 colonists carried off to Quebec, and 50 slaughtered.

Tomahawk marks can still be seen on one sturdy wooden door, but the town's lurid history is not what attracts most visitors. The draw is an extraordinary architectural cache: the carefully restored Colonial and Federal structures along "The Street," Deerfield's mile-long main thoroughfare. The treasures inside the houses, representing decades of changing decorative styles, easily equal the exteriors. Among the buildings open to the public are the Ashley House (1730), a former parson's home with intricately carved woodwork and antique furnishings; the Asa Stebbins House (1810) with early paintings, Chinese porcelain and Federal and Chippendale furniture; and the Hall Tavern (1760), where Historic Deerfield maintains its information center.

Memorial Hall Museum (Memorial Street; tel: 413-774 3768; open May–Oct daily; combination ticket or seperate admission available), houses a wonderful hodgepodge of folk art, Native American relics, needlework, and the eclectic collection of town historian George Sheldon.

It is not excelled by anything I have ever seen, not excepting the Bay of Naples.

– JOHN QUINCY ADAMS, WRITING OF DEERFIELD'S MAIN STREET

BELOW: Old Sturbridge Village.

Head south on Route 5 to **South Deerfield** ❼, home to **Magic Wings Butterfly Conservatory and Gardens** (tel: 413-665 2805; open daily; entrance fee), where thousands of butterflies flutter about in an indoor (and, in summer, outdoor) conservatory garden. A bit farther south, it's always Christmas in the Disneyesque Bavarian Village and Santa's Workshop at "the world's largest candle store," **Yankee Candle Company** (Route 5; tel: 413-665 2929; open daily).

 Map on page 188

The Pioneer Valley: a cultural nexus

Continue south on Route 5 into the heart of the region designated as Pioneer Valley (the Massachusetts section of the Connecticut River Valley) to **Northampton** ❽. Surrounded by colleges – Amherst, Hampshire, the University of Massachusetts ("U-Mass"), Mount Holyoke, and **Smith College** (tel: 413-584 2700), right in town – Northampton's lively bistros, restaurants, and galleries reflect the youthful, energetic company it keeps. Northampton has attracted hundreds of artisans and artists, who showcase their wares at craft shops throughout town and in the multi-story Thornes Marketplace complex (150 Main Street).

After a five-year, $35 million renovation, the **Smith College Museum of Art** (Elm Street, Route 9; tel: 413-585 2760; www.smith.edu/artmuseum; open Tues–Sat; Sun pm; donation) reopened in 2003. The museum exhibits one of the finest collections in the country, with a special focus on American art and on French impressionists including Degas, Seurat, Picasso, Cassatt, and Cézanne. It also exhibits an impressive collection of Asian and African and Asian pieces. The college's **Lyman Plant House** (tel: 413-585 2740; open daily), a delicate 1896 greenhouse, makes a lovely rainy-day retreat.

Calvin Coolidge (1872–1933), the governor of Massachusetts who went to

Smith College, with 2,500 undergraduates in Northampton, is the nation's largest liberal arts college for women. It was founded in 1871 with a bequest from Sophia Smith, who inherited a fortune at the age of 65.

BELOW:
Amherst Common.

Brimfield Flea Market, held three times a year, is the world's largest outdoor crafts show, with more than 5,000 dealers.

BELOW:
canoeing on the Connecticut River.

serve as 30th US President, began his law practice in Northampton and eventually died there. His reputation as a man of exceptionally few words once prompted a determined matron at a society banquet to coax him: "Mr President, I have a wager with a friend that I can persuade you to say more than two words." Coolidge's reply: "You lose." A collection of his papers is on exhibit in the **Coolidge Memorial Room** in the **Forbes Library** (20 West Street; tel: 413-584 8399; open Mon–Wed 10am–1pm). *(For more on Coolidge, see page 256.)*

A few miles to the east on Route 9 is the town of **Amherst ❾**, long a hotbed of intellectual vigor and social independence. Lexicographer Noah Webster lived here, as did a reclusive genius of American poetry.

Visitors to the **Emily Dickinson Homestead** can experience the spartan environment that housed a self-confined soul who poured her emotions solely into her poetry (280 Main Street; open Mar–mid-Dec: Apr–Oct. Wed–Sat, rest of year Wed & Sat; closed Dec 10–Feb; tours by appointment; tel: 413-542 8161).

Just off the spacious central green, **Amherst College's** stately fraternity houses flank a campus quadrangle that is a classic of early 19th-century institutional architecture; American and European works are exhibited at the college's **Mead Art Museum** (tel: 413-542 2335; open Feb–Dec 14, Tues–Sun). The skeleton of a woolly mammoth is the centerpiece at the college's **Pratt Museum of Natural History** (tel: 413-542 2165; open mid-May–mid Sept, daily; mid-Sept–mid-May, Tues–Sun), a trove of fossils and geological history.

South on Route 116, children of all ages will want to visit the home of *The Very Hungry Caterpiller*: the new **Eric Carle Museum of Picture Art** (125 West Bay Road; tel: 413-658 1100; www.picturebookart.org; open Tues–Sat and Sun pm; entrance fee) next to **Hampshire College**. The children's author/illustrator

opened the 44,000-sq.-ft (4064 sq.-meter) facility in 2002. Hampshire College alumnus Aaron Lansky is the motivating force and director of the **National Yiddish Book Center** (Hampshire College, Route 116; tel: 413-256 4900 or 800-535 3595; www.yiddishbookcenter.org; open Mon–Fri 10am–3:30pm; Sun 11am–4pm), a one million volume-plus collection of Yiddish books housed in a wooden complex designed to resemble an Eastern European *shtetl* (village). The center hosts art exhibits and special performances.

Encompassing a 7-mile (11-km) ridge that stretches from Hadley to Belchertown, **Mount Holyoke Range State Park** ❿ (Route 116, Amherst; tel: 413-586 0350; visitor center open daily) offers some of the Pioneer Valley's best scenery. Off Route 47, in nearby **J.A. Skinner State Park** on Route 47 (Hadley, tel: 413-586 0350) a road (open Apr–Nov) climbs to a viewpoint immortalized in Thomas Coles's 1830 painting, *The Oxbow*. The Summit House, a former 19th-century hotel, is open for tours on weekends from Memorial Day to Columbus Day.

South on Route 116, in nearby **South Hadley, Mount Holyoke College** ⓫ (tel: 413-538 2000) is America's oldest women's college. Its 400-acre (162-hectare) campus was the work of landscape architect Frederick Law Olmsted.

Springfield

Springfield ⓬, on the banks of the Connecticut River, was established as a trading post in 1636. In 1779 George Washington chose Springfield as the site of one of the nation's first two arsenals. The **Springfield Armory National Historic Site** (Armory Square; tel: 413-734 6478; www.nps.gov/spar; open Tues–Sun) now houses a museum featuring one of the largest collections of firearms in the world. Another product which put Springfield on the map was motorcycles:

Map on page 188

Springfield's federal armory produced its first musket in 1795 and was still turning out rifles in World War II. It finally closed in 1968.

BELOW:
face painting at a Mount Holyoke fair.

*Exhibit at the
Basketball Hall
of Fame.*

BELOW: small farms
like this one in the
Berkshires often
offer bed and
breakfast facilities.

Indian motorcycles were first manufactured here, and many early models are on exhibit at the **Indian Motorcycle Museum** (33 Hendee Street; tel: 413-737 2624; closed as we went to press – call for information).

In 1892, at the local YMCA, Dr. James Naismith invented a game celebrated in the city's major attraction: the new $103 million, interactive, state-of-the art **Basketball Hall of Fame** (1000 West Columbus Avenue; tel: 413-781 6500; www.hoophall.com; open daily; entrance fee). Max's Tavern (good steaks) is on site.

Springfield supports four more outstanding museums, all clustered around "the Quad" – the **Springfield Museums at the Quadrangle** (Chestnut and State streets ; tel: 413-263 6800 or 800-625 7738; www.quadrangle.org; open Tues–Sun, Welcome Center open daily; entrance fee). The **George Walter Vincent Smith Art Museum** features oriental decorative arts, from Persian rugs to Japanese netsuke and Chinese cloisonné. The **Science Museum** contains the first American-built planetarium and plenty of intriguing, hands-on exhibits.

The **Connecticut Valley Historical Museum** showcases local artifacts, from folk paintings to fine furniture. The **Museum of Fine Arts** has an impressively broad collection, including portraits by the noted itinerant painter Rufus Porter; contemporary shows are also mounted. And watching over all is the **Dr. Seuss National Memorial**, a fanciful outdoor sculpture park incorporating characters created by the city's favorite son, Theodor Seuss Geisel.

The 735-acre (300-hectare) **Forest Park** (Sumner Avenue; open daily; fee) has a zoo (tel: 413-733 2251) with more than 100 species and a seasonal train tour.

The city's rich cultural life is reflected in the musical offerings, ranging from classical to popular, of the Springfield Symphony Orchestra (Symphony Hall; tel: 413-733 2291; www.springfieldsymphony.org).

Across the river, in West Springfield, the **Theater Project at the Majestic Theater** (131 Elm Street; tel: 413-747 7797) mounts live theatrical performances. Down the road is the 175-acre (71-hectare) fairgrounds for the **Eastern States Exposition** (the "Big E"), New England's major agricultural fair and one of the nation's largest (tel: 413-737 2443; www.thebige.com). Every September, prize livestock and top-name talents entertain the crowds. Permanently ensconced on the grounds is the **Storrowton Village Museum**, seven transplanted 18th- and early 19th-century buildings where traditional crafts are demonstrated (1305 Memorial Avenue; tel: 413-787 0136; open mid-Jun–late Aug, with tours Tues–Sat; entrance fee). There's a good on-site restaurant.

In nearby **Agawam ⑬**, **Six Flags New England** (1623 Main Street; tel: 413-786 9300 or 877-474-3524; www.sixflags.com; open weekends in spring and fall, daily in summer; entrance fee) is New England's largest amusement park.

The Berkshires

Berkshire County encompasses valleys dotted with shimmering lakes, rolling farmlands punctuated by orchards, deep forests abundant with deer, and powerful rivers that cascade into waterfalls under the bluest of New England skies.

Everywhere one turns in this westernmost corner of Massachusetts, the horizon is piled and terraced with mountains. Though less dramatic than the mountains of New Hampshire or Vermont, these gentle ranges have nonetheless provided the Berkshire Hills with an insularity that has historically set them apart from the rest of the state.

With the Hoosac and Taconic mountains forming a natural barrier to settlement, the Berkshires remained a wilderness until 1725, when Matthew Noble built a cabin in what is now the town of Sheffield. In the years that followed, farmland was cleared and towns were established along the Housatonic River and its tributaries. During the 19th century, the Industrial Revolution brought prosperity to the Berkshires: its iron foundries smelted ore for the country's first railroads, while marble quarried from its hills graced the dome of the US Capitol.

As farming declined in the late 19th century, the Berkshires receded into a sleepy silence. But city dwellers seeking pretty scenery and respite from summer heat have periodically rediscovered the Berkshires. During the 1890s, the county became a playground for such wealthy families as the Carnegies and Vanderbilts, who built their mansions in the hills surrounding Stockbridge and Lenox. More recently, visitors have come for the renowned summer music festivals, the splendor of fall foliage, or the challenge of winter skiing.

The first settlers reached the Berkshires through the Housatonic Valley from Connecticut. The modern traveler can do the same, following US Highway 7 north along the Housatonic, or by taking the Massachusetts Turnpike from the eastern part of the state.

The South Berkshires

Just inside the Connecticut border on Route 7A is **Ashley Falls ⑭**, a village surrounded by hayfields and

Map on page 188

YMCA instructor James Naismith nailed up a pair of peach baskets to keep his charges occupied; the game was more absorbing, they discovered, once the bottoms of the baskets were removed. And so basketball was invented.

BELOW: antiques fairs are regular events.

dairy farms. The village was named for Colonel John Ashley, a prominent lawyer and Revolutionary War officer.

Off Route 7A, the **Colonel John Ashley House**, built in 1735, is the oldest structure in Berkshire County. It has been restored as a colonial museum (Cooper Hill Road; tel: 413-298 3239; grounds open year round; guided house tours Memorial Day weekend–Columbus Day weekend; entrance fee). Up the road is **Bartholomew's Cobble** (105 Weatogue Road; tel: 413-229 8600; open daily; entrance fee), a natural rock garden with hiking trails that meander along the banks of the Housatonic. It contains more species of fern than any other area in the continental United States. There's a small natural history museum.

Sheffield ⓯, established in 1733, is the oldest town in Berkshire County and boasts two of the best-preserved covered bridges in Massachusetts. Traffic still travels over the larger, a narrow, barn-red structure that spans the Housatonic just east of town, on the road to New Marlborough.

The Berkshires' true beauty lies in its backroads and small villages. **New Marlborough** and nearby **Mill River**, small communities that prospered in the heyday of the Industrial Revolution, are gems. At the Old Inn on the Green in New Marlborough, once a stagecoach stop en route from New York to Boston, visitors can dine on fresh lamb or breakfast on blueberry muffins.

Great Barrington ⓰ offers an excellent base from which to explore the towns and villages of the southern Berkshires. Although it does not have the architectural treasures of towns farther north such as Stockbridge and Lenox, Great Barrington has long been a popular vacation destination for sophisticated New Yorkers, and upscale galleries, shops, and restaurants line the main and side streets.

Head west on Route 23 and south on Route 41 to the tiny hill hamlet of **Mount**

TIP

There is excellent blueberry picking to be had on Mount Washington.

BELOW: capturing the Berkshires on canvas.

Map on page 188

Washington. This smallest of Berkshires towns offers some of the finest fall-foliage viewing and the most dramatic natural waterfall in New England: at **Bash Bish State Park ⓱** (Falls Road; tel: 413-528 0330), in Mount Washington State Forest, water plummets 80 ft (24 meters) into a deep gorge.

A literary and artistic heritage

North of Great Barrington on Route 7 is **Monument Mountain ⓲**, a craggy peak whose summit is a pleasant half-hour hike from the parking lot at its base. The mountain is a Berkshire literary landmark of considerable repute. The poet William Cullen Bryant sang its praises while practicing as a local attorney in the 1830s.

    Stockbridge ⓳ was incorporated as an Indian mission in 1739. Its first missionary was John Sargeant, a young tutor from Yale who lived among the natives for 16 years. He slept in their wigwams, shared their venison and spoke their language, while introducing them to the colonists' ways. Eventually, Sargeant helped them establish a town, build homes and cultivate the land. Some among the Mohican tribe held public office, serving alongside whites in the town government. But as more colonists moved into the area, the tribes were slowly deprived of their land. By 1783, the mission was history, and surviving Indians were forced to settle on the Oneida reservation in New York State. All that remains is the 1739 **Mission House**, now a museum on Stockbridge's Main Street (tel: 413-298 3239; open late May–mid-Oct; entrance fee).

    If Stockbridge's Main Street looks familiar, it may be because its New England essence was captured on the canvases of that remarkable illustrator of American life, Norman Rockwell. Rockwell, who created more than 300 covers for the *Saturday Evening Post,* kept a studio in Stockbridge and made his home here for

Many poets and writers have visited the Berkshires. Longfellow once hiked these trails, as did Emerson and Thoreau. Henry James visited often and, more recently, Berkshire County has been home to Thornton Wilder and Norman Mailer.

BELOW: the historic Sargeant House, Stockbridge.

Fall colors.

BELOW: Church on
the Hill, Lenox.

a quarter of a century, until his death in 1978. Located on Route 183, the stunning **Norman Rockwell Museum**, designed by Robert A.M. Stern, showcases his oeuvre and even recreates his Stockbridge studio (open May–Oct). No visitor, however sophisticated, should miss this display: Rockwell's portraits capture an age of innocence with humor and modesty (9 Glendale Road, Route 183; tel: 413-298 4100; www.nrm.org; open daily; entrance fee).

The Red Lion Inn, located in the center of Stockbridge at the intersection of Routes 7 and 102, is one of the *grandes dames* of New England country inns. Its flower-laden front porch, complete with rocking chairs, is a place of pilgrimage for Berkshires travelers.

Naumkeag, a half mile off Route 7 and Route 102 (Prospect Hill; tel: 413-298 3239; open Memorial Day weekend through Columbus Day; entrance fee), is a Norman-style mansion designed by Stanford White for Joseph Choate, US ambassador to Great Britain in 1899; the furnishings and gardens are unusually lavish.

Chesterwood, the summer home of sculptor Daniel Chester French, is 3 miles (5 km) west of Stockbridge (off Route 183; tel: 413-298 3579; open late May–mid-Oct daily; entrance fee). It was here that he created his masterpiece, *The Seated Lincoln*, focal point of the Lincoln Memorial in Washington, DC. Casts are displayed in the house.

To the southeast, off Route 102, the tiny unspoiled village of **Tyringham ⑳**, became an artists' colony in the early 20th century. **Santarella Museum and Gardens** (75 Main Road; tel: 413-243 3260; open May–Oct daily; fee), the fairytale "Gingerbread house" and studio of Sir Henry Hudson Kitson, sculptor of the Minuteman statue in Lexington, exhibits his works plus those of local artists.

Music and the Mount

Further north, off Route 7, in **Lenox**, ㉑ novelist Edith Wharton's grand neo-Classical, 1902 mansion and magnificent formal gardens at **The Mount**, (2 Plunkett Street; tel: 413-637 1899; open early-May–late Oct daily; entrance fee), have undergone a $9 million restoration and now look much as they did when she wrote *Ethan Frome, The House of Mirth,* and other works here.

Just out of town, **Tanglewood,** the 550-acre (220-hectare) summer home of the Boston Symphony Orchestra (297 West Street, Route 183; tel: 413-637 5165 or 888-266 1200; www.bso.org; open July–Aug.; entrance fee) has been a haven for performers, students and music lovers since 1937. The Boston Pops and special guest artists also perform throughout the summer season in the 6,000-seat Music Shed, designed by architect Eero Saarinen. Saturday morning rehearsals are free, as are tours of the grounds. A Visitor Center is open year-round Mon–Sat.

A replica of the little red cottage where Nathaniel Hawthorne lived and wrote *The House of the Seven Gables* and *Tanglewood Tales* is on the grounds.

The simple Shakers

"'Tis a gift to be simple," says the old Shaker hymn, and the **Hancock Shaker Village** ㉒ on Route US 20, 3 miles (5 km) west of Pittsfield, testifies to the virtues of simplicity (tel: 413-443 0188 and 800-817 1137; open year-round; self-exploration tours early April through the weekend after Columbus Day; entrance fee).

The Shakers (*see pages 300–1*) settled in Hancock in the late 1780s. The community prospered through farming, printing, selling garden seeds and herbs and making their distinctively designed furnishings. The elegance and functionalism of Shaker architecture is exemplified by Hancock's famous 1826 round stone barn. It

Map on page 188

TIP

The BSO Tanglewood season begins in late June and runs through August, with concerts on Fridays, Saturdays and Sundays.
Tel: 617-637 5135;
www.bso.org.

BELOW:
a Housatonic potter at work.

CULTURE IN THE BERKSHIRES

Tanglewood is the best-known of several Berkshires summer festivals. The South Mountain Concerts (tel: 413-442 2106), featuring chamber music by renowned performers on most Sunday afternoons at 3pm in September and October, take place south of Pittsfield, on Route 7. For Renaissance and Baroque music, head for the Aston Magna Festival (tel: 413-528 3595), in Great Barrington; performances on period instruments are given at St James Church on Saturdays at 6pm in July.

When the Jacob's Pillow Dance Festival (tel: 413-243 0745) was launched in the early 1930s, modern dance was in its infancy. Today, Jacob's Pillow (in the hilltown of Becket, southeast of Pittsfield on State 8) is a national institution and hosts a 10-week summer program.

Also impressive is the Williamstown Theater Festival (tel: 413-597 3399), which stages some of the finest summer theater in the country. Running the gamut from Greek tragedy to Restoration comedy, and from Chekhov to Pirandello, the festival also has a fine company of actors.

At Berkshire Theater Festival (tel: 413-298 5536), in Stockbridge, the emphasis is on American classics. For fans of the Bard, there's Shakespeare & Co (tel: 413-637 3353) in Lenox, performing from late May until October.

Map
on page
188

TIP

The Williamstown
Theatre Festival is held
from the third week in
June until the third week
in August. Details, tel:
413-597 3400.

BELOW:
on the Mohawk
Trail: "Hail to the
Sunrise" recalls
the Mohawk
Indians.

enabled one farmhand, standing at its center, to feed an entire herd of cattle. Shakers lived in Hancock until the 1950s, when the community had dwindled to a few staunch survivors, celibacy and changing times having led to their decline.

Returning to Route 7, the northbound traveler passes through **Pittsfield ㉓**, the Berkshire County seat and largest city (population 52,000). Herman Melville completed *Moby-Dick* (1851) while living at **Arrowhead** (off Route 7 at Holmes Road; tel: 413-442 1793; open Memorial Day–Oct Fri–Wed. First tour 11am, last tour 3pm; tours available off-season; entrance fee). A room in the **Berkshire Athenaeum** (1 Wendell Avenue; tel: 413-449 9480; open Mon–Sat) exhibits photographs, documents and memorabilia of the author. The **Berkshire Museum** (39 South Street; tel: 413-443-7171; open Mon–Sat; Sun pm; entrance fee) presents an eclectic collection of art, natural science and history exhibits.

Williamstown and the north Berkshires

Rising to 3,491 ft (1,064 meters), east of Williamstown, Mount Greylock is the tallest peak in Massachusetts. Hardy travelers can ascend on foot, while those less energetic can drive to the summit via a steep and winding access road in the **Mt. Greylock State Reservation ㉔** (off Route 7, Rockwell Road, Lanesboro; visitor center, tel: 413-499 4262). From the top, writer Nathaniel Hawthorne looked down upon Williamstown – "a white village and a steeple set like a daydream among the high mountain waves."

In the state's northwest corner **Williamstown ㉕** is among the most beautiful of New England villages. It is home to **Williams College**, founded in 1793, and the **Williams College Museum of Art** (Main Street; tel: 413-597 2429; open Tues–Sat; Sun pm). Just down the street is the exceptional **Sterling and Francine Clark Art Institute** (225 South Street; tel: 413-458 2303; www.clarkart.edu; open daily Jul–Aug; Tues–Sun rest of year; entrance fee July–Oct). Between 1918 and 1956, the Clarks amassed a superb private collection of European and American paintings, including works by Botticelli, Goya, Gainsborough and Fragonard. The museum is known for its Impressionist collection.

The **Mohawk Trail ㉖** (Route 2) winds eastwards from Williamstown, across the top of Berkshire County. An old Indian path-turned-roadway, it offers some of the most rugged and romantic scenery in the Berkshires. It is a popular leaf-peeping route in the fall. Stop in **North Adams ㉗** to visit one of the state's newest museums, the **Massachusetts Museum of Contemporary Art** (jct. Route 2/ Marshall Street; tel: 413-662 2111; daily July–Labor Day; Labor Day–Jun, Wed–Mon; entrance fee). The vast, renovated 19th-century factory complex houses a fine collection of contemporary art, including some pieces so large they've not been exhibited before. **Western Gateway Heritage State Park** (9 Furnace Street; tel: 413-663 6312; open daily), in the restored freight yard, chronicles the town's history, including the building of the nearby 4¾-mile/7.6 km Hoosac railroad tunnel. Just north on Route 8, in **Natural Bridge State Park** (tel: 413-663 6392; open daily Memorial Day–Columbus Day; entrance fee), a water-eroded bridge formed in the last ice age spans a vast chasm. ❑

Sporting Traditions

Ever since football was introduced to the nation on Boston Common in 1862 and basketballs were first stuffed into baskets in Springfield, Mass., in 1891, New England has been a sports trailblazer. Long before expansion became the buzz word, Boston was one of the only cities to boast major league teams in baseball (Red Sox and Braves), basketball (Celtics), and ice-hockey (Bruins). The Braves decamped after 1952, but football expansion led to the 1960 appearance of the Patriots.

Until recently, only the Celtics, with 16 National Basketball Association titles, and the Bruins, with five Stanley Cups in the National Hockey League, carried on a winning tradition in New England – and those teams' last championships were in 1986 and 1972, respectively. But with three recent Super Bowl triumphs for the Patriots, and the miracle victory for the Red Sox in the 2004 World Series, things changed mightily.

The Sox won the first World Series, in 1903, and clinched it four times between then and 1918. But for the next 86 years – some say because of the "Curse of the Bambino," incurred when they sold Babe Ruth to the New York Yankees – the Sox came up dry. Then came 2004. Snapping back from a three-game deficit in a seven-game league championship series – something no team had ever done – the Sox beat the New York Yankees and went on to a four-game sweep of the St. Louis Cardinals in the World Series.

The once hapless Patriots, who made it to the 1986 Super Bowl but were trounced by the Chicago Bears, won all the marbles in 2002, 2004 and 2005, setting a National Football League record for consecutive games won.

New England teams have always been generous in turning out heroes: Ted Williams, Carl Yastrzemski, Roger Clemens, and Wade Boggs in baseball; Bobby Orr in hockey; Bob Cousy and Larry Bird in basketball; and now quarterback Tom Brady in football. Homegrown sports greats include Rocky Marciano of Brockton, Mass., the heavyweight boxer who retired in 1956 as the only world champion undefeated in his professional career; Carlton Fisk, the Red Sox (and later Chicago White Sox) catcher who made his way from small-town New Hampshire and Vermont ballfields to the Hall of Fame; and John LeClair, the University of Vermont powerhouse who helped hockey's Montreal Canadiens win a Stanley Cup before joining the Philadelphia Flyers and Pittsburgh Penguins.

New England's sporting scene is enlivened by teams from its myriad colleges but mostly these have little impact nationally. Exceptions are Boston College (football and basketball) and the universities of Connecticut and Vermont (basketball); Vermont also excels in hockey. And in squash and sailing New England college teams are often in the fore.

Since 1965 oarspeople from around the globe have come to Cambridge in October for the Head of the Charles, the world's biggest one-day regatta. And each Patriot's Day in April, thousands of runners line up for the start of the celebrated Boston Marathon (tel: 617-235 4505). It's the world's oldest annual marathon, first run in 1897. ❑

RIGHT: little league baseball in Newton, Mass.

CONNECTICUT

This historic state encompasses Yale University in New Haven,
maritime traditions in Mystic Seaport, antiquing and art in
the Litchfield Hills – and, unexpectedly, America's biggest casino

Map on page 206

D riving through the neat-as-a-pin village of Guilford, a one-time resident once remarked: "Connecticut always looks as if the maid has just been in to clean." There, as in so many of Connecticut's picturesque colonial villages, the carefully kept, white clapboard homes and manicured lawns evoke an image of quiet wealth, propriety and old school ties.

Indeed, this state has always had something of a conservative mien, even though it is liberal politically. The Puritans who settled here may have been farmers and seafarers, but they were primarily involved in commerce; they understood the value of a dollar and the importance of its proper investment.

Though generations have come and gone, this aspect of the Connecticut character has not changed. It has, however, been tempered with pride for the place and a heartfelt sense of its history.

With Long Island Sound as its southern border, Connecticut roughly forms a rectangle measuring 90 miles (145 km) from east to west and 55 miles (89 km) north to south. The Connecticut River, New England's longest, bisects the state; along with the Thames and Housatonic rivers, the Connecticut was a vital avenue of settlement and industrialization.

PRECEDING PAGES:
Southbury.
LEFT: traditional
barn at Kent.
BELOW: Lake
Waramaug is one
of the state's many
boating centers.

The Constitution State

Adrian Block, a Dutch navigator, was probably the first to understand the possibilities of the region when he sailed along the coast and up the Connecticut River in 1614. Nineteen years later, the Dutch established a trading post, Fort Good Hope, near the future site of Hartford.

But it was the British, lured by fertile land and religious freedom, who finally settled the region in 1635. By that time, good farmland in the coastal areas of the Massachusetts Bay colony had mostly been claimed, and newcomers looked toward the Connecticut River. Added to population pressures were the personalities of strong-willed leaders such as the Reverend Thomas Hooker, who, unwilling to submit to Massachusetts' theocratic leaders, chose to lead his congregation to an area beyond their authority.

By 1636, settlements had been established in Hartford, Windsor and Wethersfield. Calling themselves the Hartford Colony, the three towns adopted the Fundamental Orders of Connecticut on January 14, 1639. This document is regarded by many historians as the world's first written constitution. From that historical first comes the legend on vehicle license plates, "The Constitution State."

New settlements were organized along the shores of Long Island Sound. Old Saybrook was first, followed by New Haven, Guilford, and Stamford. Later

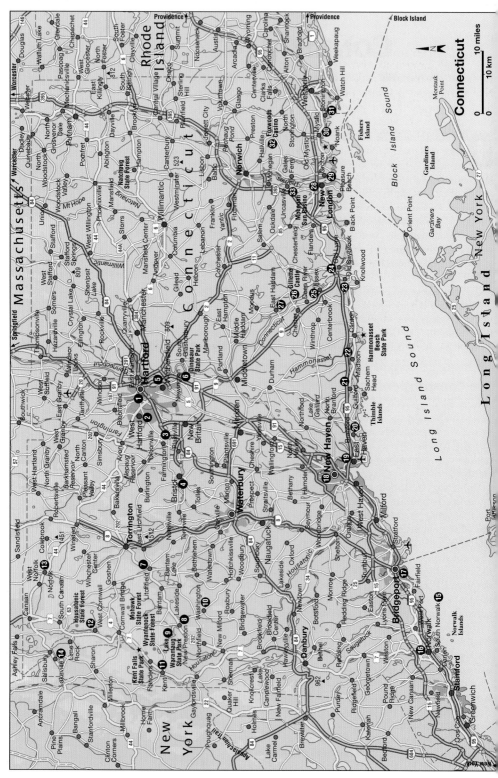

Map on page 206

towns took such Biblical names as Goshen, Sharon, Canaan, and Bethlehem.

No major battles of the American Revolution were fought on Connecticut soil, but the state had its patriots. Among them were General Israel Putnam and Ethan Allen, who made his fame as a Vermont guerrilla leader. Most famous was Nathan Hale, the Coventry, Connecticut, schoolteacher who, when hanged by the British as a spy, uttered the immortal words: "I regret that I have only one life to give for my country."

With the end of the Revolution, Connecticut turned increasingly to commerce, and from the years 1780 to 1840, the Yankee peddler reigned supreme. His sturdy wagon, loaded with tinware, soap, matches, yard goods and tools, was a familiar sight up and down the Atlantic seaboard and even beyond the Appalachians.

But it was in manufacturing that the Connecticut Yankees truly excelled. Eli Whitney, inventor of the cotton gin, first introduced the use of standardized parts at his firearms factory in New Haven. Soon, mass production was helping make Connecticut's fortune. Colt revolvers were made in Hartford, Winchester rifles in New Haven, hats in Danbury, clocks in Bristol, and fine brass in Waterbury.

New industry meant new workers, and the late 19th and early 20th centuries saw waves of immigrants settle in such manufacturing centers as Bridgeport, New Haven, and Torrington. While Connecticut may present a colonial face to the casual traveler, those who remain long enough appreciate the contributions of Italians, Germans, Portuguese, and Eastern Europeans to the essential Connecticut character. Connecticut's past is also its present, and today the state continues to rely on industry for its economic good fortune. Airplane engines are manufactured in East Hartford, helicopters in Stratford; nuclear submarines are designed and built in Groton.

Patriot John Wadsworth hides Connecticut's royal charter in an oak tree to stop the British revoking it in 1687.

BELOW:
mural painter, Mystic village.

Nevertheless, Connecticut has remained a largely rural enclave. With manufacturing concentrated along the South Shore and in Hartford, 75 percent of the state is given over to small towns and dense woodlands. Narrow, winding roads lead the visitor from one charming village to another.

Connecticut's capital

Hartford ❶ (pop. 124,000) is America's Insurance City. The skyline of Connecticut's capital is dominated by the towering headquarters of the nation's largest insurance companies. Several dozen are located in greater Hartford, and together with related financial services, employ approximately 10 percent of the total work force. The first insurance policy, covering losses in the event of shipwreck, was written in the 18th century.

Settled in 1635 and Connecticut's oldest city, Hartford has parlayed its location on the navigable Connecticut River into political, economic and social pre-eminence. In 1662, a royal charter was drawn up uniting the colonies of Hartford and New Haven, and guaranteeing their independence. Sir Edmund Andros, appointed governor of all New England in 1687, had the charter revoked. In defiance, the Hartford patriot John Wadsworth stole the charter and hid it in the trunk of an oak tree at the center of the town. Two years later, on the accession of William III, Andros was recalled to England and the charter was reinstated. A plaque at Charter Oak Place, in the south end of the city, marks the spot where the magnificent oak stood until 1856, when a windstorm felled it.

The **Greater Hartford Convention & Visitors Bureau** (One Civic Center Plaza; tel: 860-728 6789 or 800-446 7811; www. enjoyhartford.com) distributes a free, 80-page guide which includes a map and walking tour of the city. You can

Since the US Patent Office opened in 1790, Connecticut inventors have filed more patents per capita than any other state. Hats, combs, cigars, seeds, clocks, kettles, furniture and firearms – all came out of the factory stamped "Made in Connecticut."

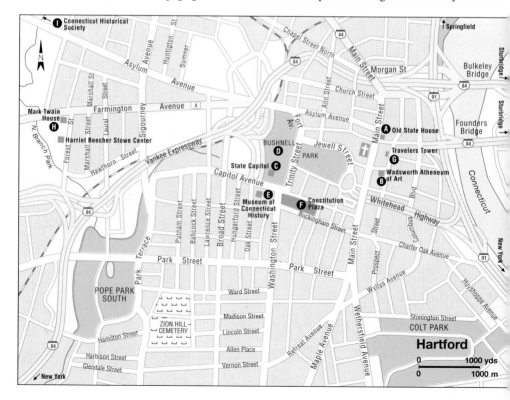

hop aboard the free, downtown Hartford Star Shuttle which passes every 10–12 minutes Mon–Fri from 7am to 11pm, and Sat 3pm–11pm.

Begin at the **Old State House Ⓐ**, at the intersection of Main Street and Asylum Avenue (800 Main Street; tel: 860-522 6766; open Mon–Sat). Built in 1796 and the nation's oldest state house, it was the first public commission for architect Charles Bulfinch, who would later design the state capitols of Maine and Massachusetts. The building was the site of the 1839 *Amistad* slave ship mutiny trial, which is re-enacted periodically in the Great Senate Chamber.

Be sure to see Gilbert Stuart's portrait of George Washington and visit the second-floor **Joseph Steward's Museum of Curiosities** (a two-headed calf, the mummified hand of Ramses, a unicorn horn – that sort of thing). A cannon is fired at opening and closing time.

Directly to the south, also on Main Street, is the **Wadsworth Atheneum of Art Ⓑ**, America's oldest continually operating public art museum (600 Main Street; tel: 860-278 2670; open Tues–Sun; entrance fee). The Gothic Revival-style Atheneum was erected to house the library and art gallery of Daniel Wadsworth. Many additions have been made, and the museum's collection now includes paintings by Goya, Rubens, Rembrandt and van Dyck, plus works by American masters such as Thomas Cole and John Singer Sargent and Meissen and Sèvres porcelains. The **Austin House**, the former home of the museum director from 1927 to 1944 and a National Historic Landmark, is open by appointment.

Perched on Capitol Hill, the white marble **Connecticut State Capitol Ⓒ**, a Gothic wedding cake of turrets, gables, porches, and towers, was designed by Richard Upjohn and opened in 1878 (210 Capitol Avenue; tel: 860-240 0222; open Mon–Fri year-round; tours begin at the neighboring Legislative Office

Maps:
Area 206
City 208

Colonial times recalled in West Hartford.

BELOW:
African-American Freedom Trail Parade in Hartford.

Building on the hour between 9:15am and 2:15pm in summer). In typical Victorian manner, its ornate interiors of hand-painted columns, marble floors and elaborate stained-glass windows were designed to reflect the prosperity of the community it served.

The Capitol overlooks 37-acre (15-hectare) **Bushnell Park** , home to a hand-carved **1914 carousel** (open May–mid-Oct Tues–Sun 11am–5pm; fee) and the **Pump House Gallery** (tel: 860-543 8874; open Tues–Fri 11–2), which hosts free summer noontime concerts. **The Bushnell Center for the Performing Arts** (166 Capitol Avenue; tel: 860-987 5900; www.bushnell.org) has an impressive program of concerts, ballet, opera and theater.

To the south of the Capitol is the State Library, the **Museum of Connecticut History** (231 Capitol Avenue; tel: 860-757 6535; open Mon–Sat). Exhibits include Connecticut's 1662 Royal Charter and the Colt Collection of Firearms manufactured in Hartford. The state's archives are housed here.

Constitution Plaza , a 12-acre (5-hectare) 1960s complex, provides Hartford with an open mall, a vast array of shops, office buildings and the starkly modern, elliptically shaped Phoenix Mutual Life Insurance Building.

Travelers Tower , the second tallest building in the city (City Place is the tallest), has an **Observation Deck**, which offers an excellent view of the Hartford area (1 Tower Square; tel: 860–277 0111; open May–Oct weekdays). The Travelers Insurance Company was founded in 1863, when Colonel James Bolter insured his life for $5,000 to cover his lunchtime trip from home to the post office.

Hartford's most famous resident, Mark Twain (1835–1910), lived in a 19-room Victorian mansion in a part of town called Nook Farm, which was a rural area and the intellectual center of Hartford in his time. Today, Nook Farm is a

developed area, but the National Historic Landmark **Mark Twain House** retains a special charm. To visit, take Interstate 84 north to exit 46 and turn right at the traffic light onto Sisson Avenue. Continue to the end and turn right at the next light onto Farmington Avenue for approximately 350 yards to the free parking lot, which is a block before the house (351 Farmington Avenue; tel: 860–247 0998; www.MarkTwainHouse.org; open May–Dec Mon–Sat and Sun pm; Jan–Apr, Wed–Mon. Guided tours only; allow two hours for a visit; entrance fee). The author's home from 1874 to 1891, designed by Edward Tuckerman Potter and decorated by Louis Comfort Tiffany, reflects the quirky character of its owner.

Outdoor porches and balconies give the impression of a Mississippi riverboat, while the interiors are grand and whimsical. Of interest is the upstairs billiard room, where Twain penned his most successful novels, including *The Adventures of Tom Sawyer* and *The Adventures of Huckleberry Finn*. The author and his family remained in Hartford until 1891, when poor investments forced them to move to Europe. They intended to return, but after the sudden death of his daughter Susy in 1896, Twain could not bear to go back. He sold the house in 1903.

Mr Twain's neighbor for many years was Harriet Beecher Stowe, author of works including *Uncle Tom's Cabin*. She lived next door in a 17-room Victorian home from 1873 until she died in 1896. Her restored house is a part of the **Harriet Beecher Stowe Center** (77 Forest Street; tel: 860-522 9258; www.HarrietBeecherStowe.org; open for guided tours Memorial Day–Columbus Day and Dec Tues–Sat and Sun pm; garden tours Jun–Oct, Wed & Sat at 10am and 1pm; combined ticket available). The center also includes the Katharine Seymour Day House, whose library includes volumes about the women's suffrage movement and African-American history.

Map on page 208

Hallowe'en pumpkin.

LEFT: Riverfest at Hartford's Constitution Plaza.
BELOW: Mark Twain's Gilded Age mansion at Nook Farm.

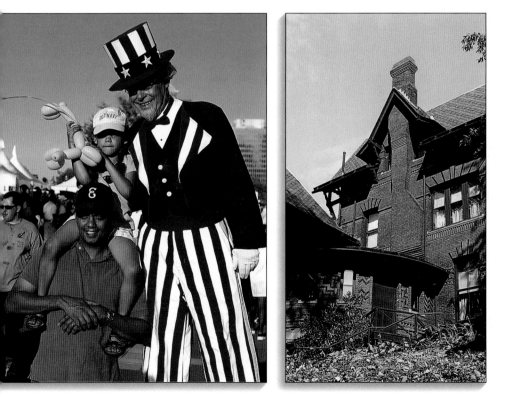

The research library at the **Connecticut Historical Society ❶** (off Asylum Avenue on campus of Connecticut Law School, 1 Elizabeth Street; tel: 860-236 5621; open daily) holds more than 3 million manuscripts and houses one of the region's finest genealogy collections. Exhibits document Connecticut history.

Side trips from Hartford

A Hartford attraction not for the faint-hearted is the Menczer Museum of Medicine and Dentistry (230 Scarborough St, tel: 860-236 5613; Mon–Fri 10am–4:30pm). It contains 18th- and 19th-century surgical instruments plus reconstructed dental and doctor's surgeries from the early 20th century.

The author of the first American dictionary lived just a few miles away in **West Hartford ❷**. The **Noah Webster House/Museum of West Hartford** (227 South Main Street; tel: 860-521 5362; open Thurs–Mon 1–4pm; entrance fee) is now the headquarters of the West Hartford Historical Society and has been restored to reflect 18th-century Connecticut life. To visit, take I-84 north to exit 81 and follow signs north for 1 mile (1.6 km).

Take Route 84 south to exit 39 to **Farmington ❸**, 10 miles (16 km) west of Hartford. Often called one of the loveliest towns in New England, its elegant 18th- and 19th-century mansions display a clarity of architectural detail seldom equaled in the area.

Hill-Stead Museum is a particular gem (35 Mountain Road; tel: 860-677 4787; www.hillstead.org; open May–Oct Tues–Sun 10am–5pm, last tour at 4pm; Nov–April Tues–Sun 11am–4pm, last tour at 3pm; entrance fee). Designed by Stanford White, the Colonial Revival home on 150 acres (60 hectares) was the retirement home of industrialist Alfred Atmore Pope, a friend of the artist Mary Cassatt and a great admirer of French Impressionism. Scattered throughout the mansion are a number of familiar canvases, including paintings from Monet's *Haystack* series, Manet's *The Guitar Lady*, and Degas's *The Tub*. Whistler and Cassatt are also well represented. The gardens are magnificent.

BELOW: the Hill-Stead Museum at Farmington.

Continue south on Route 84 to exit 34 to **Bristol ❹**, 18 miles (29 km) west of Hartford. The town was a 19th-century clockmaking capital, producing more than 200,000 clocks in a single year. The **American Clock and Watch Museum,** housed in an 1801 mansion (100 Maple Street; tel: 860-583 6070; open daily year-round; entrance fee) displays some of the region's finest and most valuable timepieces.

Maps:
Area 206
City 208

Hand-carved, antique and contemporary carousel pieces and band organs are featured at the **New England Carousel Museum** (95 Riverside Avenue, Route 72; tel: 860-585 5411; open daily year-round; entrance fee). The 1927 wooden roller coaster at **Lake Compounce Theme Park** (822 Lake Avenue; tel: 860 583 3300); open daily in July and Aug; Splash Harbor Water Park open noon–7pm; call for off-season hours; entrance fee), one of 50 rides, is rated the best of its type in the world. The state's only water park is also here.

Take Route 91 south to exit 27, and Route 314 to **Wethersfield ❺** on the Connecticut River, one of the oldest villages in the state. More than 150 of the 17th- and 18th-century "downtown" homes have been preserved. Three can be toured at the **Webb-Deane-Stevens Museum** (211 Main Street; tel: 860-529 0612; open May–Oct, Wed–Mon; Nov–Apr, weekends; entrance fee). The meticulously restored, *circa* 1710 **Buttolph-Williams House** (249 Broad Street; tel: 860-247 8996; open mid-May–mid Oct Wed–Mon; entrance fee) is a gem.

Dinosaur State Park.

Continue south on Route 91 to exit 23 to **Rocky Hill** and the National Historic Landmark **Dinosaur State Park ❻** (400 West Street; tel: 860-529 8423; open daily; exhibit center open Tues–Sun; casting area open May–Oct; entrance fee), where 200-million-year-old dinosaur tracks are housed under a geodesic dome. Visitors can make plaster casts of the tracks, but must bring materials (call for information).

BELOW:
freshly baked
bread at Litchfield.

The Litchfield Hills

In the northwest, Connecticut's wooded Litchfield Hills are dotted with quintessential New England villages, covered bridges, and the tumbling stone walls of forgotten farms. Through it runs the **Housatonic River**, crystal clear and freckled with trout, and excellent for canoeing. Hikers may want to follow the Appalachian Trail from Kent to Canaan.

Litchfield ❼, 35 miles (56 km) from Hartford is dominated by a spacious green, graced by the tall-steepled Congregational Church. Town merchants prospered during the early days of the China trade when their money backed the sailing ships of Mystic and New Haven, but industry faltered when a new railroad bypassed the town center and Litchfield was left nestled in the past. This rich history is documented at the excellent **Litchfield History Museum** (7 South Street; tel: 860-567 4501; open mid-Apr–Nov Tues–Sat; Sun pm; entrance fee). Admission includes entrance to the **Tapping Reeve House & Litchfield Law School**, the nation's first school of law (82 South Street, Route 63; open mid-Apr–Nov Tues–Sat; Sun pm; entrance fee), where visitors learn about student life in the early 19th century.

Just east of town, off Route 118, Connecticut's first winery, **Haight Vineyard & Winery** (29 Chestnut

A barn window in the quiet northwest corner of the state.

Hill Road; tel: 860-567 4045; open Mon–Sat; Sun pm) is one of 15 vineyards on the **Connecticut Wine Trail** (tel: 203-775 1616; www.ctwine.com), and offers free tours and tastings.

Head south out of Litchfield center for 3½ miles (6 km) on Route 63 to **White Flower Farm** (tel: 860-567 8789; open daily), where English tuberous begonias flourish amid 10 acres (4 hectares) of display gardens at their peak June–Sept.

White Memorial Foundation, 2 miles (3.2 km) south of town on Route 202 (tel: 860-567 0857; open Mon–Sat; Sun pm; entrance fee to museum), the state's largest nature center, encompasses 4,000 acres (1,600 hectares) and includes 35 miles (56 km) of trails and a natural history museum.

Lake Waramaug

Continue south on Route 202 for approximately 6 miles (10 km) to **New Preston** ❽, a tiny town with several fine antique shops. Continue north on Route 45 for 5 miles (8 km) to **Lake Waramaug State Park** ❾ (30 Lake Waramaug Road; tel: 860-868-2592; entrance fee May–Oct weekends and holidays), a tranquil hideaway with boating and swimming. Several fine inns and **Hopkins Vineyard** (25 Hopkins Road; tel: 860-868 7954; open Jan–Feb, Fri–Sun; Mar–Apr, Wed–Sun; May–Dec, daily) overlook the lake.

To the southeast, on Route 47 in **Washington** ❿, the historic Mayflower Inn offers luxurious accommodations and gourmet dining. Continue past the inn onto Route 199 to the turn-off for the **Institute for American Indian Studies** (38 Curtis Road; tel: 860-868 0518; open year-round, Mon–Sat; Sun pm; entrance fee), where artifacts and a simulated archaeological site interpret the 10,000-plus-year history of the region's native Americans.

BELOW: Litchfield.

Map on page 206

The Housatonic Valley has one of its most dramatic moments to the west in the now-chic town of **Kent ⓫** at **Kent Falls State Park** (Route 7; tel: 860-927 3238; entrance fee May–Oct weekends and holidays), where water tumbles some 200 ft (65 meters) down a natural stone staircase. A short distance south on Route 7, ruins of the Old Kent Furnace recall the 18th-century discovery of iron ore in the Litchfield Hills. Adjacent, the **Sloane-Stanley Museum**, (tel: 860-927 3849; open May–Oct, Wed–Sun; entrance fee) displays an extensive collection of early American tools. To the north on Route 7, in **West Cornwall ⓬**, a much photographed 1836 covered bridge spans the Housatonic.

To the north of Litchfield via Routes 63, 4, and 272, **Norfolk ⓭** is another classic town with opulent homes clustered around a tidy green. The Ellen Battell Stoeckel Estate (Routes 44 & 272; tel: 860-542 3000; www.yale.edu/norfolk; entrance fee to concerts) hosts Yale University's renowned **Norfolk Chamber Music Festival**. Purchase tickets well in advance.

Follow Route 44 west to **Lakeville ⓮**, which offers another grand display of 19th-century mansions. The **Holley-Williams House Museum** (Millerton Road; tel: 860-435 3878; open Memorial Day; July 4–Labor Day, Sat and Sun pm; rest of year Fri pm; donation) is an excellent example of a Classical Revival house built by one of the area's "Iron Barons." Professional and amateur drivers race cars at **Lime Rock Park** (497 Lime Rock Road, Route 112; tel: 800-722 3577; www.limerock.com; open Apr–Nov; entrance fee).

The southwestern shore

From the harbors of New Haven, New London, Mystic and Stonington, China clippers and Yankee whalers sailed out to seek their fortunes. Such associa-

The "Stanley" part of the Sloane-Stanley Museum comes from The Stanley Works, founded in New Britain, Connecticut, in 1843 by Frederick T. Stanley. The company now sells its hand tools and hardware around the world, employing 15,000 people and turning over $2.6 billion a year.

BELOW: white-water canoeing at West Cornwall.

Detail, Barnum Museum in Bridgeport.

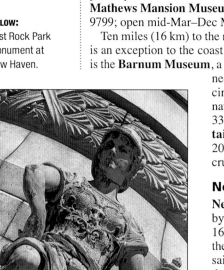

tions may be merely historical, but people along Connecticut's coast still retain a fondness for the sea. Most towns have at least one marina, and on a clear summer's day the horizon of Long Island Sound is filled with billowing sails.

Greenwich, Cos Cob, Stamford, Darien and Rowayton – to the thousands of Connecticut residents who work in New York City, this is a railroad conductor's litany. About an hour away from Manhattan by train, the Connecticut suburbs are among the most luxurious bedroom communities in the nation.

This "**Gold Coast**" has an artistic streak, too, exemplified in the galleries and shops of trendy **South Norwalk** ⑮, dubbed "SoNo" for its emulation of New York's SoHo district. Once a gritty, run-down neighborhood, it's now a great place to while away a day. The huge **Maritime Aquarium** (10 North Water Street; tel: 203-852 0700; www.maritimeaquarium.org; open daily; entrance fee) on the banks of the Norwalk River has more than 1,000 marine animals and plenty of hands-on displays relating to the marine life and maritime culture of Long Island Sound. Seal feedings are at 11:45am, 1:45pm and 3:45pm. There's also an IMAX movie theater. Hop on board a boat at Hope Dock for a scenic cruise to **Sheffield Island** and a guided tour of an 1868 lighthouse (tel: 203-838 9444; cruises daily Memorial Day–Oct; fee).

In nearby **Norwalk** ⑯, tours are offered of "America's first chateau", the partially-restored, 62-room Victorian National Historic Landmark **Lockwood-Mathews Mansion Museum** (295 West Avenue, Matthews Park; tel: 203-838 9799; open mid-Mar–Dec Mon–Fri, Sat and Sun pm; entrance fee).

Ten miles (16 km) to the northeast, **Bridgeport** ⑰, a major industrial center, is an exception to the coast's general aura of ease and affluence. One fun note is the **Barnum Museum**, a showcase for memorabilia connected to circus pioneer Phineas Barnum, with a 4,000-piece miniature circus, clown props and items relating to Bridgeport native General Tom Thumb (820 Main Street; tel: 203-331 1104; open Tues–Sat; Sun pm; entrance fee). **Captain's Cove Seaport** (1 Bostwick Avenue; tel: 203-335 1433) on Black Rock Harbor has harbor cruises, shops, a restaurant, and terrific views.

New Haven

New Haven ⑱, 18 miles (29 km) to the north, settled by Puritans in 1638, was an independent colony until 1662, when it merged with the Hartford settlement. In the early 19th century more than 100 ships regularly sailed from the town's wharves to the West Indies and the Orient. As industry took over from seafaring, New Haven pioneered such inventions as the steel fish hook, the meat grinder, the corkscrew, and the steamboat.

New Haven is best known, however, as a center of learning. **Yale University** (www.yale.edu) was founded in 1701 by a group of Puritan clergymen, and was originally located in nearby Saybrook. In 1716, the school was moved to New Haven, and two years later it took the name of benefactor Elihu Yale.

Alma mater to famous personalities such as Nathan Hale, Noah Webster, and both Presidents Bush, Yale has pursued a policy of commissioning leading architects to design its buildings. But the dominant style on the Yale campus is Gothic Revival – much of it evoking the British universities of Oxford and Cambridge. Any visit to the university should include its excellent museums and libraries. Start from the **Beinecke Rare Book and Manuscript Library** at 121 Wall Street (tel: 203-432 2972; open Mon–Sat year-round), where an edition of the Gutenberg Bible and original Audubon bird prints are displayed. Two blocks south, the **Yale University Art Gallery** (1111 Chapel Street; tel: 203-432 0600; open Tues–Sat; Sun pm) exhibits well over 100 paintings by patriot artist Jonathan Trumbull, impressive collections of African and pre-Columbian art, canvases by Manet, Van Gogh, Corot, Degas, and Matisse; and a superb collection of American paintings and decorative arts.

Across the street, is the **Yale Center for British Art**, with a vast collection of British paintings (including works by Constable and Turner), drawings and sculpture donated in 1966 by industrialist Paul Mellon (1080 Chapel Street; tel: 203-432 2800; open Tues–Sat; Sun pm).

Collections at the university's **Peabody Museum of Natural History** (170 Whitney Avenue; tel: 203-432 5050; open Mon–Sat; Sun pm; entrance fee) include dinosaur fossils, native birds, meteorites and minerals.

Holdings at the **Yale Collection of Musical Instruments** (15 Hillhouse Avenue; tel: 203-432 0822; open Sept–June Tues–Thur pm except during university vacations; entrance fee) include Western and non-Western instruments; concerts are given throughout the year.

Adjacent to the university, New Haven Green is surrounded by a trinity of churches constructed in Gothic Revival, Georgian, and Federal styles.

New Haven's cultural offerings include the Yale Repertory Theater (Chapel and York streets; tel: 203-432 1234), the Long Wharf Theater on the down-

Map on page 206

TIP

For a thorough tour of Yale University, inquire at the university's visitors' information office (149 Elm Street; tel: 203-432 2300). Tours start at 10:30am and 2pm on weekdays, 1:30pm on weekends.

BELOW:
Yale University buildings.

Guilford harvest.

town waterfront (222 Sargent Drive; tel: 203-787 4282), and the Shubert Theater (247 College Street; tel: 203-624 1825; tours Sept–June), the "Birthplace of the nation's greatest hits". The New Haven Symphony Orchestra (tel: 203-865 0831) performs at Woolsey Hall on the Yale campus.

Just off Route 95 in **East Haven** ⓳, the **Shore Line Trolley Museum** preserves some 100 trolleys, the oldest rapid transit car and a rare parlor car (17 River Street; tel: 203-467 6927; open Sun in Apr; Sat & Sun May; Memorial Day–Labor Day daily; Sat & Sun Sept–Oct; Sun. in Nov; entrance fee). Hop aboard for a 3-mile (5-km) ride on one of the vintage cars.

A short jog to the east on Route 146 off Route 1 in **Branford** ⓴, cruise boats (including Thimble Islands Cruise & Charter ; tel: 203-488 8905; and Captain Bob Milne; tel: 203-481 3345) sail from the town's nearby **Stony Creek** dock for tours of the **Thimble Islands**, a cluster of 25 mostly inhabited islands just off shore. They also offer seal watches in season.

A mile east on Route 146, **Guilford** ㉑ was settled in 1639 by the Reverend Henry Whitfield. His home, built that year, is the oldest stone dwelling in New England and now the **Henry Whitfield State Museum** (248 Old Whitfield Road; tel: 203-453 2457; open Apr–mid-Dec Wed–Sun; entrance fee). The house gives visitors a feel for how early settlers lived.

Guilford has one of the largest and prettiest town greens in New England; it's famous for its Christmas tree lighting ceremony (first weekend in Dec). Nearby are several historic house museums, including the *circa* 1690 **Hyland House** (84 Boston Street; tel: 203-453 9477; open June–Labor Day Tues-Sun; Sept–mid-Oct weekends; entrance fee) and the *circa* 1774 **Thomas Griswold House** (171 Boston Street; tel: 203-453 3176; open Jun–Sept Tues–Sun; weekends in Oct;

BELOW: the
Thimble Islands.

Nov–May by appointment; entrance fee), with a restored blacksmith shop and Colonial garden. **The Dudley Farm** (2351 Durham Road; tel: 203-457 0770; open Mon–Sat 10am–2pm), a 19th-century working farm and living history museum, has a farmers' market Saturday mornings June through October.

Five miles (8 km) east, **Madison ㉒** has some of the state's most beautiful summer and year-round homes. The *circa* 1685 **Deacon John Grave House** (581 Boston Road; tel: 203-245 4798; call for hours; entrance fee) has been a school, wartime infirmary, inn, tavern, and courtroom. **Hammonasset Beach State Park** (Route 1; tel: 203-245 2785; weekend parking fee mid-Apr–Memorial Day and Labor Day–Oct), just 2 miles (3 km) east, is the state's longest public beach.

At **Old Saybrook ㉓**, by the western mouth of the Connecticut River, **Fort Saybrook Monument Park** (Saybrook Point, Route 154) has storyboards chronicling Saybrook Colony from 1635, and offers fine estuary views, with opportunities for bird watching from the boardwalk. Stop in for a Miss James Sundae at the **James Gallery & Soda Fountain** (2 Pennywise Lane; tel: tel: 800-640 1195; open Wed–Sun pm), once managed by Connecticut's first licensed African-American pharmacist. It retains many turn-of-the-19th-century furnishings. On the second floor, period guest rooms can be rented by the night *(see margin note)*.

Of all the towns on the shore, **Old Lyme ㉔** boasts the richest artistic heritage – thanks in large part to Florence Griswold, the daughter of one of the town's many sea captains and a devoted, if impecunious, patron of the arts. Her 1817 Georgian mansion, now the **Florence Griswold Museum** (96 Lyme Street; tel: 860-434 5542; open year-round Tues–Sat and Sun pm; entrance fee) contains a stunning array of works by her illustrious American Impressionist boarders, including such notables as Childe Hassam. Some were so moved by her laissez-faire hospitality, they left painted mementos on the doors, mantels and paneled walls. Don't miss the gardens.

Cruising the Connecticut River

Beginning as a mountain stream near the New Hampshire–Canada border, the Connecticut River travels 410 miles (660 km) through four states and ends its journey to the sea as a broad and majestic tidal estuary. The Native Americans named it "Quinnituckett," which means "the long, tidal river." Throughout history, the Connecticut has linked valley residents with the outside world. A fertile floodplain nourishes crops, and water power has generated energy for small industries.

A tour of the Connecticut Valley can begin near the river's mouth in **Essex ㉕**, a seaport founded in 1645. Essex developed as an important shipbuilding center during the 18th century. The *Oliver Cromwell*, America's first warship, was launched here in 1776. Yachts and cabin cruisers still berth here, and tall masts and yards of tackle lend the town a distinctly nautical air. The **Connecticut River Museum** (67 Main Street; tel: 860-767 8269; open Tues–Sun; entrance fee), at Steamboat Dock, highlights the town's maritime heritage with exhibits, boats, and a replica of the *Turtle*, the nation's first submarine, invented by Connecticut's David Bushnell. The 1776 Griswold Inn on Main Street is one of New England's oldest hostelries.

Map on page 206

TIP

The c. 1746 Deacon Timothy Pratt B&B (tel: 860-395 1229; 325 Main Street; www.pratthouse.net), has nine antiques-filled guest rooms with jacuzzi/ whirlpool tubs, fireplaces, and four-poster or canopy beds. Rates from $120 to $180 a night.

BELOW: learning the ropes at Old Saybrook.

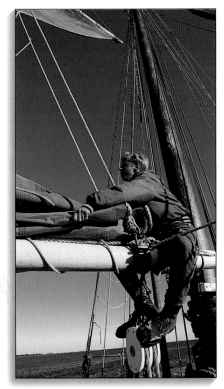

Actor William Gillette was able to develop his favorite hobby in the grounds of his castle: trains and locomotives. He constructed his very own railroad. The tracks have long since been dismantled but portions of the old roadbed make excellent hiking trails.

For a close look at the Connecticut River, take an old-fashioned journey by steam locomotive and/or riverboat. At **Essex Steam Train & Riverboat Ride** (Valley Railroad; 1 Railroad Avenue; tel: 800-377 3987 or 860-767 0103; www.essexsteamtrain.com; open May–Dec with varied schedule; fee), board a 1920s coach and ride along the river through the villages of **Chester** and **Deep River**. At Deep River, passengers may board a riverboat for a hour-and-a-half cruise. The round trip takes about 2½ hours and is recommended.

Head north on Route 154 and east on Route 148 to the **Chester-Hadlyme Ferry** (54 Ferry Road; tel: 860-443 3856 for reservations; open Apr–Nov; fee), which has been transporting passengers across the Connecticut River to East Haddam since 1769. From the opposite shore it's a short drive to the spectacularly eccentric **Gillette Castle** ㉖ at **Gillette Castle State Park** (67 River Road; tel: 860-526 2336; castle open Memorial Day–Columbus Day, daily; mid-Oct–fourth weekend after Thanksgiving, weekends; grounds open daily; entrance fee to castle). William Gillette (1853–1937) was a much admired American actor whose portrayal of Sherlock Holmes brought him fame and fortune. Gillette made the deerstalker hat a Holmes trademark; and it was he who uttered those memorable words onstage: "Elementary, my dear Watson."

For his dream house, the actor selected a hilltop aerie overlooking the Connecticut River and its surrounding countryside. Work on the 122-acre (49-hectare) site with its stone-and-concrete castle began in 1914 and took five years and more than $1 million. The results are whimsical and bizarre. The park's 184 acres (75 hectares) have hiking trails and fine views of the river.

North on Route 82, is the charming Victorian town of **East Haddam** ㉗. The 1876 **Goodspeed Opera House** (tel: 860-873 8668; www.goodspeed.org), which

BELOW: a riverboat meets the Essex Steam Train.

sits majestically on the banks of the Connecticut River, was a popular stopover in the heyday of steamboat travel. Beautifully restored, the Opera House presents musical revivals, as well as original productions, Apr–Dec. Half-hour tours are offered Jun–Oct, Mon 1–3pm, and Sat 11am–1:30pm (fee).

The American Revolutionary War patriot taught at the **Nathan Hale Schoolhouse** (29 Main Street; tel: 860-873 3399; call for hours) from 1773 to 1774.

Map on page 206

The northeastern shore

New London **㉓** was one of America's busiest 19th-century whaling ports. More than 80 ships sailed from its docks, and many a vast fortune was accumulated by its merchants. Evidence of this wealth can be seen in Whale Oil Row on Huntington Street, where four Greek Revival mansions were built in the 1830s.

When petroleum began to replace whale oil, manufacturing became New London's chief occupation. But the city maintained its ties to the sea and today is the home of the **US Coast Guard Academy** (the base is not open to the public).

It was also the boyhood home of Eugene O'Neill, the Nobel Prize-winning playwright whose works include *Long Day's Journey Into Night* and *Ah, Wilderness*. The O'Neill family's **Monte Cristo Cottage** (325 Pequot Avenue; tel: 860-443 5378, ext. 227; open Thurs–Sat; Sun pm; entrance fee) exhibits memorabilia of the author. Nearby, **Ocean Beach Park** (1225 Ocean Avenue; tel: 800-510 7263; open daily; parking fee summer months) on Long Island Sound offers excellent swimming, a boardwalk, and a swimming pool.

The two restored **Hempstead Houses** (11 Hempstead Street; tel: 860-443 7949; open mid-May–mid-Oct, Thur–Sun pm; entrance fee), built in 1678 and 1759, are furnished with period pieces that trace the evolution of colonial lifestyles.

Goodspeed Opera House, East Haddam.

BELOW:
Mystic Aquarium.

Across the Thames River from New London stands the city of **Groton ㉙**, known as the "Submarine Capital of the World" – the manufacture of nuclear submarines is its major industry. Non-claustrophobes who wish to view the interior of a submarine may visit the USS *Nautilus* Memorial at the **US Naval Submarine Base** (1 Crystal Lake Road at exit 86, off I–95; tel: 800-343 0079; www.ussnautilus.org; open May 14–Oct Wed–Mon and Tues pm; Nov–May 13, open Wed–Mon). The adjacent **Submarine Force Museum** has working periscopes, mini-subs, and mini-theaters. **Monument House**, in Groton's Fort Griswold State Park, has a collection of Civil War memorabilia.

Five miles (8 km) east, at exit 90 off I-95, in **Mystic ㉚**, Beluga whales, sharks, penguins, and sea otters are just a few of more than 3,500 creatures at the **Mystic Aquarium & Institute for Exploration** (55 Coogan Boulevard; www.mysticaquarium.org; tel: 860-572 5955; open daily; entrance fee). The Hidden Amazon exhibit recreates a rain forest, complete with crawly creatures and frogs. At Immersion Institute visitors utilize the latest deep-sea technology, including live cameras, robots, and a live web feed to dive under the sea, visit kelp beds, and watch sea otters romp. Sea explorer Dr Robert Ballard's Institute for Exploration displays many of the treasures he has brought up from the ocean floor. The Aquarium operates seasonal seal, eagle and whale-watching cruises.

Map on page 206

Mystic Seaport

Down Route 27 just a mile, **Mystic Seaport** (75 Greenmanville Avenue; tel: 888-973 2767; www.mysticseaport.org; open daily; entrance fee) is a living replica of a 19th-century waterfront community during the heyday of sailing ships. The project includes a complex of over 60 buildings covering 17 acres (7 hectares), and is so authentic, it was used as the setting for New Haven's harbor in the year 1839 in Steven Spielberg's 1997 movie *Amistad*, about a revolt aboard a slave ship sailing from Africa. A recreation of the freedom schooner was designed, built here, and launched from the seaport in June 2000. An exhibit details the project.

For serious students of maritime history, the G.W. Blunt White Library in Mystic Seaport is an incomparable resource, with thousands of books, manuscripts, ship registers, logbooks, charts and maps.

A full day and plenty of stamina are required to tour the entire seaport properly. Visitors can wander along the wharves and streets of the village, and taste the old seafaring way of life. The ***Charles W. Morgan***, the last surviving vessel of America's 19th-century whaling fleet is worth a visit (though it will be hauled out of the water for major restoration in 2007–8). Also board the ***Joseph Conrad***, which was built in 1882 by the Danish as a training vessel, and now serves as a student dormitory. You can take to the water in a rented boat or study navigation in the planetarium. A Collections and Access Research Room (10am– 5pm Mon–Fri) provides access to huge collections of maritime materials.

The village of **Mystic**, an old maritime community of trim white houses, sits at the tidal outlet of the Mystic River just down Route 27. For generations, Mystic was the home of daring mariners and fishermen, and was feared by the British during the Revolution as a "cursed little hornets' nest" of patriots. The village teemed with activity during the Gold Rush days of 1849, when shipbuilders vied to see who could construct the fastest clipper ships to travel round Cape Horn to the boom town of San Francisco. It was the *Andrew Jackson*, a Mystic-built clipper launched in 1860, that claimed the world's record: 89 days, 4 hours. The twee Olde Mistick Village has lots of "shoppes."

BELOW: under sail at Mystic Seaport.

A few miles further east is the charming old whaling port of **Stonington** ㉛, huddled at the edge of the state near the Rhode Island border. Stonington was once the third largest city in Connecticut and an important seaport. Although considerably reduced in circumstances, the village remains one of the prettiest coastal enclaves in New England. An 1823 lighthouse, the first government-operated one in Connecticut, is now the **Old Lighthouse Museum,** (7 Water Street; tel: 860-535 1440; open daily May–Oct; entrance fee) with artifacts from the Oriental trade, whaling gear and a children's room.

America's biggest casino

Ten miles (16 km) north of Stonington, on the Mashantucket Pequot Reservation, the massive **Foxwoods Casino** ㉜ has grown to become the nation's largest (*see facing page*), welcoming gamblers by the busload. On the grounds is the **Mashantucket Pequot Museum and Research Center** (110 Pequot Trail; tel: 800-411 9671; open daily 1–4pm; last admission at 3pm; entrance fee). The **Mohegan Sun** casino ㉝, a rival to Foxwoods, has been built to the southwest in **Uncasville**. ❑

How the Pequots' gamble paid off

Not so long ago, the eastern Connecticut Mashantucket Pequot Indian tribe was regarded by most New Englanders as part of the area's quaint pre-Colonial past, remembered by tongue-twisting place names such as Wequetequock and Quanaduck that outsiders find all-but-impossible to pronounce.

Then, all of a sudden, the tribe emerged from centuries-long obscurity in the mid-1980s. The reason was that, taking advantage of new legislation exempting tribal reservation land from local laws against gambling, it began developing hundreds of acres of ancestral reservation land in sleepy Ledyard, Connecticut, into a vast casino-and-hotel complex called Foxwoods.

Incredibly, it now rivals some of the gaming palaces of Las Vegas or Atlantic City. In 1998, just six years after it opened, Foxwoods was the world's highest-grossing casino. In addition to high-stakes bingo, slot machines, and dozens of other gambling games, the resort offers a regular schedule of concerts and performances by Hollywood's entertainment elite, half a dozen restaurants ranging from casual to high-roller high-style, and an ultra-plush hotel.

Most recently, the tribe has added a **Mashantucket Pequot Museum and Research Center** to the resort complex. Visitors journey back in time through a simulated glacial crevasse, complete with the sounds of creaking ice and the blast of chill air. The World of Ice sets the glacial scene; then follows the arrival of the first peoples, and has a diorama depicting a caribou kill 11,000 years ago. The exhibits include a re-created 16th-century Pequot village, a computer re-creation of a 17th-century Pequot fort excavated on the site, and a film explaining how the tribe achieved Federal recognition in 1983.

The success of Foxwoods is unquestioned, but many local residents still decry its presence in the formerly rural area. Driving up the Old Stonington Road (Route 2) into the casino complex, you are confronted with a stunning contrast: rolling countryside, stone walls, and farms versus unabashed glitz. The shining towers of the resort complex, some nearly 200 ft (60 meters) high, appear like an alarming Oz materializing out of thin air.

Just up the road in Uncasville, the Mohegan tribe has its own casino, the Mohegan Sun. A bit smaller than Foxwoods but similar in its glamorously seductive style, the Sun offers another winning hand: a slick combination of gambling, resort amenities, and Vegas-style concerts by big-name stars in its new 10,000-seat arena.

In the wake of the obvious success of both Foxwoods and the Mohegan Sun, it seemed for a while that every economically challenged small New England city was intent on rolling out a welcome mat for its own Indian-owned casino. Massachusetts and Rhode Island may yet join the party, as local tribes consider likely venues for Foxwoods competitors. There has, however, been some local opposition to opening more casinos, and a suspicion that the existing venues might have cornered the market ❑

RIGHT: Foxwoods Casino.

RHODE ISLAND

With Providence's downtown, Newport's mansions, sailing in Narragansett Bay, and Block Island's rolling pastures and beaches, this tiny state packs a diverse punch

Map on page 228

The smallest state in the nation, Rhode Island has nonetheless managed to hold on to a disproportionate share of wealth and clout. On the map, it may look more like an overgrown port than a genuine state, but that very sea-readiness accounts in large part for its long-term appeal.

Certainly, the millionaires who built their legendary summer "cottages" in Newport at the end of the 19th century recognized natural wealth when they saw it: the dramatic vistas of the Rhode Island Sound, the refreshing westerly breezes wafting in to relieve summer doldrums. The mansions they left behind still gleam atop the cliffs, jewels left over from the Gilded Age.

Centuries earlier, the reclusive Reverend William Blaxton found the area equally attractive. Blaxton, who had been living contentedly as a hermit in what would soon become Boston, fled to Rhode Island when the Puritans he'd invited to share his peninsula proved too proselytizing.

Rhode Island's official founder was a clergyman, Roger Williams. Driven out of Salem in 1635 for preaching religious tolerance, Williams headed south to establish a settlement where all were free to practice their own faith: traveling by canoe with a cadre of followers, he arrived in what is now Providence. Anne Hutchinson followed in 1637, to be joined by other dissidents. In 1663 Charles II granted a charter to the rather wordily named Colony of Rhode Island and Providence Plantations – a name it still officially retains as a state.

Soon people from even farther afield flocked to Rhode Island's shores. Many Quakers, fleeing Puritan persecution, made Newport their home, and as early as the 18th century, Jews from Portugal and Holland settled here. In the ensuing centuries came Italians, Irish, Russians, Poles, French, Swedes, Greeks, Armenians, Chinese and Cape Verdeans. By 1960 Rhode Island was the most densely populated state in America, with 859,000 inhabitants crowded into 1,214 sq. miles (3,144 sq. km). Today, with a population in excess of 1 million, Rhode Island is a bustling, multi-cultural cross-section of New England life.

PRECEDING PAGES: Rosecliff Manor, Newport. **LEFT:** sculpture in the Rosecliff gardens. **BELOW:** Villa Marina, Newport.

The Ocean State

As Rhode Island's license plate attests, **Narragansett Bay** dominates the state. Taking a dinosaur bite out of the New England coast, it gives the state a shoreline out of all proportion to its land area. Rhode Island is only 48 miles (77 km) long and 37 miles (60 km) wide, yet it claims 400 miles (640 km) of coastline.

With such an abundance of water at their disposal, Rhode Islanders have long turned to the sea for their livelihood. Two of the nation's leading seaports in the early days of the republic were Providence and Newport. Using Rhode Island as a base, pirates raided

Narragansett Bay offers good sailing.

merchant ships in the North Atlantic; the notorious Captain Kidd is rumored to have buried his cache of gold doubloons in Jamestown.

But Rhode Island is a land of contradictions. Despite the state's heritage as a sanctuary for pirates, Newport was the birthplace of the modern US Navy: President Chester Alan Arthur developed a new fleet – built of steel, rather than wood – there in the early 1880s, and enjoyed staging gun drills on the bay. (Though much of the navy pulled out in the mid-1970s, the Naval War College, founded in 1884, remains.) Founded as a haven of religious liberty, it became a world-class slave trade center.

Despite its considerable contributions to the success of the American Revolution, Rhode Island was the last holdout among states ratifying the US Constitution. Notorious for its exploitation of child labor, Rhode Island became a bastion of New Deal social ideals.

Until 1854, it couldn't even decide which city would be its capital. Each year the General Assembly packed up its belongings and moved lock, stock and

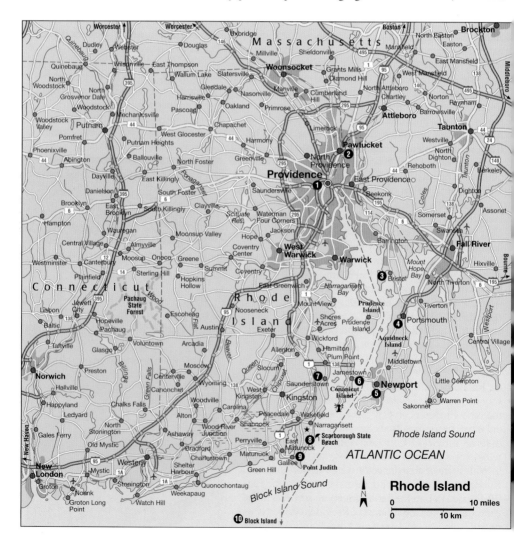

Maps:
Area 228
City 230

barrel to one of the five locales contesting for the honor. Eventually, after a raucous battle, Providence won out over Newport. It remains the capital, but Newporters contend their city is truly the heart of the state.

If little Rhode Island is a land of contradictions, it is also a land of superlatives and firsts. Among the state's distinctions are: America's first textile mill, in Pawtucket, and the only operational water-powered snuff mill in the United States, in Saunderstown. The state boasts the country's first synagogue, its first department store, and its oldest enclosed shopping mall, built in the early 19th century. And lest it be forgotten, the first two-week paid vacation on record was spent in Rhode Island. In 1524, the Italian navigator Giovanni da Verrazano, on an exploratory mission for the King of France, was investigating the North American coast when he spotted Narragansett Bay. Verrazano was "so enthralled… he lingered for a fortnight."

Rhode Island, in the singular, is actually a misnomer. In fact, there are 35 islands within the state. Within and without Narragansett Bay are the four principal islands of Aquidneck (also called Rhode, just to keep things confusing), Block, Conanicut and Prudence; others include Hen, Hog, Rabbitt, Boat, Old Boy, Patience, Hope and Despair. In and about these islands, visitors enjoy boating, sailing, surfing and fishing.

Throughout the state – generously scattered through cities and towns such as Providence, Wickford, Bristol, Little Compton and Newport – are lovely old homes representing the decorative ideals of several centuries. Despite the concentrated population, parklands are plentiful. And precisely because the state is so small – it takes less than two hours to drive from one end to the other – it's possible to enjoy its variegated offerings within a short time span. A visitor can walk historic city streets in the morning, picnic in an idyllic grove at noon and savor the delights of the seashore by moonlight.

How the state got its name is uncertain. Some believe it was called after the Greek island of Rhodes. Others think the name derived from a Dutch word meaning "red."

Revitalized Providence

Rhode Island's capital has much in its favor: it has outstanding 18th and 19th-century architecture on Benefit Street, an excitingly rejuvenated downtown, and appealingly diverse neighborhoods – Italian, Portuguese, Ivy League university, and funky places such as Hope Street. It's also easily reached from Boston, a feasible day trip by car, train or bus.

In its early days, **Providence ❶** was the port of call for ships engaged in the lucrative Triangular Trade: New England rum for African slaves for West Indies molasses. In 1781, John Brown, one of four brothers whose family would dominate Providence for some years to come, sent the first of many ships to China. The maritime trade began to decline, however, following a series of international wars which resulted in embargoes and protectionism, and public interest and investment shifted toward industry.

As a major manufacturing center in the 19th century, Providence was dubbed "the cradle of American industry." Its huge plants were known worldwide – Brown & Sharpe (machinery and tools), Nicholson (files), Grinnel (sprinkler systems), Gorham (silverware), Davol (rubber goods), and so on.

The 20th century brought hard times. With the

BELOW:
Gravity Games
at Providence.

Great Depression and the textile industry's exodus to the south, Providence lost its pre-eminence as an industrial center. Although no longer the giant it once was, Providence is now home to five colleges and universities, and has enjoyed a revitalization of business in recent decades.

The city has in turn lavished restorative attention on its variegated downtown. Artists have been given tax-free incentives to set up here; old warehouses and department stores have found new uses; I-195 is to be moved to free up more land for development close to the downtown area; and the ignored river has been beautified and made more accessible. Ironically, colorful mayor Buddy Cianci – responsible for much of the revitalization – was jailed for corruption.

Providence is a city best seen on foot. Like Rome, Providence was built on seven hills. Most people remember three: College (officially, Prospect), Federal, and Constitution. The other four seem to have melted in the metropolitan sprawl.

Adamsville, Rhode Island, claims the world's only known monument to a chicken – the prolific Rhode Island Red.

Center of town

Constitution Hill is pretty much impossible to miss because of the **State Capitol Ⓐ** that dominates its crest (Smith Street; tel: 401-222 3983; reserve ahead for tours Mon–Fri at 9, 10 & 11am). This imposing 1891–92 McKim, Mead, and White structure with one of the world's largest self-support domes is crowned with the bronze statue, "Independent Man". Exhibits inside include an historic portrait of George Washington by Rhode Island native Gilbert Stuart.

Just across the way, **Providence Place Ⓑ** (www.providenceplace.com; tel: 401-270 1017) has more than 140 stores, restaurants, and entertainment options, including a 6-story **IMAX** theater (tel: 401-453 4629).

The 4-acre (1.6-hectare) **Waterplace Park & Riverwalk Ⓒ** is evidence of

BELOW: The Arcade, Providence, dating to 1828.

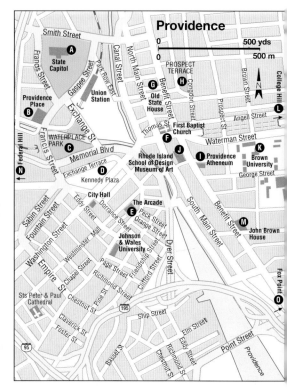

the city's waterside renaissance. The once-neglected riverside has been cleaned up, equipped with an Italian-inspired piazza, walkways, and and descriptive panels with photos of the old port days. In summer, Venetian-style gondolas offer trips and free outdoor entertainment is presented.

Map on page 230

Kennedy Plaza ◐, in the shadow of the art deco skyscraper affectionately dubbed the Superman Building (not that *Superman* was ever filmed here), is the arrival point for buses from Boston and elsewhere. To the east stands the restored Providence Station, an Amtrak stop. Around the corner from Kennedy Plaza is the **Turk's Head Building**, a 1913 landmark with an ornate stone head over its entrance; and the **Customs House** (1856), with a dome and lantern that once welcomed ships returning from China.

For shopping or snacking and a bit of history, visit the **Arcade ⓔ** (65 Weybosset Street; tel: 401-598 1199; open Mon–Fri, 10am–5pm; Sat 11am–4pm). This Greek Revival "temple of trade" and the nation's first indoor shopping mall was built in 1828. Its three-story granite columns (said to be the second largest in America, after those at the Cathedral of St John the Divine in New York) were cut from single pieces of stone, which required 15 yokes of oxen to move.

The dome of the State Capitol, Providence.

In historic East Side, **Benefit Street**, the "Mile of History," (tel: 401-831 1000) deserves walking from one end to the other. There are more than 200 restored 18th- and 19th-century buildings (many are now private homes) originally built by sea captains and merchants; many houses, churches and schools bear bronze plaques identifying their original owners and dates of construction. In the late 1960s and early 1970s the street was run down, and nearly demolished as part of a renewal program; only the efforts of the Preservation Society saved the day.

BELOW: restored sea-captains' homes on Benefit Street, Providence.

Sculpture at Rhode Island School of Design.

Benefit Street was once a twisting dirt path informally known as Back Street because it led around the back side of homes to the family graveyards. When at last a communal burial ground was marked out and ancestral bones duly transferred to it, Back Street was straightened out and "improved for the benefit of the people of Providence."

The **First Baptist Church** (75 North Main Street; tel: 401-751 2266; guided tours Mon–Fri, 10am-noon and 1–4pm; Sat 10am–2pm; and Sun at 1:15pm; donation) was established by Roger Williams in 1638, designed by Joseph Brown, and restored in 1775. It is a splendid example of the Colonial style. Joseph also designed a house for his brother, a wealthy merchant.

The **Old State House** (tel: 401-222 3103; open weekdays) at 150 Benefit Street (between North and South Court streets) is worth a peep, if only to see the modest size of the former capitol, where the Rhode Island General Assembly renounced allegiance to King George III on May 4, 1776.

Prospect Terrace , on Congdon Street a block east of the Old State House, is a tiny park that gives a fine view of the city; a statue of Roger Williams, the city's founder (who is buried here), presides. The streets hereabouts are full of imposing 19th-century industrialists' mansions.

The bookstacks of **Providence Atheneum** (251 Benefit Street; tel: 401-421 6970; open Mon–Sat; Sun pm; closed summer weekends) reputedly witnessed the courtship of Edgar Allan Poe and a local resident, Sarah Whitman. She refused to marry him, however, because she claimed he couldn't stay sober. Such literary associations apart, the 1836 Greek Revival structure is well worth a visit for its collections of rare books, prints, and paintings.

BELOW:
Brown University.

Virtually opposite is the museum of the prestigious **Rhode Island School of Design (RISD) Museum of Art** with more than 80,000 works of art, including paintings by American masters and French Impressionists, a major Oriental collection, American furniture, and decorative arts (224 Benefit Street; tel: 401-454 6500; open Tues–Sun; entrance fee except Sun 10am–1pm, Fri noon–1:30pm, and last Sat of month).

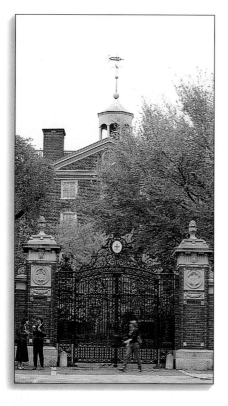

Brown University (College Hill; tel: 401-863 1000; www.brown.edu) dominates this part of Providence (open weekdays). The Ivy League establishment was founded as Rhode Island College in Warren in 1764, and moved to Providence in 1770. Among the buildings of interest on the campus: the 1770 University Hall (on the Quadrangle), used as a barracks during the Revolutionary War; the 1904 Beaux-Arts John Carter Brown Library (corner of George and Brown streets); and the Annmary Brown Memorial (21 Brown Street; open weekdays pm) with European and American paintings from the 16th to early 20th centuries.

The heart of the **College Hill** shopping area is Thayer Street, four blocks east of Benefit, packed with interesting restaurants, bars, shops, and bookstores.

John Quincy Adams called the **John Brown House** , built in 1786, "the most magnificent and elegant private mansion that I have ever seen on this continent" (52 Power Street; tel: 401-331 8575; open early Apr–early Nov Tues–Fri pm, Sat). The Brown House staff offers walking tours of historic Benefit Street. You can see period furniture, paintings, pewter, silver, porcelain, and mementos of the China Trade; a later resident added an astonishingly showy bathroom.

**Federal Hill **, just to the west on the other side of I-95, is Providence's "Little Italy." Wander along Atwells Avenue and enjoy the aroma of crusty Italian breads, cheeses, pastas, herbs and spices. Some people come to stock up on traditional delicacies such as gorgonzola, Romano, homemade pork sausages and prosciutto, others for the restaurants, espresso shops and festive ambiance. Without a doubt, Federal Hill is one of the friendliest parts of Providence.

One of Providence's best-kept secrets is **Fox Point **, home to the city's Portuguese community. Fox Point speaks with an Old World accent. On holy days, celebrants parade with statues of the Virgin Mary while children dressed in their best suits and crinolines follow along. Early morning brings to Fox Point the tantalizing scent of Portuguese sweet bread wafting from small bakeries.

Before leaving town, head south on I-95 to exit 17 and follow signs to **Roger Williams Park** (Elmwood Avenue; tel: 401-785 9450; admission to rides), a 435-acre (176-hectare) complex which encompasses an amphitheater, greenhouse, a carousel, children's train, and a highly rated **zoo** (tel: 401-785 3510; open daily; entrance fee), with more than 900 animals and exhibits.

East Shore of Narragansett Bay

In downtown **Pawtucket ❷**, 5 miles (8 km) northeast of Providence, techniques of mechanized textile production were pioneered with the construction of **Slater Mill** in 1793 by Moses Brown. The riverfront **Slater Mill Historic Site** (67 Roosevelt Avenue; tel: 401-725 8638; open daily, call for tour schedule; entrance fee) offers visitors a rare look into the earliest days of the Industrial

Maps:
Area 228
City 230

TIP

The East Bay Bicycle Path takes a level shoreline route from East Providence to Bristol, along a former railroad track, with good views for much of the way. The total distance is 14 miles (22 km).

BELOW:
carousel at Roger Williams Park.

Revolution. For more industrial history, proceed north through the **Blackstone Valley National Heritage Corridor** (Tourism Council, 175 Main Street; tel: 800-454 2882 or 401-724 2200; www.tourblackstone.com), which preserves sites in Rhode Island and across the border in Massachusetts.

In **Bristol** ❸, about 15 miles (24 km) south on Route 114, visitors can tour **Blithewold Mansion and Gardens.** The 45-room mansion was built by Pennsylvania coal magnate Augustus van Wickle in 1908 to resemble a 17th-century English country manor. The 33 acres (13 hectares) of landscaped grounds are a riot of colour in spring (101 Ferry Road; tel: 401-253 2707; grounds open daily; mansion open mid-April–mid-Oct, Wed–Sun and most Mon holidays; limited hours, Dec; entrance fee). More than 50 yachts from 1859 to 1947 and The America's Cup Hall of Fame are displayed at **Herreshoff Marine & America's Cup Museum** (1 Burnside Street; tel: 401-253 5000; open May–Oct, daily; entrance fee. Artifacts from native peoples of the Americas, Africa, Asia and the Pacific are housed at Brown University's **Haffenreffer Museum** (300 Tower Street; tel: 401-253 8388; open June–Aug, Tues–Sun; weekends rest of year; entrance fee).

Six miles (10km) south, just off Route 114 in **Portsmouth** ❹ at **Green Animals Topiary Gardens**, (Cory Lane; tel: 401-847 1000; open early Apr–early Nov daily; combined admission ticket with Newport mansions). Eighty sculpted trees and shrubs represent everything from an ostrich to a camel. The main house of the gardens' creator, Thomas Brayton, has period furnishings.

Newport claims these distinctions: first US ferry service (1657), first US synagogue (1759), first circus in the country (1774), first auto race (1895) and first automobile arrest in the US (1904, for speeding at 15mph).

Newport: domain of wealth

During World War II an anti-submarine net was strung across the entrance of the bay guarding **Newport** ❺. It was effective. But then, the elite of the city had long been expert at protecting their privacy. In the halcyon days of the Gilded Age, Newport was the domain of the very wealthy. Huge palaces built on expansive grounds were surrounded by mammoth fences and patrolled by guards and dogs. Now, however, a great many of these fiercely guarded fiefdoms are open to all comers, having become Newport's foremost tourist attractions.

Summering in Newport first became fashionable before the Revolution among Southern plantation owners intent on escaping the heat of Georgia and the Carolinas. After the Civil War, the nation's wealthiest families – Astors, Morgans, Fishers, Vanderbilts – discovered its charms. Arrivistes hoping to legitimize their newfound wealth with indisputable good taste tended to duplicate the palaces and chateaux that had so awed them on their grand tours of Europe. Edward Berwind, for instance, the son of poor German immigrants, managed to enter the ranks of this self-appointed aristocracy with The Elms *(see page 237)*. Extravagance became obligatory. Harry Lehr hosted a formal dinner at which a monkey, complete with tuxedo and princely title, numbered among the guests. James Gordon Bennett, the man who bought a Monte Carlo restaurant when it refused him a table, rode stark naked in his carriage through Newport's streets. The Coogans invited everyone who was anyone to a grand ball to celebrate the completion of their "sum-

BELOW: Ocean Drive, Newport, facing the Atlantic.

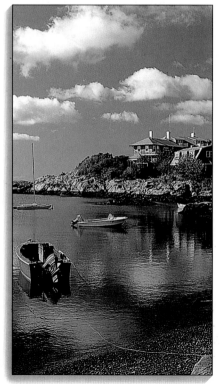

mer cottage." When no one showed up, the Coogans simply walked out – leaving all the food, drink and furniture – never to return.

A good place to begin a visit is in town at the **Museum of Newport History Ⓐ** in Washington Square (Thames Street; tel: 401-846 0813; open mid-Apr–mid-June Thurs–Sat, Sun pm ; mid-June–early Sept daily; early Sept–late Dec Thurs–Sat, Sun pm; donation) in the restored, 1762 Brick Market building.

Newport has a remarkable legacy of colonial architecture: some 200 houses pre-date 1800 – the biggest concentration in the nation. Many are to be found in the neighborhood off Washington Square. At 85 Touro Street, the Georgian **Touro Synagogue Ⓑ** (tel: 401-847 4794; tours year-round except Sats & Jewish holidays; entrance fee), built in 1763, is the nation's oldest Jewish house of worship. The mysterious Old Stone Mill in nearby Touro Park, an unexplained open-sided structure formerly said to have been left behind by the Phoenicians, Vikings, Portuguese, or Irish, is now known to be 16th- or 17th-century, and probably built by a Colonial farmer.

A landmark of Colonial Newport is the white clapboard **Trinity Church Ⓒ** (1725–26) on Queen Anne Square, said to be based on the designs of Christopher Wren (tel: 401-846 0660; open to visitors May–early July Mon–Fri; early July–Sept 1, daily; Sept 2–Oct Mon–Fri; donation).

If you're planning to tour several mansions, the **Preservation Society of Newport** (242 Bellevue Avenue; tel: 401-847 1000; www.NewportMansions.com) sells a variety of tickets for admission up to 11 properties and offers tours; seasons and hours vary greatly – call or check website. One ticket includes admission to the National Historic Landmark, dockside **Hunter House Ⓓ** (54 Washington Street; entrance fee), the 1748 home of a prosperous sea merchant.

Maps: Area 228 City 235

Touro Synagogue, Newport, the oldest in North America.

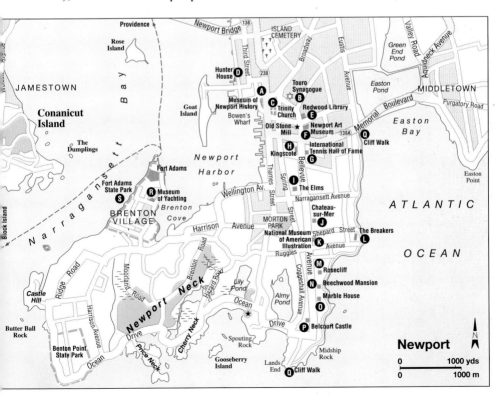

TIP

Newport is surrounded
by fine beaches. The
choice ranges from
First, Second, and
Third beaches in
Middleton (north of
Newport) to the more
exclusive Bailey's,
Hazard's, and
Gooseberry.

BELOW:
The Breakers.

The docks in town have a decidedly salty air. Watch boats being prepared and sails stitched in lofts along the wharves; admire the handsome craft tied up at yacht club slips. As night falls, head for the waterfront. The parade of strollers on Bowen's Wharf resembles a prep-school reunion. Most action centers on the bars, cafés and restaurants along Thames Street, where the fresh seafood comes accompanied by sea breezes. The White Horse is the oldest tavern in the US.

Many of Newport's attractions line Bellevue Avenue, one of the town's major thoroughfares. The 1748–50 **Redwood Library and Atheneum E** (50 Bellevue Avenue; tel: 401-847 0292; open Mon–Sat, Sun pm; donation) took its inspiration from Roman temple architecture; it is thought to be the oldest continuously used library building in the US and contains a noted collection of portraits, including works by Gilbert Stuart. The 1862 "Stick Style" **Newport Art Museum F** (76 Bellevue Avenue; tel: 401-848 8200; open Mon–Sat; Sun pm; entrance fee) designed by Richard Morris Hunt (open Mon, Tues, Thur–Sat; Sun pm; entrance fee) exhibits paintings by luminaries including Winslow Homer and George Innes as well as works by regional artists.

The state-of-the-art **International Tennis Hall of Fame G** (194 Bellevue Avenue; tel: 800-457 1144 or 401-849 3990; www.tennisfame.com; open daily; entrance fee), the country's largest tennis museum, is housed in the inappropriately-named Newport Casino, which never had anything to do with gambling, but was America's most exclusive country club when it opened in 1880. Its grass courts hosted the first Men's US Lawn Tennis Association tournament, played in 1881, and today are open to the public. Also here is the Casino Theater, designed by Stanford White, which hosts performances.

Continuing along Bellevue Avenue, the first mansion open to the public is

Kingscote (tel: 401-847 1000; check www.newport mansions.org or call for hours; entrance fee), the first of the summer cottages, built in Gothic Revival "Stick Style" – making playful use of asymmetry and varied textures, sprouting a wealth of pendants, lattices and gables. It has glass paneling by Tiffany and exquisite porcelain.

The coal-rich Edward Julius Berwind commissioned **The Elms** ❶ (tel: 401-847 1000; open 10am–4pm winter, 10am–5pm summer; entrance fee), built in French Renaissance style, based on Château d'Asnières near Paris. It borrows from a range of styles, including Chinese, Venetian and Louis XIV.

William S. Wetmore built **Château-sur-Mer** ❶ (tel: 401-847 1000; open mid-Apr–late Oct, daily; Jan–mid-Apr, weekends; entrance fee) in 1852, a confection of Victorian lavishness, and Newport's showiest mansion when it was built. Richard Morris Hunt enlarged it in the 1870s.

Works by artists including Norman Rockwell, Maxfield Parrish and NC Wyeth are exhibited at the **National Museum of American Illustration** ❶ (492 Bellevue Avenue; tel: 401-851 8949; tours May 30–Nov 3 Mon–Fri or year-round by advance reservation; $25 a person).

The Newport Preservation Society pays the grand sum of $1 a year to rent **The Breakers** ❶ (tel: 401-847 1000; open 9am–5pm summer, 9am–4pm winter; entrance fee), which recently completed a $2 million restoration. Considered the most magnificent of the Newport cottages, this opulent Italian Renaissance palace, completed in 1895, took only two years to build. Cornelius Vanderbilt II commissioned American architect Richard Morris Hunt to design the mansion, whose 70 rooms are extravagantly adorned with marble, alabaster, gilt, mosaic, crystal, and stained glass. The kitchen alone is the size of a small house.

Cornelius Vanderbilt II did not enjoy The Breakers for long. He died in 1899, aged 56, four years after its completion. Even though he had given vast amounts to charities during his life, his estate amounted to almost $73 million.

BELOW: sea kayaking along Ocean Drive.

Newport's Cliff Walk.

Further along Bellevue Avenue, Mrs Hermann Oelrichs hired Stanford White to design **Rosecliff M** (tel: 401-847 1000; check www.newport mansions.org or call for hours; entrance fee), an imitation of Versailles' Grand Trianon. It features a huge French-style ballroom and a heart-shaped staircase.

Caroline Schermerhorn Astor, the "Queen Victoria" of New York society, held court at one of the oldest "cottages", now the Astors' **Beechwood Mansion and Victorian Living History Museum N** (tel: 401-846 3772; www.astors-beechwood.com; open daily; entrance fee). Today, costumed actors show you around in your assumed role as a guest of the family. From early November to mid-December, the mansion is open for Victorian Christmas.

Marble House O (tel: 401-847 1000; open 9am–5pm summer, 9am–4pm winter, closed Jan 1– early April, daily; entrance fee), another of Hunt's designs, was built in 1892 for William K. Vanderbilt and styled after the Grand and Petit Trianons of Versailles. With scenes and figures from ancient mythology, it even manages to upstage The Breakers for ostentation, though it is not as large. A Chinese tea house stands in the grounds.

At 657 Bellevue Avenue, **Belcourt Castle P** a 1894 Gothic Revival mansion, is styled on a Louis XIII hunting lodge at Versailles (tel: 401-846 0669; one-hour guided tours 10am–4pm daily Jun–Aug; Sept Wed–Mon; Oct Thurs–Mon; closed Jan; when open, candlelight tours Fri, Sun and Mon from 6–7pm; ghosts tours Thurs and Sat 5–7pm). The castle has the largest collection of objets d'art of any of the mansions, including a full-size gold Coronation Coach.

Strollers can examine the backyards of the Bellevue Avenue mansions from the **Cliff Walk Q**, a 3½-mile (5.5-km) path that overlooks Rhode Island Sound. Crusty local fishermen saved this path for public use by going to court when

BELOW: mason at work at Anglesey on the Cliff Walk.

wealthy mansion owners tried to close it. Visitors who don't wish to walk the length of this path can start at the end of Narragansett Avenue and reach the water by way of the Forty Steps; or wander down to Brenton Point State Park on the island's southernmost tip, an ideal place to watch gulls, picnic or enjoy a sunset.

During the summer, Newport hosts a number of major outdoor music events, such as the Dunkin' Donuts Folk Festival and the JVC Jazz Festival, both held in August at Fort Adams State Park. While there, take a look at the **Museum of Yachting R** (Ocean Drive; tel: 401-847 1018; open mid-May–Oct, daily; entrance fee), which examines the pursuit through the centuries and across continents. Newport is the scene of many yachting events. The prestigious America's Cup was held in Newport waters 24 times from 1851 through 1983, when the Cup was lost (for the first time) to the Australians.

The 685-mile (1,100-km) Bermuda–Newport Race, held every other year, begins here, and the grueling Single-Handed Transatlantic Race, which starts in Plymouth, England, ends in Newport.

The National Historic Landmark **Fort Adams State Park S** (Harrison Avenue; tel: 401-847 2400; open mid-May–Oct, daily; entrance fee), built between 1824 and 1857 and decommissioned after World War II, was used to defend both the land and the sea, and offers magnificent views from the observation deck. Tours are available.

Other mansions along **Ocean Drive** include Hammersith Farm, the childhood home of John F. Kennedy's wife, Jacqueline Bouvier. The Kennedys were married here in 1953.

Just across the Newport Bridge (toll), follow signs to historic **Jamestown 6** on Conanicut Island. The southern tip of the island offers New England scenery at its most picturesque. Don't miss Mackerel Cove, Beavertail Lighthouse and museum in **Beavertail State Park** (South Main Street; tel: 401-423 9941), and the view from Fort Wetherhill. The 275-acre (110-hectare) **Watson Farm** (445 North Road; tel: 401-423 0005; open June–mid-Oct, Tues, Thurs and Sun pm; entrance fee) on Narragansett Bay has been a working farm since the late 18th century. Just down the road, the **Jamestown Windmill** (North Main Street; tel: 401-423 3650; open mid-June–mid-Sept, weekends; entrance fee), was built in 1787.

Along Block Island Sound

From Jamestown, continue west on Route 138 to Route 1A, and turn south along the coast. In **Saunderstown 7**, the renowned portrait artist was born in 1755 at the **Gilbert Stuart Birthplace** (815 Gilbert Stuart Road; tel: 401-294 3001; open May–Oct, Thur–Mon; entrance fee). Farm managers at the mid-18th century **Casey Farm** (tel: 401-295 1030; open June–mid-Oct, Sat pm; entrance fee) on Route 1A raise organic produce for homes in the area. Further south on Route 1A is the fine **Scarborough State Beach 8** (tel: 401-789-8374; parking fee).

Whale Watching tours depart from Point Judith *(see Travel Tips)*, where there's a U.S. Coast Guard Station and lighthouse. Backtrack a short distance on Route 108, past the entrance for **Captain Roger B. Wheeler**

Maps:
Area 228
City 235

TIP

For more on the Newport Mansions, see the picture feature on pages 242–43.

BELOW: Forty Steps, on the Cliff Walk.

State Beach (tel: 401-789 3563; parking fee) and follow signs to Galilee **❾**, the departure point for the ferry to Block Island as well as home port for several sightseeing boats.

Block Island

When Rhode Islanders want to get away from it all, they head for **Block Island ❿**, a 3 by 7-mile (5 by 11-km) island some 12 miles (19 km) south of Narragansett Bay. Whereas Newport is packed to the gills with hotels, shops, restaurants, and tourists, Block Island remains a hideaway holding its own, quite successfully, against developers and fast-food chains.

Block Island, discovered in 1614 by a Dutch navigator, Adriaen Block, is the least accessible of the state's islands: although regular or chartered planes fly out of Westerly, R.I., and points in Connecticut (a 10-minute hop), most people take the ferry, a 70-minute trip from Galilee, R.I. (year-round ferry service; tel: 401-783 7996 or 866-783 7996; www.blockislandferry.com), or two hours from New London, Connecticut (service mid-June–mid-Sept). A good way to explore is by bicycle; rentals are available on the island.

Greeting visitors to Block Island are fine beaches, tranquility and the romantic allure of aging Victorian hotels with huge verandahs and a sense of bygone splendor. Fishermen are attracted here by the abundant tuna, swordfish, bluefish, mackerel, cod and flounder.

The island's claim to fame in maritime annals is the large number of shipwrecks off its coast. Thousands of luckless captains saw their vessels come to misery along the coast of New England, and a great many were wrecked on the submerged rocks and sandbars around "The Block." Scavenging goods from the

Veranda detail, Block Island.

BELOW:
Fountain Square, Block Island.
RIGHT:
rides on offer at Black Rock Point, Block Island.

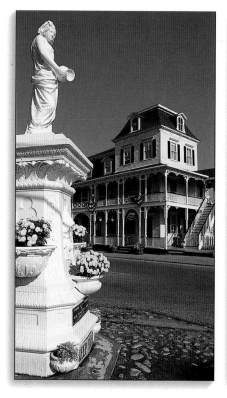

holds of wrecked ships became such a lucrative trade that some islanders helped engineer more wrecks by setting up lanterns and flares to confuse the ships. Many island place names commemorate the wrecking trade; at Cow Cove, for instance, a cargo of cows from a wrecked ship waded ashore, and on Calico Hill, bolts of cloth collected from another disaster were hung out to dry in the sun.

Life in the early days was hard. In the turbulent years of the late 17th century, the island was constantly under siege from pirates. During the Revolution, islanders – cut off from the mainland – nearly stripped Block Island of its trees building houses and ships. Tourism arrived in 1842, when the first hotel was opened, and a party of 10 men checked in. The **Spring House** opened its doors 10 years later and is still accommodating visitors to this day. To spend time in this antique of a summer hotel, with its rambling corridors and simply furnished rooms, is to be caught in a time warp. From its perch high on a hill, one can gaze out over the Atlantic Ocean and breathe the beneficent sea air just as wealthy tourists from New York and Baltimore once did.

The island has several fine sand beaches. The waves are lively at **Surfers Beach**, as its name suggests; **State Beach** and others on the east are calmer and attract the most visitors. The westerly strands are windswept and, more often than not, deserted. One trek not to be missed is the hike to **Mohegan Bluffs**. Here, the entire Mohegan tribe met its doom at the hands of the Manasees, who either enslaved them or drove them over the 200-ft (60-meter) cliffs.

Surfcasting from the beaches can absorb an entire day, as can wandering along the roads and over the hills, looking for wildflowers and Indian relics. Shops in **Old Harbor**, the island's only town, sell local specialties, such as candles, jellies, and wool watch caps. ❑

Map on page 228

State Beach.

BELOW: Mohegan Bluffs, Block Island.

NEWPORT'S "GILDED AGE" MANSIONS

Newport, a 19th-century summer playground for the rich and influential, became a showplace for America's greatest architects and designers

With the coming of the railways in the mid-19th century, vacationing became ever more popular, and the delights of Newport, set on an island with a fine summer climate, became readily accessible from New York and Philadelphia. Wealthy and influential families, began to spend their summers here. Many had made vast fortunes from industry and began to lavish unstinting funds on creating opulent summer homes, where they would entertain and impress all those who mattered.

The country's most innovative architects – names such as Stanford White and Richard Morris Hunt – were employed, creating designs that reflect the full range of styles in vogue at the time (*see also pages 235–8*). Building materials and furnishings were often imported from Europe (for Marble House, for instance, different coloured marbles were imported from Italy to be worked by Italian craftsmen in Newport). Interior decor frequently borrowed from European or Far Eastern styles; fine paintings, furnishings and objets d'art collected from around the world filled the rooms.

Eight of these mansions are now maintained by The Preservation Society of Newport County and are open to the public, as is the Astor family's Beechwood Mansion.

▷ **THE BREAKERS**
The grandest of grand dining rooms: all gold leaf, alabaster and marble – and two 12-ft (3.5-meter) chandeliers.

▽ **THE ELMS**
The Elms replicates a two-story château near Paris, with the servants' quarters behind the roof balustrade and the kitchens in a cellar.

▷ **THE ELMS**
The splendid grounds are embellished with statues, fountains, and clipped and shaped trees – but, nowadays, no elms.

THE LEGACY OF THE VANDERBILTS

The Breakers (above), was commissioned in 1893, to replace an earlier house destroyed by fire, by Cornelius Vanderbilt II, chairman of the New York Central railway, a director of 49 other railways, and the head of America's wealthiest family. His younger brother, William, had inherited equal shares in the family fortunes, some part of which he spent building Marble House, on nearby Bellevue Avenue. A serious, modest and gentle man, Cornelius II nevertheless gave free rein and an unlimited budget to Richard Morris Hunt, the architect of Marble House and of the grand Vanderbilt houses on Fifth Avenue in New York. Hunt followed the Italian Renaissance layout adopted for 16th-century palaces, where rooms were grouped symmetrically around a central courtyard. With 70 rooms, 33 of which were for resident staff and visitors' servants, The Breakers is indisputably Newport's largest "cottage".

▽ **CHATEAU-SUR-MER**
The solid granite 1850s Wetmore home was updated in the 1870s in the latest European fashions, including Arts and Crafts.

△ **ROSECLIFF**
The glittering ballroom, designed by Stanford White, witnessed many of Newport's most extravagant high-society summer balls.

◁ **MARBLE HOUSE**
The entrance hall of yellow Siena marble is dominated by a vast Venetian mirror over a bronze fountain custom-made for the house.

▷ **THE BREAKERS**
Magnificently sited on Ochre Point, The Breakers faces the Atlantic Ocean. Its grounds are skirted by Cliff Walk.

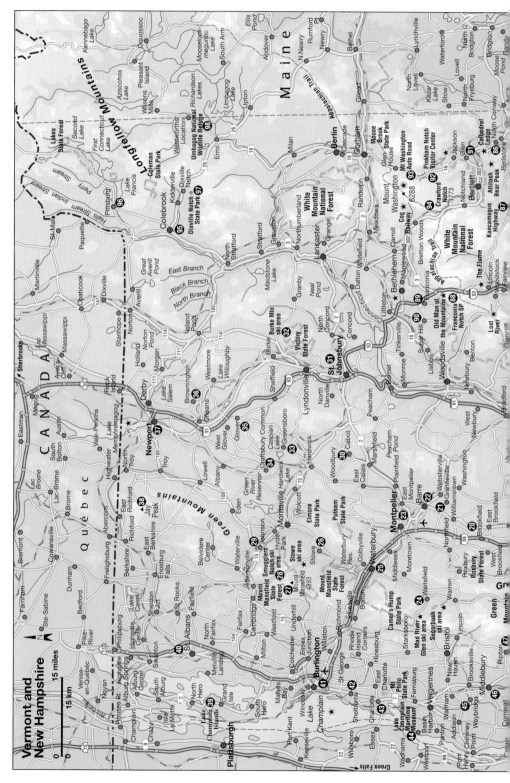

Vermont and New Hampshire

Longfellow Mountains

Green Mountains

Appalachian Trail

C A N A D A

Québec

M a i n e

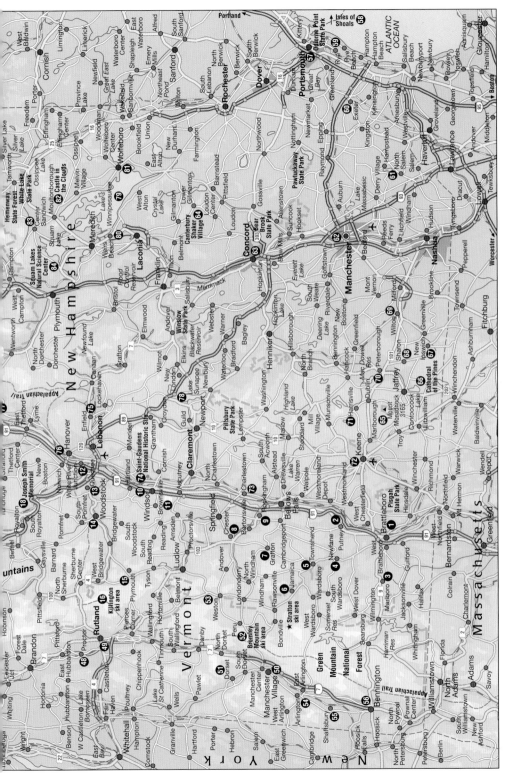

VERMONT

Map on pages 244–5

The Green Mountain State is alive with the sound of leaves crunching under foot; the sight of red barns and white steeples; the smell of country lanes and maple sugar boiling

I magine New England, and you will very likely imagine Vermont. When you round a bend to behold a valley painted in a thousand shades of green, or stand atop Mt. Mansfield to see a quilt of farm and forest rumpled against Lake Champlain; when you look towards high meadows that almost seem to cantilever off steep wooded hills, or drop down from the mountains into a white village framed in all the colors of autumn, you realize that this is the New England you already had in your mind's eye.

New England's last frontier

Tucked as it was in a corner of New England precariously close to New France and its Indian allies, Vermont was among the last parts of the region to be settled. Even after the French threat was eliminated, the lands between the Connecticut River and Lake Champlain were uncertain ground, contested by New Hampshire and New York. In the middle were Vermonters who personified the state's still-vaunted spirit of independence: this is where Ethan Allen and his Green Mountain Boys fought off "Yorker" surveyors, before turning their attention to the British during the Revolution.

Even after the war, Vermont was chary about joining the union – it had never been one of the 13 original colonies. And so for 14 years, beginning in 1777, an odd little entity called the Republic of Vermont existed on the map of North America. Not until 1791 did Vermont become the 14th state.

Much of what appeals in Vermont's human-crafted environment – the small farms, the neat villages – harks back to the state's "golden age" between that early federal era and the Civil War. Those were the peak years of local agriculture (it was sheep, not today's iconic dairy cows, that then predominated), when the state's image and character were largely created.

Things began to change in mid-century. The 1849 California Gold Rush lured some young Vermonters from their farms, and the Civil War lured many more. "Put the Vermonters ahead and keep the column well closed up," said General John Sedgewick at the Battle of Gettysburg; no other state gave as large a share of its sons to the cause of Union. Nor did all the survivors return home: too many of them heard tales of better land out west, land not burdened by the glaciers with an endless bumper crop of stones. The year 1865 marked the beginning of a decline in population, which until 1960 grew gradually older and smaller.

PRECEDING PAGES: the Green Mountains. **LEFT:** downhill skiing. **BELOW:** fall foliage.

Coming to visit – and to stay

Tourism in Vermont dates to before the Civil War – Manchester, where President Abraham Lincoln's wife and children summered in 1863, was an early resort town. Vermont lakeside retreats were popular during the late 19th century, and there was even a small hotel on top of Mt. Mansfield, the state's highest peak. There was no great cluster of palatial resort hotels such as those in New Hampshire's White Mountains, but nevertheless the word was out: Vermont was a splendid place to rusticate.

Vermont may have been able to offer fresh air, fine scenery, and good fishing, but what really kicked the state's tourism industry into overdrive was the selling of winter. The ski boom began during the 1930s, when the first mechanical tow was installed at Woodstock and the first trails were cut on Mt. Mansfield. By the early 1970s, dozens of ski areas had given rise to a burgeoning second-home industry, and new worries over rural subdivision and runaway development.

That same era brought an influx of new Vermonters, mostly young refugees from big eastern cities looking for a simpler way of life. The cliché is that they were hippie communards, but the vast majority were tradespeople, artisans, and soon-to-be professionals. What they shared was a sense that they had found someplace special, and that they wanted to keep it that way.

In alliance with progressive natives, the new Vermonters crafted a far-reaching array of environmental regulations, from a ban on off-premises billboards to controls on development in rural areas. It hasn't all gone down smoothly; there is still considerable chafing between conservative natives whose mantra is "property rights," and the "flatlanders" whom they feel have taken over the state. But no one can look at Vermont and say that it took the 20th century lying down. As for the 21st, well, stop in at a town meeting, first week of March, and see which way things are going.

BELOW: cows built to survive the harsh Vermont winters.

The Lower Connecticut River Valley

The long, lazy Connecticut River forms the entire boundary between the states of Vermont and New Hampshire. Covered today by a hydroelectric dam, Vermont's first permanent settlement – Fort Dummer, founded in 1752 – has been reduced to a mere marker on the shore. A few miles north, however, **Brattleboro** ❶, the town it was meant to protect, enjoyed resort status from 1846 to 1871, when a local physician parlayed its pure springs into a "water cure." In the 1960s and '70s, some of the more dedicated of the back-to-the-land crowd settled here, and sunk their roots deep into the community. They still support natural foods markets, alternative shops, and a worker-owned restaurant, The Common Ground, which after several decades of broad-based success seems less a restaurant than a cultural touchstone.

The 1938 **Latchis Building** on Main Street, which houses a movie theater and the Latchis Hotel, is one of only two Art Deco buildings in Vermont (the other is in Rutland). The **Brattleboro Museum and Art Center** (tel: 802-257 0124; open mid-Apr–early Mar Wed–Mon 11am–5pm; entrance fee) is in the Union Railroad Station. It hosts changing art exhibits and a history of the Estey Organ Company, which made this "the organ capital of America" from the 1850s to the 1920s.

North of the city 2½ miles (4 km), off Route 5, **Naulahka**, the shingle-style manse where Rudyard Kipling wrote the first two *Jungle Books* and *Captain Courageous* in the 1890s, has been restored by Great Britain's Landmark Trust (not open to the public, but see Tip in margin). Kipling, an Englishman born in India, built his home here after his honeymoon in 1892, and immediately warmed to the life of a country squire. His grand airs, however, didn't endear him to the locals, and in 1896 when a property dispute with his roguish brother-in-law hit the headlines, destroying his rural idyll, he and his wife fled, never to return.

A few miles further north on US 5, **Putney** ❷ predated the social experiments of the 1960s by a good 150 years: in the early 19th century, it was the site of a short-lived but sensational commune espousing free love. The countryside is still populated in part by '60s counterculture types. Many artists and craftspeople ply their trades here; look for hand-crafted signs announcing sculpture and woodworking studios and potteries.

Follow US 9 (also known as the Molly Stark Trail) west to **Marlboro** ❸ – hilltop home of small, liberal arts Marlboro College, which every summer hosts the world-renowned, chamber music **Marlboro Music Festival**, founded by the late Rudolf Serkin (book early for tickets; tel: 802-254 2394 in summer; 215-569-4690 rest of year; www.marlboromusic.org).

A few miles further west at Wilmington, turn north to reach West Dover, home to **Mount Snow/Haystack** (tel: 802-464 3333 or 800-245-SNOW; www.mountsnow .com), a behemoth ski area and summer resort.

Route 30 northwest out of Brattleboro follows the West River, past the 1872 West Dummerston Covered Bridge (there's a fine swimming hole here) to the postcard-perfect town of **Newfane** ❹. Its broad common is lined with shady elms and surrounded by stately Greek Revival public buildings – a white-columned courthouse with Congregational church to match, flanked

TIP

Kipling's house, Naulahka, is available for rent by the week from the UK's Landmark Trust. Telephone 802-254 6868 in the US or 01628-825925 in the UK for details. www.landmarktrust .usa.org

BELOW: the Art-Deco Latchis Building, Brattleboro.

Civil War monument in Newfane.

BELOW:
near Putney.

by a grange, two lovely inns, and some worthwhile antique stores *(see picture, pages 8–9)*. A flea market is held on summer Sundays in a field north of town.

Further up Route 30 the handsome town of **Townshend** ❺ has a 2-acre common whose focal point is the 1790 Congregational Church. The Black Bear Shop sells stuffed toys made next door at Mary Meyer Stuffed Toys, the state's oldest stuffed toy maker. North on Route 30, Scott Bridge – the state's longest single-span covered bridge – was built in 1870.

Just past it is the turn for **Townshend Lake Recreation Area** (tel: 802-365 7703; open late May–early Sept daily; entrance fee). Created by a dam built in the 1960s, it's a fine spot to take a swim.

There's another opportunity for swimming up the road in **Jamaica** ❻, at **Jamaica State Park** (off Route 30; tel: 802-874 4600; open late May–Columbus Day; entrance fee), where a trail leads to a 125-ft (38-meter) waterfall.

About 10 miles (16 km) north of Townshend on Route 35, **Grafton** ❼ is a Greek Revival town in an 1840s time warp: visitors wander about in blissful disbelief, sampling a slice of cheddar at the **Grafton Village Cheese Company** (tel: 800-462-3866 or 802-843 2210; open daily), and perhaps claiming a rocker on the porch of the 1801 Old Tavern, whose guests have included notables from Thoreau and Kipling to Ulysses S. Grant and Teddy Roosevelt. Once a thriving agricultural center, the town was preserved in the 1960s through the efforts of the Windham Foundation.

The **Grafton Historical Society Museum** (147 Main Street; tel: 802-843 1010; www.graftonhistory.org; open Fri–Mon Memorial Day–Columbus Day; daily during foliage season, and by appointment; donation) relates the town's fascinating history.

Route 35 winds north about 7 miles (11 km) to **Chester ❽**, a curious little strand of Victoriana on the Williams River. An 1850s stone village-within-a-village features 30 homes faced in gneiss ledgestone, built before the Civil War. The town (pop. 3,000) is a good base for cyclists and boating enthusiasts.

Chester is also the northern terminus for the **Green Mountain Flyer** (54 Depot Street; tel: 800-707 3530 or 802-463 3069; www.rails-vt.com; open daily in summer and fall; fee), a vintage diesel-powered excursion train which begins its journey 13 miles (21 km) to the southeast in Bellows Falls. The company also operates the Champlain Valley Flyer and the White River Flyer, as well as seasonal and holiday excursion trains

Between the two towns, just off Route 103 in **Rockingham ❾**, is Vermont's oldest unchanged public building, the 1787 Federal-style **Rockingham Meeting House** (tel: 802-463 3964; open Memorial Day weekend–Columbus Day, daily; entrance fee). The **Vermont Country Store** (tel: 802-463 2224; open daily), headquartered in Weston, has a branch store, along with an 1810 grist-mill, on Route 103.

Cycling in the forest.

The Upper Connecticut Valley

A center of invention during the 19th century, **Windsor ❿**, along with nearby Springfield, became home to Vermont's machine tool industry. The **American Precision Museum** at 196 South Main Street (Route 12 East; tel: 802-674 5781; open late May–Oct daily; entrance fee), housed in the National Historic Landmark, 1846 Robbins and Lawrence Armory, houses a fascinating array of the machinery that made "Yankee ingenuity" a byword.

Windsor is also famed as the birthplace of Vermont, because it was here in the

BELOW:
chicken farmer.

TIP

A fine view of the area
can be had from
Brownsville Rock, 440
yards by trail from the
3,144-ft (958-meter)
summit in Ascutney
State Park. This is also a
launch site for hang
gliding.

Old Constitution House that delegates met in 1777 to draw up a constitution for the little republic and create a Council of Safety to protect the new country as much from the other 13 states as from the Crown. The building is now a museum, with material relating to this event (tel: 802-828 3051; open late May–mid-Oct, Wed–Sun, 11am–5pm; entrance fee). Just up the road, the **Cornish Colony Museum** (Old Firehouse Building, 147 Main Street; tel; 802-674 6008; open Tues–Sat, Sun pm; entrance fee) houses an excellent collection of Maxfield Parrish paintings, as well as works by other Cornish Colony artists.

Just up Main Street, the **Windsor-Cornish Covered Bridge**, spanning the Connecticut River to lovely Cornish, New Hampshire *(see page 288)*, is the longest covered bridge in the United States.

North, just off Route 5 in the Windsor Industrial Park, **Harpoon Brewery** offers tours and tastings (Ruth Carney Drive, Windsor Industrial Park; tel: 802-674 5491; open May–Aug daily; Sept–Apr Tues–Sat; tours at 11 am, 1pm and 3 pm) and **Simon Pearce Glass** (tel: 802-674 6280; open daily) has an outpost (their main store is in Woodstock), where glass-blowing demonstrations are given.

"I live in New Hampshire so I can get a better view of Vermont," explained artist Maxfield Parrish from his home in Cornish. He did sneak a considerable piece of that view into most of his paintings, notably Mount Ascutney, which looms to the southwest of Windsor. In **Brownsville ⓫**, **Ascutney Mountain Resort** (tel: 800-243 0011; www.ascutney.com), one of the state's major downhill ski resorts, offers a full roster of outdoor activities in the summer months.

Sixteen miles (26 km) to the north, **White River Junction ⓬**, a major crossroads since railroad days, still serves as an Amtrak stop and marks the intersection of Interstates 91 and 89.

BELOW: Mount
Ascutney, with the
Windsor-Cornish
Covered Bridge in
the foreground.
RIGHT: Windsor.

A few miles west on Route 4, at **Quechee ⑬**, 162-ft (49-meter) deep **Quechee Gorge**, "Vermont's Little Grand Canyon," is best viewed from the bridge which spans it, or from trails at the Quechee Gorge Recreation Area. The **Vermont Institute of Natural Science** (6565 Woodstock Road, Route 4; www.vins.org; tel: 802-359 5000; open May–Oct daily, Nov–Apr Wed–Sun; entrance fee) runs a fascinating Vermont Raptor Center for owls, hawks, and eagles unable to survive in the wild.

In town, Irish artisan Simon Pearce has transformed **The Mill at Quechee**, an abandoned flannel factory, into an inviting complex with a distinctive glassworks. The mill sells pottery and furniture, and has a delightful restaurant. The **Quechee Polo Club** (Dewey's Mill Road; tel: 802-775 5066; entrance fee) holds matches most Saturdays in Jul–Aug at their field a half-mile (1 km) north of Route 4.

Woodstock

Woodstock ⑭, just to the west, was one of the first Vermont towns to be discovered – and given a high polish – by outsiders. Upscale shopping sprees along the refurbished downtown blocks of Cabot and French streets may have replaced placid strolls up Mount Tom as the fashionable summer pastime, but in general the enlightened despotism of philanthropist Laurance Rockefeller has preserved the tone of the town much as it must have been in the 1930s, when he met his future wife, Mary French, while summering here.

A participant in Woodstock's Wassail Parade.

A passion for maintaining a graceful balance between society and nature has long been the keynote to Woodstock's renown. Mary's grandfather, Frederick Billings, returned from his lucrative law practice in San Francisco in the 1890s to become a pioneer in reforestation and a zealous model farmer. The slopes of Mount Tom and Mount Peg and the restored **Billings Farm Museum** (Route 12 East; tel: 802-457 2355; www.billingsfarm.org; open late Apr–Oct daily, weekends Nov–Feb; entrance fee) are testaments to his love for rural Vermont and his adherence to the principles of Woodstock native George Perkins Marsh, a linguist, diplomat, and author of the seminal conservationist tract *Man and Nature*. Daily life on a late-19th-century dairy farm are depicted in the barns and farm house.

BELOW: antiques are big business in rural Vermont.

In 1998 the Billings family mansion and its surrounding 500 acres (200 hectares), were bequeathed by Laurance Rockefeller as the **Marsh–Billings-Rockefeller National Historical Park** (Route 12; tel: 802-457 3368; www.nps.gov/mabi; mansion tours by advance reservation Memorial Day–mid-Oct; entrance fee; grounds open free year-round), Vermont's only national park and the only park in the system to concentrate specifically on conservation. Tours of the grounds are also offered.

For further glimpses of Woodstock's past, visit the **Woodstock Historical Society** headquarters, nine rooms of period furnishings in the 1807 Dana House (Elm Street; tel: 802-457 1822; Memorial Day–Columbus Day, Tues–Sat; entrance fee).

The Woodstock Inn and Resort on the green remains the place to stay – and the Robert Trent Jones golf course and **Suicide Six** ski area (tel: 802-457 6661) offer year-round amusements. On the other side

of the green, a covered bridge leads to Mountain Avenue, a redoubt of old summer cottages, and a park at the base of Mount Tom. Trails to the summit overlook a guided floral walk through the Rockefeller estate.

The nation's 30th president was born and is buried at the **President Calvin Coolidge State Historic Site** in **Plymouth ⑮**, 15 miles (24 km) southwest of Woodstock. The site preserves not only "Silent Cal's" home, but his entire boyhood village, including the general store with an upstairs office that served as his summer White House, and a barn that exhibits a superb collection of 19th-century agricultural equipment (off Route 100A; tel: 8092-672 3773; open late May–mid Oct daily; entrance fee). This is one of the nation's most authentic presidential sites and is lauded by Vermonters as showing "what life in small-town America used to be like."

North and west via Routes 100 and 4, New England's largest ski area, **Killington ⑯** (4763 Killington Road; tel: 802-422 3333 or 800-621 6867; www.killington.com), covers seven peaks and encompasses 200 trails. "The Beast of the East" also ranks top among the Northeast ski resorts for nightlife. With a 4,241-ft (1,296-meter) peak reached by gondola, for sightseers as well as skiers, the resort is active year-round – the skiing often lasts from October through June and then in summer mountain bikes take over.

Visionaries, religious and commercial

The tiny village of **Strafford ⑰** was the birthplace of Vermont representative and senator Justin Morrill, author of the 1862 Morrill Acts which established America's system of land grant colleges and universities. He built his **Justin Morrill Homestead** (Route 132; tel: 802-765 4484; open year-round,

Calvin Coolidge (1872–1933) made national headlines when, as governor of Massachusetts, he used the state militia to suppress a police strike. A taciturn man and a laisser-faire president, he is best remembered for his 1925 remark: "The business of America is business."

BELOW: the Floating Bridge at Brookfield.

Wed–Sun, 11am–5pm; entrance fee), a 17-room pink Carpenter Gothic home, between 1848 and 1851. The nearby 1799 **Town House** was built for town meetings and interdenominational church services. Its steeple is one of the most beautiful in Vermont.

"A man can easily hear strange voices," said Kipling of the lonely Vermont winter, "the Word of God rolling between the dead hills; may see visions and dream dreams..." Joseph Smith, a visionary of another sort who went on to found the Mormon religion, was born a few miles away in South Royalton in 1805. Just off Route 14, Mormons maintain the **Joseph Smith Memorial and Birthplace ⓲**, with a 38½-ft (11.5-meter) obelisk made from a single block of Barre granite, and a museum (Dairy Hill Road; tel: 802-763 7742; open Mon–Sat; Sun pm). *See margin note.*

North of South Royalton on Route 10, four covered bridges span the First Branch of the White River in **Tunbridge ⓳**, which hosts the Vermont History Expo each June, and the Tunbridge World's Fair, held annually in September since 1867.

North on Route 14, the tranquil village of **Brookfield ⓴** is in the geographical center of the state. In 1812, a 320-ft (98-meter) **Floating Bridge**, supported by 380 tarred barrels, was built across Sunset Lake at the center of town, and an eighth version is in place today – albeit on plastic floats – as part of Route 65, accommodating one car at a time; it's also popular for fishing. One of the last ice harvests in the east is now the occasion for an annual festival on the lake, held the last Saturday in January. The town's Free Public Library, founded in 1791, is the oldest in Vermont.

About 10 miles (16 km) to the north, between Brookfield and Barre is the

Map on pages 244–5

Joseph Smith (1805–44) claimed that God had begun revealing the true nature of Christianity to him when he was 15, and he published these revelations in 1830 as The Book of Mormon. He said he would run for the presidency in 1844, but was jailed in Illinois. A mob broke into the jail and shot him dead.

BELOW: Brookfield's ice festival.

CRAFTS IN VERMONT

With over 1,500 professional artisans, Vermont has more artists and craftspeople per capita than any other state. Thanks in part to a bucolic setting but also to state support – the Vermont Crafts Council in Montpelier has designated three "Vermont State Craft Centers" – you'll find outstanding creative work in every major town (and in minor ones, too). Vermont's galleries exhibit and sell pottery, woodwork, jewelry, textiles, glassware, quilts and anything else you can think of.

Frog Hollow (as each of the State Craft center shops is called, after the original Middlebury location) has locations in Burlington, Manchester, and Middlebury (tel: 802-388 3177). Hundreds of "juried" artisans (those whose work has been judged to be of the highest quality) show their work at these venues.

In summer and fall, large craft fairs are held throughout the state *(see listing in the Travel Tips section)*, and on Memorial Day weekend artists participate in a statewide "Open Studio" weekend. The Vermont Crafts Council (tel: 802-223 3380; www.vermontcrafts.com) publishes a free annual studio and gallery guide, and a calendar of fairs.

This information, as well as links to member artists, is available on-line at www.vermontcrafts.com.

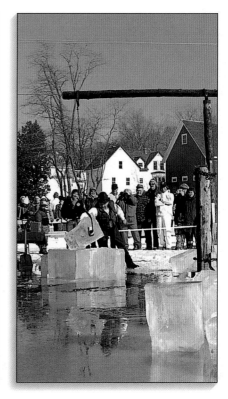

town of **Graniteville ㉑**, site of the **Rock of Ages Quarry**, the largest granite quarry in the world. Mining began soon after the War of 1812, and boomed with the influx of skilled immigrant stoneworkers between 1880 and 1910. Fed up with poor wages and working conditions (many died of silicosis), the granite workers managed to elect a Socialist mayor of Barre – many decades before liberal Burlington was ready to do the same. Today, the Rock of Ages firm owns nearly all of the Graniteville quarries, which provide the nation with one-third of its memorial stones (Visitors Center, 773 Graniteville Road; tel: 802-476 3119; www.rockofages.com; open May–Oct, Mon–Sat; Sun pm; shuttle tours June–mid-Oct, Mon–Fri; entrance fee; free self-guided tours of historic, inactive quarry daily May–Oct), with free access to the polishing and sculpting factory, and optional bus tours skirting the fully operational quarry a mile up the hill.

Many of the workers in the quarries were Italian immigrants, as evidenced by the names on the headstones at **Hope Cemetery** (off Route 14) in **Barre ㉒** (pronounced *Barry*). Quarry workers commemorated their own with often touching artwork. Among the stand-outs: a half-scale racing car, and the life-sized statue of labor leader Elia Corti, shot down in 1903 at a Socialist rally.

The workers' heritage and politics are much in evidence in downtown **Barre**. The larger-than-life statue of a mustachioed Italian stonecutter at the corner of North Main Street and Maple Avenue looks toward Granite Street, site of the National Historic Landmark, Socialist headquarters **Old Labor Hall** now being renovated by the Barre Historical Society (46 Granite Street; tel: 802-476 0567).

Barre's 1891 **Spaulding Graded School**, home to the Vermont Historical Society's **Vermont History Center** (60 Washington Street; tel: 802-479 8500; open Tues–Fri) reflects in its Romanesque grandeur the most prosperous days of the

BELOW: Robert Burns stands guard in Barre.
RIGHT: Main Street, Montpelier.

granite industry. The granite **Robert Burns Memorial** in front of the school was erected in 1899 by Scots, who also worked in the quarries.

Map on pages 244–5

The smallest capital: Montpelier

Home to about 8,200 people, **Montpelier** ㉓ (pronounced *Mont-peel-er*) is the nation's smallest state capital. The lively little downtown is dominated by the gold-leaf dome of the **Vermont State House** (State Street; tel: 802-828 2228; tours Jul–Oct Mon–Fri 10am–3:30pm; Sat 11am–2:30pm).

Initially, Vermont's capital rotated through the state, but, with the completion of the original nine-sided building in 1808, the seat of power settled here. When an imposing stone successor, built in 1838, was gutted by fire in 1857, the Doric portico and native granite walls withstood the flames to form a shell for the present structure. The Senate Chamber is rightfully considered the most beautiful room in the state.

The Italianate Pavilion Building replicates a hotel – in its day a virtual dormitory for legislators – that stood on this site adjacent to the State House. The new structure houses government offices and the **Vermont Historical Society Museum** (109 State Street; tel: 802-828 2291; www.vermonthistory.org; open Tues–Sat; May–Oct, also Sun pm; entrance fee). The extensively renovated museum contains an extensive collection of Vermont artifacts.

Montpelier is home to the **New England Culinary Institute**, whose students and teachers staff two excellent public restaurants on Main Street – the Main Street Grill and Bar (tel: 802-223 3188; open for lunch Tues–Sat; dinner Tues–Sun; and Sun brunch buffet) and the Chef's Table (tel: 802-229 9202; open for dinner Tues–Sat) – as well as La Brioche Bakery & Cafe across the way.

Montpelier was the birthplace of Admiral George Dewey (1837–1917), who became a hero during the Spanish-American War when the US fleet under his command destroyed the Spanish fleet at Manila.

BELOW:
Vermont State House, Montpelier.

North out of town via Main Street for 2½ miles (4 km), the **Morse Farm Sugar Works** (1168 County Road; tel: 800-242 2740; open daily). More than 200 years old, it offers free tours of the sugar house, tastings of maple products, and sugar-on-snow (warm maple syrup poured over snow or ice).

The Green Mountains

Some 20 miles (32 km) west of Montpelier, the Green Mountain range attains heady heights highly tempting to skiers – as well as to mountain climbers and bikers. South of I-89, the Mad River Valley towns of **Waitsfield** ㉔ and **Warren** support two ski areas, the rustic, but challenging **Mad River Glen** and more developed and extensive **Sugarbush**. Both towns are full of the pleasures – inviting restaurants and cozy inns – that outdoors enthusiasts enjoy in their off-hours.

Spectators are welcome at the **Sugarbush Polo Club** (tel: 802-496 3581 for information), which plays Wednesdays in summer (the original players, in 1962, used ski poles and a volleyball).

To get an unusual perspective on the countryside, consider a soaring excursion in a sailplane towed by **Sugarbush Soaring** (Warren-Sugarbush Airport, Route 100; tel: 802-496 2290; flights May–Oct), or try horse-trekking at the **Vermont Icelandic Horse Farm North** (Basin Road off Route 100; tel: 802-496 7141; rides year-round).

For a more conventional scenic tour, head for one of the nearby "gaps" (glacially-formed passes through the mountains). The road to **Lincoln Gap** begins on Route 100 near Warren Village and climbs for 3 miles (5 km) to 2,424 ft (739 meters) before descending into tiny Lincoln. The road through **Appalachian Gap** begins on Route 17 and winds past Mad River Glen to the

TIP

Kayaking and canoeing are popular on the Mad River and the White River between April and June, and on the Winooski River between April and September. Waitsfield has the best selection of canoe hire companies.

BELOW: adding black cherries in Ben & Jerry's ice cream factory

2,365-ft (721-meter) crest before its descent into the Champlain Valley (note: gaps can't accommodate trailers, and Lincoln Gap is closed in winter).

Fourteen miles (22 km) north via Route 100, in **Waterbury ㉕**, a pair of "flat-lander" entrepreneurs turned this famous dairy state into ice cream heaven. The **Ben & Jerry's Homemade Ice Cream Factory** offers tours and tastings daily (tours daily; tel: 866-258 6877 for schedule; **www.benjerry.com**; entrance fee for tour). If you want to actually see ice cream being made, schedule a weekday visit. The company's "small is beautiful" image was seriously dented when Ben Cohen and Jerry Greenfield sold out to the multinational giant Unilever.

Just up the road, stop for samples of the "Best Cheddar in the World" at the **Cabot Annex Store** complex (2653 Waterbury-Stowe Road; tel: 802-244 6334; open daily), which also houses Green Mountain Chocolate Co., a confiserie run by former White House pastry chef Albert Kumin.

Ben & Jerry's.

Farther north, watch cider being pressed, and browse through the huge gift shop at the **Cold Hollow Cider Mill** (3600 Waterbury-Stowe Road; tel: 800-327 7537; open daily).

In **Stowe ㉖**, the **Ski Museum** (5 South Main Street; tel: 802-253-9911; www.vermontskimuseum.org; open Wed–Mon daily; closed mid-Apr–Memorial Day and Halloween–Thanksgiving; entrance fee) chronicles the development of skiing in Vermont as well as of the sport's ever-changing technology, from the days of wooden skis and leather boots to the present. But even before skiing arrived in the 1930s, the town enjoyed a reputation as a stylish summer place. Summer or winter, sports opportunities abound, particularly along the **Stowe Recreation Path**. Ideally suited for skiers, cyclists, skaters, wheelchair racers, runners, walkers, and stroller pushers, the 5.3-mile (8.5-km) paved path skirts

RIGHT: Balloon Festival, Stowe.

the West Branch river from town all the way out to the Topnotch resort, passing a number of appealing inns, restaurants, and shops en route. Other notable Stowe inns, such as the Austrian-style Trapp Family Lodge (founded by the Baroness Maria Von Trapp of *Sound of Music* fame; *see box below*) are tucked away in the wooded hills; in summer, the meadows of the 2,700-acre (1,100-hectare) Trapp Family Lodge are alive with the sound of concerts and equestrian shows. The Trapp Family Lodge has Vermont's oldest cross-country ski trail system, part of one of the biggest networks in New England.

On **Mount Mansfield ㉗** Ralph Waldo Emerson had a bracing vacation at the Summit House, where, he recounts, his "whole party climbed to the top of the [mountain's] nose and watched the sun rise over the top of the White Mountains of New Hampshire." Hikers still favor this craggy human profile, and two shortcuts at the **Stowe Mountain Resort** (Route 108; tel: 800-253 4754; www.stowe.com) are popular: the 4½-mile (7.5-km) **Auto Road**, a century-old toll road that offers an easy way to ascend to the "nose," and an eight-passenger **gondola**, the world's speediest, zips to the 4,393-ft (1,338-meter) "chin," the state's highest point. The resort also operates an alpine slide and in-line skate park. In winter, the ski area offers long, challenging runs.

Other big summertime draws are the hot air balloon festival in July and a midsummer classic car rally; in mid-January, during the Stowe Winter Carnival, the whole town parties *(see margin caption)*.

Wintertime visitors hoping to fit in a visit to the nearby ski area at **Smuggler's Notch Resort ㉘** (Route 108 South; tel: 800-451 8752 or 802-644 8851; www.smuggs.com) (so named for its role during the War of 1812 when trade with Canada was forbidden) are in for a surprise—and a drive: the connecting

Stowe's winter carnival, first held in in 1921, is now a major nine-day event in late January and early February. Events include a range of competitive sports (including snow golf and snow volleyball), ice carving, and "the world's coldest parade."

BELOW: horse-drawn sleigh at the Trapp Family Lodge.

THE SAGA OF MARIA VON TRAPP

Maria Agusta Kutschera was born on a train in Austria in 1905. After a lonely childhood, she was sent to be governess to a sickly daughter of a retired naval captain, Georg von Trapp. In 1927, as in the best romances, she married the captain. In 1938 the entire family – by this time Maria was pregnant with their tenth child – fled from the Nazis across the Alps into Italy. As poor refugees, they tried to earn a living by singing and, while touring the US in 1939, they discovered Stowe, Vermont. Because it reminded them of home, they used their savings of $1,000 to buy an old farm. In 1947 they set up the Trapp Family Music Camp and later added a lodge to accommodate guests.

Maria told the family's story in a book, published in 1949. Naively she sold the film rights for just $9,000 to a German producer, who made *Die Trapp Familie*. This meant that she made little money from the lucrative Rodgers and Hammerstein Broadway version, *The Sound of Music*. When Hollywood later adapted the musical, it ignored her demands for a more realistic portrayal of her family, and she wasn't even invited to the film's premiere in 1965.

After spending some time on missionary work in the South Pacific, Maria returned to Stowe, where she died in 1987. She lies in the family cemetery next to the Lodge.

Map on pages 244–5

road from Stowe is closed in winter, and those who've traveled it in summer will understand why. Hundred-foot cliffs and giant boulders crowd the narrow, winding roadway – a popular staging point for mountaintop hikes. On the other side, "Smuggs" offers downhill skiing on three peaks, as well as cross-country trails, and is popular with families for its well-thought-out children's programs. In summer the attraction is hiking, horseback riding, and an assortment of water slides. The town closest to the resort, Jeffersonville, has a restaurant, several lodgings, a well-equipped general store (with a liquor outlet), and an art gallery.

About 8 miles (13 km) east on Route 15, the town of **Johnson** ㉙ has been all but taken over by the **Vermont Studio Center**, a working retreat for artists that attracts many prominent instructors. **Johnson Woolen Mills** (Main Street; tel 877-635 9665; open Mon–Sat), manufacturer of the green woolen work pants much liked by Vermont farmers, has a retail store filled with sturdy outerwear. The **Forget-Me-Not Shop** (Route 15; tel: 802 635 2335; open daily) to the west of town, with deeply discounted clothing, is a must-stop for bargain hunters.

The Northeast Kingdom

North of Route 15 is a remote and remarkable region. The Northeast Kingdom is a nearly 2,000-sq.-mile (over 5,000-sq.-km) swath of crystal lakes and deep forests, a region known for greater natural wealth and homegrown poverty than any other area in the state. The counties of Caledonia, Essex and Orleans are sparsely populated and make up Vermont's least industrialized area. *Where the Rivers Run North* is the title Orleans writer Howard Frank Mosher gave his collection of short stories (it spawned an acclaimed locally produced movie in 1994) in honor of a region known for its backwater quirks.

Only one in 10 Vermonters lives in the remote Northeast Kingdom, but it boasts 35,575 acres (14,400 hectares) of public lakes and ponds and almost 4,000 miles (6,400 km) of public rivers and streams.

BELOW: beach scene, Lake Willoughby.

The **Cabot Creamery Co-operative** in **Cabot** , founded in 1919, draws on some 500 member farms for the milk that goes into its award-winning cheddar cheese. The factory tours include cheese tastings (2870 Main Street; tel: 800-837 4261; open Jun–Oct, daily; Nov–May, Mon–Sat; cheese isn't made every day).

St Johnsbury

Vintage view of St Johnsbury Athenaeum.

The city of **St Johnsbury** ❸, the largest community in northeastern Vermont, remains a vibrant pocket of Victorian charm. From the bank buildings downtown to the Fairbanks mansion on the Plains overlooking the valley, the stamp of architect Lambert Packard and his wealthy patrons is visible everywhere. Thaddeus Fairbanks started making the world's first platform scale here in the 1830s, and he and his sons were great civic benefactors.

The handsome, Second Empire **St Johnsbury Athenaeum** (1171 Main Street;tel: 802-748 8291; open Mon–Sat; Mon and Wed till 8pm) built in 1871–73, houses both the city library and an art gallery dominated by the huge skylit panorama *Domes of the Yosemite* by artist Albert Bierstadt. This is one of the oldest intact art collections in the country ("Welcome to the nineteenth century," reads a sign at the entrance) and one of the most inviting.

With more than 4,500 stuffed birds, mammals and reptiles, old toys, exotica from around the globe, local history displays, a children's activity room, and its own vintage planetarium, the Romanesque **Fairbanks Museum and Planetarium** is a temple to Victorian curiosity erected by the Fairbanks family in 1890 (Main and Prospect streets; tel: 802-748 2372; open Mon–Sat, Sun pm; planetarium shows July and Aug, daily; Sept–Jun, weekends at 1:30pm; entrance fee).

BELOW:
exhibit at the
Fairbanks Museum.

East out of downtown St. Johnsbury on Route 2, watch for the sign for Stephen Huneck's **Dog Mountain** (Spaulding Road), where the well-known artist has created a chapel to memorialize man's best departed friends (dogs, of course, are welcome).

About 10 miles (6 km) north of St Johnsbury, the still relatively undiscovered **Burke Mountain Ski Area** ❸ (tel: 802-626 3322; www.skiburke.com) in **East Burke** offers challenging trails for both skiing and mountain biking. Owned by Burke Academy, it has consistently turned out Olympians.

West and north of St. Johnsbury via routes 15 and 16, **Greensboro** ❸, on Caspian Lake, is a peaceful retreat long favored by writers, academics, and professionals: U.S. Supreme Court Chief Justice William Rehnquist summers here. Willey's Store – the heart of the tiny village – dispenses local information and carries an astounding inventory ranging from boots to Beaujolais to the *New York Times*.

A few miles to the north, **the Craftsburys** begin. There are actually three: East Craftsbury, Craftsbury, and the Shangri-La of Vermont villages, **Craftsbury Common** ❸, a tidy collection of beautifully preserved, 19th-century homes surrounding a town green on a ridge overlooking the valley. The area is a magnet for serious athletes – the Craftsbury Sports Center offers dormitory-style accommodations, family-style meals, and year-round instruction in a variety of sports, including sculling and mountain biking.

Back toward I-91, in **Glover** ❸ the **Bread and Puppet Theater Museum** (Route 122; tel: 802-525 3031; open Jun–Nov 1 daily 10am–6pm; donation) is home base for an amazing collection of huge and fantastical creatures created by German immigrant Peter Schumann in 1963 to illustrate the horrors of war and wonders of life. Occasional Sunday afternoon shows are put on in the meadow.

Further north, off I-91, is another village that feels that like time forgot. **Brownington** ❸, a thriving community in the early 1800s when the Boston–Montreal stage stopped here, is best known for its elegant old homes and the **Old Stone House Museum** (off Route 58; tel 802-754 2022; open mid May–mid-Oct, Wed–Sun 11am–5pm; entrance fee) a collection of local miscellenia housed in the former county grammar school, built in 1827–30 by "Uncle" Alexander Twilight. He was claimed by Middlebury College as America's first black college graduate, Class of 1823, and said to be the first black legislator in the nation.

Straddling the U.S.-Canadian border, 30-mile long (48-km) **Lake Memphremagog** snakes between steep wooded hills. **Newport,** ❸ the "Border City" at the southern end of the lake," is noted for its easy mingle of Canadian day-trippers, locals, and sports fishermen in search of trout and landlocked salmon. There are a couple of local boat rental agencies; be sure to obey border regulations if you cross into Canada, where the lakeside town of Magog is attractive.

About 20 miles (32 km) to the west, Route 242 climbs to the ski area of **Jay Peak** ❸ (tel: 802-988 2611 or 800-451 4449 out of area; www.jaypeakresort.com), where an aerial tramway transports skiers, foliage peepers and summer sightseers to its 3,861-ft (1,177-meter) summit. The resort also now has an 18-hole championship golf course. The views into Canada are magnificent, and the mountain receives Vermont's greatest snowfalls.

Maple syrup – one of Vermont's specialties.

BELOW: the Black River Valley near Craftsbury.

The northwestern corner

Vermont's northwestern corner is defined by the Canadian border and the jagged, picturesque shoreline of Lake Champlain. The Vermont "mainland" here is gently rolling dairy country, growing flatter and more open as it nears the border and the great alluvial plain of the St. Lawrence River. The big lake is bisected here by the Alburg peninsula descending from Quebec (the town of Alburg is connected to the rest of the U.S. only by a causeway) and by a 22-mile (35-km) skein of islands, likewise linked by bridges and causeways. This is where Samuel de Champlain first ventured out upon the waters that would bear his name; where Iroquois raiders canoed north via Lake Champlain's outlet, the Richelieu River, to terrorize early French settlements, and where bootleggers' speedboats barreled south to the thirsty speakeasies of Prohibition days. Such excitement is long past, and today's northwest corner is one of Vermont's most enticing watery playlands.

The **Lake Champlain Islands** are strewn with arcadian preserves, lakeshore drives and sleepy little towns. Several state parks, including **Sand Bar** (Route 2; Milton; tel: 802-893 2825; open Memorial Day–Labor Day; entrance fee) and **Alburg Dunes** (off Route 129, Alburg; tel: 802-796 4170; open Memorial Day–Labor Day; entrance fee) have fine sand swimming beaches. **South Hero**, roughly on the same latitude as Bordeaux, France, is home to **Snow Farm Vineyard** (190 West Shore Road; tel: 802-372 9463; tasting room and tours May–Oct; open year round) and hosts a free Thursday evening concert series during the summer. **North Hero** is the summer stomping ground for the **Royal Lipizzaner Stallions** (Knight Point State Park, Route 2; tel: 802-372 5683; performances in July–Aug, Thurs–Sun; entrance fee), descendants of

TIP

Lake Champlain offers great scope for cruises. From Burlington, a ferry plies from to Port Kent, NY, and there are scenic trips on the *Spirit of Ethan Allen II* (College Street, Burlington Boathouse, tel: 802-862 8300) and *Northern Lights* (King Street Dock, tel: 802-864 9669).

BELOW:
beach scene,
Lake Champlain.

Map on pages 244–5

horses bred in Austria in the 16th century. On **Isle La Motte** "the oldest coral reef in the world" was left behind 10,000 years ago, when the Atlantic covered the Champlain Valley. **St Anne's Shrine** (West Shore Road; tel: 802-928 3362; open mid-May–mid-Oct, daily) honors America's first French settlement (1664).

East on Route 78 in Swanton, more than 201 avian species, including ospreys and blue heron, have been identified at the 6,345-acre (2,568-hectare) **Missisquoi National Wildlife Refuge** (headquarters on Route 78: tel: 802-868 4781).

For many years **St Albans** ❹⓿, 10 miles (16 km) south on Route 7, was headquarters of the Central Vermont Railway, and its glory days are reflected in its fine town green, imposing brick buildings, and handsome Victorian homes. St Albans was the scene of the Civil War's most northerly skirmish: in 1864 a band of Confederates infiltrated the town, robbed the banks and hightailed it to Canada. There they were caught and brought to trial; however, their exploits were excused as "legitimate" acts of war. Each April, the town hosts the Maple Festival.

Kayaking on Lake Champlain.

Burlington and environs

"The most miserable of one-horse towns," complained the young wife of an Army recruiting officer stationed here in the 1840s. "Startling incidents never occur in Burlington. None ever occurred there, and none probably ever will." Things have livened up along "New England's West Coast" since then. By the Civil War, fiercely competitive steamboat lines and a busy lumber trade were turning **Burlington** ❹❶ into a plucky little inland port of entry. By 1900, the wharves were teeming with businessmen, seekers of pleasure and ships' crews.

Today, trendy restaurants and the lively Church Street Marketplace, a pedestrian mall have further improved Burlington's outlook. But the view remains the

BELOW: a fall gathering at Peacham.

same. From Battery Park or the Cliffs, the sunset over Lake Champlain and the Adirondacks is still – as novelist William Dean Howells maintained – "superior to the evening view over the Bay of Naples," and the old workaday waterfront has been reborn with a park, bike path, marina, and sailboat rentals.

A growing influx of industry – notably, IBM – and the new metropolitan tone mingle to make the core of Vermont's "Queen City" (population 40,000) a commercial and cultural nexus that keeps turning up on polls as being one of the US's "most livable cities." Thanks in part to the presence of the University of Vermont (called "UVM" for its Latin name, *Universitas Viridis Montis*, University of the Green Mountains), the city enjoys a year-round array of cultural events, including annual Mozart and Jazz festivals.

The **Flynn Center for the Performing Arts**, a 1930 Art Deco movie palace on Main Street, hosts an impressive line-up of dance, music and theater (153 Main Street; tel: 802-652-4500; www.flynncenter.org).

Most of the city's activity is concentrated between the UVM campus, and the bustling waterfront. Many of the buildings on and surrounding the campus are architectural gems. The university offers tours (tel: 802-656 3370 for a schedule). The school's **Robert Hull Fleming Museum** (61 Colchester Avenue; tel: 802-656 0750; open May–Labor Day Tues–Sun pm; Labor Day–April Tues–Fri 9am–4pm and Sat & Sun pm; closed mid-Dec–mid-Jan; entrance fee) displays European and American paintings, and includes works by painters of the Hudson River School as well as Sargent, Homer and Fragonard. **Church Street Marketplace,** in the heart of downtown, is a lively promenade lined with, galleries, shops and restaurants. At the waterfront, visitors can rent kayaks, sailboats, or skiffs at the **Community Boathouse** (tel: 877-964 4858); take a lake cruise *(see Travel Tips)*; hop aboard a ferry to New York, or take a stroll along the Burlington Recreation Path. The lakeside **ECHO at the Leahy Center** (1 College Street; 802-864 1848; www.echovermont.org; open daily 10am–5pm; call for off-season hours; entrance fee) uses hands-on exhibits to explore the history and ecology of the Lake Champlain region.

In nearby **Winooski**, **St Michael's Playhouse** (Allen Street, Route 15; tel: 802-654 2000), on the campus of Saint Michael's College, has been mounting professional summer theater performances since 1951. Just north of downtown Burlington, off Route 127, the **Ethan Allen Homestead** (tel: 802-865 4556; open mid-May–mid-Oct, daily; call for off-season hours; entrance fee), with its restored 1787 farmhouse, was the home of Vermont's Revolutionary hero. There's an excellent exhibit on the state's history and miles of walking trails along the Winooski River.

About 7 miles (11 km) south of the city on Route 7, at **Shelburne** ㊷, is the renowned **Shelburne Museum**. (tel: 802-985 3346; www.shelburnemuseum.org; open mid-May–late Oct, daily; late-Oct–mid-May but hours can vary, guided tour of selected buildings daily at 1 pm; entrance fee). Neither a "living museum" nor a fusty historical collection, it's a 45-acre (18-hectare) complex reflecting the tastes of one very passionate and well-funded collector. Electra Havemeyer Webb developed an eye for Americana and folk art long

Albert Bierstadt (1830–1902) was part of the Hudson River School of painters, the nation's first native school of painting. Its earliest leaders worked in the wilderness areas around the Hudson River north of New York, and in nearby New England.

BELOW: a haunting Hallowe'en at Burlington.

Map on pages 244–5

before anyone else was paying attention, and managed to amass 80,000 exemplary objects – 37 buildings full, plus some train cars, a carousel and a Lake Champlain side-wheeler, the *Ticonderoga*. It takes more than a casual stroll to do the collection justice; hence admission, though pricey, is good for two days.

Shelburne's other landmark is the Webbs' 100-room Queen Anne-style "cottage" (now an inn and restaurant) on the lake. Its surrounding estate was carved from 22 lakeside farms by Frederick Law Olmsted, designer of New York City's Central Park. This 1,400-acre (570-hectare) property, **Shelburne Farms,** is now a model ecological farmstead with an award-winning cheese-making facility, extensive grounds, and a children's farmyard. (off Route 7; tel: 802-985-8686; visitor center and grounds open year-round; guided tours daily mid-May–late Oct).

Charlotte ㊸, a few miles south of Shelburne, is home to the unusual **Vermont Wildflower Farm,** a 6-acre (2.5-hectare) preserve and learning center that offers delightful strolling (Route 7; tel: 802-425 3641; open Apr–Oct daily; entrance fee to gardens).

Middlebury, Morgans, and marble

Lake Champlain's maritime traditions are preserved just west of Vergennes at the **Lake Champlain Maritime Museum ㊹** near **Panton** (Basin Harbor Road; tel: 802-475 2022; www.lcmm.org; open May–mid-Oct, daily; entrance fee). The museum, which conserves artifacts brought up from the lake bottom, chronicles its military, mercantile and recreational history with hands-on exhibits, including a replica of the Revolutionary War gunboat *Philadelphia II*.

Vermont spawned the world-famous Morgan horse, a barrel-chested steed, which, as one celebrant boasted, "can outrun, outpull, and outlast any other

Vermont hero Ethan Allen (1738–89) and his Green Mountain Boys resisted the attempts of New York and New Hampshire to gain control of the region. With Benedict Arnold, he captured Fort Ticonderoga in 1775, but soon after was jailed by the British for three years. He died two years before Vermont became a state.

BELOW: The Inn at Shelburne Farms.

breed, just as you would expect a Vermont horse to do." The **UVM Morgan Horse Farm**, off Route 23 in the village of **Weybridge ㊺**, is a working farm with training demonstrations and tours (off Route 23; tel: 802-388 2011; open May–Oct daily; entrance fee).

Middlebury ㊻, just southeast of Weybridge or directly down Route 7 for 13 miles (21 km) from Vergennes, is the ideal college town, a verdant campus of grand, well-spaced 19th-century buildings, accompanied by a lively community of shops and restaurants. The traditional arts of Vermont are highlighted at the **Vermont Folklife Center** (3 Court Square; tel: 802-388 4964; gallery open Tues–Sat). A superb collection of 19th-century Vermontiana is housed in the **Henry Sheldon Museum of Vermont History** (1 Park Street; tel: 802-388 2117; open May–Oct Mon–Sat, Sun pm; Nov–Apr Tues–Sat; entrance fee). The **Vermont State Craft Center at Frog Hollow** (1 Mill St., tel: 802-388 3177; open Mon–Sat; Sun pm) showcases and sells work by Vermont artisans *(see box, page 257)*.

In search of Robert Frost

The poet Robert Frost spent his summers writing in a log cabin seven miles (11 km) east in **Ripton ㊼**, in the northern section of the 300,000-acre (120,000-hectare) **Green Mountain National Forest.** The cabin is not far from Bread Loaf Mountain, home of the prestigious **Bread Loaf Writers' Conference**. The mile-long **Robert Frost Interpretive Trail**, beginning at his home, the Homer Noble Farm, leads to the Bread Loaf campus by way of the cabin, which has been left untouched. For great scenery, continue on State 125, through steep Middlebury Gap; you can return to Route 7 by following Route 100 for 6 miles (10 km) south and heading back west on equally scenic Route 73 through Brandon Gap.

BELOW:
Vermont Marble
Exhibit, Proctor.

About 30 miles (50 km) south, just off Routes 7 and 3, the town of **Proctor** ➍ ("Marble Center of the World") is the logical spot for the **Vermont Marble Exhibit** (52 Main Street; tel: 80-427 1396; open mid-May–Oct daily; entrance fee to exhibit). It offers a glimpse into the workings of the Vermont Marble Company factory, which flourished here for more than 100 years. There are marble samples from around the world, including the local product.

The region west of Vermont's second biggest city, Rutland, was a popular summer spot in the Victorian era, but faded after World War II, when the trains stopped coming. But wandering the back roads that link towns such as Middletown Springs, Fair Haven, and the tiny agricultural hamlets near Lake Champlain can be rewarding; there's a scattering of comfortable B&Bs; also fishing and swimming at state parks alongside lakes Bomoseen and St Catherine.

Off Route 3, a doctor built a home for his wife, an English noblewoman, in 1888. **Wilson Castle** (West Road; tel: 802-773 3284; open late May–late Oct daily; entrance fee) is an opulent stone mansion with 32 rooms, 12 fireplaces and such elegant appointments as a Louis XVI crown jewel case. The castle and its manicured walkways covering 115 acres (46 hectares) are open for tours.

Rutland ➎, a one-time thriving industrial city, is struggling hard to revitalize its downtown, and, by many accounts, is winning the battle. It's an amalgam of period architecture, ranging from palatial Victorian homes to an Art Deco mini-skyscraper to 1960s-era shopping malls.

Manchester – Vermont's original resort town

Franklin Orvis gave the local tourist industry a boost in 1849 when he began taking in summer guests at his father's house, located next to the famed 1769

A wide variety of food is the main attraction each July at the one-day Rutland Region Ethnic Festival. Various cultural events are also laid on.

BELOW: spring colors near Rutland.

Marsh Tavern in **Manchester Village** ⑩, where Ethan Allen and his "Green Mountain Boys" had plotted the Tories' overthrow. The hotel kept expanding bit by bit until it grew into The Equinox, a grand resort hotel (with the adjacent Charles Orvis Inn) named for the mountain that presides over the town, and which can be reached 4 miles (6.5 km) south of town via the 5-mile (8-km) **Skyline Drive** toll road (Route 7A; tel: 802-362 1114; open 9am–dusk May 1– October 31, weather permitting).

Vintage sports cars such as Bugattis and Bentleys stage the **Mount Equinox Annual Hill Climb** here each June.

Meanwhile, Frank's younger brother, Charles, had a clever idea, too – why not teach the leisured class to catch their supper along the banks of the abundant Battenkill River? Less than 10 years after he sold his first bamboo fly rod, Manchester had become the place to get away from it all.

By the mid-20th century, the Equinox had deteriorated into white elephanthood, but in the early 1980s it was restored to showplace luster, along with its 18-hole golf course. And the **Orvis Company**, with its core emphasis on fly fishing equipment and schools, has grown into an outdoor-lifestyle powerhouse: today it operates a thriving mail-order business, and in 2002 opened its new, $7 million, 23,000-sq.-ft (2,100 sq.-meter) retail store billed as "Vermont's largest retail attraction."

The **American Museum of Fly Fishing** (Route 7A; tel: 802-362 3300; www.amff.com; open daily 10am–4pm; entrance fee) has also moved into a new space next door.

All this brisk commerce notwithstanding, Manchester Village remains as tranquil and elegant as ever, with its marble-slab sidewalks and showy summer homes, many of them creatively converted into inns and restaurants.

Orvis's success inspired a raft of other upscale companies such as Ralph Lauren, Brooks Brothers, Joan & David, and Giorgio Armani, to open outlets in nearby **Manchester Center**, turning that one-time quaint town into a wall-to-wall shopping mall.

Although Abraham Lincoln never made it to The Equinox (several other presidents did), Mary Lincoln and son Robert *(see margin caption)* cherished fond memories of the mountains; they returned to build a 24-room estate near Manchester. **Historic Hildene** (Route 7A; tel: 802-362 1788; www.hildene.org; open Jun–Oct daily 9:30am–4:30pm; Nov–May Thurs–Mon 11am–3pm; grounds open daily; entrance fee), now opens its richly appointed Georgian Revival rooms to antiquity-lovers and its 412-acre (167-hectare) grounds to cross-country skiers and summer strollers.

Another pleasant place to visit in town is the **Southern Vermont Art Center** (West Road; ; tel: 802-362 1405; open year-round, Tues–Sat; Sun pm; entrance fee), with contemporary indoor exhibits, outdoor sculptures, and a well-marked botany trail.

The picturesque, marble-paved village of **Dorset** ⑪, approximately 8 miles (13 km) northwest of Manchester, is home to the Dorset Playhouse (tel: 802-867 5777; performances mid-June–Oct), a rustic barn that served as Vermont's first summer playhouse.

Robert Todd Lincoln (1843–1926) was 21 when his father, Abraham Lincoln, was assassinated. A lawyer, he ran the Pullman Palace Car Company, conducting business from Hildene, his stately home in Vermont, in summer and from Washington, D.C. in winter. In Vermont, he also pursued his hobbies of astronomy and golf.

BELOW:
Manchester Village.

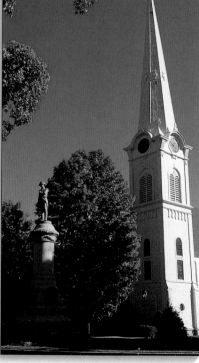

Just 6 miles (10 km) east of Manchester on Route 11, the downhill ski area at **Bromley Mountain** (tel: 802-824 5522; www.bromley.com; open weekends Memorial Day–Columbus Day; daily mid-June–Labor Day) becomes the Thrill Zone in the warmer months, with DévilKarts, a water ride, America's longest alpine slide, and a host of other activities.

One of Vermont's other venerable playhouses is about 15 miles (24 km) east of Bromley via routes 11 and 100, in the hill village of **Weston** . Weston Playhouse (tel: 802-824 5288; open late June–Labor Day, Tues–Sun evening with Wed and Sat matinees; admission fee), the oldest professional theater in Vermont, has been in operation for over 65 years. The town has also been home to the **Vermont Country Store** (tel: 802-824 3184; open daily) a purveyor of cracker-barrel atmosphere and useful (and arcane) merchandise since 1946.

Arlington

Nine miles (14 km) south of Manchester on Historic Route 7A, **Arlington** is a former Revolutionary capital and one-time home to America's most beloved illustrator. The **Norman Rockwell Exhibition** (3772 Main Street, Route 7A; tel: 802-375 6423; open May–Oct, daily) displays a large number of *Saturday Evening Post* covers and lesser-known prints, in which local uncles and grandmas figure largely. Works and papers by Rockwell and local author Dorothy Canfield Fisher are in the **Dr. George A. Russell Collection of Vermontiana** (tel: 802-375 6307; open Tues and by appointment), behind the town's Martha Canfield Public Library on Main Street.

It was in a circa 1769 stone house on Main Street in **Shaftsbury** that the poet Frost wrote his poems "Stopping by Woods on a Snowy Evening",

Map on page 244–5

Norman Rockwell (1894–1978), born in New York City, lived on a farm in Arlington from 1939 until 1953. Although best known for his sentimental "Saturday Evening Post" illustrations, he tackled everything from mail order catalogues to presidential portraits.

LEFT: a Weston-based family business that embraced mail order and the internet.

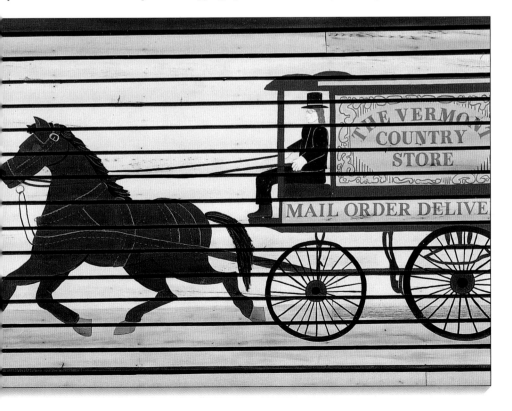

Map on page 244–5

Bennington Monument, erected in 1887–91.

BELOW:
Old First Church, Bennington.
RIGHT:
pre-Revolutionary gravestone.

and "New Hampshire," which concluded, "At present I am living in Vermont." His home is now the **Robert Frost Stone House Museum** (tel: 802-447 6200; open May–Dec, Tues–Sun; entrance fee), with exhibits about the poet on one floor, and an art gallery on another.

Just south on Route 7, **Bennington 56** is home to Bennington College, a progressive liberal arts institution occupying a bucolic campus on the outskirts of town. The town looms large in Vermont's history: the 1777 skirmish commemorated at the 306-ft-high (93-meter) **Bennington Battle Monument** (15 Monument Circle; tel: 802-447 0550; open mid-Apr–Oct, daily; entrance fee) actually took place a few miles to the west in New York State, where General John Stark and 1,800 ragtag troops forced the Redcoats back across the Walloomsac River. However, it was a colonial supply dump on this site that General John Burgoyne was after, and his failure to attain it proved a turning point in the entire British campaign.

The monument is in a section of town called **Old Bennington**, which is also the location for the **Bennington Museum** (West Main Street, Route 9; tel: 802-447 1571; open Thurs–Tues; entrance fee), exhibiting an exceptional collection of regional history and art, including the largest public collection of works by Grandma Moses. The self-taught painter's endearing primitives of rural life are exhibited in the schoolhouse she attended as a child in Eagle Bridge, New York.

Also in the National Historic District are the 1805–06 **Old First Church** (tel: 802-447 1223; open Mon–Sat; Sun pm; donations), with its unusual three-tiered steeple, and next to it, the **Old Burying Ground**, final resting place of five Vermont governors and Robert Frost, whose epitaph reads simply, "I had a lover's quarrel with the world." ❏

Ski Fever

Scandinavian immigrants introduced skiing in New Hampshire's logging camps in the 1870s. The Norwegian-speaking Nansen Ski Club was founded in Norway Village near Berlin about 1872; with six other clubs it founded the US Eastern Amateur Ski Association in 1922, and survives to this day.

Ski fever spread to the college circuit after Dartmouth's Outing Club was founded in 1909. Just five years later, Dartmouth college librarian Nathaniel Goodrich was the first to descend Vermont's highest peak, Mount Mansfield in Stowe. The sport was essentially confined to "touring" (comparable to today's cross-country), jumping off wooden chutes and the odd foray into the woods. In 1926 Appalachian Mountain Club hutmaster Joe Dodge was the first to hurtle down Mount Washington's Tuckerman Ravine.

By then, skiing was well on its way to popularity. In 1929, fresh from a Switzerland ski trip, Katharine Peckett opened the country's first organized ski school at her family's resort in Sugar Hill, New Hampshire. Soon, the Boston and Maine Railroad began running ski trains to New Hampshire. Then, in 1934, New England's first rope tow was constructed at Gilbert's Hill, in Woodstock, Vermont.

The sport was dormant during the gas-rationing of the early 1940s, but area after area sprouted up in the late '40s and '50s, among them Vermont's Mount Snow (tel: 800-245 7669), Smuggler's Notch (tel: 800-451-8752), Stratton (tel: 800-787 2886), Sugarbush (tel: 800-537 8427) and Killington (tel: 877-458 4637). For current slope conditions, call for an around-the-clock snow report (tel: 802-229 0531). The Vermont Ski Museum (Main Street, Stowe; tel: 802-253 9911) documents the state's alpine history with vintage equipment, old movies, and the Ski Hall of Fame.

It was at Killington, in the mid-'60s, that the Graduated Length Method was introduced, easing the way for the general public to approach this often intimidating sport: tyros could start on short skis, gradually increasing the length as their prowess improved.

Just to keep the challenge fresh, though, a Stratton bartender came up with an innovation in the mid '60s that has changed the landscape of skiing. Jake Burton Carpenter started experimenting secretly at night with ways to improve the "Snurfer" (as an early ancestor of the snowboarder was called). It would take years, but his Vermont-based Burton snowboard company would become a leader in the field and create a whole new skiing subculture. Today, more than one in four ticket-buyers at most resorts is a snowboarder.

Today, Maine's big downhill resorts are Sugarloaf/USA (tel: 800-843 5623) in the Carrabassett Valley and Sunday River (tel: 207-824 3000) in Bethel. Sugarloaf has 43 miles (69 km) of trails and a vertical drop of 2,820 ft (860 meters); Sunday River has 121 trails. Snowmaking is excellent at both. There are almost 20 mountains developed for skiing in New Hampshire, but the two biggies are Loon Mountain, Lincoln (tel: 800-229 5666) and Waterville Valley (tel: 800-468 2553). "Skiophiles" will want to check out the New England Ski Museum, Franconia, NH (tel: 603-823 7177), for a full regional history. ❑

RIGHT: there are resorts to suit all abilities.

NEW HAMPSHIRE

This solidly conservative state serves outdoor pleasures on a platter – by way of the dramatic and rugged White Mountains and dozens of deep lakes

Map on pages 244–5

J ust when you are about to conclude that even New England is inching towards homogenization, you come up against New Hampshire. New Hampshire is the contrarian in a contrary region, the state that has to do things just a little bit differently. It's the only state in New England that won't hear of a sales or income tax. It regularly bucks the region by voting Republican in presidential elections. And it defies any state to hold its quadrennial party primaries so much as a day before its own.

In a region famous for its reserved neighborliness, New Hampshire often stands out in stark contrast to Vermont, though they lie across the Connecticut River from each other. Vermont often seems to wring its hands over its state liquor sales and its lottery; New Hampshire was first in the nation with a state lottery, and runs liquor stores the size of Wal-Marts right on its interstate highways. And, yes, there are billboards in New Hampshire – not enough to spoil the view, but enough to let Vermont types know that business doesn't need too many regulations.

What made New Hampshire different? For one thing, it has a seacoast – all 16 miles (26 km) of it. That was just enough to get colonization started much earlier, and launch an aristocratic merchant class in Portsmouth. Later, it used water power to develop a concentration of industry, at Manchester, far beyond anything dreamed of in Vermont. It had bigger lumber interests, bigger railroads, and Boston money closer at hand to finance it all. And it had – still has – the *Manchester Union Leader*, perhaps the most consistently arch-conservative newspaper in America.

PRECEDING PAGES: Franconia Notch, in the White Mountains. **LEFT:** by rail in the White Mountains. **BELOW:** snowgiant in Hanover.

A hard-won land

Like the rest of New England, New Hampshire had little to offer in the way of good soil and easy farming. The main assets of the region at the beginning of the colonial period were the deepwater port and surrounding shores of what is now Portsmouth; and the tall, straight pines, which became highly prized in the construction of ships. Fisheries established along the coast prospered from the sale of salt cod and other catches, hauled from the Atlantic as far north as the Grand Banks off Newfoundland.

The impetus behind these first forays was provided by Sir Ferdinando Gorges, head of the council established by King James to govern all of New England, and Captain John Mason, an early governor of Newfoundland. They obtained grants to an ill-defined territory lining the coast from the Naumkeag to the Sagadahock rivers and extending roughly 60 miles (100 km) inland. Gorges and Mason proposed a variety of commercial enterprises and promised healthy

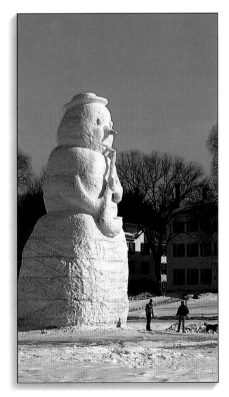

dividends to investors. The venture never really paid off. Lack of supplies limited the scheme's progress, the company eventually collapsed and the settlers simply divided the land up among themselves and proceeded to amass their own fortunes, without giving much thought to the niceties of property laws.

Settlement and Revolution

In New Hampshire it was the frontiersmen who drove the Revolution. While the merchants in coastal towns feared losing their lucrative trade with England, the frontiersmen were battle-hardened after having defended their land against the French and their Indian allies.

Strong-willed settlers, gradually pushing their way inland from Portsmouth and up the Connecticut River from the south, laid claim first to the lush valleys, then to the harsher hillsides and finally to the forbidding mountains in the north. The first man to lend the colony some cohesion was John Wentworth, a prosperous merchant appointed by the King in 1717 to govern the province of New Hampshire. Though hardly an altruist (his land grants always reserved a portion for himself, a token 500 acres/200 hectares), he did begin the process – later carried on in dynastic fashion by his son and nephew – of stabilizing the province, encouraging settlement and promoting commerce.

When the Revolution came, New Hampshire joined early in the fight – although alone of the 13 original colonies, it was spared the ravages of battle within its boundaries. Among its Revolutionary credits, New Hampshire was the first colony to assert its independence from England (establishing its own government on January 5, 1776) and the first to suggest the idea to the Continental Congress in Philadelphia (in 1775).

Following the Revolution, the people of New Hampshire went back to the task of coming to terms with their land. The push inland was by now extending up into the White Mountains, a New England "last frontier" where the logger's ax would always be more useful than the plow. Even early in the 19th

BELOW:
an old-fashioned toboggan ride.

century, though, the success of rough hostelries such as the one run by Ethan Allen Crawford in Crawford Notch pointed the way for the mountains' eventual economic path.

By the middle of that century, there were already two New Hampshires, with a buffer of small towns and farms between them: along the Merrimack River in the south, the textile mills of Manchester and Nashua were growing in output and economic power; theirs would be an urban New Hampshire, an extension of Lowell and Lawrence in Massachusetts. But up north, a far different economy was growing around a resource every bit as important as water power – mountain scenery.

The summer people

By the 1850s, "summer people" were a well-established industry. The retreats that drew them were modest at first, but as the railroads reached farther into the mountains, palatial resort hotels were built to serve clients who would arrive, servants and steamer trunks in tow, to spend a month or perhaps an entire summer season in the lap of luxury. Chairs rocked sedately on enormous wraparound verandahs, orchestras entertained at dinner, and mountain guides led tweed-suited parties along trails through the Presidential Range.

Although wonderful old arks such as the Balsams and Mount Washington remain in business, New Hampshire's tourism industry has been long since been transformed by automobile travel, shorter vacations, and a more energetic style of recreation that takes in downhill and cross-country skiing, snowboarding, backpacking, and mountain biking. And the White Mountains aren't the only draw – boaters and anglers have an array of rivers and lakes to choose

Map
on pages
244–5

Although largely forgotten, the Portsmouth-born Tom Bailey Aldrich (1836–1907) was a poet and writer of books portraying the idyllic childhood denied to so many by war. His immensely popular tales inspired his friend Mark Twain to invent Tom Sawyer and Huckleberry Finn.

BELOW: golf courses attract tourists.

*"Our liberty is
protected by four
boxes: the ballot box,
the jury box, the
soap box and the
cartridge box."*

BELOW: tugboats in
Portsmouth harbor.

from, crowned by huge Lake Winnepesaukee in the center of the state; plenty
of tidy villages and back roads lie well beyond the southeastern urban sprawl;
and there's even an 18-mile (28-km) coastline strewn with state parks. And
lovers of antiques and fine architecture can still enjoy the gracious world the
Wentworths and their contemporaries created in Portsmouth, near where New
Hampshire began. And remember, if you want to take one of those antiques
home: there still isn't any sales tax.

A sliver of seacoast: Portsmouth

Portsmouth ❺ stands at the mouth of the Piscataqua River. Graced with a
superb natural harbour, the town is the nation's third oldest English settlement
(after Plymouth and Jamestown). **Strawbery Banke** (the English settlers named
their 1623 colony for the profusion of wild strawberries that greeted them) is a
10-acre (4-hectare) living history museum that tells the story of the evolution of
the city's oldest neighborhood from 1650 to 1950. (Marcy Street; tel: 603-433
1100; www.strawberybanke.org; open for self-guided tours May–late Oct daily;
late Oct–Apr guided tours Sat & Sun 10am–2pm; 90-minute tours on the hour;
entrance fee). Restored and refurnished homes, ranging from humble to grand,
illustrate changes in architectural and living styles.

Several of the lesser abodes serve as workshops for artisans whose work harks
back to the past: open on a revolving schedule, there are studios for a cabinet-
maker, cooper, potter, and weaver. Here, also, one of the oldest boat shops in
America continues to produce dories, skiffs, and other vessels, employing archaic
copper clench nails. Strawbery Banke is literally an open-air museum: tours are
self-guided and open-ended, permitting visitors to proceed at their own pace.

Several other worthy historic manses are scattered about this enchanting, compact town. Among these is the 1763 **Moffatt-Ladd House** (54 Market Street; tel: 603-436 8221; open mid-June–mid-Oct, Mon–Sat; Sun pm; entrance fee), an imposing three-story mansion topped with a captain's walk and graced with terraced English-style gardens, a splendid carved staircase, a Gilbert Stuart portrait and choice examples of the 18th-century furniture Portsmouth was famous for.

Seek out, too, the 1716 **Warner House** (150 Daniel Street; tel: 603-436 5909; open mid-May–mid-Oct daily; entrance fee). America's first house to be registered as a National Historic Landmark back in 1962, it was the first of Portsmouth's many brick houses, and the stair hall is endowed with an intriguing array of early 18th-century murals. Rediscovered in 1852, they include depictions of Mohawk Indians and a British soldier on horseback.

Other houses of note include the 1614 **Jackson House** (143 Pleasant Street; tel: 603-436 3205; open June–mid-Oct, weekends; entrance fee), New Hampshire's oldest house; and the 1807 **Rundlet-May House** (364 Middle Street; tel: 603-436 3205; open June–mid Oct, Wed–Sun pm; entrance fee), the home of a wealthy textile merchant.

Also well worth a visit is the Port of Portsmouth **Albacore Museum and Park** (600 Market Street; tel: 603-436 3680; www.ussalbacore.org; open Memorial Day–Columbus Day daily; rest of year, Thurs–Mon; entrance fee). The *Albacore* is a grounded 1952 submarine, 205 ft (62 meters) long, which for two decades carried a crew of 55 in sardine-like quarters.

For a more pleasant experience on the water, consider a cruise to the **Isles of Shoals** ⑬, 6 miles (10 km) offshore; "barren piles of rock" charted in 1614 by Captain John Smith and long haunted by pirates and other nefarious outcasts.

Map on pages 244–5

TIP

Portsmouth's finest historic houses are linked by a popular 2½-mile (4-km) walking tour. A "Portsmouth Passport" gives reduced admission if you are visiting more than one.

BELOW: yesteryear's work and leisure at Strawbery Banke.

BELOW: the State
Capitol at Concord
with statue of John
Stark (1728–1822),
a brigadier-general
in the American
Revolution.

Improbably enough, an arts colony blossomed here at the turn of the 20th century, after poet Celia Thaxter, the daughter of an innkeeper, created a miraculous garden on Appledore which inspired no fewer than 400 paintings by the noted American Impressionist Childe Hassam.

Head out of town on Route 1B to the Portsmouth neighborhood of **New Castle**, a quaint fishing village settled in the late 1600s and home to **Fort Constitution State Historic Site** (tel: 603-436 1552). In 1774, the fort was raided by Portsmouth patriots for British guns and powder to use at the Battle of Bunker Hill.

Just off Route 1A, at 375 Little Harbor Road, is the rambling, 40-room **Wentworth-Coolidge Mansion Historic Site** (tel: 603-436 6607; open for guided tours Sat and Sun Memorial Day-Oct 15). Built between 1720 and 1760, it was the home of the state's first Royal Governor.

A few miles south on Route 1A in **Rye ❺**, **Odiorne Point State Park and Seacoast Science Center** (570 Ocean Boulevard; tel: 603-436 7406 for park and 603-436 8043 for Science Center; parking fee in summer months) has the remnants of a World War II fort, dunes, hiking trails, and a nature center (open late June–late Aug). There are several fine public beaches further to the south.

Five miles inland, just off Route 101, **Exeter ❻**, one of the state's earliest settlements, was founded in 1638. It's home to Phillips Exeter Academy, a prestigious college preparatory school whose alumni include Daniel Webster. The **American Independence Museum** documents the country's and town's experiences during the Revolutionary War (One Governors Lane; tel: 603-772 2622; Open May 31–Oct 28, Wed–Sat 10am–4pm; guided tours of the historic Ladd-Gilman House are offered; entrance fee).

The industrious Merrimack Valley

Driving north from Boston, the first site worth a detour off Interstate 93 (after it crosses the border into New Hampshire) may also be the oldest. **America's Stonehenge** in **North Salem ❻** (off Route 11 on Haverhill Road; tel: 603-893 8300; open daily; entrance fee), long known as "Mystery Hill," has purportedly been carbon-dated to about 2000 BC. Though considerably scaled down from its British namesake – its circle of standing stones measure only 3 ft (1 meter) tall – the site is thought to have served much the same purpose as Stonehenge: as a giant calendar tracing celestial movements. The identity of the builders and the purpose the site served remain matters of pure speculation. Indeed, your guess is as good as anyone's.

Further north on I-93 is **Manchester ❻**, which together with Nashua and several other New Hampshire cities, were centers of textile manufacturing, The massive, red-brick **Amoskeag Mills** was, in the early 20th century, the world's largest textile enterprise, employing 17,000 workers in 64 buildings that stretched for 1½ miles (2.5 km) along the Merrimack River. The **Manchester Historic Association** (headquarters at 129 Amherst Street; tel: 603-622 7531; www.manchesterhistoric.org; open Tues–Sat) has exhibits about the area's history, offers walking tours, and operates the **Millyard Museum** in Mill #3 (corner of Commercial & Pleasant Streets; open Tues–Sat; entrance

fee). The **See Science Center**, upstairs from the Museum (tel: 603-669 0400; open daily; entrance fee) offers a host of hands-on activities for toddlers to teens.

Amoskeag Fishways Visitor and Learning Center at Amoskeag Dam (6 Fletcher Street tel: 603-626-3474; open Mon–Sat; donation) has exhibits on the history of the river and falls. Between late April and early June, their fish ladder teems with fish making their way up stream. The mills attracted large numbers of French-Canadian immigrant workers, and comprehensive archives on French-speaking Canadians are held in the **Centre Franco-American** (52 Concord Street; tel: 603-669 4045; open Mon–Fri 9am–4pm, Sat by appointment).

The **Currier Gallery of Art** (201 Myrtle Way; tel: 603-669 6144; open Mon, Wed–Sun; Fri till 8pm; entrance fee) has fine collections of European and American paintings, New England decorative arts, and contemporary crafts; it also offers modern architecture buffs access to the **Zimmerman House**, a 1950 design by Frank Lloyd Wright. (The Currier is closed until late 2007 for refurbishment – check www.currier.org for details of Zimmerman House tours).

Some 15 miles (24 km) north of Manchester in **Concord ❸**, the capital of New Hampshire. The gold-domed 1819 **State House** (built of Concord granite by state prisoners) is fronted by statues of New Hampshire's political luminaries – Daniel Webster, Franklin Pierce, General John Stark and others – striking imperial poses in bronze. Its Hall of Flags contains 88 Civil War standards carried into battle (107 North Main Street; tel: 603-271 2154; open Mon–Fri).

The **Museum of New Hampshire History** houses the collections of the New Hampshire Historical Society, from furniture and folk art to tools and toys (Eagle Square off Main Street; tel: 603-228 6688; open Tues–Sat, Sun pm; July–mid–Oct and Dec, Mon–Sat, Sun pm; entrance fee). Among the highlights is an original

Map on pages 244–5

TIP

Located at 30 Park Street in Concord, the New Hampshire Historical Society's **Tuck Library** (open Tues–Sat 8:30am–4pm; tel: 603-856 0641; fee charged) is an invaluable resource for students of the state's history.

BELOW: covered bridges are found in most New England states.

COVERED BRIDGES

It is surmised that the covered bridges across waterways and railroads throughout New England were designed not to protect travelers from the region's brutal winters, but to safeguard the bridges' wooden supports. Other theories hypothesize that horses were more comfortable crossing covered spans than open ones where they could see the water. Although the bridges were covered, people were employed to shovel snow on to the surface since most winter travel was by sled.

Covered bridges were originally made of wood, with sides supported by triangular trestles; hardwood "tree nails" held it together. Today's renovated bridges often have metal roofs. The nation's longest covered bridge connects Cornish, NH., and Windsor, VT., and is a National Historic Civil Engineering Landmark. New Hampshire's oldest bridge, built 1829, connects Bath and Haverhill on Route 135 over the Ammonoosuc River.

New Hampshire's bridges have been more fortunate than Maine's in that 54 have survived fire, floods, ice, and modern traffic. (In Maine, only nine of 120 remain.) Most have been patiently repaired. Although many are open to traffic, most cannot take trucks and are only one-lane. For the official state highway map, tel: 1-(800) 386 4664.

Concord Coach, the 19th-century vehicle known as "the coach that won the West." Also worth a visit is the **League of New Hampshire Craftsmen** gallery at 205 North Main Street (New Hampshire was the first state officially to support its artisans, with the establishment of the New Hampshire Commission of Arts and Crafts in 1931), and the **Christa McAuliffe Planetarium** (3 Institute Drive, tel: 603-271 7827; www.starhop.com; open open Mon–Sat, Sun pm; first Fri of the month beginning at dusk they host Skywatch on the museum lawn; entrance fee; advance tickets recommended). This highly interactive museum is dedicated to the New Hampshire teacher who perished in the 1986 space shuttle *Challenger* disaster. It has one of the world's most advanced digital planetarium projection systems, capable of simulating space travel in three dimensions.

Head north on I-93 about 17 miles (27 km) to exit 18 and follow signs to **Canterbury Shaker Village** ❻ (Shaker Road ; tel: 603-783 9511; open May–Oct, daily; Apr, Nov, Dec, weekends; entrance fee), an eloquent testament to the ingenuity and gentle faith of the Shakers, one of the religious sects that sought asylum in the New World *(see pages 300–1)*. Guided tours of the grounds and 25 buildings provide a glimpse of the skill and faith of this remarkable community. Crafts on display (some reproductions of which are for sale) include basketry, tin-smithing, wood-working and "the sewing arts."

The Mount Monadnock region

Crowned by **Mount Monadnock** ❻, a rocky 3,165-ft (968-meter) peak whose 360° views attract record numbers of climbers (the ascent is surpassed in popularity only by Mount Fuji), this is a region of meandering back roads past prim white churches, innumerable antique stores, and historic inns. Trails to

Climbers of Mount Monadnock have included thinkers such as Ralph Waldo Emerson and Henry David Thoreau. Today, 125,000 hikers a year follow in their footsteps, attracted by the spectacular views and at least a dozen accessible trails.

BELOW: Canterbury Shaker Village.

the peak begin at **Monadnock State Park** (Visitor Center, off Route 12, Jaffrey Center; tel: 603-532 8862; entrance fee).

The small town of **Rindge** hosts the 2,000-seat **Cathedral of the Pines** ⑥⑥, an open-air war memorial chapel with a set of Norman Rockwell bas-reliefs (Prescott Road; tel: 603-899 3300; open daily May–Oct; July & Aug Tues– Thurs, outdoor meditations at 11am and 3:30pm; Sunday ecumenical service at 10am). It began when the Sloane family planned a small chapel to their son, a bomber pilot killed in action in Germany in 1944, and later became an interdenominational place of worship and a national memorial. Every President since Harry Truman sent a stone to built the altar, which is backed by a view of Mount Monadnock.

To the east on Route 123, in the former mill town of **New Ipswich** ⑥⑦, **Forest Hall (the Barrett House)** (Main Street; tel: 860-928 4074 or 603-878 2517; open Jun–Oct on first Sat of month; tours on the hour 11am–4pm) is an elegant Federal-style building, erected in 1800 as a wedding present to Charles Barrett from his father. The terraced grounds rise to a Gothic Revival summerhouse.

North on Route 123 in **Sharon** ⑥⑧, the **Sharon Arts Center** (tel: 603-924 7256) exhibits and sells works of regional and international artists. The Center also has a fine art gallery at 30 Grove St. in Peterboro (tel: 603-924 7676).

At the junction of Routes 123 and 101, turn right (east) to Route 45 and follow signs to visit **Frye's Measure Mill** in **Wilton** ⑥⑨, one of the country's few remaining water-powered mills and its only active measure mill (since 1858, Frye's has been making boxes designed for accurate measurement of quantities of items such as nails). There's a fine folk art shop here (12 Frye Road; tel: 603-654 6581; open Tues-Sat, Sun pm in summer; Thurs-Sat, Sun pm in winter). On Sat at 2pm from June-Oct a one-and-a-half hour tour of the mill is con-

Backroad scene.

BELOW:
Mount Monadnock.

ducted by Harland Savage, former Measure Mill owner and master box maker (fee; reservations recommended).

At the junction of Route 123, turn left (west) onto Route 101 to the handsome town of **Peterborough** , home to the McDowell Colony, the country's most prestigious artists' retreat. The village inspired *Our Town,* Thornton Wilder's 1938 Pulitzer Prize-winning play *(see margin note).* Stop at the **Chamber of Commerce** (junction Routes 101/202; tel: 603-924 7234) for a copy of *A Walking Tour of Peterborough*, which includes the town's numerous historic sites and buildings. The **Peterborough Historical Society** exhibits intriguing relics and photographs, as well as two mill houses and an early general store (19 Grove Street; tel: 603-924 3235; open pm only weekdays; entrance fee).

Head west on Route 101 for 6 miles (10 km) to **Dublin**, home of *Yankee Magazine* and the *Old Farmer's Almanac*, America's oldest continuously published periodical. Turn right at the flagpole in the center of town to the National Historic Landmark village of **Harrisville**, one of New Hampshire's best-preserved 19th-century mill towns. A self-guided tour of its beautifully proportioned brick buildings (one is now a renowned weaving center) is worth taking.

Twelve miles (20 km) to the west, **Keene** was a thriving mill town at the turn of the 19th century. Today it is primarily a market center: the restored **Colony Mill Marketplace** houses several multi-dealer antique shops, stores, and restaurants. Keene claims to have America's widest Main Street.

Along the Connecticut River valley

In **Charlestown**, about 22 miles (35 km) northwest of Keene, the **Fort at Number 4 Living History Museum** (Route 11 West; tel: 603-826 7751; open Jun–Oct daily 10am–4:30pm; entrance fee) recreates a 1740s settlement which, in its day, was the northernmost frontier of New England colonization. Within its stockade, interpreters demonstrate such crafts as candle-dipping, weaving, and the molding of musket balls and, at certain dates, re-enact skirmishes.

Some 10 miles (16 km) farther north on Route 12A in **Cornish**, the **Cornish-Windsor bridge** on the Connecticut River connects New Hampshire to Vermont and is the world's longest two-span covered bridge.

The town was a thriving artists' colony at the turn of the 20th century, and one of the most prominent to put down roots here was Augustus Saint-Gaudens, the celebrated classical sculptor whose works included *Standing Lincoln*. Today, his home, gardens and studios are the **Saint-Gaudens National Historic Site** (off Route 12A; tel: 603-675 2175; open late May–Oct, daily; entrance fee).

In West Lebanon, jog east on Routes 4 and 10 to **Enfield** and the **Enfield Shaker Museum** (24 Caleb Dyer Lane; tel: 603-632-4346; open Fri and Sat, Sun pm; entrance fee) which preserves the settlement that thrived here from 1793 to 1923 *(see page 300).* The "Great Stone Dwelling" is now The Shaker Inn; the deconsecrated chapel next to it, with its 26-rank pipe organ, is a jewel (recitals are held Sundays at 4:30 pm in July and August).

Another 5 miles (8 km) north along the river is

BELOW: near the summit of Mount Monadnock.

Hanover , home of Ivy League **Dartmouth College** (www.dartmouth.edu). Dartmouth was founded in 1769, primarily for "the education and instruction of youth of the Indian tribes in this land." The college retains much of its colonial appearance while accommodating such modern touches as the **Hood Museum of Art** (tel: 603-646 2808; open Tues–Sat; Wed until 9pm; Sun pm), whose collections run from Assyrian relief to Revere silver to Winslow Homer, and the **Hopkins Center**, with an impressive performing arts roster (Wheelock Street; tel: 603-6546 2422).

Baker-Barry Library (on the Green; tel: 603-646 2560; open daily) houses an impressive collection of rare volumes as well as a series of murals by Mexican artist Jose Orozco.

Across the river in Norwich (Vermont), the wonderful **Montshire Museum of Science** – a hit with children – addresses the whys of natural processes to all ages (Montshire Road; tel: 802-649 2200; open daily; entrance fee).

Fifteen miles (24 km) north on Route 10 in **Orford** ⑰ a string of seven mansions built between 1773 and 1889 stretch along "The Ridge" in one of the state's loveliest towns.

The Lakes Region

New Hampshire's "Lakes Region" straddles the state's central section and boasts dozens of inviting lakes and ponds. One of the prettiest, **Lake Sunapee** in Newbury has been a summer resort since the late 1800s. **Mount Sunapee Resort** (Route 103; tel: 603-763 2356; fee for lifts) includes the ski area, with a chairlift open year round; from the summit, a short trail makes the most of the views across to Mount Washington and other points some 75 miles (135 km) distant.

Map on pages 244–5

Famous alumni of Dartmouth College include Daniel Webster (1801), Theodor "Dr Seuss" Geisel (1925), Vice-President Nelson Rockefeller (1930) and writer Louise Erdrich (1976).

BELOW: Dartmouth Hall, Dartmouth College, Hanover.

If you take the 10am cruise on the *Mount Washington* from Weirs Beach, you can stop off at one of the other lakeside towns for lunch and shopping and return by a later cruise. The vessel operates from early May through the end of October.

BELOW: the Baptist Meeting House Cemetery, Center Sandwich.

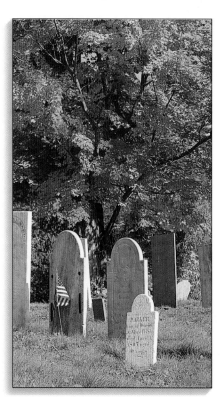

The League of New Hampshire Craftsmen *(see below)* holds its August fair at the base of the lift. There's a fine, sandy beach in **Newport** ⓦ at **Sunapee State Park Beach** (Route 103; tel: 603-271 3628; entrance fee in season)**.**

To the northeast, **Lake Winnipesaukee** ⓦ sprawls in convoluted splendor with 183 miles (294 km) of shoreline and 274 islands. According to legend, Winnipesaukee means "the smile of the Great Spirit," the name given to it by Chief Wonotan on the occasion of his daughter's marriage to a young chief from a hostile tribe. Wonotan regarded the overcast sky on their wedding day as a bad omen but, just as the two lovers were departing, the sun broke through the clouds and sparkled over the lake.

A number of towns dot the shoreline, offering various tourist attractions and services. On the western shore, **Weirs Beach** ⓧ (named for the weirs, or fishnets, which Indians once stretched across a narrow channel there) brings a touch of Atlantic City to Winnipesaukee's western shore, with its boardwalk, arcade, marina, and elaborate miniature golf links.

Other attractions include two water-slide parks and 2-hour or 2½-hour cruises on the **M/S *Mount Washington*** (tel: 888-843 6686 or, in NH 603-366 5531; www.cruise-nh.com; *see margin tip*).

The *Mount Washington* cruises across the lake to **Wolfeboro** ⓧ, on the eastern shore, the oldest summer colony in the nation. In 1769, John Wentworth, the last of New Hampshire's colonial governors, built a summer home here, and comfortable old money has been following his example ever since; a stroll around reveals a wealth of architectural styles, including Georgian, Federal, Greek Revival, and Second Empire.

The **Wolfeboro Historical Society** (233 South Main Street; tel: 603-569 4997; open July–Aug Wed–Sat; by appointment in spring and fall) maintains several historic buildings. The state's rich boating history is preserved at the **New Hampshire Antique and Classic Boat Museum** (395 Center Street; tel: 603-569 4554; open Memorial Day weekend–Columbus Day weekend, Mon–Sat; Sun pm; entrance fee).

Looking down over the lake from the north near **Moultonboro**, the **Castle in the Clouds** ⓧ (off Route 171; tel: 800-729 2468; www.castleintheclouds.org; open through mid-Oct; entrance fee) stands as an imposing monument to one man's rather megalomaniacal vision of a tranquil idyll. Built in an inventive amalgam of styles by eccentric millionaire Thomas Gustave Plant, this 1910 mansion is set in a 5,200-acre (2,100-hectare) estate with waterfalls, ponds, streams, miles of forest trails, and magnificent views out over the surrounding countryside.

A few miles to the north on Route 109 is the early 19th-century village of **Center Sandwich** ⓧ, where the **League of New Hampshire Craftsmen** (32 Main Street; tel: 603-284 6831; open May–Oct) first opened its doors in 1926 as a sales venue for the state's craftspeople.

The 1981 movie *On Golden Pond* with Katherine Hepburn and Henry Fonda was filmed on **Squam Lake**, famed for its loons. Several companies offer boat tours *(see Travel Tips)*. A few miles southwest in **Holderness** exhibits at the 200-acre (80-hectare) **Squam Lakes Natural Science Center ☷**, (Route 113; tel: 603-968 7194; open May–Nov 1, daily; entrance fee) include a nature preserve for injured animals unable to survive in the wild.

The White Mountains

Continuing north, travelers now begin their ascent into the **White Mountain National Forest**, a vast tract of almost 800,000 acres (320,000 hectares) encompassing the Franconia Range, clustered along an east-to-west axis (and dipping into Maine for a bit), and the Presidentials, running northeast and culminating in New England's tallest peak, Mount Washington. Long a forbidding wilderness, the White Mountains have evolved into an enormously popular tourist region, equally popular with hikers and motorists (particularly at foliage time).

Most of the tourist infrastructure is contained – by law and convenience – in pockets along the major highways. All the rest is reserved (and preserved) for backwoods purists.

A typical trail will lead from a parking lot along the highway directly into the forest, over gradually inclining terrain, maybe taking in a viewpoint or waterfall. Trails are well marked, with color-coded blazes cut into tree trunks at regular intervals, so there's little risk of taking a wrong turn. Eventually, towering trees give way to twisted dwarf pines and lichen-encrusted boulders. Above the tree line are the summits, from which adventurers may savor that peculiar sense of accomplishment that comes from finding oneself on top of the world.

Most of these peaks are not, for all their massive beauty, too demanding. Many summits can be reached with an hour or so of fairly leisurely walking.

Map on pages 244–5

TIP

The best time to see the blaze of color as the leaves turn in New Hampshire is during the first week of October in the northern part of the state and about a week later in the southern part. For the latest foliage report, tel: 1-800-258 3608. *See also page 299.*

BELOW: cycling in the White Mountains.

Flights over Lake Winnipesaukee.

One of the most rewarding excursions (in terms of view obtained relative to energy expended) is the short (45-minute) romp up **Mount Willard**, along an old bridle path. Those reaching the summit are rewarded with a magnificent panorama of **Crawford Notch** – particularly splendid at sunrise.

There are too many trails – some 1,200 miles (1,900 km) all told – to attempt even a partial description here; the White Mountain National Forest offices (various locations in the area; mail address: 719 North Main Street, Laconia 03246; tel: 603-528 8721; www.fs.fed.us/r9/white) and the Appalachian Mountain Club (headquarters at 5 Joy Street, Boston, Massachusetts 02108; tel: 617-523 0655; www.outdoors.org) at Pinkham Notch can provide further information. The AMC also maintains a network of "huts" (some are fairly large) offering bunk lodgings and hearty meals; it's advisable to reserve well ahead (tel: 603-466 2727). The AMC's White Mountain Guide is the "walker's bible."

Across the "Kanc" and through Franconia Notch

Alternatively, you can just enjoy the scenery from the car. One of the most rewarding routes begins in **Conway** ❸, best known as the southern end of a stretch of shopping outlets *(see page 153)* that extends 5 miles (8 km) to the bustling tourist town of **North Conway** ❻, home to the **Conway Scenic Railroad** (tel: 800-232 5251; open weekends late Apr–mid May, Nov & Dec; daily mid-May–late Oct; entrance fee), which offers excursions through Crawford Notch and the countryside aboard vintage coaches.

Conway is the eastern terminus for the 34½-mile (55-km) **Kancamagus Highway** ❼ (Route 112). The "Kanc" winds alongside the Pemigewasset and Swift rivers to Lincoln, passing numerous trailheads offering anything from short

BELOW: in the White Mountains.

Map on pages 244–5

strolls through the forest to major upland hikes. Seek out especially the signed overlooks at the western end (notably Kancamagus, Pemi and Hancock); views are at their best when the fall foliage reaches its most brilliant phase, but then you may find the traffic bumper to bumper (if you do take the drive in the fall, start early in the morning). Worthwhile short walks include the Champney Falls Trail and the Boulder Loop Trail, while pleasant roadside picnic areas are at Rocky Gorge and Sabbaday Falls.

Route 3/I-93 north from **Lincoln** winds for 8 miles (km) through **Franconia Notch State Park** ❸ (tel: 603-745 8391), between Kinsman and Franconia mountain ranges. Among the highlights en route: **The Flume** (open early May–late Oct, entrance fee to flume), an 800-ft (240-meter) gorge with granite walls attaining 90 ft (27 meters) and ending at a waterfall. It was reportedly discovered in 1803 by 93-year-old Aunt Jess Guernsey, who happened upon it while out fishing. Unfortunately, it's no longer quite as she found it – viewing platforms have been added to accommodate the busloads of sightseers – but some hint of the awe this natural wonder must have inspired remains. Off the main path is the Pool, another fine waterfall. In winter the wooden walkways are dismantled as the ice forms a massive layer.

Northward, pull into the parking lot at Profile Lake to read a plaque telling of the sad demise of the **Old Man of the Mountains**, which loomed just above the lake. Noteworthy not so much for its size – it measured 40 ft (12 meters) from top to bottom – as for the fine detailing of its features, the Old Man generated a sense of reverence over the years. The jutting brow, regal nose, lips slightly pursed as if in meditation and sharp line of the bearded chin all conspired to produce not merely a likeness, but a real sense of character. As Nathaniel Hawthorne described it in his story *The Great Stone Face*: "all the features were noble, and the expression was at once grand and sweet, as if it were the glow of a vast, warm heart, that embraced all mankind in its affection, and had room for more."

Ten thousand years of freezing and thawing cycles finally proved too much for the Old Man, who had been held together for some time with cables and iron braces. On a spring morning in 2003, the entire formation slid down the mountainside and disappeared in a pile of rubble. The Old Man survives in memory, and on the New Hampshire quarter coin in a recently issued state series.

Directly to the north is **Cannon Mountain**, a ski area (named for a cannon-shaped rock perched on its ridge. An easy year-round means of ascent is offered by the **Aerial Tramway** (tel: 603-823 8800; open late May–mid-Oct daily; fee) leading to a short trail at the summit. At the base, the **New England Ski Museum** exhibits historical paraphernalia (such as hand-crafted wooden skis from the 19th century) and various audio-visual exhibits (tel: 603-823 7177; open Memorial Day–March daily 10am-5pm) *(see box, page 275)*.

Two classic villages await the visitor just past Franconia Notch. **Franconia** ❸ was home to poet Robert Frost in 1915–20; here he "farmed a little, taught a little and wrote a lot." Looking out towards his

TIP

North Conway's outlet shops are especially attractive because New Hampshire has no sales tax. Be warned that this commercial strip is prone to bottlenecks.

BELOW: the Old Man of the Mountains, which collapsed in 2003.

The Robert Frost mailbox.

BELOW: ice coats Mount Washington Observatory, said to have the world's worst weather.

favorite three New Hampshire mountains, the modest **Robert Frost Place** ("R. Frost" still marks the mailbox) preserves manuscripts and other assorted memorabilia and hosts readings by contemporary poets (off Route 16, Ridge Road; tel: 603-823 5510; open Memorial Day–July 1 weekends; July 2–Aug Wed–Mon pm; Sept–Columbus Day Wed–Mon pm; entrance fee).

Route 117 from Franconia winds to the upscale hill town of **Sugar Hill ⑩**, home to several elegant country inns and the **Sugar Hill Historical Museum** (Main Street; tel: 603-823 5336; open July–mid-Oct, pm; entrance fee).

Pinkham Notch and Mount Washington

Nathaniel Hawthorne (who played an important role in promoting and preserving the region) accurately pointed out that the White Mountains, and particularly the Presidential Range, are "majestic, and even awful, when contemplated in a proper mood, yet by their breadth of base and the long ridges which support them, give the idea of immense bulk rather than of towering height." **Mount Washington**, at 6,288 ft (1,197 meters), is high enough to qualify as the tallest summit north of the Carolinas and east of the Rockies, and its sheer bulk is impressive, at least from the bottom, but to really appreciate its height, one must tackle the peak.

There are three ways to "climb" Mount Washington: on foot, by car, or by train. The first two options are accessible from Pinkham Notch via Route 16 north, a scenic road which passes through **Glen ⑨**, past **Story Land,** a small-scale amusement park established in 1954 to cater for the 10-and-under set (for both attractions, tel: 603-383 4186; open daily Memorial Day–Columbus Day; entrance fee). Story Land's 20 rides include Crazy Barn, Tractor Ride, Whirling Whales and Cuckoo Clockenspiel ("what just may be the world's largest cuckoo clock").

A trail to the summit via Tuckerman Ravine, a large glacial cirque famous for its spectacular scenery and dangerous but thrilling spring skiing, begins at the Appalachian Mountain Club's **Pinkham Notch Visitors Center ⑫** (tel: 603-466 2727), which offers lodgings, workshops, and trail information (tel: 603-466 2727). Across the way, the gondola at **Wildcat Mountain Ski Area** whisks off-season visitors to the top of Wildcat (tel: 800-255 6439; four-passenger gondola operates Memorial Day–mid-June Sat & Sun; daily mid-June–mid-Oct; entrance fee).

The 8-mile (13-km) climb up the **Mount Washington Auto Road ⑬**, via endless switchbacks, can be hell on radiators, the return journey tough on the best of brakes (off Route 16; open mid-May–mid-Oct, weather permitting; daily in summer 7:30am–6pm; shorter hours in spring and fall; entrance fee; tel: 603-466 3988; www.mt-washington.com), but the views along the way and at the summit make the effort worthwhile (provided the summit isn't socked in by fog). For those who'd rather spare their vehicles the ordeal (and forgo the campy "This Car Climbed Mount Washington" bumper-sticker), a tour van departs from the base.

The summit bears several chilling markers commemorating those who, like 23-year-old Lizzie Bourne in September 1855, died of exposure only a few hun-

Map on page 204-5

dred yards from the top. The destination she sought, a rustic hotel called the Tip Top House, survives as a small museum; visitors can marvel at the cramped dormitories, where travelers bunked down on crude beds cushioned with moss.

Climatically, the summit is classified as arctic. Its topographic isolation results in alarmingly abrupt changes in weather, including blizzards even in summer. The highest-velocity winds ever recorded – 231 miles (372 km) an hour – were measured here in 1934, and some of the buildings that are part of a weather observatory (founded in 1932) are tethered to keep them from blowing away.

The Sherman Adams Summit Building is surrounded by a deck with 70-mile (112-km) views; inside is the small but fascinating **Summit Museum** (tel: 603-356 2137; seasonal; entrance fee) which focuses on mountaineering history and on the summit's unusual ecology and weather.

Crawford Notch and the Cog Railway

Head west on Route 302 through **Crawford Notch** ㉔, a narrow pass named for two notable early entrepreneurs. The notch was "discovered" in 1771 (more or less accidentally) by Timothy Nash, who was tracking a moose at the time. When Nash informed Governor Wentworth of his discovery, the disbelieving governor offered to grant him a tract of land including the notch if Nash could bring a horse through it and present the animal, intact, at Portsmouth. Nash met the challenge – incidentally opening up the White Hills (as the mountains were then called) to a steady influx of settlers, and eventually tourists.

Among the first to anticipate and capitalize on the area's potential were Abel Crawford and his son, Ethan Allen Crawford. They blazed the first path to the summit of Mount Washington (in 1819), advertised both it and their services as

TIP

More than 130 people have died on Mount Washington and hikers should be aware of its fierce weather. The average daily temperature is 26.5°F (–3.1°C) and has fallen as low as –47°F (–44°C).

BELOW:
on the summit of Mount Washington.

In July 1944 delegates from 44 countries met at Bretton Woods to devise a plan to create financial stability after World War II. The meeting gave birth to the World Bank and the International Monetary Fund, and its policies, although later seen by many as instruments of US power, survived until the 1970s.

BELOW: Mount Washington Hotel.

tour guides and established inns to accommodate their clients and other travelers – thereby masterminding the White Mountains' debut as a tourist attraction. Both men were as rugged as the mountains. In his 80s, Abel is said to have hiked five mountainous miles (8 km) each morning to his son's house for breakfast. He was 75 when he made the first ascent of Mount Washington on horseback. Known as the "Giant of the Hills" – he was nearly 7 ft (2.1 meters) tall – Ethan was fond of wrestling bears and lynx and could carry a live buck home on his shoulders.

Route 302 through **Crawford Notch State Park** (tel: 603-374 2272) passes of the few remaining symbols of the mountains' resort heyday. Its genteel grandeur still surprisingly intact, the colossal **Mount Washington Hotel** (tel: 800-314 1752; www.mtwashington.com), which opened in 1902, welcomes well-heeled visitors in a manner to which most people could easily become accustomed.

Circled by a 900-ft (270-meter) verandah set with white-wicker chairs, and topped with red-tiled turrets, this elongated white-stucco wedding-cake contains some 174 rooms (many marked with plaques commemorating guests attending the famed 1944 Bretton Woods monetary conference – *see margin note*) and a voluminous lobby with 23-ft (7-meter) ceilings supported by nine sets of columns and illumined with crystal chandeliers. Without leaving the hotel grounds, guests can enjoy golf (on an 18-hole PGA course), swimming (indoor or out), tennis (12 clay courts), and horseback riding. Though the lovely formal dining room has yet to catch up with an admittedly trend-crazy age, diners can at least console themselves with the thought that, because of the room's intentionally octagonal design, they'll never be relegated to a corner table. And with a band playing throughout the dinner hour, they can work in some dancing as

well. Since 2000, the hotel has been open in winter – a boon to skiers enjoying the slopes at nearby Bretton Woods ski area (shuttle bus from hotel).

Just past the hotel, turn off Route 302 onto the access road to ride up Mount Washington on the remarkable 1869 **Cog Railway**, a testament to American ingenuity in the pursuit of diversion (operates late Apr–late May weekends; Memorial Day–Oct, daily; also operates part-way to summit for skiers in winter; tel: 800-922 8825 or, in NH, 603-846 5404; www.thecog.com; entrance fee). The train, the world's first mountain-climbing cog railway, carts tourists 3½ miles (5.5 km) up and down the mountain, but does so with an admirable inventiveness. The average grade is 25 percent, the steepest 37.4. Relying on a failsafe rack-and-pinion system, the railroad was devised by Sylvester March, a local inventor who hoped to capitalize on the tourist trade attracted to the mountain. He obtained a charter to build the railroad from skeptical Concord legislators (they offered him the right to extend it all the way to the moon) and completed it in three years. It has been outdone only once, by an even steeper version in the Swiss Alps.

The North Country

This isolated, sparsely populated region is one of New Hampshire's better-kept secrets. The landscape is as stunning as any in the state: vast stretches of forest cover most of the region and provide its primary industry – logging. A lacework of lakes, rivers, ponds, and streams offers a delicate counterpoint to the craggy hills and mountains. It is up here that the Connecticut River has its source, in a string of lakes just a few miles from the Canadian border, in a corner so out of the way that its allegiance was not decided, nor its boundary fixed (and then, by force), until 1840. The wilderness is a mecca for fishermen in search

Map on pages 244–5

In the glorious age of the grand hotel, resorts such as the Mount Washington Hotel and the Balsams (see page 298) often had private rail lines. Their wealthy guests would arrive for the season, complete with entourage of servants, in their own rail carriages.

BELOW:
Mount Washington Cog Railway.

Map on pages 244–5

of salmon and trout; and, in winter, snowmobilers attracted by miles of trails.

Route 3 is *the* road north past the Connecticut Lakes to the border. Just south of **Colebrook** ⑨⑤, where the Mohawk and Connecticut rivers meet, the Oblate fathers oversee the **Shrine of Our Lady of Grace**, notable for an unusual, life-size granite carving called "Motorcyclists in Prayer." Past Colebrook, Route 3 meanders alongside the infant Connecticut to **Pittsburg** ⑨⑥, the state's largest municipality in acreage (more than 300,000 acres/120,000 hectares), and one of its smallest in population.

From here northward to Canada, it's a world of forest, water, scattered hunting and fishing camps: a world well suited to an exploring spirit. Folks at **The Glen** (800-445 4536; open May–Oct), a handsome lakeside retreat on the western shore of the First Connecticut Lake, will be glad to provide information, as will the **Connecticut Lakes Tourist Association** (www.nhconnlakes.com).

Route 26 east out of Colebrook follows the Mohawk River through **Dixville Notch State Park** ⑨⑦. Watch for moose: the park is home to much of the state's population of these behemoths. In the heart of the Notch is **The Balsams Grand Resort Hotel** (tel: 800-255 0800; open mid-May–mid-Oct and mid-Dec–March), a sprawling 1866 establishment with some 233 rooms and recreational facilities (golf, tennis, skiing, trout-fishing, canoeing, riding) spread over an area the size of Manhattan Island; it even has its own small ski area. Its gargantuan luncheon buffets are justly famous.

At the junction of Routes 26 and 16 in **Errol**, turn north a short distance to visit the headquarters of the 13,000-acre (5,300-hectare) **Lake Umbagog National Wildlife Refuge** ⑨⑧ (tel: 603-482 3415), created in 1992 to conserve wetlands and protect migratory birds *(see margin note)*. ❑

Lake Umbagog has rapidly become too popular. On a summer weekend there can be as many as 200 boats a day on the lake. The US Fish and Wildlife Service reports that jet skis and off-road vehicles are harming wildlife habitats.

BELOW: downsizing.

The Fall

One of the most revered rituals of New England life is "leaf-peeping" – driving to see the green leaves of summer turn to vivid shades of orange, yellow and red each fall. Droves of dedicated leaf-peepers come by the car and busload from all over the US and the world (advance reservations at inns and even restaurants are essential during October). In the far northern parts of the region, the leaves usually start turning mid-September, farther south a little later; by the end of October, the show is pretty much over.

New Hampshire and Vermont are most often linked with great foliage, but all six states have favored routes for colorful fall vistas. The advantage the northern states have is their mountains: From certain routes through the Green or White Mountains (a misnomer in fall), the views across valleys to neighboring peaks can be breathtaking.

Each New England state has a toll-free foliage hotline telephone number. There's even a Maine "leaf lady" whose Web page contains frequently updated photos of the show (access the page through the state's website at www.visitmaine.com).

By trying too hard to pinpoint the absolute peak of foliage, however, you risk missing the majesty of the leaf-changing phenomenon: If you're lucky enough to be in New England in October, you're sure to see peak foliage somewhere, because each tree changes its color according to an inner timetable that's affected by moisture, temperature, and the shorter days of fall. Botanists call the color change "leaf senescence" – the process by which the green pigment chlorophyll is drawn back into the tree to nourish it, permitting other, brighter pigments in the leaves to shine through. Brightest of all are red swamp maples and sumac. Aspen and birch turn yellow, sugar maples a peachy orange.

While it can be fun to drive back roads in search of great fall color, interstates often have the best foliage. Designed to cut through swaths of forest bypassing populated areas, I-95, for example, offers some of Maine's best leaf-peeping in the 75-mile (120-km)

stretch from Augusta to Bangor. Similarly, in Connecticut, I-95, from Danielson to Waterford, always puts on a fine leaf show.

Almost any highway route designated as "scenic" on a state map will yield bountiful leaf color. In Massachusetts, one of the best foliage drives is westward along the Mohawk Trail (Route 2, Greenfield to Williamstown) in the northwestern corner of the state. Turn north on Route 7 into Vermont, then east on Route 9 and south on I-91 for an exceptionally pretty loop tour.

The state's mountains and lakes make it particularly appealing. A 340-mile (550-km) mid-state tour that takes in a little bit of mountain and lake begins at the Massachusetts border on I-93. Take Exit 24 and follow signs to Holderness on Route 25; then take Route 113 east to Route 16 north. At the Kancamagus Highway (Route 112), go west through the White Mountains National Forest back to I-93.

● **Foliage hot-line numbers:** New Hampshire, 1-800-258 3608; Vermont, 1–800-837 6668; Massachusetts, 1-800-227 6277; Maine, 1-888-624 6345. ❑

RIGHT: tupelo leaves and white pine needles.

THE SHAKERS

These disciplined people were famous for their unique way of life, their manner of worship, and a craftsmanship that permanently influenced design

The Shakers aimed for perfection in life. Devoted to orderliness and simplicity, they were also dedicated to such progressive notions as sexual equality (facilities for men and women were identical and jobs were shared on a rota), and they welcomed technological advances that might improve the quality of their work. They were inventors (of, for instance, the circular saw and clothes pegs). They ran model farms and, as keen gardeners, were the first to packet and sell seeds; they also marketed medicinal herbs. They sold their meticulously crafted baskets, boxes, chairs and textiles. By blending discipline, business acumen, ingenuity and superb craftsmanship, they achieved prosperity, both spiritual and financial.

Celibacy was a key principle, but the ranks were swelled by converts, and orphans were adopted, Numbers dwindled after the mid-1800s, however, and today just a handful of "Believers" remain, in Sabbathday Lake, Maine. The Shaker ideals of simplicity and practicality live on, however, in a legacy of architecture, furniture and crafts. The villages at Canterbury, NH, and Hancock, Mass., are preserved as museums, where visitors watch craftsmen make baskets, boxes and chairs in the Shaker manner. In the Dwelling Houses (above, at Hancock) they can see the efficient kitchens, the wall pegs on which chairs and utensils were hung, and the built-in cupboards (so no dust could accumulate on top or underneath).

▷ **THE SHAKER BOX**
Shakers did not make anything unless it served a purpose. Oval boxes of every size, with distinctive "swallowtail" joints, stored household goods.

▽ **THE ROUND BARN**
Envied by many, the round barn at Hancock, Mass., was a large one, built not only for its efficiency, but as a status symbol.

▷ **THE LADDERBACK**
These light but sturdy chairs were made for Believers by the thousand. The woven-tape seat was a Shaker innovation.

THE VISION OF MOTHER ANN LEE

The founder of the Shakers was Ann Lee, born in 1736 in Manchester, England. An illiterate factory-worker, she was a woman of deep convictions at a time of religious persecution. She became the spritual leader of a group of dissidents from the Anglican Church called the "Shaking Quakers" because of the movements they made as the holy spirit took hold of them. Persecuted and sent to jail, she had a vision that she had a mission to teach a new way of life, one where men and women were equal, free from lust, greed and violence, with their lives governed by material and spiritual simplicity. She was convinced that only through celibacy could men and women further Christ's kingdom on Earth. After a second vision, she and eight followers set sail for New York in 1770. It was not until the 1780s, however, that converts were attracted in great numbers. Mother Ann died in 1783, soon after a prosetylizing tour of New England and before the full flowering of Shakerism. At its peak in the 1840s, 6,000 members lived in 19 communities.

△ SONG AND DANCE
The Shaker dance was an integral part of worship, instituted as an ordered alternative to the whirlings and tremblings of the early Believers (above). Brothers and sisters danced in perfect unison to the sound of song. In time, thousands of songs were composed, many under divine inspiration.

▷ COMMUNAL DINING
The Hancock dining room: believers ate at fixed times, in silence, with men and women at separate tables.

MAINE

Maine is a land of jagged coastlines and vast pine woods, of remote peninsulas, fresh lobster and famed outlet shops – a state inimitably evoked in the soft canvases of Winslow Homer

Map on page 306

By New England standards, Maine – beyond its heavily trafficked southern coast – remains a mysterious wilderness. Larger in area than the other five New England states combined, the "Pine Tree State" (nine-tenths of it are covered with forest) bears little resemblance to its comfortably settled neighbors. It's little wonder, then, that residents pride themselves on their rugged independence and turn a bemused eye on the strange habits of "summer people" – or "rusticators," as they're sometimes still called. The term dates back to the late 19th century, when the first brave tourists came to reconnoiter this uncharted territory.

Henry David Thoreau explored the Mount Katahdin region in 1846 and came back raving about its savage beauty. "What is most striking in the Maine wilderness is the continuousness of the forest," he mused in *Katahdin*. "It is even more grim and wild than you had anticipated, a damp and intricate wilderness." Despite the inroads of civilization, vast stretches still fit the description.

Drowned valleys and Red Paint

Geologists refer to Maine's littoral as a "drowned" coastline: the original coast sank thousands of years ago, its valleys becoming Maine's harbors, its mountains the hundreds of islands lying just offshore. While the coastline was sinking, receding glaciers exposed vast expanses of granite, which not only gave Maine's mountains their peculiar pink coloration, but provided settlers with a valuable source of building material. The "rock-bound coast of Maine" extends only 400 miles (640 km) as the gull flies, but 3,500 miles (5,600 km) if all the coves, inlets, and peninsulas were magically ironed out.

The first known residents, 11,000 years ago, were paleolithic hunters and fishers who lived along the coast. Other tribes followed, including a race known as the Red Paint People because lumps of red ocher (powdered hematite), thought to have been part of a religious sacrament, have been found in their grave sites. The earliest European explorers, in the 15th and 16th centuries, were greeted by the Abenaki tribe, whose name means "easterners" or "dawnlanders."

John Cabot visited Maine in 1497–99 (his explorations established all future British claims to the land), but it wasn't until after Captain John Smith sounded "about 25 excellent harbors" in 1614 that the "Father of Maine," Sir Ferdinando Gorges, was granted a charter to establish British colonies. Rival French explorers also claimed parts of Maine and Canada, and territorial disputes eventually led to the French and Indian Wars of the 18th century. Maine became a part of the Commonwealth of Massachusetts and remained so until 1820, when it became, as residents still like to call it, the State of Maine.

PRECEDING PAGES: Portland Head Light. **LEFT:** Southwest Harbor, Mount Desert Island. **BELOW:** good catch.

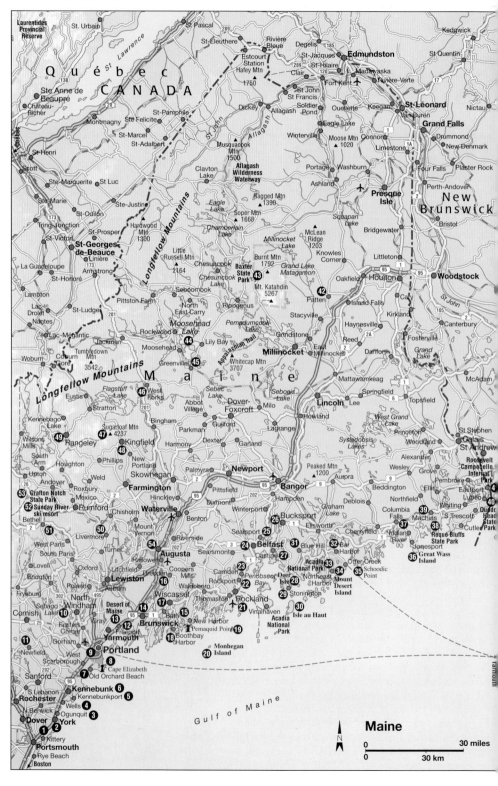

The two Maines

Maine's economy developed much in the way its future tourism industry would – with a bifurcation of interests based on geography. Coastal Mainers faced the sea in more than simply literal terms: the state's tortuous coastline offered dozens of fine natural harbors, and virtually all commerce within Maine, and between Maine and the outside world, was conducted by sea. Even in the 18th century, Massachusetts hearths depended upon Maine firewood shipped south on stout sailing vessels. The coastal seafaring life also gave Maine one of its nicknames, "Down East." Although a ship sailing northeast along the Maine coast is apparently heading "up" into higher latitudes, mariners coined the term because they were sailing "down" before the prevailing winds.

Along with trading and boatbuilding, the seaside communities of Maine depended heavily upon the fishing industry, and eventually became the home ports of New England's biggest lobster fleet. Follow any route that hugs the coast of Maine, and you'll see the doughty lobster boats, their decks piled high with the mesh traps that are marked, when deployed, by colorful bobbing floats in the cold offshore waters *(see box, page 316)*.

Inland Maine is a different story. Settlements much beyond the southern and western lakes region were always few and far between, and here the resource was timber. From the days when mast trees were marked with the broad arrow of the Royal Navy, to the modern era in which Maine's vast coniferous forests help feed the nation's appetite for paper, the logging industry has reigned supreme in northern Maine (an exception is far northern Aroostook County, a flat terrain of potato farms). A century ago, this was the land of the great log drives, when spring high water would send thousands of felled pines down the

Map on page 306

So remote are parts of northern Maine that in 1944 a camp was established at Houlton, near the Canadian border, to house around 3,000 prisoners of war, mostly Germans.

BELOW: Long Sands Beach, York, on the South Coast.

Kennebec and Penobscot rivers. Today, behemoth log trucks do the job, on a network of privately-owned roads through the northern forests. The kingdom of paper has, paradoxically, kept much of northern Maine a wild paradise for campers, canoeists, hunters, and anglers, although flux in the industry is turning more land over to potential development and shuttering mills in towns such as East Millinocket, where the overpowering aroma of paper manufacture has long been the perfume of prosperity.

The South Coast

The best way to see Maine is to start at the southern tip and head northeast along the old coastal highway, US 1. (I-95 is bigger and faster, for those who have a specific destination in mind, but utterly lacking in scenery.) Although, geographically, the coast represents only a tiny fraction of the state, 45 percent of Maine residents call it home, and the overwhelming majority of visitors are also headed for the shore.

The southernmost segment, extending from Kittery to Freeport, attracted the earliest settlers and to this day is the most heavily traveled, blending historic enclaves with built-up beaches and discount shopping malls. Just across the New Hampshire border from Portsmouth, is **Kittery ❶**, home to **Kittery Outlets** (exit 3 off I-95; tel: 888-548-8379) one of the state's largest concentrations of outlet malls. More than 120 stores are clustered around the **Kittery Trading Post** (tel: 888-587 6246; open daily) a shopping destination for outdoor equipment and clothing since 1926. The town is also home to **Portsmouth Naval Yard** – the nation's first, founded in 1806. **Kittery Historical and Naval Museum** (Routes 1 and 236; tel: 207-439 3080; open year round Tues–Sat

Kittery, settled in 1623, is Maine's oldest town and all the typical colonial architecture of early America can be seen in its older buildings.

BELOW: John Hancock Warehouse and wharf, York.

10am-4pm; entrance fee) documents the shipyard's history, from the construction of *Ranger* (the first ship ever to fly the Stars and Stripes, under the command of John Paul Jones) to today's submarines. Nearby **Fort McClary State Historic Site** (Route 103, Kittery Point; tel: 207-384 5160; open Memorial Day–Oct 1; entrance fee) was first fortified in 1715 and rebuilt repeatedly right up until the 1898 Spanish-American War. All that remains is the 1846 hexagonal wooden blockhouse, and the granite seawall – a scenic vantage point from which to view racing yachts in Portsmouth Harbor and Whaleback Light at the mouth of the Piscataqua River.

A few miles to the north, **York ❷**, one of Maine's first settlements, was a center of dissent during the Revolutionary era. The local chapter of the Sons of Liberty decided to hold their own tea party when a British ship carrying tea anchored in **York Harbor**. Being practical Mainers, however, they "liberated" the tea rather than throw it in the harbor.

The **Old York Historical Society** (207 York Street; tel: 203-363 4974, www.oldyork.org; open early June–mid-Oct Mon-Sat; entrance fee) maintains eight historic buildings, including the **John Hancock Warehouse** (a contemporary wrote that the signer of the Declaration of Independence was "more successful in politics than in business"), the 1750 **Jefferds Tavern** and the **Old Gaol**, built in 1719, thought to be the oldest public building in the US. With its 2-ft (60-cm) thick fieldstone walls and tiny windows bordered with sawteeth, the jail served its purpose until 1860. It has now been restored to its 1790s appearance, complete with dungeon. The **Elizabeth Perkins House** is a prime example of Colonial revivalism, an 18th-century farmhouse renovated by descendants of its builders in the early 20th century.

Map on page 306

TIP

To escape the bustle of town, try a contemplative – and educational – walk amid the 3,100-acre (1,250-hectare) Rachel Carson Wildlife Refuge (off Route 9). The pioneering ecologist spent many summers exploring these fertile wetlands.

BELOW: Perkins Cove, Ogunquit.

The other side of York, physically and philosophically, is **York Beach**, a narrow mile-long strip of fine sand, lined with every imaginable type of fast-seafood shack and family-entertainment facility. The Cliff Walk off York Harbor's boardwalk affords beautiful views of the coastline, and of Cape Neddick's 1879 **Nubble Light** off Route 1A; seasonal information center).

The scenic Shore Road from York to Ogunquit passes the turn-off for **The Cliff House Resort & Spa** (tel: 207-361 1000), a 70-acre (28-hectare) oceanfront resort and spa in operation since 1872. Just ahead, the **Ogunquit Museum of American Art** (543 Shore Road; tel: 207-646 4909; open July–Oct, Mon–Sat; Sun, pm; entrance fee) exhibits works by 20th-century American masters including Reginald Marsh, Edward Hopper, and Rockwell Kent. Turn right just past the museum to **Perkins Cove** in **Ogunquit ❸**, the southern terminus for **Marginal Way**, a spectacular, 1-mile (1.6-km) seaside walk along the cliffs. Several excursion boats leave from here, and there are shops and restaurants.

Charles Woodbury "discovered" the tiny fishing village of **Ogunquit** (whose Indian name meant "beautiful place by the sea") in the late 19th century, and the word soon spread to artists and vacationers. Today, tourists crowd the galleries, shops, and eateries that have taken over the fishing shacks, and frolic in the surf at the 3-mile (5-km) **town beach** (parking fee). In summer the town is so packed with visitors that reproduction trolleys are the easiest way to get around (parking is tight). Tallulah Bankhead, Bette Davis, and Helen Hayes all trod the boards at the **Ogunquit Playhouse**, a highly regarded summer theater founded in 1933 (Route 1; open June–Labor Day; tel: 207-646 5511; www.ogunquitplayhouse.org).

A few miles north on Route 1, in **Wells ❹, the Wells Auto Museum** (tel: 207-646 9064; open mid-June-Sept daily 10am–5pm; weekends Memorial Day–Columbus Day; entrance fee) exhibits more than 80 antique and classic cars. Watch for the turn-off to the **National Estuarine Research Reserve at Laudholm Farm** (Laudholm Road; tel: 207-646 1555; visitor center open mid-Jan–early Dec Mon–Fri, Memorial Day weekend–Columbus Day Mon–Sat, Sun pm; parking fee). The 1,600-acre (650-hectare) preserve has 7 miles (11 km) of hiking trails along coastal marsh, uplands, and pristine beach. There are tours in summer.

East of Wells on Route 9, **Kennebunkport ❺**, once the shipbuilding center of York County, has embraced tourism; upscale shops, galleries and restaurants are clustered around downtown Dock Square. The **Kennebunkport Historical Society** maintains historic homes (125 North Street; tel: 207-967 2751; one-hour walking tours Thurs and Sat in summer at 11am; Sept–mid-Oct, Sat at 11 am; fee). Take a drive along Ocean Avenue, past the historic Colony Hotel (tel: 800-552 2363; www.thecolonyhotel.com) and Walker's Point, the summer home of first President Bush. Continue on to visit the charming fishing village of **Cape Porpoise**.

Head up North Street about 3 miles (5 km) to the **Seashore Trolley Museum** (Log Cabin Road; tel: 207 967 2712; open weekends in May; Memorial Day–mid-Oct daily; mid-Oct–late Oct, weekends; entrance fee) which exhibits one of the world's largest collections of antique trolley cars and offers a 4-mile (6.5 km) ride.

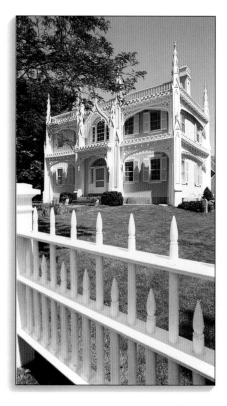

BELOW: Wedding Cake House, Kennebunk (not open to the public).

A few miles to the west, **Kennebunk's** rich shipbuilding heritage is the focus of the **Brick Store Museum** (Main Street; tel: 207-985 4802; open Tues–Sat; entrance fee) The museum offers excellent architectural walking tours from May to October. Look for the unmistakable 1826 **Wedding Cake House** (Route 53), festooned with elaborate carved wooden scrollwork. Legend has it that a sea-bound captain who married in haste had it built to compensate his wife for the lack of a cake at their rushed ceremony. **Arundel**, north of Kennebunk, has many antique shops and a summer playhouse.

Further up the coast is **Old Orchard Beach** ❼, a seaside resort popular among French Canadians. The 7-mile (11-km) beach is flanked with motels and condos and, at the Ocean Pier, there's an amusement park.

Eastward, just south of Portland on **Cape Elizabeth** ❽, is the oldest light-house *(see box, below)* on the eastern seaboard, the Portland Head Light. The **Museum at Portland Head Light** (Shore Road, Fort Williams Park; tel: 207-799 2661; open June–Oct, daily; Nov, Dec, April, May, weekends; entrance fee) documents the history of lighthouses. The sweeping views are spectacular, and largely unchanged since Henry Wadsworth Longfellow's day. The Port-land-born poet often walked here from town to chat with the keeper. His *Wreck of the Hesperus* was inspired by an actual shipwreck off Peak's Island in 1869 (but Longfellow set the poem off Gloucester, Massachusetts).

The phoenix of Maine: Portland

With a population of 230,000 in its greater area, **Portland** ❾, overlooking Casco Bay, is home to almost one-fourth of the state's population). Founded as Casco in the middle of the 17th century, the city has the advantage of being

Maps:
Area 306
City 312

Which way?

BELOW: West Quoddy Head Lighthouse, sited at the easternmost point of land in the United States.

MAINE'S LIGHTHOUSES

With thousands of miles of deep craggy coastline and treacherously rocky shores, it isn't surprising that Maine has 63 lighthouses. What's really surprising is that there aren't three times as many! These sentinels guard the entire coast – from East Quoddy Head Lighthouse on Campobello Island at the Canadian border (accessible only at low tide) to the southern Nubble Light on York Beach. You could easily structure a coastal drive with them acting as a focal point. These picturesque outposts, where sea meets shore, have long represented hope, strength, security and romance in the American imagination. Although several are privately owned, many are open to the public. Portland Head Light, Maine's oldest – built in 1791 under President George Washington's authorization – houses a charming museum in the lighthouse keepers' quarters. Pemaquid Point Light, at the tip of the eponymous peninsula, rises 79 ft (24 meters) above the water from a dramatic rock ledge. (You're guaranteed to spot painters at their easels here.) In 1934 it became the first automated lighthouse. Like others, however, it still relies on a Fresnel lens – a technology designed in 1822 that bends the light into a narrow beam by means of a magnifying lens and concentric rings of glass prisms.

100 miles (160 km) closer to Europe than any other major US seaport, and is blessed with a sheltered, deep-water harbor.

Yet Portland's success has often been choppy and beset by sudden storms. Three times the city was burned completely to the ground – by Indians in 1675, by the British in 1775, and by accident in 1866. Three times the city rose quickly from its ashes, improved and rejuvenated. After the last fire, it was reconfigured. Streets were widened, and an elaborate network of municipal parks instituted. The city stands today as a shining example of urban planning – all the more so with the revitalization, in recent decades, of the atmospheric **Old Port ❹** district, a salty warren of old brick buildings and cobbled streets, packed with sophisticated shops and restaurants. Several whale watch and cruise ships depart from the docks along Commercial Street at the edge of the Exchange. Bay Ferries (tel: 877-359 3760; www.catferry.com) operates its high-speed catamaran (passengers and cars) between Portland and Yarmouth, Nova Scotia Fri–Sun; weekdays it departs from Bar Harbor.

Spread out beyond the harbor are the Calendar Islands – so named because John Smith reported that there were 365 of them, when in fact they number only 136. The Coast Watch & Guiding Light Navigation Company (Long Wharf; tel: 207-774 6498) runs visitors out to **Eagle Island** to tour the summer home Admiral Robert Peary, who planted the American flag on the North Pole in 1909 (open late June–Labor Day and weekends in Sept).

Portland remains a thriving cultural crossroads, known for its innovative dance and theater troupes. The city is also home to the outstanding **Portland Museum of Art ❸**, designed by I.M. Pei and strong on such locally inspired artists as Winslow Homer, Edward Hopper and Andrew Wyeth, as well as Van Gogh,

TIP

For a good view of the city, it's worth climbing the 103 steps of the Portland Observatory (138 Congress St; tel: 207-774 5561; open late-May–early Oct; admission fee). Built in 1908, its purpose was to give merchants early warning that their ships were on the horizon.

BELOW: Portland's Harbor Fish Market.

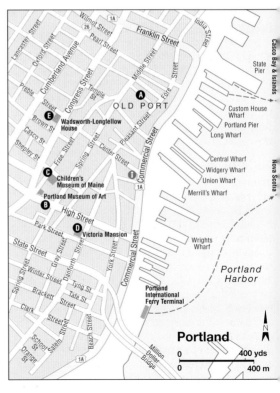

Maps:
Area 306
City 312

Degas and Picasso (7 Congress Square; tel: 207-775 6148; open Memorial Day–Columbus Day, daily; Tues–Sun rest of year; Fri until 9pm; entrance fee). Next door is the imaginative **Children's Museum of Maine** ❹ (142 Free Street; open Memorial Day–Labor Day, Mon–Sat; Sun pm; rest of year, Tues–Sat; Sun pm; entrance fee). It has a camera obscura and appeals mostly to kids up to 14.

Several Portland neighborhoods warrant strolling – especially the Western Promenade, a parade of 19th-century architectural styles. The 1859–63 brownstone Italianate villa **Victoria Mansion** ❹ (109 Danforth Street; tel: 207-772 4841; open Mon–Sat, Sun pm; entrance fee), is by far the most elaborate dwelling in town – with showpiece interiors, featuring painted ceilings and carved walls in the Rococo manner. By contrast is the somewhat restrained 1785–86 **Wadsworth-Longfellow House** ❺ (489 Congress Street; tel: 207-774 1822; open May–Oct; entrance fee), built by Longfellow's grandfather, a Revolutionary War officer. Inside are the parlor where the poet's parents were married and the room where he wrote *The Rainy Day*.

More than 3½ million visitors a year turn up at L.L. Bean's store in Freeport. World-wide mail order sales exceed $1 billion a year.

Daytrips from Portland

With its easy access from Portland, **Sebago Lake** ❿ is one of the most popular of the Western Lakes, offering swimming, boating, camping, and fishing in 1,300-acre (530-hectare) **Sebago Lake State Park** (State Park Road: tel: 207-693 6613; open May–mid-Oct; entrance fee).

On the causeway which separates Sebago from Long Lake, the *Songo River Queen II* (Route 302; tel: 207-693 6861) gives lake tours, and several marinas rent canoes, powerboats, pontoon boats, and jet skis. Head up Douglas Mountain to visit the **Jones Museum of Glass and Ceramics** (tel: 207-787 3370; open Mon–Sat, Sun pm; entrance fee), whose huge collection includes more than 10,000 pieces and spans the period from ancient Egypt to the present.

BELOW: the trail to Popham Beach.

Near the New Hampshire border off Route 11, **Willowbrook at Newfield** ⓫ (Elm Street; tel: 207-793 2784; open mid-May–Columbus Day, daily; entrance fee) is a reconstituted late 19th-century museum village of 37 buildings which captures aspects of this gentler time, from horse-drawn sleighs to bicycles built for two, from a classic ice-cream parlor to a musty general store. There's also an 1894 carousel.

Following in L.L. Bean's boots

The little town of **Freeport** ⓬ is known worldwide – all because, in 1912, a young man named Leon Leonwood Bean decided to build a better hunting boot. In his initial circular, he offered the new, improved waterproof boot with a money-back guarantee. Legend has it that 90 out of the first 100 pairs fell apart: the soles separated from the leather uppers. True to his word, Bean replaced the defective boots with pairs of a newer, improved design and – after absorbing the loss – began building the legendary **L.L. Bean** empire that he controlled until his death in 1967 at the age of 94.

Bean lived long enough to see his store grow from a humble outdoors outfitter to a purveyor of casual fashion and recreational sporting goods with an enormous mail-order business. Bean's three-story depart-

Sardines to go at Prospect Harbor.

ment store (95 Main Street; tel: 800-559 0747 x 37222; www.llbean.com), is open 24 hours, 365 days a year. Though a boon to the local economy, Bean's has inspired imitators, so that the entire village is now overrun with upscale discount outlets *(see Outlet Shopping, page 153)*.

Atlantic Seal Cruises (Main Street Wharf: tel: 207-865 6112 or 877-285 7325: Memorial Day–Oct daily) offers a variety of excursions, including a visit to Admiral Robert Peary's summer home on Eagle Island *(see page 312)*, seal and osprey watching, and a six-hour voyage to Seguin Island (Thurs only). Cruises depart from Main Street Wharf in South Freeport. Advance reservations are required for all trips.

A rather peculiar attraction in this area is the **Desert of Maine** (95 Desert Road; tel: 207-865 6962; open May–mid-Oct; entrance fee), a former farm that was over cultivated, then logged, eventually losing all its topsoil. Sand took over, eventually engulfing entire trees. It's like an overgrown sandbox.

The Mid-coast

Brunswick ⓮ is best known as the home of **Bowdoin College** (tel: 207-725 3000 for tour information). Founded in 1794, Bowdoin was originally slated to be built in Portland, but the college's benefactors found that that city offered too many "temptations to dissipation, extravagance, vanity and various vices of seaport towns" for impressionable young minds. Nathaniel Hawthorne and Henry Wadsworth Longfellow were alumni, class of 1825.

On campus, the **Bowdoin Museum of Art** houses a small but astute sampling of paintings by such notables as Stuart, Copley, Homer, Eakins, and Wyeth; as well as the Warren Collection of classical antiquities, and works by European masters (Walker Art Building; tel: 207-725 3275; open Tues–Sat; Sun pm; donations).

Also on campus, the **Peary-MacMillan Arctic Museum** (Hubbard Hall; tel: 207-725 3416; open Tues–Sat; Sun pm) heralds the accomplishments of North Pole explorers Robert E. Peary and Donald MacMillan, who achieved their objective in 1909.

The **Pejepscot Historical Society** (the Indian name for the Androscoggin River meant "crooked like a snake") oversees several fine museums in town. Their headquarters is in the **Skolfield-Whittier House** (159–161 Park Row; tel: 207-729 6606; open late May–early Oct Thurs & Sat, tours at 11am and 2pm; entrance fee), a brick Italianate "double house" built in 1859: one side houses the society's collections; the other has the original furnishings of three generations of one family. Civil War hero Joshua L. Chamberlain was living in town and teaching at Bowdoin until he enlisted. The **Joshua L. Chamberlain Museum** (226 Maine Street; open late May-late Oct, Tues-Sat, guided tours on hour from 10 am-4pm; entrance fee) exhibits memorabilia of Chamberlain, who after the war served as governor of Maine and Bowdoin's president.

East of Brunswick on US 1, **Bath** ⓯ was once the nation's fifth largest seaport, and is still a shipbuilding center. For a time during the 19th century, Maine's shipyards were responsible for one-third to one-half of all ships on the high seas. When the days of wooden ships

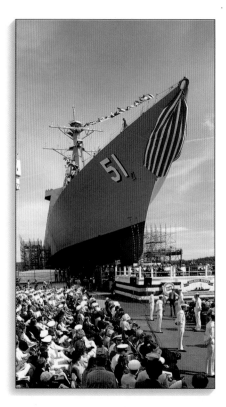

BELOW: launching the *Arleigh Burke* at Bath Iron Works.

Map on page 306

ended, the old yards gave way to the **Bath Iron Works**, today a busy producer of Navy ships. The shipyard is off-limits to civilians, but a good view of the towering cranes can be obtained from the Carleton Bridge over the Kennebec.

The history of shipbuilding in Bath and other coastal towns is preserved at the **Maine Maritime Museum** (243 Washington Street; tel: 207-443 1316; www.bath-maine.com; open daily; entrance fee), a riverside complex occupying a 19th-century shipyard, Exhibits on nautical tools and gadgets capture the flavor of seafaring days, while a working boatyard demonstrates shipbuilding techniques. The museum also maintains an authentic 142-ft (43-meter) Grand Banks schooner, the *Sherman Zwicker*, which can be boarded when in port.

Bath's historic district has fine examples of Greek Revival, Georgian and Italianate architecture among its mansions, cozy inns, and restaurants *(see Travel Tips)*. The **Southern Midcoast Maine Chamber of Commerce** (45 Front Street; tel: 207-725 8797 or 877-725 8797; www.midcoastmaine.org) distributes an excellent self-guided tour brochure.

Fourteen miles (22 km) south of Bath on Route 209 on the Phippsburg Peninsula is **Popham Beach State Park** (tel: 207-389 1335; entrance fee in season), a 4½-mile (7-km) stretch of sand which is one of the prettiest and most popular beaches in the state. Just past the park is **Fort Popham State Historic Site** (open Memorial Day-Sept), an unfinished 1861 fort with a tower and bunkers.

Just across the Kennebec River from Bath, turn north on Route 128 for approximately 10 miles (16 km) to the **Pownalborough Courthouse** (tel: 207-882 6817; open July–Labor Day, Tues–Sat; Sun pm; June and day after Labor Day–Sept, Sat, and Sun pm; entrance fee) in **Dresden ⑯**. The state's only remaining pre-Revolutionary courthouse is a handsomely- restored and magnificently-detailed three-

It was in Brunswick that Harriet Beecher Stowe wrote her 1852 masterpiece Uncle Tom's Cabin, *after having a vision while listening to her husband preach at the town church.*

LEFT: rafting on the Kennebec River. **BELOW:** a sunrise canoeing expedition.

Lobsters and Lobstering

The colorful lobster buoys dotting the coast of Maine are one of the state's hallmarks. And rightly so – more lobster is fished in Maine than in any other state. Lobstering is a $130 million business in Maine, and in one recent year more than 40 million pounds of Maine lobster were consumed throughout the US and shipped all over the world. Yet despite all this, most lobsters in Maine are still caught by independent fishermen in small boats.

A lobsterman's day starts early and goes on late: many head out before dawn, when waters are calmer, and return in the late afternoon. Traps need to be checked at least once a week, and many professional lobstermen – "high-liners" – have 1,000 to 1,500 traps or more, and may need to check several hundred a day. Although proximity to shore makes lobstering safer than other commercial fishing, it is still a dangerous profession, a year-round activity that in the bitter Maine winter can be particularly grueling. Slipping on an icy deck and going over would mean the end, so most high-liners take a helper with them in the form of a "sternman."

In Ogunquit, tourists can join Captain Eric Brazer, a lobsterman for more than 40 years, as he checks traps from his 36-ft fiberglass boat. Captain Brazer leads groups from his homeport in Perkins Cove, sharing his knowledge of the history of lobstering, the lobster life cycle, and the day in a life of a lobsterman.

Lobsters are crustaceans whose external skeletons do not grow. Every year they molt, shedding their old shells and growing larger ones. This process happens when the water is warmer, in late June or early July. Conveniently for tourists, molting brings the lobsters closer to shore, making them easier to catch during the peak summer months.

Without shells, the soft lobsters are vulnerable to predators – codfish and sharks, among others – so they migrate to shallow waters for safety. Here, they hide, absorbing sea water and expanding 15 to 20 percent in size. Over four to six weeks, the lobsters produce new shells, then return to deep water, where they shrink again. The lobsters are now known in the trade as "new-shell," or in restaurants as "soft-shell," as opposed to "hard-shell" before molting. A hard-shell lobster's meat can be up to 33 percent of its body weight, while a soft-shell's is only 25 percent; accordingly, hard-shell lobster tends to be more expensive. The taste is slightly different, and each Maine connoisseur has a preference. Some say new-shell is sweeter, some prefer hard-shell for its stronger taste. Visitors have ample opportunity to decide for themselves at the hundreds of lobster pounds along the coast, where lobsters are cooked in seawater in wood-fired barrels.

Captain Brazer's tours leave from Perkins Cove in Ogunquit June 15–August, daily except Sunday. Tours are 8am–10am, 10:30am–12:30pm, and 1pm-3pm. The boat can take up to six passengers, so reservations are requested. The cost is $30 a person. Tel: 207-646 7413 or, on the boat, 207-361 9123; www.perkinscovelobstertours.com. ❑

LEFT: at work in Corea Harbor, Down East coast.

floor riverfront building with a fascinating period cemetery on the grounds. (Note: if continuing north, to avoid backtracking continue north past the courthouse for 2½ miles/4 km to Route 27 and head south about 9 miles/14 km to Wiscasset.)

Map on page 306

The prettiest village in Maine

Wiscasset ⓱ claims, with some justification, to be the "prettiest village in Maine." Two handsome sea captains' houses maintained by the Society for the Preservation of New England Antiquities are open to visitors: the Federal-era **Nickels-Sortwell House** (Main and Federal Streets; tel: 207-882 6218) and **Castle Tucker** (overlooking the Sheepscot River (Lee and High Streets; tel: 207-882 7169), an 1807 Georgian mansion with Federal and Victorian furnishings. (Both are open June–mid-Oct, Wed–Sun, with tours on the hour 11am–4pm; entrance fee). The 1852 **Musical Wonder House** is an aptly named mansion full of vintage music boxes, player pianos, and other automata from around the world – often playing against one another in improbable euphony (18 High Street; tel: 207-882 7163; open June–Oct Mon–Sat; Sun pm; entrance fee).

Another offbeat tourist attraction is the **Old Lincoln County Jail and Museum**, an 1811 hoosegow with granite walls up to 41 inches (over 1 meter) thick (Federal Street; tel: 207-882 6817; open July, Aug Tues–Sat; Sat in June & Sept, Oct–May Mon–Fri by appointment; entrance fee). Considered a model of humane treatment in its day, because prisoners were afforded individual cells, this grim repository was used right up until 1913, and has the graffiti to prove it.

North on Route 1, just over the Sheepscot River, turn onto Davis Island to visit **Fort Edgecomb State Historic Site**, an octagonal fort of 1808–9 with commanding views of the river and beyond. Revolutionary War reenactments take

Many customers believe that Red's Eats (41 Water Street; open spring–mid-Oct; tel: 207-882 6128) serves up the state's best lobster roll. The tiny diner hasn't changed its recipe since 1938: the meat of one whole lobster served in a buttered and toasted hot dog bun, with melted butter or mayonnaise on the side.

BELOW: Fort Edgecomb.

place on some weekends in summer (Fort Road; Edgecomb; tel: 207-882 7777; open Memorial Day–Labor Day, daily; entrance fee).

Although certainly subdued compared to the commercial excesses of the south coast, **Boothbay Harbor** ⑱, to the south on Route 27, is decidedly touristy. In summer, tens of thousands of visitors throng the streets of this former fishing village to inspect the shops, sample seafood delicacies, charter boats to explore offshore islands with names such as the Cuckolds and the Hypocrites, and book passage on whale watches and deep-sea fishing trips. There are yacht and golf clubs, flower shows, auctions, and clambakes.

Boothbay Railway Village (Route 27, 472 Wiscasset Road; tel: 207-633 4727; open June–early Oct, daily; entrance fee) features a narrow-gauge, coal-fired railroad, encircling a range of reconstructed buildings of yesteryear, including a barbershop, bank and country store.

Pemaquid Point

Farther to the north off Route 1, Route 130 cuts south through Damariscotta to **Pemaquid Point** ⑲, a rocky peninsula whose Indian name meant "long finger." Early explorers couldn't miss it, and in fact there's some evidence to support a claim – unsubstantiated as yet – that a settlement here may have predated Plymouth. Its cellar holes filled in by 19th-century farmers, this "Lost City" was entirely unknown until the early 1960s, when Helen Camp, a Rutgers University professor, noticed clay pipes and other detritus in a freshly plowed field. Some 40,000 artifacts have been unearthed so far. The more remarkable ones – such as a 16th-century German jug – are displayed in the state-run museum, **Colonial Pemaquid State Historic Site**, alongside a diorama recreating the

BELOW: Pemaquid Point Lighthouse.

settlement (off Route 130; open late May–early Sept, daily; tel: 207-677 2423; entrance fee to museum). Admission also includes **Fort William Henry**, a 1907 replica on the site of several unsuccessful stockades. The 1630 original was burned by pirates, and a 1677 replacement, thought impregnable, was destroyed in 1689 by the French and Indians.

At the tip of this peninsula on Route 130, in Lighthouse Park (open Memorial Day-Columbus Day, daily; entrance fee) stands the **Pemaquid Point Lighthouse** (closed to public), which was commissioned in 1827 by John Quincy Adams. With powerful surf constantly breaking on the rocks, the point is a favorite spot for painters and photographers, as well as families who enjoy poking around the tide pools. The lighthouse is shown on the Maine quarter coin.

Monhegan, an island in time

An early European explorer, David Ingram, astounded Europe with tales – most rather tall – of the marvelous peoples and cities he encountered on a journey from the Gulf of Mexico to Canada. Lured by such promising reports, a group of Germans settled Waldoboro in 1748, with, as a plaque at the center of town attests, "the promise and expectation of finding a prosperous city, instead of which they found nothing but wilderness." Another Ingram allusion, to "a great island that was backed like a whale," was naturally dismissed as fantasy.

However, the cliffs of **Monhegan Island ⑳**, 12 miles (19 km) south of Port Clyde, do indeed lend the island the appearance of a whale. And an otherworldly air still pervades this 700-acre (280-hectare) isle, little changed in the past century. Cars have made no inroads, and many residents are perfectly content without electricity. A magnet first for fishing fleets and later for artists (the

Map on page 306

TIP

For information on Maine's 63 surviving lighthouses, visit the Fishermen's Museum, in the old keeper's residence, next to the Pemaquid Point Lighthouse (open mid-May–mid-Oct daily). *See also page 320.*

BELOW: artist on Monhegan Island.

most famous summer resident is the painter Jamie Wyeth, son of Andrew Wyeth), most of the island remains undeveloped.

Visitors can explore the Cliff Trail circling the island, and the Cathedral Woods Trail, where the island children are in the habit of constructing tiny "fairy houses" out of twigs and moss. Monhegan is served by ferries from Boothbay Harbor (Balmy Days Cruises, tel: 800-298 2234, www.balmyday-cruises.com; June–late Sept, daily), Port Clyde (Mohegan Boat Line, sailing from late May–mid-Oct; www.moheganboat.com), and New Harbor (Hardy Boat Cruises, tel: 800-278 3346; mid May–mid-Oct). Although it's possible to make the round-trip in one day, an overnight is advised for those who wish to ease back into a less stressful age.

Penobscot Bay

On the west end of Penobscot Bay is the town of **Rockland ㉑**, once a great limestone producer and now the world's largest distributor of lobsters, as well as the "Schooner Capital of Maine". These two- or three-masted schooners are a wonderful way to discover the coast as the earliest explorers encountered it. Weekend and weeklong excursions may be booked aboard more than a dozen venerable vessels. The **Maine State Ferry Service** (general information: tel: 207-596 2202; www.state.me.us/mdot/opt/ferry/ferry.htm) transports passengers and vehicles to **Matinicus**, a quiet island populated primarily by lobstermen and their families; **Vinalhaven**, where old granite quarries make fine swimming holes and the paved roads are ideal for day-tripping bicyclists, and **North Haven**, which is mainly given over to vacation homes.

Thanks to the 1935 bequest of "Aunt" Lucy Farnsworth, a frugal spinster who lived in but three rooms of her family mansion and left the town $1.3 million to start a museum, Rockland has a world-class collection of art. The **Farnsworth Art Museum and the Wyeth Center** (16 Museum Street; tel: 207-596 6457; www.farnsworthmuseum.org; open late May–mid-Oct, daily; mid-Oct–late May, Tues–Sun; Sun, pm; entrance fee) counts among its holdings many noted 19th- and 20th-century works, including paintings by Winslow Homer and John Marin, and sculpture by Louise Nevelson, who grew up in a Bath lumberyard. Paintings by all three Wyeths – N.C., Andrew, and Jamie – are exhibited in a former church across from the **Farnsworth Homestead**, an 1850 Greek Revival home next to the museum (admission to both buildings is included in the museum fee).

Another pleasant venue is the **Maine Lighthouse Museum** at Maine Discovery Center (One Park Drive; tel: 207-594 3301; open daily in season, Thurs–Mon winter–early spring; entrance fee to museum).

To view an interesting assortment of vehicles, airborne and otherwise, visit the **Owl's Head Transportation Museum**, housed in a spiffed-up hangar at the Owl's Head airport south of Rockland (off Route 73; tel: 207-594 4418; open daily; entrance fee). They range from vintage bicycles to a 1910 Harley, a Model T Ford and a Model F plane (a Wright Brothers prototype). On summer weekends, some of the displays are taken off their blocks and sent for a spin.

The weathered house featured in Andrew Wyeth's signature painting Christina's World *still stands in Cushing, and is the site of many a reverential pilgrimage. The house – and the painting – belong to the Farnsworth Art Museum.*

BELOW:
often the most practical transport.

The works of some of the state's finest contemporary artists are exhibited at the **Center for Maine Contemporary Art** (162 Russell Avenue; tel: 207-236 2875; open year-round Tues–Sat, Sun pm; entrance fee) a few miles up the coast in the quiet village of **Rockport** ㉒. The fine gift shop is worth visiting.

Map on page 306

Camden

Camden ㉓ ("Where the Mountains Meet the Sea") has enjoyed a long reign as the ultimate in genteel summering spots. It was here, as a chambermaid at the gracious Whitehall Inn, an 1834 home turned hotel in 1901, that Rockland native Edna St Vincent Millay (1892–1950) first began to polish her poetry, and even recite some aloud (one of the guests, noting her talent, arranged for a scholarship to Vassar).

One of her verses was penned after climbing to the summit of 800-ft (244-meter) Mount Battie in the **Camden Hills State Park** (off Route 1; tel: 207-236 3109; open mid-May–mid-Oct; entrance fee), now accessible on foot or via a toll road: "*All I could see from where I stood / Was three long mountains and a wood / I turned and looked another way / And saw three islands in a bay.*"

Souvenirs of Down East.

A modern statue of the poet stands watch in a waterfront park overlooking the Megunticook River falls; it's a pleasant place to catch one's breath amid the hubbub of town. Camden is once again in full flower as a summer destination, and the port is packed with restaurants and shops. Many of the grander "cottages" gracing the hilltops have become luxurious B&Bs.

Several overnight (and longer) windjammer schooners set sail from Camden: for information contact the **Maine Windjammer Association** (P.O. Box 1144, Blue Hill 04614; tel: 800-807 9463; www.sailmainecoast.com). Several cap-

BELOW: Camden from Mount Battie.

tains also offer two-hour sails from late May to mid-October. Contact the Chamber of Commerce for information (tel: 800-223 5459 or 207-236 4404; www.visitcamden.com).

The 19th-century captains and shipbuilders of **Belfast** ㉔ built their stately mansions in a variety of architectural styles that makes the town at the mouth of the Passagassawaukeag River a fascinating place to take a stroll. Stop at the **Belfast Area Chamber of Commerce**'s (tel: 207-338 5900; www.belfast-maine.org) seasonal booth on Main Street for a Walking Tour brochure.

A few miles to the north on Route 1, **Searsport** ㉕, lined with dazzling white sea captains' homes, calls itself "the antiques capital of Maine," and the pickings are indeed unusually good. Between 1770 and 1920, this one town produced more than 3,000 vessels, and evidence of its rich history, along with China Trade treasures, can be found on Route 1 in the **Penobscot Marine Museum** (5 Church Street; tel: 207-548 2529; open late May–late-Oct, Mon–Sat; Sun, pm; entrance fee). There's a good collection of 19th-century marine art.

Farther along the coastal road, **Bucksport** ㉖ is dominated by the vast Fort Knox at **Fort Knox State Park** (Route 174 off Route 1; tel: 207-469 7719; open May–Nov; entrance fee), built 1844–69 to defend Maine from Canada during the Aroostook War (actually a boundary dispute), but never completed.

Detours "down east"

Intent on getting to the justly famed Mount Desert Island, many tourists never veer from US 1 and thus miss one of the most scenic areas in Maine. The peninsulas along the eastern side of Penobscot Bay well warrant some poking around, but be forewarned: the roads can be confusing, even with a road map.

The Alamo Theater in Bucksport (85 Main St; tel: 207-469 0924; www.oldfilm. org) houses Northeast Historic Film, which has built up a huge collection of films (including many amateur movies) tracing New England's history.

BELOW: conductors on the Belfast to Moosehead Lake railroad.

Established as a trading post by the Plymouth Pilgrims, **Castine** ㉗ became one of the most hotly contested chunks of property in New England: changing hands nine times, it was owned by the French, Dutch, British, and, eventually, Americans (it was a Tory outpost during the Revolution, and the British managed to take it over again after the War of 1812). Plaques around town, as well as a free walking-tour brochure distributed by the Castine Merchants' Association, fill in the details, but it's enough to wander around, beneath a canopy of elms, taking in the array of fine white houses.

Some of these houses belong to the **Maine Maritime Academy** (founded in 1941 and one of five such schools nationwide that train merchant mariners). Their 1952 ship, the decommissioned *T/V State of Maine*, serves as a floating classroom (tel: 800-464 6565 in Maine; 800-227 8465 out of state; hourly tours, early-July–Aug, daily; early Sept–early May, Sat–Sun).

Take a detour off this detour to make a circuit of **Deer Isle** ㉘, where the principal occupations are lobstering and fishing, and tourists, though welcome, won't find themselves catered to unduly. On the eastern side of the isle is the prestigious **Haystack Mountain School of Crafts**, whose 1960 "campus" is a cluster of small modern buildings perched precipitously on a piny bank overlooking Jericho Bay (Sunshine Road; tel: 207-348 2306; www.haystack-mtn.org). Special evening presentations are open to the public during the summer, and tours are offered Wednesdays at 1pm.

For a true getaway, take the **Isle-au-Haut Company mailboat** (tel: 207-367 5193; www.isleauhaut.com) from the picturesque port of **Stonington** ㉙ to the sparsely inhabited 5,800-acre (2,300-hectare) **Isle au Haut** ㉚. Half is privately owned and occupied primarily by lobstermen and their families; the other half

Map on page 306

Wild lupins.

BELOW: Stonington, Deer Isle.

Potatoes are a staple crop in Maine.

BELOW: the Claremont Hotel, Southwest Harbor, Mount Desert Island.

part of Acadia National Park. For information, contact the Park: P.O. Box 177, Bar Harbor 04609; tel: 207-288 3338.

Heading northeast to hook up with US 1 again, you'll pass through **Blue Hill** ㉛, long the choice of blueblood summerers who didn't care for the showy social season in Bar Harbor. Long a shipbuilding center, the town is also renowned for its pottery, finished with glazes made from nearby copper mines and quarries. Several potters welcome visitors, including Rowantrees Pottery (Union Street; tel: 207-374 5535) and Rackliffe Pottery (Route 172; tel: 207-374 2297).

Mount Desert Island

The reason there's so much territory to explore in Mount Desert Island is that 41,409 acres (16,765 hectares) of the 16 by 13-mile (26 by 34-km) island belong to **Acadia National Park**, which draws over 5 million visitors a year. "Society" discovered this remote spot in the mid-19th century, and by the time the stock market crashed in 1929, millionaires had constructed more than 200 extravagant "cottages." (Only a few survive, some as institutions or inns: many were destroyed in 1947's devastating fire.) Fortunately, Harvard University president Charles W. Eliot had the foresight to initiate the park in 1916, and many of his peers contributed parcels. John D. Rockefeller Jr. threw in 11,000 acres (4,400 hectares) crisscrossed with 50 miles (80 km) of bridle paths he built to protest against the admission of horseless carriages onto the island in 1905. The trail network makes for great mountain-biking, cross-country skiing, and just plain walking. And **Frenchman Bay**, just to the northeast, is still one of America's great sailing waters.

Bar Harbor ㉜ is Mount Desert Island's main town – a bit over commer-

Map on page 306

cialized, but with a pretty town green, a marvelous Art Deco cinema, and some exceptional crafts stores, along with appealing restaurants, and a good choice of accommodations. Numerous whale watches, cruise boats and sailing charters set sail from the town's wharf, and **Bay Ferries** (tel: 207-288 3395 or 888-249 7245; www.catferry.com) offers a high-speed catamaran car and ferry service from Bar Harbor to Yarmouth, Nova Scotia (late May–mid-Oct Mon–Thurs).

The **Abbe Museum** (26 Mount Desert Street; tel: 207-288 3519; open late May–mid-Nov daily; entrance fee), displays an extensive collection of Indian artifacts from Maine's Native people, the Wabanaki.

Spotting the 17 exposed pink granite peaks of **Mount Desert Island**, now the main part of Acadia National Park ㉝, in 1604, Samuel de Champlain described the place as *"l'île des monts deserts"* – and the French pronunciation still holds, more or less, so accentuate the final syllable, as in "dessert."

Exploring Acadia

Off Route 3 in Hulls Cove is the National Park's **Visitor Center** (open mid-Apr–Oct, daily; tel: 207-288 3338; www.nps.gov/acad). Pick up a park map and a schedule of naturalist activities here; there are excellent hiking maps on sale. Most visitors will want to experience the view from Cadillac Mountain, whose form dominates the park, and to drive or cycle the Park Loop Road, but there are many other possibilities, including horse and carriage tours from Wildwood Riding Stables, kayaking, sailing, and hiking in the less frequented areas. Even the shorter trails tend to be over uneven rock, so suitable footwear is essential.

Car traffic is kept under control by a permit system covering the mostly one-way 27-mile (43 km) Park Loop Road, a toll road which makes a clockwise

Bar Harbor's heyday as a fashionable summer resort was in the 19th century, when a railroad from Boston and a steam-boat service lured the wealthy. A forest fire in 1947 destroyed 60 of the grand summer cottages and finally ended the resort's gilded age.

BELOW:
Bar Harbor.

circuit of all the more scenic spots along the eastern coast; the reasonably priced permits are good for a week. Close to the Visitor Center, the **Acadia Wild Garden** shows a range of flora that can be found at a variety of park sites, such as mountain heath and bog; adjacent are the Nature Center, with exhibits on the cultural and natural history of Acadia, and a branch of the **Abbe Museum** (off Route 3 and Park Loop Road; open May–Oct, daily; entrance fee). Sweeping views follow, from the Champlain Mountain Overlook across Frenchman Bay to the distant Gouldsboro Hills. The road passes the start of the Precipice Trail, which features iron rungs and ladders for the steep sections, and further on are Sand Beach – edged by low cliffs, and Acadia's one sandy beach – and the Beehive Trail, which gets superb panoramas but involves some potentially dizzying sections. Thunder Hole needs a wind to stir things up; in the right conditions, the spray blasts up through this chink on the coastline. Otter Point provides another memorable coastal outlook before the road heads inland, past Jordan Pond, with walks along the lakeside or on the short trail past Bubble Rock, a huge boulder transported and dumped by glacier, to South Bubble Summit.

Reached by road or on foot, the tallest peak, 1,530-ft (466-meter) **Cadillac Mountain**, is the highest point along the Atlantic coast north of Rio de Janeiro, and affords glorious 360° views stretching inland as far as Mount Katahdin, Maine's highest summit, and seaward to encompass myriad smaller islands – a particularly lovely vista when bathed in the orange glow of sunset.

On the other side of Somes Sound, the only fjord on the East Coast, the landscape on the "Quiet Side" is just as lovely and quite a bit less traveled. In **Northeast Harbor 34**, visit the spectacular seaview **Thuya Gardens** (tel: 207-276 3727; open July–Labor Day; donation), the 215-acre (87-hectare) garden of

Readily viewed wildlife in Acadia National Park include white-tailed deer, beavers, red foxes, sea urchins, porpoises, bald eagles, herring gulls, and humpback, finback and minkie whales.

BELOW: biking on one of Acadia's carriage roads.

landscape artist Joseph Henry Curtis. Boats leave from here and nearby South-west Harbor for tours to **Little Cranberry Island**, a scenic, 400-acre (160-hectare) island 20 miles (32 km) offshore. At the most southerly point of the island, **Bass Harbor Head Lighthouse** is a classic Maine cameo.

Map on page 306

To the Canadian Border

It's worth a detour to the small, unspoiled fishing village of Winter Harbor and nearby **Schoodic Point** ㉟, a little-visited portion of Acadia National Park with fine views of Cadillac Mountain across the bay.

North on Route 1, in Washington County – also known as "Sunrise County" for its easterly location – tourism takes a back seat to lobstering and growing blueberries and Christmas trees. The patient will be rewarded with a vision of the true Maine, much as it looked 50 years ago.

South on Route 187 about 12 miles, continue through Jonesport and Beals Island to the 1,580-acre (640-hectare) **Great Wass Island** ㊱. The Nature Conservancy property is one of the state's natural treasures. Just off Route 1 in **Columbia Falls** ㊲, tour the elegant, 1818 **Ruggles House** (Main Street; tel: 207-483 4637; open June–mid-Oct; entrance fee), with its magnificent flying staircase. A few miles north turn south onto Roque Bluffs Road for about 5 miles (8 km) to **Roque Bluffs State Park** ㊳ (Tel: 207-255 3475; open mid-May–mid-Sept; entrance fee), which offers fabulous views, a beach (with incredibly cold water), and a much warmer freshwater pond.

Machias ㊴ on Route 1, was the site of the first naval battle of the Revolutionary War. In June 1775, a month after the Battle of Lexington, the *Margaretta* set anchor off Machias to stand guard over a freight ship collecting wood with

BELOW:
a frequent sight
in northern Maine.

Unlike a deer, a moose can do substantial damage to a car and cause serious injury. Be alert when you see these signs.

BELOW:
a lake camp.

which to build British barracks in Boston. After debating their course of action at **Burnham Tavern** (now restored and open as a museum; Main and Free Streets; tel: 207-255 4432; open mid-June–Labor Day, Mon–Fri; entrance fee), the townspeople successfully attacked. *Margaretta*'s captain died of his wounds when brought back to the tavern, but the crew, nursed back to health there, vowed revenge – and followed through, with subsequent attacks and conflagrations.

North on Route 1 and east on Route 189 about 18 miles (29 km), **Lubec** is the easternmost town in the United States, and the easternmost American soil is West Quoddy Point, a dramatic landscape of rocky cliffs and crashing surf graced with a candycane-striped 1858 lighthouse (closed to the public). Hiking trails wander past a peat bog, through stances of wild roses and day lilies. The lighthouse is part of 600-acre (240-hectare) **Quoddy Head State Park** �40 (Tel: 207-733 0911; open mid-May–mid-Oct; entrance fee)

From Lubec, cross over the Franklin D. Roosevelt Memorial Bridge to **Roosevelt Campobello International Park** �41 on New Brunswick, Canada's Campobello Island. Franklin Delano Roosevelt summered here from 1905 to 1921, when he was crippled by polio. After a self-guided tour of the 34-room Roosevelt house, which remains as the family left it, visitors can enjoy 8 miles (13 km) of walking trails, including a 2-mile (3-km) stroll along the ocean (Tel: 506-752 2922; Visitor Center and cottage open late May–Columbus Day; trails open year-round). Note that New Brunswick is one hour ahead of Maine's Eastern Standard Time.

The North Woods

Much of the northernmost part of Maine consists of millions of acres of softwood forest, owned by a couple of dozen corporations who sometimes admit visitors onto their gravel logging roads for a fee. For an overview of the logging boom that swept the area in the mid-19th century, when papermakers turned to timber in lieu of rags, visit the **Lumberman's Museum** (Route 159; tel: 207-528 2650; open Memorial Day–June Fri–Sun; July & Aug Tues–Sun; Sept–Columbus Day Fri & Sun; entrance fee) in **Patten** �42. Here nine buildings of exhibits include a reconstructed 1860s cabin and a blacksmith shop.

Continue west on Route 159 to **Baxter State Park** �43 (tel: 207-723 5140; www.baxterstateparkauthority.com), the legacy of Percival Baxter, governor from 1920 to 1925. When the state legislature refused to purchase and protect this land, he bought a total of 201,018 acres (81,211 hectares), and deeded them to the state, requiring only that the tract remain "forever wild." The park contains 45 peaks over 3,000 ft (900 meters) high, including 5,267-ft (1,605-meter) Baxter Peak, the tallest of Mount Katahdin's three peaks and the second highest point in New England. Baxter is connected to nearby Pamola Peak by a narrow, mile-long strip of rock known as the Knife Edge. Only a few feet wide in spots, the Knife Edge is an acrophobe's nightmare – 3,000 ft (900 meters) straight down on one side, 4,000 ft (1,200 meters) on the other. Would a person fall straight down to the bottom? No, a park ranger reassures: they'd bounce a couple of times. Don't try to cross in high winds.

Map on page 306

Running northward from the northwest corner of Baxter State Park, the **Allagash Wilderness Waterway** provides 92 miles (150 km) of America's most scenic canoeing; the trip takes a week to 10 days. South of the park, the Penobscot River's West Branch offers hair-raising whitewater rafting, through granite-walled Ripogenus Gorge. To the west of the park, accessible only by boat or float plane *(see below)*, is the preserved 19th-century logging town of **Chesuncook**. The Chesuncook Lake House (tel: 207-745 5330) in this lovely little village welcomes outdoors-oriented guests eager to leave the 21st century behind.

Several dozen such "camps," unchanged for decades, are tucked away in this region pocked with lakes and ponds, where the fish are plentiful and moose and black bear still roam. Many are clustered around **Moosehead Lake ❹**, the largest body of fresh water entirely in New England, with 320 miles (512 km) of shoreline.

Although tiny **Greenville ❺**, at the southern end of the lake, has grown into a year-round vacation destination with several fine B&Bs, fishing resorts, and restaurants, it still retains its air of a wilderness hideaway. Three-hour lake tours are offered aboard the *Katahdin*, a restored 1914 lake steamboat (center of town; tel: 207-695 2716; www.katahdincruises.com; check schedule for cruise times). The vessel also provides five-hour cruises to Mount Kineo, a peninsula whose 763-ft (233-meter) cliff was sacred to early Native Americans.

The **Moosehead Marine Museum** (open July–Columbus Day; donation) next to the boat contains fascinating displays on Greenville's history. Another great way to get a full grasp of this mammoth lake is to take a float-plane tour; several operators offer "fly-and-canoe" packages, including Folsom's Air Service (Greenville; tel: 207-695 2821) and Currier's Flying Service (Greenville Junc-

Here immigration is a tide which may ebb when it has swept away the pines.

— HENRY DAVID THOREAU
ON CHESUNCOOK

BELOW:
Baxter State Park.

tion; tel: 207-695 2778). **Lily Bay State Park** (tel: 207-695 2700; open mid-May–mid-Oct; fee), 8 miles (13 km) north of Greenville, has a fine sandy beach and an excellent spot to picnic.

About 20 miles (32 km) southwest of Greenville as the crow flies (or thrice that distance by car), **West Forks** ⓯ attracts thousands of amateurs eager to try whitewater rafting along the Kennebec and Dead rivers. Suitable for anyone over the age of 10 and in reasonably good health, these thrilling descents take only a day and alternate roiling rapids with placid floats. Several outfitters organize trips and provide lodging and meals. Among them: Northern Outdoors, Inc. (tel: 800-765 7238; www.northernoutdoors.com), New England Outdoor Center (tel: 800-766 7238; www.neoc.com), and Wilderness Expeditions (tel: 800-825-9453; www.wildernessrafting.com)

The western lakes and mountains

In the heart of Carrabassett Valley, the ski area at **Sugarloaf/USA** ⓱ (Route 27; tel: 207-237 2000; www.sugarloaf.com) on Maine's second highest peak, has a treeless top offering superb views (including Mounts Katahdin and Washington), and boasts a greater vertical descent (2,820 ft/860 meters) than any other winter resort in New England (tel: 207-237 2000). The area is a year-round resort, with an 18-hole golf course, fly-fishing, and hiking and mountain-biking trails

A useful base for Sugarloaf is **Kingfield** ⓲, 18 miles to the south, which has been a magnet for sporting types since the mid-18th century. The renovated but decidedly funky 1818 Herbert Hotel in the center of town offers basic but comfortable rooms and moderately-priced dining. The town fostered a family of homegrown geniuses, whose accomplishments are showcased in the **Stanley**

BELOW: winter scene: Sugarloaf and the Carrabassett Valley.

Museum (40 School Street; tel: 207-265 2729; open Nov–May Tues–Fri pm or by appointment; entrance fee). The twins, F.O. and F.E., invented the Stanley Steamer, which wowed enthusiasts at the first New England auto show in 1898 and set a land-speed record of 127 mph (203 km/h) in 1906. Three restored, working samples are garaged in this Georgian-style schoolhouse, which the family built for the town in 1903. On display are the photographs of their younger sister, Chansonetta, who had an eye for rural customs now all but forgotten.

About 15 miles (24 km) to the west of Sugarloaf is the low-key resort town of **Rangeley ㊾**, the main service area for the **Rangeley Lakes**, popular with outdoors enthusiasts for more than a century. The town was also the unlikely home of one-time Freud protégé Wilhelm Reich. His renegade theories on sexual energy ended in his ignominious death in jail – the victim, many believe, of an overzealous Food and Drug Administration. Some of the "orgone energy accumulators" he built stand at his remote home and laboratory, Orgonon, at the **Wilhelm Reich Museum** (off Routes 4 and 16; tel: 207-864 3443; open July, Aug, Wed–Sun pm; Sept, Sun pm; entrance fee). The tour is fascinating, the view of Rangeley Lake inspiring.

To the south of the lake region, in **Livermore ㊿**, the **Norlands Living History Center** (Norlands Road; tel: 207-897 4366; www.norlands.org; open July–Labor Day; Labor Day–early Oct, Sat & Sun pm; early Oct–June Mon–Fri 2:30–4pm or by appointment; entrance fee) offers a rare opportunity to time-travel back to 19th-century farm life when the prominent Washburn family lived and worked their 445-acre (180-hectare) farm. Most visitors content themselves with a 1½-hour tour (arrive by 2:30pm for the full tour), which includes the restored mansion, schoolhouse, church, and barn, but true aficionados can

Map on page 306

The Farm and Home Museum in Wilton (entrance behind Key Bank; tel: 207-645 2091; open Jul–Aug Sat 1–4pm) contains a life-size replica of Sylvia Hardy, a local woman billed by P.T. Barnum's circus as The Tallest Lady in the World. When she died in 1888, she weighed 400lb (180 kg) and was 7ft 10½ ins tall (2.4 meters).

BELOW: ready to take to the canoe.

Map on page 306

sign up for a weekend "live-in" program, in which they'll enact historic characters associated with the farm – and carry out all their chores.

West Paris, about 12 miles (19 km) west, might prove more attractive to those with "get rich quick" inclinations: **Perham's** of West Paris (Jct. Routes 26/219; tel: 207-674 2342), founded in 1919, is a rockhound's mecca, not just for its store, but for the chance to poke around in the five quarries it owns within 10 miles (16 km). Gem-quality tourmaline – striated in a watermelon-like color scheme – is fairly common in these hills, and even gold is not unheard of.

Augusta was incorporated in 1797 but was soon renamed after Pamela Augusta, the daughter of the Revolutionary War general Harry Dearborn.

Bethel (51) takes its name, which means "House of God," from the Book of Genesis. It gained prominence as a spa town when Dr John Gehring attracted to his clinic many Harvard academicians suffering from nervous disorders. The hotel he built in 1913 on the pretty town green, the Bethel Inn (tel: 800-654 0125), is still a restorative treat. Also in town, the National Historic Register **Moses Mason House** (10–14 Broad Street; tel: 207-824 2908; open July–early Sept, Tues–Sun pm; entrance fee), an 1813 Federal manse maintained by the Bethel Historical Society, is a treasure house of American primitive painting: the itinerant muralist Rufus Porter decorated the entryway and second-floor landing with, respectively, a seascape and forest tableau.

North of town, in **Newry,** the **Sunday River ski resort** (52) (Sunday River Road; tel: 207-824 3000 or 800-543 2754; www.sundayriver.com) covers seven mountains and has the largest snow-making system in New England. Off-season, chairlifts carry mountain bikers to the top for an exhilarating ride and spectacular views. The nearby 1872 Artists' Covered Bridge (closed to traffic) is a delightful spot for a swim or a picnic.

BELOW: Augusta's State House. **RIGHT:** lobstering. **PAGE 336:** lighthouse lens.

Head north on Route 26 which climbs into the fabulously scenic **Grafton Notch State Park** (53) (tel: 207-824 2912), passing by numerous trailheads and the parking lot for Screw Auger Falls.

The Capital City

Augusta (54), Maine's modest-sized capital (population 22,000), stands on the Kennebec River and began its days in 1628 as a trading post. Although its website describes it as "a world-class capital city," the locals tend to head for Portland when they seek urban excitement. It has a gold-domed **State House** (State and Capitol streets; tel: 207-287 1400; open weekdays) designed by Charles Bulfinch in 1832, but substantially altered and enlarged in 1909–10.

The superb **Maine State Museum** in the State House complex (tel: 207-287 2301; open Mon–Sat; Sun pm) has displays on "12,000 years of Maine," plus the "Made in Maine" exhibition, which includes prehistoric arrowheads, a water powered woodworking mill and hundreds of Maine-made items.

The city's other major sight is **Old Fort Western**, built close to the river in 1754 and America's oldest wooden fort (City Center Plaza; tel: 207-626 2385; open Memorial Day–Labor Day, daily in pm; Labor Day–Columbus Day, Sat & Sun pm; Nov–Jan, first Sun of month 1–3pm; entrance fee). The stockade and blockhouses have been evocatively re-created, complete with replica cannons. ❑

FOREST, LAKE AND MOUNTAIN WILDLIFE

New England's wilderness areas are one of its big draws. Hunting, fishing, photography and simply enjoying nature attract both locals and visitors

It's obvious from the air and just as clear from the freeways: trees cover more than three-quarters of New England, cloaking the mountains of New Hampshire, Maine, and Vermont. These woods and mountains ring with birdsong and are carpeted with wild flowers; particularly enthralling are the alpine flowers on Mount Washington (above and far right).

The most exciting animal to see in the forests is moose. Desperately ungainly, and sporting hairy dewlaps beneath large snouts, they can often be spotted in northern New England, especially in and around lakes and marshes – or licking the salt that runs off the roads in winter. A bull can grow to well over 6 feet (2 meters) tall, with huge antlers, and can weigh half a ton (give him a wide berth). You may see moose as you drive around, particularly at dawn or dusk; if not, join one of many moose-watching trips organised locally.

Black bears are shy denizens of the deep forests. They seldom attack humans, but don't feed them or leave food scraps on the ground. Keep food in sealed containers and *never* approach cubs – their mothers are firecely protective.

In the lakes and streams that lace the forests, beavers fell trees with their teeth, building lodges and dams and creating ponds. Their lodges built of mud and sticks, may be up to 6 ft (2 meters) tall. Also look out for raccoons, chipmunks, and porcupines.

△ **BEAVERS AT WORK**
A beaver dam (above) is an amazingly effective construction of mud and sticks. Sticks stripped of their bark are a give-away sign of a beaver colony.

▽ **THE LOON**
The loon is the state bird of New Hampshire and, some say, the oldest bird on Earth. The diver is often to be seen on Squam Lake, New Hampshire (above).

◁ **WHITE-TAIL DEER**
White-tailed deer are common in forested areas, and hunting them is a popular pastime in the fall. This fawn wears its white-spotted, spring-time coat.

▽ BIRDLIFE
Waders include American egret (below) and black-crowned night heron. Forest birds include pine siskin, blue jay, golden-crowned kinglet and chickadee.

▽ FOREST FLOOR
In the cool, moist forests, pine seedlings grow up through a silver-gray carpet of mosses and lichens, some of which are native to Arctic tundra regions.

△ DAWN OUTING
A sunrise canoe trip on a lake or river (look out for advertisements locally in Maine and New Hampshire) is often the time to see beavers and moose.

▷ DRIVERS BEWARE!
A collision with a moose could cause serious damage not only to your car, but also quite possibly to you and your passengers. Go slowly if you see one by the road.

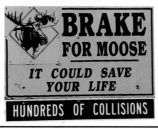

BRAKE FOR MOOSE
IT COULD SAVE YOUR LIFE
HUNDREDS OF COLLISIONS

ALPINE FAUNA AND FLORA

Mount Washington in New Hampshire, subjected to three continental storm systems, has some of the worst weather in the world, and the treeline occurs as low as 1,400 feet (420 meters). This arctic zone supports a few mammals – voles and shrews, for instance, living in deep crevices – and some 100 species of alpine plants, many of which grow only here, on Mount Katahdin in Maine's Baxter State Park, and in Labrador and the Arctic. These plants have successfully adapted to dessication caused by biting winds, poor soil, minimal sunlight, and a short growing season. For some, it is 25 years before they flower. It's a fragile ecology. These exquisite plants, growing in and around the lichen-covered rocks with sedges and dwarfed balsam firs, include gold thread, fireweed, alpine bearberry, starflower, arnica, mountain cranberry, wren's egg cranberry, skunk currant and the dwarf cinquefoil *Potentilla robbinsiana*, unique to Mount Washington. Their vibrant colors are best seen mid-June to August.

Travel Tips

CONTENTS

Getting Acquainted

Following this general introduction, information is given state by state.

The Place

Situation: New England's six states form the northeastern tip of the US, bordering Canada to the north and the Atlantic Ocean to the East.

Language: Though English is the national language, some communities speak other tongues, including French (northern Maine), Portuguese (Gloucester, New Bedford and coastal towns), and Italian (Boston's North End). Many notices in the Boston area are printed in English, Portuguese, Spanish, Vietnamese and Cambodian.

Time Zone: New England is within the Eastern Time Zone (1 hour ahead of Chicago and 3 hours ahead of California). On the last Sunday in April the clock moves ahead 1 hour for Daylight Saving Time, and on the last Sunday in October it moves back 1 hour.

Currency: US dollar.

Weights and Measures: English pounds, feet, etc; metric only for spirits, wine, and some soft drinks.

Electricity: most wall outlets have 110-volt, 60-cycle, alternating current. If using European-made appliances, step down the voltage with a transformer and bring a plug adaptor as sockets are two-prong.

International Dialing Code: 001 (*see page 333 for codes for each state*).

Government

New England's six states are all politically separate, with senators and representatives in Congress. Each also has an elected governor. Small towns have annual town meetings, open to the whole adult population, at which anyone can air their views, and the town's business and finances are decided; larger communities have representative government.

Doing Business

Most offices are open Mon– Fri 9am–5pm. Many businesses have free 800 numbers (some operate 24 hours a day), and virtually all use voice-mail or answering machines. Fax machines are also ubiquitous.

Climate

New England's climate is as varied as its landscape, with large variations from state to state and from season to season:

Massachusetts Pittsfield in the west has an average annual temperature of around 7.2°C (about 45°F), while Boston in the east is about 10.8°C (about 51.5°C) and Nantucket about 9.7°C (49.5°F).

Connecticut Winters are just below freezing, and summers are warm and humid. Average yearly temperature along the coast is 10.6°F (51°F), while in the northwest it is 7.2°C (45°F); for most of the rest of the state the yearly mean is 8.3–9.4°C (47–49°F).

Rhode Island Summer temperatures are moderated by proximity to the ocean, but winters are quite cold. Providence has an average January temperature of about –2°C (about 28°F) and an average July temperature of about 22°C (about 72°F); Block Island has a mean January temperature of about –1°C (about 31°F) and a mean July temperature of about 21°C (about 70°F).

Vermont There are considerable variations in temperature depending on proximity to the mountains (which have heavy snows).Saint Johnsbury, in the northeast, has an average January temperature of about –8.1°C (about 17.5°F) and an average July temperature of about 20.8°C (about 69.5°F); Rutland, in the central part of the state, has a mean January temperature of around –5.8°C (about 21.5°F) and a mean July temperature of around 20.8°C (about 69.5°F).

New Hampshire Concord has an average July temperature of about 21°C (around 70°F) and a mean January temperature of about –6°C (about 21°F); atop Mount Washington, on the other hand, the average July temperature is around 10°C (about 50°F) and the mean January temperature about –14°C (about 6°F). In April 1934, winds of 231 mph (372 kph) were recorded on the summit of Mount Washington.

Maine Being on the coast, the state has a maritime climate. Winter temperatures are much milder than those inland; summer temperatures are cooler. In the north, however, it is extremely cold with a high snowfall. In 1925, Maine's lowest recorded temperature of –44.4°C (–48°F) was observed. The south is the warmest part of the state.

Planning the Trip

Passports and Visas

To enter the United States most foreign visitors need a passport (which should be valid for at least six months longer than their intended stay). You should also be able to provide evidence that you intend to leave the United States after your visit is over (usually in the form of a return or onward ticket).

Visa requirements

Most foreign nationals (except Canadians and Mexicans) also require a visa to visit the US.

Citizens of the UK, New Zealand, Japan and European Union nations do not need a visa, however, as long as they are staying for less than 90 days and have a round-trip or onward ticket. Before entering the US, they must sign a Non-Immigrant Visa Waiver form, declaring, among other things, that they are not seeking to work during their stay.

Anyone wishing to stay longer than 90 days must apply for a visa. This can be done by mail to the nearest US Embassy or Consulate. Visa extensions can be obtained in the US from the United States Immigration and Naturalization Service offices.

HIV

Anyone who is HIV positive or has Aids must also obtain a visa (unless they are the spouse, partner or child of a US citizen or have a green card). Although being HIV-positive is not grounds for exclusion from the States, the US Immigration and Naturalization Service requires proof of your current state of health, medication and so on. Failure to provide correct information on the visa application is grounds for deportation.

Immunization requirements

Visitors from some countries need to supply proof of immunization against yellow fever and cholera.

Money Matters

Travelers' checks

Despite the small fee (generally 1 percent of the cash value), travelers' checks are the best way to bring money into New England, as they can be replaced if lost or stolen. These should be in US dollars, as other currencies may be difficult to exchange. Most hotels, restaurants and stores will cash them for you or accept them as payment without charging commission. Make sure you have plenty of small-denomination checks, though, as stores may not cash $100 checks.

Foreign currency

Visitors may encounter problems exchanging foreign currency. Many banks in larger cities throughout New England offer a foreign-exchange service (don't forget to take your passport), but this is not universal.

Banks

Many banks have only one branch in smaller towns; more in large cities. Most banks open around 10am and close between 3pm and 5pm on weekdays; few are open on Saturday and if so, only in the morning.

Most banks have ATMs that give cash and accept most credit cards.

Credit cards

These are widely accepted. If you rent a car, a credit card is essential.

Health

INSURANCE

Most visitors to New England have no health problems during their stay: sunburn is the main nuisance for the majority. Even so, foreigners should never leave home without travel insurance to cover themselves and their belongings. It's not cheap to get sick in the United States. Your own insurance company or travel agent can advise you on policies, but shop

around as rates vary. Make sure you are covered for accidental death, emergency medical care, cancellation of trip, and baggage or document loss.

HAZARDS

Lyme disease (borne by deer ticks hiding in high grass) is a potentially dangerous chronic condition. Starting with a rash, it develops into flu-like symptoms and joint inflammation, and possible long-term complications such as meningitis and heart failure. Precautions are in order, particularly along the coast (so far, it is extremely uncommon in the northern interior). When hiking in grass or brush, wear light-colored pants tucked into socks, and spray the clothing with an insecticide. Inspect your skin afterwards: if a tick has attached itself, disinfect the area with alcohol and visit a doctor or clinic immediately. An undetected bite may result in a red-ringed rash; again, see a doctor. If you suffer any of the symptoms described after exposure to ticks, a doctor can prescribe antibiotics.

Poison ivy causes only temporary discomfort, but this can be avoided by keeping an eye out for the shiny three-leaf clusters and washing immediately upon accidental contact. Camomile lotion is good for soothing the skin. **Tap water** is perfectly safe to drink, but avoid stream water as it can cause giardia, an intestinal disorder spread by wild animal wastes. Use a filter or purification tablets, or boil water, when hiking or camping.

What to Wear/Bring

Clothing styles in New England vary from state to state, as well as from region to region. In New Hampshire, Maine, Vermont and the Berkshires in

Customs

Visitors aged 21 or over may bring the following to the US:
● 1 liter of duty-free alcohol
● 200 duty-free cigarettes, or 2 kg tobacco or 100 cigars
● Gifts worth $100 if non-US citizens or $800 if US citizens
● up to $10,000 in US or foreign cash, travelers' checks or so on; any more must be declared. Import of meat, seeds, plants, and fruit is forbidden.

Massachusetts people tend to dress in casual clothes geared towards outdoor life, whereas attire in cities in Massachusetts, Connecticut and Rhode Island is more traditional.

To cover all occasions, bring a variety of clothing . For men, a jacket and tie, although not necessarily a suit, is standard dress for more formal restaurants and may in fact be required; women have more latitude, in terms of pants versus dresses, but be warned that some urban or resort bars and nightclubs may ban jeans and T-shirts.

Some warm clothing, such as sweaters, jackets, and windbreakers, should be packed even during the summer, when evening temperatures tend to dip, especially in the mountains and on the coast. Winters necessitate heavy outerwear, including hats, scarves, gloves, and boots.

Getting There

Flying is by far the easiest way to get to New England from abroad. If you come overland from elsewhere in the US, cars are the preferred mode of travel. Trains are less frequent than flights, and although buses connect most cities and several major towns, they are not much cheaper than a discount airfare, take substantially longer, and are less comfortable.

BY AIR

Most major US carriers service the New England states. A variety of discount fares and special deals are offered, so shop around.

Logan International Airport in Boston is the 15th-busiest airport in the world, and smaller airports – many of them served by Delta or US Air – are scattered throughout New England, near larger cities such as Hartford, Bangor, and Burlington.

Some 15 international airlines fly direct to New England. Alternatively, you can fly into New York and catch one of the many connecting flights to

Tourist Information Abroad

There is no American Tourist Office in the UK, US or Australia. If you have a business or visa enquiry, information can be obtained from the US Embassies in each country:
Australia: 21 Moonah Place, Yarralumla, ACT 2600
Tel: 02 6214 5600
www.usembassy-australia.state.gov/embassy/contact.html
UK: 5 Upper Grosvenor Street, London W1A 1AE
Tel: 020 7499 9000
www.usembassy.org.uk

For holiday information, the tourist organisation Discover New England supplies a color brochure with sights, useful telephone

numbers and accommodation, plus maps of each state.
UK: Sellet Public Relations, 16 Dover Street, London W1F 4LR
Tel: 0870 264 0555
Other countries:
Discover New England,
P.O. Box 3809,
Stowe, Vermont 05672, US
Tel: 802-253 2500
Fax: 802-253 9064
e-mail: DNE@together.net
www.discovernewengland.org

There is a Massachussetts Office of Travel and Tourism in the UK at: Molasses House, Clove Hitch Quay, Plantation Wharf, York Place, London SW11 3TN. Tel: 020 7978 7429.

the New England area, or the hourly shuttle to Boston (no reservations required, tickets can be bought just before boarding). Boston's Airport has a bureau de change and hotel reservation desk (which charges no commission), plus car hire outlets.

During holidays (see panel below) it may be difficult to find a flight, especially at Thanksgiving, when most of the US seems to be on the move and discount tickets are virtually non-existent.

BY LAND

Train

Amtrak (tel: 800-872 7245) offers efficient rail services to New England from Washington, DC, and New York, routing through Connecticut and Rhode Island and terminating in Boston; another route extends from Washington and New York to New Haven, Connecticut, Springfield, Massachusetts, and St Albans, Vermont. Amtrak's Downeaster runs between Boston and Portland, Maine. Various commuter trains link Boston with smaller towns in Massachusetts, and Rhode island.

Bus

Large air-conditioned buses connect New England to most other US tourist destinations (see page 342).

Car

Driving is by far the best way of exploring and experiencing New England (see page 342).

Tour Operators

The following companies specialise in tailormade New England itineraries:

In the UK
North America Travel Service
7 Albion Street, Leeds LS1 5ER
Tel: 0113 243 1606
Fax: 0113 243 0919
www.americatravelservice.com
In the US
CST International
22 Moon Penny Lane
Centerville, MA 02632
Tel: 508-771 1423/800-966 9445
www.newenglandtours.com
Tourco
29 Bassett Lane
Hyannis, MA 02601
Tel: 800-537 5378
www.tourco.com

Practical Tips

Media

Newspapers

As well as the US nationals such as USA Today and the financial Wall Street Journal, New England has many local newspapers. The Boston Globe is a highly regarded daily; the Boston Herald a tabloid daily, with listings on Thursday and Friday respectively, and the Boston Phoenix is a Saturday-only paper. The New York Times is widely distributed in New England, and larger towns have their own dailies such as the Hartford Courant. Alternative papers, often with excellent events and entertainment listings, thrive in college towns. The Advocate series of free weeklies is very good for listings. Foreign magazines and papers are sold on newsstands in the larger cities.

Television and radio

Flick through the channels on both TV and radio, and you'll experience the gamut of American life, from game show to in-depth news. Most hotels receive the three major national networks (ABC, CBS and NBC), plus many cable networks including CNN and Fox. The Public Broadcasting System (PBS) has some of the better-quality programs. National Public Radio (NPR), at the low and high ends of the FM scale, carries excellent news, classical music, and jazz.

Postal Services

There are post offices in most New England villages and towns. Opening hours vary between central big city branches and those in smaller places, but hotel personnel can tell you when the nearest post office is open.

If you do not know where you will be staying in a particular town, you can receive mail simply by having it addressed to you, care of General Delivery, at the main office in that town – but you must pick up such mail personally (within 10 days). Check with postal officials about charges and the variety of mail-delivery services available.

Stamps may be purchased from vending machines installed in hotel lobbies, in shops and airports, and at bus and train stations.

To facilitate quick delivery within the US, include the five-digit zip code when addressing communications. Zip code information may be obtained from any post office.

Telecommunications

Telephone

Public telephones are to be found in hotel lobbies, restaurants, drugstores, street corners, garages, convenience stores, and other general locations. Long-distance call rates decrease after 5pm, going down still further after 11pm, and are lowest on weekends. Many countries can be dialed directly from New England, without operator assistance. For all specific information concerning telephone rates and conveniences, simply call the local operator (0) and inquire.

All 800, 877, and 888 numbers are toll-free. For emergencies, dial **911**.

Email

Internet cafes, where you can retrieve email from your account, are increasingly popular. However, don't count on finding one in small towns. It's best to rely on faxing messages unless you are in a big city.

Fax

All but the smallest of hotels and B&Bs offer access to a fax machine; there's generally a fee for outgoing faxes (often exorbitant), but incoming are usually free.

Public Holidays

During the holidays listed below, some or all state, local and federal agencies may be closed. Local banks and businesses may also close on the following days.
● **January 1:** New Year's Day
● **Third Monday in January:** Martin Luther King Jr. Day
● **Third Monday in February:** Presidents Day, celebrating Lincoln's and Washington's birthdays
● **Third Monday in April:** Patriots' Day (Massachusetts only)
● **Last Monday in May:** Memorial Day
● **July 4:** Independence Day
● **First Monday in September:** Labor Day
● **Second Monday in October:** Columbus Day
● **November 11:** Veterans Day
● **Fourth Thursday in November:** Thanksgiving
● **December 25:** Christmas Day

Telephone Codes

Dial the following codes, preceded by 1, when phoning from a different state or area:
Connecticut (southwest) 203
Connecticut (elsewhere) 860
Maine 207
Massachussets (western) 413
Massachussets (central and east) 508, 978, 351, 774, 857, 781, 339
Massachussets (Boston area) 617
New Hampshire 603
Rhode Island 401
Vermont 802

Alcohol

The legal age for both the purchase and consumption of alcoholic drinks is 21. Liquor stores are state-owned or franchised in Vermont, New Hampshire and Maine; privately owned in southern New England. Laws on Sunday purchase and consumption vary between states.

Often a restaurant without a liquor license will permit customers to bring their own beer or wine; but some communities have elected to remain "dry", and if they do, you must, too. If you are driving, keep bottles of alcohol unopened and out of sight in the car.

Medical Treatment

Pharmacies stock most standard medication (though some painkillers that are available over the counter in other countries may be prescriptions only in the US), and staff are trained to help with most minor ailments.
Hospitals are signposted on highways with a white H on a blue background. Major hospitals have 24-hour emergency rooms – you may have a long wait before you get to see the doctor, but the care and treatment are thorough and professional. Boston's hospitals are highly regarded.

Walk-in clinics are commonplace in cities, where you can consult a nurse or doctor for a minor ailment without an appointment. If cost is a concern, turn first to clinics offering free or pro-rated care (look under "Clinics" in the *Yellow Pages*).

Security and Crime

Crimes against persons and property are quite uncommon in rural New England and in parts of big cities frequented by visitors. However:
● Keep a firm grip on bags. Don't sling them over the back of a chair.
● Whenever possible, travel with another person, especially at night.
● When not driving, lock your car and never leave valuables in view. At night, park in lighted areas. When returning to your car, have your keys ready.
● Never leave luggage unattended. Never leave valuables in your room.
● Do not carry more cash than you need. Whenever possible, use credit cards and travelers' checks.

Gay Travelers

Boston has a vibrant gay community, as do, to a lesser extent, other cities and college towns. Northampton, Massachusetts, for instance, emerged as a lively enclave for lesbians in the late 20th century, and Provincetown on Cape Cod has long been a popular gay summer vacation spot. The town even has a gay counterpart to the Chamber of Commerce: the Provincetown Business Guild (tel: 508-487 2313, 800-637 8696, www.ptown.org).

Information concerning gay-oriented activities and businesses can be found in alternative weeklies such as northern Vermont's *Seven Days* or western Massachusetts and Connecticut's *The Advocate*, and in Boston's *Bay Windows*, a gay newspaper, and in the *One in Ten* supplement produced by the alternative weekly the *Boston Phoenix*.

A good in-town networking source,

for those visiting Boston, is the We Think the World of You bookstore at 540 Tremont Street (tel: 617-267 3010; books@wethinktheworld ofyou.com).

Disabilities

Federal regulations have promoted handicapped accessibility, but the work is by no means complete. Many B&Bs, mindful of their elderly clientele, have done adaptive retrofitting. If in doubt, call ahead.

Taxes

All states levy taxes on meals and accommodation, and all but New Hampshire on all sales. When restaurants and hotels quote prices, these taxes are not normally included – so ask, as they can bump up the cost by up to 11 percent. Ticket prices for transport have the tax included.

Tipping

Tip appropriately or it will be interpreted as an insult. For meals, hairdressers, bartenders, and taxi drivers, around 15 percent is the norm (20 percent for exceptional waiter service or if the bill is $100 or more). Don't tip on the tax portion of the bill. Give a few dollars to the doorman and bellhop; housekeepers should get $2 per day.

Dates

The convention for writing dates in the US is to put the month first, so 2/12/2006 is 12 February 2006.

Smoking

Smoking is banned in most indoor public places and on transport. Some states ban smoking in restaurants; others specify non-smoking areas. Hotels have non-smoking rooms; many inns and B&Bs ban smoking.

Tourist Information in New England

The following state tourist agencies provide ample information on attractions, restaurants, lodgings, recreational options, and events. They can also refer you to local chambers of commerce, if required.

Connecticut
505 Hudson Street
Hartford, CT 06106
Tel: 860-270 8080/800-282 6863
www.ctbound.org

Maine
State House Station 59
Augusta, ME 04333
Tel: 207-287 5711/888-624 6345
www.mainetourism.com
Massachusetts
10 Park Plaza, Suite 4510
Boston, MA 02116
Tel: 800-227 6277
www.mass.vacation.com
New Hampshire
Box 1856
Concord, NH 03302

Tel: 603-271 2343/800-386 4664
www.visitnh.gov
Rhode Island
1 West Exchange Street
Providence
RI 02903
Tel: 401-222 2601/800-556 2484
www.visitrhodeisland.com
Vermont
6 Baldwin Street
Montpelier, VT 05633
Tel: 802-828 3237/800-837 6668
www.travel-vermont.com

Getting Around

Information

The best source of information for travelling around New England is the tourist board of each specific state, which may also be able to book tickets for you *(see page 333)*.

By Air

Internal flights are expensive, but if you want to hop from place to place by air, airlines serve the following New England towns and cities:
Massachusetts Boston, Hyannis, Martha's Vineyard, Nantucket, New Bedford, Worcester
Maine Bangor, Portland, Bar Harbor
Connecticut Bradley Airport (near Hartford), Bridgeport, Groton, New Haven
Vermont Burlington, Rutland
New Hampshire Lebanon-Hanover, Manchester
Rhode Island Providence

AIRLINES

Major domestic airlines include:
Continental Tel: 800-525 0280
Cape Air Tel: 800-352 0714
Delta Tel: 800-221 1212
JetBlue Tel: 800-538 2583
Northwest Airlines Tel: 800-225 2525
USAir Tel: 800-428 4322

By Bus

Most New England cities and tourist sights can be reached by bus. Greyhound has the most comprehensive coverage of the US, and the following companies operate local services:
Bonanza Tel: 800-556 3815. Based in Providence, RI, with connections to New York and Massachusetts, and several routes within Rhode Island.
C&J Trailways Tel: 800 258 7111. Services northeastern Massachusetts, New Hampshire, and southern Maine.
Concord Trailways Tel: 603-228 3300/800-639 3317. Services mainly New Hampshire and based in Concord.

Greyhound Tel: 617-526 1800/800-231 2222. The most extensive bus network, with offices in Boston, MA, and elsewhere, and long-distance routes throughout the US.
Peter Pan Tel: 800-343 9999. Based in Springfield MA.
Plymouth & Brockton Tel: 508-746 0378. Routes mainly within Massachusetts and Connecticut.
Vermont Transit Lines Tel: 802-864 6811/800-451 3292. The main Vermont service, based in Burlington.
Some bus terminals are in "problem areas", so take care when traveling to and from stations.

By Train

The most extensive train service is offered by **Amtrak** Tel: 800-872 7245, www.amtrak.com.
Connecticut is served by **Metro North**, with trains between New York and New Haven. Tel: 800-638 7646/212-532 4900.
Boston has a commuter line (**MBTA**) from North Station traveling north and west, with stops at Concord, Rockport, Gloucester, Salem, and Newburyport. Tel: 617-222 3200, www.mbta.com.

By Car

A car offers the most popular and convenient means of getting around New England. Although the network of airplanes, buses, trains, ferries, and taxis is reliable, having your own car is the easiest way to get around (except in the congested heart of Boston), and it also offers the greatest leeway for getting off the beaten path.
Highways A number of well-maintained interstate highways (ranging from four to eight or more lanes) make covering New England's distances easy. To get an idea of the range, picture a radius from Boston to Burlington, in northwestern Vermont – a trip which, on Routes 93 and 89, would take only about five hours. That radius, extended across New England, would cover all but the northernmost regions of Maine (beyond Bangor).
Secondary roads Travel on secondary roads is time-consuming, but all the more scenic. However, beware of dirt roads – usually represented by a

Drunk Driving

Regulations are very strict. If you fail a breath test after drinking, your license will be removed on the spot. Fines are exemely high. Avoid drinking and driving and keep alcohol inaccessible and unopened in the car.

broken line – in mud season (typically, March into May). Note that mountain roads may be closed in winter.

CAR HIRE

Visitors wishing to rent or lease a car on arrival will find offices of all the major US firms at airports (usually more expensive than elsewhere) and convenient city locations. Toll-free arrangements can be made in advance. The most reputable firms are:
Hertz Tel: 800-654 3131
Avis Tel: 800-331 1212
Budget Tel: 800-527 0700
It's also worth calling around, referring to the *Yellow Pages* (under "Automobile Renting & Leasing"), for the best rates. Sometimes local rental firms may offer low rates, especially for lower-quality cars (franchise chains, such as Rent A Wreck, cater for just this market). But be sure to check insurance coverage provisions.
The cheapest rates tend to be from Thursday noon until Monday noon.

Legal requirements

Most car-rental agencies require drivers to be at least 21 years old (sometimes 25), to hold a major credit card and a driver's license that is current and has been valid for at least a year; some will accept a cash deposit, sometimes as high as $500, in lieu of a credit card.
Foreign travelers may need to show an international driver's license or a license from their own country.

Insurance

Liability is not included in the terms of your lease, so advertised rates usually do not include additional fees for insurance. Collision Damage Waiver (CDW) is recommended, as it covers you if someone else causes damage to your car.

RULES OF THE ROAD

States and municipalities have specific laws and regulations regarding parking, speed limits and the like; most are clearly posted.

Seatbelts

These are obligatory for all front-seat occupants. Children under six must be buckled into safety belts, safety seats, or a proper child restraint. Many rental firms supply child seats for a small extra cost.

Fuel

Petrol, or gas, is lead-free and stations are plentiful, and often open 24 hours a day near major highways (otherwise, usually 5 or 6am until 10 or 11pm). British travelers should note, however, that the US gallon is 17 percent smaller than the English equivalent. Metric users note that 1 gallon equals 3.8 litres.

Special considerations
Rotaries (roundabouts), especially in Boston, pose a particular challenge. The official rule is that the cars already in the circle have the right of way in exiting, but this rule is rarely observed in practice. It's best to proceed cautiously, whether entering or exiting. Unless otherwise posted, a right-hand turn at a red light is permitted throughout New England. On sighting a school bus that has stopped to load or unload children, drivers in both directions must stop completely before reaching the bus and may not proceed until the flashing red warning signals on the school bus have been switched off, or until directed to do so.

Hitching and car-jacking
Hitchhiking is discouraged; so is picking up hitchhikers. Car-jackings are rare, but a growing threat. Learn what areas of cities to avoid before starting out. Ask your rental clerk when you pick up your vehicle.

Breakdown
Some highways have emergency phones every few miles. Otherwise, park up with your bonnet raised and a police patrol will soon arrive. The American Automobile Association (tel: 800-222 4357) offers reciprocal breakdown services for some affiliated firms in other countries.

Parking
You must park in the direction of traffic, and never by a fire hydrant. A yellow line or yellow curb means no parking is allowed. In some towns a white line along the curb shows where you can park.

Speed Limits

New England states maintain their interstate highway system in good condition. Highway speed is mostly 65 mph (104 kph), although along portions in built-up areas – check the roadside signs – the maximum is 55 mph (89 kph) or lower.

On interstates, fellow drivers may be cruising along at about 10 miles more per hour than the posted limit, on the presumption that police will allow that much leeway. Join them at your own risk. Enforcement, if sporadic, can be strict, with high penalties.

Where to Stay

New England has an especially diverse set of accommodation alternatives. The options vary in terms of location, price, amenities, atmosphere, and orientation, and can be anything from low-budget B&Bs and youth hostels, through roadside motels, to full-service grand hotels such as Boston's Ritz Carlton. For details in each state, see *Where to Stay* sections below.

COUNTRY INNS
Perhaps the most uniquely New England lodging is the famed country inn. If you are tired of motels and hotels, and willing to forego certain conveniences (such as an in-room phone or TV) for more simple pleasures, country inns are a wonderful option. They range from weathered farmhouses, with huge fireplaces and relaxing music, to grand elegance. Most are warm and welcoming, though a few can seem slightly pretentious or effete.

In the UK, New England Inns & Resorts specialises in country inns. Tel: 01923 821469; fax: 01923 827157.

B&BS
B&B accommodation is widespread. Companies specializing in B&Bs include: **Bed & Breakfast Agency of Boston** Tel: 800-248 9262; in UK, 0800-895 128.

HOLIDAY HOMES
UK firms specializing in renting out New England houses include:
Bridgewater's Holiday Homes 217 Monton Road, Monton Manchester M30 9PN Tel: 0161 707 8547 Massachusetts, all year round.
Four Seasons in New England 2 Higher St. Hatherleigh EX20 03JD Tel: 01837 711267 www.nelodgings.com Houses and inns in all states.
New England Connection Vincent House, Vincent Lane,

Dorking RH4 1AR Tel: 01306 877600 Vermont, New Hampshire and Massachusetts. All year round.
North American Vacation Homes 45 Perrymount Rd Haywards Heath W. Sussex R141 63BN www.usahomes.co/uk Tel: 01444 450034 Houses in Massachusetts, New Hampshire, Maine and Vermont.

Hotel Chains

Among the large chains that have hotels throughout the New England states are:
Best Western Tel: 800-528 1234; www.bestwestern.com
Comfort Inn/Choice Hotels Tel: 800-424 6423; www.comfortinn.com
Days Inn Tel: 800-325 2525; www.daysinn.com
Hilton Tel: 800-445 8667; www.hilton.com
Holiday Inn Tel: 800-465 4329; www.basshotels.com
Howard Johnson Tel: 800-654 2000; www.hojo.com
Hyatt Tel: 800-233 1234; www.hyatt.com
Marriott Tel: 800-872 9563; www.marriott.com
Quality Inn Tel: 800-228 5151; www.qualityinn.com
Radisson Tel: 800-333 3333; www.radisson.com
Ramada Tel: 800-272 6232; www.ramada.com
Red Roof Inn Tel: 800-843 7663; www.redroof.com
Sheraton Tel: 800-325 3535; www.sheraton.com
Super 8 Tel: 800-800 8000; www.super8.com

Where to Eat

"Land of the bean and the cod"
New England's culinary standing made a stratospheric leap during the 1990s. Once bemoaned as the land of "the bean and the cod", Boston started the region's culinary renaissance rolling with a group of world-class chefs who trained their sous-chefs so well that their ranks kept expanding. Where once the highest quality you could expect was provincial and stodgy, now the offerings are fresh, flavorful and sophisticated.

New England's chefs have not only come up with brilliant new uses and combinations for the area's renowned bounty (especially seafood), they've developed their own network for securing new native delicacies, from farmstead cheeses to locally raised game birds.

Traditional fare revisited

If you've never tried the classics, by all means try them. These range from thick, wholesome soups, to seafood specialties including lobster bisque and broiled scrod, to old-timers such as boiled dinner (a hotpot of boiled beef, cabbage, carrots and potatoes), to wicked desserts including Indian pudding (a cornmeal bake flavored with milk, molasses, ginger, cinnamon and sometimes raisins), and pies made with fresh seasonal apples, blueberries, and raspberries. For regional traditions see the *Where to Eat* section for each state.

But be prepared for some surprises. New England's ingenious cooks – from executive chefs at the four-star hotels to the hardworking chef/owners at country inns – are having a year-round field day with seasonal specialties, and lucky customers are in for an ever-changing array of treats.

Entertainment

New England offers a wide range of entertainment. Rural areas tend to be more slow-paced and relaxed during the evening, while Boston supports a varied, exciting nightlife.
Boston outgrew its staid image long ago. At night, the city sparkles with lively and sophisticated activity. The Boston Symphony Orchestra has earned an international reputation; it's less formal offshoot, the Boston Pops, also commands a great following.
Music permeates the region, ranging from rural chamber groups to big-city rock and jazz. Comedy clubs are also increasingly popular.
Theater thrives not only in Boston and New Haven (proving grounds for Broadway) but in myriad regional repertory companies and "straw-hat" summer theaters.
Dance Professional modern dance and ballet can be seen in bucolic settings, as well as in towns. The larger cities have dance clubs where it's easy to meet and mingle.

Listings For more specific information, check the listings in local papers, such as the *Boston Globe*'s Thursday Calendar section, *phoenix* (various editions cover Boston, Providence and Worcester), *Advocate* (Pioneer Valley), and *Seven Days* (Burlington, Vermont). See also *Nightlife* and *Culture* for each state, below.

Special Events

State tourist boards will gladly provide detailed lists of seasonal festivals, fairs, and other annual events large and small – from teddy-bears' picnics to antique car rallies. Many are so appealing it makes sense to plan a trip around them – or at the very least commit yourself to a detour.

Shopping

New England provides as great a range of shopping opportunities as can be found anywhere in the country: large department stores, enormous malls, local country auctions, antique shows, craft stores and bargain factory outlets. Whether you want bargains or works of art, the six states have much to offer.

ANTIQUES

Antiques stores abound and antiquing in these shops can be fun and, depending on the level of the stock, relatively inexpensive.

HANDICRAFTS

US handicrafts are experiencing a renaissance. There are more quality craft items being produced now than at any time since the Industrial Revolution. Crafts, whether pottery, weaving, or woodworking, are less expensive and higher quality when bought directly from the artisans, at their studios or juried crafts fairs.

FACTORY OUTLETS

Discount and "factory outlet" stores are increasingly popular in this area. The prices aren't always that much lower than you would find in a regular store, but there is the convenience of having a lot of goods in one location, and sometimes there are "end of range" lines at bargain prices.

Filene's Basement The world-famous store in Boston (with dozens of branches throughout the country) initiated off-price retailing in 1908. The original store, at the corner of Winter and Summer Streets, is still a wild, lucrative place to shop: you might find a designer original reduced to a fraction of its original price.

Dozens of factory outlets have sprung up in **Freeport, Maine**, around the flagship store of outdoor clothing and equipment specialist L.L. Bean.

Manchester, Vermont is another outlet center, specializing in top-end fashion labels.

Children

New England is a paradise for children. They can be kept entertained with amusements as simple as observing a tide pool, or take in history at such "hands-on" and accessible living museums as Plimoth Plantation or Old Sturbridge Village. Staff members at these sites are skilled at engaging children's interests.

Boston

Boston's Children's Museum is one of the most appealing museums in the country, and smaller facilities with similar agendas are scattered through the surrounding countryside. Other Boston attractions sure to thrill little ones include the Museum of Science, the New England Aquarium, and the Swan Boats in the Public Garden.

Bernice Chesler's excellent book, In and Out of Boston with (or without) Children can provide leads on lesser-known but equally rewarding attractions.

Seaside attractions

Cape Cod might as well be a giant sandbox, and the calm, shallow waters on the bay side offer optimal swimming and splashing for those still acquiring their sea legs.

Children's reaction to the many whalewatching excursions offered on the Cape and along the coast up into Maine is invariably "Awesome!"

Resorts

A number of resorts – most notably Smuggler's Notch in northern Vermont – have made a specialty of catering for kids and the parents they hold in thrall. In summer, this ski area basically becomes a camp for all ages, with waterslides, special outdoors events, and a real sense of camaraderie.

Some of New England's family-oriented resorts, such as The Balsams, in remote northern New Hampshire, date back to around 1900 or earlier, and are attracting a fifth generation for mannered meals and unstructured enjoyment of the great outdoors.

Accommodations

Regrettably, many of New England's fussier B&Bs shun the company of children. If you're blessed with particularly well behaved youngsters, you might try pushing the envelope, but then again, it's no fun to go where you're not welcome. Fortunately, there are plenty of inns where their presence is not only tolerated but actively courted.

If in doubt, call ahead or check the detailed listings in Best Places to Stay in New England, by Kimberly Grant and Christina Tree.

Restaurants

The fancier restaurants may also exercise their own unpublished strictures regarding children – claiming, for instance, that the place is booked solid when you can see plainly that it's half-empty. Here, the best solution is a reservation. On the other hand, you may enjoy an equally pleasant and educational repast at a ramshackle lobster pound or a nostalgic diner.

Outdoor Activities

Whatever your age and whatever the season, New England offers plenty of active outdoor adventures. From urban walking to thrill-a-minute rafting, from downhill skiing to mountain biking, from fly fishing to gliding a canoe through the salt marshes, New England is an outdoor playground. Within each state are recommendations for outfitters who will help you enjoy the outdoors more fully.

Massachusetts

The Place

Known as: The Bay State.
Motto: Ense Petit Placidam Sub Libertate Quietem (By the sword we seek peace, but peace only under liberty).
Origin of name: May derive from an Algonquian Indian village meaning "place of big hills".
Entered Union: 6 February 1788, the sixth of the 13 original states.
Capital: Boston.
Area: 10,555 sq. miles (27,337 sq. km).
Highest point: Mount Greylock.
Population: 6.1 million.
Population density: 570 people per sq. mile (220 per sq. km).
Economy: Financial services; high technology; healthcare; academe.
Annual visitors: 33 million.
National representation: 2 senators and 10 representatives to Congress.
Famous citizens: Samuel Adams, Louisa May Alcott, Emily Dickinson, Ralph Waldo Emerson, John Hancock, Nathaniel Hawthorne, Oliver Wendell Holmes, Edgar Allen Poe, Henry David Thoreau.

Where to Stay

BOSTON

Boston Harbor Hotel
70 Rowes Wharf, 02110
Tel: 617-439 7000/800-752 7077
Fax: 617-330 9450
www.bhh.com
With 230 standard rooms and one- and two-bedroom suites, this is a modern beauty with old-world charm, perched on the harbor. $$$$
The Millennium Bostonian Hotel
Faneuil Hall Marketplace, 02109
Tel: 617-523 3600/800-343 0922
www.millennium-hotels.com
A mix of modern and historic, overlooking Quincy Market with 201 rooms. $$$$
Copley Square Hotel
47 Huntington Avenue, 02116
Tel: 617-536 9000/800-225 7062
Fax: 617-267 3547
www.copleysquarehotel.com

Older, centrally located, European-style hotel with 143 rooms; often more affordable than neighboring hotels. **$$$$**

Courtyard Boston Tremont Boston
275 Tremont Street, 02116
Tel: 617-426 1400/800-331 9998
www.marriott.com
Handsomely-restored, 15-story historic hotel offers 322 nicely refurbished rooms in the thick of the theater district. **$$$-$$$$**

Eliot Suite Hotel
370 Commonwealth Avenue, 02215
Tel: 617-267 1607/800-443 5468
Fax: 617-536 9114
www.eliothotel.com
Well-appointed European-style hotel built in 1925 has 95 comfortable one-bedroom suites and a popular first-class restaurant. Convenient for both Back Bay and the Fenway. **$$$$**

Fairmont Copley Plaza Hotel
138 Saint James Avenue, 02116
Tel: 617-267 5300/800-527 4727
Fax: 617-247 6681
www.fairmont.com/copleyplaza
A 1912 grand hotel with 379 rooms, 54 suites, and plenty of romance. **$$$-$$$$**

Four Seasons
200 Boylston Street, 02116
Tel: 617-338 4400/800-332 3442
Fax: 617-423 0154
www.fourseasons.com/boston
The standard-setter for luxury and service. The hotel has 274 rooms and overlooks the Public Garden. **$$$$**

Langham Boston
250 Franklin Street, 02110
Tel: 617-451 1900/800-543 4300
Fax: 617-423 2844
www.langhamhotel.com
A modern hotel with old-world ambiance; 314 rooms built atop a Renaissance Revival 1922 bank. Fabulous French food. **$$$$**

The Lenox
61 Exeter Street, 02116
Tel: 617-536 5300/800-225 7676
Fax: 617-236 0351
www.lenoxhotel.com
An historic, newly-remodeled 212-room hotel well situated for shopping,

Price Categories

A very approximate guide to current room rates for a standard double per night is:
$$$$ = over $200
$$$ = $150–200
$$ = $100–150
$ = under $100

with Copley Place and Newbury Street on either side. Standard units and suites; some with fireplaces. **$$$$**

Boston Omni Parker House
60 School Street, 02108
Tel: 617-227 8600/800-843 6664
Fax: 617-742 5729
www.omni.hotel.com
Hawthorne, Whittier, Emerson and Longfellow conducted literary salons at this grand 551-room hotel soon after it opened in 1854. **$$$$**

Ritz-Carlton Hotel
15 Arlington Street, 02117
Tel: 617-536 5700/800-241 3333
Fax: 617-536 1335
www.ritzcarlton.com
Classic Bostonian white-glove elegance, with the lovely Public Garden at its doorstep and a total of 275 rooms. The Ritz franchise is also represented in a new hotel around the corner, on Boston Common. **$$$$**

Boston Park Plaza Hotel & Towers
64 Arlington Street, 02116
Tel: 617-426 2000/800-225 2008
Fax: 617-423 1708
www.bostonparkplaza.com
A huge, 15-story hotel with 950 standard units and one- and two-bedroom suites near the Boston Common and downtown. **$$$-$$$$**

Gryphon House
9 Bay State Road, 02215
Tel: 617-375 9003/877-375 9003
Fax: 617-425 0716
www.innboston.com
Near Kenmore Square and Boston University, this bowfront brownstone has been converted to a small luxury hotel with just eight rooms. Voice mail, fax machines, two phone lines,

CD players, and other high-tech amenities. **$$$-$$$$**

Hyatt Regency Boston
1 Avenue de Lafayette, 02111
Tel: 617-912 1234/800-621 9200
Fax: 617-451 2198
www.regencyboston.hyatt.com
Around 500 rooms offering modern luxury in a convenient location for the financial and theater districts. **$$$-$$$$**

Harborside Inn
185 State Street, 02109
Tel: 617-723 7500/888-723 7565
Fax: 617-670 6015
www.harborsideinnboston.com
A renovated mercantile warehouse near Faneuil Hall, the financial district, and the waterfront. All 54 modern rooms have exposed brick and Victorian-style furnishings. **$$-$$$$**

Mid-Town Hotel
220 Huntington Avenue, 02115
Tel: 617-369 6240/800-343 1177
Fax: 617-262 8739
www.midtownhotel.com
One of Boston's better deals, a motel-style building with 159 rooms and an outdoor pool, near the Prudential building and the Christian Science Center. Parking included in rate. **$$-$$$$**

82 Chandler Street
82 Chandler Street, 02116
Tel: 617-482 0408/888-482 0408
Fax: 617-482 0659
www.82chandler.com
A five-room B&B in a 19th-century brownstone with bay windows and fireplaces in the revitalized South End neighborhood. Credit cards not accepted. **$$-$$$**

John Jeffries House
14 David G. Mugar Way, 02114
Tel: 617-367 1866
Fax 617-742 0313
www.johnjeffrieshouse.com
Red-brick inn at the foot of Beacon Hill. The 46 rooms are small and simply appointed, but many have kitchens or sitting areas. **$-$$**

Newbury Guest House
261 Newbury Street, 02116
Tel: 617-437 7666/800-437 7668
Fax: 617-670 6100
www.newburyguesthouse.com
A trio of 1882 townhouses converted into a Victorian-style inn right on the "street of dreams". With a total of 32 rooms, this guest house offers excellent value for the location, so book far in advance. **$-$$$**

Brookline

Bertram Inn
92 Sewall Avenue, 02446
Tel: 617-566 2234/800-295 3822
www.bertraminn.com
Comfortably elegant Victorian mansion

Getting Around Boston

Boston is the only New England city with a subway system (the MBTA, or "T" for short); the cost is low (especially compared to other cities), the transit rapid, and the experience is on the whole fairly pleasant.

The Boston Passport, offering one, three or seven days of unlimited rides, can be purchased at the Boston Common Visitor Information Center at 147 Tremont

St, tel: 617-426 3115. Alternatively, contact the MBTA on 617-222 5568 (www.mbta.com), for further information.

The Association for Public Transportation advocacy group publishes an excellent and comprehensive low-cost guide called *Car-Free in Boston*, available at newsstands and bookstores; it actually covers, in lesser detail, all of New England.

Boston B&Bs

B&B Agency of Boston
47 Commercial Wharf, 02110
Tel: 617-720 3540/800-248 9262.
From UK free on 0800-895 128
Fax: 617-523 5761
www.boston-bnbagency.com
This is the largest B&B agency in
Boston, with rooms and self-
catering apartments in Beacon Hill,
Back Bay, North End, and near the
waterfront.

with a grand staircase and 14 rooms.
Situated on a quiet street, it is
convenient for the Green Line MBTA
trolleys that go to downtown Boston.
$$$–$$$$

Cambridge
The Charles Hotel
1 Bennett Street, 02138
Tel: 617-864 1200/800-882 1818
Fax: 617-864 5715
www.charleshotel.com
A modern hotel with 293 rooms right
in Harvard Square, with airy,
traditional-style rooms, some
overlooking the river. Home to the
popular Regattabar jazz club, which
draws nationally known jazz
performers. **$$$$**
The Inn at Harvard
1201 Massachusetts Avenue, 02138
Tel: 617-491 2222/800-458 5886
Fax: 617-520 3711
www.theinnatharvard.com
Graham Gund designed this intimate
four-story inn encircling a peaceful
atrium (113 rooms). **$$$$**
The Hotel at MIT
20 Sidney Street (off Massachusetts
Avenue), 02139
Tel: 617-577 0200/800-222 8733
Fax: 617-494 8366
www.hotelatmit.com
Business-class hotel (opened in
1998) between Central and Kendall
Squares. Occasional quirky decorating
touches in the 210 rooms, such as
armoires with circuit-board inlays, play
up the hotel's location near the
Massachusetts Institute of Technology
campus. **$$$$**
A Cambridge House B&B
2218 Massachusetts Ave, 02140
Tel: 617-491 6300/800-232 9989
Fax: 617-868 2848
www.acambridgehouse.com
B&B with 15 rooms in a quiet, lavishly
restored 1892 Victorian house with
carved cherry paneling and immense
fireplaces in the common areas.
Located about one mile (1½ km) north
of Harvard Square, but only four
blocks from a subway stop. **$$–$$$$**
Mary Prentiss Inn
6 Prentiss Street, 02140

Tel: 617-661 2929
Fax: 617-661 5989
www.maryprentissinn.com
Tastefully appointed Greek Revival
B&B with a spacious deck. Some of
the 20 rooms have antique armoires
and four-poster beds. Situated
between Harvard and Porter Squares.
$$–$$$$
Irving House
24 Irving Street (off Cambridge
Street), 02138
Tel: 617-547 4600/800-854 8249
Fax: 617-371 1533
www.irvinghouse.com
Basic but comfortable 44-room B&B.
Just a short walk from Harvard
Square. **$$–$$$**

BOSTON DAY TRIPS

Concord
Concord's Colonial Inn
48 Monument Square, 01742
Tel: 978-369 9200/800-370 9200
Fax: 978-369 2170
www.concordscolonialinn.com
A 1716 inn on Concord's town
common with 56 rooms. **$$**
Hawthorne Inn
462 Lexington Road, 01742
Tel: 978-369 5610
Fax: 978-287 4949
www.concordmass.com
B&B with seven rooms (some with gas
fireplaces) in the historic district,
opposite Hawthorne's Wayside.
$$–$$$$
Longfellow's Wayside Inn
Wayside Inn Road
South Sudbury, 01776
Tel: 978-443 1776/800-339 1776
Fax: 978-443 8041
www.wayside.org
A mid-18th-century tavern with 10
rooms, close to Lexington and
Concord. The restaurant serves
Yankee fare. **$$–$$$**

Fall River
Lizzie Borden Bed and Breakfast
92 2nd Street, 02720
Tel: 508-675 7333
Fax: 508-673 1545
www.lizzie-borden.com
This B&B is the house where the
infamous Lizzie Borden allegedly
hacked her father and stepmother to

death in 1892. The eight rooms in the
1845 Greek Revival-style home are
small but feature Borden family
memorabilia. **$$$**

Gloucester
Bass Rocks Ocean Inn
107 Atlantic Road, 01930
Tel: 978-283 7600/800-528 1234
Fax: 978-281 6489
www.bassrocksoceaninn.com
bassrocksoceaninn
A 48-room, Georgian colonial-style
motel looking straight out to sea.
Breakfast is served on the sun porch.
Outdoor pool. **$$–$$$**
Harborview Inn
71 Western Avenue, 01930
Tel: 978-283 2277/800-299 6696
Fax: 978-282 7397
www.harborviewinn.com
A comfortable house-turned-B&B near
the Fishermen Memorial statue. Six
rooms, some with ocean views. **$–$$**

Marblehead
Harbor Light Inn
58 Washington Street, 01945
Tel: 781-631 2186
Fax: 781-631 2216
www.harborlightinn.com
A formally decorated inn, built around
an 18th-century house with a 19th-
century addition. Decor in the 21
rooms ranges from traditional to
contemporary. **$$–$$$$**
Marblehead Inn
264 Pleasant Street, 01945
Tel: 781-639 9999/800-399 5843
Fax: 781-639 9996
www.marbleheadinn.com
A stately 1872 Victorian with 10 cozy
two-bedroom suites, all with private
baths. **$$$–$$$$**

New Bedford
Days Inn
500 Hathaway Road, 02740
Tel: 509-997 1231/800-329 7466
Fax: 508-991 5095
www.daysinn.com
A full-service chain hotel with 153
rooms. **$$–$$$**

Newburyport
Clark Currier Inn
45 Green Street, 01950
Tel: 978-465 8363

Sightseeing in Boston

Guided Tours
You can hop on and off a tram-style
wooden bus for a sightseeing tour of
the historic parts of the city and
most of the Freedom Trail. Start your
tour at any stop, buy tickets on the
bus and get on and off wherever you
wish.

Boat Cruises
Without doubt the most colorful way
of doing Boston is onboard a Duck,
or renovated World War II
amphibious landing vehicle. The
tours (with commentary) start in the
back bay area and include a mini-
cruise on the Charles River.

www.clarkcurrierinn.com
A dignified, three-story 1803 shipbuilder's home in the Federal mode. Many of the eight rooms feature wide-board floors, pencil-post beds and other antique furnishings. **$$–$$$$**
Windsor House
38 Federal Street, 01950
Tel: 978-462 3778/888-873 5296
Fax: 978-465 3443
www.bbhost.com/windsorhouse
B&B in a 1786 house with a British bent (four rooms). **$$$**
Garrison Inn
11 Brown Square, 01950
Tel: 978-499 8500
Fax: 978-499 8555
www.garrisoninn.com
1803 former residence-turned-inn has 24 rooms with reproduction antiques and 6 suites with lofts; some fireplaces. **$$$**

Plymouth

John Carver Inn
25 Summer Street, 02360
Tel: 508-746 7100/800-274 1620
Fax: 508-746 8299
www.johncarverinn.com
An immaculate modern hotel, with 85 rooms and suites (with fireplaces); near the sights; indoor theme pool with water slide. **$$–$$$**
Governor Bradford Motor Inn
98 Water Street, 02360
Tel: 508-746 6200/800-332 1620
Fax: 508-747 3032
www.governorbradford.com
A motel with 94 rooms right on the historic (and heavily trafficked) harbor. **$–$$**
Pilgrim Sands Motel
15 Warren Avenue, 02360
Tel: 508-747 0900/800-729 7263
Fax: 508-746 8066
www.pilgrimsands.com
Oceanfront motel with standard units and oceanfront housekeeping apartments directly across from Plimoth plantation. Private beach; indoor and outdoor pools. **$–$$$**

Rockport

Seaward Inn & Cottages
44 Marmion Way, 01966
Tel: 978-546 3471/877-473 9273
Fax: 978-546 7661
www.seawardinn.com
A welcoming summer house-turned-B&B on a beautifully landscaped seaside ledge. There are 38 rooms available in the main inn building, two nearby houses, and adjacent cottages. **$$$–$$$$**
Yankee Clipper Inn
127 Granite Street, 01966
Tel: 978-546 3407/800-545 3699
Fax: 978-546 9730

www.yankeeclipperinn.com
A total of 16 rooms in three buildings: a Georgian mansion (where John and Jackie Kennedy once stayed) on an ocean promontory, an 1840 neo-classical-style house across the street designed by Charles Bulfinch, plus a modern waterside building with large picture windows. Facilities include a heated saltwater pool. **$$$–$$$$**
Eden Pines Inn
48 Eden Road, 01966
Tel: 978-546 2505
www.edenpinesinn.com
A cliffside mansion with dramatic ocean views. Seven large bedrooms, many with private balconies. Continental breakfast. **$$$**
Addison Choate Inn
49 Broadway, 01966
Tel: 978-546 7543
Fax: 978-546 7638
www.addisonchoate.com
Lovely summery decor and a quiet in-town setting for this Greek Revival inn with six rooms and two apartments; breakfast in the fireplaced dining room. **$$–$$$**
Seacrest Manor
99 Marmion Way, 01966
Tel: 978-546 2211
www.seacrestmanor.com
A 1911 clapboard mansion that is now a quiet, comfortable B&B with eight rooms, well-tended gardens, sea views, some private decks. **$$**
Linden Tree Inn
26 King Street, 01966
Tel: 978-546 2494/800-865 2122
www.linden-tree.com
A captain's home with 18 well-priced B&B rooms and an innkeeper who loves to bake. **$–$$**
Sally Webster Inn
34 Mount Pleasant Street, 01966
Tel: 978-546 9251/877-546 9251
www.sallywebster.com
Small antiques-filled town inn. Several of the seven rooms have wide-board pine floors, (non-working) brick fireplaces, or canopy beds. **$–$$**
The Tuck Inn B&B
17 High Street, 01966
Tel: 978-546 7260/800-789 7260
www.tuckinn.com
Comfortable in-town accommodations in a 1790 Colonial home. Some of the nine rooms have separate entrances and/or decks. All have A/C and Cable

TV. Apartment with full kitchen and studio also available. Outdoor pool. **$–$$**

Salem

Hawthorne Hotel
18 Washington Square West, 01970
Tel: 978-744 4080/800-729 7829
Fax: 978-745 9842
www.hawthornehotel.com
A 1920s hotel with 89 rooms and harbor views from the top floors. **$$–$$$$**
Amelia Payson Guest House
16 Winter Street, 01970
Tel: 978-744 8304
www.ameliapaysonhouse.com
1845 Greek Revival B&B with four bright, airy rooms. Convenient for the museums and sites. **$$**

CAPE COD AND THE ISLANDS

Barnstable

Charles Hinckley House
8 Scudder Lane, 02630
Tel: 508-362 9924
Fax: 508-362 8861
A B&B with four period rooms in an 1809 Federal house. Lavish breakfasts. **$$**
Crocker Tavern Bed and Breakfast
3095 Main Street (Route 6A), 02630
Tel: 508-359 9100
Fax: 508-362 5562
A tastefully renovated 1754 B&B. The five rooms are furnished with canopy or four-poster beds and also have quilts, claw-foot tubs, and antique sinks. **$–$$**

Brewster

Captain Freeman Inn
15 Breakwater Road, 02631
Tel: 508-896 7481/800-843 4664
Fax: 508-896 5618
www.captainfreemaninn.com
A luxurious 1860 shipbuilder's home with 14, antiques-filled spacious rooms (some with whirlpool tubs) and a heated, outdoor pool. Bicycles for guests. **$$–$$$$**
Bramble Inn
2019 Route 6A, 02631
Tel: 508-896 7644
Fax: 508-896 9332
www.brambleinn.com
Historic country inn in two buildings (1792–1861) offering eight rooms with distinctive decor. **$$$**
Old Sea Pines Inn
Route 6A, 2553 Main Street, 02631
Tel: 508-896 6114
Fax: 508-896 7387
www.oldseapinesinn.com
A 1907 Shingle-style mansion that once served as a girls' boarding school. There are 24 rooms, and the modern annex is wheelchair accessible. **$–$$**

Chatham

Captain's House Inn of Chatham
371 Old Harbor Road, 02633
Tel: 508-945 0127/800-315 0728
Fax: 508-945 0866
www.captainshouseinn.com
The 16 B&B rooms have luxurious traditional decor; silver-service tea is served in the garden room, as are full breakfasts. **$$$$**

Chatham Bars Inn
297 Shore Road, 02633
Tel: 508-945 0096/800-527 4884
Fax: 508-945 5491
www.chathambarsinn.com
A 1914 private hunting lodge-turned-grand hotel/resort has 205 nicely-furnished rooms. The private Atlantic beach has resort activities. **$$$$**

Wequassett Inn
Pleasant Bay, Route 28, 02663
Tel: 508-432 5400/800-352 7169
Fax: 508-432 1915
www.wequassett.com
104 rooms, in a country club-style setting. There are facilities for tennis, a pool and a bay beach. **$$$$**

Pleasant Bay Village Resort Motel
1191 Route 28, 02633
Tel: 508-945 1133/800-547 1011
Fax: 508-945 9701
www.pleasantbayvillage.com
A complex of 58 rooms with elaborate gardens. Not your average motel. **$$$–$$$$**

Dennis area

Lighthouse Inn
1 Lighthouse Road
West Dennis, 02670
Tel: 508-398 2244
Fax: 508-398 5658
www.lighthouseinn.com
An old-fashioned seaside resort B&B with 61 rooms on a private beach comprising cottages and a 1855 lighthouse-turned-inn. There are supervised activities for children during the months of July and August. **$$$–$$$$**

Isaiah Hall B&B Inn
152 Whig Street, Dennis, 02638
Tel: 508-385 9928/800-736 0160
Tax: 508-385 5879
www.isaiahhallinn.com
Stars from the Cape Playhouse favor this lovely 1857 farmhouse, with its 10 rooms furnished with country antiques, on a residential street. **$$–$$$**

Beach House Inn
61 Uncle Stephen's Way
West Dennis, 02670
Tel: 508-398 4575
This gray shingled house right on the beach is simply furnished with practical oak and wicker pieces. There are 7 bright and airy rooms. No credit cards. **$–$$$**

Eastham

Whalewalk Inn
220 Bridge Road, 02642
Tel: 508-225 0617
www.whalewalkinn.com
This B&B in an 1830s Greek Revival captain's house has 16 luxurious rooms decorated with breezy panache. Gourmet breakfasts are served, and there are cottages, too. **$$–$$$**

Inn at the Oaks B&B
3085 Route 6, 02642
Tel: 508-225 1886
www.innattheoaks.com
Scottish hospitality in a colorful 1869 Victorian 11-room B&B near the Salt Pond Visitors Center. **$$**

East Orleans

Nauset House Inn
143 Beach Road, 02643
Tel: 508-255 2195
Fax: 508-240 6276
www.nausethouseinn.com
A convivial 1810 farmhouse B&B with 14 rooms and stylish 1900s conservatory. Good situation near the magnificent Nauset Beach. **$$**

Falmouth Area

Inn at West Falmouth
Off Blacksmith Shop Road
West Falmouth, 02574
Tel: 508-540 7696
Fax: 508-540 9977
www.innatwestfalmouth.com
Six rooms in a luxuriously renovated 1898 Shingle-style summer house with tennis court, small heated pool, and views of Buzzards Bay. **$$$–$$$$**

Mostly Hall
27 Main Street
Falmouth, 02540
Tel: 508-548 3786
Fax: 508-457 1572
www.mostlyhall.com
1849 National Register Italianate villa built by a seafarer to please a homesick wife has large, handsome, high-ceilinged rooms, and friendly, knowledgeable hosts. **$$$$**

Inn on the Sound
313 Grand Avenue South
Falmouth Heights, 02540
Tel: 508-457 9666/800-564 9668
Fax: 508-457 9631
www.innonthesound.com
A B&B in an 1880 shingled cottage on a bluff overlooking Vineyard Sound. A large porch offers great water views,

as do four of the 10 rooms with private decks. **$$$–$$$$**

Harwichport area

Augustus Snow House
528 Main Street
Harwichport, 02646
Tel: 508-430 0528/800-320 0528
Fax: 508-432 6638
www.augustussnow.com
Victorian splendor in a five-room B&B in a 1901 Queen Anne mansion near the Sound. The two-bedroom suite has a whirlpool. **$$$–$$$$**

Winstead Inn & Beach Resort
4 Braddock Lane, 02646
Tel: 508-432 4444/800-870 4405
Fax: 508-432 9152
www.winsteadinn.com
Four rooms with all the comforts of home including air-conditioning, color TV and much more. Great location, right on the beach. **$$$–$$$$**

Commodore Inn
30 Earle Road, West Harwich, 02671
Tel: 508-432 1180/800-368 1180
Fax:508-432 3263
www.commodoreinn.com
A seaside motel with 27 rooms, only yards from the sandy beaches and warm waters of Nantucket Sound. Pretty country decor. **$$**

Hyannis

Anchor In Cape Cod Hotel
One South Street, 02601
Tel: 508-775 0357
Fax: 508-775 1313
www.anchorin.com
Some of the luxurious rooms overlooking Lewis Bay have private decks and jacuzzis. Close to downtown and ferries. Heated outdoor pool. **$–$$$**

Four Points by Sheraton Hyannis Resort
35 Scudder Avenue, 02601
Tel: 508-775 7775
www.starwoodhotels.com/fourpoints
This full-service resort on 54 landscaped acres has it all: 224 guest rooms, an 18-hole golf course, fitness center, spa,indoor and outdoor pools, and restaurants. **$$$–$$$$**

Hyannis Inn Motel
473 Main Street, 02601
Tel: 508-775 0255/800-922 8993
Fax: 508-771 0456
www.hyannisinn.com
Right in the center of town, with rooms ranging from standard to deluxe, and a heated indoor pool and saunas. **$–$$$**

MARTHA'S VINEYARD

Edgartown

Charlotte Inn
27 S Summer Street, 02539
Tel: 508-627 4751

Fax: 508-627 4652
An exquisite country inn encompassing five buildings (from 18th century to new) and a total of 25 rooms, all romantically decorated in various styles. **$$$$**

Harbor View Hotel
131 N Water Street, 02539
Tel: 508-627 7000/800-225 6005
www.harbor-view.com
A lavishly renovated 1891 shingled grand hotel, with 124 rooms and a heated pool, near Lighthouse Beach.
$$$$
Colonial Inn
38 N Water Street, 02539
Tel: 508-627 4711/800-627 4701
Fax: 508-627 5904
www.colonialinnmvy.com
Nicely updated and centrally located, this shingled 1911 hotel has 43 rooms. **$$$–$$$$**

Menemsha
Menemsha Inn and Cottages
off North Rd, 02552
Tel: 508-645 2521
Fax: 508-645 9500
www.menemshainn.com
Peaceful simplicity in 27 rooms and cottages, on 10 green acres with water views. **$$$**

Oak Bluffs
The Oak House
Seaview Avenue, 02557
Tel: 508-693 4187/800-245 5979
Fax: 508-696 6293
www.vineyardinns.com
A lavish, wedding-cake Queen Anne Victorian B&B with 10 rooms overlooking Nantucket Sound. Rates include afternoon tea. **$$$–$$$$**

Vineyard Haven
Martha's Place
114 Main Street
Tel: 508-693 0253
Fax: 508-693 1646
Handsome 1840 Greek Revival B&B with six immaculately designed and spacious bedrooms (some with jacuzzis). **$$$–$$$$**

West Tisbury
Lambert's Cove Country Inn

Lambert's Cove Road, 02575
Tel: 508-693 2298
Fax: 508-693 7890
www.lambertscoveinn.com
A 15-room 1790s farmhouse on seven pastoral acres with an English garden. Gourmet fare is served in the restaurant. **$$$–$$$$**

Nantucket
The Wauwinet Inn
120 Wauwinet Road
Wauwinet, 02584
Tel: 508-228 0145/800-426 8718
www.wauwinet.com
A fabulously refurbished 1850 hotel with 35 rooms. Luxurious, secluded, and expensive. **$$$$**
Jared Coffin House
29 Broad Street, 02554
Tel: 508-228 2400/800-248 2405
Fax: 508-325 7752
www.jaredcoffinhouse.com
Grand 1845 mansion with 60 rooms and several adjoining buildings make up this popular island inn. **$$$**
Martin House Inn
61 Centre Street, 02554
Tel: 508-228 0678
www.martinhouseinn.net
Reasonably priced, this 13-room 1803 mariner's home is one of the prettiest and most congenial of the many historic B&Bs in town. Some rooms have shared bath; some with fireplaces. **$–$$$$**
Tuckernuck Inn
60 Union Street, 02554
Tel: 508-228 4886/800-228 4886
Fax: 508-228 4890
Nineteen rooms with country furnishings, in-room phones, air conditioning, and TVs just a short walk from Main Street. **$–$$$**

North Truro
Beachfront White Sands Resort
North Truro 02652
Tel: 508-487 0244
www.provincetownlodging.com
Just minutes from Provincetown, the resort has 51 beachfront and poolside rooms with kitchen units, private beach, heated indoor and outdoor pool, spa, and sauna. **$$$**

Provincetown
Best Inn
698 Commercial Street, 02657
Tel: 508-487 1711/800-422 4224
www.capeinn.com
Motel in the East End a mile from town center with 78 comfortable rooms and ample parking. Some rooms have harbor views. **$$–$$$**
White Horse Inn
500 Commercial Street, 02657
Tel: 508-487 1790
Twelve rooms and six apartments in an 18th-century captain's house inn

shaped by Provincetown's 20th-century artistic history. Located in the East End. **$–$$**
Captain Lysander Inn (B&B)
96 Commercial Street, 02657
Tel: 508-487 2253
An 1850s captain's house in the sedate West End (13 rooms). **$–$$$$**

Sandwich
Belfry Inn
8 Jarves Street, P.O. Box 2211, 02563
Tel: 508-888-8550/800-844-4542
www.belfryinn.com
The property consists of three restored, period buildings, The Painted Lady, The Abbey & Bistro, and The Village House. All rooms are unique, and many have fireplaces and whirlpool tubs. **$$–$$$$**
Dan'l Webster Inn
149 Main Street, 02563.
Tel: 508-888 3622/800-444 3566
Fax: 508-888 5156
A large 53-room luxury hotel on the site of a historic tavern. **$$–$$$**
Inn at Sandwich Center
118 Tupper Road, 02563
Tel: 508-888 6958/800-249 6949
Fax: 508-888 2746
www.innatsandwich.com
A 1750s saltbox, with five bright bedrooms decorated with Laura Ashley bedding; across from the Sandwich Glass Museum. **$$**
Wingscorton Farm (B&B)
11 Wing Boulevard, East Sandwich, 02537
Tel: 508-888 0534
Fax: 508-888 0545
A working farm with four rooms for B&B located about five minute's walk from the beach. The 1763 main house with original paneled bedrooms was once a stop on the Underground Railroad. **$$**

Woods Hole
Nautilus Motor Inn
539 Woods Hole Road, 02543
Tel: 800-654 2333
Fax: 508-457 9674

National Parks

An extensive selection of accommodation is available in and around America's National Parks. For details of where to stay in the Freedom Trail area in Boston and Maine's National Park, contact:
The National Park Reservation Service
Public Inquiry
Department of the Interior
18th and C Streets NW
Washington, DC 20013
Tel: 800-365 2267
www.reservations.nps.gov

www.nautilusinn.com
Waterfront motel has 54 one-bedroom units on two floors. Swimming pool surrounded by gardens. **$$**

Woods Hole Passage
186 Woods Hole Road, 02540
Tel: 508-548 9575/800-790 8976
Fax: 508-540 4771
A 1890s carriage house and barn converted into a romantic B&B with five room. "Breakfast in a bag" for early risers. **$$**

Yarmouth Port

Liberty Hall Inn B&B
77 Main Street (Route 6A), 02675
Tel: 508-362 3976/800-821 3977
Fax: 508-362 6485
www.libertyhillinn.com
Handsomely-preserved 1825 Greek Revival shipwright's house has five rooms with private baths, air conditioning, and TV in the main house, and four luxury rooms with gas fireplaces in the carriage house. **$$–$$$$**

One Centre Street Inn
One Centre Street, 02675
Tel: 508-362 9951/866-362 9951
Restored Colonial inn (1824) has five guest rooms and a one-bedroom suite in three-story building. **$$–$$$**

CENTRAL MASSACHUSETTS

Amherst

The Lord Jeffery Inn
30 Boltwood Avenue, 01002
Tel: 413-253 2576/800-742 0358
Fax: 413-256 6152
www.lordjefferyinn.com
A traditionalist Colonial Revival-style inn with 48 rooms. Situated on the town green, near the Amherst College campus. **$$–$$$**

The Allen House Victorian Inn
599 Main Street, 01002
Tel: 413-253 5000
www.allenhouse.com
Meticulously restored inn of the Aesthetic period, blending Victoriana with Japanese influences. Seven B&B bedrooms. **$–$$$**

Deerfield

Deerfield Inn
81 Old Main Street, 01342
Tel: 413-774 5587/800-926 3865

Fax: 413-775 7221
www.deerfieldinn.com
Historic, 1884 inn on the town's historic street has 23 large rooms furnished with antiques and period reproductions. Afternoon tea is served. **$$$–$$$$**

Greenfield

Brandt House Country Inn
29 Highland Avenue, 01301
Tel: 413-774 3329/800-235 3329
Fax:413 772 2908
www.brandthouse.com
An 1890s Victorian B&B with eight comfortable, simply decorated rooms and huge porches. Facilities include a tennis court. Pets are welcome. **$$–$$$**

Hadley

Ivory Creek B&B
31 Chmura Road, 01035
Tel: 413-587 3115/866-331 3115
www.ivorycreek.com
A large, comfortable house with decks, balconies, porches, nooks, and spacious, antiques-filled guest rooms. The family room is filled with toys and games, and there are 24 landscaped acres to explore. **$$$–$$$$**

Northampton

Clarion Hotel
One Atwood Drive, 01060
Tel: 413-586 1211/800-582 2929
Fax: 413-586 0630
www.hampshirehospitalitygroup.com
On the edge of town, this place has 122 well-appointed motel rooms. There are indoor and outdoor pools, tennis courts, a restaurant, and a whirlpool spa. **$$–$$$**

Hotel Northampton
36 King Street, 01060
Tel: 413-584 3100
Fax: 413-584 9544
Handsomely-appointed historic inn in the center of town has 99 one-bedroom units and six suites with whirlpool baths. There's an exercise room and a lively restaurant which serves New England fare. **$$$**

Northfield

Centennial House
Main Street, 01360
Tel: 413-498 5921/877-977 5950
Fax: 413-498 2525
www.thecentennialhouse.com
Handsome 1811 Colonial home in the center of town with five antiques-filled guest rooms (three with private bath) and a third floor suite that sleeps up to four people. Extensive landscaped grounds. **$$**

Sturbridge

Publick House Historic Resort
Route 131, The Common, 01566

Tel: 508-347 3313/800-782 5425
Fax: 508-347 5073
www.publickhouse.com
A cluster of historic houses, plus a modern motel-style annex offering 125 rooms in all. Good situation near Old Sturbridge Village. **$$–$$$**

Worcester

The Beechwood Hotel
363 Plantation Street, 01605
Tel: 508-754 5789/800-344 2589
Fax:508-752 2060
www.beechwoodhotel.com
A handsome new 73-room hotel overlooking the lake. **$$–$$$**

THE BERKSHIRES

Blackinton Village

Blackinton Manor
1391 Massachusetts Avenue
Blackinton Village
Tel: 413-663 5795
www.blackintonmanor.com
Equidistant between North Adams and Williamstown, this 1849 Federal-style mansion is owned by classical musicians, and each of the five elegantly-furnished, antiques-filled guest rooms, and the common rooms, are finished with musical accents. The owners often host concerts. **$$**

Great Barrington

Windflower Inn
684 S Egremont Road, 01230
Tel: 413-528 2720
Fax: 413-528 5147
www.windflowerinn.com.
A B&B in an early 20th-century country estate with gardens and a pool. The 13 rooms have four-poster beds and are decorated with antiques; some have fireplaces. **$$–$$$$**

Lanesboro

Bascom Lodge
Mount Greylock Reservation
Tel: 413-743 1591
The fieldstone lodge at the summit of Mount Greylock offers private rooms and dormitories, all with shared bath. Breakfast and dinner served family-

Camping

New England has many campsites. Government-run sites (open mid-May to October) are fairly spartan with flush toilets and hot showers (at extra cost). Private campsites (mainly for RVs) have shops and snack bars and offer extensive recreation facilities, incuding playgrounds, swimming pools and even mini-golf courses. Book well in advance in July and August, fall foliage season, and weekends.

Price Categories

A very approximate guide to current room rates for a standard double per night is:

$$$$ = over $200
$$$ = $150–200
$$ = $100–150
$ = under $100

style. Open mid-May–late Oct. No credit cards **$**

Lenox

Apple Tree Inn
10 Richmond Mountain Road, 01240
Tel: 413-637 1477
Fax: 413-637 2528
www.appletree-inn.com
A 22-acre hilltop estate with heated pool, within earshot of Tanglewood; some 32 motel units **$$$–$$$$**

Blantyre
16 Blantyre Road (off Route 20), 01240
Tel: 413-637 3556
Fax: 413-637 4282
www.blantyre.com
An opulent mock-Tudor castle on 100 manicured acres with a heated pool, sauna, tennis courts, croquet lawns, and gourmet dining. The sky-high prices help ensure luxury and impeccable service in this 25-room hotel. **$$$$**

Canyon Ranch
165 Kemble Street, 01240
Tel: 413-637 4100/800-742 9000
Fax: 413-637 0057
www.canyonranch.com
New England's most elaborate spa occupies an 1890s building modeled on Versailles's Petit Trianon. 126 rooms. **$$$$**

Cliffwood Inn
25 Cliffwood Street, 01240
Tel: 413-637 3330/800-789 3331
Fax: 413-637 0221
www.cliffwood.com
An antiques-filled 1890 colonial mansion with seven bedrooms and an outdoor swimming pool on a quiet residential street. **$$$–$$$$**

Rookwood Inn
11 Old Stockbridge Road, 01240
Tel: 413-637 9750/800-223 9750
Fax: 413-637 1352
www.rookwoodinn.com
An 1885 "painted lady" B&B at the center of town. Comfortably elegant Victorian furnishings in the 20 rooms, creative modern breakfasts. **$$$–$$$$**

The Summer White House
17 Main Street, 01240
Tel: 413-637 4489/800-372 8491
Fax: 413-637 4489
www.thesummerwhitehouse.com
An original Berkshire Cottage built in 1885 in the heart of town has lavishly decorated rooms and porches to sit on and watch the world pass by. **$$–$$$$**

The Village Inn
16 Church Street, 01240
Tel: 413-637 0020/800-253 0917
Fax: 413-637 2196
www.villageinn-lenox.com
A 1771 inn, with 31 comfortably furnished rooms. **$$–$$$$**

Garden Gables
135 Main Street, 01240
Tel: 413-637 0193
www.lenoxinn.com
Country charm in this 18-room B&B in a 1780s house. One of Lenox's better deals. **$–$$$$**

Walker House
64 Walker Street, 01240
Tel: 413-637 1271/800-235 3098
Fax: 413-637 2387
www.walkerhouse.com
This B&B with eight rooms is a cultural mecca. Private recitals. **$$$**

New Marlboro

Old Inn on the Green
Village Green (Route 57), 01230
Tel: 413-229 7924
www.oldinn.com
Chef/owner Peter Platt and his wife, Meredith Kennard have created a lodging/dining destination. There are five comfortable rooms above the restaurant and six second-floor rooms in the restored Thayer House. **$$$–$$$$**

North Adams

The Porches Inn at MASS MOCA
231 River Street, 01247
Tel; 413-664 0400
www.porches.com
This lodging, in a renovated building that once housed mill workers, bills itself as "ultra savvy": all of the 46 rooms are furnished in contemporary-retro décor and fully wired for computer use; some two-room suites

Youth Hostels

American Youth Hostels
733 15th Street, Suite 840,
Washington, DC 20005
Tel: 202-783 6161
Fax: 202-783 6171
www.hiayh,org
This organisation can supply a list of youth hostels in New England. The group's publication *Hostelling North America* is available in bookstores.

have spiral staircases to loft sleeping areas. **$$$$**

Sheffield

Birch Hill B&B
254 S Undermountain Road
(Route 41), 01257
Tel: 413-229 2143/800-359 3969
www.birchhillbb.com
Casual, sprawling, simply furnished country inn with pool, set in 20 acres. Seven rooms with fireplaces. Full breakfast. **$$$**

Staveleigh House
59 Main Street, 01257
Tel: 413-229 2129
A B&B with seven rooms in an 1821 parson's home. Spacious grounds beside the Housatonic. **$$**

Stockbridge area

Red Lion Inn
30 Main Street, Stockbridge, 01262
Tel: 413-298 5545
Fax: 413-298 5130
www.redlioninn.com
A classic old inn (est. 1773) at the center of a Norman Rockwell town. Many guest rooms in the main inn are quite small; accommodations in the adjacent buildings offer a little more space. 111 rooms. **$$–$$$$**

Merrell Tavern Inn
1565 Pleasant Street (Route 102)
South Lee/Stockbridge, 01260
Tel: 413-243 1794/800-243 1794
Fax: 413-243 2669
www.Merrell-Inn.com
A ten-room B&B in an authentically restored 1794 stagecoach tavern, in a rural riverside setting. **$$–$$$**

Williamsville Inn
Route 41
West Stockbridge, 01266
Tel: 413-274 6118
Fax: 413-274 3539
www.williamsvilleinn.com.
A 16-room B&B in a restored 1790s farmhouse and barn on landscaped grounds. Summer sculpture garden. **$$–$$$**

Williamstown

The Orchards
222 Adams Road (Route 2), 01267
Tel: 413-458 9611/800-225 1517

Stay in a Lighthouse

Lighthouses are dotted along the whole New England coast, a memorial to the area's maritime past. A few of these are now B&Bs, and at some of them you can get a taste of how life was as a lighthouse keeper – complete with record-keeping jobs. For details contact:
New England Lighthouse Foundation, PO Box 1690, Wells, Maine, 04090. Tel: 800-758 1444; www.lighthousedepot.com

Fax: 413-458 3273
www.orchardshotel.com
A modern hotel with antique appointments in its 49 rooms. This is a peaceful, elegant oasis despite its location on an unappealing commercial strip of Route 2. **$$$–$$$$**

Field Farm Guest House
554 Sloan Road (off Route 43), 01267
Tel: 413-458 3135
Fax: 413-412 2556
www.thetrustees.org
This 1948 American Modern mansion B&B set in over 250 acres of conservation land has five large rooms with modern furnishings and views of the grounds or the hills. Outdoor amenities include a pool, tennis courts, pond (with fishing poles available), and trails for hiking or cross-country skiing. **$$–$$$**

River Bend Farm
643 Simonds Road, 01267
Tel: 413-458 3121
A painstakingly restored 1770 colonial house. Furnishings are simple, even rustic, as befits the colonial period in this four-room B&B. No credit cards. **$**

Steep Acres Farm
520 White Oaks Road, 01267
Tel: 413-458 3774
A four-room B&B on a 50-acre hilltop, with orchards and animals. **$**

Where to Eat

BOSTON

Ambrosia on Huntington
116 Huntington Avenue
Tel: 617-247 2400
Bold new American cuisine in a dramatic windowed dining room. Decide whether the patrons or plates are dressed more fancifully? Near the Prudential Center. **$$$–$$$$**

Antico Forno
93 Salem Street
Tel: 617-723 6733
A wood-burning brick oven and sawdust-covered floors set the mood for this rustic Neapolitan-style trattoria. Just about everything is cooked in the oven, including a delicious chicken with garlic and herbs and a variety of pizzas. **$$–$$$**

Aujourd'hui
Four Seasons Hotel
200 Boylston Street
Tel: 617-338 4400
The decor is corporate-opulent, the cuisine invariably artful. The best power tables overlook the Public Garden. **$$$$**

Azure
Lenox Hotel, 61 Exeter St.
Tel: 617-933-4800
Contemporary American menu, with an emphasis on fresh seafood, draws inspiration from French, Asian, Latin and Mediterranean flavors. **$$$$**

Clio
Eliot Hotel
370A Commonwealth Avenue
Tel: 617-536 7200
Creative food but not excessively trendy in a polished spot for business or a night out. Specials include roast suckling pig and Moscovy duck with kumquats. Tasting menu. Dinner Tues–Sun. **$$$$**

Excelsior
The Heritage on the Green,
272 Boylston Street
Tel: 426-7878
A glass elevator whisks patrons up to renowned Boston restaurateur Lydia Shire's newest creation, overlooking the Public Garden. The cuisine is contemporary American, highlighted by Lydia's lobster pizza. Pub menu in second-floor Crystal Bar. **$$$$**

L'Espalier
30 Gloucester Street
Tel: 617-262 3023
This ultra-elegant, ultra-romantic, ultra-expensive Victorian townhouse stays two steps ahead of the culinary cutting edge with its *prix-fixe* French-inspired menu. Popular spots for marriage proposals. *Prix-fixe* menu. Dinner Mon–Sat. **$$$$**

Julien
Le Meridian Boston
250 Franklin Street
Tel: 617-956 8751
First-class French cuisine, amid the marble grandeur of the former Federal Reserve Building. Dinner Tues–Sat. **$$$$**

Meritage
Boston Harbor Hotel
70 Rowes Wharf
Tel: 617-439 3995
Superb harbor views and superior contemporary American cuisine. **$$$$**

Grill 23
161 Berkeley Street, Back Bay
Tel: 617-542 2255
Upscale steak house with an old-world ambiance, with specialties such as a 24-ounce porterhouse steak, a 3 lb. baked stuffed lobster, and the special Grill 23 meatloaf. Dinner only. **$$$–$$$$**

Hamersley's Bistro
553 Tremont Street
Tel: 617-423 2700
This pioneer on the now-hopping South End restaurant row remains the standard for other eateries to match. Deft and imaginative touches dress up this excellent, sophisticated comfort food. Dinner only. **$$$–$$$$**

Pignoli
79 Park Plaza
Tel: 617-338 7500
A stylish, ultra-modern Back Bay haunt for imaginative Italian/Mediterranean creations featuring pasta, meat, fish, and wild game. Dinner only. **$$$–$$$$**

Sonsie
327 Newbury Street
Tel: 617-351 2500
A trendsetter's cafe, with exotic fare. Also a good spot for a light breakfast. **$$$–$$$$**

Aquitaine
569 Tremont Street
Tel: 617-424 8577
A happening French bistro and wine bar (although the "bar" is the size of a postage stamp) in the trendy South End restaurant district. **$$$**

Hampshire House
84 Beacon Street
Tel: 617-227 9600
Unparalleled Sunday jazz brunch with a view of the Public Garden. Above the bar made famous in the long-running television series *Cheers*. **$$$**

Lala Rokh
97 Mount Vernon Street
Tel: 617-720 5511
Refined Persian cuisine in an intimate, romantically appointed Beacon Hill townhouse. The staff are happy to explain the intriguing, comforting dishes. **$$$**

Legal Sea Foods
Boston Park Plaza Hotel
64 Arlington Street
Tel: 617-426 4444
Part of a chain, but serves the freshest of fish, served the moment it's done. Other Legal branches are located in the Prudential Center, Copley Place, Logan Airport, and across the river in Cambridge's Kendall Square. **$$$**

Restaurant Guidelines

Prices are approximate, but for a three-course meal for one (excluding beverages, tax, and tip), the following guidelines may prove helpful:

$$$$ = over $40
$$$ = $28–40
$$ = $15–28
$ = under $15

Meal tax varies from state to state, but it is customary to tip 15 to 20 percent on the pre-tax total.

Credit cards Most moderate to expensive establishments generally accept credit cards, but call ahead to check just in case.

Reservations Most restaurants, except for the clearly casual, appreciate reservations (some require them).

Ristorante Toscano
47 Charles Street
Tel: 617-723 4090
True Tuscan delicacies in a
handsome upscale trattoria on
Beacon Hill. **$$$**

Sage
69 Prince Street
Tel: 617-248 8814
Hidden away on a North End side
street, this tiny storefront, where
there is barely any room to walk,
blends warm service and New Italian
cuisine. Closed Sunday. **$$$**

Skipjack's
199 Clarendon St
Tel: 617-536 3500
Native seafood with a modernist bent
in the shadow of the massive John
Hancock tower. **$$$**

Tremont 647
647 Tremont Street
Tel: 617-266 4600
Adventurous American "melting pot"
cuisine in a hip South End dining spot.
Wear black. **$$$**

29 Newbury St
29 Newbury St
Tel: 617-536 0290
A perennially popular bistro, with a
strategic sidewalk cafe for assessing
the passing fashion parade. **$$$**

Cottonwood Café
222 Berkeley Street
Tel: 617-247 2225
Upscale Tex-Mex fare served in a
trendy setting, with dishes such as
deep-fried jalapenos with shrimp and
cheese. Note that you can request
"not too *caliente*" if you prefer.
$$–$$$

Artu
6 Prince Street
Tel: 617-742 4336
Friendly, bustling trattoria in the North
End. Offers very good value for fresh
pastas, roasted vegetables, and
updated Italian classics. **$$**

The Daily Catch
323 Hanover Street
Tel: 617-523 8567
Superb calamari and other seafood in
the North End. The room is tiny and
always jammed. **$$**

Durgin Park
Faneuil Hall Marketplace
Tel: 617-227 2038
One of the city's oldest restaurants
serves well-prepared New England
classics (chowder, pot roast, baked
beans), with good-natured service. **$$**

East Ocean Seafood
25 Beach Street
Tel: 617-542 2504
Fresh-from-the-tanks Hong Kong-style
seafood served in a low-key
Chinatown eatery. **$$**

Ginza Japanese Restaurant
16 Hudson Street
Tel: 617-338 2261

A Meal with a View

Look out over Boston's night lights
when you dine on the 52nd floor at
the Top of the Hub restaurant. Y

Top of the Hub
Prudential Center, Back Bay
Tel: 617-536 1775
Great seafood and delicious
Sunday brunches.

One of Boston's best sushi spots,
tucked away in Chinatown. The
unusual *maki* rolls are particularly
tasty. **$$**

Sakura-bana
57 Broad Street
Tel: 617-542 4311
Unparalleled sushi in the financial
district. **$$**

Barking Crab
88 Sleeper Street, at Northern Avenue
Tel: 617-426 2722
Seaside clam shack transported to
the city. Fried clams and other simple
seafood with great harbor and city
vistas. **$–$$**

No Name Restaurant
17 Fish Pier
Tel: 617-423 2705
Since the 1920s, the casual
waterfront spot has been of the best
and least expensive places in the city
to get off-the-boat fresh seafood.
$–$$

Empire Garden
690 Washington Street
Tel: 617-482 8898
Waitresses circle this large room with
carts filled with snack-size dim sum
such as steamed dumplings and
barbecue pork buns. Diners pay by the
number of plates have stacked up at
the end of the meal. **$–$$**

Jumbo Seafood
7 Hudson Street
Tel: 617-542 2823
Unusual seafood dishes are the
specialty at this Chinatown spot; the
catches of the day are swimming in
the aquarium and can be cooked in
various styles. **$**

Sorellina
1 Huntington Avenue
Tel: 617-412 4600
One of the city's newest and most
gracious dining destinations offers
high-concept Italian fare prepared with
a hint of the Asian. Look for treats
such as kobe beef meatballs and
homemade cannoli. **$$$$**

Sultan's Kitchen
116 Broad Street
Tel: 617-570 9009
A popular downtown take-out shop
(with a few upstairs tables) serving
fresh Turkish/Middle Eastern shish
kebabs, salads, and the Greek sweet
baklava. **$**

Cambridge

Chez Henri
1 Shepard Street (off Mass Avenue)
Tel: 617-354 8980
Modern French fare with a Cuban
accent in a snug bistro north of
Harvard Square. The spinach salad
fired up with spicy duck *tamale* is
destined to become a classic.
$$$–$$$$

Rialto
Charles Hotel
I Bennett Street
Tel: 617-661 5050
Provincial French, Italian and Spanish
dishes in a chic, sophisticated, and
elegant dining room. **$$$–$$$$**

East Coast Grill & Raw Bar
1271 Cambridge Street
(Inman Square)
Tel: 617-491 6568
A stylish, wildly popular spot – and
deservedly so – for innovative grilled
seafood (often topped with exotic
spice rubs or fruit salsas), creative
salads, barbecue and fiery "pasta
from hell". Margaritas help ease the
often long waits for a table. **$$$**

Harvest
44 Brattle Street
Tel: 617-868 2255
One of Harvard Square's most reliably
innovative bistros, with prime meat
and seafood dishes and an award-
winning wine list. The garden terrace
is delightful. **$$$**

Atasca
50 Broadway at Columbia Street
Tel: 617-621 6991
Way off the beaten path (between
Central and Inman Squares), this cozy
storefront brings a satisfying taste of
Portugal to Cambridge. **$$**

Casablanca
40 Brattle Street
Tel: 617-876 0999
Harvard Square's oldest restaurant
serves a Turkish/Moroccan menu
within reach of student budgets. Go
just for David Omar White's murals of
the movie, but the comfortable bar is
a fine spot for appetizers, too. **$$**

Cambridge Ice Cream

Toscanini's Ice Cream
899 Main Street
Tel: 617-491 5877
In the ice cream-crazy Boston area,
this is the Mecca. As well as
excellent versions of the basics, it
serves many more unusual flavors
such as mango, green tea and
ginger. The flagship store (which
often hosts small art exhibits) is just
off Massachusetts Avenue between
Central and Kendall Squares.
Another (smaller) location is on
Mass Ave in Harvard Square. **$**

Green Street Grill
280 Green Street
Tel: 617-876 1655
French tropical Caribbean dishes with
South and Latin American influences
(especially grilled fish) and suitable
live music nightly. **$$**
Brother Jimmy's BBQ
96 Winthrop Street, Cambridge
Tel: 547-7427
"Put some South in Yo' Mouth" at this
student-friendly spot which specializes
in Blues, St. Louis-style ribs, and
other Southern treats. Sunday is the
all-you-can-eat and all-you-can drink
beer night. **$$**
John Harvard's Brew House
33 Dunster Street
Tel: 617-868 3585
Surprisingly refined pub grub including
the house special chicken pot pie, and
made-on-the-premises beers. In
Harvard Square. **$$**
Algiers Cafe and Restaurant
40 Brattle Street
Tel: 617-492 1557
Serves Turkish coffee, *shish kabob*,
cous-cous and *tabbouleh* to the
intelligentsia in Harvard Square.
Breakfast all day. **$**
Mr. Bartley's Burger Cottage
1246 Massachusetts Avenue
Tel: 617-354 6559
For more than 40 years this casual
eatery has been serving up terrific
burgers, sweet potato fries, and onion
rings. Closed Sunday. **$**
Spice Thai Cuisine
24 Holyoke Street
Tel: 617-868 9560
A student hot spot for well-prepared
pad Thai, curries, satays and other
regional dishes. **$**

Charlestown
Olives
10 City Square
Tel: 617-242 1999
Avid patrons put up with long lines
and often-deafening hubbub to savor
Todd English's first-class Tuscan
country cuisine. Among the
specialties: veal saltimbocca, paella,
and braised lamb shank. Dinner
Monday–Saturday. **$$–$$$$**
Figs
67 Main Street
Tel: 617-242 2229
Olives' pizza-parlor cousin, still up-
scale, only slightly less mobbed. **$–$$**

Somerville
Dali
415 Washington Street (at Beacon
Street)
Tel: 617-661 3254
Robust Spanish specialties (try the
signature fish baked in salt) and
particularly fine tapas in a lively
atmosphere worthy of Hemingway. On

Restaurant Prices
Prices are approximate, but for a
three-course meal for one
(excluding beverages, tax and tip),
the following guidelines may prove
helpful:
  $$$$ = over $40
  $$$ = $28–40
  $$ = $15–28
  $ = under $15

the Cambridge/Somerville line.
$$–$$$
The Elephant Walk
2067 Massachusetts Avenue
Tel: 617-492 6900
Cambodian and French dishes meet in
a light and airy restaurant of wood
and brick. Dinner only. **$$–$$$**
eat
253 Washington Street
Tel: 617-776 2889
Creative comfort food – roast chicken,
grilled fish with intriguing sauces – in
a homey Union Square storefront.
Dinner; no reservations. **$$**
Redbone's
55 Chester Street (off Elm Street)
Tel: 617-628 2200
The place to go when you're hungry
for massive plates of barbecued ribs.
A loud and rowdy Davis Square dive
with an extensive beer list and valet
parking for bicycles! **$–$$**
The Burren
247 Elm Street
Tel: 617-776 6896
Comfortable Davis Square Irish pub
draws locals, yuppies and students.
Stop in for a Guiness or some fish
and chips. **$**

BOSTON DAY TRIPS
Concord
Colonial Inn
48 Monument Square
Tel: 978-369 2000
A 1716 inn serving traditional New
England fare as well as fresh grilled
fish, baked stuffed lobster, and a
selection of international favorites.
High tea is served Friday–Sunday
3–5pm (reservations recommended).
$$–$$$
La Provence
105 Thoreau Street
Tel: 978-371 7428
A self-serve, informal bistro with
upscale luncheon treats such as
salmon in champagne sauce, beef
bourgougnon, and quail. A great place
to pick up a picnic. Open Mon–Fri
7am–7pm; Sat 7am–5:30pm. **$–$$**
Walden Grille
24 Walden Street
Tel: 978-371 2233
Contemporary cuisine such as wild

mushroom ravioli and grilled shrimp in
a handsomely-renovated, old brick
firehouse. **$$–$$$**
Essex
Jerry Pelonzi's Hearthside Restaurant
109 Eastern Avenue, Route 133
Tel: 978-768 6002
Fresh seafood, thick chowders, and
sirloin steak share the menu at this
casual, fireplaced restaurant in a *c.*
1680 farmhouse. **$$**
Woodman's
The Causeway
Tel: 978-768 6451
Home of the original fried clam,
invented in 1915. Also on the menu at
this very informal spot: fresh fish, a
raw bar, and chowder. No credit cards.
$

Fall River
Estoril
1577 Pleasant Street
Tel: 508-677 1200
A white-tablecloth introduction to
classic Portuguese fare. **$$**
Tabacaria Açoriana Restaurant
408 S Main Street
Tel: 508-673 5890
A casual Portuguese cafe downtown
with authentic dishes such as kale
soup, marinated pork and steamed
octopus, and a fine selection of
regional wines. **$**

Gloucester
White Rainbow
65 Main Street
Tel: 978-281 0017
Rich, evolved Continental-style food
served in a dramatic granite-walled,
1800s hideaway. The café wine bar
offers a lighter menu. Dinner
Tuesday–Sunday. **$$$**
Passports
110 Main Street
Tel: 978-281 3680
Foods from around the world are on
offer here, including fresh fish dishes
from the Adriatic, sushi from Japan,
and creative pastas from across Italy.
Closed Sunday. **$$–$$$**
Evie's Rudder
73 Rocky Neck
Tel: 978-283 7967
A rollicking tavern in the Rocky Neck
artists' colony. **$$**

Lexington
Dabin
10 Muzzey Street
(Off Mass Avenue)
Tel: 781-860 0171
Traditional Japanese and Korean fare
in a peaceful shelter from the bustle
of Lexington Center. A small patio for
outdoor dining in warm weather. **$$**
Lemon Grass
1710 Massachusetts Avenue

Tel: 781-862 3530
A low-key Thai storefront café where the food is tempered for American palates. **$–$$**

Lowell
La Boniche
143 Merrimack Street
Tel: 978-458 9473
An intimate French-style bistro in a landmark Art Nouveau building serving creative fare. Lunch Tuesday–Friday; dinner Tuesday–Saturday **$$–$$$**
The Olympia
453 Market Street
Tel: 978-452 8092
A friendly, family-run Greek restaurant. Lunch Monday–Friday; dinner nightly. **$–$$**

Marblehead
The Landing
81 Front Street
Tel: 781-639 1266
New England seafood in a cheerful dining room overlooking Marblehead Harbor. Opt for the deck in nice weather. **$$–$$$**
Maddie's Sail Loft
15 State Street
Tel: 781-631 9824
Standard fried or broiled seafood and fine chowder in a lively, often-crowded casual room. Located between Front and Washington streets. **$$**

New Bedford
Antonio's
Coggeshalle and N Front streets
Tel: 508-990 3639
Enormous portions of Portuguese classics that draw crowds to this nondescript dining room. Situated near the intersection of Routes 95 and 18. **$$**
Davy's Locker
1480 E Rodney French Boulevard
Tel: 508-992 7359
Traditional seafood preparations, since 1962, right on the harbor near the Martha's Vineyard ferry docks. **$$**

Newburyport
Glenn's Restaurant
Merrimack Street
Tel: 978-465 3811
"World class cuisine in a funky casual atmosphere" – actually a former shoe factory. Try a dish from the wood-fired grill. **$$**
The Grog
13 Middle St.
Tel: 978-465 8008
For more than 30 years, this 200-year-old brick row building has housed the city's premier rendezvous for burgers, seafood, chowder, and drinks in a laid-back atmosphere. Live music (rock, folk, blues) weekends. **$–$$**

Szechuan Taste & Thai Café
19 Pleasant Street
Tel: 978-463 0686
A superb selection of ethnic dishes, with a particularly deft touch with seafood dishes, in a handsomely-decorated spot off State Street. **$–$$**

Plymouth
Mayflower Restaurant
14 Union Street
Tel: 508-747 4503
Seafood and beef specialties at a pleasant spot whose deck looks out on the Mayflower II. **$$$**
Bert's Cove
140 Warren Avenue, Route 3A
Tel: 508-746 3330
Fresh seafood and steak are on the menu at this local landmark with a waterfront view near the beach. **$$**
Lobster Hut
on the Town Wharf
Tel: 508-746 2270
Basic fried seafood served on the waterfront. **$**

Rockport
Brackett's Oceanview Restaurant
25 Main Street
Tel: 978-546 2797
A small storefront opens up into a spacious dining room overlooking the harbor. Seafood is the specialty, and the emphasis is on solid, reasonably-priced Yankee fare. **$–$$**
Portside Chowder House
Bearskin Neck
Tel: 978-546 7045
A basic seafood hole-in-the-wall located in the heart of Rockport's tourist bustle. Specializes in chowder, but serves up sandwiches, burgers, and seafood plates, too. Lunch and dinner in summer; lunch all year. **$**

Salem
Grapevine
26 Congress Street
Tel: 978-745 9335
A peaceful, elegant spot for northern Italian fare sparked with an occasional fusion influence. Dinner only. **$$–$$$**
Lyceum Bar & Grill
43 Church Street
Tel: 978-745 7665
Seafood, chowder and grilled meats

Restaurant Prices

Prices are approximate, but for a three-course meal for one (excluding beverages, tax and tip), the following guidelines may prove helpful:

$$$$ = over $40
$$$ = $28–40
$$ = $15–28
$ = under $15

are on offer at this converted, 19th-century theater overlooking the Green. Lunch and dinner Sunday–Friday; Sat, dinner only. **$$–$$$**
Red's Sandwich Shop
15 Central Street
Tel: 978 745 3527
A terrific spot for hearty breakfasts and lunches. **$**
Salem Beer Works
278 Derby Street
Tel: 978-745 2337
This is Salem's contribution to the microbrewery fad. Upscale bar food and fresh-brewed beers are served in a renovated warehouse building. **$–$$**

CAPE COD AND THE ISLANDS
Barnstable
Mattakeese Wharf
271 Mill Way
Tel: 508-362 4511
A classic wharfside seafood haven. Open May–October. **$$–$$$**

Brewster
Chillingsworth
2449 Route 6A
Tel: 508-896 3640/800-430 3640
Chillingsworth's splendid seven-course *prix-fixe* menu, a feast of classic French food, is among the ultimate dining experiences that the Cape has to offer. Dinner Tuesday–Sunday. **$$$$**
Bramble Inn
2019 Route 6A
Tel: 508-896 7644
Four-course dinners featuring continental dishes with an emphasis on fresh seafood are served in the intimate rooms of a restored 1861 house. **$$$**
Brewster Fish House
2208 Route 6A
Tel: 508-896 7867
Creative fresh seafood and pasta, snazzy desserts, and long waits. **$$**

Chatham
Chatham Bars Inn
Shore Road
Tel: 508-945 0096/800-527 4884
A grand old inn dining room with French and regional cuisine. **$$$$**
Christian's Restaurant
443 Main Street
Tel: 508-945 3362
A lively New American bistro downstairs and an inviting, library-like piano bar upstairs. Dinner only. **$$–$$$**
Vining's Bistro
595 Main Street
Tel: 508-945 5033
A wood grill with a taste for exotic spices. **$$$**

Impudent Oyster
15 Chatham Bars Avenue
Tel: 508-945 3545
International takes on local seafood.
Popular and packed. **$$**

Cotuit
Regatta of Cotuit at the Crocker House
4631 Falmouth Road
Tel: 508-428 5715
Sophisticated New American cuisine
with French, Continental and Asian
accents served in an 18th-century
stagecoach inn with eight, intimate
candlelit dining rooms. **$$$–$$$$**

Dennis
Gina's by the Sea
134 Taunton Avenue
Tel: 508-385 3213
Hearty classics characterize this lively
cafe set amid the Cape's "Little Italy".
Seasonal. **$$$**
The Red Pheasant
905 Route 6A
Tel: 508-385 2133
Daring New American cuisine served
in an 18th-century ship's chandlery.
Dinner only. **$$$**
Scargo Cafe
799 Route 6A
Tel: 508-385 8200
Traditional New England favorites, plus
a few eclectic wild cards, in a retro-
fitted captain's house. **$$**
Captain Frosty's
219 Route 6A
Tel: 508-385 8548
A casual clam shack with exceptional
lobster rolls. **$**

Eastham
Eastham Lobster Pool
4360 Route 6
Tel: 508-255 9706
No frills, just unbeatable fresh fish.
$$$

Falmouth
**Coonamessett Inn Cahoon
Dining Room**
311 Gifford Street
Tel: 508-548 2300
Classic country inn serves elegant
fare, with an accent on fresh seafood
and prime meats. Dress is semi-
formal, and Sunday brunch is superb.
$$$–$$$$
Chapoquoit Grill
Route 28A
Tel: 508-540 7794
New American cuisine, grilled seafood,
and wood-fired, brick oven pizza
served in a casual environment. The
desserts are all homemade. **$$–$$$**
Clam Shack
227 Scranton Avenue
Tel: 508-540 7758
A shack (albeit very picturesque), right
on the water. **$**

Shaker Meals
Hancock is Massachusetts' best-
kept Shaker village, now a living
museum. You can watch
craftspeople at work and cooks
preparing meals using herbs from
the original-style herb garden. On
Friday and Saturday in the fall,
and at Thanksgiving and
Christmas time, visitors can enjoy
candlelit dinners, featuring dishes
from Shaker cookbooks. But
guests should take heed: the
expression "shaker your plate"
derives from the fact that
leftovers were frowned upon by
the Shakers. Tel: 413-443 0188;
www.hancockshakervillage.org

Hyannis
Alberto's Ristorante
360 Main Street
Tel: 508-778 1770
Northern Italian fare with a flair, with
homemade pastas and entrées such
as seafood ravioli stuffed with lobster,
scallops, shrimp and ricotta. **$$–$$$**
Baxter's Boat House
177 Pleasant Street
Tel: 508-775 4490
Perched over the harbor, a 1950s
clam shack with a very lively blues
bar. **$**
Naked Oyster Bistro and Raw Bar
20 Independence Drive
Tel: 508 778 6500
Flopping fresh fish and prime grilled
beef are specialties, but for a real
taste of the sea belly up to the raw
bar for a platter of fresh oysters or
shrimp, or superb tuna sashimi. Open
for Lunch Tues–Fri; dinner nightly
July–Aug, and Mon–Sat the rest of the
year. **$$–$$$**
The Original Gourmet Brunch
517 Main Street
Tel: 508-771 2558
Brunch is the focus, and omelets are
the specialty, with offerings such as
an onion and cheddar omelet, and–for
the daring–a peanut butter and jelly
omelet. Also on the menu: Belgian
waffles, eggs Benedict,and a full
luncheon menu. Open Mon–Sat
7am–midday; Sun until 2pm. **$–$$**
Tugboats
21 Arlington Street
Tel: 508-775 6433
Fun food and great harbor views,
especially at sunset. **$$**

MARTHA'S VINEYARD
Edgartown
Atria
Old Post Office Square
Tel: 508-627 5850
Contemporary fare in a house just out

of town. Among the specialties: ahi-
tuna tempura and seared filet mignon.
A lighter menu is served in the pub.
Terrace dining in the summer.
Reservations; dinner only. **$$$$**
L'Etoile
Charlotte Inn
27 S Summer Street
Tel: 508-627 5187
Superlative French cuisine served in a
candlelit conservatory. Dinner only.
$$$$
Among the Flowers Cafe
Mayhew Lane
Tel: 508-627 3233
Omelets, quiches, pasta, and other
filling, inexpensive fare. **$**
The Newes from America
23 Kelley Street
Tel: 508-627 4397
Well-prepared pub grub in a 1742
tavern. A vast range of beers is
available in sampler "racks". **$**

Mashpee
Bleu
Mashpee Commons
7 Market Street
Tel: 508-539 7907
Award-winning French cuisine, with
classic bistro offerings such as
choucroute, cassoulet, planked
salmon, and chicken Provencal. And,
for dessert, a caramelized apple tart
tatin. Lunch Mon-Sat, dinner nightly,
and Sun jazz brunch. **$$–$$$**

Menemsha
Homeport
512 North Road
Tel: 508-645 2679
Overlooking the harbor and one of the
best spots on the island for fresh fish:
eat on the lawn or the deck. No credit
cards. BYOB. Dinner only; closed mid-
October–mid-April. **$–$$$**

Oak Bluffs
Papa's Pizza
Upper Main Street Mobil Station
Tel: 508-627 7784
Pizza, pasta, subs. **$**

Vineyard Haven
Black Dog Tavern & Bakery
Beach Street Extension
Tel: 508-693 9223
One of the island's most popular
restaurants serves up fresh seafood,
homemade breads and pastries, and
a children's menu. **$–$$$**
Le Grenier
96 Main Street
Tel: 508-693 4906
A Vineyard favorite for classical French
cuisine for more than 25 years. Table-
side preparations include lobster
Normande flambéed with calvados,
and banana flambé. **$$$$**

Nantucket

American Seasons
80 Centre Street
Tel: 508-228 7111
Adventurous dining from around the country in a romantic atmosphere amid colorful murals, well-chosen folk art. Reservations. Dinner only; closed late December–May. **$$$$**

Boarding House
12 Federal Street
Tel: 508-228 9622
Bold New American cuisine, and the island's most sophisticated sidewalk café. **$$$$**

Chanticleer Inn
9 New Street, Siasconset
Tel: 508-257 6231
High-class traditional French cuisine served in an opulent auberge-like setting. **$$$$**

Rope Walk
Straight Wharf
Tel: 508-228 8886
Seafood with *nouvelle* splashes, on the harbor. Raw bar daily 3–10pm. **$$$$**

Straight Wharf Restaurant
Straight Wharf
Tel: 508-228 4499
Elegant regional fare in a handsome loft space. **$$$$**

21 Federal
21 Federal Street
Tel: 508-228 2121
Sensational new and traditional American fare cuisine in a tastefully spare 1847 Greek Revival house. Lunch is served on the patio in season. **$$$$**

Brotherhood of Thieves
23 Broad Street
No phone
Great burgers, live music, and a nice crowd in an 1840 whaling bar. **$$**

Espresso To Go
1 Toombs Court
Tel: 508-228 6930
Cheap, scrumptious international grazing. **$**

North Truro

Adrian's
Route 6
Tel: 508-487 4360
Irresistible neo-Italian treats plus spectacular views. **$$**

Orleans

Captain Linnell House
137 Skaket Beach Road
Tel: 508-255 3400
One of Cape Cod's most respected restaurants, housed in an 1811 sea captain's home, serves continental treats including bourbon lobster bisque, scrod in parchment, and rack of lamb. Dinner only. **$$$$**

Mahoney's
28 Main Street

Tel: 508-255 5505
Classy, contemporary US cuisine. Live jazz is played on Thursday nights. **$$$$**

Land Ho!
38 Main Street
Tel: 508-255 5165
A pub known mostly to locals, who keep it packed. **$$**

Capt. Cass Rock Harbor Seafood
117 Rock Harbor Road
No phone
No-frills seafood shanty. **$**

Provincetown

Cafe Edwige
333 Commercial Street
Tel: 508-487 2008
The candlelit contemporary dishes, with specialties such as crab cakes and Wellfleet scallops over pasta, are among the best in town. Closed November–May. **$$$**

Front Street
230 Commercial Street
Tel: 508-487 9715
Italian dishes, with a Mediterranean accents, are cutting-edge, the ambiance is intimate, and the wine list is excellent. **$$$**

Martin House
157 Commercial Street
Tel: 508-487 1327
A *c.* 1750 shingled house with intimate, rustic dining rooms and a skilled regional-cuisine chef. **$$$**

Napi's
7 Freeman Street
Tel: 508-487 1145
A colorful institution built of architectural salvage. The menu spans the world. **$$$**

Sal's Place
99 Commercial Street
Tel: 508-487 1279
Romantic classic Italian. **$$$**

Mews and Cafe Mews
429 Commercial Street
Tel: 508-487 1500
Beach-side elegance and creative cuisine. **$$–$$$**

Cafe Blase
328 Commercial Street
Tel: 508-487 9465
A sidewalk café that is perfect for people-gazing. **$**

Restaurant Prices

Prices are approximate, but for a three-course meal for one (excluding beverages, tax and tip), the following guidelines may prove helpful:
   $$$$ = over $40
   $$$ = $28–40
   $$ = $15–28
   $ = under $15

Cafe Heaven
199 Commercial Street
Tel: 508-487 9639
The best burgers in town. Good breakfasts, too. **$**

Spiritus
190 Commercial Street
Tel: 508-487 2808
A pizza mecca, and a magnet for the late-night crowd. **$**

Sandwich

Dan'l Webster Inn
149 Main Street
Tel: 508-888 3622
Offers surprisingly sophisticated cuisine for a restaurant on so large a scale. **$$**

Dunbar Tea Shop
1 Water Street (Route 130)
Tel: 508-833 2485
English tearoom serving pastries, light lunches and, of course, tea. **$**

Wellfleet

Bayside Lobster Hut
Commercial Street
Tel: 508-349 6333
Shore dinners in an 1857 oyster shack. **$**

Woods Hole

Fishmonger Cafe
56 Water Street
Tel: 508-540 5376
Lively wharfside café with inventive natural foods and fresh seafood. **$$**

Landfall
Luscombe Avenue
Tel: 508-548 1758
Seafood in a loft-like space festooned with nautical salvage. **$$**

Shuckers World Famous Raw Bar & Cafe
91A Water Street
Tel: 508-540 3850
The freshest of seafood, to be slurped dockside. **$$**

Yarmouthport

Abbici
43 Route 6A
Tel: 508-362 3501
This 1775 house sports drop-dead modern decor and serves knockout Northern Italian cuisine. **$$$$**

Inaho
157 Route 6A
Tel: 508-362 5522
A superb Japanese restaurant, with the freshest sushi imaginable. **$$$**

Jack's Outback
161 Main Street
Tel: 508-362 6690
Looking for local color? You'll find it here in spades, along with tasty, affordable old-favorites food. **$**

CENTRAL MASSACHUSETTS

Amherst

Amherst Chinese
62 Main Street
Tel: 413-253 7835
A casual restaurant known for hearty portions at low prices. **$**

Lord Jeffrey Inn
30 Boltwood Avenue
Tel: 800-742 0358
Continental dishes including beef Wellington and grilled venison are served in the formal, dark-paneled, fireplaced dining room of this historic, in-town inn. **$$–$$$**

Deerfield

Deerfield Inn
81 Old Main Street
Tel: 413-774 5587/800-926 3865
The setting, an antiques-filled, historic inn, is appropriately sedate, the Continental menu with New England accents is surprisingly forward thinking. **$$$**

Sienna
6 Elm Street
South Deerfield
Tel: 413-665 0215
An informal but intimate atmosphere and a menu that changes often but never disappoints, with dishes such as wild-mushroom crêpes and grilled duck breast, and creative desserts. Reservations. Dinner Wednesday–Sunday. **$$–$$$**

Northampton

Spoleto
50 Main Street
Tel: 413-586 6313
Italian classics in a lively contemporary cafe. **$$$**

East Side Grill
19 Strong Street
Tel: 413-586 3347
Wildly popular Cajun-influenced grill. The food may not convince you that New Orleans has come north, but the room is always bustling. **$$**

Springfield

Student Prince and Fort Restaurant
8 Fort Street
Tel: 413-734 7475
Established in the 1940s, this spot offers stout German cuisine and an authentic beer-hall ambience. Dinner only. **$$–$$$**

Sturbridge

Whistling Swan
502 Main Street
Tel: 508-347 2321
Continental cuisine in three formal dining rooms in a Greek-Revival mansion; more casual fare is available in the converted barn. Closed Monday. **$$**

West Brookfield

Salem Cross Inn
Route 9
Tel: 508-867 2345
New England favorites including baked stuffed scallops and broiled lamb chops are specialties at this handsomely-restored, 1705 home amid 600 acres. Prime rib slow-roasted in a pit is served during special Drover's Roasts. **$$–$$$**

Worcester

Coney Island Lunch
158 Southbridge Street
Tel: 508-753 4362
Folks have been flocking to this tiny spot for hot dogs since 1918: look for the sign – a hand holding a wiener. Closed Tuesday. **$**

Restaurant at Tatnuck Bookseller Marketplace
335 Chandler Street (Route 122)
Tel: 508-756 7644
Located on the West Side in the city's largest bookstore, this comfortable café serves light dishes such as salads and stir fry pastas. **$$**

Viva Bene
144 Commercial Street
Tel: 508-797 0007
A casual downtown spot serving Italian dishes ranging from basic pizza and calzones to more creative chicken or veal dishes. **$–$$$**

Charlie's Diner
32 West Main Street
Tel: 508-885-4033
A classic diner, manufactured in 1941 by the Worcester Lunch Company serving classic diner fare. Breakfast and lunch Mon–Sat. **$**

CENTRAL MASSACHUSETTS

Great Barrington

Boiler Room Cafe
405 Stockbridge Road (Route 7)
Tel: 413-528 4280
Contemporary American/ Mediterranean food. **$$–$$$**

Castle Street Cafe
10 Castle Street
Tel: 413-528 5244
An American/Continental bistro with big-city flair. **$$–$$$**

Pearl's
47 Railroad Street
Tel: 413-528 7767
Meat is a specialty at this upscale and bustling spot with pressed-tin ceilings exposed brick walls. Among the offerings: huge steaks, thick chops, and oysters on the half shell. Dinner only. **$$–$$$**

Lenox

Blantyre
off Route 20
Tel: 413-637 3556
Contemporary French cuisine in the formal dining rooms of a Tudor mansion. Summer only. **$$$$**

Village Inn
16 Church Street
Tel: 413-637 0020
New American artistry in a venerable 1771 inn. **$$$**

Church Street Cafe
65 Church Street
Tel: 413-637 2745
American bistro fare and whimsical decor. **$$**

New Marlboro

Old Inn on the Green
Village Green (Route 7), 01230
Tel: 413-229 7924
Chef/owner Peter Platt serves dishes such as roast duck and lamb shank in the candlelit, fireplaced dining rooms of a c. 1760 stagecoach inn. A 4-course, prix-fixe dinner is offered Sat evenings. Dinner only. **$$–$$$**

West Stockbridge

Williamsville Inn
Route 41
Tel: 413-274 6118
Candlelight, fireside dining featuring regional American cuisine with Italian and Mediterranean accents, prepared with produce from the garden. **$$$**

Truc Orient Express
3 Harris Street
Tel: 413-232 4204
A handsome dining room, fine service and creatively-presented Vietnamese fare, with specialties such as Shaking Beef and Happy Pancake. **$–$$$**

Williamstown

The Orchards
222 Adams Road
Tel: 413-458 9611
Accomplished New American cuisine with a creative flair in a setting of studied elegance. **$$$**

Culture

DANCE

Boston Ballet (tel: 617-695 6950/800-447 7400) are world renowned and perform regularly at the Wang Center for the Performing Arts. **Dance Complex** (tel: 617-547 9363; 536 Massachusetts Avenue, Central Square, Cambridge) performs throughout the area.

CLASSICAL MUSIC

Boston Symphony Orchestra and **Boston Pops** are heard at the acoustic and aesthetic **Symphony Hall** (tel: 617-266 1492/888-266 1200; 301 Massachusetts Avenue). **New England Conservatory's Jordan**

Hall (tel: 617-536 2412; 30 Gainsborough Street) hosts its own classical concerts.
Berklee College of Music Performance Center (tel: 617-266 7455; 136 Massachusetts Avenue, Boston) excels in jazz performances by faculty and students, many international. On the North Shore, the **Great House** at Ipswich's Castle Hill (tel: 978-356 4351; 290 Argilla Road) presents a season of classical, pop and folk music.

OPERA

Boston Lyric Opera Company (tel: 617-542 4912/800-447 7400; 114 State Street) produces three operas per season at the Shubert Theater.

ROCK AND POP

Boston Big-name national rock and alternative talent can be heard at **Mama Kin** (tel: 617-536 2100; 36 Lansdowne Street) books a variety of rock bands on three stages.
Beverly North Shore Music Theater (tel: 978-922 8500; 62 Dunham Road, off Route 128) hosts acts from April through December.
Cambridge Try the incomparable Johnny D's (tel: 617-776 2004; 17 Holland Street near Davis Square) for everything from blues jams to Cajun music.
Hyannis Cape Cod Melody Tent (tel: 508-775 9100) hosts national comics and musicians throughout the summer on the Cape.

JAZZ

Sculler's Jazz Club (tel: 617-783 0811; 400 Soldiers Field Road, Guest Quarters Suites Hotel, Cambridge) features blues, Latin, and jazz in a cozy setting.
Regattabar (tel: 617-864 1200/ 617-876 7777 for tickets; Bennett and Eliot Streets, Charles Hotel, Harvard Square, Cambridge) presents

Buying Tickets

BosTix (tel: 617-262 8632; www.bostix.org), with booths in Copley Square and Faneuil Hall Marketplace, is a major entertainment information center. Half-price tickets can be bought at 11am on the day of the event. Cash and travelers' checks only.
Ticketmaster (tel: 617-931 2000; www.ticketmaster.com), dispenses tickets for theaters and nightclubs.

traditional, big-name jazz personalities.
Bank of Boston Celebrity Series (tel: 617-482 2595) hosts jazz performances throughout the area.
Ryles Jazz Club (tel: 617-876 9330; 212 Hampshire Street, Inman Square, Cambridge) features local jazz talent and a jazz brunch on weekends.

THEATER

Boston's theater district, at the intersection of Tremont and Stuart streets has many first-rate and historic theaters, including the **Wang Center, Schubert, Colonial,** and **Wilbur.** High-quality drama is found across the city, however, with performances on show at the **Boston Center for the Arts** (tel: 617-426 5000; 539 Tremont Street) and Boston University's **Huntington Theater** (tel: 617-266 0800; 264 Huntington Avenue), with Boston's largest professional company in residence.
American Repertory Theater Company (tel: 617-495 2668; 64 Brattle Street, Harvard Square, Cambridge), a highly acclaimed award winner, has two stages at the Loeb Drama Center. On the north shore, the **Firehouse Center for the Performing Arts** (tel: 978-462 7336; Market Square, Newburyport) produces year-round plays, and specializes in children's theater. **Merrimack Repertory Theater** (tel: 978-454 3926; 50 East Merrimack St, Lowell) has professional productions. **Cape Playhouse** (tel: 508-385 3838; off Route 6A, Dennis) offers some of the best summer stock on the Cape; check local listings for other current shows. The **Center for Arts in Northampton** (tel: 413-584 7327; 17 New South Street) presents theater, dance, music and art.

CINEMA

Brattle Theater (tel: 617-876 6837; 40 Brattle Street) and the **Harvard Film Archive** (tel: 617-495 4700; 24 Quincy Street), both in Cambridge, show classic, foreign, nostalgic, and art films.
The Art Deco **Kendall Square Cinema** (tel: 617-499 1996; Kendall Square, Cambridge) offers frothy cappuccino with its foreign and art movies.
Pleasant Street Theater (tel: 413-586 0935; 27 Pleasant Street, Northampton) runs independent, foreign, and art films.
Cape Cinema (tel: 508-385 2503; off Route 6A, Dennis) was built in 1930

as a movie theater and is still true to its mission.
A trip to the **Wellfleet Drive-In** (tel: 508-349 7176; Route 6, Wellfleet) is one of the best remembrances of a sultry, relaxing summer holiday.

COMEDY

Boston's Faneuil Hall Market Place has several comedy clubs, including **Comedy Connection** (tel: 617-248 9700). Also of note is **Nick's Comedy Stop** (tel: 617-482 0930; 100 Warrenton Street), in the theater area.

ART GALLERIES

Most of Boston's largest art galleries can be found on Back Bay's Newbury Street, while a number of upstarts have moved to the Fort Point Channel area near South Station. Also try Tremont Street in the South End.
The north shore town of Rockport has more than two dozen art galleries, as does Northampton in western Massachusetts.
In Lowell, **Brush Art Gallery and Studios** (tel: 978-459 7819; 256 Market Street) showcases the studios of 12 working artists.
On Cape Cod, head to Wellfleet and Provincetown and simply wander the streets from gallery to gallery.

Nightlife

NIGHTCLUBS/DISCOS

Boston's Lansdowne Street, behind Fenway Park in Kenmore Square, is the city's largest conglomeration of nightclubs. **Axis** (tel: 617-262 2437; 13 Lansdowne Street), one of the city's largest clubs with a capacity of 1,000 people, has music on several floors.

LIVE MUSIC

In Cambridge, head to **The Middle East** (tel: 617-354 8238; 472 Massachusetts Avenue, Central Square), an eclectic club with nightly jazz, rock and world music on two floors, and **Club Passim** (tel: 617-492 7679; 67 Palmer Street, Harvard Square) is a venerable folk establishment where Joan Baez and other legends first made their names.
The venerable **Iron Horse** (tel: 413-584 0610; 20 Center Street, Northampton) puts on both live folk and jazz music. Also in town, **Pearl Street Nightclub** (tel: 413-584 0610; 10 Pearl Street) hosts live music.
In Springfield, **Theodore's** (tel: 413-736 6000; 201 Worthington Street) presents "booze, blues & BBQ".

GAY & LESBIAN VENUES

At **Avalon** (tel: 617-262 2424; 15 Lansdowne Street, Boston), Sunday is gay night. **Club Café and Lounge** (tel: 617-536 0966; 209 Columbus Avenue) offers chic surroundings to the area's gays.

Provincetown is the East Coast's main center (perhaps tied with Key West) for gays and lesbians. It's best to ask around for the current "in" club, but you can count on tea dances at **The Boatslip** (tel: 508-487 1669; Commercial Street), every summer afternoon on the waterfront deck. Northampton has several clubs for lesbians: the local paper has listings.

CABARET

Zeiterion Performing Arts Center (tel: 508-997 5664; 684 Purchase Street, New Bedford), a handsomely-restored all-vaudeville theater, stages theme performances.

LATE-NIGHT VENUES

Although Boston is notorious for shutting down early, its large student population usually keeps things rolling, at least on Friday and Saturday. Most nightclubs on Lansdowne Street are open until 2.30am, but don't forget: the "T" stops running at 12.30am.

DANCING

In Boston's Theater District, **Venu** (tel: 617-388 8061; 100 Warrenton Street) is one of the new hot spots to dance the wee hours away. The fashionable **Gypsy Bar** (tel: 617-482 7799; 116 Boylston Street) attracts Boston's chic dance set. **Aria** (tel: 617-338 7080; 246 Tremont Street), beneath the Wilbur Theater, rocks after the theater ends.

MUSIC

During the summer, Boston has several free outdoor concert series at the **Hatch Shell** on the Charles River Esplanade. Check the *Boston Globe* for listings.

Generally, the New England states are represented by Boston's teams: basketball's **Boston Celtics** (tel: 617-624 1000; Fleet Center, September–May), baseball's Boston **Red Sox** (tel: 617-267 1700; Fenway Park, April–October) and hockey's **Boston Bruins** (tel: 617-624 1000/617-931 2222 for tickets; Fleet

Information Sources

Boston
The Phoenix (published weekly) contains a large Arts and Entertainment section. *The Boston Globe*'s pull-out Calendar section (published every Thursday) is devoted to cultural events around the city.
Western Massachusetts
For cultural events, consult the *Five College Calendar of Events*, published monthly, or *The Advocate*, a free weekly paper.

Center, October–March).

The major exception is football, which the **New England Patriots** (tel: 508-543 1776/800-543 1776 for tickets, Foxboro Stadium, August–December) play in the southern suburb of Foxboro.

For up-to-date information on schedules and locations, check the sports section of any local daily.

Outdoor Activities

BIKING

In Eastern Massachusetts, mountain bikers can explore the trails of **Blue Hills Reservation** (tel: 617-698 1802) in Milton, just south of Boston, or in **Maudslay State Park** in Newburyport on the North Shore. In the western part of the state, **Mount Greylock State Reservation** (tel: 413-499 4262) near Williamstown has a number of mountain biking trails.

Bikers also flock to the **Cape Cod Rail Trail**, a scenic 30-mile (48-km) paved path along the former Penn Central Railway route from South Dennis to South Wellfleet *(see page 160)*. In Provincetown, the paved **Province Lands Trail** winds for 7¼ miles through the dunes.

A classic urban bike path is Boston's **Dr. Paul Dudley White Bikeway**, an 18-mile (29-km) loop that follows both sides of the Charles River. **The Norwattuck Rail Trail** (tel: 413-586 8706) extends 10 miles (16 km) from Northampton to Belchertown.

CANOEING/KAYAKING AND RAFTING

In Boston and the nearby suburb of Newton, **Charles River Canoe and Kayak Center** (tel: 617-965 5110) rents canoes and kayaks on the Charles River for an hour or more.

South Bridge Boat House in historic Concord (tel: 978-369 9438) has canoes for rent on the lazy Sudbury and Concord Rivers.

At Nickerson State Park on Cape Cod, **Jack's Boat Rentals** (tel: 508-896 8556) rents canoes, kayaks, sunfish, pedal boats, sailboards and seacycles.

Sportsmen's Marina Boat Rental Company in Hadley (tel: 413-586 2426; Route 9) rents canoes and kayaks, as does the **Northfield Mountain Recreation and Environmental Center** (tel: 800-859 2960). In western Massachusetts, **Zoar Outdoor** (tel: 800-532 7483), based along the Mohawk Trail in Charlemont, organizes whitewater rafting expeditions for all levels on the Deerfield River. They also run two- or three-day learn-to-kayak or canoe clinics.

FISHING

For salt-water fly-fishing, check with **Orvis Saltwater School** (tel: 800-235 9763; Chatham) on Cape Cod. They run a 2½-day course that teaches basic saltwater techniques. Also on the Cape, **Patriot Party Boats** (tel: 508-548 2626), operating out of Falmouth Harbor, offers deep-sea fishing trips.

The Orleans-based **Rock Harbor Charter Fleet** (tel: 508-255 9757) also run fishing excursions.

On Cape Ann, **Yankee Deep Sea Fishing** (tel: 978 283 0313/800-942 5464; 75 Essex Avenue, Gloucester) journeys out to Stellwagen Bank and Jeffrey's Ledge.

HIKING

Close to Boston, hikers can explore the 150 miles of trails at **Blue Hills Reservation** (see *Biking* above). More ambitious hikers head west to **Mount Tom State Reservation** in Holyoke or **Mount Greylock State Reservation** (see *Biking*, left), which includes a stretch of the Appalachian Trail.

SAILING

Boston's **Community Boating** (tel: 617-523 1038), America's oldest public sailing program, sells two-day (and longer) memberships for sailing along the Charles River.

Cape Cod Museum of Natural History (tel: 508-896 3867/800-479 3867; Brewster) offers nature explorations in Orleans' Nauset Marsh on a motorized catamaran.

The schooner **Bay Lady II** (tel: 508-487 9308) makes two-hour sails from Provincetown into Cape Cod Bay.

SKIING

Massachusetts' best downhill skiing is in the Berkshires. Two of the major

Massachusetts Festivals

Spring

Spring officially arrives with the **Boston Marathon** (tel: 617-236 1652), held on **Patriot's Day** (the third Monday in April). Modern-day Minutemen stage **Revolutionary War Reenactments** in Boston at the Paul Revere House (tel: 617-536 4100) and in Lexington and Concord (tel: 781-861 0928).

In late April, a colorful **Daffodil Festival** is held on Nantucket (tel: 508-228 1700). In mid-May (and again in July and September), flea-market fevers sweeps tiny Brimfield for the three **Brimfield Outdoor Antiques Shows** (tel: 413-283 6149/800-628 8379), mega-swap meets that attract over 1,000 dealers and serious antiquaries.

Summer

Summer is music time, beginning in mid-June with the **Boston Globe Jazz Festival** (tel: 617-929 2649).

From mid-June to late August, the Boston Symphony Orchestra presides over the world-famous **Tanglewood Music Festival** (tel: 413-637 5165/800-274 8499) in Lenox. Following roughly the same schedule are two fellow Berkshires institutions: the **Jacob's Pillow Dance Festival** (tel: 413-243 0745) in nearby Becket, and the outstanding **Williamstown Theatre Festival** (tel: 413-597 3400) in Williamstown.

While the BSO is off to the country, the Boston Pops wow the masses with a free **Fourth of July Concert** (with fireworks) at the Hatch Shell on the Charles River Esplanade (tel: 617-266 1492).

Later in July, the Lowell National Historical Park holds the **Lowell Folk Festival** (tel: 978-970 5000), the largest free folk fest in the country, a melange of traditional music and ethnic foods.

Summer is also a good time to

catch up with local artisans. Five hundred of the country's very best (including a sizable New England contingent) exhibit in West Springfield at the **ACC Crafts Fair** (tel: 800-836 3470) in mid-June.

A smaller sampling show at the **Old Deerfield Craft Fair** (tel: 413-774 7476) in mid-June and late September.

Fall

Harvest festivals mark the foliage season, including extravaganzas such as Springfield's **Big E** (tel: 413-737 2443), and one of the nation's oldest county fairs, the **Topsfield Fair** (tel: 978-887 5000).

Also in October, college crew teams and spectators come to Cambridge for the **Head of the Charles Regatta** (tel: 617-864 8415), while in Salem, the annual **Haunted Happenings** week climaxes on Halloween (tel: 978-744 0013).

Winter

Communities across Massachusetts ring in the New Year with First Night festivities. Started by Boston artists in 1977, **First Night** has spread to more than 70 communities nationwide and offers a moveable feast of music, theatre, ice sculptures, parades and fireworks.

Towns in which First Night celebrations are held include the following:
Boston (tel: 617-542 1399),
Salem (tel: 978-744 0004),
several Cape Cod towns
(tel: 508-709 2787),
and Northampton
(tel: 413-584 7327).

For further information about venues and timings of the events listed above, consult the local tourist offices or newspapers with listings.

areas are **Jiminy Peak** in Hancock (tel: 413-738 5500) and **Brodie Mountain** in New Ashford (tel: 413-443 4752; Route 7). **Northfield Mountain Recreation and Environmental Center** (tel: 800-859 2960; 99 Miller's Falls Road) has 26 miles (42 km) of trails.

However, weather permitting, there are options for skiing in the eastern part of the state; the largest area is **Wachusett Mountain** in Princeton, about an hour west of Boston (tel: 978-464 2300/800-754 1234).

The Berkshires are the most reliable for cross-country skiing. **Northfield Mt.**

XC Center (tel: 413-659 3715) has around 25 miles (40 km) of trails.

Closer to Boston, two smaller but still popular areas are **Weston Ski Track** (tel: 781-891 6575) and in Carlisle, **Great Brook Farm** (tel: 978-369 7486).

Shopping

WHERE TO SHOP

Boston Downtown Crossing, a pedestrian-only zone, is Boston's largest shopping area, complete with

outdoor kiosks. The popular Faneuil Hall Marketplace has more than 150 small shops and foodstands, and attracts over a million visitors a month. With everything from funky sportswear to vintage street signs on offer, it's a handy place to pick up last-minute gifts. Boston's version of Fifth Avenue is Newbury Street, eight-block stretch of expensive clothing stores, salons, and art galleries. **Cambridge** Harvard Square has more than 150 stores within a small radius. **Nantucket** Good for shopping if you have money to burn; an excellent and dense concentration of shops.

MALLS

Boston's **Copley Place** (tel: 617-369 5000; Copley Square) has almost 100 upscale stores and restaurants, while **Cambridgeside Galleria** (tel: 617-621 8666; 100 Cambridgeside Place, Cambridge) is a three-story mall with over 100 shops and three department stores. **Cape Cod Mall** (tel: 508-771 0200; Routes 132 and 28, Hyannis) isn't particularly distinctive, but it does have a very wide range of stock on offer. The **Holyoke Mall**, just off I-91 in Holyoke, is one of the biggest in western Massachusetts.

MARKETS

Boston's historic **Haymarket**, selling inexpensive fruits and vegetables, meat, and seafood, is open Friday and Saturday near Faneuil Hall Marketplace.

Gourmet Outlet (tel: 508-999 6408; 2301 Purchase Street) in New Bedford has a wonderful selection of unusual foods from around the world. Open Tuesday–Saturday.

FASHION & ACCESSORIES

Chic Newbury Street in Boston is the place for high fashion, with stores such as **Brooks Brothers** at no. 46 (tel: 617-267 2600), **Alan Bilzerian** at no. 34 (tel: 617-536 1001), and **Ann Taylor** at no. 18 (tel: 617-262 0763). One of Boston's oldest men's store, **Louis Boston** (tel: 617-262 6100; 234 Berkeley Street) also sells women's apparel now.

BOOKS

Boston and Cambridge are havens for buyers and browsers of new and used books. Check out **Wordsworth** (tel: 617-354 5201; three stores in Harvard Square, Cambridge) as well as the various branches of the big chains: **Borders** (10 School Street and 300 Boylston Street in Boston, and CambridgeSide Galleria in Cambridge);

and **Barnes & Noble** (395 Washington Street, and 800 Boylston Street/ Prudential Center).

As for used bookstores, **Trident Booksellers and Cafe** (tel: 617-267 8688; 338 Newbury Street), **Brattle Book Shop** (tel: 617-542 0210; 9 West Street), and **Commonwealth Books** (tel: 617-338 6328; 134 Boston Street), all in Boston, are great.

Schoenhof's (tel: 617-547 8855; 76a Mount Auburn Street, Cambridge) sells foreign-language materials, as well as fiction and many dictionaries.

Tatnuck Bookseller Marketplace in Worcester (tel: 508-756 7644; 335 Chandler Street) is the largest independent bookseller in the state, carrying over 500,000 volumes. Northampton has a particularly dense concentration of shops.

ANTIQUES

Boston's Charles Street has a large number of antique dealers, including the **Boston Antique Co-op** (tel: 617-227 9810; 119 Charles Street). Also try the **Boston Antique Center** (tel: 617-742 1400; 54 Canal Street, near North Station) and the **Cambridge Antiques Market** (tel: 617-868 9655) at 201 Monsignor O'Brien Highway in Cambridge.

On the north shore, Gloucester's Main Street has lots of interesting antiques shops; in Essex there is the excellent **White Elephant** (tel: 978-768 6901; 32 Main St), one of the town's 40 antique dealers.

Antique Center of Sturbridge (tel: 508-347 5150; 462 Main Street, Sturbridge) has dealers on two floors.

On Cape Cod, the whole stretch of Route 6A from Sandwich to Orleans is lined with antique shops. Brewster has the most and generally the best.

The **Antique Center of Northampton** (tel: 413-584 3600; 9½ Market Street) and the **Hadley Antique Center** (tel: 413-586 4093; 227 Russell Street) offer plenty of opportunity for browsing.

Department Stores

The huge **Macy's** on Washington Street in Boston (tel: 617 357 3000; 450 Washington Street) is the city's largest department store. Be sure to go next door to **Filene's Basement** (tel: 617-348 7848; 426 Washington Street) for some unbelievable bargains. There's also a smaller Filene's Basement in the Back Bay at 497 Boylston Street (617-424 5520).

CHINA AND GLASS

Fellerman & Raabe Glassworks
Main Street, Sheffield
Tel: 413-229 8533
Sells glassware of every shape, size, and color.
The Berkshire Center for Contemporary Glass
6 Harris Street, West Stockbridge
Tel: 413-232 4666
Has glassblowers at work during summer months. Both are in the Berkshires.
Martha's Vineyard Glass Works
State Road, West Tisbury
Tel: 508-693 6026
Carries an exceptional selection of glassware; you can also watch the master craftspeople at work.
Pairpoint Crystal
Route 6A, Sagamore
Tel: 508-888 2344/800-899 0953
Glassmakers use a variety of techniques developed in nearby Sandwich, world-renowned in the 1800s for its innovative glassmaking.

JEWELRY

Shreve, Crump & Low
330 Boylston Street, Boston
Tel: 617-267 9100
One of Boston's oldest and most venerated shops, the store sells a dazzling array of fine jewelry, as well as exceptional china, crystal, and silverware.
Tiffany & Co
Copley Place, Boston
Tel: 617-353 0222
World famous and exceptional.

ARTS AND CRAFTS

Society of Arts and Crafts
175 Newbury Street, Boston
Tel: 617-266 1810
A prestigious, non-profit institution with high-quality handmade items.
Worcester Center for Crafts
25 Sagamore Road, Worcester
Tel: 508-753 8183
One of America's oldest crafts complexes.
Great Barrington Pottery
Route 41
Tel: 413-274 6259
Sells pieces glazed in Japanese wood-burning kilns, and performs a tea ceremony Wednesdays in July and August.

Children

THEME PARKS
Whalom Park
Route 13, Lunenburg
Tel: 978-342 3707
A waterslide, 50 carnival-style rides and a beach on Whalom Lake. Closed Monday.

ZOOS
Franklin Park Zoo
Blue Hill Ave at Columbia Rd
Boston
Tel: 617-541 5466
Has a free-flight aviary and African Tropical Rain Forest exhibit, along with animals including giraffes and zebras.

STEAM TRAIN JOURNEYS
Berkshire Scenic Railway
10 Willow Creek Road
Lenox
Tel: 413-637 2210
Train rides May through October.

THEATER
Priscilla Beach Theater
Rocky Hill Road
Plymouth
Tel: 508-224 4888
Presents children's shows on Friday and Saturday. Performing arts camp throughout the summer.

MUSEUMS
Children's Museum
Museum Wharf
300 Congress Street
Boston
Tel: 617-426 8855
A delight. Fun with learning.
Museum of Science
Science Park at the Charles River Dam, Boston
Tel: 617-723 2500
Hundreds of hands-on exhibits to spark the excitement of children aged three and up; also an Omni Theater.
New England Aquarium
Central Wharf
Boston
Tel: 617-973 5200
A world-class facility that supports serious marine research.
Thornton W Burgess Museum
4 Water Street
Sandwich
Tel: 508-888 6870
This museum is dedicated to the creator of Peter Rabbit and many other children's books.

Connecticut

The Place

Known as: The Constitution State, because its delegates played a crucial role in drawing up the US Constitution in 1787
Motto: *Qui Transtulit Sustinet* (He who transplanted still sustains)
Origin of name: probably derived from Algonquian Indian term thought to mean "place of the long river"
Entered Union: 9 January 1788, the fifth of the original 13 states.
Capital: Hartford.
Area: 5,544 sq. miles (14,358 sq. km).
Highest point: Mount Frissell, 2,380 ft (725 meters).
Population: 3.29 million.
Population density: 593 people per sq. mile (229 per sq. km).
Economy: Hartford is a a major insurance centre. Also aircraft engines, helicopters, submarines, and firearms.
National representation: 2 senators and 6 representatives to Congress
Famous citizens: Phineas T. Barnum, Samuel Colt, Katharine Hepburn, J. Pierpoint Morgan, Harriet Beecher Stowe, Mark Twain, Noah Webster, Eli Whitney.

Where To Stay

AVON

Avon Old Farms Hotel
279 Avon Mountain Road, Routes 44 and 10, 06001
Tel: 860-677 1651/800-836 4000
Fax: 860-677 0364
www.avonoldfarmshotel.com
160 modern rooms with traditional furnishings in several red-brick buildings spread across 20 acres. Swimming pool. **$$–$$$**

BRISTOL

Chimney Crest Manor
5 Founders Drive, 06010
Tel: 860-582 4219
Fax: 860-584 5903
Five-room B&B in an elegantly

appointed 1930s, National Historic Register 32-room Tudor-style mansion with views of the Farmington Valley, 20 minutes west of Hartford. **$$–$$$**

CHESTER

Inn and Vineyard at Chester
318 West Main Street, 06412
Tel: 860-526 9541
Fax: 860-526 1607
www.innatchester.com.
Modern amenities in a 42-room inn built around an original 1776 farmhouse. Located between Essex and East Haddam. Tennis courts, tavern. **$$$–$$$$**

EAST HADDAM

Bishopsgate Inn
7 Norwich Road, 06423
Tel: 860-873 1677
Fax: 860-873 3898
www.bishopsgate.com
Six-room B&B in an 1818 shipwright's home with six fireplaces. **$$–$$$**

ESSEX

Griswold Inn
36 Main Street, 06426
Tel: 860-767 1776
Fax: 860-767 0481
www.griswoldinn.com
Open since 1776. Historical appointments in the 31 rooms include ancient firearms, antiques, and Currier & Ives prints. Eight of the 14 suites have fireplaces. There's a fine art collection in the Tap Room. **$$$**

FARMINGTON

Centennial Inn Suites
5 Spring Lane, 06032
Tel: 860-677 4647/
800-852 2052 outside CT
Fax: 860-676 0685
112 one and two-bedroom suites with kitchen, living room, fireplace and TV on 12 wooded acres. Whirlpool, exercise room. Pets welcome. **$$$–$$$$**
Farmington Inn
827 Farmington Avenue, 06032
Tel: 860-677 2821
Fax: 860-677 8332
www.farmingtoninn.com
A handsomely renovated motel with 72 traditionally decorated rooms furnished with fresh flowers, antiques,and local art work. **$$**

GLASTONBURY

Butternut Farm
1654 Main Street, 06033
Tel: 860-633 7197
Fax: 860-659 1758

www.butternutfarmbandb.com
B&B with five rooms in a 1720 colonial house with eight fireplaces, period antiques, herb gardens, and a barn housing goats, chickens (for fresh eggs), ducks, pigs, and a llama. Full breakfast served in the original dining room or an intimate breakfast room. **$**

HARTFORD

Goodwin Hotel
1 Haynes Street, 06103
Tel: 860-246 7500/800-922 5006
www.goodwinhotel.com
A historic, luxury urban inn with 124 rooms, including 11 suites, in the heart of town. There's a 24-hour fitness center, and good discounts are often available at weekends. Valet parking. **$$$–$$$$**
Hilton Hartford
315 Trumbell Street, 06103
Tel: 860-728 5151
Fax: 860-240 7247
The renovated, 22-floor, downtown hotel connected to the Hartford Civic Center has 390 rooms, a restaurant, a workout room, and an indoor pool. **$$–$$$$**
The 1895 House B&B
97 Girard Avenue, 06105
Tel: 860-232 0014
Bay-windowed Victorian home with two bedrooms in the west end of town. **$**

IVORYTON

Copper Beech Inn
46 Main Street, 06442
Tel: 860-767 0330/888-809 2056
www.copperbeachinn.com
Luxuriously appointed 1890 Victorian home and carriage house on 7 acres (3 hectares). Nine of the 13 rooms have whirlpool tubs. **$$$–$$$$**

LAKEVILLE

Interlaken Inn
74 Interlaken Road, Route 112, 06039
Tel: 860-435 9878/800-222 2909
Fax: 860-435 2980
For more than 100 years, this romantic country retreat has been taking in guests. There are rooms in the main inn – an English Tudor house – as well as the Townhouse and a private lakefront cottage. Pets welcome in some rooms. There's a spa on the premises. **$$$–$$$$**
Wake Robin Inn
Sharon Road (Route 41), 06039
Tel: 860-435 2000
Fax: 860-435 6523
www.wakerobininn.com
A Georgian, colonial-style inn and motel with 38 rooms set on 15 acres (6 hectares). **$$–$$$**

LEDYARD

Stonecroft
515 Pumpkin Hill Road, 06339
Tel: 860-572 0771
Fax: 860-572 9161
Close to the casinos but a world away, this 1807 Georgian colonial, a National Register of Historic Places property on six-and-a-half acres, has 10 rooms with private baths; three have fireplaces. **$$–$$$$**

Foxwoods
Tel: 800-369 9663
www.foxwoods.com
The world's biggest casino has three hotels with a total of 1,416 rooms and suites, including the 24-floor Pequot Tower, the Great Cedar Hotel, and, a short drive away by the 24-hour courtesy van, Two Trees Inn, designed to feel and look like a country inn. **$$$–$$$$**

LITCHFIELD

Abel Darling B&B
102 West Street, 06759
Tel: 860-567 0384
1782 Colonial overlooking the Green in the historic district has three antiques-filled guest rooms. **$$$**

Litchfield Inn
432 Bantam Road (Route 202), 06759
Tel: 860-567 4503/800-499 3444
Fax: 860-567 5358
www.litchfieldinnct.com
Central location is a plus at this reproduction inn, with its 32 rooms traditionally decorated in the Colonial style. The parlor has a baby grand piano and fireplace. **$$–$$$**

Tollgate Hill Inn
Tollgate Road and Route 202, 06759
Tel: 860-567 4545/800-445 3903
Fax: 860-567 4545
A romantically appointed 1745 Federal inn supplemented by a renovated schoolhouse. Many of the 20 rooms have canopy beds. **$$$–$$$$**

MADISON

Tidewater Inn B&B
949 Boston Post Road (Route 1) 06443
Tel: 203-245 8457
Fax: 203-318 0265
A former, shorefront stage coach stop turned cozy, antiques-filled B&B with nine rooms (some with fireplaces). Walking distance to Madison village. **$$$–$$$$**

Madison Beach Hotel
94 West Wharf Road, 06443
Tel: 203-245 1404
Fax: 203-245 0410
www.madisonbeachhotel.com

An old-fashioned, Victorian wooden hotel with a wraparound porch, right on the Sound. 35 rooms and six suites. **$$$–$$$$**

MYSTIC AREA

Steamboat Inn
73 Steamboat Wharf, Mystic, 06355
Tel: 860-536 8300
Fax: 860-536 9528
www.steamboatinnmystic.com
Ten waterfront rooms, some with fireplaces and whirlpools, in an elegant inn in the historic district. **$$$–$$$$**

House of 1833 B&B
72 N Stonington Road, Mystic, 06355
Tel: 860-536 6325/800-367 1833
www.houseof1833.com
Elegant, 1833 Greek-revival mansion has five antiques-filled guest rooms, some with canopy beds and private porch or balcony and wood burning fireplaces. Swimming pool and tennis court. **$$–$$$$**

Inn at Mystic
Routes 1 and 27, Mystic, 06355
Tel: 860-536 9604/800-237 2415
www.innatmystic.com
Choose from motel units, guest houses, or the National Historic Register Colonial Revival mansion at this 15-acre (6-hectare) property overlooking Mystic Harbor. Outdoor pool, tennis, boating, and kayaking. **$$$–$$$$**

Red Brook Inn
2750 Gold Star Highway
Old Mystic, 06372
Tel: 860-572 0349
www.redbrookinnmystic.com
B&B in a pair of National Historic Register classic colonials on seven acres. Rooms furnished with American period antiques. Seven of the ten rooms have working fireplaces. **$$$–$$$$**

Whaler's Inn
20 E Main Street (Route 1)
Mystic, 06355
Tel: 860-536 1506/
800-243 2588 outside CT
Fax: 860-572 1250
www.whalersinnmystic.com
Several 19th-century homes transformed into a homey inn with 41 rooms, clustered near the docks. **$$–$$$**

Price Categories

A very approximate guide to current room rates for a standard double per night is:
  $$$$ = over $200
  $$$ = $150–200
  $$ = $100–150
  $ = under $100

Harbour Inne & Cottage
15 Edgemont Street, Mystic, 06355
Tel: 860-572 9253
www.harbourinne-cottage.com
A family-friendly pine-paneled 1950s bungalow on the Mystic River, with six nautical-themed rooms and a three-room cottage. Walking distance to the seaport and boat dock. **$$**

NEW HAVEN

Three Chimneys Inn
1201 Chapel Street, 06511
Tel: 203-789 1201
Fax: 203-776 7363
www.threechimneysinn.com
A 10-room B&B in a luxurious restored 19th-century urban inn near Yale University. **$$$**

Colony Inn
1157 Chapel Street, 06511
Tel: 203-776 1234/800-458 8810
Fax: 203-772 3929
www.colonyatyale.com
Located near the Yale campus, this European-style inn features a lobby with a grand chandelier and 86 comfortable guest rooms furnished with Colonial reproductions. **$$–$$$**

New Haven Hotel
229 George Street, 06510
Tel: 203-498 3100/800-644 6835
Fax: 203-498 0911
www.newhavenhotel.com
A seven-story, 92-room city-center hotel with the feel of an exclusive inn. Amenities include an indoor swimming pool, in-room data ports, and a health club. **$$**

NEW LONDON

Lighthouse Inn
6 Guthrie Place, 06320
Tel: 860-443 8411/888-443 8411
Fax: 860-437 7027
www.lighthouseinn-ct.com
Restored in 2002, this 1902 mansion has 51 nicely-furnished rooms; some with water views. There's a private beach and lovely grounds. Located a few blocks from Ocean Beach Park. **$$–$$$**

NEW PRESTON

Boulders Inn
East Shore Road, Route 45, 06777
Tel: 860-868 0541/800-552 6853
Fax: 860-868 1925
www.bouldersinn.com
17 rooms in an elegant 1895 stone mansion and carriage house overlooking Lake Waramaug. Also, eight fireplaced guesthouses. B&B or MAP. **$$$$**

Hopkins Inn
22 Hopkins Road, 06777
Tel: 860-868 7295

Price Categories

A very approximate guide to current room rates for a standard double per night is:

$$$$ = over $200
$$$ = $150–200
$$ = $100–150
$ = under $100

www.thehopkinsinn.com
1847 Federal-style country inn perched high above Lake Waramaug has 11 comfortable, simply-furnished rooms and two apartments. **$–$$**

NORFOLK

Blackberry River Inn
538 Greenwoods Road, Route 44W, 06058
Tel: 860-542 5100/800-414- 3636
www.blackberryriverinn.com
Eight rooms–some with fireplaces–in a 240-year-old Colonial inn on 27 acres in the Berkshire foothills. Also rooms in the Carriage House. **$–$$$$**

Manor House
69 Maple Avenue, Route 44, 06058
Tel/fax: 860-542 5690
www.manorhouse-norfolk.com
An opulent 1898 Tudor summer home B&B with 20 Tiffany stained-glass windows. Some of the nine rooms have whirlpool tubs, fireplaces and balconies. **$$–$$$$**

NORWALK

Silvermine Tavern
194 Perry Avenue, 06850
Tel: 203-847 4558
Fax: 203-847 9171
www.silverminetavern.com
A 1785 country inn with 11 antiques-filled bedrooms set by a waterfall; some have fireplaces. **$$**

OLD LYME

Bee & Thistle Inn
100 Lyme Street, 06371
Tel: 860-434 1667/800-622 4946
Fax: 860-434 3402
www.beeandthistleinn.com
A 1756 Colonial home with 11 rooms and a cottage, set peacefully beside a river. **$–$$$$**

Hotel Meal Guide

B&Bs supply a complimentary full breakfast and are often quite sophisticated
MAP (Modified American Plan) rates include both breakfast and dinner
FAP (Full American Plan) supply all three meals

OLD SAYBROOK

Saybrook Point Inn and Spa
2 Bridge Street, Route 154, 05475
Tel: 860-395 2000/800-243 0212
Fax: 860-388 1504
www.saybrook.com
Well-appointed 81-room nautical luxury hotel, with water views, indoor and outdoor pools, and a spa, offering luxury services from exercise programs to massages and facials. A lighthouse suite has a kitchenette. **$$$–$$$$**

SALISBURY

White Hart Inn
Village Green (Routes 44 and 41) 06068
Tel: 860-435 0030/800-832 0041
Fax: 860-435 0040
www.whitehartinn.com
A century-old landmark offering 26 rooms and suites at the center of a timeless town. **$$$$**

STONINGTON

Inn at Stonington
60 Water Street, 06378
Tel: 860-535 2000/860-535 2000
Fax: 860-535 8193
www.innatstonington.com
A contemporary inn overlooking Stonington Borough harbor. All 18 rooms and suites have fireplaces; 10 have jacuzzis. Exercise room and, for the nautical, a 400-ft pier. **$$–$$$$**

WASHINGTON

Mayflower Inn
118 Woodbury Road (Route 47), 06793
Tel: 860-868 9466
Fax: 860-868 1497
www.mayflowerinn.com
The ultimate in romantic country luxury. A new building with 25 rooms built on the site of an old country inn on 28 secluded acres with gardens, woods, and ponds. Facilities include a pool, tennis courts, health club, and a highly regarded restaurant. **$$$$**

WEST CORNWALL

Hilltop Haven
175 Dibble Hill Road, 06796
Tel: 860-672 6871
www.hilltopbb.com
A stone house on a 64-acre hilltop estate, perched over the village, with lovely views of the Housatonic Valley and Taconic Mountains. Two antiques-filled rooms only. **$$$–$$$$**

WESTPORT

Inn at National Hall
2 Post Road West, 06880

Tel: 203-221 1351/800-628 4255
www.innatnationalhall.com
An elegant inn, styled like an English manor house and fashioned from a 19th-century Historic District building on the banks of the Saugatuck. There are 16 lavishly decorated rooms and suites and a first-class restaurant. **$$$$**

Inn at Longshore
260 Compo Road South, 06880
Tel: 203-226 3316
Fax: 203-227 5344
www.innatlongshore.com
The handsome 12-room inn on 52 acres, a former country club, overlooks Long Island Sound and has an 18-hole golf course and a popular restaurant open for dinner nightly. **$$$**

WETHERSFIELD

Chester Bulkley House B&B
184 Main Street, 06109
Tel: 860-563 4236
Five-room B&B (three with private bath) in an elegant 1830 Greek Revival home located in an historic town 5 miles (8 km) from Hartford. **$–$$**

WOODBURY

Longwood Country Inn
1204 Main Street South 06798
Tel: 203-266 0800
Fax: 203-263 3474
www.longwoodcountryinn.com
A rambling 1789, National Historic Register B&B, decorated in an English country style, in Connecticut's "antiques capital", has four guest rooms, including a spacious suite. Located on four wooded acres near the Pomperaug River. **$$–$$$$**

Where to Eat

AVON

Seasons Restaurant
Avon Old Farms Hotel
1 Nod Road, Routes 44 and 10
Tel: 860-677 0240
Continental favorites including Long Island roast duck in an elegant room overlooking a stream. Sunday brunch is a stand-out. A lighter menu in The Pub. **$$$**

Max A Mia
70 East Main Street
(Route 44)
Tel: 860-677 6299
A lively northern Italian spot; good for pizza, risotto, and seafood. **$–$$**

BETHEL

Roadside Chili House
44 Stony Hill Road
Tel: 203-790 5064
Fry a foot-long wiener, put it on a soft bun, and top it with spicy chili, melted cheese, and raw onion. Hot dog perfection. **$**

CANAAN

Cannery Cafe
85 Main Street
(Routes 44 and 7)
Tel: 860-824 7333
"American bistro" fare, including creative fish dishes, grilled lamb, and a fine Sunday brunch. Dinner; Sunday brunch. **$$–$$$**

CHESHIRE

Deli 66
1152 Meriden-Waterbury Road
Tel: 203-271 2464
A genuine New York-style deli specializing in corned beef, pastrami, and homemade chicken soup. **$–$$**

CHESTER

Restaurant du Village
59 Main Street
Tel: 860-526 5301
Superb formal French cuisine, with specialties such as filet mignon and escargot, is served in this charming country auberge. Dinner Wednesday–Sunday. **$$$–$$$$**

EAST LYME

Flanders Fish Market & Restaurant
22 Chesterfield Road, Route 161
(Route 161)
Tel: 860-739 8866/800-638 8189
This humble roadside restaurant consistently wins accolades for its ultra-fresh, very good-value fish. Sunday seafood buffet is served 11am–3pm. **$–$$**

ESSEX

Griswold Inn
36 Main Street
Tel: 860-767 1776

Well-prepared, traditional, New England fare with a touch of the sophisticated in an historic, 250-year-old country inn. The Tap Room offers a lighter menu. **$$–$$$**

FARMINGTON

Ann Howard's Apricots
1593 Farmington Avenue
Tel: 860-673 5903
Award-winning, creative New American dishes in an elegant Colonial home with river and garden views. More casual pub fare is available downstairs. **$$–$$$$**

GLASTONBURY

Glas Restaurant
2935 Main Street
Tel: 860-657 9251
A modern American café serving updated American favorites include grilled steak and seafood, along with some classic Latin dishes. Lunch Mon-Fri, dinner nightly. **$$–$$$**

J. Gilbert's
185 Glastonbury Boulevard
Tel: 860-659 0409
Steakhouse with southwestern and Mediterranean influences. Club-like dining room done in dark woods. **$$–$$$**

Max Amore
Somerset Square Shopping Arcade
Tel: 860-659 2819
A marriage of well-prepared Northern Italian dishes, oak-grilled meats, and seafood, and a handsome yet casual dining room make the bistro environment a perennially popular spot for both lunch and dinner. **$$–$$$**

GROTON

Fun 'n' Food Clam Bar
283 Route 12
Tel: 860-445 6186
Tasty chili dogs, clams, chowder, and milkshakes. All at a very fair price. **$**

Norm's Diner
171 Bridge Street
Tel: 860-445 5026
A 1950s diner serving breakfast all day. The house cheesecake enjoys local acclaim. **$**

GUILFORD

Guilford Tavern
2455 Boston Post Road
Tel: 203-453 2216
The ambience in this one-time foundry is rustic, and the focus of the food is fresh seafood and prime beef. Pub fare also available. **$$–$$$**

HARTFORD AREA

Butterfly Restaurant
831 Farmington Avenue, West Hartford
Tel: 860-236 2816
Szechuan and Cantonese dishes are artfully presented in elegant surroundings at one of the state's best Chinese restaurants. Live piano music nightly. **$$**

Max Downtown
185 Asylum Street, Hartford
Tel: 860-522 2530
Upscale power dining. The Contemporary menu emphasizes fish, pasta, and meat dishes. Cigar bar draws a business crowd. Lunch weekdays; dinner nightly. **$$$–$$$$**

Grants Restaurant, Bar & Patisserie
977 Farmington Avenue
West Hartford
American fare with a few twists in one of the city's hottest new spots: among the steaks and chops, prosciutto-wrapped sea bass. Lunch Monday–Friday; dinner. **$$$–$$$$**

Arugula
953 Farmington Avenue
West Hartford
Tel: 860-561 4888
Contemporary Italian cuisine – from roasted eggplant Napoleon to grilled polenta with portobello mushrooms, and asparagus-filled sun-dried tomato ravioli to wild mushroom lasagna – served in a small, intimate dining room. Closed Sun and Mon. **$$$**

Carbone's
588 Franklin Avenue, Hartford
Tel: 860-296 9646
The city's premier Italian restaurant has been winning awards since it opened in 1938. Tableside preparations are a specialty, as is the "bocce ball" dessert. Lunch Monday–Friday; dinner nightly. **$$**

Costa Del Sol Restaurant
901 Wethersfield Road
Tel: 860-296 1714
Spanish cuisine, with specialties such as paella, garlic soup, and the house special flan, in a pleasant spot near the airport. **$$–$$$**

Quaker Diner
319 Park Road, West Hartford
Tel: 860-232 5523
Restored 1931 diner cooking up "made from scratch" breakfasts and homestyle food. Breakfast, lunch. **$**

IVORYTON

Copper Beech Inn
46 Main Street
Tel: 860-767 0330/888-809 2056
One of Connecticut's best-known restaurants serves classic French cuisine in a setting of studied elegance. Specialties include *moules aux épinards, homard à la Provençale*. Jacket and tie. Dinner Tues–Sun.
$$$$

LAKEVILLE

Morgan's
Interlaken Inn
74 Interlaken Road, Route 112
Tel: 860-435 9878/800-222 2909
New American cuisine, with organic/hormone and antibiotic-free ingredients, in the dining room of an elegant country inn. Breakfast daily, lunch Fri-Sun, dinner nightly. **$$–$$$**

LITCHFIELD

Village Restaurant
25 West Street
Tel: 860-567 8307
Reasonably priced New England fare, including burgers, pot roast, and homemade desserts, served up in ample portions in this popular local eatery. **$–$$**
West Street Grill
43 West Street
Tel: 860-567 3885 (Route 202)
On the town green, this is the local favorite for a host of specialties including homemade soups, tuna tartare, steaks, and grilled fish.
$$–$$$$

MADISON

Café Allegre
Inn at Lafayette
725 Boston Post Road (Route 1)
Tel: 203-245 7773/866-623 7498
Once a church meeting house, now an elegant spot for great, Southern Italian food with a French flair. Closed Monday. **$$$**

MANCHESTER

Cavey's Restaurant
45 East Center Street
Tel: 860-643 2751
A casual Italian menu is offered upstairs; award-winning French cuisine is offered in the more formal restaurant downstairs. **$$$$**

MYSTIC

Flood Tide Restaurant
The Inn at Mystic
Routes 1 and 27

Tel: 860-536 8140
Fax: 860-536 9604
Contemporary continental food served with water views. **$$$**
Seamen's Inne Restaurant and Pub
105 Greenmanville Road
Tel: 860-536 9649
Regional American and New England fare convenient to Mystic Seaport.
$$

NEW HAVEN

Barkies
220 College Street
Tel: 203-776 0795
Casual American grill and rotisserie serving up seared chops, chicken, fish, and vegetarian sausages. **$$$**
Fire
7 Elm Street
Tel: 203-787 9000
Modern Italian-inspired fare with an extensive wine list. Sophisticated and upscale, but not stuffy. Lunch Mon–Fri; dinner Mon–Sat. **$$–$$$**
Ibiza Tapas Café
39 High Street
Tel: 203-865 1933
Authentic Spanish tapas elevate group-grazing to a high art. Lunch Wednesday–Saturday; dinner Tuesday–Sunday. **$$**
Sandra's Place Soul Food
636 Congress Ave and 46 Whitney Ave
Tel: 203-787 4123
The name says it all: terrific barbecued pork and beef ribs, chicken 'n' dumplings, fried catfish, chitlins, and all the other treats from the South. Congress Avenue location: open for lunch Sat and Sun; dinner Wed–Sun. Whitney Avenue location: open for breakfast Sat; Sun brunch buffet; lunch and dinner daily. **$–$$**
Quattro's
172 Temple Street
Tel: 203-787 6705
Ecuadorian chefs prepare traditional Italian dishes, with surprising good results. The pasta is homemade, the daily specials are creative. Reservations advised. **$$–$$$**

NEW LONDON

Timothy's at the Lighthouse Inn
6 Guthrie Place
Tel: 860-443 8411/888-443 8411

Mystic Pizza

Connecticut cuisine hit the map in curious way when the 1988 movie *Mystic Pizza* was named after a fast-food parlor in downtown Mystic. Filming took place in a nearby lobster warehouse.

Home of the Burger

Louis' Lunch
261 Crown Street
Tel: 203-562 5507
This homely, family-run burger joint in New Haven claims the distinction of being the birthplace of the original 1900 hamburger. Today's burgers are still served in time-honored style on toast, *sans* frills), amid period decor and Tiffany lamps. Lunch Tuesday–Saturday; dinner Thursday–Saturday. **$**

Traditional American fare with a seafood emphasis in a restored Victorian mansion overlooking the water. House specialties include lobster and crabmeat bisque and homemade pastas. **$$–$$$**

NEW MILFORD

Adrienne
218 Kent Road (Route 7)
Tel: 860-354 6001
Chef-owned restaurant featuring New American fine, fireside dining in a pretty white, 19th-century farm house. Dinner only. **$$$**
Forsythia's
31 Bank Street
Tel: 860-355 3266
Contemporary American fare in a relaxed atmosphere. **$$$**

NEW PRESTON

Boulders Inn
Route 45
Tel: 860-868 0541
Overlooking Lake Waramaug, the inn's elegant restaurant features a menu that changes with the season, but might include chicken breast stuffed with goat cheese, or braised lamb shanks. **$$$**
Hopkins Inn
22 Hopkins Road
Tel: 860-868 7295
www.thehopkinsinn.com
Austrian and Swiss specialties – including sweetbreads – are offered in the dining room of an 1847 Victorian inn overlooking Lake Waramaug.
$$–$$$

NORWALK

Meigas
10 Wall Street
Tel: 203-866 8800
Tapas, fish and other artfully-prepared Spanish dishes have earned this restaurant (formerly Meson Galicia) high accolades. Lunch Tues–Fri; dinner Sat and Sun. **$$$–$$$$**

NOANK

The Fisherman
937 Groton Long Point Road
Tel: 860-536 1717
Seafood is the order of the day here.
Good steaks and a water view, too.
$–$$

Abbott's Lobster in the Rough
117 Pearl Street
Tel: 860-536 7719
A classic lobster shack on the water.
Summer only. **$**

OLD LYME

Bee & Thistle Inn
100 Lyme Street
Tel: 860-434 1667/800-622 4946
Award-winning American cuisine is
elegantly served in one of
Connecticut's most romantic historic
inns. Sun brunch is excellent. Closed
Tues. **$$$–$$$$**

Old Lyme Inn
85 Old Lyme Street
Tel: 860-434 2600
Creative American dishes served with
aplomb in the lovely dining room of a
white clapboard 1850s farmhouse in
the historic district. **$$$–$$$$**

OLD SAYBROOK

The Terra Mar Grille
Saybrook Point Inn & Spa
2 Bridge Street
Tel: 860-388 1111
Traditionalist decor, continental fare
with emphasis on fresh fish and prime
meats, and lovely water views. Try the
blue corn-encrusted oysters. **$$$**

RIDGEFIELD

Elms Restaurant and Tavern
500 Main Street
Tel: 203-438 9206
Renowned chef Brendon Walsh
prepares sophisticated Yankee cuisine
such as lobster shepherd pie, along
with an award-winning wine list in his
four-star restaurant in a 1799 Colonial
inn. Terrace dining in season.
$$$–$$$$

SALISBURY

White Hart Inn
Village Green (Routes 44 and 41)
Tel: 860-435 0030/800-832 0041
Country dining, with dishes such as
braised lamb shank osso bucco, in
the Colonial-era Tap Room or the
fireplaced Garden Room. Dinner also
served on porch in fine weather.
$$$–$$$$

SOUTHINGTON

R.G. Brannigan's Restaurant
176 Lansing Street
Tel: 860-621 9311
The place for barbecued spare ribs
with all the fixin's **$$**

SOUTH NORWALK AREA

Silvermine Tavern
194 Perry Avenue
Norwalk
Tel: 203-847 4558
An historic country inn with a Colonial
dining room serves up New England
classics beside a mill pond. Live jazz
Thursday–Saturday; buffet dinner
Thursday. **$$–$$$**

Barcelona Restaurant and Wine Bar
63 N Main Street
South Norwalk
Tel: 203-899 0088
Savory Spanish tapas are on offer at
this stylish dining room and sidewalk
cafe. Dinner only. **$$**

Pasta Nostra Trattoria
116 Washington Street
South Norwalk
Tel: 203-854 9700
A convivial contemporary Italian café;
homemade pastas a specialty. Dinner
Wednesday–Saturday. **$$**

VERNON

Rein's New York-Style Delicatessen
435A Hartford Turnpike, Route 30
(I-84, Exit 65)
Tel: 860-875 1344
The most authentic – and tasty – deli
fare available north of Manhattan is
located just east of Hartford.
Breakfasts are a knock-out. **$**

WASHINGTON

Mayflower Inn
118 Woodbury Road, Route 47
Washington
Tel: 860-868 9466
The regional American cuisine is far,
far from being rustic: it is every bit as
rarefied, in fact, as this fine country
inn. Reserve a table on the terrace
overlooking the garden.
$$$–$$$$

Restaurant Prices

Prices are approximate, but for a
three-course meal for one
(excluding beverages, tax and tip),
the following guidelines may prove
helpful:

        $$$$ = over $40
        $$$ = $28–40
        $$ = $15–28
        $ = under $15

G.W. Tavern
20 Bee Brook Road
Washington Depot
Tel: 860-868 6633
A restored colonial tavern honoring
the first president with updated New
England classics: clam chowder, slow-
roasted duck, and homemade cherry
pie. **$$**

WESTPORT

Acqua
43 Main Street
Tel: 203-222 8899
Italian/Mediterranean fare in wildly
popular, sometimes clamorous, two-
story riverside villa. Lunch Monday–
Friday; dinner nightly. **$$–$$$**

Sakura
680 Post Road East
Tel: 203-222 0802
One of Connecticut's favorite sushi
spots also serves hibachi-style
tableside dishes and a terrific
tempura. Lunch Monday–Friday; dinner
nightly. **$$–$$$**

WOODBURY

Good News Cafe
694 Main Street
Tel: 203-266 4663
A cheerful spot whose well-known
chef, Carole Peck, uses local bounty
to prepare creative healthful but
tasty fare such as onion bundles,
braised veal shanks and wok-seared
shrimp. Coffee and desserts are
served in an adjoining room. Closed
Tues. **$$**

Culture

DANCE

Hartford Ballet (tel: 860-525 9396;
166 Capitol Avenue, Hartford) stages
both classical and modern dance
productions.

CLASSICAL MUSIC

Hartford Symphony performs at The
Bushnell (tel: 860-244 2999; 166
Capitol Avenue).
New Haven Symphony Orchestra, the
fourth oldest in the States, holds a
concert series at Yale University's
Woolsey Hall (tel: 203-865 0831; 33
Whitney Avenue).

CHAMBER MUSIC

The renowned **Norfolk Chamber
Music Festival** (tel: 860-542 3000;
Route 44 and 272, Norfolk) includes
chamber music and choral concert.

OPERA

The famous **Goodspeed Opera House** (tel: 860-873 8668; Goodspeed Landing, East Haddam) showcases operas, musicals and revivals from April to December.

ROCK AND POP

Concerts are held year-round at the huge **Hartford Civic Center** (tel: 860-727 8010; 1 Civic Center Plaza). **Arch Street Tavern** (tel: 860-246 7610) presents live acts. The **Webster Theater** in Hartford (tel: 860-246 8001; 31 Webster Street) is one of the city's hottest venues for live rock and roll.

THEATER

Hartford Stage Company (tel: 860-527 5151; 50 Church Street), an award-winning ensemble, produces new plays, as well as classics. **Theaterworks** (tel: 860-527 7838; 233 Pearl Street, Hartford) features more experimental theater. The **Bushnell Center for the Performing Arts** (tel: 860-987 5900; 166 Capitol Avenue) is one of the city's premier performing arts centers, presenting Broadway and off-broadway shows, films, and music. **The Little Theater** (tel: 860-645 6743; 177 Hartford Road, Manchester), Connecticut's oldest theater, presents local talent.

Two Tony-award-winning theater companies reside in New Haven: The **Long Wharf Theater** (tel: 203-787 4282; 222 Sargent Dr) premiered Arthur Miller's *The Crucible* and still produces many prize-winning shows. **Yale Repertory Theater** (tel: 203-432 1234; 222 York Street) shows experimental work by Yale students. **Westport Country Playhouse** (tel: 203-227 4177; 25 Powers Court) launches six productions every summer in a renovated barn.

CINEMA

Cinestudio (tel: 860-297 2463; 300 Summit Street, Trinity College, Hartford) shows both first-run and art films.

COMEDY

City Steam (tel: 860-525 1600; Hartford), a brew pub, features comedians from both Boston and New York on Thursday, Friday and Saturday nights. Reserve in advance.

ART GALLERIES

"SoNo" (short for South Norwalk and a take-off of SoHo in New York City) has revitalized itself with art galleries, chichi cafés, and shops. Kent also has more than a dozen galleries. In Hartford, The **Artists' Collective** (tel: 860-527 3205; 1200 Albany Avenue) exhibits the arts and culture of the African Diaspora. In Kent, the **Bachelier-Cardonsky Gallery** (tel: 860-927 3129; 10 Main Street) exhibits works by some of the country's finest contemporary artists.

Nightlife

NIGHTCLUBS AND DISCOS

Hartford's popular **Bourbon Street North** (tel: 860-525 1014; 70 Union Place) features a large dance floor and a variety of music styles.

The **"SoNo"** area of downtown South Norfolk contains a variety of tavernlike nightclubs.

LIVE MUSIC

The **Arch Street Tavern** (tel: 860-246 7610; 85 Arch Street) in Hartford presents local rock bands. **Toads Place** (tel: 203-624 8623; 300 York Street, New Haven) is a popular club that books major acts.

CASINOS

Foxwoods Resort (tel: 800-363 9663; Route 2 in Ledyard between I-395 and I-95), which is housed on what was formerly a small Native American reservation, is now the largest gambling casino in the US. The massive, 115,000 sq.-ft casino at **Mohegan Sun Resort Casino** (tel: 888-226 7711; Route 2A, Montville), situated 10 miles south of Foxwoods, rivals that of Foxwoods.

Outdoor Activities

BIKING

Winding Trails Recreation Area off Route 4 in Farmington (tel: 860-677 8458) and **Woodbury Ski Area** (tel: 203-263 2203) are big with Connecticut mountain bikers.

For a free Connecticut Bicycle Map, write to the Connecticut Department of Transportation, 2800- Berlin Turnpike, P.O. Box 317546, Newington, CT 06131-7546.

CANOEING, KAYAKING, AND RAFTING

For whitewater rafting or canoeing, head for the Housatonic River. **North American Outdoor Adventures** (tel: 800-727 4379) organizes Housatonic rafting trips. In New Hartford, **Main Stream Canoe and Kayaks** (tel: 860-693 6791) rents canoes and kayaks and conducts day trips on the Farmington River.

Canoe can be rented at several state parks; the **Connecticut State Bureau of Parks and Recreation** (tel: 860-424 3200) has details.

SIGHTSEEING CRUISES

Deep River Navigation Company (tel: 860-526 4954; Saybrook Point) offers narrated cruises along the Connecticut River shoreline. Among companies that offer cruises along the Thimble Islands are **Volsunga IV** (tel: 203-488 9978) and **Sea Mist II** (tel: 203-488 8905). **Captain John's Dock** (tel: 860-443 7259) in Waterford gives lighthouse, seal and bald eagle cruises.

FISHING

All along the Connecticut coast, charter boats run half-day or full-day fishing expeditions. The best thing to do is get a list of operators from the **Connecticut State Tourism** Office (tel: 888-288 4748) or head to the harbor where you want to go out and talk to the captains directly.

Catch-and-release fly fishing is popular on the Housantanic River.

HIKING

The **Appalachian Trail**, a 2,000-mile (3,200-km) trail linking Maine and Georgia, traverses about 50 miles (80 km) of western Connecticut and the Appalachian Mountain Club (tel: 617-523 0636; Boston) provides detailed trail information.

At **Talcott Mountain State Park** in Simsbury, hikers who reach the peak of the 1½-mile (2.5 km) walk are rewarded with panoramic vistas of the Farmington River Valley. On clear days, visibility can sometimes be up to 50 miles (80 km).

Macedonia Brook State Park in Kent and **Sleeping Giant State Park** in Hamden run scenic day hikes. Contact **The Connecticut State Parks** (tel: 860-424 3200) for details.

SAILING

Mystic is a center for sailing activity. The **Offshore Sailing School** (tel: 800-221 4326) conducts five-day learn-to-sail courses in the town.

SKIING

There are several small downhill areas in the Litchfield Hills region: **White Memorial Foundation** (tel: 860-678 9582) in Litchfield, **Mohawk Mountain** in Cornwall (tel: 860-672 6100), **Mount Southington** in Southington (tel: 860-628 0954), and **Powder Ridge Ski Area** in Middlefield (tel: 860-349 3454).

For cross-country skiing, try the **Woodbury Ski & Racquet Area** (tel: 203-263 2203) or Farmington's **Winding Trails Cross Country Ski Center** (tel: 860-678 9582).

CRUISES

Voyager Cruises' Argia (tel: 860-536 0416), a replica of a 19th-century schooner, offers half-day excursions from Mystic to Fisher's Island. **The Mystic Whaler** (tel: 800-697 8420), a classic schooner, sails for one- to five-day trips along the New England coast. **Mystic Seaport** (tel: 888-973 2767) offers cruises from Mystic on the 61-ft (19-meter) schooner *Brilliant*.

Shopping

MALLS

Hartford Civic Center (tel: 860-249 6333; 1 Civic Center Plaza) has more than 60 shops. The huge **Danbury Fair Mall** (tel: 203-743 3247; Backus Ave, off I-84, Danbury) has 240 shops, including five department stores. The **Olde Mistick Village** (tel: 860-536 4941; Exit 90 off I-95, Mystic), has 60 Colonial-style shops. **West Farms Mall** (tel: 860-561 3024)

in Farmington has many upscale department stores.

BOOKS

In West Hartford, **Bookworm** (tel: 860-233 2653; 968 Farmington Avenue). **Yale University Bookstore** (tel: 888-730 9253; 77 Broadway) has text and trade books. Farmington's charming **Millrace Bookshop in the Gristmill** (tel: 860-677 9662; 40 Mill Lane) hosts numerous readings and book signings.

ANTIQUES

New Haven sports over 30 antique dealers, among them **Antique Corner** (tel: 203-387 7200; 859 Whalley Ave.).

The Litchfield Hills are often referred to as the "antique capital" of the country (slight hyperbole, but there are an impressive number), with almost every village having multiple shops. Try **The Bittersweet Shop** (tel: 860-354 1727; Route 7, New Milford) and **Old Carriage Shop Antiques** (tel: 860-567 3234; 920 Bantam Road, Bantam). Both have over 15 dealers. With 500 exhibitors in 17 shops, downtown Putnam (tel: 800-514 3448) has the state's largest antiques district. Dealers in Mystic and Stonington are on Main and Water Streets.

The large **Old Saybrook Antiques Center** (tel: 860-388 1600; 756 Middlesex Turnpike, Route 154, in Old Saybrook) has more than 100 dealers of 18th- and 19th-century pieces.

ARTS AND CRAFTS

Dozens of pottery and crafts shops are located in the Litchfield Hills; try

either of these on Route 128 in West Cornwall: **Cornwall Bridge Pottery & Store** (tel: 860-672 6545) and **Ingersoll Cabinetmakers** (tel: 800-237 4926). **O'Reilly's Irish Gifts** (tel: 860-677 6958; 248 Main Street, Farmington) is the largest purveyor of Irish goods in the US.

Children

THEME PARKS

Lake Compounce (tel: 860-583 3631; 822 Lake Avenue, Bristol), America's oldest amusement park.

CAROUSELS

The Carousel (tel: 860-246 7739; Bushnell Park, Hartford) is a 1914 merry-go-round, with hand-carved horses.

ZOOS

Beardsley Zoological Gardens (tel: 203-394 6565; 1875 Noble Avenue, Beardsley Park, Bridgeport) has over 120 species, a carousel, and a New England farmyard petting zoo.

JOURNEYS BY STEAM TRAIN

Naugatuck Railroad of New England (tel: 203-575 1931; 83 Bank Street, Waterbury) offers a historic ride through Black Rock State Park. **Essex Steam Train** (tel: 860-767 0103; Railroad Avenue, Essex) runs an old-fashioned service that can be combined with a riverboat ride.

Connecticut Festivals

Spring
Lime Rock Park (tel: 800-722 3577) is the venue for the largest sports car race in North America in May. Meriden's annual **Daffodil Festival** (tel: 203-630 4259) in April is one sign that spring is on the way. In May, the **Mystic Lobsterfest** (tel: 860-572 5312/888-973 2767) draws lobster lovers to the seaport for an old-fashioned outdoor lobster bake.

Summer
Summer is arts festival time, beginning in June with New Haven's **International Festival of Arts & Ideas** (tel: 888-278 4332) commissioned works.

In July, the **Hartford Riverfest** (tel: 860-293 0131) celebrates

Independence Day with entertainment for everyone, culminating in spectacular fireworks over the Connecticut River. The **SoNo Arts Celebration** (tel: 203-866 7916) in August, a two-day outdoor festival of the performing and visual arts, draws visitors to historic South Norwalk. **Mark Twain Days** (tel: 860-713 3131) celebrate the author's legacy and Hartford's heritage with frog jumping contests, concerts, and house tours at the end of August.

Fall
Connecticut's harvest festivals begin in August with the **Brooklyn Fair** (tel: 860-779 0012), the oldest continuously active agricultural fair in the US, followed in September by the

Woodstock Fair (tel: 860-928 3246), the nation's second oldest. In October, Southington hosts the annual **Apple Harvest Festival** (tel: 860-628 8036).

Sample the best of local chefs at Mystic Seaport's **Chowderfest** (tel: 860-572 5315) in October.

Winter
First Night Hartford (tel: 860-722 9546) is the New Year's Eve festival of the arts. In February, skiers head for the Litchfield Hills for the **Salisbury Invitational Ski Jump** and the **US Eastern Ski Jump Championships**, an Olympic-level competition on the site of the nation's oldest ski jumping program (tel: 860-435 9729).

Rhode Island

The Place

Known as: The Ocean State.
Motto: Hope.
Origin of name: unknown. Perhaps reminded an early explorer of Rhodes in Greece. Or maybe derived from the Dutch for "red" after the color of its soil.
Entered Union: May 29, 1790, the last of the 13 original states.
Capital: Providence.
Area: 1,545 sq. miles (4,002 sq. km).
Highest point: Jerimoth Hill, 812 ft (247 meters).
Population: 1 million.
Population density: 649 people per sq. km (251 per sq. km).
Economy: manufacturing (fabricated metals, precision instruments, apparel and textiles, printed materials, rubber and plastic items, industrial machinery, primary metals, electronic goods, transportation equipment, chemicals, and processed foods.
Annual visitors: 29 million
National representation: 2 senators and 2 representatives to Congress.
Famous citizens: George M. Cohan, Nelson Eddy, Christopher and Oliver La Farge.

Where to Stay

BLOCK ISLAND

Atlantic Inn
High Street, Old Harbor, 02807
Tel: 401-466 5883/800-224 7422
Fax: 401-466 5678
www.atlanticinn.com
An 1879 white-clapboard hotel, Block Island's *grande dame*, with a spacious porch in a hill overlooking the sea. 21 pleasant Victorian-style rooms and two tennis courts. **$$$–$$$$**
Spring House Hotel
Spring Street, Old Harbor, 02807
Tel: 401-466 5844/800-234 9263
Fax: 401-466 2633
www.springhousehotel.com
A classic 49-room hotel (built in 1852) with Victorian furnishings, a cupola-topped mansard roof and a

wraparound porch. Set on 15 acres above the ocean. **$$$–$$$$**
Hotel Manisses and The 1661 Inn
Spring Street, Old Harbor, 02807
Tel: 401-466 2421/800-626 4773
Fax: 401-466 3162
www.blockislandresorts.com
Victorian inns with ocean views; there are 53 old-fashioned rooms in the main inns and cottages. An animal farm on the property is home to llamas and emus. **$$$–$$$$**

BRISTOL

Bradford Dimond Norris House
474 Hope Street, 02809
Tel: 401-253 6338/888-329 6338
Fax: 401-253 4023
www.bdnhouse.com
Handsomely-restored downtown Federal-style B&B, built in 1792, has four air-conditioned guest rooms with four-poster or canopy beds. **$$**
Bristol Harbor Inn
259 Thames Street, 02809
Tel: 401-254 1444/866-254 1444
Fax: 401-254 1333
www.bristolharborinn.com
The East Bay's only waterfront inn, in downtown Bristol, has 40 well-appointed rooms, many with views of Narragansett Bay.
$$–$$$$

JAMESTOWN

Bay Voyage Inn
150 Conanicus Avenue, 02835
Tel: 401-423 2100
Fax: 401-423 3209
www.bayvoyageinn.com
Formerly a country house in Newport, this 32-room inn was transported across the bay in 1899. It's now an all-suite inn overlooking the harbor.
$$–$$$$

LITTLE COMPTON

Stone House Club
122 Sakonnet Point Road, 02837
Tel: 401-635 2222
A stone farmhouse overlooking the ocean, now a private club, that rents 15 simply furnished rooms. **$–$$**

NARRAGANSETT

Stone Lea
40 Newton Avenue (off Ocean Road), 02882
Tel: 401-783 9546
A Victorian summer "cottage" designed in 1884 by McKim, Meade & White, located on a cliff over-looking the ocean. This formal inn B&B – many of the nine rooms have ocean views – is set on a broad lawn that extends to the sea. **$$–$$$**

The Richards
144 Gibson Avenue, 02882
Tel: 401-789 7746
Fax: 401-783 7168
An 1884 stone English manor B&B surrounded by gardens. All four antique-furnished rooms have working fireplaces. Private access to the rocky coast. No credit cards. **$$–$$$**

NEWPORT

Castle Hill Inn
590 Ocean Drive, 02840
Tel: 401-849 3800/888-466 1355
www.castlehillinn.com
Scientist and explorer Alexander Agassiz's 1874 estate is now a first-rate resort which encompasses his mansion along with several other lodgings. The property, on 40 acres at the west end of Ocean Drive, has one of the area's most magnificent views.
$$$$
Cliffside Inn
2 Seaview Avenue, 02840
Tel: 401-847 1811/800-845 1811
Fax: 401-848 5850
www.cliffsideinn.com
Near the Cliff Walk, an 1880 Victorian villa, carved into grand, dramatic quarters. The 15 rooms in this B&B are light and airy, and some have working fireplaces and whirlpool tubs.
$$$$
Francis Malbone House
392 Thames Street, 02840
Tel: 401-846 0392/800-846 0392
Fax: 401-848 5956
www.malbone.com
A 1760 Colonial brick mansion B&B on the harborfront. Twenty lavishly appointed rooms with period reproduction furnishings. **$$$–$$$$**
Victorian Ladies Inn
63 Memorial Boulevard, 02840
Tel: 888-849 9960
www.victorianladies.com
A pair of *circa* 1850s vintage lovelies, in period style, offering 11 B&B rooms and elaborate gardens. Near First Beach and the Cliff Walk. **$$$–$$$$**
Ivy Lodge
12 Clay Street, 02840
Tel: 401-849 6865/800-834 6865
www.ivylodge.com
Seven-room B&B in a Victorian home in the mansion district, designed by Stanford White. Dramatic old-English

Price Categories

A very approximate guide to current room rates for a standard double per night is:
$$$$ = over $200
$$$ = $150–200
$$ = $100–150
$ = under $100

entryway, wraparound porch, and 11 fireplaces. **$$–$$$**

Melville House
39 Clarke Street, 02840
Tel: 401-847 0640
Fax: 401-847 0956
www.melvillehouse.com
A 1750 Colonial B&B on a gas lamp-lit street on Historic Hill. Seven small, but comfortably appointed guest rooms (some with shared bath), plus a fireplace suite. **$$–$$$**

PROVIDENCE

Providence Biltmore Hotel
Kennedy Plaza, 02903
Tel: 401-421 0700/800-294 7709
Fax: 401-455 3040
www.providencebiltmore.com
A downtown, 1922 Art Deco-style grand hotel with 238 nicely-restored and very spacious rooms and suites. **$$–$$$$**

The Old Court B&B
144 Benefit Street, 02903
Tel: 401-751 2002
Fax: 401-272 4830
www.oldcourt.com
Near the Rhode Island School of Design, an 1863 rectory retrofitted as an elegant Victorian-style inn. Ten spacious rooms with high ceilings, chandeliers, phones, and cable TV. **$$–$$$**

State House Inn
43 Jewett Street, 02908
Tel: 401-351 6111
Fax: 401-351 4261
www.providence-inn.com.
An 1889 Colonial Revival home, renovated in 1990, located near the State House. The 10 B&B rooms are furnished with Shaker and American folk art; some have canopy beds and working fireplaces. **$$**

WEEKAPAUG

Weekapaug Inn
25 Spray Rock Road, 02891
Tel: 401-322 0301
Fax: 401-322 1016
www.weekapauginn.com
A classic FAP inn (65 rooms) with a wraparound porch sheltering well-heeled families since 1938 (the original inn was built in 1899). On a peninsula surrounded on three sides by Quanochontaug Pond in a coastal village 6 miles (9.6 km) from Westerly. Summer programs for ages 3–10. No credit cards are not accepted. **$$$$**

WESTERLY

Shelter Harbor Inn
10 Wagner Road (Route 1), 02891
Tel: 401-322 8883/800-468 8883

Fax: 401-322 7907
www.shelterharborinn.com
Once a working farm, now a luxury 24-room getaway for B&B in a rural setting near the beach. The roof deck has a barbecue grill and a hot tub. **$$–$$$**

Andrea Hotel
89 Atlantic Aveue, Misquamicut
Tel: 401-348 8788
www.andreahotel.com
Old-fashioned hotel directly on the beach offers 25 very basic rooms, but some have private balconies and fabulous water views. In-season nightly entertainment and restaurant. **$–$$**

Grandview Bed and Breakfast
212 Shore Road, 02891
Tel: 401-596 6384/800-447 6384
Fax: 401-596 3036
www.grandviewbandb.com
A comfortable turn-of-the-20th-century house with 9 cozy guest rooms (some with ocean views), gardens, and a stone wraparound porch. **$–$$**

Where to Eat

BLOCK ISLAND

Atlantic Inn Restaurant
High Street, Old Harbor
Tel: 401-466 5883
The dining room in this Victorian resort overlooking the water serves well-prepared, *prix-fixe* seafood and continental dinners. The breakfast buffet is excellent. Dress is more casual than the food. **$$$$**

Hotel Manisses
1 Spring Street
Tel: 401-466 2421
The place to go for a big night out. Elegantly-prepared and sophisticated fare might include lobster bisque, seared fois gras, roasted rack of wild boar, or a *bouillabaisse* of swordfish, scallops, mussels, littleneck clams, and and ouille sausage. **$$$$**

Spring House Hotel
Spring Street, Old Harbor
Tel: 401-466 5844
Seafood, pastas, and all-you-can-eat barbecues overlooking Block Island Sound. **$$–$$$**

Finn's
Ferry Landing
Tel: 401-466 2473
The food is ample and well-prepared, and the views are incomparable. Great burgers, bluefish pate, and fried seafood platters. No reservations. Seasonal. **$$–$$$**

Juice 'n Java
235 Dodge Street, Old Harbor
Funky coffee house serving sandwiches and pastries. Large supply of magazines and board games. **$**

Restaurant Prices

Prices are approximate, but for a three-course meal for one (excluding beverages, tax and tip), the following guidelines may prove helpful:

$$$$ = over $40
$$$ = $28–40
$$ = $15–28
$ = under $15

BRISTOL

Quito's
411 Thames Street
Tel: 401-253 4500
Well-established spot for casual seafood, overlooking the bay. **$–$$**

Lobster Pot
119–21 Hope Street, Route 114
Tel: 401-253 9100
On the harbor, this local institution has been serving up American fare including fresh fish, steaks and poultry, since 1929. **$$**

Aidan's Pub
5 John Street
Tel: 401-254 1940
Irish pub serving fish and chips, bangers and mash and the like. **$**

JAMESTOWN

Bay Voyage Inn
150 Conanicus Avenue
Tel: 401-423 2100
American standbys – lobster thermidor, rack of lamb, filet mignon – and bountiful Sunday brunch with harbor views. **$$$**

Jamestown Oyster Bar
22 Narragansett Avenue
Tel: 401-423 3380
Fresh fish, burgers, and quahogs in a popular local spot. Lunch Wed–Sun, dinner nightly. **$**

LITTLE COMPTON

Stone House Club
122 Sakonnet Point Road
Tel: 401-635 2222
A private club in an old farmhouse whose Tap Room, an English tavern, is open to non-members for dinner. Traditional American fare includes Sat evening Soup and Sandwich buffet for $12 (summer only). **$–$$$**

The Commons Lunch
Tel: 401-635 4388
A downhome diner fit for gentleman (and lady) farmers. **$**

NARRAGANSETT

Basil's
22 Kingstown Road
Tel: 401-789 3743

Continental fare, with an accent on French, in an intimate and elegant Victorian restaurant near the pier. Dinner. **$$–$$$**
Aunt Carrie's
1240 Ocean Road, Point Judith
Tel: 401-783 7930
A classic seaside clam shack. **$**
Champlin's Seafood
256 Great Island Road
Tel: 401-783 3152
Diners can sit on the outside deck and watch fishermen unload their catches; the self-service spot serves flopping-fresh fish, has a great raw bar, whole belly fried clams, and homemade clam chowder. **$–$$$**
Woody's
21 Pier Marketplace
Tel: 401-789 9500
This place does savory tapas-style appetizers and substantial contemporary entrées. Dinner. **$$**

NEWPORT
Le Bistro
Bowen's Wharf
Tel: 401-849 7778
A charming French café in a loft above the bustling harbor has been serving fresh local seafood, pastas, and prime steaks for almost 30 years. **$$$$**
Clarke Cooke House
Bannister's Wharf
Tel: 401-849 2900
Formal, waterview dining in a 1790 Colonial house. Eclectic Continental fare is served by waiters in tuxedos. Al fresco dining in warm weather. **$$$$**
The Black Pearl
Bannister's Wharf
Tel: 401-846 5264
A classic harborside tavern serving classical French and new American dishes, including the house special clam chowder. Jackets and reservations are required in the formal Commodore Room. **$$$–$$$$**
Castle Hill Inn
590 Ocean Avenue
Tel: 401-849 3800
The 1874 one-time summer "cottage" overlooking Narragansett Bay specializes in New England cuisine with a menu that changes seasonally. Sunday brunch *al fresco* is not to be missed. **$$$–$$$$**
The Mooring Restaurant
Sayer's Wharf
Tel: 401-846 2260
Award-winning chowder, fish, and braised beef loin are on the menu at this family-friendly restaurant with an enclosed patio overlooking the harbor. **$$–$$$**
Puerini's Restaurant
24 Memorial Boulevard West
Tel: 401-847 5506
The extensive menu of innovative

Italian specialties includes homemade pastas, *tortellini* with seafood, veal, and a reasonably-priced wine list. No reservations. Dinner only. **$$**
Scales & Shells
527 Thames Street
Tel: 401-848 9378
For an incredibly large selection of fresh fish dishes, including wood-grilled specialties, this is the place. For a more peaceful meal – and higher prices – sit upstairs. **$$–$$$**
White Horse Tavern
26 Marlborough Street
Tel: 401-849 3600
Reputedly the oldest continually operating tavern in the US (est. 1687), American and continental classics such as Chateaubriand, grilled lobster, and other native seafood in candlelit rooms with cavernous fireplaces and beamed ceilings. Lunch Thur–Sat; jackets required at dinner. **$$–$$$**

PROVIDENCE
Al Forno
577 S Main Street
Tel: 401-273 9760
Arguably New England's preeminent temple of *nuova cucina*. Northern Italian specialties include grilled pizza, clams *Al Forno*, and baked pasta. Dinner only Tuesday–Saturday. **$$$$**
The Capital Grille
1 Union Station
Tel: 401-521 560
Premium dry-aged beef, fresh seafood, an extensive wine list in a renovated railroad station that gleams of brass. **$$$**
Hemenway's Seafood Grill & Oyster Bay
1 Providence Washington Plaza
Tel: 401-351 8570
Superb seafood, along with steak, chicken and pasta in upscale surroundings overlooking the Providence River. **$$$**
Walter's Historical Fine Dining
265 Atwells Ave (DiPasquale Plaza)
Tel: 401-273 2652
Choose from Italian regional cuisine using ancient clay cookery techniques or recipes of Italian-Jewish origin in a comfortably

Restaurant Prices

Prices are approximate, but for a three-course meal for one (excluding beverages, tax and tip), the following guidelines may prove helpful:

    $$$$ = over $40
    $$$ = $28–40
    $$ = $15–28
    $ = under $15

upscale Federal Hill location. A seven-course tasting menu is available. Dinner only. **$$$–$$$$**
Rue de L'Espoir
99 Hope Street
Tel: 401-751 8890
Chic, modern bistro fare in a pretty room near Brown University. Closed Monday. **$$–$$$**
Olga's Cup and Saucer
103 Point Street
Tel: 401-831 6666
Well-established bakery serves their muffins, scones and pastries as well as homemade soups, sandwiches and salads. Breakfast and lunch Monday–Saturday. **$**

WATCH HILL
Olympia Tea Room
Bay Street
Tel: 401-348 8211
A classic 1916 luncheonette with a menu far more ambitious than its surroundings. Among the chef's specialties: stuffed quahogs and the "world-famous Avondale swan", a dessert incorporating puff pastry, ice cream and chocolate sauce. **$$**

WESTERLY
Shelter Harbor Inn
Route 1
Tel: 401-322 8883
A changing menu of well-priced regional specialties and an outstanding Sunday brunch. **$$$**
Three Fish
37 Main Street
Tel: 401-348 9700
Seafood and top desserts in a former mill by the Pawcatuck River. **$$–$$$**

Culture

MUSIC
Rhode Island Philharmonic (tel: 401-831 3123; 222 Richmond Street, Providence) gives concerts throughout the year.
The 1928 **Providence Performing Arts Center** (tel: 401-421 2787; 220 Weybosset Street) presents concerts, Broadway shows, and other events.
Theatre-by-the-Sea (tel: 401-782 8587; Cards Pond Road off Route 1, South Kingston) hosts musicals and plays in a National Register of Historic Places building.

ROCK AND POP
Providence Civic Center (tel: 401-331 6700; 1 LaSalle Square) hosts big-name touring rock bands.
On Block Island, **Captain Nick's Rock and Roll Bar** (tel: 401-466 5670) on

Ocean Avenue rocks nightly in season with live bands.

THEATER

Trinity Square Repertory Company (tel: 401-351 4242; 201 Washington Street, Providence). This Tony-award-winning group always puts on among the country's finest and most innovative productions.
Brown University (tel: 401-863 2838; Leeds Theater, 77 Waterman Street, Providence) stages contemporary to classical and everything In between.
Sandra Feinstein-Gamm Theatre (tel: 401-831 2919; 31 Elbow Street) presents classic and contemporary plays in its 75-seat hall.
Astors' Beechwood (tel: 401-846 3772; 580 Bellevue Avenue, Newport) stages murder-mystery plays once a week in-season.

CINEMA

Cable Car Cinema (tel: 401-272 3970; 204 S Main Street, Providence) has seen better days, but perhaps that's the point.
Art films, old couches from which to watch the flicks, and cheap popcorn continue to survive in college towns.

ART GALLERIES

Providence's Wickenden Street has a number of galleries, including **Alaimao Gallery** (tel: 401-421 5360; 301 Wickenden Street) which has an unusual number of prints, playbills, and posters.
Galleries line the streets and wharfs of Newport.

ALL-IN-ONE

AS220 (tel: 401-831 9327; 115 Empire Street, Providence) caters to so many interests: at various times it is a performance art space, gallery, theater, and musical venue for tastes as diverse as techno and folk.

Nightlife

The free *Providence Phoenix* can be found around town in shops and restaurants, and is slanted towards a younger, hip crowd.
Thames Street is where it's happening in Newport.

LIVE MUSIC

Sh-na-na's (tel: 401-732 7437; 731 Airport Road, Warwick) puts on regular dance-music nights.
Monet Lounge (tel: 401-580 4847;

115 Harris Avenue, Providence) offers New York City-style clubbing.
On Block Island, both **The National Hotel** (tel: 401-466 2901; Water Street) and **Govern's Yellow Kittens Tavern** (tel: 401-466 5855; Corn Neck Road) have music every night in summer. Govern's agenda is the more diverse of the two, with reggae and R&B included.
Chan's Fine Oriental Dining (tel: 401-765 1900; 267 Main Street, Woonsocket) hosts blues, jazz and folk groups. Reservations required.

GAY & LESBIAN VENUES

David's (28 Prospect Hill Street, Newport) is primarily a men's bar, as is **Mirrabar** (tel: 401-331 6761; 35 Richmond Street, Providence).

LATE NIGHT VENUES

The Hot Club (tel: 401-861 9007; 575 S Water Street, Providence) is a popular waterfront hang-out.

Rhode Island Festivals

Spring
In Bristol, the Blithewood Gardens & Arboretum sponsors the **Annual Spring Bulb Display** (tel: 401-253 2707) in April and May; it's one of New England's largest daffodil exhibitions.

Summer
Bristol claims the nation's oldest **4th of July Parade** (tel: 401-253 0445). In August, Newport's gilded mansions scintillate to classical strains of the **Newport Folk Festival** (tel: 401-847 3700), followed by the legendary **JVC Jazz Festival** (tel: 401-847 3700).
Later in the month, Native Americans gather in Charlestown for their annual **Narragansett Indian Pow Wow** (tel: 401-364 1100).
In late August and early September, more than 100 wooden classic yachts built between the 1800s and 1955 gather in Newport's Narragansett Bay for the **Classic Yacht Regatta and Parade** (www.moy.org).

Outdoor Activities

BIKING

The 14½-mile (23-km) **East Bay Bicycle Path** follows Narragansett Bay and winds through several towns between Providence and Bristol.
On Block Island and in Tiverton and Little Compton, the relatively quiet roads are popular with bikers.
Bikers can also follow Newport's **Bellevue Avenue** and **Ocean Drive** for about 15 miles (24 km) past the mansions and along the shore.
For a free *Guide to Cycling in the Ocean State*, call 401-222 4203, extension 4042.

CANOEING, KAYAKING, AND RAFTING

Coastal sea kayaking is popular and the **Kayak Centre** (tel: 401-295 4400 in Wickford) leads a variety of excursions, including a Newport tour with ocean glimpses of mansions; the company also runs a multi-day trip to Block Island. **Adventure Sports** (tel: 401-849 4820) rents sailboats, kayaks and canoes on Newport's Long Wharf.
In Providence, for information about canoeing the 45-mile (72-km) long Blackstone RIver, request a free copy of the *Blackstone River Canoe Guide* (tel: 800-454 2882).
On Block Island, both **New Harbor**

Fall
The **Newport International Boat Show** (tel: 401-846 1115) in September, the country's only show which features half sail and half power boat exhibits, attracts more than 650 exhibitors. Later in the month, more than 40 of the state's restaurants set up booths at Newport's **Aquafina Taste of Rhode Island** (tel: 401-846 1600).
In October, more than 200 artists and antique dealers display their wares at the annual **Scituate Art Festival** (tel: 401-647 0057).

Winter
The 10-day **Newport Winter Festival** (tel: 401-849 8048) in January and February lures visitors with food, music, ice carving, and snow sculptures.
First Night Providence (tel: 401-521 1166) is a city-wide celebration of the arts, with musicians, artists, and dance ensembles performing at venues throughout the city.

Kayak (tel: 401-466 2890) and **Oceans & Ponds** (tel: 401-466 5131) rent kayaks.

SAILING

Newport, "the Sailing Capital of the World", is a good base for short harbor excursions and learn-to-sail vacations.
Sightsailing of Newport (tel: 401-849 3333) offers harbor sails, rentals and instruction.
America's Cup Charters (tel: 401-846 9886) runs evening sails and half- or full-day sailboat charters. Other charters include **Flyer** (tel: 401-848 2100), a 57-ft catamaran; **Spirit of Newport** (tel: 401-849 3575); and the 72-ft schooner **Madeline** (tel: 401-847 0298).
Newport Sailing School (tel: 401-848 2266) runs narrated one- and two-hour sailing tours plus classes.
Sail Newport (tel: 401-846 1983) in Newport's Fort Adams State Park rents sailboats hourly.
Offshore Sailing School (tel: 800-221 4326; Newport) conducts a learn-to-sail vacation program. **Block Island Club** (tel: 401-466 5939) offers comprehensive sailing instruction and one-week family memberships.

FISHING

Saltwater Edge (tel: 401-842 0062; Newport) offers fly-fishing lessons as well as guided saltwater fishing outings. Several charter fishing boats are based in Narragansett, including **Persuader** (tel: 401-783 5644).
On Block Island, **Oceans & Ponds** (tel: 401-466 5131) organizes charter fishing boat trips, as do myriad boats lined up near the ferry terminal. Buy bait at **Twin Maples** (tel: 401-466 5547; Beach Avenue)

HIKING

Rhode Island Audubon Society (tel: 401-949 5454) leads various nature hikes. On Block Island, contact the **Nature Conservancy** (tel: 401-466 2129; Ocean Avenue) for the best places to hike.

Shopping

WHERE TO SHOP

In Providence, **The Arcade** (tel: 401-598 1199; 65 Weybosset Street, Providence) was the country's first indoor mall, built in 1828. Architecturally, it's a beauty to behold. It's still a bastion of consumerism, although styles have changed over the years. **Gasbarro's** (tel: 401-421 4170;

Useful Listings

The daily *Providence Journal* and glossy *Rhode Island Monthly* have all the up-to-date information on what's happening culturally in and around Rhode Island.

361 Atwells Avenue) sells one of – if not the – largest wine selections in the state.

MARKETS

Route 77 to Little Compton is blessed with many roadside farm stands offering extra-fresh produce. **Costantino's Venda Ravioli** (tel: 401-421 9105; 275 Atwells Avenue) sells more than 50 varieties of fresh made pasta, as well as fresh baked bread and Italian cold cuts. They serve lunch Monday–Saturday.

BOOKS

Map Center (tel: 401-421 2184; 671 N Main Street, Providence) sells every kind of imaginable map. **Borders Books** (tel: 401-270 4801) is on Level B of Providence Place. **Armchair Sailor Books** (tel: 401-847 4252; 543 Thames Street, Newport), purveyors of maritime titles, is appropriately located in this sailing center.

ANTIQUES

In Providence antiques hunters should head straight to Wickenden Street. In Newport, you'll find clusters of antiques shops on Thames, Franklin, and Spring streets. **The Armory** (tel: 401-848 2398), 365 Thames Street, situated in a sprawling 19th-century complex, sells the wares of more than 125 antiques, jewelry, and art dealers.

CHINA AND GLASS

Thames Glass (tel: 401-846 0576; 688 Thames Street and 8 Bowen's Wharf, Newport) blows glass in a neighboring studio and sells firsts and seconds from the shop.

SOUVENIRS & GIFTS
Jewelry

Copacetic Rudely Elegant Jewelry (tel: 401-273 0470; The Arcade, 65 Weybosset Street, Providence) is a determinedly eclectic place, thanks to the diverse work of a very distinct group of artisans.
The Platinum House (tel: 401-848 7528; 137 Swinburne Row, Brick

Market Place, Newport) is a goldsmith and designer of fine jewelry.

Arts and Crafts

MacDowell Pottery (tel: 401-846 6313; 220 Spring Street, Newport) displays the work of many state- and New England-wide potters.
Newport Scrimshanders (tel: 800-635 5234; 14 Bowen's Wharf, Newport) sells Nantucket lightship baskets, handmade scrimshaw, and handwoven baskets.

Children

THEME PARKS

Flying Horse Carousel (no phone; Bay Street, Watch Hill), with beautiful hand-carved horses, lays claim as the oldest merry-go-round in the country.

ZOOS

Roger Williams Park Zoo (tel: 401-785 3510; Elmwood Avenue, Providence), a 400-plus-acre park with an antique carousel, tiny train, and lots of animals to keep the children entertained, and a quiet Japanese garden for adults.

Vermont

The Place

Known as: The Green Mountain State.
Motto: Freedom and unity.
Origin of name: from the French *vert* (= green) and *mont* (= mountain).
Entered Union: March 4, 1791, the 14th state.
Capital: Montpelier
Area: 9,615 sq. miles (24,903 sq. km).
Highest point: Mount Mansfield, 4,393 ft (1,339 meters).
Population: 589,000
Population density: 59 per sq. mile (23 per sq. km).
Economy: once agricultural, now relies increasingly on tourism.
Annual visitors: 7.9 million.
National representation: 2 senators and 1 representative to Congress.
Famous citizens: Ethan Allen, Calvin Coolidge and Admiral George Deweys.

Where to Stay

Many Vermont inns take a break between foliage and the holidays, and again during "mud season," so check first if you plan to visit in the late fall or early spring. Many inns require a two–three night minimum stay during busy times.

ARLINGTON

West Mountain Inn
River Road (off Route 313), 05250
Tel: 802-375 6516
Fax: 802-375 6553
www.westmountaininn.com
A family-friendly 1840s farmhouse turned 18-room inn with mountain views on 150 country acres. Trails for hiking or cross-country skiing, children's game room, and the resident llama ranch amuse all ages. MAP available. **$$$–$$$$**
Arlington Inn
Route 7a, 05250
Tel: 802-375 6532/800-443 9442
Fax: 802-375 6534
www.arlingtoninn.com
An elegant Greek Revival mansion with comfortable Victorian-style interior furnishings in the 19 guest

rooms in the inn and three annexes. **$$–$$$**

BENNINGTON

Four Chimneys Inn and Restaurant
21 West Road (Route 9), 05201
Tel: 802-447 3500
Fax: 802-447 3692
www.fourchimneys.com
French Provincial decor in a grand Georgian Revival manse with 11 rooms for B&B. The restaurant serves continental, fixed price dinners. **$$–$$$$**
Molly Stark Inn
1067 E Main Street, 05201
Tel: 802-442 9631/800-356 3076
Fax: 802-442 5224
www.mollystarkinn.com
A friendly, homey B&B in an 1890 Victorian house. The six cozy guest rooms have New England country-style furnishings, antique quilts and clawfoot tubs. The three cottages have jacuzzis. **$$–$$$**

BOLTON VALLEY

Bolton Valley Resort
Bolton Access Road, 05477
Tel: 802-434 3444/877-926 5866
Fax: 802-434 2131
www.boltonvalleyvt.com
After a multimillion-dollar renovation, this family-friendly ski resort is better than ever. There's now a complex of condos and inn rooms at the base of the mountain, a sports center, six lifts, night skiing, and an excellent complex of cross-country and snowshoe trails. **$$–$$$**
The Black Bear
Bolton Access Road, 05477
Tel: 802-434 2126/800-395 6335
Fax: 802-434 5161
www.blkbearinn.com
Cozy countrified decor (with bear-adorned quilts) in a lodge located amid the Bolton Valley Resort. Some of the 24 rooms have balconies, hot tubs, and firestoves. The owner is a chef, and the restaurant is a popular *après-ski* dinner spot. On-site kennel. **$**

BRATTLEBORO

Forty Putney Road B&B
192 Putney Road, Route 5, 05301
Tel: 802-254 6268/800-941 2413
Fax: 802-258 2673
www.fortyputneyroad.com
French chateaux-style, 1930s home on the West River has four nicely-furnished guest rooms with air conditioning and TV, and lovely grounds down to the riverfront. **$$$–$$$$**

Latchis Hotel
50 Main Street, 05301
Tel: 802-254 6300
Fax: 802-254 6304
www.latchis.com
A 1938 Art Deco hotel, right in the heart of downtown. Some of the 30 rooms have refrigerators, some have views of Main Street or the Connecticut River. **$–$$**

BRIDGEWATER CORNERS

October Country Inn
Upper Road, 05035
Tel: 802-672 3412/800-648 8421
Fax: 802-672 1163
www.octobercountryinn.com
A cozy, 19th-century farmhouse with 10 rooms on a back road, about 5 miles (8 km) from the Killington ski area. MAP available, and dinners feature ethnic menus. **$$**

BROOKFIELD

Green Trails Inn
Main Street, 05036
Tel: 802-276 3412
www.greentrailsinn.com
A sprawling 13-room inn and lodge B&B, built around 1790 and 1830 farmhouses, on 17 acres overlooking Sunset Lake. The owners maintain 19 miles (30 km) of trails for cross-country skiing and hiking. **$–$$**

BURLINGTON

Willard Street Inn
349 S Willard Street, 05401
Tel: 802-651 8710/800-577 8712
Fax: 802-651 8714
www.willardstreetinn.com
Built for a state senator in the 1880s, this stately, formally appointed house in Burlington's historic hill area has views of Lake Champlain. The 14 rooms are furnished with antiques and down comforters. Guests can walk downtown. **$$–$$$$**

CHITTENDEN

Mountain Top Inn
Mountain Top Road, 05737
Tel: 802-483 2311/800-445 2100
Fax: 802-483 6373

Price Categories

A very approximate guide to current room rates for a standard double per night is:
   $$$$ = over $200
   $$$ = $150–200
   $$ = $100–150
   $ = under $100

www.mountaintopinn.com
A large, comfortable, fully-contained family resort deep in the countryside north of Rutland. The 52 rooms are in the inn and outlying cottages. Outstanding Nordic skiing. MAP available. **$$$–$$$$**

Fox Creek Inn
Chittenden Dam Road, 05737
Tel: 802-483 6213/800-707 0017
www.foxcreekinn.com
An electricity magnate's 1920s' retreat 10 miles (16 km) north of Rutland. Five of the eight rooms have whirlpool tubs. MAP available. **$$–$$$$**

CRAFTSBURY COMMON AND ENVIRONS

Inn on the Common
Main Street (Route 14)
Craftsbury Common, 05827
Tel: 802-586 9619/800-521 2233
Fax: 802-586 2249
www.innonthecommon.com
A 17-room MAP with luxurious decor, including plush carpets, quilts, historic wallpaper reproductions, as well as a swimming pool, tennis court, and mountain views. Pets welcome (cleaning fee). MAP available. **$$$–$$$$**

Craftsbury Outdoor Center
Craftsbury Common, 05827
Tel: 802-586 7767
Fax: 802-586 7768
www.craftsbury.com
The 47-room FAP facility offers dormitory-style accommodations, with skilled training available in various outdoor sports. There are more than 100 miles (160 km) of cross-country ski trails, plus sculling, running camps, mountain biking, and canoeing on offer. **$–$$$**

Craftsbury Inn
Main Street (Route 14)
Craftsbury, 05826
Tel: 802-586 2848/800-336 2848
Fax: 802-586 8060
www.craftsburyinn.com
Country comfort in an 1850 Greek Revival inn. Ten rooms with wraparound verandahs overlooking lavish gardens. Just down the road from Craftsbury Common. **$$–$$$**

DORSET

Barrows House
Route 30, 05251
Tel: 802-867 4455/800-639 1620
Fax: 802-867 0132
www.barrowshouse.com
An 18th-century Federal-style inn and carriage house with homey touches in the 28 rooms and a well-regarded restaurant. Pool and tennis courts. Located 6 miles (10 km) north of

Snow Tours

The following places offer cross-country ski tours led by ski instructors, or guided snowmobile tours:
● Killington, Wells and Post Mills in Vermont
● Bartlett, Colebrook, East Conway, Littleton, and Tamworth in New Hampshire
● Rangeley in Maine

Manchester. MAP available. **$$$$**
Dorset Inn
Church & Main Streets, 05251
Tel: 802-867 5500
Fax: 802-867 5542
www.dorsetinn.com
One of the state's oldest – and reliably commendable – inns (MAP), opened in 1796, with 31 rooms. **$$$–$$$$**

Marble West Inn
Dorset West Road, 05251
Tel: 802-867 4155/800-453 7629
www.marblewestinn.com
An elegant, eight-room B&B in a marble-columned 1840s Greek Revival manse. The rate includes a candlelit, gourmet breakfast. **$$–$$$**

EAST BURKE

Inn at Mountain View Farm
Darling Hill Road, 05832
Tel: 802-626 9924/800-572 4509
Twelve lovely guest rooms with private baths and antiques in an 1890 Georgian inn on the grounds of a one-time creamery. With 440 acres of grounds, there are miles of cross-country, hiking, and mountain biking trails. Excellent restaurant on the premises. **$$–$$$**

Old Cutter Inn
143 Pinkham Road, 05832
Tel/fax: 802-626 5152/800-295 1943
www.oldcutterinn.com
A small farmhouse close to the ski area has been converted into a quaint 10-room inn by owner/chef Fritz Walther, who prepares Swiss specialties in his charming restaurant. Closed April and November. **$**

ESSEX JUNCTION

Inn at Essex
70 Essex Way (off Route 15), 05452
Tel: 802-878 1100/800-727 4295
Fax: 802-878 0063
www.vtculinaryresort.com
A Colonial-style inn with 120 rooms (30 with fireplaces), a swimming pool and outstanding cuisine (provided by the New England Culinary Institute); near the Essex Outlet Center and convenient to Burlington. **$$$–$$$$**

FAIR HAVEN

Maplewood Inn
1108 Route 22A South, 05473
Tel: 802-265 8039/800-253 7729
Fax: 802-265 8210
www.maplewoodinn.net
A three-room B&B in a former dairy farm with fanciful decor and hearty breakfasts. Located west of Rutland near the New York border. **$–$$**

GRAFTON

Old Tavern at Grafton
Route 121, 05146
Tel: 802-843 2231/800-843 1801
Fax: 802-843 2245
www.old-tavern.com
One of New England's oldest inns was built in 1801 as a stagecoach stop. There are 11 rooms in the inn furnished with country antiques, plus 11 additional properties scattered around the grounds. Swimming pond, tennis courts, ice skating, and cross-country ski trails. **$$–$$$$**

HIGHGATE SPRINGS

Tyler Place Family Resort
Route 7, 05460
Tel: 802-868 4000
Fax: 802-868 5621
www.tylerplace.com
A popular family destination since the 1930s, accommodations at the FAP "camp" include cottages, an 1820 farmhouse, a Victorian guest house, and a modern inn with 60 rooms. The 165 acres (67 hectares) of lakefront property includes a private beach and boating. Special children's programs. **$$$$**

JAY

Jay Peak Ski & Summer Resort
Route 242, 05859
Tel: 802-988 2611/800-451 4449
Fax: 802-988 4049
www.jaypeakresort.com
48 simple, ski lodge-style hotel rooms and 140 modern one- to three-bedroom condos, most right on the slopes. **$–$$$**

KILLINGTON

Cortina Inn
Route 4, 05751
Tel: 802-773 3333/800-451 6108
Fax: 802-775 6948
www.cortinainn.com
Some 97 surprisingly lush and spacious rooms with air conditioning and balconies. Facilities include an indoor pool, tennis courts, a health club, ice skating, and horseback riding. **$$–$$$**

Inn of the Six Mountains
Killington Road, 05751
Tel: 802-422 4302/800-228 4676
Fax: 802-422 4898
www.sixmountains.com
Just a few minutes from the lifts, this 103-room modern hotel has a Rockies feel. Everything, including the central fieldstone hearth, is lavishly overscale. Facilities include indoor and outdoor seasonal pools, a fitness room, outdoor hot tubs, and tennis courts. **$$-$$$$**

Inn at Long Trail
Route 4, 05751
Tel: 802-775 7181/800-325 2540
Fax: 802-747 7034
www.innatlongtrail.com
A 1938 rustic 19-room ski inn/B&B constructed around an enormous boulder, which intrudes picturesquely into the dining room and Irish Pub. (The pub has Guiness on tap and, often, Irish music.) It's in a good location near the Pico ski area and the Appalachian Trail. **$$-$$$$**

Mountain Meadows Lodge
Thundering Brook Road, 05751
Tel: 802-775 1010/800-370 4567
Fax: 802-773 4459
www.mtmeadowslodge.com
A large lakeside farmhouse offering 20 rooms (MAP), with extensive cross-country trails. There's a child care center with a playground, and farm animals. **$$**

LAKE CHAMPLAIN ISLANDS

Henry's Sportsman's Cottages Inc.
218 Poor Farm Road, Alburg 05440
Tel: 802-796 3616
Fourteen lakefront, one- two- and three-bedroom housekeeping cottages with screened porches. Private beach; boat and motor rentals. **$-$$**

Terry Lodge
54 West Shore Road, Isle LaMotte 05463
Tel: 802-928 3264
www.geocities.com/terry_lodge
Old-fashioned lakeshore lodge has seven rooms (two with private bath) and four motel units. MAP available. **$$**

North Hero House Inn & Restaurant
Route 2
North Hero, 05474
Tel: 802-372 4732/888-525 3644
Fax: 802-372 3218
www.northherohouse.com
Historic inn complex with three annexes overlooking Lake Champlain offers well-furnished rooms, many with jacuzzi tubs and fireplaces. Boat rental. **$-$$$**

Shore Acres Inn and Restaurant
237 Shoreacres Drive, North Hero 05474
Tel: 802-372 8722
www.shoreacres.com
A sedate 23-room lakeside motel with a vast verandah affording a 40 mile (64 km) view. Clay tennis courts. Open April–November; B&B open year-round. **$-$$$**

LOWER WATERFORD

Rabbit Hill Inn
Route 18, 05848
Tel: 802-748 5168/800-762 8669
Fax: 802-748 8342
www.rabbithillinn.com
A Greek Revival stagecoach inn on 15 wooded acres near Street. Johnsbury. There are 20 ultra-romantic rooms, a superb and elegant restaurant, and lots of pampering personal touches. Trails for walking or cross-country skiing; canoes can also be arranged. MAP available. **$$$$**

LUDLOW

Governor's Inn
86 Main Street, 05149
Tel: 802-228 8830/800-468 3766
www.thegovernorsinn.com
This nine-rooms inn has formal Victorian decor, a romantic ambiance, and solicitous hospitality, and is located just 10 minutes from the Okemo Mountain ski area. French-influenced cuisine is served in the well-regarded dining room on antique china and sterling silver. MAP available. **$$-$$$$**

LYNDONVILLE

Wildflower Inn
Darling Hill Road, 05851
Tel: 802-626 8310/800-627 8310
Fax: 802-626 3039
www.wildflowerinn.com
This 21-room, cheerfully renovated 1796 B&B farmhouse (with modern carriage house annex) is great for families. There's a petting zoo, pool, and panoramic views to boot. It's also just a short drive from the Wildflower to the Burke Mountain ski area. **$$-$$$$**

MANCHESTER

The Equinox & The Charles Orvis Inn
Route 7a, 05254
Tel: 802-362 4700/800-362 4747

Fax: 802-362 1595
www.rockresorts.com
A grand old hotel with 183 finely refurbished rooms and suites in the main inn and nine suites in the elegant next-door inn. Fitness center and spa, indoor and outdoor pools, stocked trout pond, tennis court, and one of Vermont's finest 18-hole golf courses. **$$$$**

Village Country Inn
Route 7a, 05254
Tel: 802-362 1792/800-370 0300
Fax: 802-362 7238
www.villagecountryinn.com
A rambling 32-room old inn with romantic French country decor. Suites have fireplaces and canopy beds. MAP available. **$$-$$$$**

Wilburton Inn
River Road (off Route 7a), 05254
Tel: 802-362 2500/800-648 4944
Fax: 802-362 1107
www.wilburton.com
A railroad baron's 100-year-old brick mansion set on 20 acres of lawn, with contemporary outdoor sculpture. The 30 elegantly appointed guest rooms for B&B feature canopy beds, fireplaces, and whirlpool tubs. Cottages are also available. **$$-$$$$**

1811 House
Route 7a, 05254
Tel: 802-362 1811/800-432 1811
Fax: 802-362 2443
www.1811house.com
A Federal manse (former minister's home) at the north end of Manchester Village. The building has been an inn/B&B for most of its history and currently has 14 spacious, antiques-filled guest rooms, plus additional rooms in a separate cottage. Scottish pub. **$$-$$$$**

MARLBORO

Whetstone Inn
550 South Road, 05344
Tel: 802-254 2500
www.whetstoneinn.com
A 200-year-old farmhouse with 12 bedrooms (four with shared bath) decorated with a mix of Colonial appointments and contemporary Scandinavian furnishings. Pond for swimming, skating. No credit cards. **$**

MIDDLEBURY

Middlebury Inn
14 Court House Square, 05753
Tel: 802-388 4961/800-842 4666
Fax: 802-388 4563
www.middleburyinn.com
An 1825 inn (plus 1827 annex and modern motel extension, offering a total of 80 rooms) overlooking the village green. Dining room serves traditional New England fare. **$-$$$$**

Swift House Inn
25 Stewart Lane, 05753
Tel: 802-388 9925
Fax: 802-388 9927
www.swifthouseinn.com
A former governor's estate, this elegantly detailed 1815 Federal house has 21 luxurious guest rooms. The Carriage House has spacious suites with whirlpool baths. **$$–$$$$**

MIDDLETOWN SPRINGS

Twin Mountain Farms B&B
549 Coy Hill Road, 05757
Tel: 802-235 3700
Fax: 802-235 3701
www.twinmountainsfarmbb.com
Three comfortable rooms with private baths in a home nestled on 150 acres; on-site spa services are available. Pets welcome by prior arrangement. **$–$$**

MONTGOMERY

Black Lantern Inn
Route 118, 05470
Tel: 802-326 4507/800-255 8661
Fax: 802-326 2024
www.blacklantern.com
Built in 1803 to house mill workers, now a country-style inn with 15 rooms for B&B near Jay Peak. Suites have whirlpool baths and fireplaces. **$–$$**

English Rose Inn
Route 242, Montgomery Center, 05471
Tel: 802-326 3232
Fax: 802-326 2001
www.theenglishroseinn.com
1850s farmhouse just 3½ miles (6 km) from Jay Peak has 14 guestrooms and suites decorated with Victorian furnishings. The restaurant serves British and American cuisine. **$–$$$**

Inn on Trout River
Main Street, 05471
Tel: 802-326 4391/800-338 7049
Fax: 802-326 3194
www.troutinn.com
A late 1800s inn with 10 B&B rooms that are furnished in English and Victorian country styles with down quilts and flannel sheets (in winter). The living/dining room has a large wood-burning stove; the downstairs recreation room has a pool table. Near Jay Peak. **$–$$**

MONTPELIER

Betsy's Bed & Breakfast
74 East State Street, 05602
Tel: 802-229 0466
Twelve rooms and suites in two adjacent homes and a carriage house near town. Five suites have full kitchens. **$–$$**

Capitol Plaza Hotel & Conference Center
100 State Street, 05602
Tel: 802-223 5252/800-274 5252
Fax: 802-229 5427
www.capitolplaza.com
Full-service hotel adjacent to State House has nicely-furnished motel-type rooms and J. Morgan's Steakhouse on the premises. **$–$$$**

Inn at Montpelier
147 Main Street, 05602
Tel: 802-223 2727
Fax: 802-223 0722
www.innatmontpelier.com
A pair of adjoining Federal mansions make a restful in-town retreat (19 rooms) for both business travelers and vacationers. The main inn has a wide wraparound porch and a formal sitting room. Both buildings have small guest pantries with coffee makers and snacks. **$$–$$$**

NEWFANE AREA

Four Columns Inn
230 West Street, Newfane, 05345
Tel: 802-365 7713/800-787 6633
Fax: 802-365 0022
www.fourcolumnsinn.com
A majestic white-columned Greek Revival inn beside one of New England's most photogenic greens. The 16 Colonial-style guest rooms have been updated, and there is a pool and trout ponds. **$$–$$$**

River Bend Lodge
Route 30, 05345
Tel: 802-365 7952
Fax: 802-365 5004
www.riverbendlodgevt.com
18 newly redecorated rooms with A/C and cable TV in a sprawling lodge on 30 acres with mountain views and private trails. **$**

PUTNEY

Hickory Ridge House
Hickory Ridge Road, 05346
Tel: 802-387 5709/800-380 9218
Fax: 802-387 5387
www.hickoryridgehouse.com
An 1808 National Register of Historic Places brick Federal manor with six country-style rooms and two cottages on 12 pastoral acres. Vegetarian breakfasts, with soufflés and homemade breads, are a specialty of this B&B. **$$–$$$**

The Putney Inn
Depot Road, 05346
Tel: 802-387 5517/800-653 5517
www.putneyinn.com
Great care has been take to preserve the charm and integrity of this 1790s farmhouse. There are rooms in the inn as well as a new, motel-type unit. **$–$$**

QUECHEE

Quality Inn at Quechee Gorge
US Route 4, 05059
Tel: 802-295 7600/800-732 4376
Fax: 802-295 1492
www.qualityinnquechee.com
Pleasant chain motel accommodations just a minute from the highway. Facilities include an indoor pool, fitness center, and restaurant. **$–$$$**

Quechee Inn at Marshland Farm
Clubhouse Road, 05059
Tel: 802-295 3133/800-235 3133
Fax: 802-295 6587
www.quecheeinn.com
An historic, 1793 farmstead with 24 rooms in a bucolic riverside setting. MAP available. Cross-country skiing, hiking, canoeing. **$$$–$$$$**

RUTLAND

Inn at Rutland
70 N Main Street, 05701
Tel: 802-773 0575/800-808 0575
Fax: 802-775 3506
A 10-room B&B in a renovated, 1889 Victorian mansion with views of the surrounding mountains and valleys. Traditional appointments include an ornate oak staircase, carved ceiling moldings, and botanical prints. **$–$$$**

SHELBURNE

Inn at Shelburne Farms
Harbor Road, 05482
Tel: 802-985 8498
Fax: 802-985 1233
www.shelburnefarms.org
Lila Vanderbilt's turn-of-the-20th-century Tudor-style mansion (24 rooms, MAP) set amid a grandiose working farm beside Lake Champlain. Tennis, boating, and fishing available. A gem. Open mid-May–mid-Oct. **$$$$**

SHOREHAM

Shoreham Inn
51 Inn Street, 05770
Tel: 802-897 5861/800-255 5081
Ten-room B&B in a personable village farmhouse, with sophisticated hosts. Near Larabees Point on the southern end of Lake Champlain. **$**

STOWE

Stone Hill Inn
89 Houston Farm Road, 05672
Tel: 802-253 6282
www.stonehillinn.com
One of the area's newest luxury lodgings emphasizes the romantic, with fireside jacuzzis for two, king-size beds, and lovely landscaped grounds to stroll. Adults only. **$$$$**

Topnotch at Stowe Resort and Spa
Mountain Road, 05672
Tel: 802-253 8585/800-451 8686
Fax: 802-253 9263
www.topnotch-resort.com
A luxury 105-room establishment with
inn rooms and chalets, a world-class
spa, plus tennis and stables.
$$$–$$$$

Trapp Family Lodge
700 Trapp Hill Road, 05672
Tel: 802-253 8511/800-826 7000
Fax: 802-253 5740
www.trappfamily.com
On 2,800 acres, this modern,
European-style lodge is a replacement
for the original lodge, which was lost
to fire. There are also rooms in
adjacent townhouses. There's a first-
rate xc ski area, fitness center, indoor
pool, and tennis courts. $$$

Green Mountain Inn
Route 100, 05672
Tel: 802-253 7301/800-455 6629
A rambling 1833 in-town inn with 64
rooms, nicely restored. Facilities
include a year-round outdoor heated
pool and sauna. $$–$$$

**Stowe Mountain Resort's inn at the
Mountain**
5781 Mountain Road
Stowe, 05672
Tel: 800-253 4754
Fax: 802-253 3659
www.stowe.com
At the foot of Mount Mansfield, the
tastefully-decorated motel and condo
complex is surrounded by state forest.
Amenities include clay tennis courts,
an outdoor pool, and fitness center.
$$$–$$$$

Stowehof Inn and Resort
Edson Hill Road, 05672
Tel: 802-253 9722/800-932 7136
Fax: 802-253 7513
www.stowehofinn.com
A hilltop hotel with intentionally
eccentric decor in the 45 rooms and
an outdoor pool with the best view in
town. $$–$$$

Alpenrose Motel
2619 Mountain Road, 05672
Tel: 802-253 7277/800-962 7002
Fax: 802-253 4707
www.gostowe.com/members/
alpenrose
Small motel on the recreation path
and halfway between the village and
Mount Mansfield. Standard rooms and
efficiencies with all the amenities,
plus an outdoor pool. German spoken.
$

VERGENNES

Basin Harbor Club
Basin Harbor Road, 05491
Tel: 802-475 2311/800-622 4000
Fax: 802-475 6545
www.basinharbor.com

A classic lakeside summer colony,
built around an old farmhouse, full of
timeless pleasures. Most of the 138
accommodations are in newer
cottages, many with fireplaces and
refrigerators. The 700-acre property
includes a beach, swimming pool, golf
course, tennis courts, and a
playground. Extensive children's
activities. FAP July and August; B&B
available other times. $$$$

WAITSFIELD

Inn at Round Barn Farm
1161 E Warren Road, 05673
Tel: 802-496 2276/800-721 8029
Fax: 802-496 8832
www.theroundbarn.com
A luxuriously retrofitted farmhouse
B&B on 245 acres with 12 plush
guest rooms with canopy beds, some
with whirlpool baths. The unusual 12-
sided Shaker-style barn is used for
summer concerts and parties.
$$–$$$$

Lareau Farm Country Inn
Route 100, 05673
Tel: 802-496 4949/800-833 0766
Fax: 802-496 7979
www.lareaufarminn.com
This 13-room B&B has an authentic
farmhouse atmosphere, with country-
style rooms and a dining room with
many windows. On 67 acres of woods
and pasture, near the Mad River.
$–$$$

Knoll Farm Inn
Bragg Hill Road, 05673
Tel: 802-496 3939
A functioning farmhouse with four
rooms on 150 acres; home-grown
meals, and a pond for swimming or
skating. $$

Inn at Mad River Barn
Route 17, 05673
Tel: 802-496 3310/800-631 0466
www.madriverbarn.com
A 1948 ski lodge with 15 rooms with
a vintage game room. Extensive
grounds include a swimming pool and
trails. MAP available. $–$$

WARREN

Pitcher Inn
Warren Village, 05674
Tel: 802-496 6350/888-867 4824
www.pitcherinn.com

Each of the 11 elegant rooms and
suites at this white clapboard Relais &
Chateaux property has been designed
by a different architect. All have
jacuzzis, and many have steam
showers and fireplaces. $$$$

WATERBURY

Inn at Blush Hill
Blush Hill Road, 05676
Tel: 802-244 7529/800-736 7522
Fax: 802-244 7314
www.blushhill.com
An exemplary B&B high on a hill with
sweeping mountain vistas. Five
cheerful rooms and gourmet
breakfasts in a 1790s room with its
original open hearth fireplace. $–$$

The Old Stagecoach Inn
18 North Main Street, 05676
Tel: 802-244 5056/800-262 2206
www.oldstagecoach.com
Beautifully-restored 19th-century
stagecoach stop has eight
comfortable guest rooms and three
efficiency suites. Several rooms have
fireplaces and sitting areas; some
share bath. $–$$

WEATHERSFIELD

Inn at Weathersfield
Route 106, 05151
Tel: 802-263 9217/800-477 4828
Fax: 802-263 9219
Twelve guest rooms in an 18th-
century country inn where Early
American style blends with modern
amenities, with the promise of
romance at every turn. Located south
of Windsor. MAP available. $$$–$$$$

WEST DOVER

Inn at Sawmill Farm
7 Crosstown Road, Route 100, 05356
Tel: 802-464 8131/800-493 1133
Fax: 802-464 1130
www.the inn atsawmillfarm.com
A Relais & Chateaux property with 20
guest rooms and a first-rate
restaurant in an old farmstead jazzed
up with bold decorative touches. This
is country elegance at its best, plus
superb regional cuisine. Convenient to
Mount Snow and Haystack Mountain
ski areas. $$$$

WEST TOWNSHEND

Windham Hill Inn
311 Lawrence Drive, 05359
Tel: 802-874 4080/800-944 4080
Fax: 802-874 4702
www.windhamhill.com
An elegantly appointed 1825
farmhouse-cum-cross-country-ski-
center. 21 MAP rooms, set right in the
heart of the country. An extensive CD

collection entertains music-loving guests. Facilities include a pool, tennis courts, skating pond. Located 10 miles (16 km) north of Newfane and 10 miles (16 km) east of Stratton Mountain ski area. **$$$–$$$$**

WILMINGTON

Trail's End, A Country Inn
Smith Road, 05363
Tel: 802-464 2727/800-859 2585
Fax: 802-464 5532
www.trailsendvt.com
The 15 lovely rooms and suites at this B&B on 10 acres (4 hectares) branch off from a cathedral-ceiling living room with fieldstone hearth. Convenient for Mount Snow and Haystack Mountain ski areas. **$$–$$$$**

WINDSOR

Juniper Hill Inn
153 Pembroke Road, 05089
Tel: 802-674 5273/800-359 2541
Fax: 802-674 2041
www.juniperhillinn.com
An 100-year-old Greek Revival-style, hilltop mansion set on a broad lawn near Ascutney Mountain. The 16 elegant rooms are furnished with Queen Anne and Edwardian pieces; some have working fireplaces. Extensive grounds include beautiful gardens and a pool. **$$–$$$**

WOODSTOCK AREA

Jackson House Inn and Restaurant
37 Route 4 West, Woodstock, 05091
Tel: 802-457 2065/800-448 1890
www.jacksonhouseinn.com
A lovingly restored 1890s clapboard house, now a 15-room B&B. Has an award-winning restaurant, serving five-course breakfasts, and *hors-d'oeuvres* with champagne. **$$$–$$$$**
Woodstock Inn & Resort
14 The Green (Route 4)
Woodstock, 05091
Tel: 802-457 1100/800-448 7900
Fax: 802-457 6699
www.woodstockinn.com
The Rockefellers' homage to country inns past, full of Americana. The decor is corporate/country with modern furniture and patchwork quilts. The impressive facilities include 144 rooms, indoor and outdoor pools, tennis courts, golf, a health club, and racquet ball and squash courts. **$$$–$$$$**
Kedron Valley Inn
Route 106
South Woodstock, 05071
Tel: 802-457 1473/800-836 1193
Fax: 802-457 4469
www.kedronvalleyinn.com
Heirloom quilts line the walls and

dress up the 28 prettily decorated rooms of this B&B. Some rooms have fireplaces, jacuzzis, and decks. The ski lodge-style building situated just behind the main inn attracts families, with a swimming pool as an extra attraction. The restaurant is first-rate. **$$–$$$$**
Applebutter Inn
Happy Valley Road
Woodstock, 05091
Tel: 802-457 4158/800-486 1734
Fax: 802-457 4158
www.applebutterinn.com
Five-room B&B in an 1840 Federal house full of fluffy comforters; three fireplaced sitting rooms. **$$–$$$**
The Lauren Inn
3 Church Street, Woodstock, 05091
Tel: 802-457 1925
Fax: 802-457 9181
www.thelaureninn.com
10 luxurious standard rooms, studios, and suites in a gracious early 19th-century house near the common, with a tennis court and pool. **$$$$**

Where to Eat

ARLINGTON

West Mountain Inn
River Road (off Route 313)
Tel: 802-375 6516
Fixed-price, New American cuisine featuring fresh fish and prime meat in a low-beamed paneled dining room at a romantic and family-friendly inn. Dinner only. **$$$$**
Arlington Inn
Route 7A
Tel: 802-375 6532
A formal candlelit restaurant with French Continental dishes – rack of lamb, roast duck – all prepared with local meats and produce. Fixed-price menu offered week nights off-season. Dinner only. **$$$**

BENNINGTON

Four Chimneys
21 West Road (Route 9)
Tel: 802-447 3500
American and continental cuisine in the gracious dining room of a beautifully-restored 1910 Colonial Revival inn. Dinner only. **$$$$**

Blue Benn Diner
Route 7
Tel: 802-442 5140
A classic 1940s diner serving unconventional ethnic dishes as well as traditional fare. Breakfast is served all day. **$**
Pangaea
1&3 Prospect Street, North Bennington
A sophisticated menu and an award-winning wine list make this spot a favorite in this corner of the state. Among the house specialties are sautéed veal sweetbreads and filet mignon à la Rossini. Dinner only. **$$$–$$$$**

BRATTLEBORO

Common Ground
25 Eliot Street
Tel: 802-257 0855
One of the country's oldest natural food restaurant-co-ops serves up vegetarian fare, home made desserts, and wine and beer. Call for hours. **$**
T.J. Buckley's
132 Eliot Street
Tel: 802-257 4922
Upscale cuisine in a 1920s Worcester diner. Diners choose from 4 creative entrées – usually a fish, chicken, beef, and vegetarian. *Prix-fixe* dinners include salad. Dinner only Wednesday–Sunday. Reservations required. **$$$**
Peter Havens
32 Eliot Street
Tel: 802-257 3333
The locals' favorite New American bistro; a tiny art-filled space whose kitchen turns out dishes such as roasted boneless duck breast and home made pastas. Dinner only Tuesday–Saturday. **$$–$$$**
Riverview Café
Bridge Street
Tel: 802-254 9841
A child-friendly place with two levels of outdoor decks overlooking the Connecticut River and crowd pleasers such as all-you-can-eat fish and chips, macaroni and cheese with Grafton cheddar cheese and Vermont ham, and pizza. **$**

BURLINGTON AREA

Bove's
68 Pearl Street
Tel: 802-864 6651
Both the tiny, narrow restaurant with its tin ceilings and wooden booths, and the Neapolitan fare, are unpretentious. Possibly the last place in town where one can dine for under $3. Closed Sunday and Monday. **$**
Peking Duck House
79 West Canal Street, Winooski
Tel: 802-655 7474

This restaurant just over the Winooski Bridge consistently wins awards for the best Chinese food around. Both the dishes and the atmosphere are upscale; the prices are down to earth. **$–$$**

Pauline's Cafe and Restaurant
1834 Shelburne Road
(Route 7 S)
South Burlington
Tel: 802-862 1081
Deft American dishes and regional specialties, including wild mushrooms, Vermont cheeses, and organic greens, in an elegant little restaurant improbably located in a strip mall. The downstairs café offers a lighter and less expensive menu at lunch and dinner; the main dining room serves dinner only. **$$–$$$**

Daily Planet
15 Center Street
Tel: 802-862 9647
World-beat cuisine: Mediterranean with Asian influences in a cheerful solarium in the center of town. Specialties include soups and tapas. **$$**

Sakura
2 Church Street
Tel: 802-863 1988
One of the first – and still the best – Japanese restaurant in town serves artfully-arranged and skillfully prepared specialties including *tempura* and *sashimi*. Sushi bar. **$$–$$$**

Sweet Tomatoes
83 Church Street
Tel: 802-660 9533
A boisterous trattoria with a wood-fired oven that turns out scrumptious pizzas and other Tuscan-inspired fare. **$–$$**

Trattoria Delia
152 Street Paul Street
Tel: 802-864 5253
Award-wining, authentic Italian trattoria specialties include handmade pastas, hardwood-grilled chops, and finely-prepared veal specialties. Dinner only. **$$–$$$**

Mirabelle's
198 Main Street
Tel: 802-658 3074
An inviting cafe/patisserie with light lunches. **$**

Restaurant Prices

Prices are approximate, but for a three-course meal for one (excluding beverages, tax and tip), the following guidelines may prove helpful:

$$$$ = over $40
$$$ = $28–40
$$ = $15–28
$ = under $15

CHESTER

Country Girl Diner
Route 11
Tel: 802-875 2650
A traditional 1950s diner with better than expected food on the western end of town. **$**

CRAFTSBURY

Craftsbury Inn
Main Street
Tel: 802-586 2848
Well-prepared, Continental dishes are lovingly prepared and handsomely-presented by the talented chef-owner in the elegant dining room of an 1850 Greek Revival village inn. Wed–Sun by reservation. **$$$**

DORSET

Barrows House
Route 30
Tel: 802-867 4455
New American seasonal specialties such as Maine crab cakes and pan roasted veal tenderloin served in an intimate setting with formal touches; the tavern serves lighter fare. **$$$**

Chantecleer
Route 7A, East Dorset
Tel: 802-362 1616
The Swiss chef at one of the area's finest restaurants skillfully prepares Swiss and French provincial cuisine in a handsomely-renovated dairy barn. Reservations required. Dinner Wednesday–Sunday. **$$$–$$$$**

Dorset Inn
Route 30
Tel: 802-867 5500
Superb New England regional cooking might include turkey croquettes or Welsh rarebit: a choice of formal dining or tavern feasting in a 1796 hostelry. **$$$**

EAST BURKE

Old Cutter Inn
Tel: 802-626 5152
Chef-owner Fritz Walther's native Swiss specialties, including irresistible *rosti*, *rahmschnitzel*, and rack of lamb. **$$**

River Garden Cafe
Route 114
Tel: 802-626 3514
Bruschetta and *tiramisu* come to the Northeast Kingdom, along with rack of lamb and local smoked trout. Closed Monday. **$$**

GRAFTON

Old Tavern at Grafton
Route 121
Tel: 802-843 2231

Hearty New England dishes, perhaps venison stew, or grilled quail, served in two dining rooms: one more formal, the other rustic tavern-style. **$$–$$$**

KILLINGTON

Hemingway's
Route 4
Tel: 802-422 3886
Truly inspired American cuisine, which is regularly hailed as among the nation's best, in an 1860 country house. Closed most Mondays and Tuesdays. **$$$$**

Cortina Inn
Route 4
Tel: 802-773 3333
Chefs from the New England Culinary Institute ensure deft and innovative fare at this Killington institution. **$$$**

LAKE CHAMPLAIN ISLANDS

Blue Paddle Bistro
Route 2, South Hero
Tel: 802-372 4814
A cozy destination for Island gourmets, who return for gorgonzola-stuffed meatloaf, half-pound burgers with hand-cut fries, and, at Sunday brunch, lobster Benedict. Lunch Wed–Sat, dinner nightly. **$$–$$$**

LOWER WATERFORD

Rabbit Hill Inn
Route 18
Tel: 802-748 5168
Dazzling New American cuisine served amid rural understated elegance in a country inn that has been accommodating guests since 1795. **$$$–$$$$**

LUDLOW

Nikki's
Route 103
Okemo Mountain
Tel: 802-228 7797
The New American cuisine is delicious, and the decor is delightful. Dinner only. **$–$$$**

The Governor's Inn
86 Main Street
Tel: 802-228 8830/800-468 3766
Prix-fixe dinners prepared by one of the state's finest chefs in the dining room of her Victorian inn. Dinner begins at 7pm with *hors d'oeuvres* and cocktails. Dinner only Friday and Saturday by reservation. **$$$$**

MANCHESTER

The Equinox
Route 7A
Tel: 802-362 4700
Spectacular regional cuisine in a

formal barrel-vaulted dining room looking out on Mount Equinox. **$$$–$$$$**
Bistro Henry's
Route 11/30
Tel: 802-362 4982
A spacious dining room on the edge of town preparing authentic Mediterranean cuisine. Extensive wine list. **$$$**
Mother Myrick's Confectionery and Ice Cream Parlor
Route 7A
Tel: 802-362 1560
The place to indulge your sweet tooth with a slice of freshly baked pie, homemade fudge, or an ice-cream treat. **$**

MIDDLEBURY

Fire and Ice
26 Seymore Street
Tel: 802-388 7166/800-367 7166
Prime rib and fresh fish, a 55-item salad bar (with peel-and-eat shrimp), and an intimate atmosphere attract couples as well as families with small children, who opt for the "Children's Corner", complete with a VCR and cartoons. **$$**

MONTGOMERY

Black Lantern Inn
Route 118, Montgomery Village
Tel: 802-326 4507
Contemporary fare served by candlelight at this old inn near Jay Peak. **$$**
Paddington's
English Rose Inn
Route 242, Montgomery Center
Tel: 802-326 3232
British tourists will be right at home at one of the area's newest restaurants, with dishes such as Lord Nelson rack of lamb, Cornish pasties, and prime rib with Yorkshire pudding. Dinner Thursday–Sunday. **$$–$$$**

MONTPELIER

The Chef's Table
118 Main Street
Tel: 802-223 9240
This New England Culinary Institute enterprise is thoroughly elegant, and culinarily eloquent. Dinner only. **$$$**
Main Street Grill
118 Main Street
Tel: 802-223 3188
Adventurous grazing courtesy of the highly skilled students of the New England Culinary Institute. **$$**

NEWFANE

Four Columns Inn
230 West Street

Tel: 802-365 7713
Creative European/American cuisine with fresh, Vermont ingredients in the formal dining room of an historic country inn. Dinner only. **$$$–$$$$**

NEWPORT

The East Side Restaurant
47 Landing Street
Tel. 802-334 2340
Extremely popular lakefront restaurant serves up large portions of American dishes such as chicken and biscuits, roast turkey, and fried scallops in a large, cheerful dining room. Opt for the deck in nice weather. **$–$$**
Lago Trattoria
95 Main Street
Tel: 802-334 8222
One of the town's nicest surprises: a genuine Italian trattoria with creatively-prepared dishes, an open kitchen, and extremely reasonable prices. Lunch Friday; dinner Monday–Saturday. **$–$$**

PUTNEY

Curtis' Barbecue
Just off Route 5
Tel: 802-387 5474
Good ol' barbecue, slow-cooked and served up from an old school bus. Seating is at outdoor picnic tables. Divine. Open Apr–Oct, Wed–Sun. **$**
Front Porch Café
133 Main Street
Tel: 802-387 2200
A cozy spot with a welcoming hearth, a British ambiance, and – in nice weather – a porch to dine al fresco. Breakfasts might include home baked pastries or corned beef hash; lunch treats include buffalo and black bean chili and home made soup. **$**

QUECHEE

Parker House Inn
16 Main Street
Tel: 802-295 6077
Tasteful, upscale American fare with a continental flair in an 1857 brick Victorian mansion overlooking the Oattauquechee River. Outdoor terrace. Dinner only. **$$$–$$$$**
Simon Pearce Restaurant
The Mill, Main Street
Tel: 802-295 1470
Fine country cuisine, with some Irish touches, in a modern café in an old riverside mill. Extensive wine list. **$$–$$$**

ST JOHNSBURY

Anthony's Restaurant
50 Railroad Street
Tel: 802-748 3613
Burgers, homemade potato chips, pie

and other American fare served up in a family-friendly spot. A St Johnsbury institution. **$**
Element Food & Spirit
98 Mill Street
Tel: 802-748 8400
"Creative comfort food" in a 150-year-old mill might include house specials such as red curry mussels or smoked trout and apple cakes; there's a nightly blue plate special. **$$**

SHELBURNE

Cafe Shelburne
Route 7
Tel: 802-985 3939
One of the area's most popular upscale restaurants has been serving French bistro fare for more than 30 years. Dinner Tuesday–Sunday. **$$$**
Inn at Shelburne Farms
Harbor Road
Tel: 802-985 8498
Gourmet dining in the elegant dining room of Queen Anne-style manor overlooking Lake Champlain. Sunday brunch is a local institution. Reservations required. **$$$**

STOWE

Ten Acres Lodge
Luce Hill at Barrows Road
Tel: 802-253 7638
Skilled regional cuisine, in handsome old farmhouse set amid a meadow. **$$$–$$$$**
Cliff House
Mount Mansfield
Tel: 802-253 3000
Board the gondola to the top of the mountain for dishes such as turkey club sandwich, shepherd's pie, and a genuine fondue. Buy a one-way ticket and stroll back down. Lunch only. **$$**
Edson Hill Manor
1500 Edson Hill Road
Tel: 802-253 7371
Critically-acclaimed restaurant with majestic views in an elegant inn, with entreés such as seared rare tuna loin and pan broiled duck breast. Dinner only. **$$$–$$$$**
Topnotch at Stowe
Mountain Road
Tel: 802-253 8585
A formal dining room and casual grill offer skilled contemporary cuisine, some calibrated for the health-conscious. **$$$**
Blue Moon Café
35 School Street
Tel: 802-253 7006
A creative menu of international treats, with appetizers such as Malpegue oysters and entrées including seared roast scallops and wasabi rice cakes with Asian stirfry in a bistro atmosphere. Dinner. **$$$**

Trapp Family Lodge
Luce Hill Road.
Tel: 802-253 8511
Gemütlich treats with fine valley views in the Austrian tea room for lunch. Formal continental dining at night in the dining room. **$$–$$$$**

Trattoria La Festa
Mountain Road
Tel: 802-253 8480
Authentic Italian cuisine in an 1859 farmhouse. **$$**

Miguel's Stowe Away
Mountain Road
Tel: 802-253 7574
Decent Mexican fare in a small restaurant with a large bar, complete with pool table . **$**

WAITSFIELD

The Steak Place
Tucker Hill Lodge
65 Marble Hill Road
Tel: 802-496 3983
Tucker Hill Lodge offers steakhouse fare in its restaurant and lighter food in the pub. **$$**

WARREN

Pitcher Inn
Warren Village
Tel: 802-496 6350
Elegant dining and an outstanding wine list in one of the area's finest inns. **$$$$**

Chez Henri
Sugarbush Village
Tel: 802-583 2600
An authentic romantic French bistro in the middle of a bustling ski resort. **$$$**

The Common Man
German Flats Road
Tel: 802-583 2800
Country-sophisticate fare is served in this delightful, atmospheric old barn; a Vermont landmark for 30 years. Dinner only. **$$$**

WEATHERSFIELD

Inn at Weathersfield
Route 106
Tel: 802-263 9217
Fine regional fare in a library

Restaurant Prices

Prices are approximate, but for a three-course meal for one (excluding beverages, tax and tip), the following guidelines may prove helpful:

$$$$ = over $40
$$$ = $28–40
$$ = $15–28
$ = under $15

---

illuminated by candlelight. Piano accompaniment. **$$$**

WEST DOVER

Inn at Sawmill Farm
Off Route 100
Tel: 802-464 8131
Superb, seemingly simple, cuisine is served in the elegant dining room of an elegant inn. The wine list is outstanding. Dinner only. **$$$$**

WEST TOWNSHEND

Windham Hill Inn
Windham Hill Road
Tel: 802-874 4080
Prix-fixe classic French cuisine in a romantically appointed inn. **$$$$**

WILMINGTON

The Hermitage Inn
Coldbrook Road
Tel: 802-464 3511
Elegant surroundings, finely-prepared treats such as homemade venison sausage and game birds raised on the grounds, and a legendary wine cellar. **$$$$**

WINDSOR

Juniper Hill Inn
Juniper Hill Road
Tel: 802-674 5273
Updated classics are served by candlelight in the traditional-style dining room of this equally traditional inn. **$$$**

Windsor Station
Depot Avenue
Tel: 802-674 2052
Classic American fare in a family-oriented spot in a converted railroad station, where the booths were constructed from the depot's railroad benches. Dinner only. **$$**

WOODSTOCK AREA

The Prince & the Pauper
24 Elm Street, Woodstock
Tel: 802-457 1818
Fine Nouvelle and Continental fare and exquisite desserts in a candlelit but comfortably rustic atmosphere. A lighter bistro menu is also available. Dinner only. **$$$$**

Woodstock Inn & Resort
Route 4 on The Green, Woodstock
Tel: 802-457 1100
Regional and New American cuisine in an ultra-formal setting. **$$$**

Kedron Valley Inn
Route 106, South Woodstock
Tel: 802-457 1473
One of the area's finest inns has one of its finest restaurants, serving

---

regional specialties with a Vermont accent. Award-winning wine list. A lighter menu is available in the tavern. Dinner only. **$$$$**

The Jackson House Restaurant
Route 4W
Tel: 802-457 2065
Highly-rated, award-winning, creative cuisine, with a variety of *prix-fixe* menus to choose from. Dinner only. **$$$$**

Bentley's Restaurant
3 Elm Street, Woodstock
Tel: 802-457 3232
Eclectic, antique-ish decor and international dishes; a popular spot. Live music (jazz or blues) on the weekends. **$$**

Culture

Call **Burlington City Arts** (tel: 802-865 7166) for up-to-the-minute information on what's happening in this hip and lively city, or pick up the free weekly newspaper *Seven Days*.

CLASSICAL MUSIC

Marlboro Music Festival (tel: 802-254 2394; www.marlboromusic.org, Marlboro Music Center) has one of the most renowned line-ups in New England. Concerts given in summer. **Vermont Symphony Orchestra** (tel: 802-864 5741) performs in Manchester, Woodstock, and Brattleboro in the summer and Bennington, Arlington, and Rutland during the winter. **Vermont Mozart Festival** (tel: 802-862 7352; www.vtmozart.com) presents classical music in indoor and outdoor venues July and Aug; winter series in and around Burlington.

OPERA

Vermont Opera Theater (tel: 802-223 8610; P.O. Box 869, 05601) in Montpelier features local talent in shows ranging from classical to cabaret.

FOLK

Vermont Pub and Brewery (tel: 802-865 0500; College and Street Paul Sts, Burlington) is one of the more popular places in this young college town, and hosts a range of folk musicians.

THEATER

St Michael's Playhouse (tel: 802-654 2281; Burlington) is Vermont's oldest equity playhouse, and you can almost always count on them for top-quality productions.

Flynn Theater for the Performing Arts (tel: 802-863 8778; 153 Main Street, Burlington) is the big venue for big-name and big-audience productions. **Weston Playhouse Theater Company** (tel: 802-824 5288; Weston) is home to Vermont's oldest summer theater. **Dorset Playhouse** (tel: 802-867 5777; Dorset) stages professional performances in the summer, but in the winter a fine consortium of community folks takes to the stage.

CINEMA

Catamount Arts (tel: 802-748 2600; 60 Eastern Avenue, St Johnsbury) brings a little bit of everything to this remote corner of Vermont: art films, dance, classical music. Stop by if you're in the area and something's on tap. **Majestic 10** at Maple Tree Place in Williston (tel: 802-878 2010) and **Essex Cinemas** in Essex (802-879 6543) are two multiplexes with stadium seating.

Nightlife

LIVE MUSIC

Club Metronome (tel: 802-865 4563; 188 Main Street, Burlington), above Nectar's, has a beat all its own: reggae, blues, or whatever the newest musical beat just happens to be. **Mulligan's** (tel: 802-297 9293) on Stratton has year-round music. **Common Ground** (tel: 802-257 0855; 25 Eliot Street, Brattleboro) has jam dance bands on most weekends, while more mellow guitarists play during brunch. **Purple Moon Pub** (tel: 802-496 3422; Route 100) in Waitsfield presents a full roster of live performers.

LATE-NIGHT VENUES

All of the big ski mountains have a phalanx of nightly live music from which to choose. You're bound to find something to your liking. **Bentley's** (tel: 802-457 3232; 3 Elm Street, Woodstock) has DJs on the weekends.

Outdoor Activities

BIKING

Many of the downhill ski areas are converted into mountain-biking centers after the winter season ends. **Mount Snow** (tel: 802-464 3333), home to the first American mountain bike school, has 45 miles (72 km) of bike terrain and runs one-day coaching programs, leads mountain tours, and hosts family bike weekends.

At **Killington** (tel: 802-422 6232), mountain bikers can cruise 50 miles (80 km) of trails. Vermont is a popular destination for upscale inn-to-inn tours. **Bike Vermont** (tel: 802-457 3553/ 800-257 2226) puts together tours throughout New England.

CANOEING, KAYAKING, AND RAFTING

Vermont Canoe (tel: 802-257 5008; Brattleboro) rents canoes and kayaks and conducts guided paddling tours. Burlington-based **Paddleways** (tel: 802-238 0674) teaches kayaking fundamentals and runs kayaking trips, as does **True North Kayak Tours** (tel: 802-860 1910).

FISHING

Anglers flock to the trout-laded Battenkill River near Manchester,

where **Orvis** (tel: 802-362 3622/800-235 9763) runs a program of popular two-and-a-half day fly-fishing classes. **Battenkill Anglers** (tel: 802-379 1444) organize fly-fishing vacations and schools.

Fishing guides at **Strictly Trout** (tel: 802-869 3116) work all Vermont rivers but specialize in the Connecticut River.

HIKING

Vermont's topography offers everything from easy day hikes to multi-day mountain jaunts. Long-distance hikers gravitate to the **Appalachian Trail**, which cuts across southern Vermont, and to the **Long Trail**, a 270-mile (435-km) traverse across Vermont's highest peaks between the Massachusetts state line and the Canadian border.

Green Mountain Club (tel: 802-244 7037) has specific trail information and publishes the *Day Hiker's Guide to Vermont*.

To mix serious hiking with country-inn comforts, contact **Country Inns Along the Trail** (tel: 326 2072/800-838 3301), which organizes inn-to-inn tours. **Wonder Walks** (tel: 802-453 2076/877-897 7175), headquartered in Bristol, also offers inn-to-inn tours.

SAILING

Lake Champlain and **Lake Memphremagog** are the main sailing lakes. **Burlington Community Boathouse** (tel: 802-865 3377) both rents sailboats and runs charters and "bareboats" on Lake Champlain. **Tudhope Sailing Center** (tel: 802-372 5320; Grand Isle) rents sailboats on the Champlain Islands. **Winds of Ireland** (tel: 802-863 5090; Burlington Boathouse) runs day and sunset sailing cruises. On Lake Memphremagog, you can rent pontoon boats at **Newport Marine** (tel: 802-334 5911).

SKIING

For many, Vermont is synonymous with New England skiing. In the south, the largest downhill mountains are: **Stratton** (tel: 802-297 4000/800-787 2886; Jamaica), **Okemo** (tel: 802-228 4041/800-786 5366; Ludlow), and **Mount Snow** (tel: 800-245 7669). **Killington** (tel: 802-422 3261/800-621 6867; Rutland) is monumental

In the north, check out: **Stowe** (tel: 802-253 3600), **Sugarbush** (tel: 802-583 2381/800-537 8427; Warren), and **Jay Peak** (tel: 802-988 2611/800-451 4449; Jay).

Skiing Tour Operators to Vermont

Companies offering tailormade skiing package holidays to Vermont from the UK include the following:
Ski the American Dream
38–44 Gillingham Street
London SW1V 1HU
Tel: 0870-350 7547
Crystal Holidays
Kings House
12–42 Wood Street
Kingston-upon-Thames
KT1 1JY
Tel: 020-8241 4000
Inghams
10–18 Putney Hill
London SW15 6AX
Tel: 020-8780 4400

North America Travel Service
7 Albion Street
Leeds LS1 5ES
Tel: 0113-243 1606
Thomas Cook Retail
63 Queensgate
Peterborough PE1 1NH
Tel: 0845-308 9497
United Vacations
United House, Southern Perimeter Road, Heathrow Airport,
Middlesex TW6 3LP
Tel: 020-8750 9674
Virgin Holidays
The Galleria, Station Road
Crawley RH10 1WW
Tel: 0870-220 2788

One of Vermont's largest cross-country skiing areas is **Craftsbury Nordic Center** (tel: 800-729 7751), but Stowe also boasts several excellent centers, including **Edson Hill** (tel: 802-253 8954), **Topnotch** (tel: 802-253 8585), and **Trapp Family Lodge** (tel: 802-253 8511).

Serious Nordic skiers may ski the 280-mile (450-km) **Catamount Trail**, which runs nearly the entire length of the state; contact the Catamount Trail Association (tel: 802-864 5794; Burlington).

Shopping

WHERE TO SHOP

Vermont's largest city, Burlington, has its most diverse and sophisticated offerings. The **Burlington Square Mall** on downtown's Church Street and **University Mall** on Dorset Street just off Route 2 have the greatest concentration of shops.

Manchester has many upscale, discount outlets, with famous-name retailers such as Ralph Lauren, Brooks Brothers, and Giorgio Armani.

COUNTRY STORES

Vermont Country Store (tel: 802-824 3184; Route 100, Weston), the venerated institution that country stores all over the country aspire toward, might as well be a department store, for the impressive range of merchandise you can get here. From Vermont-made food stuffs to folk remedies to flannel shirts. They also

Amber Nectar

One of Vermont's specialties is maple syrup, which comes in three grades:

A (Light Amber) Light gold colour.
A (Dark Amber) Stronger and darker than Light Amber.
B Stronger still and a deep amber shade, best for cooking.

During the maple season, from March to April, visitors are welcome at farms listed in *Maple Sugarhouses Open to Visitors*, published by the Vermont Department of Agriculture, tel: 802-828 2500.

have a branch store in Rockingham.

Shelburne Country Store (tel: 802-985 3657; on the green, Shelburne) is a scaled-down version of the above, but still a very fine one at that.

The classic **Warren Store** in Warren Village serves home baked treats on a deck overlooking the waterfall.

MARKETS & FOODSTUFFS

Equinox Valley Nursery (tel: 802-362 2610; Route 7A south of Manchester) sells homegrown products; they always have a scarecrow display and other seasonal displays that make you want to take out your camera.

Harlow's Sugar House (tel: 802-387 5852; Route 5, Putney) takes kids and adults on horse-drawn sugaring rides. In the fall you can pick apples here, and in the summer, berries.

Cold Hollow Cider Mill (tel: 802-244 8771; Route 100, Waterbury Center) offers up glasses and cartons of fresh-pressed cider and other goodies grown in Vermont.

The Cabot Annex Store (tel: 802-244 6334; Route 100, Waterbury) has samples galore of their fine cheeses. **Lake Champlain Chocolates**, next door, sells the stuff of children's dreams and dentist's nightmares.

MARKETPLACES

Church Street Marketplace (tel: 802-863 1648; Main and Pearl Sts, Burlington) encompasses a pedestrian-only section of downtown lined with lively cafés and interesting shops.

Historic Marble Works (tel: 802-388 3701; Middlebury) is a warren of individual shops in a renovated marble factory.

BOOKS

Chain stores are well represented in Burlington by **Borders** (tel: 802-865 2711; 29 Church Street) and **Barnes & Noble** (tel: 802-864 801; 102 Dorset Street). For used books, **North Country Books** (tel: 802-862 6413; 2 Church St) has a fine selection, as does **Rivendell Books** (tel: 802-223 3928; 100 Main Street) in Montpelier.

Northshire Bookstore (tel: 802-362 2200; Main Street, Manchester) is one of the better shops in the state. **Stowe Books** in Stowe Village has a fine selection of local authors.

Vermont Festivals

Spring
Over 90 varieties of lilacs offer a fragrant setting for family activities and musical entertainment at the **Shelburne Museum's Lilac Festival** (tel: 802-985 3346) in May.

Also in May, artists across the state open their studios to visitors during the annual **Open Studio Weekend** (tel: 802-223 3380).

Summer
The hills come alive with the sound of music as soon as summer arrives, starting with Burlington's **Discover Jazz Festival** (tel: 802-863 7992) in early June.

In July, Marlboro College, on a bucolic hilltop, welcomes the month-long, internationally renowned **Marlboro Music Festival** (tel: 802-254 2394).

Meanwhile, Burlington-area towns host the **Vermont Mozart**

Festival (tel: 802-862 7352/800-639 9097).

Circus Smirkus (tel: 800-532 7443) – the world's only international youth circus, with participants recruited from as far afield as Russia and China – raises its one-ring big top throughout Vermont mid-July to mid-August.

The **Vermont Festival of the Arts** comprises more than 100 performing and visual arts events in the Mad River Valley (Warren-Waitsfield area) during the first two weeks of August (tel: 800-517 4247; www.vermontartfest.com).

Fall
The state's wide variety of autumn fairs and festivals includes the huge **Champlain Valley Fair** in Essex Junction (tel: 802-878 5545), the **Stratton Arts Festival** – the state's oldest and largest juried exhibition of

contemporary crafts (tel: 802-297 3265), and the **Vermont State Fair** (tel: 802-775 5200; www.vermonttatefair.net), held during the first week of September at the historic Rutland fairgrounds.

Winter
Vermonters celebrate New Year's Eve with **Burlington's First Night** festivities (tel: 802-863 6005/800-639 9252). Then in mid-January, the ski town of Stowe, which views the frigid weather as one more excuse to party, hosts the **Stowe Winter Carnival**, a week-long bash featuring dog-sled races, ice sculptures, and fireworks (tel: 802-253 7321).

Other ski areas also sponsor various special events to spice up the season.

For further details about events, contact the local tourist office.

ANTIQUES

In Brattleboro, **Twice Upon a Time** (tel: 802-254 2261; 63 Main Street) showcases the wares of more than 100 dealers. North of Brattleboro on Route 30 there are more than two dozen antiques shops. *(See also page 255 for information on crafts in Vermont.)*

ARTS AND CRAFTS

Vermont State Craft Centers in Manchester, Burlington and Middlebury exhibit works by many of the finest craftspeople throughout the state.

Vermont Artisan Design (tel: 802-257 7044; 115 Main Street, Brattleboro) is one of the state's best shops for handmade goods.

Bennington Potters (tel: 802-447 7531; 324 County Street, Bennington and 127 College Street, Burlington) sells seconds (as well as the best, of course) from the well-known (and expensive) Bennington Potters.

Newfane Country Store (tel: 802-365 7916; Route 30, Newfane) is the place to go for quilts.

Green Mountain Spinnery (tel: 802-387 4528; Exit 4 off I-91, Putney) offers home-grown, home-spun wool and mohair.

Northern Kingdom Artisans' Gallery (tel: 802-748 0158; 430 Railroad Street, St. Johnsbury) showcases the works of local craftspeople.

ICE CREAM

Ben & Jerry's Ice Cream Factory, Route 100, north of I-89, near Waterbury, is still a big draw. As well as producing more than 30 "euphoric flavors" of ice cream, Ben Cohen and Jerry Greenfield made their name by plowing back 7½ percent of their profits into social causes and donating half the proceeds of their factory tours to Vermont charities. Then they sold the company to the multinational Unilever.

For schedule of daily tours daily; tel. 866-258 6877; www.benjerry.com; entrance fee for tour). If you want to see ice cream actually being made, schedule a weekday visit.

GLASS

Simon Pearce (tel: 802-295 2711; Main Street, Quechee and Industrial Park, Windsor), perhaps the most famous glass emporium-owner in New England, employs a number of highly talented mastercraftsmen to carry out his vision, and you can watch them

work here. The shop sells first- and second-quality glassware and other fragile items.

Luminosity Studios (tel: 802-496 2231; Route 100, Waitsfield) sells stained glass from former church.

GIFTS

Scotland by the Yard (tel: 802-295 5351; Route 4, Quechee) sells everything Scottish, and although you came to Vermont not the Highlands, you might just find a warm sweater for an unusually early fall day.

TOYS

Vermont Teddy Bear Company (tel: 802-985 3001; 2236 Shelburne Road, Shelburne), which sells furry handmade creatures for significant sums of money, turned a small cottage industry into a multi-million dollar enterprise. Tours offered daily.

Children's Museums

ECHO at the Lahey Center
One College Street
Burlington
Tel: 802-864 1848
Teaches youngsters and "oldsters" about the lake's history and ecology.
Montshire Museum of Science
Montshire Road
Norwich
Tel: 802-649 2200
Arguably second only to Boston's Museum of Science, is a fine place to explore and discover both the natural and man-made world.

New Hampshire

The Place

Known as: The Granite State.
Motto: Live free or die.
Origin of name: Named in 1629 by Captain John Mason of Plymouth Council for his home county in England.
Entered Union: June 21, 1788, the ninth of the 13 original states.
Capital: Concord.
Area: 9,351 sq. miles/24,219 sq. km.
Highest point: Mount Washington, 6,288 ft (1,917 meters).
Population: 1.172 million.
Population density: 119 people per sq. mile (46 per sq. km).
Economy: Manufacturing (industrial machinery, precision instruments, and electronic equipment) and services (including tourism).
National representation: two senators and two representatives to Congress.
Famous citizens: Mary Baker Eddy, Robert Frost, Horace Greeley, and Daniel Webster

Where to Stay

BEDFORD

Bedford Village Inn
2 Village Inn Lane, 03110
Tel: 603-472 2001/800-852 1166
Fax: 603-472 2379
www.bedfordvillageinn.com
Some 14 luxury suites, with four-poster beds and marble bathrooms, carved out of a three-story barn, south of Manchester. **$$$–$$$$**

BETHLEHEM

Adair Inn
80 Guider Ln (at Route 302), 03574
Tel: 603-444 2600/888-444 2600
Fax: 603-444 4823
www.adairinn.com
A 1927 Georgian Colonial mansion with 200 acres encompassing gardens and tennis courts, now a nine-room B&B. The common areas include a tap room with an honor bar, fireplace, and vintage pool table. The

guest rooms are furnished with elegant antiques or reproductions. All rooms have either garden or mountain views. **$$$–$$$$**
Mulburn Inn
2370 Main Street, 03574
Tel: 603-869 3389/800-457 9440
Fax: 603-869 5633
www.mulburninn.com
A Tudor mansion constructed for the retail magnate Woolworths in 1908, with stained glass windows, ornately carved mantles, and imported fireplace tiles. This B&B has seven spacious and individually decorated guest rooms. **$$–$$$**

BRETTON WOODS
Mount Washington Hotel and Resort
Route 302, 03575
Tel: 603-278 1000/800-314 1752
www.mountwashington.com
A National Historic Landmark grand hotel (195 rooms, MAP), preserved in all its glory since 1902. There's a formal atmosphere (jackets are required in the dining room in the evenings), but the hotel is still family friendly. There are kids' camps and other children's programs, plus swimming pools, tennis courts, horseback riding, movies, and a fitness center. A 900-foot-long verandah looks out across the Presidential Range. In winter, there's xc skiing on the grounds or alpine skiing at the nearby Bretton Woods Ski Area. MAP. **$$$$**
Bretton Arms Country Inn
Route 302, 03575
Tel: 603-278 1000
Fax: 603-278 8868
A small, handsome, 1896 country inn with 34 elegantly furnished guest rooms on the grounds of the Mount Washington Resort. **$$–$$$$**

CENTER HARBOR
Kona Mansion
50 Jacobs Road, P.O. Box 458, 03226
Tel: 603-253 4900
This Tudor-style, 1900s mansion on 100 acres has 10 guest rooms, four one-and two-bedroom housekeeping cottages, and two three-bedroom chalets. Breakfast and dinner are served in the ornate, Victorian dining room. Nine-hole golf course, tennis courts, private beach. MAP available. **$$–$$$**

CONCORD
Centennial Inn
96 Pleasant Street, 03301
Tel: 603-227 7102/800-360 4839
Fax: 603-225 5031

www.someplacesdifferent.com
Restored, 1892 Victorian mansion has 32 individually-appointed guest rooms and suites with all the modern conveniences. **$$–$$$**
Wyman Farm
22 Wyman Road
Loudon, 03307
Tel/fax: 603-783 4467
An 18th-century Cape on a 60-acre hilltop, about a 10-minute drive from Canterbury Shaker Village. There are just three bedrooms, with B&B offered. **$**

DIXVILLE NOTCH
Balsams Grand Resort Hotel
Route 26, 03576
Tel: 603-255 3400/800-255 0600
Fax: 603-255 4221
www.thebalsams.com
A sprawling, 19th-century resort hotel, set in its own natural preserve. Activities include dancing and entertainment nightly, pool, tennis courts, skiing, fishing, and children's programs. Opulent lunch buffets, creative dinners. 215 rooms. FAP. Open mid-May–mid-October. **$$$$**

EATON CENTER
Inn at Crystal Lake
Route 153, 03832
Tel: 603-447 2120/800-343 7336
Fax: 603-447 3599
www.innatcrystallake.com
An 1884 Victorian in a sleepy lakeside village. Comfortable and relaxing B&B with 11 rooms, just minutes from Conway in a tranquil village on Crystal Lake. Walk to the beach. Snacks and cocktails. **$–$$$**
Rockhouse Mountain Farm Inn
off Route 153, 03832
Tel: 603-447 2880
An established family resort offering 15 MAP rooms on a 450-acre farm. There are resident horses, llamas, cows, chickens, and pigs, to keep the kids happy. **$**

ETNA
Moose Mountain Lodge
Moose Mountain Highway, 03570
Tel: 603-643 3529
www.moosemountainlodge.com

Price Categories
A very approximate guide to current room rates for a standard double per night is:
$$$$ = over $200
$$$ = $150–200
$$ = $100–150
$ = under $100

Leaf Peeping
For up-to-date information on where you can catch foliage at its most magnificent in the fall during September and October, call the states' Autumn Foliage Hotlines on the following numbers:
Connecticut 800-282 6863
Maine 800-533 9595
Massachusetts 800-227 6277
New Hampshire 800-258 3608
Rhode Island 800-354 4595
Vermont 800-828 3239

A classic 1938 ski lodge, with stone hearth and dizzying views. Located right off the Appalachian Trail, only 7 miles (11 km) from the Dartmouth College green. 12 rooms. FAP. **$$$**

FRANCONIA
Bungay Jar Bed & Breakfast
Easton Valley Road, 03580
Tel: 603-823 7775
www.bungayjar.com
An imaginatively retrofitted 18th-century barn on 8 private acres with great views. 6 rooms. B&B. **$–$$$$**
Franconia Inn
1300 Easton Valley Road, 03583
Tel: 603-823 5542/800-473 5299
Fax: 603-823 8078
www.franconiainn.com
A rambling, 19th-century 36-room inn-turned-resort with 107 acres to explore on foot, by ski, or on horseback. Other amusements include a pool, hot tub, tennis courts, and ice skating. 34 rooms. MAP. **$$**

GLEN
The Bernerhof
Route 302, 03838
Tel: 603-383 9132/800-548 8007
www.bernerhofinn.com
A Victorian, European-style inn with nine antiques-filled B&B rooms. Modern additions include double whirlpools. The restaurant serves "Middle European" fare. **$$**
Covered Bridge House B&B
Route 302, 03838
Tel: 603-383 9109/800-232 9109
www.coveredbridgehouse.com
A basic Colonial with six B&B rooms on the banks of the Saco River, near North Conway. Rooms are country-style with quilts, braided rugs, and rocking chairs. Guests can use the beach on the river for swimming. **$–$$**

GORHAM
Appalachian Mountain Club
Tel: 603-466 2727
The AMC operates two roadside dorms

and six high-mountain "huts" in the White Mountain National forest; reservations needed. 10 dorms. MAP. **$**

HAMPTON BEACH

Ashworth by the Sea
295 Ocean Boulevard, 03842
Tel: 603-926 6762/800-345 6736
(outside NH)
www.ashworthhotel.com
Year-round oceanfront accommodations directly across from Hampton Beach. 105 rooms with one queen or two double beds; TV, and air conditioning. **$–$$$$**

HANOVER

Hanover Inn at Dartmouth College
Main Street, 03755
Tel: 603-643 4300/800-443 7024
Fax: 603-646 3744/643 4433
www.hanoverinn.com
An integral part of the Dartmouth campus, a four-story, traditionally decorated Georgian brick house with 92 rooms and rockers on a long porch overlooking the common. **$$$–$$$$**

HENNIKER

Colby Hill Inn
3 The Oaks, 03242
Tel: 603-428 3281/800-531 0330
Fax: 603-428 9218
www.colbyhillinn.com
A rambling late 18th-century inn with a perennial garden and swimming pool. The 16 rooms. are furnished with antiques and Colonial reproductions; four rooms have fireplaces. Located west of Concord, near the Pat's Peak ski area. B&B. **$–$$$**

HOLDERNESS

The Manor on Golden Pond
Route 3 and Shepard Hill Road
03245
Tel: 603-968 3348/800-545 2141
Fax: 603-968 2116
www.manorongoldenpond.com
A 1903 English manor-style stone mansion overlooking Squam Lake with a clay tennis court, swimming pool, private beach, and canoes. Some of the 21 rooms have fireplaces. MAP. **$$$$**

JACKSON

Inn at Thorn Hill
Thorn Hill Road, 03846
Tel: 603-383 4242/800-289 8990
Fax: 603-383 8062
www.innatthornhill.com
Walk to the village from this 1895, Stanford White designed this gambrel-roofed summer house, on a secluded slope with views of Mount Washington. Romantically decorated rooms, suites, and cottages. Adjacent to Jackson cross-country trail network. 19 rooms. MAP. **$$$–$$$$**
The Wentworth
Route 16A, 03846
Tel: 603-383 9700/800-637 0013
Fax: 603-383 4265
www.thewentworth.com
An 1869 grand hotel and rental houses in the center of the village adjoining an 18-hole golf course and cross-country ski center. 54 rooms. MAP. **$$$**
Whitney's Inn
Route 16b, 03846
Tel: 603-383 8916/800-677 5737
Fax: 603-383 6886
www.whitneysinn.com
A simply furnished comfy inn (with three cottages and 30 rooms for B&B), geared towards families. The inn is situated on 9 acres at the foot of Black Mountain, in a small-scale ski area. Extras include a pub and game room. **$$–$$$**
Wildcat Inn & Tavern
Route 16A, 03846
Tel: 603-383 4245/800-228 4245
A 12-room B&B with delightful, albeit tiny, suites in the social center of town. There's a fine informal restaurant which serves lunch and dinner. **$**

JAFFREY

Benjamin Prescott Inn
Route 124, 03452
Tel/fax: 603 532 6637
A sprawling 1820 B&B, decorated with handmade quilts and ship models, set amid a working dairy farm. Near Mount Monadnock. Ten rooms and suites. **$–$$**

KEENE

Carriage Barn
358 Main Street, 03431
Tel: 603-357 3812
www.carriagebarn.com
A Civil War-era barn that is simply furnished with antiques and handmade quilts in the four rooms. Situated just across the street from Keene State College. **$–$$**
E. F. Lane Hotel
30 Main Street, 03431
Tel: 603-357 7070/888-300 5056
Fax: 603-357 7075
www.someplacesdifferent.com
In part of an historic, c. 1890s complex in Central Square, the full-service hotel has 40 rooms and suites with original exposed brick walls and oversize windows, some with whirlpools. **$$$**

LINCOLN

Innseason Resorts South Mountain
Route 112, 03251
Tel: 800-654 6183
Fax: 603-745 6896
www.innseasonsresorts.com
A three-inn complex built around an old mill. Properties include: the Rivergreen Resort Hotel, a riverside condominium hotel; The Lodge at Lincoln Station, with hotel rooms, studios and suites with kitchenettes; and the Mill House Inn, a country inn with rooms and suites, a fitness sauna, and walkway to the Millfront Marketplace. **$$–$$$**

LITTLETON

Beal House Inn
2 West Main Street, 03561
Tel: 603-444 2661/888-616 2325
Fax: 603-444 6224
www.bealhouseinn.com
Restored 1833 Federal-style inn close to town has eight antiques-filled and cozy rooms and suites with four-poster beds and some fireplaces. The Flying Moose Cafe specializes in wood-grilled cuisine. **$$–$$$**
Thayer's Inn
111 Main Street, 03561
Tel/Fax: 603-444 6469
The white-columned Greek Revival inn in the center of town is one of New Hampshire's oldest hostelries. The 36 rooms range from small and simple to quite plush, but are all comfortable and reasonably priced. **$–$$**

MANCHESTER

Ash Street Inn
118 Ash Street 03104
Tel: 603-668 9908
Fax: 603-629 9532
www.ashstreetinn.com
Built in 1885 and renovated in 2000, the Queen City's premier intown B&B, a three-story Victorian, has many of its original 19th-century accents, including magnificent stained-glass windows. The antiques-filled guest rooms feature thick quilts, Egyptian cotton sheets, and down pillows. **$$**

NEW CASTLE

Wentworth by the Sea
Wentworth Road, 03854
Tel: 603-422 7322
www.wentworth.com
After extensive renovations, one of the seacoast's premier destination inns, a Victorian confection, has been brought into the Marriott fold and offers first-class accommodations. Most of the 161 rooms and suites have water views; there's a full-service spa and a

Price Categories

A very approximate guide to current room rates for a standard double per night is:

$$$$ = over $200
$$$ = $150–200
$$ = $100–150
$ = under $100

fine restaurant. Golf course adjacent. **$$$–$$$$**

NEW LONDON

New London Inn
140 Main Street, 03257
Tel: 603-526 2791/800-526 2791
www.newlondoninn.us
An in-town, 25-room 1792 inn with lots of antiques, an eclectic decor, a well regarded restaurant, and an inventive chef/innkeeper. **$$**

Inn at Pleasant Lake
Pleasant Street, 03257
Tel: 603-526 6271/800-626 4907
Fax: 603-526 4111
www.innatpleasantlake.com
A 1790 inn with 12 guest rooms on 5 acres overlooking the lake and Mount Kearsarge. Fixed-priced gourmet meals are served in the candlelit dining room; and tea is served daily. There are canoes and a rowboat for guests. **$$–$$$**

Maple Hill Farm
200 Newport Road, 03257
Tel: 603-526 2248/800-231 8637
www.maplehillfarm.com
A family-friendly, comfortably furnished 1824 farmhouse/B&B near Little Lake Sunapee (canoes and rowboats available) has 10 basic guest rooms (four with shared baths) with antiques and handmade quilts. Owners raise chickens, sheep and rabbits; younger guests may help gather eggs or watch yarn being spun. **$–$$**

NORTH CONWAY

The 1785 Inn
Route 16, 03860
Tel: 603-356 9025/800-421 1785
Fax: 603-356 6081
www.the1785inn.com
One of the oldest buildings in the Mount Washington valley, this colonial inn with spectacular mountain views is comfortably furnished with colonial, Victorian, and country-style pieces. 17 rooms with some shared baths. Outdoor pool. MAP available. **$$–$$$**

Farm By The River B&B
2555 West Side Road, 03860
Tel/fax: 603-356 2694/888 414 8353
www.farmbytheriver.com
A 1785 classic country farmhouse set on 70 acres, with gardens, a sugar

maple orchard, and a beach on the Saco River. Jacuzzis and year round horseriding. Located on a back road parallel to Route 16/302, one mile (1.6 km) from Echo Lake State Park. Eight rooms. B&B. **$$–$$$**

Stonehurst Manor
Route 16, 03860
Tel: 603-356 3113/800-525 9100
Fax: 603-356 3217
www.stonehurstmanor.com
A 100-year-old mansion amidst 33 acres of pine forest, once part of the summer estate of carpet baron Erastus Bigelow, has 25 rooms (seven with fireplaces), an outdoor pool, hot tub, and tennis court. MAP available. **$–$$**

NORTH SUTTON

Follansbee Inn on Kezar Lake
Route 114, 03260
Tel: 603-927 4221/800-626 4221
Fax: 603-927 6307
www.follansbeeinn.com
A cozy, 1840s lakeside inn with 2½ acres of land on the beach. There are 20 rooms for B&B, including two one-bedroom suites. **$–$$$**

NORTH WOODSTOCK

Woodstock Inn
Main Street (Route 3), 03262
Tel: 603-745 3951/800-321 3985
Fax: 603-745 3701
www.woodstockinnnh.com
Three Victorian inns in a bustling tourist town. The 21 rooms vary from romantic to family-friendly. Outdoor hot tub and beer garden brewery. **$–$$**

PITTSBURG

The Glen
First Connecticut Lake, 03592
The region's premier resort, a mile down a private road, offers full service, a lodge with spacious rooms or rustic log cabins, and maid service for all. Hiking, boats, motors, and guides. Open May–October. FAP. **$$$–$$$$**

PORTSMOUTH

Sise Inn
40 Court Street, 03801
Tel: 603-433 1200/877-747 3466
Fax: 603-431 1200
www.siseinn.com
An elegant, 1881 Queen Anne Victorian inn with 34 rooms in the center of town. Amenities include antique furnishings, fireplaces, whirlpool baths, and stereos in some rooms. **$$$–$$$$**

Inn at Strawbery Banke
314 Court Street, 03801

Tel: 603-436 7242/800-428 3933
www.innatstrawberybanke.com
1800 sea captain's house adjoining the historic preserve has seven handsome guest rooms and elegant gardens. B&B. **$$**

Martin Hill Inn
404 Islington Street, 03801
Tel: 603-436 2287
www.martinhillinn.com
An 1812 Colonial main house and a country-style 1850 guest house across the perennial gardens. Solicitous hosts and lavish breakfasts. 7 rooms. B&B. **$$**

Inn at Christian Shore
335 Maplewood Avenue, 03801
Tel: 603-431 6770
An antique appointed 1800s-Federal house, near the historic district. 5 rooms. B&B. **$$**

SNOWVILLE

Snowvillage Inn
92 Stuart Road, Off Route 153, 03832
Tel: 603-447 2818/800-447 4345
Fax: 603-447 5268
www.snowvillageinn.com
Austrian motifs pervade this high-perched eyrie. The 18 rooms are in the New England farmhouse-style main house, an old carriage barn, and a new lodge. Located south of Conway, near Crystal Lake. Tennis courts, hiking trails, sauna, cross-country skiing (including lessons), snowshoeing. MAP available. **$$–$$$$**

SUGAR HILL

Sugar Hill Inn
Route 117, 03580
Tel: 603-823 5621/800-548 4748
Fax: 603-823 5639
www.sugarhillinn.com
An 18th-century country inn on the side of Sugar Hill. Comfortable, country-style rooms in main house and cottages. 16 rooms. B&B. **$$$**

Sunset Hill House
Sunset Hill Road, 03585
Tel: 603-823 5522/800-786 4455
Fax: 603-823 5738
www.sunsethillhouse.com
Built in 1880, this inn (with a 30-ft deck and 30 B&B rooms) sits on a 1,700-foot ridge with sweeping views of the Presidential Range. The homey rooms all have mountain views, and some have bay windowed reading nooks. Facilities include pool, a golf course, and cross-country ski trails. **$$$–$$$$**

Hilltop Inn
Route 117, 03585
Tel: 603-823 5695/800-770 5695
Fax: 603-823 5518
www.hilltopinn.com

Price Categories

A very approximate guide to current room rates for a standard double per night is:

$$$$ = over $200
$$$ = $150–200
$$ = $100–150
$ = under $100

A homey 1895 Victorian inn serving large country-style breakfasts. Located 10 minutes from Franconia Notch. Six rooms. B&B. Pets welcome (fee). **$$–$$$**

SUNAPEE

Dexter's Inn and Tennis Club
Stage Coach Road, 03782
Tel: 603-763 5571/800-232 5571
A secluded yellow clapboard 1801 house with three all-weather courts and an outdoor pool. 17 rooms. Pets welcome (fee). MAP. **$$–$$$**

The Burkehaven
179 Burkehaven Road, 03782
Tel: 800-567 2788
Fax: 603-763 9065
www.burkehaven.com
Ten pleasant motel units overlooking Sunapee Harbor; outdoor pool. Pets welcome. **$**

TEMPLE

Birchwood Inn
Route 45, 03084
Tel: 603-878 3285
Fax: 603-878 2159
www.thebirchwoodinn.com
An 1800-brick inn with Rufus Porter murals. Guest rooms each have a theme: the Editorial Room displays newspapers (with noteworthy headlines), and the Train Room has photos and models of trains (of course). Convenient to Cathedral of the Pines. 7 rooms. B&B. **$**

TROY

The Inn at East Hill Farm
460 Monadnock Street
03465
Tel: 603-242 6495/800-242 6495
www.east-hill-farm.com
This 150-acre resort/working farm has cottages and inn rooms with mountain views. There are indoor and outdoor pools, a sauna, and facilities for tennis and horse-riding. Special programs for children are also on offer. **$$–$$$**

WATERVILLE VALLEY

Waterville Valley Resort
Waterville Valley, 03223

Tel: 800-468 2553
Fax: 603-236 4344
www.waterville.com
A resort complex with more than 700 rooms. cupped in a high valley, with skiing in winter, hiking, tennis, and other sports the rest of the year.
$–$$$$

WEST CHESTERFIELD

Chesterfield Inn
Route 9, 03466
Tel: 603-256 3211/800-365 5515
Fax: 603-256 6131
www.chesterfieldinn.com
A 1798 house, originally a tavern, converted to a luxurious 15-roomed B&B. Attractions include wet bars, whirlpool tubs, and antique fireplaces.
$$–$$$$

WHITEFIELD

Mountain View Grand
Mountain View Road, 03589
Tel: 603-837 2100/8866-484 3843
www.mountainviewgrand.com
The White Mountains' "newest" grand resort hotel is a faithfully-restored, four-seasons 1865 hostelry with 146 modern guestrooms, a European-style spa, a fine restaurant with unparalled views, and a Ralph Barton-designed 18 hole golf course fully renovated in 1999. **$$$–$$$$**

Spalding Inn
199 Mountain view Road, 03598
Tel: 603-837 2572/800-368 8439
Fax: 603-837 3062
www.spaldinginn.com
A quiet but full-scale family resort on 200 acres, operating since 1926, with golf course, tennis courts, and heated pool. Accommodations in the main inn, a lodge, and separate cottages. 45 rooms. B&B or MAP. **$$–$$$**

WOLFEBORO

Wolfeboro Inn
90 North Main Street, 03894
Tel: 603-569 3016/800-451 2389
Fax: 603-569 5375
www.wolfeboroinn.com
A luxury lakeside inn since 1812. Located a short walk from the village, the inn has a private beach, excursion boat, and fishing. 49 rooms. **$$–$$$$**

Where to Eat

BEDFORD

Bedford Village Inn
2 Old Bedford Road
Tel: 603-472 2001
Country club atmosphere in an elegantly-updated 18th-century inn south of Manchester. Lobster and

New Hampshire Trivia

The longest wooden bridge in the United States and longest two-span covered bridge in the world links Cornish, New Hampshire with Windsor, Vermont. It was built in 1866 and cost the princely sum of $9,000.

Atlantic salmon are often on the menu, which features continental fare. Sunday brunch is an event. **$$$–$$$$**

BRETTON WOODS

Mount Washington Hotel
Route 302
Tel: 603-278 1000
Old-fashioned and sometimes uneven fare in a formal dining room, but a fascinating glimpse of luxury past. An orchestra plays nightly. Reservations essential. **$$$**

CENTER SANDWICH

Corner House Inn
Main Street
(Routes 109 and 113)
Tel: 603-284 6219
Continental fare, antiques, and candlelight in a delightful 1849 house. Try the lobster and mushroom bisque and the double-thick lamb chops. Lunch June–October; dinner nightly. **$$**

DIXVILLE NOTCH

Balsams Grand Resort Hotel
Route 26
Tel: 603-255 3400/800-255 3400
Lavish buffet spreads are on offer at this impressive resort hotel. Reservations are required and the place is only open mid-May–mid-Oct. **$$$**

EATON CENTER

Palmer House Pub
Inn at Crystal Lake
Route 153
Tel: 603-447 3599
Belly up to the bar that was once in Boston's Ritz-Carlton for a bone-dry martini, or enjoy a sit-down bowl of chili, a pork porterhouse steak, or rack of lamb. **$$$–$$$$**

FRANCONIA

Franconia Inn
1300 Easton Valley Road
Tel: 603-823 5542
Ambitious Continental cuisine served in a formal dining room with mountain views. **$$$**

Lovett's Inn by Lafayette Brook
Profile Road
Tel: 603-823 7761
A mix of traditional favorites and more adventurous fare in an 18th century inn. Roast pork, duck and chicken Forestiere are among the house specialties. Dinner only. **$$**

GLEN

The Bernerhof
Route 302
Tel: 603-383 9132/800-548 8007
Alpine delights, including spaetzle and Provimi veal, are on offer at the ski-country Bernerhof. Other specialties include Wiener schnitzel and cheese fondue for two. A Taste of the Mountains Cooking School has been an institution here for almost 20 years. **$$$**

Red Parka Pub
Route 302
Tel: 603-383 4344
Offering "good food and good times" for more than 30 years. The steaks are aged, the prime rib prime, the fish fresh, and the salad bar salads all homemade. Couples without kids might opt to dine on the porch or in the Skiboose, a 1914 railroad car. **$$–$$$**

HANOVER

The Hanover Inn at Dartmouth College
Main Street
Tel: 603-643 4300
Classic Contemporary American cuisine in "Edwardian elegance and intimacy". Rack of lamb and pan-seared tuna are among the entrées. Sunday brunch is a local tradition. The restaurant has an outstanding wine list. Al fresco dining is available on The Terrace in season. Main dining room open for breakfast Mon–Sat; lunch weekdays; dinner Tues–Sat. **$$$**

HENNIKER

Colby Hill Inn
3 The Oaks, Henniker
Tel: 603-428 3281
A late 18th-century inn with country views and Continental cuisine with New England accents. Try the house signature Chicken Colby Hill, a boneless breast stuffed with lobster, leeks and boursin cheese. Dinner only Tuesday–Saturday. **$$$**

HOLDERNESS

The Manor on Golden Pond
Route 3 and Shepard Hill Road
Tel: 603-968 3348
Excellent New American cuisine and a

menu that changes daily in a baronial setting. *Prix-fixe* three or five course dinners are available; the wine list is superb. Breakfast and dinner. **$$$**

JACKSON

Inn at Thorn Hill
Thorn Hill Road
Tel: 603-383 4242
A four-course *prix-fixe* menu of country-sophisticate cuisine in a handsome country house. Reservations required. **$$$**

Wentworth Resort Hotel Dining Room
Route 16a
Tel: 603-383 9700
Exceptional Continental cuisine with New England ingredients in a fancy French provincial dining room. The more casual lounge serves mountain specialties including fondues and raclette. **$$$**

Thompson House Eatery
Routes 16a and 16
Tel: 603-383 9341
Innovative salads and sandwiches, and luscious entrées, in an 1800s barn with flowery patio. Closed Tues. **$$$–$$$$**

Wildcat Inn & Tavern
Route 16a
Tel: 603-383 4245
The owner/chef Marty Sweeney prepares treats such as baked scallops, lasagna, and lobster fettuccini in one of the area's most popular restaurants, which serves three meals daily. **$$**

KEENE

One Seventy Six Main
176 Main Street
Tel: 603-357 3100
Upscale pub grub (burgers, pasta, and seafood) and a good beer list in a National Register of Historic Places building across from Keene State College. **$$**

LITTLETON

Flying Moose Café
Beal House Inn
2 West Main St (Routes 302 and 28)
Tel: 603-444 2661.

Restaurant Prices

Prices are approximate, but for a three-course meal for one (excluding beverages, tax and tip), the following guidelines may prove helpful:

$$$$ = over $40
$$$ = $28–40
$$ = $15–28
$ = under $15

Wood-grilled steaks, fresh seafood, and fabulous, homemade desserts in a historic inn close to town. **$$–$$$**

MANCHESTER

Fratello's Ristorante Italiano
155 Dow Street
Tel: 603-624 2022
Traditional Italian dishes including veal piccata and Caesar salad in a renovated, turn of the 20th-century textile mill. **$$**

Red Arrow Diner
61 Lowell Avenue
Tel: 603-626 1118
A 1903 luncheonette, open 24 hours. **$**

MOULTONBORO

The Woodshed
Lee's Mill Road
Tel: 603-476 2311
New England classics – clam chowder, scrod, prime rib, and Indian pudding – plus a raw bar in an 1860s barn. **$$–$$$**

NEW LONDON

The New London Inn
140 Main Street
Tel: 603-526 2791
Good for inventive New England cuisine, with dishes such as popovers, fresh Atlantic season and prime steaks, along with Caesar salad and home baked breads. **$$–$$$**

NORTH CONWAY

Stonehurst Manor
Route 16
Tel: 603-356 3113
Continental cuisine such as smoked roasted duck, veal Oscar and pastas, plus wood-fired, oven-baked pizzas. **$–$$$**

NORTH WOODSTOCK

Woodstock Inn
Main Street (Route 3)
Tel: 603-745 3951
A variety of appealing options, at a range of prices. Continental cuisine is served in the Victorian parlor, casual fare from meatloaf to fajitas is on offer at the Woodstock Station cafe, and microbrews are served in the Woodstock Inn Brewery. **$–$$$**

PINKHAM NOTCH

Appalachian Mountain Club
Pinkham Notch Camp
Route 16
Tel: 603-466 2727
Hearty dinner for hikers. **$**

PORTSMOUTH

Library Restaurant at the Rockingham House
401 State Street
Tel: 603-431 5202
International cuisine (rack of lamb, filet mignon) served amid carved mahogany paneling and masses of books in a former luxury hotel (now converted to condominiums). **$$$**

Muddy River Smokehouse
21 Congress Street
Tel: 603-430 9582
Great BBQ, homemade chili, and a large selection of beers. Blues club downstairs. **$–$$**

The Wellington
67 Bow Street
Tel: 603-431 2989
A small, intimate restaurant with harbor views and creative American fare. **$$–$$$**

Dolphin Striker
15 Bow Street
Tel: 603-431 5222
A riverfront tavern in a restored, 18th-century warehouse specializing in New American dishes including seafood and beef, as well as a variety of pastas. Lunch Wed–Sat; dinner. **$$**

Portsmouth Brewery
56 Market Street
Tel: 603-431 1115
A microbrewery with international munchies as well as burgers, sandwiches, and salads. **$–$$**

Cafe Brioche
14 Market Square
Tel: 603-430 9225
Tasty French pastries including croissants, brioches, and quiches are served at this friendly sidewalk cafe. **$**

SNOWVILLE

Snowvillage Inn
92 Stuart Road (Off Route 153)
Tel: 603-447 2818
Candlelight dinners include dishes including roast rack of lamb and filet of beef tenderloin, along with inspiring, unparalleled views. **$$**

SUGAR HILL

Polly's Pancake Parlor
Route 117
Tel: 603-823 5575.
The place to go for tasty – if somewhat expensive – pancakes. **$**

TEMPLE

London Tavern
Birchwood Inn
Route 45
Tel: 603-878 3285
The classic English menu includes traditional dishes such as steak and ale pie, bangers and mash, shepherd's pie, and, for dessert, spotted dick and custard. Dinner Wed–Sun. **$$–$$$**

WOLFEBORO

The Wolfeboro Inn
44 North Main Street
Tel: 603-569 3016
New England fare along with a few northern Italian dishes are served in the 1812 Dining Room; the tavern serves sandwiches, salads, soups, and a full dinner menu. Ask for a table overlooking Wolfeboro Bay. **$–$$$**

Culture

CLASSICAL MUSIC

The Music Hall (tel: 603-436 2400; 28 Chestnut Street) features international classical musicians, while **Music in Market Square** is a classical summer series (tel: 603-436 9109; North Church); both are located in Portsmouth.

North Country Chamber Players (tel: 603-444 0309) performs world-class chamber music throughout the area from mid-July to mid-August.

ROCK AND POP

Gaslight Restaurant (tel: 603-430 8582; 64 Market Street, Portsmouth) features rock, hiphop and techno acts Thurs–Sat.

OPERA

Opera North (tel: 603-643 1946; 511 North Park Street, Lebanon) performs at the historic Lebanon Opera House.

THEATER

Seacoast Repertory Theater (tel: 603-433 4472; 125 Bow Street, Portsmouth) features adult and children's productions year-round.

Colonial Theater (tel: 603-352 2033; 95 Main Street, Keene) showcases live performances and films.

Palace Theater (tel: 603-668 5588;

Live Music

Press Room
77 Daniel Street, Portsmouth
Tel: 603-431 5186
Has live folk, Irish and blues music, with a country-western jam session every Friday.

The Music Hall
28 Chestnut Street, Portsmouth
Tel: 603-436 2400
Offers a variety of musical performances all year.

Hopkins Center for the Arts
Dartmouth College, Hanover
Tel: 603-646 2422
Arts venue with live music all year round.

80 Hanover Street, Manchester) puts on six productions a year, including dinner theater by its resident company **Stage One Productions**.

Hopkins Center for the Arts (tel: 603-646 2422; Dartmouth College, Hanover) stages multiple musicals and various other theater productions.

New London Barn Playhouse (tel: 603-526 4631; 290 Main Street), the state's oldest consecutively-operated theater, presents plays and musicians in a renovated barn in the summer.

Many theaters present special children's productions throughout the season.

CINEMA

Hopkins Center for the Arts (tel: 603-646 2422; Dartmouth College, Hanover) shows classic and experimental films, while **Nugget Theater** (tel: 603-643 2769; S Main Street, Hanover) shows current films.

ART GALLERIES

Your best bets are in Portsmouth: **New Hampshire Art Association-Robert Lincoln Levy Gallery** (tel: 603-431 4230; 136 State Street) exhibits paintings, photographs, and prints, while **Pierce Gallery** (tel: 603-436 1988; 105 Market Street) offers New Hampshire and Maine coastal scenics.

Outdoor Activities

BIKING

Several ski areas offer summer and fall mountain biking. **Loon Mountain** attracts novice through advanced riders to 21 miles (34 km) of trails, where lifts serve the steepest biking routes. Nearby, the self-guided **Franconia Notch Bike Tour** starts at

Echo Lake, passes the Old Man of the Mountain, and ends at the Loon Mountain ski area.

Near Mount Washington, **Great Glen Trails** (tel: 603-466 2333) offers learn-to-mountain-bike courses, ranging from a short introductory class to more in-depth skill-building. If inn-to-inn touring is more your speed, call Harrisville- based **Monadnock Bicycling Touring** (tel: 603-827 3925).

CANOEING, KAYAKING, AND RAFTING

Saco Bound River Outfitters (tel: 603-447 2177) runs a river kayaking school, and leads canoeing expeditions, guided kayak trips, and white-water rafting excursions at several New Hampshire and Maine locations.

North Star Canoe Livery (tel: 603-542 6929), based in Cornish, conducts canoe trips on the Connecticut River. Appalachian Mountain Club's New Hampshire chapter (tel: 603-466 2725; www.amc-nh.org) offers a **Spring Whitewater Canoe School** one weekend each April. **Seacoast Kayak** (tel: 603-474 1025; 210 Ocean Boulevard, Seabrook Beach) rents kayaks for flatwater and ocean access.

FISHING

Great Glen Trails *(see Biking, page 395)* offers introductory fishing classes and arranges guided fly fishing excursions. **North Country Angler** (tel: 603-356 6000), also based in the White Mountains, runs

guided fly-fishing weekends.

For ocean fishing, several charter companies operate on the seacoast, including **Atlantic Fishing Fleet** (tel: 603-964 5220; Rye) and **Al Gauron Deep Sea Fishing** (tel: 603-926 2469; Hampton Beach).

HIKING

The 86 major peaks of the White Mountains provide plenty of hiking challenges. The **US Forest Service** (tel: 603-528 8721; Laconia) provides specific trail information.

The **Appalachian Mountain Club** (tel: 603-466 2725) has detailed hiking trail information; this group maintains a network of huts in the White Mountains providing overnight accommodations. For hut reservations, tel: 603-466 2727.

For inn-to-inn hiking tours, contact **New England Hiking Holidays** (tel: 603-356 9696, 800-869 0949) in North Conway. For guided hiking tours (and canoe and kayaking adventure tours), contact **Outdoor Escapes New Hampshire** (tel: 603-528 0316).

SAILING

Marinas abound on Lake Winnipesaukee, the state's largest lake. Although it's a popular power boating spot, some marinas rent sailboats, including **Fay's Boat Yard** (tel: 603-293 8000; Guilford).

SKIING

Major areas include: **Waterville Valley** (tel: 603-236 8311), **Loon Mountain** (tel: 603-745 8111; Lincoln), and

Cannon Mountain (tel: 603-823 5563; Franconia).

Smaller areas include: **Attitash Bear Peak** (tel: 603-374 2368 or 800-223 7669; Bartlett), **Bretton Woods** (tel: 603-278 5000) and **Wildcat** (tel: 603-466 3326/800-255 6439), both in Jackson.

The state's largest cross-country ski centers are **Jackson Ski Touring Foundation** (tel: 800-927 6697) and **Mt Washington Valley Ski Touring** (tel: 603-356 9920; off Route 16, Intervale).

South of the White Mountains you'll find the **Nordic Center** (tel: 603-236 4666; Waterville Valley) and **Franconia Village Cross Country Center** at the Franconia Inn (tel: 603-823 5542/800-473 5299).

Shopping

WHERE TO SHOP

Shops fill Portsmouth's revitalized waterfront area near Market, Bow and Ceres Streets. Route 16 in North Conway – a collection of more than 200 outlet stores – is also good for general shopping.

MALLS

The 19th-century **Colony Mill Marketplace** (tel: 603-357 1240; 222 West Street, Keene) houses 33 stores. **Mall of New Hampshire** (tel: 603-669 0433; 1500 S Willow Street, Manchester) has 88 shops and three department stores.

New Hampshire Festivals

Spring
The town of Lisbon, near Cannon Mountain, bids farewell to winter in May with the annual **Lilac Festival** (tel: 603-838 6397).

The Sheep and Wool Festival (tel: 603-746 4191) at the fairgrounds in Hopkinton, readies in a different way – with shearing, spinning and weaving, as well as border collie demonstrations.

Summer
Portsmouth's **Market Square Days** (tel: 603-436 1118) in June draw over 100,000 people to an outdoor street fair with concerts, a 10km road race, and other festivities.

In early July, the **Seacoast Jazz Festival**, held in Prescott Park (tel: 603-436 1118), showcases local performers.

Motorcycle fans may want to visit the **Laconia Motorcycle Rally and Race Week** (tel: 603-366 2000) for eight days in June.

For a different sort of excitement, the annual **Mount Washington Road Race** (tel: 603-466 3988; www.gsrs.com for entries) takes runners up the 6,288-ft (2,000-meter) peak along the historic Auto Road.

With about 200 artists exhibiting at Mount Sunapee State Park, the **League of New Hampshire Craftsmen's Fair** (tel: 603-224 3375) in August draws thousands of visitors interested in traditional New England crafts.

Fall
In September, Hopkinton looks like Scotland when the **New Hampshire**

Highland Games (tel: 603-229 1975), with Scottish music, dances and other cultural events, come to the state fairgrounds.

During the annual **Hampton Seafood Festival** (tel: 603-926 8717), also in September, local restaurants take their seafood creations to the streets for a two-day food fair.

Winter
Both Portsmouth and Wolfeboro host **First Night** celebrations on New Year's Eve.

In March, more than 50 sugarhouses statewide open their doors for syrup-making demonstrations (and free samples) during the **Maple Weekend**.

BOOKS

In Portsmouth, **Gulliver's Books** (tel: 603-431 5556; 7 Commercial Alley) is an excellent outlet for regional and general travel books, maps, and globes. Upstairs, **Second Run** (tel: 603-431 2000) has a fine selection of used books. **River Run Book Store** (tel: 603-431 2100) carries general fiction and nonfiction.

In the Lakes Region, **Black's Paper Store and Gift Shop** (tel: 603-569 4444) on Main Street in Wolfeboro has a fine selection of local authors.

Eagle Books (tel: 603-357 8721; 19 West Street, Central Square, Keene) specializes in writer's projects books, and **Toadstool Bookshop** (tel: 603-352 8815; Colony Mill, Keene) carries general titles and also has a large café. **Dartmouth Bookstore** (tel: 643 3616; 33 S Main Street, Hanover) stocks upwards of 130,000 titles.

ANTIQUES

The **New Hampshire Antiques Dealers Association** (www.nhada.org) has a comprehensive list of antique dealers.

Antique stores, including **Antiques at Colony Mill** (tel: 603-358 6343; West Street, Keene), which represents more than 100 dealers, abound in the Monadnock region.

Several shops line the Main Street (Route 302) of Bethlehem, and the town hosts a free flea market Saturdays from June–October.

Route 4 west of Durham is known as Antiques Alley; the road is lined with antiques stores selling a huge assortment of collectibles.

ARTS AND CRAFTS

League of New Hampshire Craftsmen (tel: 603-224 1471; 205 North Main Street, Concord, and other locations throughout the state) has a gallery of handmade crafts.

The **Artisan's Workshop** (tel: 603-763 5226; in Sunapee Harbor and at 186 Main Street in New London) sells local crafts.

Hampshire Pewter (tel: 603-569 4944; 43 Mill Street,Wolfeboro) hand crafts pewter items and offers weekday tours.

The **Dorr Mill Store** (tel: 800-846 3677; Hale Street) in Guild is a national craft center for hand hooking, braiding, and wool quilting.

GIFTS

Littleton Grist Mill (tel: 603-444 8489/999-284 8489; 18 Mill Street) in Littleton, in a restored, waterwheel-powered 1798 working grist mill, sells fine crafts, gifts, and organically-grown whole grains and stone-ground flour.

Children

JOURNEYS BY STEAM TRAIN

Winnipesaukee Railroad (tel: 603-279 5253; S. Main Street, Weirs Beach) runs historic coaches around the lake. **Conway Scenic Railroad** (tel: 603-356 5251/800-232 5251; North Conway) offers excursions from the 1874 station. **Mount Washington Cog Railway** (tel. 603-278 5404) has the second-steepest railway track in the world.

AMUSEMENT/THEME PARKS

Children can explore caves carved by the Ice Age at **Lost River Gorge & Boulder Caves** (tel: 603-745 8031; Route 112) in North Woodstock. **Clark's Trading Post and the White Mountain Central Railroad** (tel: 603-745 8913; Route 3, Lincoln) has live bear shows, a family circus, and train excursions.

Christmas is alive all summer at **Santa's Village** (tel: 603-586 4445; Route 2, Jefferson), with rides and live reindeer. Next door, bumper boats, waterslides, and go karts are just part of the fun at **Six Gun City & Fort Splash Water Park** (tel: 603-586 4592). Theme rides, shows, and storybook characters are all part of the fun at **Story Land** (tel: 603-383 4186), on Route 16 in Glen.

Whale Watching

Whale watching and cruises to the nine Isles of Shoals are some of New Hampshire's big attractions. Firms offering these include:
The Isles of Shoals
Tel: 800-441 4620/603-431 5500
New Hampshire Seacoast Cruises
Tel: 603-964 5545
Portsmouth Harbor Cruises
Tel: 800-776 0915/603-436 8084

Maine

The Place

Known as: The Pine Tree State.
Motto: *Dirigo* (I direct).
Origin of name: called after ancient French province.
Entered Union: March 15, 1820, when it was separated from Massachusetts to form the 23rd state.
Capital: Augusta.
Area: 33,215 sq. miles (91,653 sq. km).
Highest point: Mount Katahdin, 5,268 ft (1,606 meters).
Population: 1.24 million.
Population density: 35 people per sq. mile (13 per sq. meter).
Economy: services (including tourism) and manufacturing (paper and paper products, footwear and other leather goods, lumber), plus fishing, agriculture, and forestry.
Annual visitors: 8 million.
National representation: two senators and two representatives to Congress.
Famous citizens: Longfellow, Sir Hiram and Hudson Maxim, and Edna Street Vincent Millay.

Where to Stay

Note that many of Maine's hotels and inns are open only in summer.

ADDISON

Pleasant Bay B&B
386 West Side Road, P.O. Box 222, 04606
Tel: 207-483 4490
Fax: 207-483 4653
www.pleasantbay.com
On the shores of Pleasant River, this 110-acre working llama farm has four guest rooms with shared or private baths, and splendid views. Room four, a two-room suite, has a TV, microwave, and fridge. **$–$$**

BAR HARBOR

The Tides
119 West Street, 04609
Tel: 207-288 4968
www.barharbortides.com
An 1887 Greek Revival manor B&B

with views of Frenchman's Bay. Three elegant suites with working fireplaces and ocean vistas. **$$$$**

Bar Harbor Inn
Newport Drive, 04609
Tel: 207-288 3351/800-248 3351
Fax: 207-288 5296
www.barharborinn.com
For more than 125 years, a Bar Harbor institution; 153 rooms in three buildings in town. Most rooms have fireplaces and views; some have private decks. **$$$–$$$$**

Manor House Inn
106 West Street, 04609
Tel: 207-288 3759/800-437 0088
Fax: 207-288 2974
www.barharbormanorhouse.com
An 1887 Victorian inn with 14 one- and two-bedroom units and a carriage house surrounded by gardens. **$$–$$$**

Edgewater Motel & Cottages
Salisbury Cove
Tel: 207-288 3491/888-310 9920
www.edgewaterbarharbor.com
Oceanfront lodging, with seven fireplace units with kitchens and a motel with porches or balconies. Private pebble beach. **$$**

BATH

Inn at Bath
969 Washington Street, 04530
Tel: 207-443 4294/800-423 0964
Fax: 207-443 4295
www.innatbath.com
An elegant, comfortable antiques-filled 1810 inn/B&B with nine guest rooms with wood-burning fireplaces and whirlpool baths. **$$–$$$**

Fairhaven Inn
North Bath Road, 04530
Tel: 207-443 4391/888-443 4391
www.maincoast.com/fairhaveninn
A 1790 Colonial inn B&B set in 20 acres overlooking the Kennebec river. The eight guest rooms furnished with four-poster beds and handmade quilts. Trails for hiking and cross-country skiing. **$–$$**

The Galen C. Moses House
1009 Washington Street, 04530
Tel: 207-442 8771
Fax: 207-442 0808
www.galenmoses.com
National Register of Historic Homes, 1874 pink Victorian mansion has five antiques-filled guest rooms: one has a marble fireplace and bay windows. **$$**

BELFAST

Harbor View House of 1807
213 High Street, 04915
Tel: 207-338 3811/877-393 3811
www.harborviewhouse.com
Vintage Federal mansion offers views of Penobscot Bay and six well-

furnished rooms with working fireplaces (five have views of the water) and TV. **$$**

The Jeweled Turret Inn
40 Pearl Street, 04915
Tel: 207-338 2304/800-696 2304
1890s home with gables and turrets has seven antiques-filled bedrooms, a handsomely-fireplaced den, and several verandahs. **$–$$**

BETHEL

Bethel Inn & Country Club
Village Common, 04217
Tel: 207-824 2175/800-654 0125
Fax: 207-824 2233
www.bethelinn.com
A rambling yellow clapboard 1913 country inn and townhouses, with tennis, golf, and a lake for water sports. MAP available. **$$$–$$$$**

Telemark Inn
RFD 2, Box 800, 04217
Tel: 207 836 2703
www.telemarkinn.com
A secluded 1900 Adirondack-style lodge with six B&B rooms. The lodge is 10 miles (16 km) west of Bethel, and outdoor activities include llama treks and "skijoring", cross-country skiing pulled by dogs. **$$–$$$$**

The Ames Place
46 Broad Street, 04217
Tel: 207-824 3170
Fax: 207-824 0276
Two-room B&B in a lovely 1850 home with personable hosts; bookstore attached. **$**

Holidae House
85 Main Street, 04217
Tel: 207-824 3400/800-882 3306
A bargain seven-room Victorian B&B, considering the in-town location. **$–$$**

Sunday River Inn
23 Skiway Road, 04217
Tel: 207-824 2410/866-232 4354
Fax: 207-824 3181
www.sundayriverinn.com
A handsome ski dorm with its own cross-country center. MAP. **$**

BLUE HILL

Blue Hill Inn
Union Street, 04614
Tel: 207-374 2844/800-826 7415
Fax: 207-374 2829
www.bluehillinn.com
A 12-room MAP inn in an 1830s Federal-style inn with six fireplaces one block from Blue Hill bay in a lovely village. Cocktails are served in the garden during clement weather. **$$–$$$**

Blue Hill Farm Country Inn
Route 15, 04614
Tel: 207-374 5126
Fax: 207-374 5126
www.bluehillfarminn.com
A 14-room B&B (seven rooms in the

farmhouse, seven in a renovated barn) in a rural retreat on 48 acres 5 miles (8 km) from Blue Hill village. **$**

BOOTHBAY HARBOR AREA

Spruce Point Inn
Grandview Avenue, Boothbay Harbor, 04538
Tel: 207-633 4152/800-553 0289
Fax: 207-433 7138
www.sprucepointinn.com
An 100-year-old MAP inn and resort (including cottages and condominiums, totaling 92 rooms) on a 100-acre peninsula. Activities include swimming pool, tennis court, fitness room, croquet, badminton, and a putting green. Shuttle bus into town. **$$$$**

Fisherman's Wharf Inn
22 Commercial Street, Pier 6, 04538
Tel: 207-633 5090/800-628 6872
Fax: 207-633 5092
www.fishermanswharfinn.com
Rooms and suites overlooking the harbor in a downtown complex. The restaurant has outside dining. Open mid-May–late October. **$$–$$$**

Five Gables Inn
Murray Hill Road
East Boothbay, 04544
Tel: 207-633 4551/800-451 5048
www.fivegablesinn.com
This 16-room B&B in a spiffed-up 1865 summer hotel has views of Lineken Bay and the ocean from the broad verandah (complete with hammock). **$$–$$$**

Linekin Bay Resort
Wall Point Road
Boothbay Harbor, 04538
Tel: 207-633 2494/866-847 2103
Fax: 207-633 0580
www.linekinbayresort.com
An old-fashioned seaside resort with complimentary sailing instruction. 70 rooms FAP. **$$–$$$**

BROOKSVILLE

Oakland House
Herrick Road, 0461
Tel: 207-359 8521/800-359 7352
Fax:207-359 9865
www.oaklandhouse.com
A casual 1889 complex with waterside cottages offering 33 MAP rooms set in 50 acres near Blue Hill. **$$–$$$$**

Price Categories

A very approximate guide to current room rates for a standard double per night is:
$$$$ = over $200
$$$ = $150–200
$$ = $100–150
$ = under $100

BRUNSWICK

Captain Daniel Stone Inn
10 Water Street, 04011
Tel/fax: 207-725 9898/877-573 5151
www.captaindanielstoneinn.com
An upscale Federal inn overlooking the
Adroscoggin River. 34 rooms, many
with whirlpool baths. **$$$–$$$$**

Brunswick Bed and Breakfast
165 Park Row, 04011
Tel: 207-729 4914/800-299 4914
Fax: 207-725 1759
www.brunswickbnb.com
An historic house decorated with
handmade quilts, within walking
distance to the Bowdoin College
campus. Five simply furnished guest
rooms. **$–$$**

CAMDEN

Camden Harbor Inn
83 Bayview Street, 04843
Tel: 207-236 4200/800-236 4266
Fax: 207-236 7063
www.camdenharborinn.com
A porch-encircled 1874 B&B. The 22
rooms are furnished with period
antiques; some have fireplaces and
decks, balconies, or patios. **$$–$$$$**

Norumbega
63 High Street (Route 1), 04843
Tel: 207-236 4646/877-363 4646
Fax: 207-236 0824
www.norumegainn.com
13 rooms. B&B. A grand 1880s
Victorian stone castle overlooking the
bay. Furnished like an English country
house, the inn has a three-story turret
and seven fireplaces. Much
photographed. **$$$–$$$$**

Lord Camden Inn
24 Main Street, 04843
Tel: 207-236 4325
www.lordcamdeninn.com
Restored, four-story, 1893 Masonic
Hall right in town has modern rooms
and suites with balconies overlooking
the harbor. **$$$**

Windward House
6 High Street, 04843
Tel: 207-236 9656
Antiques, an English garden and all-
out breakfasts in this eight-room B&B.
$$–$$$

Lodge at Camden Hills
P.O. Box 794, Camden, 04843,
(Route 1)
Tel: 207-236 8478/800-832 7058
Fax: 207-236 7163
www.thelodgeatcamdenhills.com
Twenty units, including suites and
jacuzzi cottages, in park-like setting
with views of woods. **$$**

Maine Stay Inn
22 High Street (Route 1), 04853
Tel: 207-236 9636
Fax: 207-236 0621
www.camdenmainestay.com

An 1802 house with period
furnishings, a five-minute walk from
the town center. Two parlors have
wood-burning fireplaces; a glass-
enclosed porch overlooks the
gardens. 8 rooms. B&B. **$$–$$$**

Whitehall Inn
52 High Street (Route 1), 04843
Tel: 207-236 3391/800-789 6565
Fax: 207-236 4427
www.whitehall-inn.com
A venerable 1834 home, converted
into an inn/B&B in 1901. The 39
rooms are small and simple and some
share baths, but are all quite
charming. **$$–$$$**

CAPE ELIZABETH

Inn by the Sea
40 Bowery Beach Road
(Route 77), 04107
Tel: 207-799 3134/800-888 4287
Fax: 207-799 4779
www.innbythesea.com
A superb inn and resort connected by
boardwalk to Crescent Beach. Rooms,
suites and cottage condominiums with
Chippendale-style pieces, plus wicker
and white pine. Pool and tennis
courts. Pets welcome. **$$$$**

CAPE NEWAGEN

Newagen Seaside Inn
Route 27, 04552
Tel: 207-633 5242/800-654 5242
Fax: 207-633 5340
www.newagenseasideinn.com
An old-fashioned full-service resort,
with saltwater and freshwater pools,
tennis, and rowboats at the tip of
Southport Island, 6 miles (10 km)
from Boothbay Harbor. 26 rooms and
shorefront cottages. MAP available.
$$–$$$

CASTINE

Pentagoet Inn
Main Street at Perkins Street, 04421
Tel: 207-326 8616/800-845 1701
www.pentagoet.com
Castine's oldest, original "summer
hotel" is a turreted, 1894 Queen Anne
Victorian beauty with 16 rooms for
B&B. It overlooks the harbor and has
a wonderful wrap-around porch for
people-watching. **$$–$$$**

Castine Inn
Main Street, 04421
Tel: 207-326 4365
Fax: 207-326 4570
www.castineinn.com
A simply furnished 1898 clapboard
inn with 20 rooms for B&B. The
comfortable living room has a
fireplace and there's also a
distinguished restaurant. **$$–$$$**

Village Inn
6 Water Street, 04421
Tel: 207-326 9510
The four rooms at this B&B are very
simple but there's a wonderful in-
house bakery. **$**

CHEBEAGUE ISLAND

Chebeague Island Inn
Box 492, 04017
Tel: 207-846 5155
Fax: 207-846 4265
www.chebeagueinn.com
Constructed in 1925 after the original
structure was destroyed in a fire, this
three-story clapboard inn with 21
rooms for B&B is a classic summer
hotel, accessible only by ferry, just
north of Portland. **$$**

CHESUNCOOK

Chesuncook Lake House
Box 656, Route 76, 04441
Accessible only by boat, air or
snowmobile, this 1864 farmhouse in
the middle of an abandoned lumbering
camp has four guest rooms with
shared bath. Rate is Full American
Plan. **$$**

DEER ISLE

Pilgrim's Inn
Main Street (Route 15 A), 04622
Tel: 207-348 6615/888-778 7505
www.pilgrimsinn.com
A four-story, 1793 inn with antique-
filled guest rooms and seaside
cottages. Pleasant views over the
harbor and a mill pond. 15 rooms.
MAP. **$$–$$$**

EASTPORT

Weston House
26 Boynton Street, 04631
Tel: 207-853 2907/800-853 2907
Fax: 207-853 0981
www.westonhouse-maine.com
This 1802 Federal manse (former
minister's house), at the easternmost
town in Maine near Campobello
Island, is now a four-room B&B. One
room has a fireplace and YV. The inn
once hosted the naturalist John
James Audubon (1785–1851). **$**

FREEPORT

Harraseeket Inn
162 Main Street, 04032
Tel: 207-865 9377/800-342 6423
Fax: 207-865 1684
www.harraseeketinn.com
Luxury in a town of bargains. An 1850
Greek Revival home with modern
appointments, an indoor pool, and
elegant gardens. Many of the 84

rooms have fireplaces. **$$$–$$$$**
Royalsborough Inn at the Bagley House
1290 Royalsborough Road
(Route 136), 04222
Tel: 207-865 6566/800-765 1772
Fax: 207-353 5878
www.royalsboroughinn.com
A 1772 Colonial B&B with eight rooms in the country, 10 minutes from town. Breakfasts are served in the kitchen with its massive brick fireplace and beehive oven. **$–$$**

GEORGETOWN

Grey Havens Inn
Reid Park Road, 04548
Tel: 207-371 2616
Fax: 207-371 2613
www.greyhavens.com
A Shingle-style 1904 inn with a wraparound verandah on an oceanfront hillside near Bath. 14 rooms. B&B. **$$$–$$$$**

GREENVILLE

Chalet Moosehead Lakefront Motel
Route 15, Greenville Junction, 04442
Tel: 207-695 2950/800-290 3645
www.mooseheadlodging.com
The deluxe units at this modern, intown motel have private balconies; there are also standard units and efficiencies that permit pets ($10/nightly). Open all year. **$–$$**
Lodge at Moosehead Lake
Lily Bay Road, 04441
Tel: 207-695 4400
Fax: 207-695 2281
www.lodgeatmooseheadlake.com
An eminently civilized wilderness retreat in a 1917 summer estate. Rooms have four-poster beds and whirlpool baths, some have private decks and spectacular lake views. 8 rooms. B&B. **$$$–$$$$**
Greenville Inn
Norris Street, 04441
Tel: 207-695 2206/888-695 6000
Fax: 207-695 0335
www.greenvilleinn.com
A lumber baron's opulent 1895 mansion, plus six simpler cottages, on a hill in town overlooking Moosehead Lake. Ornate woodwork and stained glass set a formal tone in the inn's common rooms. **$$–$$$**

ISLE AU HAUT

The Keeper's House
Stonington, 04681
Tel: 207-367 2261
A 100-year-old lighthouse keeper's house, on an island off Stonington, accessible only by mailboat. No electricity – light comes from gas lamps – but indoor plumbing and hot

Price Categories

A very approximate guide to current room rates for a standard double per night is:
$$$$ = over $200
$$$ = $150–200
$$ = $100–150
$ = under $100

water are part of the package. The house has 6 rooms and offers FAP. **$$$$**
The Inn at Isle au Haut
Stonington, 04681
Tel: 207-335 5141
www.innatisleauhaut.com
Four simple rooms in a gracious home overlooking the water. The first floor room has its own bath and ocean views; three on the second floor share a bath. All meals, including a picnic lunch, included in rate. No TV or phone. **$$$$**

ISLESBORO

Dark Harbor House
Jetty Road, 04848
Tel: 207-734 6666
Fax: 207-734 6938
www.darkharborhouse.com
A waterside 1890s mansion with an elegant double staircase and spacious guest rooms. Set up on a hill on an island accessible by ferry from Lincolnville Beach, on Route 1 north of Camden. 11 rooms. B&B. **$$–$$$$**

KENNEBUNK

The Lodge at Kennebunk
95 Alewive Road, Route 35N, 04043
Tel/fax: 207-985 9010/877-918 3701
www.lodgeatkennebunk.com
Family- and pet-friendly resort on eight wooded acres; one, two- and three-room suites, heated pool, game room, BBQ grills. **$–$$**

KENNEBUNKPORT

Captain Lord Mansion
Pleasant and Green Streets, 04046
Tel: 207-967 3141
Fax: 207-967 3172
www.captainlord.com
In Kennebunkport's historic district, an elegant formally decorated 1812 inn topped by an octagonal cupola. 16 rooms. B&B. **$$$–$$$$**
Inn at Harbor Head
Pier Road, 04046
Tel: 207-967 5564
Luxury lodgings and gourmet breakfasts, alongside quaint Cape Porpoise harbor. 5 rooms. B&B. **$$$–$$$$**

Old Fort Inn
Old Fort Avenue, 04046
Tel: 207-967 5353/800-828 3678
Country decor in a converted barn and brick carriage house. 16 rooms. B&B. **$$$–$$$$**
The Colony Hotel
140 Ocean Avenue , 04046
Tel: 207-967 3331/800-552 2363
Fax: 207-967 8738
www.thecolonyhotel/maine.com
A coastal grand hotel built in 1914. Many of the 123 antiques-filled rooms have splendid ocean views. FAP. Private beach and heated saltwater pool. Open May–October. **$$–$$$$**
White Barn Inn
37 Beach Avenue, 04046.
Tel: 207-967 2321.
www.whitebarninn.com
Relais et Château-level luxury in an 1820 farmhouse and adjoining complex between town and the beach. Some of the 25 rooms have fireplaces: all are elegantly furnished. **$$$$**
Bufflehead Cove
Bufflehead Cove Road, 04046
Tel/fax: 207-967 3879
www.buffleheadcove.com
A comfortably appointed early 20th-century summer home overlooking the Kennebunk River. Private dock with rowboats available for guests. 5 rooms. B&B. **$$–$$$**
Green Heron Inn
Ocean Avenue, 04046
Tel: 207-967 3315
www.greenheroninn.com
Plain and pleasant lodgings; excellent breakfasts. 10 rooms and a cottage. B&B. **$$**
Captain Jefferds Inn
Pearl Street, 04046
Tel: 207-967 2311
Fax: 207-967 0721
An antique-filled 1804 Federal mansion, with 11 rooms; the four carriage-house suites allow dogs ($30/night), and a pet-sitting service is available. B&B. **$–$$$$**

KINGFIELD

Sugarloaf/USA
RR 1, Box 5000, 04947
Tel: 207-237 2000/800-843 5623
www.sugarloaf.com
New England's largest ski village with two hotels and hundreds of condominiums (with over 400 rooms) attracts hikers, mountain-bikers, and golfers when the snow subsides. **$$–$$$**
The Herbert Grand Hotel
246 Main Street, P.O. Box 67, 04947
Tel: 207-265 2000/888-656 9922
Fax: 207-265 4594
www.herbertgrandhotel.com
This somewhat funky but decidedly

charming columned hotel, which was heralded upon its 1918 debut as "A Palace in the Wilderness", is now the unofficial heart of town. 27 simple rooms. **$–$$**

Inn on Winter's Hill
33 Winterhill Street, 04947
Tel: 207-265 5421/800-233 9687
Fax: 207-265 5424
www.wintershill.com
An 1895 Georgian Revival mansion with a total of 20 rooms in the main house and the simply furnished former barn. Pool, tennis, hot tub, and cross-country skiing. **$–$$**

Three Stanley Avenue
3 Stanley Avenue, 04947
Tel: 207-265 5541
Six comfy rooms (three with private bath) in a Victorian home designed by one of the Stanley brothers. There's fine restaurant next door. B&B. **$**

KITTERY

Portsmouth Harbor Inn and Spa
6 Water Street, 03904
Tel: 207-439 4040
Fax: 207-438 9286
www.innatportsmouth.com
An 1889 brick Victorian B&B close to the town green and overlooking Portsmouth Harbor and the Piscataqua River. Five nicely-furnished rooms with cable TV and data ports; some clawfoot tubs. **$$–$$$**

LUBEC

Home Port Inn and Restaurant
45 Main Street, P.O. Box 50, 04652
Tel: 207-733 2077/800-457 2077 (outside Maine)
www.homeportinn.com
An 1880s home in the village, with seven guest rooms with private baths. There's a spacious and cheery livingroom for TV watching or reading. The restaurant ($$–$$$) serves seafood specialties. **$–$$**

MILBRIDGE

Guagus River Inn
376 Kansas Road, 04658
Tel: 207-546 9737
www.guagusriver.com
A contemporary home overlooking the Narraguagus River; six themed guest include the log cabin room, the fish room overlooking the blueberry fields, and the master suite, which overlooks the river. Indoor lap pool. **$–$$$**

MONHEGAN ISLAND

The Island Inn
Ocean View Terrace, 04852
Tel: 207-596 0371
Fax: 207-594 5517

www.islandinnmonhegan.com
Hundred-year-old simplicity on a painter's dream of an island. 30 rooms and four suites; 15 with private bath. Some rooms overlook the ocean. MAP. Open Memorial Day–mid-October. **$–$$$$**

The Monhegan House
1 Main Street, 04852
Tel: 207-594 7983
Fax: 207-596 6472
www.monheganhouse.com
Four-story, 1870s inn with 33 small, basic, but cheerful rooms with shared baths. There's a fireplaced lobby and pleasant porch with rocking chairs. **$$–$$$$**

NEW HARBOR

Gosnold Arms
Northside Road, 04554
Tel: 207-677 3727
Fax: 207-677 2662
www.gosnold.com
Shoreside rusticity at Pemaquid Point since 1925. The inn's glassed-in dining room overlooks the water. Rooms are available in the main inn and in 14 cottages. 26 rooms. B&B. Open mid-May–mid-October. **$–$$**

NORTHEAST HARBOR

Asticou Inn
Route 3, 04662
Tel: 207-276 3344
Fax: 207-276 3373
www.asticou.com
A cultured carryover from Bar Harbor's heyday as Society's summer playground. Elegant, 1885 Victorian-style inn and three annexes overlooking Great Harbor. 47 rooms. MAP. **$$–$$$$**

Harbourside Inn
Northeast Harbor 04662
Tel: 207-276 3272
www.harboursideinn.com
A Shingle-style 1889 inn with 14 guest rooms beside Acadia National Park. **$$–$$$$**

OGUNQUIT

Anchorage by the Sea
55 Shore Road, 03907
Tel: 207-646 9384
Fax: 207-646 6256
www.anchoragebythesea.com
A modern oceanfront resort on the Marginal Way offering 242 rooms (some with jacuzzis). Indoor and outdoor pools, hot tubs, a poolside cafe, and gazebos. **$$$–$$$$**

Sparhawk Oceanfront Resort
85 Shore Road, 03907
Tel: 207-646 5562
Fax: 207-646 9143
87 rooms, suites, and apartments at a luxury motel on the Marginal Way and within walking distance of town. The oceanfront rooms with private decks are almost in the ocean. Pool, croquet, tennis. **$$$–$$$$**

Cliff House Resort & Spa
Shore Road (off Route 1), 03907
Tel: 207-361 1000
Fax: 207-361 2122
www.cliffhousemaine.com
A classic New England summer resort since 1872. Several buildings on the 70-acre oceanfront resort house 164 spacious and well-appointed rooms: some look directly onto the ocean. Amenities include swimming pools, tennis courts, a full service spa, indoor and outdoor pools, and a fitness center. MAP available. **$$–$$$$**

Gorges Grant Hotel
449 Main Street, Route 1, 03907
Tel: 207-646 7003/800-646 5001
www.ogunquit.com/gorgesgrant/
A sleek contemporary hotel with traditionalist furnishings, just north of the town center. 81 rooms, indoor and outdoor pools, a jacuzzi, and fitness center. **$$–$$$**

The Dunes on the Waterfront
518 Main Street, Route 1, 03907
Tel: 207-646 2612
www.dunesonthewaterfront.com
A 1930s cottage complex with 19 cottages and 17 guest rooms on the tidal Ogunquit River, 200 yards from Ogunquit Beach and situated on the trolley line to the town center. Swimming dock, with rowboats. **$–$$$$**

Morning Dove
13 Bourne Lane, 03907
Tel: 207-646 3891
www.themorningdove.com
A lovingly decorated 1860s Victorian

farmhouse on a quiet street close to town. Five of the seven comfortable rooms have private baths; all have small refrigerators and air conditioning. One room has a private deck. B&B. **$–$$$**

PORTLAND

Portland Regency Hotel
20 Milk Street, 04101
Tel: 207-774 4200/800-727 3436
Fax: 207-775 2150
www.theregency.com
A snazzily refurbished, five-floor, 19th-century armory in the Old Port. Amenities in the 95 rooms include extended cable TV, high-speed internet, and honor bars. **$$$–$$$$**

Pomegranate Inn
49 Neal Street, 04102
Tel: 207-772 1006/800-356 0408
Fax: 207-773 4426
www.pomegranateinn.com
One of the city's most elegant inns – an art- and antiques-filled home with eight bedrooms for B&B in Portland's upscale residential West End. All rooms have phones and TV, five with gas fireplaces. **$$$–$$$$**

Eastland Park Hotel
157 High Street, 04101
Tel: 207-775 5411/888-671 8008
Fax: 207-775 2872
www.eastlandparkhotel.com
Portland's landmark, 12-story, 1927 hotel has 204 rooms with all of the modern amenities, old-fashioned service, and harbor views. The rooftop lounge is a fine spot to watch the sunset. **$$–$$$**

PROUTS NECK

Black Point Inn Resort
510 Black Point Road, 04074
Tel: 207-883 2500/800-258 0003
Fax: 207-883 9976
www.blackpointinn.com
An 1870s resort, on a peninsula favored by Winslow Homer. Located between Old Orchard Beach and Cape Elizabeth, 10 miles (16 km) south of the Portland airport. Facilities include an 18-hole golf course, 14 tennis courts, two beaches, indoor/outdoor pools, boating, nature trails, health club. 84 rooms. FAP. Age restriction in peak summer months. **$$$$**

RANGELEY

Country Club Inn
Mingo Loop Road, 04970
Tel/fax: 207-864 3831
www.rangeleyme.com/ccinn
A 1920s inn, plus 1950s-era motel units. The inn's grand living room has two fireplaces, a cathedral ceiling, and game trophies, and there are lovely

views of the lake. Amenities include a swimming pool and golf course. B&B. Closed April and November. **$$**

Rangeley Inn and Motor Lodge
Main Street, 04970
Tel: 207-864 3341/800-666 3687
Fax: 207-864 3634
www.rangeleyinn.com
An old-fashioned three-story inn in the heart of town with 50 guest rooms (built around 1907), some in modern motel units. Some rooms have water views, kitchenettes whirlpool baths, and woodstoves. MAP available. **$–$$**

Grant's Kennebago Camps
Kennebago Lake Road, 04970
Tel: 207-864 3608
Secluded, waterfront rustic cabins with woodstoves and porches for fishermen and those wanting a true Maine camp experience. Boat, sailboat and canoe rentals; floatplane rides. FAP. **$$$**

ROCKLAND

Captain Lindsey House Inn
5 Lindsey Street, 04841
Tel: 207-596 7950/800-523 2145
Fax: 207-596 2758
www.lindseyhouse.com
A three-story, 1837 antiques-filled inn with nine spacious guest rooms with air conditioning, phone and television. **$$–$$$$**

LimeRock Inn
96 Limerock Avenue, 04841
Tel: 207-594 2257/800-546 3762
Fax: 207-594 1846
www.limerockinn.com
Elegantly decorated Queen Anne Victorian B&B on a residential street near the Shore Village and Farnsworth Museums. Some of the rooms have whirlpool tubs and private decks. **$$–$$$**

ROCKPORT

Samoset Resort
220 Warrenton Street, 04856
Tel: 207-594 2511/800-341 1650
Fax: 207-594 0722
www.samoset.com
A full-scale, 230-acre golf resort overlooking Penobscot Bay, with 178 rooms. Sports facilities include two swimming pools, a fitness center, and four tennis courts. **$$$$**

ROCKWOOD (MOOSEHEAD LAKE)

The Birches
off Route 15, 04478
Tel: 207-534 7588
Fax: 207-538 8835
www.birches.com
A rustic 1940s lakeside lodge with log cabins and wood-burning stoves or

Price Categories

A very approximate guide to current room rates for a standard double per night is:
$$$$ = over $200
$$$ = $150–200
$$ = $100–150
$ = under $100

fireplaces. Amenities include boating on the lake, saunas, and hot tubs. 33 rooms. B&B. **$**

Maynard-in-Maine
Rockwood 04478
Tel: 207-534 7703
www.maynardinmaine.com
A classic hunting camp, founded in 1919. 13 rooms. FAP. **$**

Rockwood Cottages
Route 15, 04478
Tel/fax: 207-534 7725
www.connectmaine.com/rockwood
Eight lakeside cottages with screened porches and fully equipped kitchens. Sauna and boating facilities. **$**

SEARSPORT

The Homeport Inn
121 E Main Street (Route 1), 04974
Tel/fax: 207-548 2259/800-742 5814
www.homeportbnb.com
10 rooms, and two oceanfront Victorian cottages. B&B. A cupola-topped 1860s captain's house filled with Victorian appointments in the "antiques capital" of Maine. Some rooms have private decks and views of the bay. **$–$$$**

SOUTH CASCO

Migis Lodge on Sebago Lake
P. O. Box 40, 04077
Tel: 207-655 4524
Fax: 207-655 2054
www.migis.com
A rustic, elegant, and old-fashioned 100-acre resort with 32 rooms for FAP. There are rooms in the main lodge and in cottages, all overlooking the lake. Sports facilities include sailing, canoeing, waterskiing, and tennis courts. In the dining room, you can enjoy traditional New England fare, including steamers, clam chowder, and lobster. **$$$–$$$$**

SOUTHWEST HARBOR

The Claremont Hotel
P. O. Box 137,04679
Tel: 207-244 5036/800-244 5036
Fax: 207-244 3512
www.theclaremonthotel.com
Mount Desert Island's oldest grand hotel, built in 1884. Rooms in the main inn, two guest houses, and a

dozen cottages. Waterfront location for swimming, boating. Also tennis and croquet. 41 rooms. MAP. **$$–$$$**

Inn at Southwest
371 Main Street, 04679
Tel: 207-244 3835
Fax: 207-244 9879
www.innatsouthwest.com
Seven elegant, romantic rooms with antique furnishings in an 1884 Victorian home overlooking the harbor. B&B. **$$**

SPRUCE HEAD

Craignair Inn at Clark Island
St George, 04859
Tel: 207-594 7644/800-320 9997
Fax: 207-596 7124
www.craignair.com
A basic, cheerful shorefront B&B inn near a nature preserve between Rockland and Tenant's Harbor. Originally built in 1928 to house workers from the nearby quarries. The 20 rooms in the main inn share baths, the somewhat more upscale rooms in the annex have private baths. **$–$$**

STONINGTON

Inn on the Harbor
Main Street, 04681
Tel: 207-367 2420/800-942 2420
Fax: 207-367 5165
www.innontheharbor.com
Fifteen comfortable rooms with phones and cable TV in a waterside lodging. Some rooms have water views, fireplaces, full kitchens, and private decks. **$–$$$$**

SUNSET

Goose Cove Lodge
Deer Isle, 04683
Tel: 207-348 2508/800-728 1963
Fax: 207-348 2624
www.goosecovelodge.com
An informal family resort with a rustic, simply furnished lodge and cottages in a remote natural setting. The lodge overlooks Penobscot Bay, adjacent to nature conservatory land. There are 22 rooms, offering MAP. **$$$–$$$$**

TENANTS HARBOR

East Wind Inn
Mechanic Street (Route 131) 04860
Tel: 207-372 6366/800-241 8439
Fax: 207-372 6320
www.eastwindinn.com
This is a simply decorated, harborside inn with a wraparound porch in an unspoiled fishing village south of Rockland. There are 26 antiques-filled rooms and suites with ocean views, some with fireplaces. The Friendship

A very approximate guide to current room rates for a standard double per night is:
$$$$ = over $200
$$$ = $150–200
$$ = $100–150
$ = under $100

sloop *Surprise* sails daily from the private dock. B&B. **$$–$$$**

VINALHAVEN

Tidewater Motel
Main Street, 04863
Tel: 207-863 4618
A simple harborside motel, right on the water, on a scenic and quite uncrowded island ideal for biking. 11 rooms. **$–$$**

WISCASSET

Squire Tarbox Inn
1181 Westport Island Road, Route 144, 04578
Tel: 207-882 7693
Fax: 207-882 7107
www.squiretarboxinn.com
A colonial country farmhouse on a working farm where the owners raise goats. Delicious home-grown dinners feature the farm's goat cheese. 11 rooms. B&B. **$$–$$$**

Marston House
Main Street, 04578
Tel: 207-882 6010
Fax: 207-882 6965
A small private carriage house with just two rooms, simply appointed with Shaker- and Colonial-style furnishings and fireplaces. No public spaces so breakfast (continental) is delivered to your room. **$$**

YORK AREA

View Point Hotel
229 Nubble Road
York Beach, 03910
Tel: 207-363 2661
Fax: 207-363 6788
www.viewpointhotel.com
Nine luxury 1–3 bedroom suites with gas fireplaces and full kitchens at this inn with 300 feet of frontage on the rocky shore. Views of Nubble Light. **$$$$**

Stage Neck Inn
8 Stage Neck Road off Route 1 A, York Harbor, 03911
Tel: 207-363 3850/800-340 2243
Fax: 207-363 2221
www.stageneck.com
A contemporary seaside resort known for its 60 low-key luxury. Queen Anne-style rooms with refrigerators, many

with ocean views. Indoor pool with whirlpool spa. **$$$–$$$$**

York Harbor Inn
Route 1A
York Harbor, 03911
Tel: 207-363 5119/800-596 4926
Fax: 207-363 7151
www.yorkharborinn.com
A seaside inn, which accrued around a 1637 sail loft. There are 55 Colonial-style rooms, some with fireplaces, jacuzzi spa tubs, and ocean views with decks. **$$–$$$$**

The Union Bluff Hotel
8 Beach Street
York Beach, 03910
Five, story oceanfront hotel has 63 guest rooms, some with whirlpools, decks, and ocean views. **$–$$$**

Dockside Guest Quarters
Harris Island Road
(Off Route 103)
York, 03909
Tel: 207-363 2868/888-860 7428
Fax: 207-363 1977
www.docksidegq.com
Classic 19th-century seacoast home flanked by cottages. 27 rooms. **$$–$$$$**

BANGOR

Momma Baldacci's
12 Alden Street
Tel: 207-945 5813
One of Bangor's oldest Italian restaurants serves well-prepared traditional dishes at a reasonable price. **$–$$**

BAR HARBOR

Jordan Pond House
Park Loop Road
Tel: 207-276 3316
A classic spot for popovers, homemade ice cream, and tea served on the lawn of a landmark building daily in season from 11.30–5.30pm. The restaurant, is on the Loop Road in Acadia National Park. Jackets suggested at dinner. **$$**

Lompoc Café and Brew Pub
36 Rodick Street
Tel: 207-288 9392
A brew pub and restaurant with its signature Bar Harbor Real Ale, international dishes, delicious pizza, a porch, weekend entertainment. **$$**

Epi's Sub and Pizza
8 Cottage Street
Tel: 207-288 5853
An informal spot for terrific pizza, homemade calzones and pizza. **$**

BATH

Beale Street Barbecue & Grill
215 Water Street
Tel: 207-442 9514
A comfortable, affordable barbecue joint, with choices ranging from a basic pulled pork plate to a New York sirloin. **$–$$**

Mae's Café and Bakery
160 Centre Street (Route 209)
Tel: 207-442 8577
A popular spot for light for eclectic fare, Maine microbrews, and pecan sticky buns. Outdoor patio; entertainment. Breakfast, lunch and dinner. **$–$$**

BETHEL

Bethel Inn & Country Club
Village Common. 04217
Tel: 207-824 2175
Yankee classics and impressive mountain views in the formal dining room of an old-fashioned inn. Breakfast and dinner. **$$**

S.S. Milton
Upper Main Street
Tel: 207-824 2589
A cozy house is the setting for this fine restaurant which specializes in creatively-preparedfresh fish dishes. Children's menu. **$$–$$$**

BLUE HILL

Arborvine Restaurant
Main Street, Tenney Hill
Tel: 374 2119
Romantic, candlelight dining in several rooms of an 1823 Cape Cod-style house. Traditional American fare includes roast duck, native fish, and lamb, all prepared with the freshest seasonal ingredients. Lighter fare in The Vinery; piano bar Wed–Sun. **$$$–$$$$**

Blue Moose Restaurant
50 Main Street
Tel: 207-374 4374
A diverse menu, family-friendly atmosphere, and reasonable prices pack in the locals as well as tourists. Entrées come in two sizes, and there's a children's menu. Lunch, dinner, and weekend breakfast buffet. **$$**

BOOTHBAY HARBOR AREA

Robinson's Wharf
Route 27, Southport Island
Traditional Maine lobster pound serves lobster in a variety of ways, as well as chowders, fried fish and homemade desserts. Seating is at picnic tables. **$–$$**

Ebb Tide
67 Commercial Street

Tel: 207-633 5692
A stylish restored diner serving a wide variety of classic comfort foods, including lobster rolls, seafood platter, and homemade desserts; and breakfast all day. **$–$$**

BRUNSWICK

The Great Impasta
42 Main Street
Tel: 207-729 5858
A small storefront serving – true to its name – pasta of all types, as well as other Italian treats including stuffed eggplant and homemade lasagna. **$–$$**

CAMDEN

Cappy's Chowder House
Main Street
Tel: 207-236 2254
Homemade chowders, croissant sandwiches, great burgers and pasta dishes, home baked goodies, and a lively pub atmosphere. Quieter fare is available in upstairs dining room. **$$**

Sea Dog Brewing Company
43 Mechanic Street
Tel: 207-236 6863
A brew pub situated in a former wool mill, with great views and hearty portions of American favorites. **$**

CAPE NEDDICK

Cape Neddick Lobster Pound
Shore Road, Route 1A
An extremely popular spot, with indoor and outdoor seating. Lobster and clams are house specialties, but there are lots of choices for landlubbers. **$–$$$**

CAPE PORPOISE

Cape Porpoise Lobster Company
15 Pier Road
Tel: 207-967 0123/800-967 4268
Oceanfront lobster shanty cooks up ocean-fresh lobsters and fried clams. Seasonal. **$**

CASTINE

The Pentagoet Inn
Main Street
Tel: 207-326 8616
New England specialties, such as lobster pie or Spanish seafood stew, served in the intimate, candlelit dining room of a turreted Victorian inn. Reservations are required. **$$$**

Castine Inn
Main Street
Tel: 207-326 4365
Creative, regional delicacies served in a dining room painted to depict the town. The crabmeat cakes in mustard

sauce are a house specialty. Breakfast and dinner. **$$$–$$$$**

Dennett's Wharf
Sea Street
Tel: 207-326 9045
Casual harborside seafood, salads, and a good selection of microbrews. **$–$$**

DEDHAM

The Lucerne Inn
2517 Main Road
Tel: 207-843 5123/800-325 5123
With an outstanding view and a convenient location between Bangor and Bar Harbor, this little bit of Switzerland, a 200-plus-year-old lakefront inn, offers pleasant fare including chicken parmesan and truffled salmon. **$$$–$$$$**

DEER ISLE VILLAGE

Whale's Rib Tavern
Pilgrim's Inn
Main Street, Route 15A
Tel: 207-348 6615
A casual and cozy spot, with true tavern fare such as fish and chips, pot pies, and chowder. Local musicians stop by to play. Dinner. **$–$$**

FREEPORT

Harraseeket Inn
162 Main Street
Tel: 207-865 9377
Fabulous local produce, seafood, and game. The buffets are especially renowned. More casual fare – hamburgers, steamers, and simple fish dishes – are on offer in the tavern room, which has a hunting lodge-style ambiance. **$$–$$$$**

Harraseeket Lobster Company
Main Street
South Freeport
Tel: 207-865 3535
Seafood basics in the rough: lobster dinners, fried clams, and other fried seafood. Next to the town landing in South Freeport. Picnic tables outside for al fresco munching in fair weather. **$–$$**

GARDINER

A-1 Diner
Route 201
Tel: 207-582 4804
A 1946 Worcester diner, south of
Augusta, serving the standards. **$**

GEORGETOWN

Robinhood Free Meetinghouse
Robinhood Road off Route 127
Tel: 207-371 2188
An 1855 Greek Revival meeting-house
near Bath transformed into a simple
yet elegant temple of classic and
fusion cuisine. Think American bistro
fare blended with Italian, Chinese,
Thai, and Caribbean influences. The
chef's signature dessert is
"Obsession in Three Chocolates".
$$$–$$$$

GREENVILLE

Greenville Inn
Norris Street
Tel: 207-695 2206
Bountiful dinners accompanied by
giant popovers in an opulent mansion
overlooking Moosehead Lake. **$$$**
Blue Moose Café
Main Street
Tel: 207-695 0786
American seafood and meat dishes
prepared with a Caribbean-French
accent in a cozy dining room. Dinner
Monday–Saturday. **$$–$$$**

KENNEBUNKPORT

White Barn Inn
37 Beach Avenue
Tel: 207-967 2321
One of the state's most highly-
regarded restaurants is housed in the
beautifully appointed barn of a Relais
& Chateaux inn. The five-course, *prix-
fixe* menu changes often, but
emphasizes nouvelle cuisine. Service
is formal and impeccable. **$$$$**
Windows on the Water
Chase Hill
Tel: 207-967 3313
A modern restaurant known for its
inventive treatments of lobster, which
may appear in half-a-dozen succulent
guises. Reservations essential. **$$$$**
Kennebunkport Inn
Dock Square
Tel: 207-967 2621
Delightful regional cuisine with French
accents in an elegant, lace-filled
dining room. The *bouillabaisse* is a
house specialty. Breakfast and dinner.
$$$–$$$$
Cape Arundel Inn
Ocean Avenue
Tel: 207-967 2125
The skilled chef creates dishes such

as lobster Chardonnay risotto and
sauteed lobster in wild mushrooms in
an elegant dining room overlooking
the ocean, with views of the Bush
estate on Walker Point. **$$$–$$$$**
Grissini
27 Western Avenue (Route 9)
Tel: 207-967 2211
Fine contemporary northern Italian
fare – such as grilled lamb with
Tuscan white beans, *gnocchi* (potato
dumplings), and grilled salmon served
on sweet potato polenta – in a
casually upscale room. **$$–$$$**

KINGFIELD

One Stanley Avenue
Tel: 207-265 5541
The indigenous foods of Maine,
artfully prepared in one of the region's
finest restaurants for more than 30
years. The service is excellent, the
atmosphere delightful. **$$$–$$$$**
Longfellow's
Main Street
Tel: 207-265 4394
A casual riverside cafe with solid,
American fare and good prices across
from The Herbert. **$**

KITTERY

Warren's Lobster House
Route 1
Tel: 207-439 1630
On the water just north of
Portsmouth, a local institution serving
lobster and other seafood. Hefty salad
bar, too. **$$**
Bob's Clam Hut
315 Route 1
Tel: 207-439 4233
Next to the Kittery Trading Post, this
local institution knows how to fry fish.
$

LINCOLNVILLE BEACH

Lobster Pound Restaurant
Route 1
Tel: 207-789 5550
One of the most popular spots along
the shore for lobster, seafood, and
traditional American fare. Sit in the
vast dining room or, better, at one of
the picnic tables on the beach. **$$**

Restaurant Prices

Prices are approximate, but for a
three-course meal for one
(excluding beverages, tax and tip),
the following guidelines may prove
helpful:
$$$$ = over $40
$$$ = $28–40
$$ = $15–28
$ = under $15

LITTLE DEER ISLE

Eaton's Lobster Pool
Blastow Cove
Tel: 207-348 2383
Water views and fresh-off-the-boat
seafood. **$–$$**

MADAWASKA

Gateway Motel and Restaurant
An unpretentious spot just across
from New Brunswick serving American
fare as well as French Canadian and
Acadian regional dishes: poutine–
fresh fries covered with gravy and
cheese curds– is a local favorite.
$–$$

NORTHEAST HARBOR

Asticou Inn
Tel: 207-276 3344
Yankee standards in a grand old
dining room overlooking the sea.
Reservations required, jackets
recommended at dinner. **$$$–$$$$**

OGUNQUIT

Arrows Restaurant
Berwick Road (off Route 1)
Tel: 207-361 1100
Consistently named one of the top 50
restaurants in America," this exquisite
restaurant housed in an 18th-century
farmhouse has appetizers such as
Beluga caviar, and paillard of foie gras
with caramelized Belgian endive; and
entrées such as sautéed John Dory
with a Maine Peekytoe crab timbale.
The desserts, too, are fabulous. A six-
course tasting menu is available ($89).
Dinner only. **$$$$**
Barnacle Billy's
Perkins Cove
Tel: 207-646 5575
Classic seafood, chicken and beef at
a great location, right on the water.
$$–$$$
Ogunquit Lobster Pound
Route 1
Tel: 207-646 2516
Another terrific lobster pound – this
one in a 1930s log building with huge
cauldrons out front. Order up some
mussels on the side, and blueberry
pie for dessert. There's chicken, beef
and pasta for non-lobster lovers. **$–$$**

PORTLAND

Back Bay Grill
65 Portland Street
Tel: 207-772 8833
Sophisticated decor, sensuous New
American dishes, and an outstanding
crème brulée to finish. The five-course
lobster-tasting menu is a great way to
go. Dinner Monday–Saturday. **$$$**

Commissary
25 Preble Street
Tel: 207-228 6667
A contemporary spot in the city's
Public Market, with American dishes
with a Maine accent prepared in an
open kitchen and in wood-burning
rotisseries. There's a seasonal
outdoor patio. **$$$**
Street & Company
33 Wharf Street
Tel: 207-775 0887
Fresh fish and seafood served in the
pan right on one of the dozen copper-
topped tables. You can choose a
vegetarian alternative if you must, but
seafood is the reason to be here.
Dinner only. **$$–$$$**
Uffa! Restaurant
190 State Street
Tel: 207-775 3380
An eclectic bistro emphasizing
vegetarian dishes and fish. Microbrews,
too. Dinner Wed–Sat; Sun brunch.
$–$$

RANGELEY
Country Club Inn
Mingo Loop Road
Tel: 207-864 3831
Traditional white-tablecloth fare in a
glassed-in dining room with lake and
mountain views. Reservations
required. **$$$–$$$$**

ROCKLAND
Jessica's
2 S Main Street (Route 73)
Tel: 207-596 0770
European bistro-style cuisine, such as
pasta, risotto, and paella, served in
four cozy dining rooms in a Victorian
house. Located at the far southern
end of town. **$$**
The Water Works
Lindsey Street
Tel: 207-596 2752
A former waterworks with two distinct
personalities: on one side, an upscale
dining room with dishes such as
lobster stew and broiled seafood; on
the other side, a pub serving comfort
food, ranging from roast turkey and
fish 'n' chips, through grilled
sausages to meatloaf, and
microbrews. **$–$$$**

ROCKPORT
Marcel's at the Samoset Resort
220 Warrenton Street
Tel: 207-594 0774
Million-dollar views, a formal
atmosphere, and eclectic cuisine
priced to match. From rack of lamb
and Chateaubriand to more
contemporary fare with French and
Italian influences. Jackets

recommended at dinner. Breakfast,
dinner and Sunday brunch. **$$$$**

ROCKWOOD
The Birches
(Off Route 15)
Tel: 207-534 7305
Seafood, steaks, and pasta in a stone
hearthed dining room overlooking
Moosehead Lake at this north woods
resort. Among the specialties: prime
rib and grilled chicken. **$$–$$$**

SOUTHWEST HARBOR
The Claremont
Clark Point Road.
Tel: 207-244 5036.
The formal dining room of this
venerable 1884 inn has an ambitious
modernist menu. Jackets are required
for men; "corresponding attire" for
women. **$$$**
Beal's Lobster Pier
Clark Point Road
Tel: 207-244 7178
A good old classic wharfside lobster
shack. **$**

WELLS
Maine Diner
Route 1
Tel: 207-656 4111
Surprisingly good food in a classic
diner just before the turn-off to
Kennebunkport. The clam chowder
and chicken pot pie are specialties of
the house. Open for breakfast, lunch,
and dinner. **$**

WISCASSET
Le Garage
Water Street
Tel: 207-882 5409
Regional American fare in a
converted, 1920s garage overlooking
the Sheepscot River; tables on the
porch have the best view. **$$$**
Squire Tarbox Restaurant
Route 144
Tel: 207-882 7693
A colonial farmhouse inn serves five-
course, candlelight dinners by
reservation with one seating only.
Dinner, after cocktails, include home-
raised delicacies, including farm's
own goat cheese, and entrées such
as roast rack of lamb. Dinner only.
$$$$

YORK AREA
York Harbor Inn
Route 1A, York Harbor
Tel: 207-363 5119
Well-considered continental/
regional fare with a seafood focus in a

"big night out" room. **$$$–$$$$**
The Restaurant at Dockside
Guest Quarters
Harris Island Road
(Off Route 103), York
Tel: 207-363 2868
From fried clams and steamed
lobsters to "swordfish Pacific Rim"
and pesto chicken – all with a water
view. **$$$**
Chef Mimmo's
Route 1A, York
Tel: 207-363 3807
An unprepossessing café with an
exuberant Tuscan chef just across
from Long Sands Beach. BYOB. Dinner
only. **$$**
Clay Hill Farm
220 Clay Hill Road
Tel: 207-362 2272
This bird sanctuary-wildlife refuge-tree
farm is also one of the area's most
popular restaurants, a romantic spot
with outstanding regional fare
including the house specialty prime
rib, and lobster pie. The early-bird
special serviced Sun–Fri at 5:30pm is
under $20. Piano entertainment.
$$–$$$$

Culture

CLASSICAL MUSIC

Portland Symphony Orchestra (tel:
207-773 6128; 20 Myrtle Street,
Portland). Performs year-round except
during September.
Maine Center for the Arts (tel: 207-
581 1805) at the University of Maine
in Orono hosts classical concerts, as
well as dance and children's theater.
**The Pierre Monteux School for
Conductors and Orchestra Musicians**
(tel: 207-546 4495) in Hancock
presents faculty and student concerts
in their concert hall in June and July.

MUSIC FESTIVALS
Bowdoin International Music Festival
(tel: 207-725 3895; Brunswick) hosts
a popular and renowned six-week
series of concerts.
Kneisel Hall Chamber Music Festival
(tel: 207-374 2811; Route 15, Blue
Hill), dating back to 1902, has a
developed a fine reputation for its
summer concerts.

THEATER
Center for Cultural Exchange (tel:
207-761 0591; Longfellow Square,
Portland) is a multi-purpose venue
offering space for a variety of cultural
events. Also in Portland, check the
local newspapers for anything
mounted by the Portland Stage
Company (tel: 207-774 0465).

Ogunquit Playhouse (tel: 207-646 5511; Route 1, Ogunquit) stages musicals, theater, and plays during the summer only. It's one of the oldest playhouses in the US.

Arundel Barn Playhouse (tel: 207-985 5552; 53 Old Post Road) in Arundel presents professional classic summer theater June through late August.

Hackmatack Playhouse (tel: 207-698 1807; Route 9, Beaver Dam, Berwick) launches plays with local performers.

ART GALLERIES

Bayview Gallery (tel: 207-773 3007, 800-244 3007; 75 Market Street, Portland) represents preeminent Maine artists.

Eclipse Gallery (tel: 207-288 9048; 12 Mount Desert Street) in Bar Harbor exhibits contemporary handblown glass, ceramics, and furniture. There are excellent galleries along Northeast Harbor's Main Street; clustered around the Farnsworth Museum in Rockland; and throughout downtown Ogunquit.

The **Leighton Gallery** (tel: 207-374 5001; Parker Point Road) in Blue Hill houses three floors of contemporary art.

LIVE MUSIC

Left Bank Bakery and Cafe (tel: 207-374 2201; Route 172, Blue Hill) brings folk music to the already-musical town.

The Big Easy Blues Club (tel: 207-871 8817; 55 Market Street) offers live entertainment in Portland's Old Port.

GAY & LESBIAN VENUES

Ogunquit has a growing number of gay-friendly establishments including **Inside Out** (tel: 207-646 6655; 237 Main Street), a dance club/adult musical comedy venue. In Augusta, **P.J.'s Lounge** (tel: 207-623 4041; 80 Water Street) presents live music. **Portland's Blackstones** (tel: 207-775 2885; 6 Portland Street) is the city's oldest neighborhood gay bar.

LATE-NIGHT VENUES

It doesn't have to be late to pop into the **Sea Dog Tavern & Brewery** (tel: 207-236 6863; 43 Mechanic Street, Camden), which features its own microbrews in a lively setting within a former wool mill.

Sunday River in Bethel is a hoping kind of place (both slopeside and in town) during ski season. Check out

the **Sunday River Brewery** (tel: 207-824 4253; Route 2) and **The Shipyard** (tel: 207 824 3000; on the mountain), which both have rock bands.

DANCING

The Pavillion (tel: 207 773 6422; 188 Middle Street), Portland's historic ballroom, offers dancing, and, some nights, a Manhattan-style night club. **Asylum** (tel: 207-772 8274; 121 Center Street) is one of Portland's most popular high-tech dance clubs.

BIKING

When the snow melts after winter, the Sunday River Ski area turns into the **Sunday River Mountain Bike Park** (tel: 207-824 3000), where bikers can ride the lifts up and then bike down.

Boston-based **Bike Riders' Tours** (tel: 800-473 7040) is one of several companies offering bicycle tours in the state of Maine. Their week-long Penobscot Bay trip stops off in Camden, Islesboro and Castine.

BOAT CRUISES

Beal & Bunker (tel: 207-244 3575) and **Islesford Ferry** (tel: 207-276 3717) set sail from Northeast Harbor to Little Cranberry Island. **Island Cruises** (tel: 207-244 5785) in Bass Harbor cruises to Frenchboro, Placentia and Black Islands and Great and Little Gott Islands.

En route to whale watching, **Bar Harbor Whale Watch Company** (tel: 207-288 9800/888-533 9253; 1 West Street) visits Petit Manan National Wildlife Refuge and puffins on their 3½-hour cruise. **Balmy Day Cruises** (tel: 207-633 2284/800-298 2284; Pier 8, Bar Harbor) offers harbor tours.

CANOEING, KAYAKING, AND RAFTING

With more than 2,000 coastal islands and their protected waters, Maine has

A tour with a difference... Guided sea-kayaking excursions are conducted in the Acadia area by two Bar Harbor-based companies: **National Park Kayak Tours** Tel: 207-288 0342/800-347 0940, www.acadiakayak.com
Coastal Kayaking Tours Tel: 207-288 9605

become a center for sea kayaking. The **Maine Island Kayak Company** (tel: 800-796 2373), based at Peaks Island near Portland, runs a range of sea-kayaking trips and instructional courses. **Old Quarry Ocean Adventures** (tel: 207-367 8977; Oceanville Road) in Stonington rents kayaks, canoes, and sailboats and organizes boat trips.

H2Outfitters (tel: 207-833 5257), on Orr's Island near Brunswick, offers one-day sea kayaking classes, as well as multi-day trips.

The Kennebec, Dead, and Penobscot Rivers offer some of New England's most challenging whitewater rafting. **North American Outdoor Adventure** (tel: 800-727 4379) organizes Maine river rafting trips for novices through experts. The Allagash Wilderness Waterway, a 92-mile (150-km) corridor of lakes and rivers from Baxter State Park to the Canadian border, is another canoeing and rafting destination.

Outfitters in this area include **Allagash Canoe Trips in Greenville** (tel: 207-695 3668), **Mahoosuc Guide Service**, based in Newry (tel: 207-824 2073), and the Birches Resort in Rockwood (tel: 207-534 2242).

For more sedate paddling excursions, the **Maine Audubon Society** (tel: 207 781 2330) offers guided canoe trips and rentals in Scarborough Marsh, the state's largest salt marsh.

On Mount Desert Island, **National Park Canoe Rentals** (tel: 207-244 5854) has canoes for hire on Long Pond.

Bus 1 takes passengers round the Eastern and Western Promenades and the rest of downtown Portland. **Bikes** Forest City Mountain Bike Tours operate guided two- to six-hour tours of Portland, South Portland, Cape Elizabeth and elsewhere.
51 Melbourne Street, Portland.
Tel: 207-879 2512.

Cruises Casco Bay, to the east of Portland town, is the starting point for cruises to Maine's islands. Casco Bay Lines (tel: 207-774 7871) runs mail/delivery motorboats that you can hop on for cruises of various lengths up to just under two hours. From the Ferry Terminal at 56 Commercial Street at Franklin Street.

FISHING

The Rangeley area is a popular destination for those who fly-fish. Fish for smallmouth bass, brook trout, pickerel, and landlocked salmon in the Belgrade Lakes region. **Days Store** (tel: 207-495 2205) in Belgrade Village is a good place for information and supplies. In Kennebunkport, **Chick's Marina** (tel: 207-967 2782) offers fishing cruises for up to six people. In the Boothbay region, **Catch 22 Sport Fishing** (tel: 207-785 2408) operates from the Boothbay Region Boatyard.

HIKING

Baxter State Park (tel: 207-723 5140) in Maine's North Woods draws thousands of hikers annually who tackle the day-long climb to the summit of **Mount Katahdin**, the state's highest peak (5,267 ft, or 1,755 meters). Eighteen mountains in the park exceed 3,000 ft (900 meters).

SAILING

The Rockport-Camden area is Maine's center for windjammer cruising. The **Maine Windjammer Association** (tel: 800-807 9463), headquartered in Blue Hill, represents a number of windjammers that offer multi-day excursions. **Maine Classic Schooners** (tel: 888-807 6921/207-549 3908) and **Maine Windjammer Cruises** (tel: 888-692 7245) are also good bets.

Do-it-yourself sailors can contact **Manset Yacht Service** (tel: 207-244 4040), near Acadia National Park, to arrange sailboat rentals. Boats can also be hired on Sebago and Long Lakes: try **Moose Landing Marina** (tel: 207-693 6264) or **Sun Sports Plus** (tel: 207-693 3867), both in Naples.

SKIING

Maine's largest areas for downhill skiing are:
Sunday River in Bethel (tel: 207-824 3000/800-543 2754).
Sugarloaf/USA in Kingfield (tel: 207-237 2000/800-843 5623).
Saddleback in Rangley (tel: 207-864 5671).

Bethel is also home to several cross-country ski centers including:
The Bethel Inn Ski Center (tel: 207-824 6276).
Carter's Cross Country Ski Centers (tel: 207-539 4848).
Sunday River Inn Ski Touring Center (tel: 207-824 2410).

Other Nordic skiing spots include the **Harris Farm Cross Country Ski Center** in Biddeford (tel: 207-499 2678).

WHERE TO SHOP

Between the towns of Freeport and Kittery, Maine has cornered the market in outlet stores *(see also page 153)*. You'll also find outlet stores on Route 1 between Kittery and Wells.

If heavy foot traffic is any indication of good shopping, it's readily apparent that the Dock Square area in Kennebunkport offers it in spades.

Portland's Old Port, a dense few blocks along Fore and Exchange Streets, is great for browsing and buying.

SHOPPING MALLS

Maine Mall (tel: 207-774 0303), 5 miles (8 km) south of Portland, has almost 150 stores, including large anchor department stores. The **Bangor Mall**, exit 49 off I-91, is the area's pre-eminent shopping area.

BOOKS

DeLorme's Map Store (tel: 207-846 7000; Yarmouth) stocks an outstanding range of Maine and New England specialty maps, as well as travel guides.
Owl and Turtle Bookshop (tel: 207-236 4769; 8 Bay View Street, Camden) has two floors of Maine maritime and children's books.
Port in a Storm (tel: 207-244 4114; Main Street, Somesville, near Acadia National Park), regardless of the weather, is one of the best bookstores on the Maine coast. The **Big Chicken Book Barn** (tel: 207-667 7308), on Route 1 just a few miles south of Ellsworth houses the state's largest used book store.

ANTIQUES

You can often find silver for the price of flatware at flea markets, if you know what you're looking for. Route 1 through Searsport is lined with semi-permanent seasonal flea markets, as well as the more traditional antiques shops. Bargain hunters should do well here.

For those must-have mementos, downtown Boothbay Harbor (along with Camden and Bar Harbor, situated further to the north) is absolutely chock-a-block with shops that will draw the money from your pockets like magnets to steel.

Maine State Ferry Service runs ferries from the mainland to most of Maine's major islands.
Tel: 800-491 4883;
www.state.me.us/mdot/opt/ferry/ferry.htm.
Bay Ferries operates a car and passenger ferry service from Portland to Yarmouth, Nova Scotia, Fri–Sun. Tel: 877-259 3760; www.catferry.com.
Northumberland/Bay Ferries operates a car and passenger ferry from Bar Harbor to Yarmouth, Nova Scotia.
Tel: 888-249 7245;
www.nfl-bay.com.

NAUTICAL

The Wooden Boat School (tel: 207-359 4651/800-273 7447; Brooklin) has an outstanding store for all things nautical, including books and charts.

ARTS AND CRAFTS

Handworks Gallery (tel: 207-374 5613; Main Street) and **North Country Textiles** (tel: 207-374 2715), both on Main Street in Blue Hill, are just two of many shops in town that carry excellent hand-made crafts. Don't miss **Rackliffe Pottery** (tel: 207-374 2297; Route 172) and **Rowantrees Pottery** (tel: 207-374 5535; Union Street), also both in Blue Hill.

Although you may visit studios by only appointment, many alumni of the **Haystack Mountain School of Crafts** (tel: 207-348 2306; off Route 15 south of Deer Isle) have settled in the area and have their own studio/shops.

Dow Studio Showroom (tel: 207-348 6498; 19 Dow Road, Deer Isle) exhibits works of nationally-known artists and craftspeoople. **Deer Isle Artists Association** (no phone; Route 15, Deer Isle) mounts revolving shows of area artists.

Edgecomb Potters (tel: 207-882 9493; Route 27) and **Sheepscot River Pottery** (tel: 207-882 9410; Route 1) are both located in Edgecomb and sell distinctive pottery. Sheeposcot also offers a wide variety of other hand-crafted goods.

THEME PARKS

Palace Playland (tel: 207-934 2001; Old Orchard Street, Old Orchard Beach) features an old carousel and

Ferris wheel and lots of other rides. **Seacoast Fun Park** (tel: 207-892 5952) in Windham has a 100-foot free-fall ride, driving range, bumper boats, go karts, and mini golf. A wooden roller coaster is one of the main attractions at **Funtown/Splashtown** (tel: 800-878 2900) on Route 1 in Saco. There's also a water park with slides, a tube river run and play area.

ZOOS

Rescue and rehabilitation are the focus at **Maine Wildlife Park** (tel: 207-657 4977; www.state.me.us/ifw) in Gray.
Acadia Zoological Park (tel: 207-667 3244; Route 3, Trenton) is small (just 15 acres) but it will occupy the kids.

JOURNEYS BY STEAM TRAIN

Belfast & Moosehead Lake Railroad (tel: 207-948 5500/800-392 5500; Unity) operates two scenic trains: one passes along a river, another by villages. Kids will particularly like the open-air cars.
Seashore Trolley Museum (tel: 207-967 2800; Log Cabin Road, Kennebunkport) offers a 4-mile trolley tips aboard one of their restored antiques.

Maine Coast Railroad (tel: 207-882 8000/800-795 5404; Route 1, Wiscasset) travels to Newcastle on vintage trains.
Boothbay Railway Village (tel: 207-633 4727; Route 27, Boothbay) offers just a 1½-mile narrow-gauge steam train ride, but it's picturesque as it travels through a re-created New England village.

Dozens of antique steam locomotives, coaches and cars are housed in an historic waterfront building at **Maine Narrow Gauge Railroad** in Portland (tel: 207-828 0814; 58 Fore Street); there's also a three-mile ride on a two-foot narrow gauge train along Casco Bay.

MUSEUM

The highly interactive **Children's Museum of Maine** (tel: 207-828 1234; 142 Free Street, Portland) will keep even the most boisterous youngsters occupied for hours – hauling in traps on a lobster boat, broadcasting the news, making stained glass, and more.
Bangor's **Maine Discovery Museum** (tel: 207-262 7200; 74 Main Street) has three floors of interactive, fun exhibits for kids.

Maine Festivals

Spring
"Mush" is the cry that rings through Farmington when the town hosts the annual **sled dog races** in early February (tel: 207-778 4215).

Summer
Portland kicks off the summer season with the **Old Port Festival** (tel: 207-772 6828) in early June, while later in summer, Wiscasset hosts its **Strawberry Festival** (tel: 207-882 7184).
Other summer celebrations of Maine food include **Rockland's Lobster Festival** (tel: 800-562 2529) in late July, and the mid-August **Wild Blueberry Festival** (tel: 207-255 6665) down east in Machias.
Also in late June, Gardiner, Augusta, and surrounding towns host the **Great Kennebec Whatever Family Festival** (tel: 207-623 4559) including fun-filled "Day in Capitol Park" (Augusta) with lots of kids' activities.
During **Windjammer Days** (tel: 207-633 2353), late June in Boothbay Harbor, graceful sailing vessels crowd the harbor.
In July and August, musicians

assemble in Hamilton for the **Sebago-Long Lake Chamber Music Festival** (tel: 207-583 6747), while the **Bar Harbor Music Festival** (tel: 207-288 5744) comes to Mount Desert Island.

Fall
Several towns honor the season's colors in October with **fall foliage, crafts, and harvest festivals,** including events in Camden (tel: 207-236 4404), Boothbay (tel: 207-633 4743) and York (tel: 207-363 4422).
Portland toasts the season in a different way at the annual **Maine Brewers' Festival** (tel: 207-771 7571).

Winter
For two December weekends, the Kennebunk area hosts holiday crafts fairs with tree-lighting and caroling during the annual **Christmas Prelude** (tel: 207-967 0857).
In January, all of the cross-country ski areas thumb their noses at winter throughout the statewide **Ski Fest** events (tel: 800-754 9263).

Further Reading

Not all the books cited are currently in print, but it can be fun tracking them down in New England's atmospheric secondhand bookshops.

History and Culture

Paul Revere and the World He Lived In by Esther Forbes. Boston, 1942.
Boston: A Topographical History, rev. 3rd ed. by Walter Muir Whitehill and Lawrence R. Kennedy. Cambridge, Mass. 2000.
The Flowering of New England by Van Wyck Brooks. New York, 1936.
New England: Indian Summer, 1865–1915 by Van Wyck Brooks. New York, 1940.
History of the White Mountains by Lucy Crawford. Boston, 1846.
The New England Mind: From Colony to Province by Perry Miller. Cambridge, 1953.
The Proper Bostonians by Cleveland Amory. New York, 1947.
The Enduring Shore: A History of Cape Cod, Martha's Vineyard, and Nantucket by Paul Schneider. New York, 2001.
The Outermost House: A Year of Life on the Great Beach of Cape Cod by Henry Beston. New York, 1928.
The Lobster Chronicles by Linda Greenlaw. New York, 2002.

Landscape and Natural History

These Fragile Outposts: A Geological Look at Cape Cod, Martha's Vineyard and Nantucket by Barbara B. Chamberlain. New York, 1964.
A Guide to New England's Landscape by Neil Jorgensen. Barre, VT, 1971.
Hands on the Land: A History of the Vermont Landscape by Jan Albers. Cambridge, Mass, 2000.

Architecture

Cityscapes of Boston: An American City through Time by Robert Campbell and Peter Vanderwarker. Boston, 1992.
Preserving New England by Jane Holtz Kay and Pauline Chase-Harrell. New York, 1986.

Fiction

Writing New England: An Anthology from the Puritans to the Present edited by Andrew Delbanco.

Cambridge, Mass, 2001.
Contemporary New England Stories by Michael C. Curtis, ed. Old Saybrook, CT, 1992.
The Late George Apley by John P. Marquand. Boston, 1936.
The Last Hurrah by Edwin O'Connor. Boston, 1956.
String Too Short to Be Saved: Recollections of Summers on a New England Farm by Donald Hall. Boston, 1979.
Imagining Boston: A Literary Landscape by Shaun O'Connell. Boston, 1990.

Other Insight Guides

More than 190 *Insight Guides* cover every continent. In addition, a companion series of more than 120 *Insight Pocket Guides* provides selected, carefully timed itineraries for the traveler with little time to spare and include a full-size fold-out map.

And more than 130 *Insight Compact Guides* provide ideal on-the-spot companions, with text, maps and pictures all carefully cross-referenced. Titles which highlight destinations in New England include:

Insight City Guide: Boston (above) is a comprehensive and lavishly illustrated companion to the present book, and comes with a very useful pull-out restaurant map. *Pocket Guide: Boston* provides recommendations and a full-size city map.

Boston, Cape Cod, and *Martha's Vineyard & Nantucket* are covered in detail by three Compact Guides. These extremely portable "mini-encyclopedias" are the ideal guides to carry while on the road.

● As a complement to the guides, *Insight FlexiMap: Boston* contains detailed and clear cartography plus destination information, and comes with a laminated finish for durability and easy folding.

ART & PHOTO CREDITS

Photo Features

Cartography Editor Zoë Goodwin.
Maps Colourmap Scanning Ltd.
© 2007 Apa Publications GmbH & Co. Verlag KG (Singapore branch)

Index

Numbers in italics refer to photographs

n

A
B
C
D
E
F
G

I
J
a

c
d

f
g
h
i
j
k
l

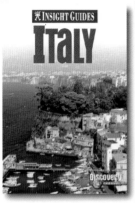

Insight Guides Website
www.insightguides.com

*Don't travel the
planet alone.
Keep in step with
Insight Guides'
walking eye,
just a click away*

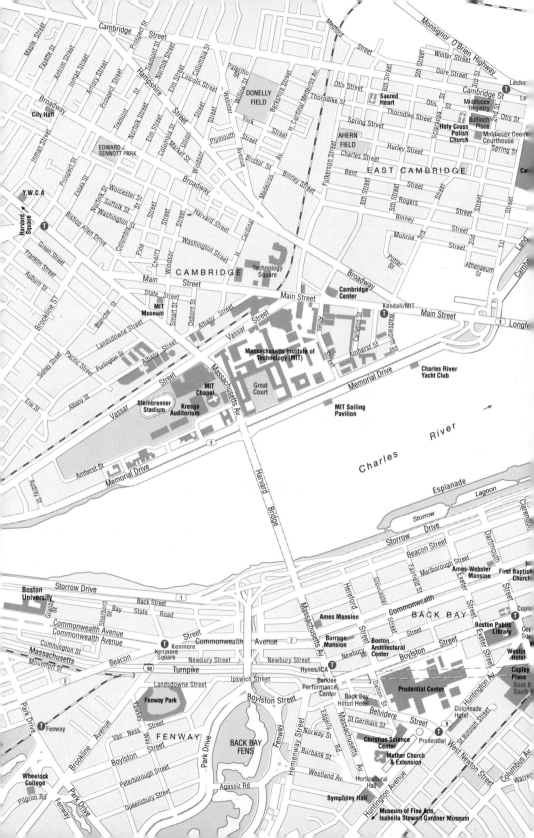